**Readings
in Business Policy
and Strategy from
BUSINESS WEEK**

McGraw-Hill Series in Management

KEITH DAVIS and FRED LUTHANS
Consulting Editors

ALLEN: Management and Organization
ALLEN: The Management Profession
ARGYRIS: Management and Organizational Development: The Path from XA to YB
BECKETT: Management Dynamics: The New Synthesis
BENTON: Supervision and Management
BROWN: Judgment in Administration
BUCHELE: The Management of Business and Public Organizations
CAMPBELL, DUNNETTE, LAWLER, AND WEICK: Managerial Behavior, Performance, and Effectiveness
CLELAND AND KING: Management: A Systems Approach
CLELAND AND KING: Systems Analysis and Project Management
CLELAND AND KING: Systems, Organizations, Analysis, Management: A Book of Readings
DALE: Management: Theory and Practice
DALE: Readings in Management: Landmarks and New Frontiers
DAVIS: Human Behavior at Work: Organizational Behavior
DAVIS AND NEWSTROM: Organizational Behavior: Readings and Exercises
DAVIS, FREDERICK, AND BLOMSTROM: Business and Society: Concepts and Policy Issues
DeGREENE: Systems Psychology
DUNN AND RACHEL: Wage and Salary Administration: Total Compensation Systems
EDMUNDS AND LETEY: Environmental Administration
FIEDLER: A Theory of Leadership Effectiveness

FINCH, JONES, AND LITTERER: Managing for Organizational Effectiveness: An Experiential Approach
FLIPPO: Personnel Management
GLUECK: Business Policy and Strategic Management
GLUECK: Strategic Management and Business Policy
GLUECK AND SNYDER: Readings in Business Policy and Strategy from *Business Week*
HAMPTON: Contemporary Management
HICKS AND GULLETT: Management
HICKS AND GULLETT: Modern Business Management: A Systems and Environmental Approach
HICKS AND GULLETT: Organizations: Theory and Behavior
JOHNSON, KAST, AND ROSENZWEIG: The Theory and Management of Systems
KARLINS: The Human Use of Human Resources
KAST AND ROSENZWEIG: Experiential Exercises and Cases in Management
KAST AND ROSENZWEIG: Organization and Management: A Systems and Contingency Approach
KNUDSON, WOODWORTH, AND BELL: Management: An Experiential Approach
KOONTZ: Toward a Unified Theory of Management
KOONTZ, O'DONNELL, AND WEIHRICH: Essentials of Management
KOONTZ, O'DONNELL, AND WEIHRICH: Management
KOONTZ, O'DONNELL, AND WEIHRICH: Management: A Book of Readings
LEE AND DOBLER: Purchasing and Materials Management: Text and Cases
LEVIN, McLAUGHLIN, LAMONE, AND KOTTAS: Production/Operations Management: Contemporary Policy for Managing Operating Systems
LUTHANS: Introduction to Management: A Contingency Approach
LUTHANS: Organizational Behavior
LUTHANS AND THOMPSON: Contemporary Readings in Organizational Behavior
McNICHOLS: Policymaking and Executive Action
MAIER: Problem-Solving Discussions and Conferences: Leadership Methods and Skills
MARGULIES AND RAIA: Conceptual Foundations of Organizational Development
MARGULIES AND RAIA: Organizational Development: Values, Process, and Technology
MAYER: Production and Operations Management
MILES: Theories of Management: Implications for Organizational Behavior and Development
MILES AND SNOW: Organizational Strategy, Structure, and Process
MILLS: Labor-Management Relations
MITCHELL: People in Organizations: An Introduction to Organizational Behavior
MOLANDER: Responsive Capitalism: Case Studies in Corporate Social Conduct
MONKS: Operations Management: Theory and Problems
NEWSTROM, REIF, AND MONCZKA: A Contingency Approach to Management: Readings
PETIT: The Moral Crisis in Management
PETROF, CARUSONE, AND McDAVID: Small Business Management: Concepts and Techniques for Improving Decisions
PORTER, LAWLER, AND HACKMAN: Behavior in Organizations
PRASOW AND PETERS: Arbitration and Collective Bargaining: Conflict Resolution in Labor Relations
REDDIN: Managerial Effectiveness
SARTAIN AND BAKER: The Supervisor and the Job
SAYLES: Leadership: What Effective Managers Really Do . . . and How They Do It
SCHROEDER: Operations Management: Decision Making in the Operations Function
SHORE: Operations Management
SHULL, DELBECQ, AND CUMMINGS: Organizational Decision Making
STEERS AND PORTER: Motivation and Work Behavior
STEINHOFF: Small Business Management Fundamentals
SUTERMEISTER: People and Productivity
TANNENBAUM, WESCHLER, AND MASSARIK: Leadership and Organization
WALKER: Human Resource Planning
WERTHER AND DAVIS: Personnel Management and Human Resources
WOFFORD, GERLOFF, AND CUMMINS: Organizational Communications: The Keystone to Managerial Effectiveness

McGRAW-HILL BOOK COMPANY

New York   St. Louis   San Francisco   Auckland
Bogotá   Hamburg   Johannesburg   London
Madrid   Mexico   Montreal   New Delhi   Panama
Paris   São Paulo   Singapore   Sydney   Tokyo   Toronto

READINGS in BUSINESS POLICY and STRATEGY from

READINGS IN BUSINESS POLICY AND STRATEGY FROM *BUSINESS WEEK*

Copyright © 1982 by McGraw-Hill, Inc.
All rights reserved.
Formerly published under the title of "Readings in Business Policy from *Business Week*,"
copyright © 1978 by McGraw-Hill, Inc. All rights reserved.
Printed in the United States of America.
Except as permitted under the United States Copyright Act of 1976,
no part of this publication may be reproduced or distributed
in any form or by any means, or stored in a data base or retrieval system,
without the prior written permission of the publisher.

1234567890 SMSM 8 9 8 7 6 5 4 3 2

ISBN 0-07-059540-2

This book was set in Century Expanded by University Graphics, Inc.
The editors were Kathi A. Benson and Scott Amerman;
the designer was Nicholas Krenitsky;
the production supervisor was Phil Galea.
The cover photograph was taken by DeMarco/Tamaccio.
Semline, Inc., was printer and binder.

Library of Congress Cataloging in Publication Data
Main entry under title:

Readings in business policy and strategy from
    Business week.

   (McGraw-Hill series in management)
   Rev. ed. of: Readings in business policy from
Business week. 1st ed. c1978.
      1. Industrial management—United States—Addresses,
essays, lectures.   2. United States—Commerce—Ad-
dresses, essays, lectures.   I. Glueck, William F.
II. Snyder, Neil H.   III. Business week (McGraw-Hill
Book Company)   IV. Series.
HD70.U5R43   1982   658.4'012   81-23622
ISBN 0-07-059540-2   AACR2

To
Katie, Melanie, and Rebekah

Contents

PREFACE	xiii
CROSS-TABULATION MATRIX	xv
HOW TO USE THE BOOK	xix
INTRODUCTION	xxi

1
The Concept of Strategy and Policy — 1

Texas Instruments Shows U.S. Business How to Survive in the 1980s (September 18, 1978)	2
Wanted: A Manager to Fit Each Strategy (February 25, 1980)	12
Sun and Arco: How Contrasting Strategies Made Different Companies (June 2, 1980)	14
Trans World Corp.: The Strategy Squeeze on the Airline (May 19, 1980)	20
What Caused the Decline: The Penalties of Short-Term Corporate Strategies (June 30, 1980)	25
A New Social Contract: How Companies Can Lengthen Their Sights (June 30, 1980)	27
Corporate Culture: The Hard-to-Change Values That Spell Success or Failure (October 27, 1980)	30

2
The Strategy Makers — 36

Following the Corporate Legend (February 11, 1980)	38
Managers Who Are No Longer Entrepreneurs (June 30, 1980)	44
ITT: Groping for a New Strategy (December 15, 1980)	48
The Pains of Turning Firestone Around (September 8, 1980)	54
Richard J. Ferris: Flying a Risky New Route for United (August 18, 1980)	55
After Years of Hoarding Cash Hearst Is Spending Big (September 15, 1980)	59
The Man behind Kraft's Merger (August 25, 1980)	64
How a New Chief Is Turning Interbank Inside Out (July 14, 1980)	66
Trautman: A Goal Eludes a Willful Manager (October 27, 1980)	68
First of Chicago: New Management to Bring Back the Past (August 4, 1980)	70

3
Environmental Opportunities and Threats to Enterprise Strategy — 76

Magazines Targeted at the Working Woman (February 18, 1980)	78
The Investor Excitement over New City Hotels (March 17, 1980)	80
The Microchip Revolution: Piecing Together a New Society (November 10, 1980)	82
The Shrinking Standard of Living (January 28, 1980)	84
Southeast Banks: Set for a Slump (January 28, 1980)	90
Antibusiness Forces Aim at Corporations (February 11, 1980)	92
A U. N. Space Treaty That Could Zap Industry (March 10, 1980)	93
U.S. Autos: Losing a Big Segment of the Market—Forever? (March 24, 1980)	94
Luxury Car Sales Skid to New Lows (May 19, 1980)	100
Detroit's High-Price Strategy Could Backfire (November 24, 1980)	101

Tight Credit Slams Car Dealers Two Ways (April 14, 1980)	103
What Caused the Decline: Inflation Skews the Profit Incentive (June 30, 1980)	104
What Caused the Decline: Expectations That Can No Longer Be Met (June 30, 1980)	106
Maine's Nuclear Vote Has the Industry Jumpy (September 22, 1980)	107
A Skewed Recession Has Hidden Strengths (December 15, 1980)	108
Cable TV: The Race to Plug In (December 8, 1980)	109
The Implications of Oil Company Profits (August 18, 1980)	115
Videodiscs: A Three-Way Race for a Billion-Dollar Jackpot (July 7, 1980)	118
U.S. Home: Defying a Slowdown By Continuing to Expand (March 10, 1980)	125

4
Two Environmental Sectors of Special Importance in Formulating Strategy: Government and Unions   128

A GOVERNMENT

Truckers Quietly Get Set for Deregulation (March 24, 1980)	130
Tax Credits That Could Save Industry Billions (April 7, 1980)	131
Senate Energy Gets a Friend of Industry (December 8, 1980)	133
Using the Market in Regulation (December 15, 1980)	134
The New Case for Monopolists (December 15, 1980)	135
How Washington Spurs High Technology Companies (November 10, 1980)	136
The Court Leaves OSHA Hanging (July 21, 1980)	137
What Trade Sanctions Will Cost (January 28, 1980)	138
Here Comes the Credit Crunch (March 31, 1980)	140
Credit Curbs Push Sales toward a Tailspin (April 28, 1980)	142
A Product Liability Bill Has Insurers Uptight (March 31, 1980)	143
Canada's Oil Policy Is Starting to Hurt (December 8, 1980)	144
States Seek a Slice of Oil Company Profits (November 10, 1980)	145
Justice Takes Aim at Dual Distribution (July 7, 1980)	146
A Bill That Will Give the Fed More Power (March 24, 1980)	147

B UNIONS

A New Social Contract: A Partnership to Build the New Workplace (June 30, 1980)	148
The UAW's About-Face on Import Controls (January 28, 1980)	151
How the Changing Auto Market Threatens the UAW, Too (March 24, 1980)	152
The Risk in Putting a Union Chief on the Board (May 19, 1980)	153
Can Chrysler Squeeze More from the UAW? (December 17, 1979)	155
The Price of Peace at Chrysler (November 12, 1979)	156
Ailing AMC Seeks Relief from the UAW (August 25, 1980)	158
Steel Talks: A Costly Pact, Even with Restraint (February 18, 1980)	159
Steel Labor Is Adding Insurance (March 31, 1980)	161
Labor Cools It with Big Steel (April 28, 1980)	162
When Steel Wages Rise Faster than Productivity (April 21, 1980)	164
Edgy Steelworkers Set Their Goals High (December 24, 1979)	167

5
Assessing Strategic Advantages and Disadvantages   170

The Decline of U.S. Industry: A Drastic New Loss of Competitive Strength (June 30, 1980)	172
A Policy for Industry: Technology Gives the U.S. a Big Edge (June 30, 1980)	175
Will It Work? What the U.S. Can Learn from Its Rivals (June 30, 1980)	179
Can Canon Copy Its Camera Coup? (January 28, 1980)	183
Ford Rests Its Future on Tough Cost Controls (March 31, 1980)	184

Why Consumer Products Lag at Texas Instruments (May 5, 1980)	185
Tandy's Next Big Drive into Home Electronics (June 2, 1980)	187
Where K Mart Goes Next Now That It's No. 2 (June 2, 1980)	188
Wang's Game Plan for the Office (December 15, 1980)	191
Key Pharmaceuticals: Bidding for Growth through New Products (November 3, 1980)	193
Mobil's Successful Exploration: Making People Remember It Is an Oil Company (October 13, 1980)	194
Iowa Beef: Moving in for a Kill by Automating Pork Processing (July 14, 1980)	200
PPG Industries: Still Relying on Glass—But Now in Growth Areas (January 21, 1980)	202

6
Considering and Choosing Strategies — 204

An Oil Giant's Dilemma: Investing a Mountain of Cash before the Oil Runs Out (August 25, 1980)	206
Deere: A Counter-Cyclical Expansion to Grab Market Share (November 19, 1979)	212
LTV: On the Acquisition Trail Again, but Now in Aerospace and Energy (November 3, 1980)	214
Nabisco: Diversifying Again, but This Time Wholeheartedly (October 20, 1980)	216
Baker International: A Growth Wizard Divides to Conquer (April 28, 1980)	218
Western International: A $1 Billion Expansion in the Face of Recession (April 28, 1980)	220
Ramada Inns: Renovating Rooms and Rushing into Gambling (January 14, 1980)	221
Citibank: A Rising Giant in Computer Services (August 4, 1980)	223
Caterpillar: Sticking to Basics to Stay Competitive (May 4, 1981)	226
Why Esmark Sold a Profitable Subsidiary (September 8, 1980)	230
Kaiser Steel: The Strategic Question Is Whether to Liquidate (September 8, 1980)	231
The Chores Facing Polaroid's New CEO (March 24, 1980)	233
Could Bankruptcy Save Chrysler? (December 24, 1979)	234

7
Implementing and Evaluating the Strategic Decisions: The Policy Process — 238

Ashland Oil: Scrambling for Crude after a Premature Sell-Off (February 4, 1980)	240
Republic Air Takes on a New Merger Problem (March 24, 1980)	242
Volkswagen of America: Facing a Head-On Challenge from Detroit (April 14, 1980)	243
Anheuser's Plan to Flatten Miller's Head (April 21, 1980)	245
Open for Business: IBM's Computer Store (December 1, 1980)	247
Hart Schaffner and Marx: Expanding Boldly from Class to Mass Markets (October 20, 1980)	248
AT&T's Fast Move on Baby Bell (September 8, 1980)	249
Washington Post: New Ventures Get Off to an Uncertain Start (September 22, 1980)	251
Beatrice Foods: Adding Tropicana for a Broader Nationwide Network (May 15, 1978)	253
Why IBM Reversed Itself on Computer Pricing (January 28, 1980)	255
Quaker Oats Retreats to Its Food Lines (February 25, 1980)	256
American Can: Diversification Brings Sobering Second Thoughts (March 24, 1980)	258
McGraw-Edison: Paying the Price of the Studebaker Acquisition (March 31, 1980)	260
GE Moves to Correct Its Error in Chips (September 22, 1980)	261

8
Summary and Conclusions — 263

Preface

Traditionally, courses in the field of business policy and strategic management have relied almost exclusively on the case method. The logic behind using cases in the business policy course is sound. Business policy, the capstone course in the business curriculum, focuses on the general manager's or top manager's job; cases familiarize students with the problems faced by these top managers and permit them to make strategy decisions under conditions of uncertainty.

There are, however, problems associated with most cases.

1. Most policy cases are long and are the result of lengthy interviews, field observation, and document search and compilation. Because of the time and energy required to prepare a case, many are used for years after they are written. The issues addressed in the cases become less relevant over time, but instructors continue to use them because nothing better is available.

2. Many cases describe sensitive subjects, so frequently the cases are disguised, but the disguising process prevents students from follow-up analysis after the case description ends.

In recent years, many books on business policy and strategic management have appeared that contain text material to supplement the cases or that use text material instead of cases. Sometimes the text material is theoretical and the author does not illustrate the theoretical points with examples from the current business scene. This book is designed to compensate for the shortcomings of the present materials in the field:

- *Business Week*'s articles are uniquely suited to the study of business policy and strategic management. They provide *timely* descriptions of companies and events which can enrich the understanding of older, lengthier cases.

- *Business Week*'s articles provide descriptions of real, not disguised, companies. Thus, they can be used for classroom discussion and they can be used as a launching pad for more in-depth study.

- *Business Week*'s articles help illustrate the theories discussed in many business policy and strategic management texts.

This edition of the text is significantly different from the previous edition. Its new features include the following:

- Articles on firms in a wide variety of industries (such as steel, automobiles, electronics, newspapers, etc.)
- Special emphasis on several newly emerging fields (such as microchips, videodisks, etc.)
- A chapter devoted exclusively to government-business and union-business relationships.

This book will promote thoughtful discussion in the classroom since it deals with such *timely* and *important* issues. Additionally, it will provide a foundation about business in general and business policy and strategic management in particular upon which students can build for the remainder of their careers. Finally, this book is a powerful tool for use in executive education programs. It provides opportunities for discussion based on situations and events to which business executives can relate.

This is the plan of the book:

The introduction of the book provides a conceptual framework. This framework provides the rationale for the organization of the book.

Each of the seven sections begins with an introduction tying the specific section to the conceptual framework and the rest of the book.

The book concludes with a summary and conclusions.

For the convenience of those using this volume in conjunction with other texts in business policy and strategic management, a cross-tabulation matrix between this book's sections and parts or sections of other texts is provided.

Many thanks to *Business Week* for the opportunity to reprint their articles; colleagues at the McIntire School of Commerce of the University of Virginia and the University of Georgia for their esprit de corps and good fellowship; Dean William Shenkir, Associate Dean Bernie Morin, Professor Tom Wheelen, Professor Dave Hunger, and Professor Hank Odell at the McIntire School of the University of Virginia and Dean William Flewellen, Dr. Richard Huseman, and Associate Dean Archie Carroll at the University of Georgia for their administrative support and for creating a stimulating work climate. Finally, I wish to thank Linda Kiser, research assistant, for her help in meeting the publication deadline.

The following reviewers of the early manuscript helped considerably with their comments and suggestions: Professor Hale Bartlett, University of Illinois at Chicago Circle; Professor H. Kurt Christensen, Purdue University; Professor Fred Luthans, University of Nebraska; Dr. Warren S. Martin, The University of Alabama, Birmingham; Professor Michael McGinnis, Shippensburg State College; Professor Tim Mescon, Arizona State University; Professor Israel Unterman, San Diego State University; and Professor John L. Ward, Loyola University of Chicago.

I sincerely hope that readers of this volume will find it helpful in understanding the challenging field of business policy and strategic management.

NEIL H. SNYDER

Cross-Tabulation Matrix

1. Bates, D. L., and D. L. Eldredge, *Strategy and Policy: Analysis, Formulation, and Implementation.* (Wm. C. Brown Company Publishers, 1980)

2. Bennett, E. D., et al., *Business Policy: Case Problems of the General Manager.* (Charles E. Merrill Publishing Co., 1978, 3d ed.)

3. Bridges, F. J., et al., *Management Decisions and Organizational Policy.* (Allyn and Bacon, Inc., 1977, 2d ed.)

4. Christensen, C. R., et al., *Business Policy: Text and Cases.* (Richard D. Irwin, Inc., 1978, 4th ed.)

5. Christensen, C. R., et al., *Policy Formulation and Administration.* (Richard D. Irwin, 1980, 8th ed.)

6. Glueck, W. F., *Business Policy and Strategic Management.* (McGraw-Hill Book Company, 1980, 3d ed.)

7. Higgins, J. M., *Organizational Policy and Strategic Management.* (The Dryden Press, 1979)

8. Hodgetts, R. M., and M. S. Wortman, *Administrative Policy.* (John Wiley & Sons, Inc., 1980, 2d ed.)

9. McNichols, T. J., *Policymaking and Executive Action.* (McGraw-Hill Book Company, 1977)

10. Newman, W. H., and J. P. Logan, *Strategy, Policy, and Central Management.* (South-Western Publishing Co., 1981)

11. Paine, F. T., and W. Naumes, *Organizational Strategy and Policy.* (W. B. Saunders Company, 1978, 2d ed.)

12. Steiner, G. A., and J. B. Miner, *Management Policy and Strategy.* (Macmillan Publishing Company, 1977)

13. Thompson, A. A., and A. J. Strickland, *Strategy and Policy.* (Business Publications, Inc., 1981)

14. Uyterhoeven, H., et al., *Strategy and Organization.* (Richard D. Irwin, 1977, rev. ed.)

CROSS-TABULATION MATRIX

Glueck and Snyder: *Readings in Business Policy and Strategy from Business Week*, 2d ed.	Bates and Eldredge	Bennett, Brandt, and Klasson	Bridges, Olm, and Barnhill	Christensen, Andrews, and Bower	Christensen, Berg, and Salter
Chapter 1: The Concept of Strategy and Policy	Chapter 1	Section 3, Part A	Pages 5–8 and Article 1	Pages 125–143	Pages 3–10
Chapter 2: The Strategy Makers	Chapter 2			Pages 13–23	
Chapter 3: Environmental Opportunities and Threats to Enterprise Strategy	Chapters 3 and 4		Article 2	Pages 247–254	Pages 15–24
Chapter 4: Government and Unions					

CROSS-TABULATION MATRIX (*Continued*)

Glueck and Snyder: *Readings in Business Policy and Strategy from Business Week*, 2d ed.	Bates and Eldredge	Bennett, Brandt, and Klasson	Bridges, Olm, and Barnhill	Christensen, Andrews, and Bower	Christensen, Berg, and Salter
Chapter 5: Assessing Strategic Advantages and Disadvantages	Chapter 5		Article 2	Pages 254–278	Pages 24–29
Chapter 6: Considering and Choosing Strategies	Chapter 7	Section 3, Part B	Article 2	Pages 448–454 and 524–537	Pages 29–51
Chapter 7: Implementing and Evaluating the Strategic Decisions	Chapters 9, 10, 11, and 12	Section 3, Part C	Article 3	Pages 593–603	

Glueck and Snyder: *Readings in Business Policy and Strategy from Business Week*, 2d ed.	Glueck	Higgins	Hodgetts and Wortman	McNichols	Newman and Logan
Chapter 1: The Concept of Strategy and Policy	Chapter 1	Chapter 1	Chapter 1	Chapters 5 and 7	Pages 1–13
Chapter 2: The Strategy Makers	Chapter 2		Chapters 3 and 4		Pages 1–13, 629–638
Chapter 3: Environmental Opportunities and Threats to Enterprise Strategy	Chapter 3	Pages 62–64	Chapter 5	Chapter 9	Pages 22–41, 71–91
Chapter 4: Government and Unions					
Chapter 5: Assessing Strategic Advantages and Disadvantages	Chapter 4	Pages 62–64	Chapter 5	Chapter 3	Pages 42–70
Chapter 6: Considering and Choosing Strategies	Chapters 5 and 6		Chapter 5	Chapters 7 and 8	Pages 92–109, 352–378
Chapter 7: Implementing and Evaluating the Strategic Decisions	Chapters 7 and 8	Chapters 6 and 7	Chapters 6 and 7		Part 5

Glueck and Snyder: *Readings in Business Policy and Strategy from Business Week*, 2d ed.	Paine and Naumes	Steiner and Miner	Thompson and Strickland	Uyterhoeven, Ackerman, and Rosenblum
Chapter 1: The Concept of Strategy and Policy	Chapter 5, pages 144–151	Chapters 2 and 3	Chapter 2	
Chapter 2: The Strategy Makers	Chapter 8	Chapters 6 and 10	Chapter 1	Chapters 1, 2, and 15
Chapter 3: Environmental Opportunities and Threats to Enterprise Strategy	Chapter 9, pages 276, 405–463	Chapters 4 and 5	Chapter 3	Chapters 3, 4, and 5
Chapter 4: Government and Unions				
Chapter 5: Assessing Strategic Advantages and Disadvantages	Pages 781–812	Chapters 7 and 8	Chapter 3	Chapter 6
Chapter 6: Considering and Choosing Strategies	Pages 152–176, 601–720	Chapter 9	Chapter 3	Chapters 7 and 9
Chapter 7: Implementing and Evaluating the Strategic Decisions	Chapter 8, pages 240–243	Chapters 14 and 15	Chapters 4, 5, 6, and 7	Chapter 8

How to Use the Book

The purpose of this book is to increase your knowledge about top management decision making—the focus of the business policy course. The book is divided into seven sections paralleling the model of strategic management used here. Each section contains an overview which relates the material in the section to the strategic management model and to the other parts of the book. Also, each section contains a number of *Business Week* articles describing real-life situations appropriate for the part of the model on which the section focuses. Three criteria were used in selecting *Business Week* articles for inclusion in this book. They are

1. The timeliness of the issues addressed.

2. The long-run relevance of the issues for our economy.

3. The importance of the issues for discussions in business policy classes.

This book can be used alone. The model description and articles can be used to improve your understanding of business policy and strategic management, and related articles in various sections can be studied simultaneously to focus in on particular issues, industries, or firms. Additionally, this book can be used in conjunction with other business policy and strategic management texts. In the cross-tabulation matrix are listed the books with which this text is most likely to be used. The chapters in this book are cross-tabulated with sections in other books. Thus, it is easy to tie this book to other texts for a richer and more rewarding learning experience.

The *Business Week* articles in this book cover some of the most important issues with which today's top managers must deal. Additionally, in selecting the *Business Week* articles for inclusion in this book, a special effort was made to find related articles which would enable you to study these issues from a number of different perspectives. Thus, reading these articles will enlarge your understanding of business policy and strategic management.

It is hoped that you will find this volume helpful in preparing you to meet the challenges confronting managers in the 1980s.

Introduction

This book is about business policy and strategic management. Various terms have been used to describe this subject (that is, long-range planning, strategic planning, strategic management, and business policy). The latter two terms are the ones used most frequently today.

Strategic management is a process which includes a set of decisions leading to the development of an effective strategy for a firm. Business policy has a similar meaning. A strategy, on the other hand, is a unified, comprehensive, and integrated plan which helps the firm achieve its objectives.

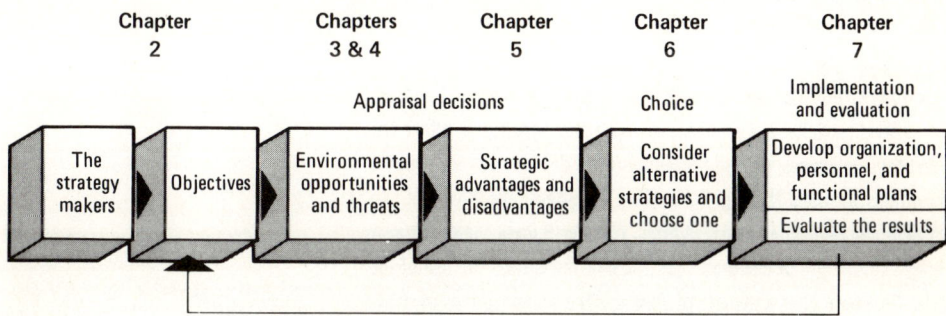

Exhibit 1
A MODEL OF THE BUSINESS POLICY AND STRATEGIC MANAGEMENT PROCESS

Exhibit 1 is a simplified model of the business policy and strategic management process. Although Exhibit 1 implies that there are a number of separate decisions involved in business policy, in fact, appraisal, choice, implementation, and evaluation are interactive and overlapping. Let us briefly define each of the items in the model.

- The strategy makers are those persons involved in the business policy and strategic management decisions.
- The objectives are the ends which the enterprise seeks to achieve.
- Environmental opportunities are those factors emerging outside the firm which can be exploited by the firm to produce positive outcomes if the firm mobilizes its resources properly.
- Environmental threats are those factors emerging outside the firm which can result in negative outcomes for the firm if they are not perceived and accounted for by the firm's strategy makers.
- Strategic advantages are the firm's internal strengths or distinctive competences which give the firm a competitive edge.
- Strategic disadvantages are the firm's internal weaknesses which make the firm vulnerable to competitive actions and environmental threats.
- Choice is the process of selecting a grand strategy to respond to threats or opportunities in the environment, after considering the firm's strengths and weaknesses. The strategy chosen should match the firm's strengths and weaknesses with opportunities and threats in its external environment. There are four grand strategies. They are: stability, growth, retrenchment, or a combination of two or more of these.

- Implementation is the process of
    - Designing an organization's structure and climate to match the strategy.
    - Assuring that the top managers heading major divisions and functional managers of the firm have the right experience, education, personality, and background for the new strategy.
    - Designing the appropriate policies (hence the term business policy) to make the strategy work. The major functional policies are

        1. Financial/accounting
        2. Marketing/logistics
        3. Operations/production management
        4. Research and development
        5. Personnel/labor relations
        6. Risk management

- Evaluation is the process by which management examines how closely the results of the chosen strategy meet the objectives set for the strategy. Note the linkage in the model between evaluation and objectives. The objectives are the standards against which performance is measured, and information generated in the evaluation process is used as input in formulating new objectives.

This book follows the pattern of the model shown in Exhibit 1. The *Business Week* articles in Chapter 1 address the concept of strategy and policy. The *Business Week* articles in Chapter 2 describe how strategists affect the formulation and implementation of strategy. Chapter 3 examines environmental appraisal decisions as exemplified in a series of *Business Week* cases. Chapter 4 contains *Business Week* articles which investigate the effects of two important environmental factors (that is, government and unions) on business firms. Chapter 5 gives some *Business Week* descriptions of firms examining their strategic advantages or disadvantages and how this affects the rest of the business policy and strategic management process. Chapter 6 gives a number of *Business Week* descriptions of strategies considered and/or chosen by business firms. Chapter 7 includes a number of *Business Week* cases describing how strategies are being implemented and several cases which describe firms evaluating the effectiveness of past strategies.

It is important to remember that the subparts of the business policy and strategic management process overlap and are interactive and that many of the *Business Week* descriptions include several aspects of the process within the article. The articles are placed where they are within the book based on the primary emphasis of the article. The total business policy and strategic management process is introduced in the beginning of the book and summarized again at the end. Each chapter of the book contains articles which focus on subparts of the business policy and strategic management process. The process should be clear when you have completed the entire book.

Readings in Business Policy and Strategy from BUSINESS WEEK

One.

before objectives are formulated, strategists make appraisal decisions. The business policy and strategic management process continues as the strategy makers choose and implement a strategy. After implementation, the strategy is evaluated periodically (weekly, monthly, quarterly, and so on) to determine if the firm is on schedule in achieving its objectives. In Exhibit 1-1, evaluation appears as the final step in the business policy and strategic management process. However, evaluation can be viewed as a new beginning. Information obtained in the evaluation process is used to make decisions about

process used in firms such as Texas Instruments—a maker of calculators, computers, and other electronic products. Additionally, they describe specific problems which firms experience as they develop and implement strategy (that is, the tendency to focus on short-term objectives and the difficulty of forecasting future happenings). Finally, the *Business Week* article entitled "Corporate Culture: The Hard-to-Change Values That Spell Success or Failure" stresses the importance of consistency between the strategy chosen by a firm's strategy makers and the prevailing values in the organization.

These *Business Week* articles should make clear how a number of factors (external and internal) influence the development of strategy. Such factors are

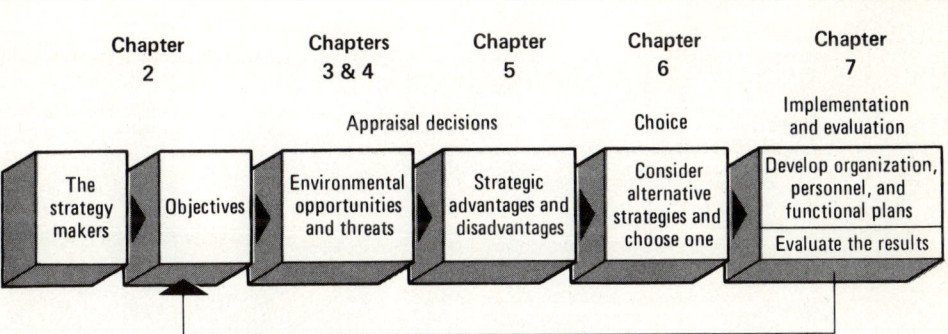

Exhibit 1-1: A MODEL OF THE BUSINESS POLICY AND STRATEGIC MANAGEMENT PROCESS.

This book begins by providing the reader with an overview of the business policy and strategic management process as a whole, and it concludes with a summary of the process. The intervening chapters look at specific subparts of the process (that is, analysis, choice, implementation, and so on), but the reader should remember that these subparts cannot be separated easily in reality.

Together, they represent an ongoing, comprehensive, and integrated process.

The business policy and strategic management process begins as a firm's objectives are formulated by its strategy makers. However, objectives are not formulated in a vacuum. They must reflect what is attainable for the firm given the opportunities and threats in its environment and its strengths and weaknesses. Thus,

the appropriateness of the firm's objectives, strategy, and implementation plan.

The *Business Week* articles in this chapter illustrate the business policy and strategic management

- The strategists' personalities, values, experiences, and education.
- The firm's past history, size, and location.
- The objectives (past and present) of the firm.
- The firm's environment.
- The firm's strategic advantages and disadvantages.

The Concept of Strategy and Policy

1

TEXAS INSTRUMENTS SHOWS U.S. BUSINESS HOW TO SURVIVE IN THE 1980s

The 1980s loom as a bloody battlefield for U. S. industry. America, which so often led the world in its ability to mass-produce and market innovative products, is fast losing its edge, many experts feel. These same experts worry about a disappearance of innovation and the increasingly minuscule gains in U. S. productivity. But no U. S. company is working harder than Texas Instruments Inc. to foster innovation and to focus an entire corporation on boosting productivity—a crucial factor in an era of seemingly endemic inflation.

Today the Dallas electronics giant leads the world in such fast-moving, high-technology markets as semiconductors, calculators, and digital watches. And it is now building its production machine to move even faster in the 1980s. TI is doing this with a very complex system designed to stimulate and manage innovation (page 76), a system that helped it accomplish what no other U. S. company has been able to do in the 1970s—build a world-leading consumer electronics business from scratch. TI's struggle to the top and its game plan for the hot trade competition of the 1980s with Japan, certainly America's chief adversary (page 84), stand as strong examples of what other U. S. companies must do if they, too, are to survive in the next decade.

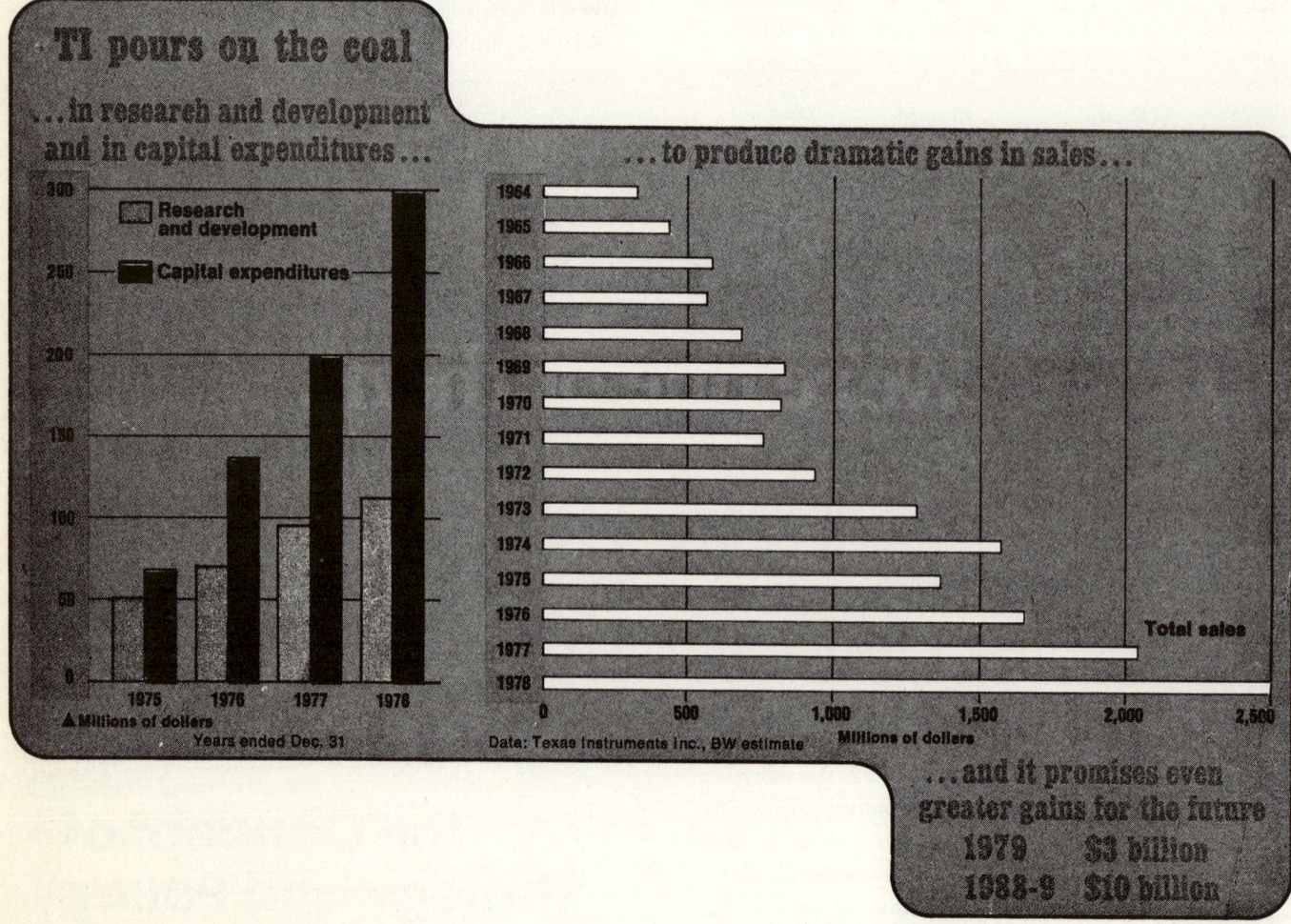

Steve Hart

2 / Readings from *Business Week*

The strategy that took TI to the top

Texas Instruments Inc. is now "the most feared competitor in the consumer electronics business," concludes a recent, major market study. Indeed, no manufacturer—short of the Japanese—could so thoroughly disrupt a marketplace as TI has done by driving down prices to gain market share. The calculator and watch markets are prime examples.

But it has certainly paid off. The Dallas electronics giant has accomplished what 100 or more other U.S. companies tried and failed to do in recent years: It has built a flourishing, profitable business in consumer electronics. In doing so, TI has beaten the Japanese at their own game and probably is now No. 1 in worldwide revenues in both calculators and digital watches. Some experts believe that TI has more potential in consumer electronics than any company in the world.

Sustaining TI's drive is a complex, but highly successful, management system that tightly controls one of the most intensive efforts in the U.S. to increase the productivity of an entire company—from the worker on the production line to the office worker writing invoices. As a result, TI's productivity improvement over the past five years has slightly more than offset the combined impact of its wage and benefit increases (averaging 9.2% annually) and its price decreases (averaging 6.4% per year).

Still, the outcome of the company's risky thrust into the consumer business was often in doubt. The huge entry dues and early operating losses probably would have stopped even a General Electric Co. or an RCA Corp. And TI's pricing strategies and marketing ineptness infuriated most of the nation's retailers. The all-out effort to establish the consumer business also diverted both management's attention and the funds needed for TI's growth in semiconductors and minicomputers. Consequently, TI had nearly as many setbacks as it did successes during the early 1970s.

But in recent months, the company has begun to make significant strides toward getting its entire corporate act together. "TI learns very slowly," acknowledges Peter Bonfield, who heads the Professional Calculator Div., "but we don't easily forget." Now the company's rapidly building momentum, orchestrated by one of the world's most finely tuned management systems, is causing some observers to point to TI as the prototype of what a U.S. company must be to compete in the surging, worldwide electronics markets of the 1980s.

"I think we'll need lots of TIs to compete in the 1980s with Japan," declares Richard L. Petritz, former research and development head at TI and now managing director of Inmos Ltd., a new semiconductor company that the British government is backing. "Like IBM, TI is an enormous asset to the U.S.," he says. "If it wasn't for TI, the whole U.S. consumer electronics business would be going down the drain."

An enigma on Wall Street

TI's 1972 move into consumer electronics with the hand-held calculator turned out to be a "very judicious one," agrees Benjamin M. Rosen, veteran industry analyst at Morgan Stanley & Co. "It was a controversial decision," he says, "because TI did it at the expense of early leadership in semiconductor memories and microcomputers"—products that were to become the two most important in the industry's history. But because the company gambled and won, Rosen predicts that TI and the Japanese "are going to share the huge, consumer electronics business in the 1980s—they'll be the two major suppliers."

For a company that is making such waves in the electronics marketplace, TI is still something of an enigma, a company often misread by the outside world—particularly Wall Street. Until recently, TI seemed to like it that way. Earlier this year, though, J. Fred Bucy, TI's president, ordered a major push to promote the company's image as a leader in technology. He even showed up recently at a press conference in California, the first time that Bucy has done that, he admits, "in at least 10 years."

Nothing gets the scrappy, hard-nosed TI president angrier than to hear that his company is no longer regarded as a leader in technology. "The image we want is of a high-technology innovator—it's the key to our strategy," snaps Bucy. "Because of our highly visible successes, people say that our strategy is to come in second in a market and overwhelm the competition with our manufacturing power. That's not our fundamental strategy," he insists. But he adds: "We will use it if necessary."

What TI really is, maintains Glenn E. Penisten, a longtime TI executive who is now president of American Microsystems Inc. (AMI), "is an innovator in applying technology and exploiting it." TI, in fact, is the only semiconductor producer that is building end-user products and developing new applications for all market areas—consumer, military, and computers. "What's peculiar to TI among technology companies is that this company's driving force is innovating markets," says Jerry Wasserman, an industry expert at Arthur D. Little Inc.

It is clear now that TI long ago concluded that the Japanese were going to be its chief competitor worldwide. "With the Japanese, it's a war," declares Ronald J. Ritchie, the TI vice-president who heads consumer products. "They train their management that way." TI is fighting the same kind of war, and it is no accident that TI closely resembles a Japanese company in its highly structured organization, its management style, and its market approach.

TI will be able to compete strongly with the Japanese, declares Bruce D. Henderson, president and founder of the Boston Consulting Group, because it "follows the same underlying competitive approach the Japanese have used. TI combines scale, technology, and capital intensity," he says, "and once you have these three factors in combination, it's tough for competitors to catch up."

From the beginning, TI was willing to take the long-term point of view, according to Henderson. The company would commit itself to a 25% to 30% growth rate by building new plants while its first plant for a product was not yet going full tilt. TI assumed, he says, that it could then capture a big share of a growth market by taking advantage of declining unit costs to price its products below the competition's. The Japanese government, with an export-or-die outlook, sees such a strategy as logical, Henderson adds, but the U.S. government frequently takes an opposite point of view with its antitrust policies.

"TI has much of the style of the Japanese, such as the employee identification with the firm," agrees TI watcher Arnoldo C. Hax, of the Sloan School of Management at the Massachusetts Institute of Technology. Like Japanese companies, he says, TI stresses a strong spirit of belonging, a strong work ethic, competitive zeal, company loyalty, and rational decision-making. "The TI style creates a TI culture, and for the kind of people there, it works," he says.

"There is a certain similarity to the Japanese companies," acknowledges TI's Bucy. The company's planning and management systems "institutionalize the TI culture—it's a way to ensure our growth," he says. "Whatever other corporations call it, they will have to come up with something similar. If we [the U.S. companies] don't do that," Bucy states bluntly, "the overseas competition will take us."

The electronics slugfest to come

The battle with the Japanese is shaping up as a fierce one for the U.S. electronics industry, which still clearly dominates the booming world markets for both computers and semiconductor

Under its ten-gallon hat, a Japanese-style culture

The overpowering culture of Texas Instruments Inc., so vital to the success of the Dallas company's management systems, has its roots buried deep in a soil of Texas' pioneer work ethic, dedication, toughness, and tenacity. Says one former TI manager: "Everybody in that organization is either from Texas or just out of school. And they honestly believe—I used to believe it myself—that the company can do anything."

"The TI culture is a religion," pronounces one TI vice-president. As such, "the climate polarizes people—either you are incorporated into the culture or rejected," declares Arnoldo C. Hax, who has studied the company at the Sloan School of Management of the Massachusetts Institute of Technology. Some of his students who have gone to work at TI fit right in, but others quickly bail out.

Glenn E. Penisten, president of American Microsystems Inc., and a former TI executive, agrees. "I've seen people brought in at reasonably high levels and not survive . . . the culture tends to reject 'strange' individuals."

'Involvement teams.' TI figures that it takes five years to train a full-fledged TI manager. For those who survive the course, it is as a cog in a demanding, no-nonsense world. The management takes itself and the company very seriously. "There's not a helluva lot of frivolity over there," says another former TI executive. In fact, the company is developing its culture in a way that causes both competitors and admirers to compare TI to Japanese companies.

When J. Fred Bucy, TI president, described his Japanese competition recently, he could have just as easily been describing what he wants in his own company. "Japan has a culture and society well suited to achieving increased productivity and the growth that results from it," said Bucy. "They are hardworking, dedicated people. . . and are highly motivated, in part, because of a culture that assigns personal responsibility for the quality of work." And, he added, "there is a strong tendency in the Japanese culture to align personal goals with goals set by their companies. . . ."

Looking at TI, the similarities can be startling. More than 83% of all TI employees, for example, are now organized into "people involvement teams" seeking ways to improve their own productivity. At TI, "the employee is subservient to the success of the corporate entity," says a former TI manager. Adds another: "The company looks at its people as being completely interchangeable—kind of like auto parts."

---

devices. Japan, the world leader in consumer electronic products, knows that it must beat the Americans in the worldwide computer market if the island nation is to keep its export earnings growing in the 1980s. Five Japanese companies are hard at work on a $300 million, government-sponsored program to develop a new generation of semiconductor chips intended to leapfrog U. S. products and provide the essential building blocks for a new class of very-low-cost computers.

The unified effort has panicked some U. S. semiconductor producers. They wonder how Japan Inc., as the Japanese government-industry partnership is often called, can be stopped from taking over their business as it has already done in radios, stereos, television sets, and motorcycles. Bucy is concerned, but hardly panicked. There is a basic distinction, he feels, between TI and the U. S. companies that ran into the Japanese buzz saw earlier. "The big difference," Bucy told shareholders recently, "is that TI is the first major non-Japanese company [the Japanese] have run into that understands and uses the learning curve." And he added: "This is absolutely mandatory to compete successfully with the Japanese."

The learning curve certainly is chapter one in the TI "bible." The concept is fundamental to the success of TI's strategy in driving for the leadership position in a high-volume market because, the gospel goes, the company with the largest share of the sales has the best opportunity for profit.

The theory says simply that manufacturing costs can be brought down by a fixed percentage, depending on the product, each time cumulative volume is doubled. "It is not just spreading overhead over a larger volume of product produced," Bucy says. "It also involves constantly forcing manufacturing costs down through design improvement of the product and the production process." So the faster a producer can get into volume production, the earlier he can drop the price.

10 million functions on a chip?

The learning curve theory has never been better proven than in the semiconductor business, and TI has applied the same philosophy with great success in both the calculator and digital watch markets. Under TI's competitive pressure, the rest of the U. S. semiconductor industry is using the learning curve, too. Coupled with a high level of R&D, this should permit the U. S. to keep its lead in semiconductors, Bucy believes.

AMI's Penisten agrees. "I don't think Japan will do to the U. S. semiconductor industry what it's done to other [U. S. industries]," he says. "Our industry is too strong and moving too fast."

The premier learning curve at TI—and the cornerstone of most of the company's business—charts the declining cost of an electronic function. In 1960 the simplest functional circuit needed two transistors and five other parts. Today, 20,000 functions fit on a single chip of silicon. This incredible growth in circuit density has driven the cost of an electronic function to less than 1¢ today from nearly $10 in 1960. TI expects this trend, which reflects both technology and manufacturing learning curves, to continue through the 1980s. That means a single chip in 1990 could contain 10 million or more functions and cost less than a hundredth of a cent per function.

TI: Creating new, billion-dollar markets

With up to a two-year lead in mass producing the bubble memory, TI expects the device to take over the $3 billion-plus, mechanical disc-memory business in the same way that semiconductors wiped out the magnetic cores formerly used in all computer memories. The market—which is peanuts now—could exceed $1 billion by the mid-1980s. TI not only pioneered the electronic, educational device business—products that teach spelling, math, and how to tell time—but it still has little or no competition. TI will soon introduce, perhaps in early 1979, a line of home computers—an embryonic market that could soar to $3.5 billion by the early 1980s. Says one forecaster: "TI is the single company that is most likely to stimulate [that] phenomenal growth rate."

The power of this radically changing semiconductor technology cannot be overestimated. It has reduced the retail price of an electronic calculator to less than $10 from $1,600 in a single decade, and it transformed the 3-ton, $200,000 computer of 23 years ago into a 12-oz. hand-held unit priced at $300 today.

4 / Readings from *Business Week*

But just as in Japan, TI employees do not normally get fired—particularly those who have worked at the company for five years or more. "There's lots of yelling and screaming, but not much ripping off of badges," says one former TI employee. TI is not compassionate toward the manager who is not meeting the goals that he set for himself. "He'll be moved to the side, or down, or put on special assignment," comments a former TI manager. "But TI doesn't cut a guy's throat and put him out on the street."

The work ethic. Corporate loyalty is big at TI. In "Silicon Valley" south of San Francisco, where many of TI's semiconductor competitors are concentrated, "you've got a group of very bright people whose loyalty is focused on the industry, not on the company they work for," says Jack R. Yelverton, a veteran San Francisco executive recruiter for the industry. "At TI, it's the other way around."

Most of the experienced professionals that TI hires from other companies do not have a great deal of success. Says one who left after two years: "TI doesn't want experienced people; they want to hire them young and train them." Over the past five years, in fact, TI has hired 5,604 graduates right out of college.

The work ethic is a cornerstone of the TI culture. "If you didn't work overtime you were ostracized—at least in the early days," comments Bruce D. Henderson, president of the Boston Consulting Group. And it has not changed much since then. "When you're a professional and work for TI, long hours come with the territory," says one competitor. "They demand, and get, a lot of mileage out of their people."

TI still works a 42½-hour week, and 5:30 p.m. meetings "are rather common," says one former employee. "The office is certainly a good place to meet people on Saturday mornings. People show up because it's expected."

Keeping employees happy. Seniority is another common denominator with the Japanese. "Seniority is all-important at TI," says Jerry Wasserman, an industry consultant at Arthur D. Little Inc. "Other companies have badges where color denotes levels of authority, but at TI, your badge color shows your years at the company."

And like the Japanese, TI works to keep its employees happy. "TI tries hard to keep you in the fold by covering all aspects of life," says one former employee who is still impressed with the company's efforts. "They have this fantastic 'rec' center, with a gymnasium and baseball diamonds; they have a rod and gun club; and they have 75 acres on Lake Texoma, where a lot to build a cabin, or put a trailer on, costs you $43—and a nickel a year."

This is the primary force behind the "electronics revolution," which increasingly is being recognized as a force that will have a far greater impact on society than the industrial revolution had 200 years ago. As far as TI is concerned, the revolution has just begun.

Powered by continuing reductions in the cost of electronic logic, the world electronics industry will grow from about $100 billion last year to about $325 billion in the late 1980s, according to TI's predictions. But if the next generation of chips—called VLSI (very-large-scale integrated) circuits because each packs more than 100,000 functions—has a major impact on products by that time, TI believes that the world market could reach $400 billion. In either case, electronics in 10 years would be the world's fourth largest industry. Only automobiles, steel, and chemicals—each totaling about $500 billion—would be larger.

Four years ago, TI decided what size company it wanted to be by the late 1980s. It set $10 billion as its sales goal. That was a brash forecast for a company that had reached only $1.3 billion the year before. But TI has always set ambitious sales targets. As far back as 1949, when TI was only a $5 million petroleum exploration company, it set a goal of becoming a "good, big company"—one with $200 million in sales. In 1960 the next big goal became $1 billion by the early 1970s; that was reached in 1973. By 1966, the sales target for the late 1970s was put at $3 billion. This goal seems elusive since TI cracked $2 billion only last year. But based on a strong first half, analysts peg 1978 sales at $2.5 billion. If TI can do this, it might make its $3 billion target on schedule.

TI: Beating the Japanese at their own game

TI is already putting together the radically new production line—first in the world, it claims—needed to build the next generation of integrated circuits. It is here that a $300 million, Japanese government-industrial effort is trying to leapfrog the U.S. and take over world leadership. With its vigorous cost-cutting efforts, TI not only now dominates the U.S. market for calculators—beating the Japanese at the low-priced end and Hewlett-Packard Co. at the high end—but also is No. 1 in the worldwide, $1.8 billion market. TI is No. 1 in revenues in the fast-growing digital watch market, too. It is about the only company still assembling watches in the U.S.

Even some of TI's major competitors are believers now. "Hell, TI will make $6 billion by 1983," declares one company president, "so it will easily hit $10 billion in the 1980s." Adds one longtime TI senior executive who is now a very active competitor: "I'm convinced that TI will achieve $10 billion, but maybe not in their time frame, because so much depends on the economy."

To meet its ambitious goal, TI is Devices Inc., "and the cheaper memory becomes, the more we sell."

Nowhere is that better illustrated than in the "dynamic RAM," a random-access memory that in the past five years has taken the computer main-memory business away from magnetic cores. Each time that semiconductor makers quadrupled the amount of data storage on a chip, the chip price remained about the same, but total market dollars continued to soar. TI is a major producer of the first two such memories—4K and 16K—but it had to "brute force" the development of both devices to make up for bad initial chip designs. And TI came close to missing the boat with the current star, the 16K (16,384 bits of storage). TI got its second chance with the 16K only because of "bad planning" by Mostek Corp., the market leader, says Petritz of Inmos. Mostek did not expand its manufacturing capacity fast enough and was caught short when the market took off.

For TI, it was essential to be a leader and volume producer in 16K memories. "It is extremely difficult to go to the next big product if you haven't made it in the previous big part," says List. And the next big part for the industry is the incredible 64K memory. On one chip, it will store 65,536 bits of data—the basic memory size of a minicomputer in the early 1970s.

An embarrassing failure

The stakes are huge. Rosen of Morgan Stanley estimates that, by 1983, the market for this part alone will be 40 million units annually, with a market value of a quarter billion dollars. The new TI management is going all out for a leadership role, and Rosen says that the company "does seem to have more going for it this time around."

The Concept of Strategy and Policy / 5

For one thing, it may be first into production. TI built a big, highly automated module at Lubbock, Tex., specifically designed for volume production of the wafers for the 64K chips in 1979. According to List, that module is already working, making parts ahead of schedule. "We'll have the capacity to keep the lead in 64K," says List.

TI is announcing its 64K memory on Sept. 8, which puts it several months ahead of its competitors. That is important, because profit margins are much higher initially, and there is a good chance of the part becoming the industry standard, forcing competitors to redesign their products to be compatible.

That is exactly what Intel achieved in the mid-1970s with its medium-performance (8-bit) microprocessor. As a result, the California company has the lion's share of a market segment that amounts to nearly two-thirds of the entire computer-on-a-chip business. For TI, that represents a somewhat embarrassing failure, because the computer-on-a-chip is clearly the single most important reason why electronics will become so pervasive throughout society in the 1980s. Sales already are rising at 45% annually, which would put the 1980 market at a cool $1.1 billion.

There is irony in TI's failure in the so-called 8-bit microprocessor market. The company showed the brilliance of its strategic planning in 1975 when it introduced a new computer family that tied together both minicomputers and high-performance (16-bit) microprocessors by using the same architecture and software. But three years ago, List says, "we got too optimistic on how fast the 16-bit microprocessor would take over the market." In 1988, List now predicts, 35% of the market will still be 8-bit units, and TI is restudying its options in this Intel-dominated business.

As part of its catch-up game, TI is spending almost as much on R&D as it expects to gain in total microprocessor sales this year, and List figures that it will take no more than two years for TI to grab the technology leadership in microprocessors. But he is still juggling management, and his competition is divided over how fast TI can move.

Microprocessors cannot be "brute-forced," declares an executive from one microprocessor producer. "That's a hole in TI's strategy, and it may take four or five years to fix it." But a senior executive from another TI competitor disagrees. "Success in the microprocessor market is a software problem," he says. "For TI, it's now a matter of deciding their strategy and amassing the software to support it." TI's strategy could be to go after the high-performance Intel microprocessor, the executive suggests, "and in that case, look out, Intel."

If TI was overly optimistic with its 16-bit microprocessor, then the 8-bit makers certainly overestimated their ability to penetrate the oldest microprocessor market, which exploits the relatively slow-operating 4-bit model. Here, TI claims virtually the entire market with its TMS-1000 family, a fallout from its calculator business. Competitors call TI's product a "calculator chip," but List says he does not care. "With the profits we've got, they can call it anything."

Including internal sales, TI must be building close to 1 million of the small microprocessors a month. In just two years the price dropped to less than $2 from $5. "And it will be $1 next year," List predicts. "It certainly shows the power in that learning curve." Because of the low price, TI has been capturing markets, such as appliances and toys, that soak up huge numbers of units. This year alone it will ship 700,000 microprocessor game modules to the Parker Bros. Div. of General Mills Inc.

TI's major thrust into the distributed computing market could be called the company's second try to gain a major share of this hotly competitive business. The company started bragging "Texas-style" about making it big in the minicomputer business as far back as 1971, when the market was really beginning to take off. TI executives talked about becoming a $1 billion computer company and beating out Digital Equipment Corp. for the top spot. But for a number of reasons, it never came off. Nowadays, mention TI to one of the minicomputer leaders, and their reaction is likely to be no more than a yawn.

But that could be a mistake. The signs are multiplying that TI is moving on the distributed-computing front. "This company is a sleeping giant in computers—never underestimate TI," declares Charles T. Casale, an industry analyst for Bache Halsey Stuart Shields Inc. He reckons that the $150 million in minicomputers and terminals that the company sold last year will increase to $200 million or more this year.

Distributed computing

Other developments are even more impressive. One reason TI did not make it big in computers earlier was that it did not invest sufficient resources. In contrast, TI now has more than 500,000 sq. ft. of plant space under construction just for its distributed-computing business. Major centers are situated in Austin and Temple, Tex., in addition to Houston, which was the group's only location three years ago.

Two other problems that TI faced with distributed computing in the past were a critical lack of software and too few products. But software is rolling out now, and TI is rapidly filling out its entire product line. In June, for example, the TI group added six new terminals, including three "intelligent" models.

The broadening product line and the massive investment in plants are beginning to gain TI more attention from the rest of the distributed-computing industry. "We see TI more than we used to, and they've gotten a lot more aggressive in the marketplace," says Edward P. Gistaro, marketing vice-president of Datapoint Corp., one of the fastest growing manufacturers in distributed computing. "TI is as close as any of Datapoint's competitors to having a full family of machines," he acknowledges. "I think TI will be formidable."

This growing apprehension of TI as a competitor might be something new in distributed computing, but it is a well-understood feeling in the semiconductor industry. Penisten, the AMI president, for one, figures that TI always has its plans in place and its resources committed, "and you know they'll be a factor."

As a result, he is basing AMI's strategy on the premise that TI, International Business Machines, and Japan Inc. will be the primary forces in the semiconductor industry. "They will tend to shape the way the industry moves," Penisten explains, "and we work hard to continually understand the direction of those three so we can align our strategies with theirs." He adds: "We'll be in competition with them, but I prefer not to go head-on with them in a marketplace they intend to dominate, because you'll get run over if you do."

TI: Unleashing a flood of innovative new products

On Sept. 8, TI is introducing its "64K" memory, storing 65,536 bits of data on a single chip. The company expects to be the first into production, giving it an important several-month lead over competitors with a product expected to hit $250 million in annual sales in five years. With the bulk of the watch market still in analog-style models, TI in September will begin shipping the first all-electronic analog watch, using a display to create the image of "hands." Also this month, retailers will start selling Speak & Spell, a $50 learning aid from TI that teaches children how to spell by pronouncing each word, then interactively grading and scoring them. It is built around a voice synthesizer on a single chip, a technology that will spawn a flood of new TI products that can talk.

---

6 / Readings from *Business Week*

TI's magic in managing innovation

Running any $2 billion company with 68,000 workers in 45 plants spread throughout 18 countries is a tough management task. But when such a company is expected to grow 15% annually in a worldwide business keyed to rapid technology change and declining unit costs, the job of managing might seem all but impossible. To meet that challenge, Texas Instruments Inc. has successfully evolved one of the most formal planning systems in existence.

"If we hit $10 billion [by the late 1980s], it will be because we planned every foot of the way," emphasizes TI President J. Fred Bucy. Innovation is the lifeblood of the company, and the key to TI's success has been its novel, highly complex system to stimulate and manage innovation.

"It requires an extraordinary amount of coordination to work," says Arnoldo C. Hax, who follows TI at the Sloan School of Management at the Massachusetts Institute of Technology. But, he adds, "I think it has worked at TI."

Indeed it has. TI has grown at an average rate of 15% annually for the past 15 years and yet has kept the innovation juices flowing. "I would think that TI would be getting old and a little bit creaky at this point," comments Richard L. Petritz, an early research and development manager at TI who now heads Inmos Ltd. "But it is not happening."

George H. Heilmeier, who saw a large amount of cutting-edge technology during the three years that he ran the Pentagon's Defense Advanced Research Projects Agency, got his first, close-up look at TI recently when he joined the company as a vice-president, the first corporate officer TI has ever elected from the outside. "This is a large company that still has the esprit of a small company, and I'm not sure I understand that," he says. "It may be because they're all Texans," Heilmeier adds, "and it may be because it's a company run by engineers rather than by lawyers and accountants."

That kind of environment was precisely what Patrick E. Haggerty, then president and now honorary chairman, was aiming for when he decided in 1962 that TI was getting too big for all of its managers to sit down together and hammer out strategies. He formalized his own strategic planning style, but it took more than a decade of hard work before this "objectives, strategies, and tactics" (OST) system became an integral part of the TI culture. "Haggerty understood what it took to motivate people, and he worked hard to keep the company from becoming insensitive as it got bigger," says Glenn E. Penisten, a 16-year TI veteran who is now president of American Microsystems Inc. (AMI).

It was Mark Shepherd Jr., Haggerty's successor as president, who really made the OST system work. In the late 1960s, he split TI's annual expenditures into separate strategic (OST) and operating budgets, placing the strategic funds under the control of a corporate committee that was to set the guidelines for spending them. Under OST, a project-oriented management structure focuses entirely on tomorrow's growth, while a more conventional operating hierarchy concentrates entirely on today's profitability. Shepherd set up this dual reporting structure to ensure that managers did not underplay or postpone long-range strategic programs in favor of short-range profits.

OST is a highly decentralized "bottom-up" planning system, where more than 250 funded projects called tactical action programs—TAPs in TI jargon—drive more than 60 strategies that support the company's dozen business objectives. The objectives are now set up to build TI into a $10 billion company in 10 years. One TAP manager, for example, is responsible for developing a new liquid-crystal display (LCD) watch for the watch strategy manager, who, in turn, reports to the consumer objectives manager.

'Management by objective'

This OST pyramid is overlaid across TI's operating hierarchy of 32 divisions (ranging in annual sales from $50 million to $150 million each) and more than 80 product-customer centers ($10 million to $100 million each). The centers (PCCs) are roughly equivalent to departments, except that they are more self-sufficient. Many of them have their own engineering, manufacturing, and marketing units. TI pulls together a tactics program from whatever PCCs are required. "The real power of OST," says Inmos' Petritz, "is that it enables you to get into a new business without reorganizing your company to do it."

One 10-year TI veteran, now a major competitor, liked TI's system so much he patterned his own management structure after it. But he adds: "Frankly, TI's OST program is a label for management by objective, Haggerty's naval strategy system." Unlike military program management systems, however, at TI most TAP managers also manage PCCs, and strategy managers typically are division heads. In this way, TI gets away from the "handoff" problem between a separate development or planning group and the operating organization.

OST is a highly visible program where all managers are constantly measured against documented goals. There are monthly reviews, and TI's computerized scheduling, or PERT, system, is updated by status reports on every TAP. That gives top management a window deep into the company. "I don't believe in the hierarchy system where you have to funnel information through several management levels," says Bucy.

TI's Heilmeier observes: "It's impossible to bury a mistake in this company; the grass roots of the corporation are visible from the top. There's no place to hide in TI—the people work in teams, and that results in a lot of peer pressure and peer recognition." Adds Bucy: "An outside manager joining TI would be surprised at how much upper management knows. We communicate so thoroughly through OST that [managers] don't need day-to-day guidance."

On the other hand, Wilfred J. Corrigan, chairman of Fairchild Camera & Instrument Corp., a TI competitor, declares that "the middle manager [at TI] often finds that the system is really a tool to manage him, not the other way around." But Bucy says: "As long as the guys are on course, they don't get interfered with."

Even so, some managers do find the tight control stifling. "[Bucy] sets policies and procedures, and the consequences of not following them are quite severe," notes one longtime TI manager. While this executive believes that TI's management system is overdone, and at times serves to work against the company, he also sees it as a real strength of TI. "Companies need to be well-managed and disciplined," he says, "and though TI has gone overboard, I'd rather err that way than be like the many companies that go the opposite route."

AMI's Penisten is currently trying to transplant much of the TI planning system to his Santa Clara (Calif.) semiconductor company. But he worries that "you can quickly spend too much time on detail and spend all your energies on planning and reporting." Some of the questions that Penisten is still wrestling with: How does he get control without stifling creativity and interfering with decision-making, and how does he avoid creating a bureaucracy?

A constant search for ideas

TI officials believe that OST can be transplanted to other companies, but they warn that the system has grown in

The Concept of Strategy and Policy / 7

the TI culture, and its success depends partly on that structure. Professor Hax of MIT does not think it can be transplanted. "TI's formal structure and management systems can't be understood apart from the culture," he says.

Former TI managers generally give the company's structure high marks. "There are a lot of middle managers running around TI talking about 'growth share matrices' and 'learning-curve pricing,'" says one. "You don't get that depth of planning in other companies." Says a 17-year TI veteran who is now a competitor: "TI has numerous systems for getting people to think and to make their ideas known—management is constantly seeking ideas."

Just about now, TI managers are submitting more than 400 tactical proposals for OST money next year that range in thrust from product development and feasibility testing to cost reduction and new marketing techniques. Because TI uses zero-based budgeting—it was the first company to employ the concept—managers must rank their proposals in order of priority. Next March the process will culminate in a full week's strategic planning conference in Dallas attended not only by 500 managers but also by TI's board of directors. Together they will decide on the corporate plan and allocate funds.

TI is constantly refining the OST. In 1975, "we realized we had a problem; we were slighting the more speculative development efforts," says Charles H. Phipps, an assistant vice-president heading OST. So TI now asks its objectives managers to decide how much OST money TI should spend on such programs and to rank those proposals separately. Haggerty called them "wild hare" ideas, and the name has stuck.

Wild hare seems to be solving TI's problem. It funded the company's highly successful portable computer terminal, the first product on the market using magnetic-bubble memory devices.

Such funding has even started new businesses. TI's entry into the marine electronics market last fall was kicked off two years earlier by a wild hare grant. The result was a navigation receiver that was introduced at $2,095, a full $1,000 below its closest competitor.

Like any strategic planning effort, the original OST thrust was aimed externally at developing and building new technologies, products, and businesses. But TI has successfully turned the system inward as well. "We're using OST to look hard at internal funding programs that will impact productivity," Phipps says. Called people and asset effectiveness (P&AE), the system is aimed not only at reducing manufacturing costs but at paring indirect costs as well.

Like the OST program, P&AE took an entire decade to get fully accepted into the TI culture. But now the company has 83% of its employees organized into teams to participate in the planning and control of their own work to improve productivity. TI believes that P&AE has played a major role in good employee relations. One measure of its effectiveness, as well as that of TI's broad benefits package, was that TI is the "third largest, nonunionized corporation in the U.S.—after IBM and Kodak," Senior Vice-President James L. Fischer noted recently.

The OST spinoff is spawning a host of successful productivity improvements. Last year TI gave one of its $300 programmable calculators, along with six hours of training, to each of 8,000 technical and administrative personnel. In six months, the $3 million P&AE program had paid for itself by boosting the productivity of those people by 3.5% to 4%.

But most of the P&AE programs, which have to compete with other OST programs for funding, are closely tied to advanced manufacturing techniques. Factory automation is high on TI's list, and programs are under way to automate the assembly of calculators, large-scale integrated (LSI) circuits, and a host of other products.

Passing out $25,000 grants

Any large company, especially one with formal management systems, sooner or later finds that it is freezing out some innovation, and TI is no exception. But in 1973, the company started a program dubbed IDEA to further encourage innovation. TI splits up $1 million annually among 40 IDEA representatives—usually senior technical staffers, not managers—who pass out grants of up to $25,000 to employees with ideas for a product or process improvement.

If an employee is turned down by one IDEA representative, he can take his idea to another. "We've found that about a third to a half eventually get funded," says Vice-President Bernard H. List. "And once the guy gets his money, no one—not even Bucy—can take it away from him." Half of the ideas funded end up paying off. "But aside from the payoff," List says, "the motivational effect has been very positive."

With the IDEA program, TI employees avoid the massive presentation and documentation that OST requires. "We're just learning how to use it at the working and management levels," says Hector A. Cardenas, consumer technology head. "Like many institutionalized things, it was slow to get started."

But already, IDEA is starting an amazing number of innovative products, particularly in the consumer area. The $19.95 digital watch that tore apart the market in 1976 got its start as an IDEA program in the Semiconductor Group. "The people running the watch division figured it wouldn't work," Phipps recalls. "They were convinced that the watch was a jewelry business."

And in June, 1977, Cardenas himself went to an IDEA representative for money after his managers turned him down for OST funding because they did not believe that it was possible to manufacture a new type of watch. For less than $25,000, Cardenas and his team proved that TI could. And a year later, they were in New York announcing it—the first all-electronic, analog watch that uses a new type of liquid-crystal display to show the traditional hands.

Gene A. Frantz' idea was a low-cost speech synthesizer built on one tiny chip with voice quality equal to that of the telephone system. His team won a $25,000 award and "then spent a month convincing corporate research that we could implement its speech technology with our semiconductor technology," he says. The Frantz team did it, and the first product using their breakthrough technology was announced in June—a talking, learning aid to teach spelling. The $50 Speak & Spell is the first of what is expected to be a flood of products over the next several years using the revolutionary chip.

With these kinds of innovative products spilling out of TI now, it seems clear that the company is solving much of the problem of stimulating and managing innovation in a large company. There will always be room for many management styles, and other companies may not have to emulate the TI strategy to survive in the 1980s. "But TI seems to have discovered the style that allows a multibillion-dollar corporation to grow at 15% a year," points out TI's Heilmeier. "To match that, companies are going to have to share information with more people. They're going to have to maintain entrepreneurial spirit, and management is going to have to have good visibility into all of the company."

What gives TI its consumer clout

If "made in Texas" becomes as pervasive in the consumer electronics business in the 1980s as "made in Japan" is now, then the consumer electronics capital of the U.S.—perhaps even the world—will be the town of Lubbock, 350 lonely miles west of Dallas in the hot, arid, always windy plains of West Texas. For it was this agricultural town that Texas Instruments Inc. picked in 1976 to be the headquarters of its fledgling consumer operations.

The whole expansion out of Dallas was a very risky and costly experiment, even though TI did not call it that. The company's biggest gamble, by far, was that it could build consumer products in the U.S. that would be competitive in price with Japanese products. It was also the company's first attempt to set up the entire management and technology center of a group at one site, with the intention of adding nearby satellite assembly plants as needed. And Lubbock was the first test of a new factory design that made super-fast expansion possible because standard production modules could be added to an existing, central spine structure.

Surprisingly, the whole thing worked—a credit perhaps to Texan tenacity as well as to TI strategic planning. In fact, the successful way that TI is pursuing its strategic and tactical plans here should make Lubbock a textbook case of how to grow a major consumer business.

Because of the success of this tightly managed, intensive planning effort, TI has been able to build in just six years a consumer electronics operation with estimated sales of $400 million annually. And it was all the more remarkable because, at the same time, the company's two primary consumer markets—calculators and watches—were rapidly turning into classic, mature businesses. Today, no more than a handful of viable competitors are left, worldwide, from the hundreds that tried.

But the pace at Lubbock has not slackened; if anything, it is building in tempo as the company commits more and more money to creating innovative products and building the competitive production machine needed for its drive for global leadership. Nearly 500,000 sq. ft. of plant has been added in West Texas during the past two years. In Lubbock alone, 6,500 employees are now at work, a total that grows seasonally by as many as 3,000 more. Last year a satellite plant in Midland-Odessa started up, and watches and printer calculators are now being turned out in two 60,000-sq.-ft. modules. And just a few months ago, a second satellite went on line in Abilene.

TI is pushing automated assembly. Four automated lines working three shifts are now assembling TI's lowest-priced calculator. "They are the first of many such lines," says a TI manager, "and the only way we can build the low-end products in the U.S." By next year, 75% of all TI hand-held calculators will be built on such lines. The payoff is a 40% gain in productivity and a 35% reduction in floor space.

One key to automated assembly was a switch from rigid circuit boards to flexible film circuits on reels. This eliminated separate handling of the integrated circuit, the keyboard, and the display. The continuous lines also employ several robot arms that do "pick and place" tasks. At one work station, for example, a television camera locates the calculator on the conveyor for a robot, which picks it up and loads it into a carousel that applies foot pads and the date code. A second robot off-loads the calculator. Farther down the line, a similar setup loads a completed calculator into a test system that pushes the keys with bursts of air while a camera-equipped minicomputer "reads" the calculator display in a check for errors.

Just as important as automation are TI's vigorous "design to cost" efforts on all of its products. A good example is the company's lowest-priced calculator. It retailed for $45 in 1974 when it contained 119 parts. A 1976 redesign cut the number of parts to 22 and dropped assembly costs dramatically to make possible a $10 price tag. The latest redesign pares the number of assembly operations from 44 to 26 and cuts the number of parts to just 17.

Cutting the price in half

TI is taking a similar path with its printing calculators as part of a two-year campaign to wrest market share away from the Japanese. The U.S. company started with one big advantage: Its thermal print head, which uses integrated-circuit technology to burn the characters into heat-sensitive paper, enabled it to build its printer with just 90 parts, compared with 150 for an impact printer. Now TI has cut the part count to 35 by designing a snap-together assembly. By reducing assembly costs this way, TI hopes to crack the market wide open by 1980, with new units "you can hold in your hand that will sell for $30 to $40," says a TI executive. TI's printer model now sells for $80 to $90, and "the price has to be cut in half to grow that market," he says.

TI has also tackled the potentially awesome problem of handling repairs in impressive fashion. It has gotten rid of all the paperwork by turning to a computer-based information system at its central calculator and watch repair facility in Lubbock. A bar-code label, similar to that used in supermarkets, is stuck on each incoming product. Hand-held "wands" that optically read the bars keep track of the product as it moves from station to station.

The system not only slices TI's repair shop space and the cost of repair but also provides better customer service. TI can find any product being repaired by looking up its serial number, or the customer's name and zip code. "When a customer calls us wondering what's happened to his calculator, we can tell him immediately where it is in our repair cycle," says Gordon C. Chilton, customer services manager. The operation has generated so much interest from other companies that TI is likely to offer the internally developed system as a commercial product.

Its own efforts aside, TI's competitive position has been aided a great deal this year by the soaring value of the Japanese yen in relation to the U.S. dollar. Japanese makers of consumer products have had to increase prices of their exports to the U.S. across the board.

That, in turn, has allowed TI to raise its prices by about 10% on several calculator models this year. Since the company is still coming down the cost-learning curve on those models, the price increases should do a lot for profits. "The yen has helped us," says one TI manager. "We haven't had to make price moves that didn't make a whole lot of sense from a business point of view."

TI has not dropped watch prices this year either. Because all new watches introduced this year carry higher prices, "the average price of everything we sell is going up now," says Thomas D. George, manager of the Time Products Div. This is because the company is expanding its product line into the medium-price watch market, an area that died out two years ago in the great price wars. "Now TI and Casio are moving in to fill the void," says John McDonald, president of Casio Corp., a major Japanese-owned competitor.

The switch to liquid-crystal display (LCD) watches from the push-to-see LED models is happening faster than TI had expected, which is causing some short-term bumps for the company, since it only started selling LCD watches a year ago. Even so, TI's watch sales should exceed $100 million this year. The company has broadened its digital line to 80

The Concept of Strategy and Policy / 9

models and will soon be selling its first analog watch, an all-electronic version that uses an LCD to display the hands. It is aimed at the fast-growing, quartz-analog watch market now dominated by K. Hattori & Co.'s Seiko brand.

Without a doubt, the most exciting consumer electronics product in history is the personal computer. And no company has launched a more meticulous planning effort than TI has, supported as it is by dozens of development and test projects. Nearly everyone in the business believes that TI's entry is only a matter of time, and they are plenty worried over the prospect. Even though TI has yet to introduce a product, Creative Strategies International, a San Jose (Calif.) market research firm, predicts that by next year the company will dominate the market.

Mass-producible software

The personal computer has a good chance of becoming the most important consumer product of the 1980s. Retail sales of personal computers, both for home and nonhome use, will rise to nearly $3.5 billion in 1982, predicts Creative Strategies. "TI is the single company," according to the research firm, "that is capable of stimulating the phenomenal growth rates" that it has forecast.

To turn the personal computer into its kind of high-volume, low-cost business, TI knows that it will be necessary to change the nature of the computer business. Currently, computer hardware is cheap enough, but the customized software to run the machines is too high in price for consumers. TI has to make the software mass-producible, and it not only has found a way but also has been testing the concept for a year with its SR-59 programmable calculator.

Called "solid-state software," tiny modules containing a permanent semiconductor memory are simply plugged into the back of the calculator to turn it into a powerful special-purpose machine for such jobs as statistics and security analysis. TI will use the plug-in modules for all of its small computers, which it believes will make them easy enough for the average person to use.

TI also has been working hard to develop and test software application packages for small businessmen and to find the best way to distribute and service its personal computers. The company is drawing heavily from test programs conducted with the SR-59. The prototype Houston Learning Center, where TI gives training courses on how to use the programmable, was a rousing success. Now TI is expected to start adding significant numbers of these centers to train small businessmen as well as consumers in how to use its upcoming small computer line.

Network of learning centers

A few years ago, TI seriously considered building a worldwide network of its retail stores to sell the company's expanding line of consumer products. TI Supply Co., its wholly owned distributor, still operates several stores, but it looks as if the company has given up that approach. "TI will play a big role," says Ronald J. Ritchie, vice-president for consumer products, "but we won't set up a large number of retail outlets." Instead, TI will set up the network of learning centers, where the buying public can see products demonstrated and learn how to use them. "Then," he says, "they can buy [at the retailer] where they can get the best deal."

While TI's timetable is not set, the company is likely to introduce several personal computers in the next year. The first, designed to operate with a home television set, will probably be priced in the $300 to $400 range and may be called a home information center. "We're not necessarily positioning it as a computer," Ritchie says.

A small business computer selling for $700 to $900 is expected to follow, and it will have larger data storage to handle such things as inventories. This model will be sold off the shelf by retailers and business-equipment dealers and will operate with plug-in software modules that have self-instructing programs. That means the computer would "ask" the operator for entries or decisions. Such "very small business computers" will account for more than $1 billion in revenues by 1982, according to Creative Strategies.

The personal computer is not the only high-growth consumer market for the mid-1980s, as far as TI is concerned. The company figures that personal communications will be a $3 billion annual market by then. Some companies in the telephone autodialer business are convinced that TI will move into their business, marketing an electronic telephone with a built-in autodialer. TI stubbed its toe in the communications market last year when it announced, but never marketed, a "smart" citizens band radio (BW—May 23, 1977). As innovative as this product was, TI's timing into the failing CB market was awful. "This was a case," a TI executive admits, "where we violated our own strategic planning rules—and paid for it."

The real sleeper in TI's bag of consumer tricks for the 1980s, however, could easily be its learning aids, already one of its fastest-growing product segments. The company kicked off this business two years ago with the Little Professor, a calculator-like math trainer and game player that, so far, has had sales of more than 1.6 million units. Five more learning aids have followed—three this year alone—that teach math, spelling, and how to tell time. "TI has created a new product category in electronic educational devices," says Benjamin M. Rosen, an analyst with Morgan Stanley & Co.

Speak & Spell, just now getting into stores, is one of the most innovative products to come out of TI in years. The unique product stores more than 200 words in its semiconductor memory and employs a patented, one-chip voice synthesizer that some scientists had believed was years off. It pronounces a word, and the child, using a keyboard, attempts to spell the word on a display. If the child fails after two tries, Speak & Spell says: "That is incorrect," and goes on to spell it, pronouncing each letter and the entire word. The learning aid will sell for $50, and TI does not expect to catch up this year with the flood of incoming orders.

Speak & Spell is another good example of TI strategic planning. It opens up a new market of potentially high growth that TI might well dominate. It draws heavily on other parts of the company for technology. And it has a high parts commonality with other products. TI, in fact, has almost no competition in any learning-aid products. "The Japanese have pretty much stayed away," says Kirk Pond, Calculator Div. manager.

The voice-synthesizer product is just the beginning. "We're doing research to build a whole product line," Pond says. Late this year, in a move to position Speak & Spell as a mass consumer item, TI will start selling $15 plug-in modules that expand the product's vocabulary and offer adult spelling games. TI is also thinking about giving an interactive voice to its math learning aids.

In fact, the voice synthesis and semiconductor technology behind Speak & Spell has so much market potential that it has stunned competitors. "It's a marketing breakthrough," says Arthur E. Fury, vice-president at Siliconix Inc. Fury sees it as evidence that TI shares his view of a near future in which spoken words will replace warning lights as safety devices in cars and airplanes, or just about any place where recorded messages and answering systems are needed.

One promising near-term application is in the teaching of foreign languages. Morgan Stanley's Rosen predicts that TI will come out next January with the first machine to teach languages. And the technology also should give a voice to TI's upcoming home computer.

"By taking the normal cost-performance curve in the semiconductor industry," Rosen says, "we should easily be able to get up to 20,000-word products in the next 10 years." That would provide a vocabulary for a wide variety of products, including dictionaries that could pronounce a word as well as spell it and directories for telephone numbers, addresses, and the like.

The reverse side of the speech-synthesis coin is speech recognition. Rosen predicts that speech-recognition devices with the ability to understand thousands of words could be available in the 1980s. "With 3,000 to 5,000 words of speech recognition," he says, "you could dictate rough drafts into a home computer and have it print the draft out." It is hardly surprising, then, to learn that TI is currently going all out to develop speech-recognition technology. ∎

WANTED:
A Manager to Fit Each Strategy

Manpower planning and strategic planning have become two of the most popular catchphrases in management parlance. Of chief executives responding to a recent survey, 85% listed manpower planning as one of the most critical management undertakings for the 1980s. The popularity of strategic planning—and particularly the phase known as product portfolio analysis—is pointed up by the growing practice of diversified companies to identify products by market share and growth potential, and to base long-range capital allocations and operational goals on individual product life cycles. Under this concept, products with a high market share but a low growth potential, for example, are used as cash cows to fund star performers that may not yet be self-sufficient in cash flow.

A joint concept. All too often, however, chief executives speak of manpower and strategic planning as though they were separate functions. Management experts warn that corporations failing to link the two concepts may be sounding a death knell for both. The problem, as these experts perceive it, is that corporate manpower officers still tend to weigh specialized, product-line knowledge more heavily than general management skills in making executive assignments. They ignore the fact that the entrepreneurial type of manager who brought a product line from only, say, a

Meshing strategic planning with executives' skills. A guard isn't a quarterback

2% share of market to 20% in three years may not be the right person to continue managing that line with equal effectiveness once it becomes a mature product with little growth potential. Very likely the entrepreneurial type's forte is risk-taking and innovating, while cost-cutting and pushing productivity—the essence of operating a mature, cash-generating business—may well be anathema to him.

"Too often it's like trying to put your best guard into the quarterback's slot—it just can't work," says consulting psychologist Harry Levinson, of Belmont, Mass. Adds Richard J. Hermon-Taylor, vice-president of Boston Consulting Group: "I just don't think companies give a lot of explicit attention to the personality attributes of management when they are considering significant changes in strategy."

But some companies do recognize the link between manpower and strategic planning and are striving to match a manager's personal orientation or style with operating strategy.

CHASE MANHATTAN BANK. When the trust manager retired, corporate management decided that the department, whose operations had been essentially stable, should focus on a more aggressive growth strategy. Instead of seeking a veteran banker, Chase hired a man whose main experience had been with International Business Machines Corp. "We felt he had that strong IBM customer marketing orientation," explains Alan F. Lafley, Chase's executive vice-president for human resources. Similarly, when Chase reoriented its retail banking business from a low-margin operation, in which the stress was on keeping down costs, to a more expansionary enterprise offering broader consumer financial services, it hired—because of his entrepreneurial skills—an executive who had been a division chief for a small industrial firm overseas. The former head of retail banking, who was viewed as a strong cost-cutter, is now successfully whipping some of Chase's European operations into better financial shape.

HEUBLEIN'S UNITED VINTNERS INC. The subsidiary split its wine operations in two in 1977, forming a premium wine division to stress quality over volume and a standard division to emphasize aggressive pricing and efficient volume production. The company chose a wine professional, Robert M. Furek, its previous marketing vice-president for all wines, to run the premium wine business. But it tapped Harold G. Spielberg, formerly personal products manager for Gillette Co., to be general manager of United's new Standard Wines Div. The sales staff was drastically reshuffled along similar quality-vs.-volume lines. "People in our premium wine company tend to have more wine background, while those in our standard wine company come out of consumer products and food companies," an official concedes.

CORNING GLASS CO. It had projected fast growth for its fledgling optical fibers business over the next decade, and it shifted the head of the company's television tube business to direct the new venture. The growth of the tube business had leveled, and its manager had shown himself to have entrepreneurial flair, says Richard A. Shafer, Corning's director of management and professional personnel. "Optical fibers is clearly an entrepreneurial thing," Shafer explains. "We don't know what the i's and t's are, so we can't get someone who dots i's and crosses t's." A manager from Corning's more mature electronics business replaced the television tube head.

In December, ironically, Corning reshaped its electronics strategy, deciding that the market was starting to expand again, and that it needed a growth-oriented manager. It placed a manufacturing specialist who had "shown a great deal of flair in working with customers" in the top marketing slot for electronics, and, says Shafer, "it looks like he's turning it around."

Although such moves sound simple to arrange, many companies are reluctant to choose managers primarily on the basis of managerial orientation or personality traits. Appointing outsiders as managers can be demoralizing for executives who assumed they were next in line. Finding a challenging spot for a competent manager whose only fault is that his department's strategy has changed can also be a problem, particularly for companies that do not have the luxury of numerous divisions and products. Moreover, appraising an individual's managerial orientation or style and determining the type needed for a specific job are imprecise tasks at best. "Too few people are keeping adequate records of their employees' behavior patterns, and too few companies are writing job descriptions focusing on needed behaviors," Levinson says.

The TI story. It can be a hit-or-miss proposition. For example, Texas Instruments Inc. has adopted a manpower planning policy that sounds as if it comes out of a behavioral science textbook. "As a product moves through different phases of its life cycle, different kinds of management skills become dominant," says Charles H. Phipps, manager of strategic planning. "It may be in the nature of an entrepreneurial manager to continue to take risks, but if the business gets too large, then top management can no longer tolerate wide swings in performance."

But although TI takes great pains to

assess its managers in terms of personal orientation, it failed to capitalize on its early lead in integrated circuits largely because it misjudged the style needed to manage the product line. The story goes back two decades. Jack Kilby, one of TI's foremost researchers and a pioneer in integrated circuit technology, had been pegged as a brilliant scientist but not a strong manager. In 1959, when TI formally launched its IC development program, it placed an executive skilled in administrative chores in charge, with Kilby subordinate to him. The company ignored Kilby's "strong desire to lead his brainchild into the marketplace," Phipps recalls.

To placate Kilby, TI moved the new manager elsewhere in 1961 and let Kilby manage the fledgling IC department. Not surprisingly, Kilby stressed innovation and research at the expense of financial controls, and a few years later he was gently eased out of the department and back to research. Top management brought in managers from TI's technically mature germanium transistor department to provide tighter cost controls.

The tighter controls were introduced, but TI failed to recognize that Kilby's research orientation was really what the IC department needed at that stage. The new management team did not provide the technical push needed to get the IC operation, still in the development phase, off to a fast commercial start. When J. Fred Bucy became head of TI's semiconductor operations in 1967, he swept out most of the IC management and again put in technically oriented people. The result: TI went on to pioneer brilliantly in bipolar integrated circuits and became a competent follower, though not a leader, in the newer metal oxide semiconductor technology.

A chastened TI has since redoubled its

But does all the scientific selection matter? Old-style managers still win points

efforts to match management orientation with job needs. Bucy, now president, personally reviews the records of the top 20% of TI's managers. But Phipps admits that the company still has no all-encompassing answer as to how to fit the manager to the strategy.

Several companies are trying hard to formalize programs that will at least keep them heading in the direction of making perfect managerial meshes. Chase's Lafley, a 27-year veteran of General Electric Co. who was recruited in 1975 to set up a strategic manpower planning program, says his group has "started at the top of the bank and addressed every one of the positions, checked the strategy of the division, and checked whether the people leading the divisions had the proper [behavioral] criteria." It has not been painless. Lafley says that 200 to 300 people have left the bank, "at least half of whom were encouraged to leave because their skills didn't fit our strategies."

'Growers' vs. 'undertakers.' At GE, an adherent of product portfolio analysis, strategic objectives for the company's wide-ranging products are defined as "grow," "defend," and "harvest," depending on the product life cycle. Now its general managers are being classified by personal style or orientation as "growers," "caretakers," and—tongue-in-cheek—as "undertakers" to match managerial type with the product's status. Notes one consultant and GE-watcher: "I hear they have a shortage of growers, but they are making great efforts to remove the undertaker types who are heading up growth businesses."

A look at the game of musical chairs recently played in GE's Lighting Business Group in Cleveland tends to support that observation. "The lighting business is mainly mature, but we just designated international operations as a growth area in our five-year forecast," explains Harry T. Rein, the group's manager for strategic planning. John D. Hamilton, the manager responsible for its manpower planning, says he and the executive manpower staff at corporate headquarters "looked at the whole pool of corporate talent." They decided to move in a manager from GE's motor division who had an industrial rather than lighting background, but who seemed to show an entrepreneurial flair.

Corning's match-ups. Perhaps the most formal integration of personal managerial styles and strategic objectives is being done by Corning Glass. A personnel director has been assigned specifically to assess the company's top 100 managers for such qualities as entrepreneurial flair. Each of 11 other personnel development managers is responsible for gathering skills data for about 300 lower-echelon managers. "We're asking incumbents and their bosses what you need to have on the job, because we want to know what goes into success," Richard Shafer says.

The process is easier for small companies, which can assess the types of managers employed by larger competitors and emulate their approach to staffing. In 1974, Prime Computer Inc., a Wellesley Hills (Mass.) minicomputer maker, had sales of only $6.5 million and was operating in the red. The next year, Kenneth G. Fisher left Honeywell Inc. after 20 years to become Prime's president, and he immediately started to hire new managers from companies like his former employer.

"We wanted people from big companies that had already been through what we were going through," Fisher explains. "We assumed that we were going to succeed extraordinarily, and we needed men who had been through all the plateaus before." Fisher has since increased the managerial staff from 15 to 260 people. Last year, Prime's sales were up to $153 million and net income to $17 million, but Fisher is still looking for managers from much larger companies. "We're building a management substructure that can manage a $500 million company," he says.

Doubts about it all. Fisher notes that recruitment of executives with the sophistication gained at giant companies induced Prime to automate its process for laying out printed circuit boards much earlier than competitors of its own size. Similarly, Prime computerized factory scheduling, material control, and other functions long before sales volume justified such an investment. This has let the company operate with an administrative staff at least one-third smaller than would otherwise have been required. Fisher boasts that Prime gets revenues of about $70,000 per employee, compared with an average in the minicomputer industry of about $35,000.

Despite such successful results from strategic manpower planning, many companies remain uninterested in the concept. Says Chairman James L. Ketelsen of Tenneco Inc., who prefers versatile, jack-of-all-trades managers: "It doesn't make that much difference to us whether it's a growth business or a stable business per se. Most good managers can run any kind of business." Many behavioral scientists shudder at such views, but they hope that 10 years from now fewer chief executives will hold them. ∎

SUN AND ARCO
HOW CONTRASTING STRATEGIES MADE DIFFERENT COMPANIES

Just 15 years ago the forerunners of Atlantic Richfield Co. and Sun Co. were neck-and-neck competitors, amazingly similar in size, in business mix, in management style, and even in location. Today they are vastly dissimilar. ARCO is No. 8 in income among the U. S. oil giants, Sun is No. 12. Over the years they have chosen strikingly different strategies, but none so sharply delineated as in their recently announced capital plans for the future. For ARCO there is a bold, five-year, $20 billion program, 60% of which goes to prospecting and developing U. S. oil fields. For Sun, there is a more modest, three-year, $3.6 billion plan, half of which goes for exploration and development. And with its recent $2.3 billion agreement to buy the U. S. assets of Texas Pacific Oil Co., Sun will get more oil and exploratory lands.

That both are going after oil is unremarkable. At $28 a bbl., oil is the most valuable asset a company can have. But the size of the two programs and the nature of their thrust is remarkable because it shows the differing ways each views its future. As a result of those differences, the gap between the two companies may widen rather than narrow over the next decade.

Both have grown staggeringly by any measure. Much of the growth can be attributed to the meteoric rise in the price of oil. And certainly, the relative size of ARCO vs. Sun is partly a reflection of ARCO's luck in finding North Slope oil. But it is also a result of the differing strategies of the two companies.

Exposure to risk

At ARCO the plan has had one major guideline: to find oil in the U. S. The company has changed tactics frequently; it has looked for partners, taken on high debt, made use of multiple technologies, and managed multiple risks to accomplish its goal. Sun has been more conservative, sticking with a difficult technology to produce oil in Canada even at the risk of losing momentum elsewhere. It has stayed with its investments longer, and it has made fewer plays. On the surface, this conservative path ironically appears to have exposed Sun to more risks than ARCO's entrepreneurial way.

In 1965 both companies were regional, medium-size refiners eager to compete in the big leagues. Both were crude-short when crude was cheap and foreign supplies relatively stable. Both managements came out of the Philadelphia Main Line conservative mode that produced paternalistic employers, slow change, and unexciting results. Atlantic Refining Co. (ARCO's name at that time) had recently been taken over by a Western wildcatter and entrepreneur, Robert O. Anderson, who was its largest shareholder and who had become its chairman and chief executive. Sun Oil Co. (Sun's former name) had just taken a major gamble—betting one-third of its assets on syncrude from Alberta's Athabasca tar sands. Sun was then slightly larger than Atlantic; at $925.2 million, its revenues were 12% higher, and its net income of $84.8 million was 28% greater than that of its rival.

The contrast today is dramatic. Although ARCO grossed 54% more than Sun's $10.8 billion, its net exceeded Sun's $699.9 million by $466 million, or some 67%, making it far more efficient on the bottom line. Roughly 16% of the gross assets of both companies are in nonenergy diversifications. But ARCO earned 8.3% of its net before taxes on these assets, while Sun earned only 1%.

Numbers are only one facet of the difference between the two companies. In nonenergy ventures, for example, Sun has elected to wet its feet in a series of diversifications that ranged from trucking and industrial distribution to real estate and leasing operations, culminating in its abortive attempt to gain control of the medical instrument manufacturer, Becton, Dickinson & Co. ARCO has made one bold move into other natural resources with its 1977 acquisition of Anaconda Co. (copper and aluminum).

On one point both managements do agree. Both entered the coal business by small acquisitions, and both are beefing up that business right now. Sun already is earning money from its coal—some $31 million last year. ARCO, much smaller in coal, lost $12 million. Both companies see coal as the next major energy venture, but each regards it as an alternate play to its main goal.

It is in energy ventures, however,

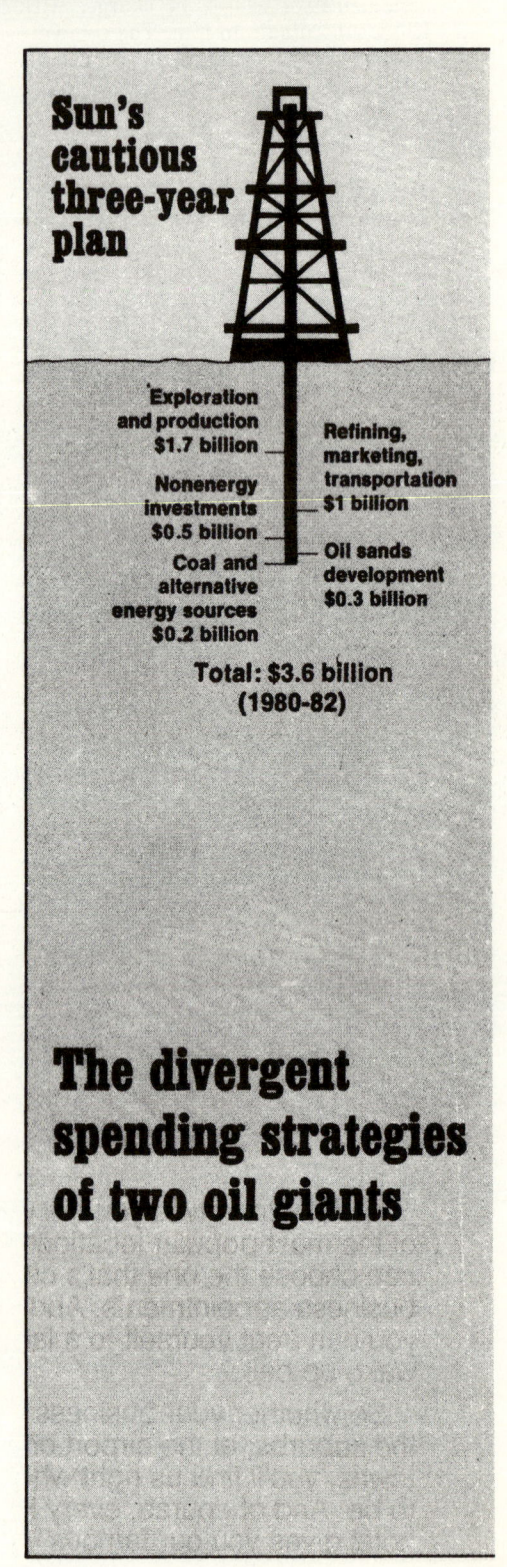

Sun's cautious three-year plan

Exploration and production $1.7 billion

Nonenergy investments $0.5 billion

Coal and alternative energy sources $0.2 billion

Refining, marketing, transportation $1 billion

Oil sands development $0.3 billion

Total: $3.6 billion (1980-82)

The divergent spending strategies of two oil giants

14 / Readings from *Business Week*

ARCO's bold five-year plan

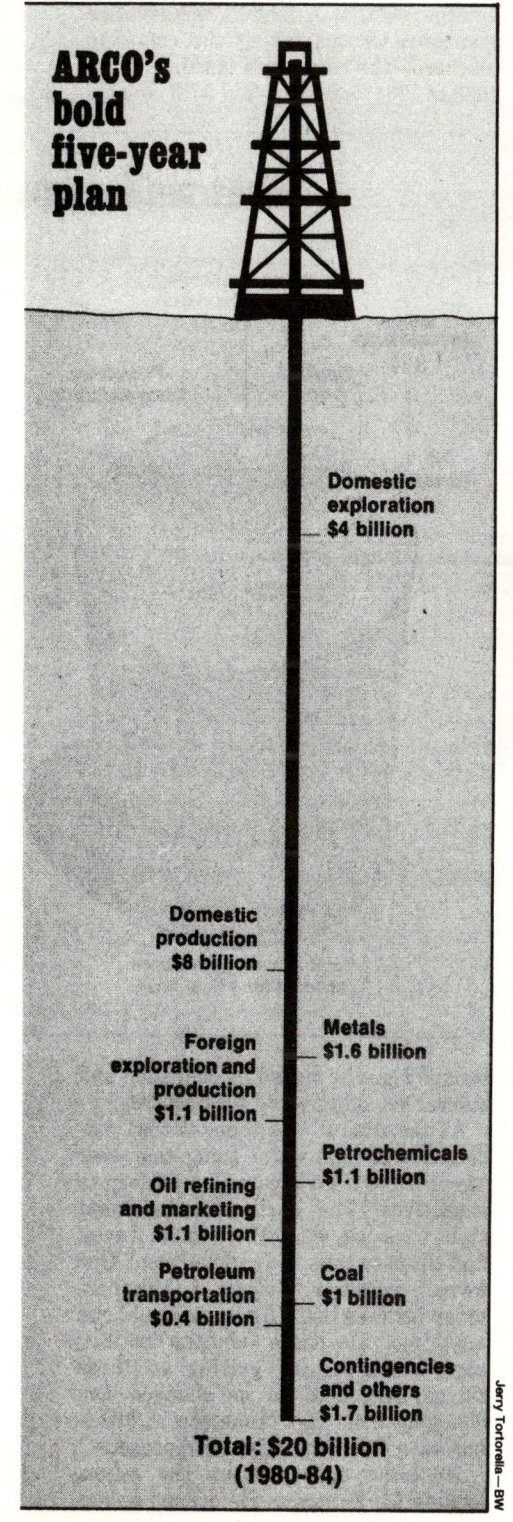

- Domestic exploration $4 billion
- Domestic production $8 billion
- Foreign exploration and production $1.1 billion
- Oil refining and marketing $1.1 billion
- Petroleum transportation $0.4 billion
- Metals $1.6 billion
- Petrochemicals $1.1 billion
- Coal $1 billion
- Contingencies and others $1.7 billion

Total: $20 billion (1980-84)

Jerry Tortorella—BW

where the major differences between the two companies' strategies appear. Both companies agreed on the same basic facts about oil in 1965. U.S. supplies were dwindling as its consumption was rising. There would be a U.S. shortfall in the 1970s, and oil would become more valuable as the shortfall increased. As prices went up for the essential resource, inflation would rise, although neither company (nor any economist) predicted its magnitude. Both needed to grow rapidly to compete for the remaining oil plays that were still around. Indeed, both looked to acquire the same Midwestern refining and marketing company, Sunray DX Oil Co., to grow large enough to make those plays. And both looked for stable areas in which to bet.

On this last point, however, the two parted company. Anderson was convinced that as oil became more valuable, governments inevitably would become increasingly protective of their supplies. Accordingly, he accelerated the move, begun by his predecessor, Henderson Supplee Jr., to withdraw from foreign dependency and move toward domestic self-sufficiency.

J. Howard Pew, Sun's chairman in 1964, stuck with the strategy of foreign ventures, relying on stable political regimes and on his friendly relations with Alberta Premier Ernest C. Manning and Venezuela's chief, Romulo Betancourt, to provide the long-term resources his company needed. Sun also held leases on the Persian Gulf in Iran.

ARCO: DOMESTIC SELF-SUFFICIENCY

ARCO's primary strategy, to become domestically self-sufficient in oil, is still under way. Today ARCO gets 95% of its 568,000 bbl. of oil per day of production from U.S. sources. That still leaves a shortfall of 31% at its refineries—one that Anderson is trying to fill largely by fielding more seismic exploration crews than any other company in the U.S. The other parts of ARCO's long-range plans—to diversify into other natural resources and into petrochemicals—are also in progress. Its big move into Anaconda puts it squarely among the top producers of copper, aluminum, and uranium. Its $1 billion planned investment in coal, now a relatively small operation, is designed to make the company the No. 5 producer by 1990. And its $2.1 billion petrochemical investment, already in place, is expected to become far more valuable as oil becomes too expensive to burn.

Even though ARCO has dropped its present shale plans, selling its 60% interest in a major venture in May, and scaled down its ambitious petrochemical plans by 50% (it had planned to build two more refineries in the mid-1970s, but the plan was dropped in 1977), Anderson insists that ARCO is on track. "Our strategy has never changed," he says, "and I don't think it's apt to."

But Anderson believes that soaring oil prices and new exploration technology, which permits much deeper drilling in rugged environments, have dramatically shifted the odds back in favor of its traditional business. To grab more than its share of the potential rewards, ARCO's $20 billion capital program is aimed at outspending other oil companies its size by 50%—and overwhelming its $3 billion-per-year cash flow. Although loaded down with more debt than such industry giants as Gulf, Standard Oil of California, and Sun, ARCO plans to keep it that way. "We expect to refinance $2 billion in debt which comes due in the next four years, and to do a considerable amount of borrowing beyond that," says Claude O. Goldsmith, vice-president of finance.

To concentrate on conventional oil, ARCO slashed $1.2 billion from its budget for the shale oil plant. With construction almost under way, Anderson decided that "oil shale is the type of resource you can't force the timing with. It's much closer [to being economic] now than it has ever been, but I'm still not sure it's totally here yet."

Capital dollars thus freed will be quickly dropped into oil and gas exploration and production, which is scheduled for a $12 billion infusion by 1984. "That's more money than we knew existed in history," says one gleeful ARCO oil and gas man. To some extent, the com-

The Concept of Strategy and Policy / 15

pany will be playing catch-up in areas that already have become hot plays, such as the Rocky Mountain Overthrust Belt and the Tuscaloosa Trend in Louisiana and East Texas. ARCO is eager to test its own acreage nearby.

But in other frontier areas, ARCO will be breaking new ground. "We don't intend to be tag-alongs," says Vice-Chairman William F. Kieschnick. "In some areas we'll just have to have faith that we're doing the right thing now." Last year, ARCO was high bidder on $140 million in tracts in the Beaufort Sea off Alaska's North Slope, where a single exploratory well may cost $50 million. The award of the tracts has been held up by environmental suits, but ARCO expects to proceed with seismic work this summer. The company also amassed more than 2 million acres in the Appalachian Overthrust Belt, which stretches from Mississippi to New York, and it is likely to begin a major exploration program in the eastern Kentucky part of this zone soon.

Although more and more domestic companies are turning to secondary and tertiary production—in wells that bring up as little as 30 bbl. of oil a day from 8,000-ft. depths—the word has come down from Anderson that he wants more wildcats and more aggressive spending in new basins. Executive Vice-President Edward M. Benson Jr. tells of a discussion he and Kieschnick had with exploration people in Dallas: "We told them there was too much emphasis on bread-and-butter [known fields] than there should be, and we expect them to develop major new plays to search for big reserves."

Other companies are upping their ante in domestic petroleum. But much of this money is going to buy existing reserves, such as Getty's $267 million purchase of some Ashland wells, Shell's awesome $3.7 billion acquisition of Belridge's heavy oil fields in California, and Sun's giant Texas Pacific buy. Argues Anderson: These transactions are "simply banking ventures for someone who wanted to tie up known amounts of domestic petroleum. We're just not in the banking business." Another company executive says flatly, "It's cheaper to find oil than buy it."

ARCO is counting on the golden touch it has had in the past. The company made the first strike at Alaska's Prudhoe Bay, which at 10 billion bbl. is the largest domestic discovery on record. Owned also by Exxon Corp. and Standard Oil Co. (Ohio), the field is producing more than 1.5 million bbl. a day, some 16% of U. S. production.

The corollary to this domestic strategy is the reduction of foreign risk, the nature of which ARCO has learned the hard way. Oil properties it acquired earlier in Venezuela, Algeria, Libya, and Iran were all expropriated in the last decade. The most recent blow, the cutoff last year of 100,000 bbl. a day of Iranian crude, reduced the self-sufficiency of ARCO's four domestic refineries from 79% in 1978 to 69% last year.

"Its exploration budget outside the U. S. is practically nil," complains Charles C. Cahn Jr., an analyst with Sanford C. Bernstein & Co., who believes

Sun Chairman Burtis: After the aggressive bid for Texas Pacific, he is likely to play it safe.

ARCO's refusal to go abroad is causing it to lose out on some excellent foreign plays. ARCO is raising its budget abroad to $1.1 billion over the next five years, but that will represent only 5% of its total investments, and the company is taking an extremely conservative stance. It will only explore where it believes it can get a full payback in five years, and when the foreign government involved shows promise of remaining in place. Moreover, it likes to sign up the foreign government as a full partner. "Sooner or later some government involvement is almost inevitable," claims Anderson. "You might as well ask them to share some of the hair-tearing and birth pains." The company is now exploring some tracts in Indonesia, Dubai, Somalia, and Norway.

'An instinctive entrepreneur'

Anderson, 62, has stamped his imprint on every aspect of the company's development. He first became a director of the Philadelphia-based Atlantic Refining Co. in 1963, when the company purchased his New Mexico-based Hondo Oil & Gas Co. for stock. Within a year he determined that Atlantic's conservative management was taking the company nowhere—the company's earnings from 1960 to 1964 were flat—and with characteristic vigor he ousted its chairman and several key officers and took control.

At the time it was thought that Anderson was "the worst thing that ever happened to the company," recall former executives. The earlier management style, says one, was: "Don't make waves; find the easy time to do something." One former executive, Eugene J. Minahan, today believes that "Anderson could run anything." He has a fabulous instinct, says Minahan, for getting to those things that need to be changed and changing them fast. Anderson is, Minahan says, "an instinctive entrepreneur."

Anderson did speed up the action, looking for a merger. He opened unsuc-

What makes up

- Other investments 3%
- Refining, marketing, and petrochemicals 24%
- Coal 2%
- Petroleum transportation
- Oil sands 8%
- Oil and gas 58%

SUN
Net income: $699.9 million

Total nonenergy ventures account for 1% of total

16 / Readings from *Business Week*

cessful talks with Pure Oil Co. Then he looked at Sunray DX and next Union Oil Co., but Union was better managed than Atlantic, with one of the best rates of return in the industry while Atlantic's was among the worst. So he streamlined his own management, setting up profit centers to make each division more accountable, and then he went after a merger with Richfield Oil Corp. Richfield was No. 4 in West Coast marketing, and it had just outbid Atlantic for some lease acreage on Alaska's North Slope. Cash short, Richfield had already turned to Humble Oil & Refining Co. (now Exxon) for $3 million to explore the North Slope. In return, Humble became a 50% partner there. Richfield stock was held by Sinclair Oil Corp. and Cities Service Co., but they were under a Justice Dept. order to divest it. The chemistry was right between Anderson and Charles S. Jones, Richfield's chief, who was also an ardent wildcatter. In January, 1966, the two companies joined forces, moving Atlantic up from 15th place in the industry (in sales) to 13th.

Within three years, ARCO was on the acquisition trail again, this time to fill in marketing and refining between the East and West coasts. It looked at Sunray once more, but its hopes were dashed when Sun made its move. Instead, it took over Sinclair, which was struggling to escape from a bid by Gulf & Western Industries Inc. The Sinclair acquisition, however, proved to be a mixed blessing. Before the Justice Dept. and the Federal Trade Commission got through, ARCO had to sell off $400 million worth of Sinclair's marketing operations on the East Coast, its Marcus Hook (Pa.) refinery and bulk terminal operations, and ultimately its Wyoming refinery and acreage. Its grand plan to set up Chicago offices to oversee Midwestern marketing and refining went down the drain, and it sold off its East Chicago (Ind.) refinery for $80 million. What ARCO got from the $1.6 billion deal was Sinclair's Houston refinery (its largest), its first step into petrochemicals, the basic component of its pipeline system, and some additional acreage in Alaska on the North Slope.

The latter property proved especially valuable after the strike at Prudhoe Bay in 1968. From that time on, ARCO's management and financial energies were involved in getting North Slope oil to market, overcoming delays by environmentalists, engineering problems, and the increasingly massive commitment of dollars caused by the delay in building the Trans-Alaska pipeline. For the third time ARCO willingly put itself in hock, with total debt rising to $4.7 billion to finance its share of development and pipeline costs. Meanwhile, the delays meant no return on its investment, and no Alaskan oil coming to its refineries.

Instead of resting from its efforts, however, Anderson had the company on the move physically and figuratively. As part of his plan to streamline the company, he moved headquarters first to New York City and then to Los Angeles, dropping those executives who lacked a commitment to the enterprise. Even without the oil from the North Slope, he was planning for its use by opening the most modern refinery in the U.S. at Cherry Point, Wash., to handle the high-sulfur Alaskan oil. And he began the Houston petrochemical complex.

Not content with oil alone, Anderson's strong conviction that all natural resources would ultimately be in short supply had caused him in 1968 to look at Anaconda as a possible acquisition. The costs of the North Slope had tabled that action, but when his old friend, Thomas Mellon Evans, pointed out in 1976 that Anaconda, with heavy losses, was seeking a merger with Tenneco Inc. (partly to escape from Evans, whose Crane Co. held a 19% interest), Anderson outbid the pipeline company with an $800 million offer. Anderson rapidly revamped Anaconda's management. He fired or transferred from New York to Colorado all but 45 of the 180-member corporate staff, replaced two of its three top officers, closed four of Anaconda's high-cost mines, and sold off some brass and valve operations.

The efficiency moves were to prepare Anaconda for the huge investment planned in copper, aluminum, and molybdenum. Meanwhile, Anderson won his bet that natural resource prices were sure to rise as inflation soared. Anaconda earned $179 million before taxes last year, up from $16.7 million in 1976, on a 51% rise in sales since then to $2.2 billion.

ARCO's timing has not always been so good. It brought two giant olefin plants on line in 1976 and 1977, just as the market for their output began to weaken severely. Last year, despite strong foreign demand, ARCO's petrochemical investments were still only eking out a 5.6% pretax return on assets, compared to a 15.5% level of return on assets company-wide. The company dropped its plans to add two more such plants in 1977, but Anderson is convinced that as petroleum supplies diminish in the next decades, oil will become too valuable to burn as fuel. By that time, Anderson believes, ARCO will have the investment

the bottom line

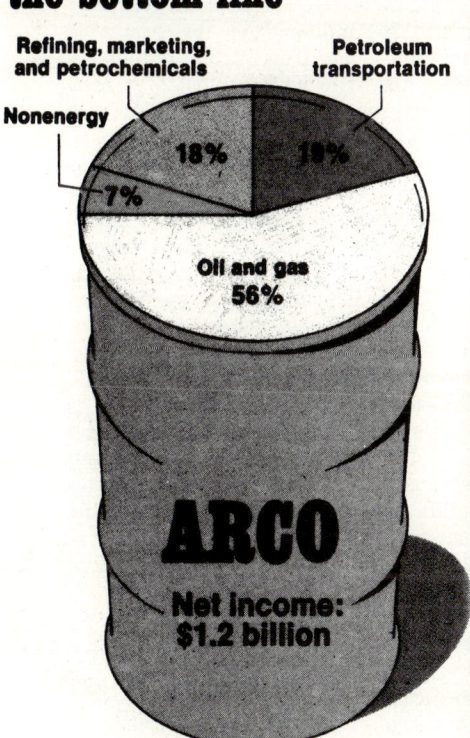

ARCO
Net income: $1.2 billion

- Refining, marketing, and petrochemicals 18%
- Petroleum transportation 19%
- Nonenergy 7%
- Oil and gas 56%

Coal produces loss of less than 1% of total net

ARCO Chairman Anderson: Despite heavy spending, he is unafraid to increase debt for expansion.

The Concept of Strategy and Policy / 17

in place and the expertise to upgrade intermediates into higher-value specialty chemicals.

Although ARCO has faced several such setbacks, it has switched tactics, often in midstream, to take chances it found along the way. It has not hesitated to reverse decisions if they prove wrong. And it is clearly willing to spend heavily to back its bets.

Even its balance sheet demonstrates that disposition. At yearend, ARCO's debt-to-equity ratio was more than double Sun's 0.2 to 1. Sun's ratio will rise this year nearly to ARCO's level, as a result of its Texas Pacific purchase. But Sun Chairman Theodore A. Burtis' goal is to reduce that ratio quickly, while ARCO's plan is to increase its total debt for expansion.

SUN: A BELATED RETURN TO OIL

When Theodore Burtis reported his Texas Pacific move to Sun shareholders two weeks ago, there was genuine applause. One longtime stockholder rose to praise the Sun chairman for his role in the acquisition. Indeed, there is a sense of family at Sun, reinforced each year at its annual meeting, when Sun choristers serenade executives, shareholders, and retirees.

But Burtis inherited a company in 1978 that lacked the continuity that ARCO has had. In the last 15 years, Sun has had four chief executives: J. Howard Pew, a member of the founding Pew family; Robert G. Dunlop, now a board member at Sun and a director of the Pew family's Glenmede Trust, which holds 28% of Sun's stock; H. Robert Sharbaugh; and Burtis. Moreover, the company had been torn by a debate on Sharbaugh's policies, which sought to take Sun far afield from oil.

Burtis quickly set about repairing the damage from the debate. He rapidly settled a suit brought by Becton Dickinson and the SEC over Sun's earlier attempt to gain control of that company. Then, with his aggressive and preemptive bid for Texas Pacific's U.S. assets, he clearly signaled to his staff, employees, and shareholders that Sun now sees oil as its main chance, at least for the next several years. His stepped-up program to explore and develop new resources reinforces that point. By his quick decisions and his willingness to pay high prices for what he wants, he has shown himself to be persuasive and resolute with his board.

But Burtis will have to move farther and faster than even the Texas Pacific purchase to catch up in the oil game. Sun's refinery system is now operating at only 39% self-sufficiency, which forces it to buy expensive oil. Texas Pacific's 120 million-bbl. reserves are currently pledged to other refiners. To fill its system efficiently, Sun will need a big oil find, or a shutdown or sell-off of some of its refineries. William G. Kay Jr., one of three executive vice-presidents who share the chairman's office, notes that Sun has been engaged in an 18-month study of worldwide refinery capacity. Within the next two months it will reach its conclusions, and almost certainly they will show too much capacity for future needs.

Says Kay: "It is possible that some part of our refinery system would be more valuable to others." He notes that the government has a "small-refiner bias," permitting higher profits for such operations.

As a refiner, Sun has other problems as well. Its major refinery at Marcus Hook, Pa., with a capacity of 190,000 bbl. a day, is dependent on low-sulfur oil, primarily from abroad, because it has never been modernized to include a desulfurization unit. All told, the cost of modernizing all six of Sun's refineries is $500 million, an investment that Sun is unwilling to make now, according to Kay.

It is in finding oil, however, that Sun has been notably unlucky. "There was major attention directed toward finding big reserves [in the early 1970s]," says Marion "Zeke" Noble, Sun's president of exploration and development in Dallas. "Sun turned offshore to the international area, because it knew it was not going to find any big reserves onshore." But in some four years of drilling in 22 countries from the Far East to West Africa, Sun was still unsuccessful.

Meanwhile, it was saddled with a $400 million investment in tar sands in Canada that J. Howard Pew had started in 1964 and that had brought no profits. Pew had run Sun until 1970 and was regarded by the Pew family with the same reverence as Anderson is at ARCO. His long-term dream for Sun was nearly as entrepreneurial as Anderson's, but he was unwilling to reverse his course when it proved a long risk.

Pew's goal was to protect Sun's oil supplies with the giant venture in syncrude. The 1964 project sank one-third of Sun's assets into Canada in the hope that Sun's pioneering technological abilities to squeeze the oil out of the sands would supply Sun's present and future refineries. The investment would be in place early, thus avoiding future inflation.

What Pew did not reckon on was that Sun had no expertise in mining, and that the tar sands would be so intractable to move, particularly in cold weather. "From startup to 45,000-bbl.-per-day production took five years," says Robert McClements Jr., executive vice-president. But even then the plant was not profitable. Plant breakdowns, technological snags, and an oil price of $2.50 when $2.75 oil was needed for a profit kept the program in the red. Yet Pew, and his successors, Robert Dunlop and Sharbaugh, refused to abandon the project, which finally broke even in 1975. "Profitability was always just in front of us," according to McClements.

Neither Pew nor Dunlop anticipated the Canadian government's actions to limit oil prices once the plant was in shape. Those limitations were lifted last year under Prime Minister Joe Clark, but this year, with Pierre Trudeau back in power, Sun has just been notified that the Canadian government is reviewing Clark's policy of allowing those prices to remain at world oil levels. Last year, Sun earned $64 million from its Athabasca operations, up from $13.7 million in 1978. And it is in the midst of a $185 million expansion of its plant to increase capacity by 29%.

The decision to move into tar sands as a hedge against shortages and inflation led to other moves at Sun, even before Athabasca was profitable. The purchase of Sunray DX in 1969, for example, was part of a four-pronged strategy, in which Sun's Puerto Rican refinery would handle Venezuelan and Iranian crude, and Sunray's Toledo (Ohio) refinery would process Canadian crude for Sunray's Midwest outlets. Sunray also provided a Gulf Coast refinery that turned out lubricants and chemicals.

But Sunray brought little oil, and there was none forthcoming from Canada. After the Organization of Petroleum Exporting Countries quadrupled crude prices in 1974, Sun started phasing down its international activities. "We had pretty much phased down already domestically," says Noble, noting Sun's reduction of exploratory lands by nearly 1 million acres between 1971 and 1974. TP adds 3 million acres to Sun's current 4.8 million holding.

Sharbaugh, who had succeeded Dunlop in 1974, was worried. In 1975 he began restructuring Sun, looking closely at the profitability of individual segments of the business. A possible goal: the sale of some oil operations.

Sharbaugh decided to use Sun's oil operations as a cash cow to diversify away from oil. He reasoned that it was only a matter of time before all oil companies were in the same boat. By taking Sun's investments out of oil early, it would have the edge on others less educated to manage nonenergy businesses.

Accordingly, Sharbaugh began to make small acquisitions in trucking, real estate, and industrial distribution. But his board, looking at Sun's flat earnings, pushed for clearer and faster action. When investment bankers offered Bec-

18 / Readings from *Business Week*

The risky race for oil: How Sun and ARCO have evolved

1965

	Sun	ARCO
Oil and natural gas liquids production	227,000 bbl. per day	199,600 bbl. per day
Refinery runs	256,000 bbl. per day	217,600 bbl. per day
Sales	$925.2 million	$826.9 million
Net income	$ 84.8 million	$ 66.2 million

1979

	Sun	ARCO
Oil and natural gas liquids production	236,900 bbl. per day	568,000 bbl. per day
Refinery runs	607,500 bbl. per day	823,000 bbl. per day
Sales	$ 10.8 billion	$16.7 billion
Net income	$699.9 million	$ 1.2 billion

ton Dickinson as a large potential acquisition, Sharbaugh bit. He moved ahead in a surprise, overnight purchase of 34% of BD for $293 million from private parties, offering a 37% premium over the market price. The uproar raised by other BD shareholders, its management, and ultimately the SEC brought lawsuits and ended Sharbaugh's reign. This year Sun settled its suit by agreeing to divest itself of BD over 25 years through the sale of debentures convertible into BD shares. The settlement is awaiting court approval. When that comes, Sun will have three years to issue the debentures.

Sun must also sell between 15% and 20% of its Canadian oil and tar sands venture to Canadians as part of its agreement with Canada. The two sales could bring in some $800 million between now and 1983, but that money is currently earmarked to pay the second installment on the Texas Pacific acquisition—some $900 million in three-year notes, according to John P. Neafsey, Sun's senior vice-president for finance.

Sun still needs an increased oil supply. The Texas Pacific acreage may be a starting point. Secondary and tertiary recovery brings in some oil, but Sun needs more. It has chosen not to go into the U.S. side of the Beaufort Sea because it has holdings on the Canadian side. Nevertheless, its slowdown under Sharbaugh's regime makes some rapid catching up essential. "When you phase down like this," says Noble, "you can't rejuvenate yourself overnight. You can turn it off fast, but if you leave it off, you can't turn it back on fast."

Now Sun is trying to increase its activity in the North Sea, Libya, and Algeria. "There's a political risk," Noble concedes, "but so far there's been a lot of rhetoric but not much impact. Libya is not all that bad a place to be, and the profit margins have been good."

Libya now requires its oil purchasers to agree to explore for new reserves. Sun is willing. "We're waiting for them to notify us right now to go there and sign the agreement," says Noble. But while Sun can pass the exploration costs through on its oil purchases, if it discovers oil in Libya and develops a field, the costs could run to $1 billion. That would indeed be a political risk.

After the turmoil

Right now, Burtis is unwilling to commit himself past his three-year program. He has promised his board he will not push another deal the size of Texas Pacific "any time soon." Nor has he abandoned the idea of Sun's remaining a diversified energy company. "I don't want to be 95% in anything," he says adamantly. Neither is he willing to repeat Pew's plan of betting one-third of his company's assets on any single play. It is not surprising that after all the turmoil at Sun, with its troubles in finding oil, its political risks, and its recent woes with BD, Burtis is likely to play it safe.

What that means in terms of future growth remains to be seen. ARCO has taken a riskier path that brings it more opportunities but more danger as well. Much of ARCO's success so far has been directly related to Anderson's ability to manage risk. Although Anderson now plans to retire when he reaches 65 in three years, most insiders believe he will stay on through the mid-1980s. He worries, as Burtis does, that eventually the oil industry will phase out as supplies end. And, although ARCO has done more than Sun to protect itself against that exigency, he nevertheless recognizes that someday it will happen. Says Anderson: "I don't know of any industry that successfully converted from one line of endeavor to another. Most companies have simply phased out with their industries." For ARCO to avoid that, he adds, "it will still take years of planning, and decades for the actual transition." ∎

Trans World Corp.
THE STRATEGY SQUEEZE ON THE AIRLINE

As their first-quarter earnings statements painfully show, the nation's airlines are in a sickening dive. Unable to cope with the ruinous effects of last year's 50% increase in jet fuel prices or with the fierce competition caused by congressional deregulation of air travel 19 months ago, four of the top six carriers were stung with pretax losses in the three months ended Mar. 31. The losses were huge: $69.2 million for industry leader United Airlines, $55.9 million for second-ranked American Airlines, $83.3 million for fourth-ranked Pan American World Airways, and $59 million for Trans World Airlines. With the 1980 recession deepening and competition from foreign carriers increasing on international routes, many experts believe that the consolidation of the U. S. airline industry will greatly accelerate.

All airlines are now making tough choices to survive, but the most difficult strategic decisions are likely those that must be made in the Manhattan offices of Trans World Corp. (TW), the holding company that owns TWA. The reason is that Trans World, by far the most diversified of airline companies, may have to choose whether even to remain a major air carrier or focus instead on its more stable nonairline operations, which offer better growth potential. Diversification, initially seen as a way to make TWA a more viable airline, now provides some compelling reasons for the company to pull back—or even withdraw altogether—from that business.

TWA's shrinking share

Actually, the retreat has been under way, although only gradually, for some time. Trans World, with revenues of $4.3 billion in 1979, has built itself into the largest holding company in the airline business, but TWA is barely holding onto its third-place position among U. S. carriers, and its share of domestic air travel has fallen from 13.2% a decade ago to 11.4% last year.

In 1967, when Howard Hughes was still the principal owner of Trans World Airlines Inc., the company set forth on a long-term business plan that seemed not only logical but also distinctive from all other U. S. airlines. TWA that year traded $86 million of stock to buy Hilton International Co., the foreign hotel chain that had been spun off earlier from the domestic Hilton Hotels Corp., as the first step in a major diversification program. The company's objective—then and now—has been to build nonairline businesses that would smooth the wild, cyclical fluctuations common in the airline industry, and especially vexing to TWA, because it depends on seasonal transcontinental and transatlantic routes.

This strategy reached full bloom last year. Trans World spent $82 million in cash to buy Spartan Food Systems Inc., a fast-food chain, and paid $92 million to buy Century 21 Real Estate Corp., the nation's largest real estate brokerage chain. In 1973 the company had acquired Canteen Corp., the largest purveyor of vending machines in the U. S.

Three other U. S. airlines—United, American, and Pan Am—also have acquired hotels, but none is now even half as reliant on nonairline revenues as is TW. So important have the diversification ventures become to Trans World that last year the company was reorganized into a holding company, and L. Edwin Smart, chairman of TWA, became chairman and chief executive of TW instead. Now, Smart notes sharply: "Our company is Trans World Corp. One of our subsidiaries is an airline." Indeed, TW's nonairline businesses in 1979 contributed 31.6% of its total revenues and provided $93.3 million in pretax earnings. In 1980, the nonairline companies may easily contribute 35% of total TW revenues.

But TW's diversification plan has really never accomplished its purpose of smoothing out the horrendous earnings cycle created by the company's airline operations. In 1970 the company lost $93.2 million, and in 1975, $91.9 million. Last year, TWA pretax losses of $27.2 million pulled down the nonairline gains to leave TW, which also subtracts corporate costs after arriving at pretax figures for its subsidiaries, with net income of just $8.6 million. In the first quarter of 1980, nonairline profits offset only part of TWA's $59 million loss, and TW thus suffered a net loss of $49.3 million.

Right now, there is increasing evidence that the strategic balancing act may never work because the airline and nonairline operations are not nearly as compatible or mutually supportive as Trans World's managers had hoped they would be. On the surface, the diversifica-

Trans World's strategy that didn't fly

20 / Readings from *Business Week*

tion seemed well designed to produce a symbiotic relationship. The airline would throw off cash to fund acquisitions of less capital-intensive and less cyclical service businesses. Those, in turn, would provide more profit stability and ensure TW of a home for its investment tax credits from airplane purchases. (Such credits now total $73 million.)

But that theoretical business fit could not be further from reality at the moment. For one thing, TW's nonairline businesses may all enter a recessionary downturn this year, even as the airline dips into its own severe trough. The general recession has already shut down auto and other industrial plants, where TW's Canteen subsidiary has up to 85% of its vending machines and 70% of its cafeterias. Hence, Canteen saw its pretax earnings in the first quarter plunge 72% to $1.4 million on sales of $178 million. High mortgage interest rates drove first-quarter earnings down 50% to $1 million at Century 21. And as the year progresses, high fuel prices are expected to hurt not only the airline but also Hilton, which is dependent on foreign travel, and Spartan, whose franchised Hardee's Food Systems Inc. hamburger restaurants and Quincy's Family Steak House chain depend on auto traffic.

Moreover, the acquired businesses now are looking to spend surprisingly large amounts of capital to seize growth opportunities or respond to competitive challenges in their markets. At the same time, however, TWA, which operates one of the oldest and most fuel-inefficient fleets among trunk carriers, has been forced to embark on a massive $1.2 billion equipment purchase program to meet the two major challenges of its business in the early 1980s—price competition and fuel conservation. "We will have as efficient, if not the most efficient, aircraft of any company in the industry by 1985," boasts Chairman Smart.

The problem is that TW's attempt to rescue its ailing airline could jeopardize its nonairline businesses. The company has a debt-equity ratio of 2.1 to 1, much lower than it used to be but still third highest among large airlines. And C. E. Meyer Jr., TWA's president, declares that the $1.2 billion is just the beginning of a total $5 billion he will need for modernization by 1990. How these new planes will be financed is unclear, but knowledgeable sources say half of the recent orders have been financed by Boeing Co., which is manufacturing 10 767 aircraft for delivery in 1982 or 1983.

If it strains to buy all the equipment TWA needs, the corporation seems certain to restrain growth at its other subsidiaries, all of which have ambitious expansion plans of their own. Canteen wants to acquire a youth-oriented restaurant chain, and Century 21 wants to buy back regional franchises it sold in the 1970s to speed its nationwide development. Meanwhile, Hilton is trying to follow an industry trend among foreign hotel chains by building luxury units in the U. S.

At Spartan, Chairman Charles J. Bradshaw described plans just last year to build 250 new Quincy's units within five years to add to his modest chain of 40. Now, in the wake of TWA's first-quarter loss, Bradshaw has scaled down the program, even though Spartan showed a quarter-to-quarter pretax earnings increase of 36%. Spartan now proposes to build just 50 Quincy's in two years. "We can't make money in this business borrowing money at more than 12% interest to build restaurants," gripes Brad-

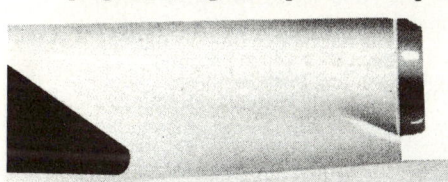

Seeking profit stability, it diversified more than other airlines...

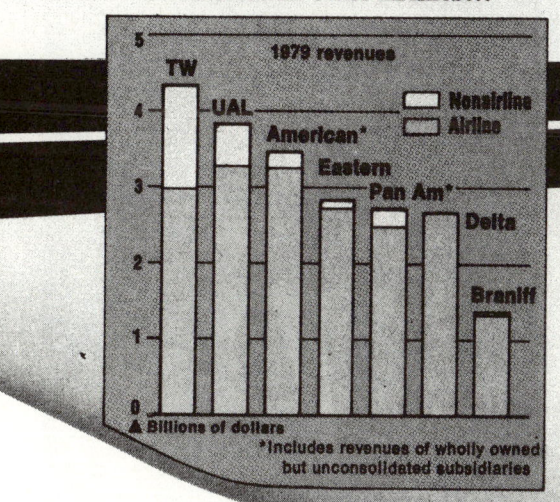

...but TW's corporate profits still gyrated...

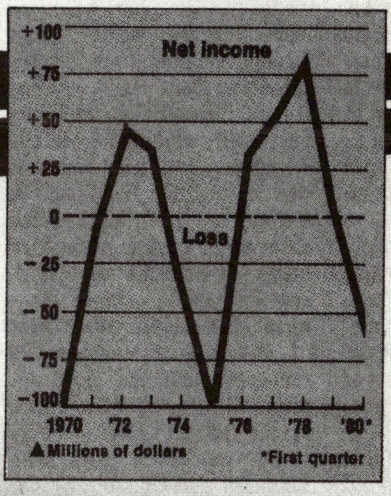

...and as recession begins, results of its new ventures are already spotty

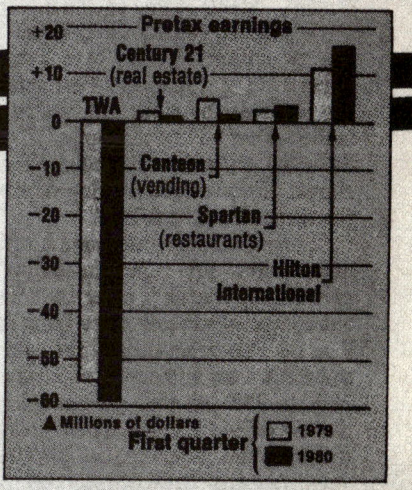

Illustration by James Humphrey—BW
Charts by Steve Hart—BW

The Concept of Strategy and Policy / 21

Trans World Corp.'s Smart: His nonairline companies may account for 35% of revenues this year.

shaw. And, he adds tellingly: "We might rely on internal funds, depending on what kind of deal we can cut with TW in terms of capital spending. [But] I have to leave that a little nebulous."

Bradshaw is not alone in his frustrations. Another high-ranking nonairline executive is known to be so irritated by his subsidiary's connection to faltering TWA that he is job-hunting. Holding company executives are caught in the middle of the vying financial needs of their two business sectors, and they face the morale problems caused by this rivalry. Increasingly, some are looking with skepticism at the extent to which the airline's turnaround should be funded, unless TWA chief Meyer can show positive results fairly soon. Snaps one TW officer: "I don't care how many billions Ed Meyer wants. Performance is the name of the game, and we've got to make money to buy airplanes." Frank L. Salizzoni, TW's chief financial officer, declares: "Future fleet buildup depends on the airline's profitability."

Chairman Smart, although he publicly underscores his commitment to TWA, nonetheless makes it clear that the parent company expects more from its airline. On Feb. 1, he slashed the salaries of some 800 TWA managers, making cuts of 10% to 25% on that portion of annual pay exceeding $35,000. These reductions will save the company just $900,000 this year, causing little impact on overall performance, but Smart says the pay cuts were meant to be a "symbolic gesture" to TWA employees.

None of TW's officers or directors is suggesting that the company should abandon the airline business. Besides, TW might have lost its best chance to get out of the airline business last year, when it turned a cold shoulder to an acquisition inquiry from Francisco A. Lorenzo, chairman of Texas International Airlines Inc.

Lorenzo never made a formal offer to purchase TWA, but he met with Smart over breakfast last Sept. 14 and asked whether he would consider selling the airline. Smart declined. Texas International bought 4% of TW's stock and threatened to purchase the holding company instead, but it gave up the takeover effort and unloaded its Trans World stock when it met with publicly expressed opposition from TW's board.

If TWA could be turned around, of course, its parent's diversification strategy could still be viable. But even without skyrocketing fuel costs and deregulation of the airline industry, the restoration of TWA would have required herculean efforts. The airline's long-standing problem has been that it flies in highly competitive markets: 48% of its traffic is derived from transcontinental and transatlantic routes. TWA has thus suffered from the nation's population shift from the North to the Sunbelt—a major cause of the decline in its domestic market. The company has steadily held roughly 20% of the transatlantic market, but company officials complain that the profitability of these routes has been hurt badly by increasing competition from foreign airlines that receive subsidies from their governments. Beyond this, TWA has never fully emerged from the criticism that, ever since it was owned by Hughes, the airline has been milked for short-term profits instead of being fed with the most modern aircraft to achieve long-term efficiencies. TWA's fleet of 194 aircraft includes 72 fuel-inefficient and now unprofitable Boeing 707s, and a stable of 81 Boeing 727s whose economics have been rendered questionable by the increases in jet fuel prices. Already, the airline has grounded seven unprofitable DC-9s. The fuel price spurt has hurt all airlines badly. But at TWA, annual fuel costs jumped 55% from 1978 to 1979—higher by at least 10 percentage points than at most major competitors—because of the inefficient nature of the airline's fleet. In addition, the fleet suffers from high maintenance costs because it contains planes of many varieties.

TWA got stuck with such an inefficient fleet because management decided during the latter half of the 1970s to reduce the company's burdensome debt load, which resulted in a debt-equity ratio of 6.4 to 1 in 1975. That year the company sold 12 of its Boeing 747s to Iran for $150 million to improve liquidity ratios and satisfy covenants contained in agreements with its major lenders. Since then, the company has improved cash flow further by depreciating existing planes and postponing the purchase of new ones. Last year, TWA took delivery on seven modestly efficient Boeing 727-200 aircraft, but it was the airline's first addition of new equipment since 1975. Such moves improved the balance sheet, but they left TWA in a weak competitive position as the airline business enters a new era. "With deregulation, airlines have become commodities businesses, and fares will reflect the expenses of the lowest-cost companies," observes Michael R. Armellino, airline analyst at Goldman, Sachs & Co.

TWA executives believe they have developed plans that will make the airline a low-cost and effective competitor by the mid-1980s. Even now, TWA President

TWA's Meyer: Guiding a $1.2 billion program to replace an aging and fuel-inefficient fleet.

22 / Readings from *Business Week*

Meyer maintains that the airline's fleet is in the midst of a turnaround that will surprise industry-watchers. This year, he says, the company will take delivery of 10 more 727-200s, four 747s, and two L-1011s. Moreover, in the last two years the company has ordered two additional L-1011s as well as the 10 Boeing 767s. The new 767 will use 21% less fuel per hour and yet carry more passengers than the 707 it will replace. Even though TWA will not receive all of this equipment until 1983, Meyer maintains he is "not the least bit concerned about our position on airplanes." Nevertheless, some industry observers remain unconvinced that TWA will be financially able to modernize its fleet fast enough. Says one analyst: "The airlines that have the best fleets and are able to maintain or expand their share of the business in the future will be those with the most money to spend and the highest operating efficiencies, and that will not be TWA."

More competitive

Still, TWA has taken some major steps to become more competitive even before the new aircraft are delivered. For example, the airline inaugurated service from 10 Northern cities to Florida last December to offset the normal seasonal declines of its traditional East-West routes. Backed by a "kids fly free" promotion, the new service has managed to capture an estimated 5.4% of the air traffic to Florida, and company officials say the Florida service did comparatively well during the winter by nearly breaking even.

To come to grips with its fuel efficiency problems for the short term, TWA has also revamped its schedules—eliminating some flights and adding others—to fly its newer planes as much as possible while all but putting its inefficient 707s in mothballs. On average, these older craft now are used only about five to six hours a day, about half of their potential. As a result of these cutbacks, 5,000 of the airline's 39,000 employees have been laid off in the last eight months.

So far, such efforts have produced mixed results and received equally mixed industry reviews. For their part, TWA officials argue that while the airline lost $59 million pretax during the first quarter of this year, that quarter is typically the carrier's worst. TWA's passenger volume during August, its peak month, is normally 45% higher than traffic in February, its slowest. Viewed from that perspective, TWA believes that it has dealt with the industry's recent troubles better than its competitors, since its 7.5% decline from the results of the first quarter of 1979—when the airline lost $54 million pretax—was easily the smallest decline of any of the major carriers. Even Delta Air Lines Inc., which is built around strong North-South winter routes, suffered a 17% profit decline in the quarter ended on Mar. 31, although it remained the most profitable of the major carriers. "I'm not at all proud of our operating loss," notes Meyer, "but if you look what happened to us vs. last year, and what happened to our principal competitors, our record is pretty good."

Many industry analysts, however, do not completely buy that argument, because they say TWA has lately benefited from some extraordinary and temporary circumstances. Most significant among these is that TWA's fleet contains no DC-10 aircraft, still burdened by the stigma from last year's crashes. By contrast, American Airlines Inc. TWA's biggest competitor in crucial transcontinental markets, has been losing passenger volume to TWA because, through March, it had committed three DC-10s on New York-to-Los Angeles routes. But TWA's advantage in this respect has come to a sudden end. On Apr. 27, American pulled all DC-10s from the New York-L.A. run and began widely promoting its use of nothing but 747s.

The newly enforced efficiencies at TWA have also produced some hidden costs. Meyer, for example, is already walking a tightrope in handling employee morale. He contends that the across-the-board pay cuts at TWA will produce no ill effects on work performance, and he even maintains that five pilots recently laid off have called him to say they understand the reasons. But of the pay cuts, another airline industry executive remarks: "If I were running the company and decided to cut the budget by 15%, I would get rid of the deadwood and give everyone else a raise. You ought to be motivating them."

In addition, Meyer either is not receiving or not reporting a cross section of opinion from his laid-off pilots. Another pilot layoff of as yet unspecified size has been tentatively scheduled for June, and some TWA employees are blaming inept airline management rather than the industry's recessionary fall. Says Captain James A. Schmitt, a 23-year TWA veteran: "Last fall, a lot of pilots were in favor of Texas International buying the company. TI's management is young, aggressive, and fighting. At TWA, we see no growth." A decade ago, Schmitt was a leader in a pilots' program called "Go TWA," designed to improve morale.

Among other things, the pilots say that TWA's decision to use 707s sparingly has involved substantial labor cost. One 707 captain says he recently worked two hours in two days, flying a 37-minute route one way each day. For that brief productive time, he was paid $800 in salary. " I like the money, and I took a book along with me to read in the hotel," he says. "But this kind of scheduling is scary."

Such comments add to long-standing criticism of the quality of TWA management. Most questionable is the degree to which the diversification program penalized the airline by diverting not only cash but also top management attention from the company's basic business. Some observers, for example, believe that TW Chairman Smart, despite his 13 years in airline management, is far more interested in growing the new ventures than in overseeing the nation's third largest airline. Says a source who was close to the proposed Texas International acquisition, "The people [at TW] don't believe in airlines. If they did, you'd think they would spend their time and effort on the business, rather than keeping the airline around as a tax loss and diversifying instead."

He notes that Trans World's airline assets alone, which have a book value of $930 million, vastly exceed the market value of the company's 16 million shares of common stock, which recently sold at $12.88 a share. "The market price for years has reflected the fact that with existing management the place isn't worth anything," he says.

Regardless of the merits of TWA's past management, it will have to perform much better in the future, because deregulation has compounded the burden of high fuel costs. Officially, air fares have increased domestically by about 35% in the last year, but discounting has reduced average realized fare increases to 30%. Invasions of markets once closely held by a few competitors in the days of regulation are increasing. In March, fuel consumption by all airlines was up 7% from a year earlier, even though paid passenger miles were down 8%—a clear indicator that route competition is exploding. Just as TWA's move into Florida has put it in new competition with Eastern Air Lines Inc., Eastern on June 1 will launch its first New York-to-L.A. service to take share from TWA. Even TWA's ebullient executives admit they are fearful of Eastern's move. "It will hurt our profitability," concedes Meyer. Notes Willis Player, senior vice-president at Pan American World Airways Inc.: "When everyone shifts to the same profitable route, they all have the pleasure of losing money together." Charles C. Tillinghast Jr., Smart's predecessor as Trans World's chief executive, predicts that "there will be a shakeout" in the airline industry.

To survive the new competition in air travel, Trans World management will almost certainly have to pay closer attention to the day-to-day operations of its airline and be more responsive to

The Concept of Strategy and Policy / 23

events in the industry. Lackadaisical management may well explain why TWA failed to join the half-fare coupon war that United touched off last summer in an effort to regain market share it lost during a two-month strike. Smart now concedes TWA erred in not offering the coupons, and by outside estimates the airline lost $100 million in revenues by not joining United and American in the coupon promotion. "It was a bad mistake not to get into that battle," fumes Tillinghast, TWA's CEO from 1961 to 1976.

Now, Smart seems to recognize that because of the new pressures on the airline and the company's accelerated diversification beyond that business, his management team is stretched thin. Last year's reorganization presumably is intended to provide better management oversight of both the airline and nonairline subsidiaries. "We are in a state of suspense as far as further acquisitions are concerned," says Smart. "We've grown very substantially in a very short time, and we now need an elaborate organization to deal with everyone properly."

But there is a serious question whether better management alone can overcome the capital constraints on TW's group of businesses. The nonairline companies will have to forgo their growth plans if they want to match the original corporate goal that they not be capital-intensive. But, ironically, each of TW's subsidiaries now sees a need for capital to fund its own diversification.

At Canteen, President Howard C. Miller says he wants to acquire a chain of "concept" restaurants whose menu quality and prices would be higher than in fast foods but lower than in white-tablecloth restaurants. Miller is looking to reduce Canteen's overdependence on industrial customers and at the same time to lessen its reliance on vending machines, which typically yield the lowest margin in the food service business. Such dependence explains Canteen's meager pretax return of 3.6% on sales of $716.4 million in 1979.

Meanwhile, Spartan wants to expand because of competitive pressures. Its 228-unit Hardee's chain (Spartan is Hardee's largest franchisee) is restricted to Southeastern states, where there is the greatest concentration of fast-food hamburger restaurants. Spartan benefited from Hardee's introduction last year of breakfast menus, but this "will probably not continue to improve Spartan in the future," observes Donald W. Mitchell, a management consultant and former director of strategic planning at Heublein Inc., which owns Kentucky Fried Chicken. Spartan's way out of its predicament is to expand rapidly its Quincy's steakhouse chain, which it acquired in 1977. But because these restaurants are company-owned, not franchised, the expansion program requires a lot of capital. "Spartan," adds Mitchell, "was a company starved for capital when TW bought it. To me, the purchase of Spartan just adds to the rumor that TW plans eventually to get out of the airline business. Otherwise, there is an internal conflict over the use of capital." The 250 Quincy's units Spartan wants to build would cost some $125 million.

Hilton, meanwhile, has stood by and watched as prime competitors, such as Pan Am's Intercontinental chain, have moved into a huge new market—the U.S. Although Hilton's pretax profits were up 25% to $55.5 million in 1979, the company nevertheless is already experiencing some recessionary softness at its European hotels, and it wants to launch a major assault of its own on the American market. Hilton's first venture is the Vista International hotel now being built at the World Trade Center in New York, scheduled to open this year. But Hilton will only manage this hotel, and it has hopes to both manage and own some equity in other hotels it plans to build in Washington, Kansas City, Houston, and Atlantic City. Uncertainty over interest rates has caused Hilton this year to stretch out its construction timetable on these units.

At Century 21, company officials will need an estimated $60 million to complete the repurchasing of regional franchises sold in the 1970s. TW's newest subsidiary set up a two-tiered franchising system in 1972 that made it by far the biggest U.S. real estate brokerage chain. It sold territorial franchises—encompassing one or more states—to businessmen who in turn sold franchises to local brokers. But the attraction in repurchasing these regional franchises has become apparent. The 13 territorial franchises Century 21 had already repurchased by 1979 contributed about $10 million in pretax profits last year, but during the same period, 20 remaining independent franchisees took in profits of about $30 million.

'Acquisitions in the future'

Beyond this, Smart himself has visions of new ways he would like to use the company's network of real estate offices. He suggests Century 21 would like to become a mortgage financer and offer mortgage insurance as well. As with TW's other nonairline businesses, a spreading of Century 21's business interests is also being forced by competitive pressure. Since 1970, the number of national real estate brokerage franchising companies has grown from less than a dozen to more than 30, and new heat is coming from independents, who are organizing to fight the chains. On May 1, for example, 33 leading independents gathered in Tarpon Springs, Fla., to inaugurate a national home buyer referral system designed to garner a larger part of the market for the estimated 275,000 families that move every year because of job relocations—a customer group more recession-proof than any other segment of home buyers.

Originally purchased just to shore up the airline, TW's nonairline operations are thus—by virtue of both need and opportunity—pressuring the holding company to invest in them at an accelerating rate. And although Smart says Trans World has bought enough nonairline companies for the time being, one outsider suggests, "TW will certainly make further nonairline acquisitions in the future." While the company may be able to do that without leaving the airline industry altogether, it will, at the least, be pressed to reduce the scope of TWA's operations. Confirms one TW insider: "The market share trends at TWA may be expected to continue." ∎

WHAT CAUSED THE DECLINE

The penalties of short-term corporate strategies

On June 4, Thomas A. Murphy, chairman of General Motors Corp. and the perennial optimist of the auto industry, made a speech that was uncharacteristically critical. "The 1970s were all but a disaster" for auto executives as well as for leaders of other sectors of business and government, Murphy declared. "We seem to have spent most of our time not making decisions but postponing them."

While atypical, Murphy's remarks are understandable. Imported cars by May had usurped 28.4% of the U.S. market, up from about 15% in 1970. This erosion already threatens the death of Chrysler Corp. and has shaken GM, Ford, and American Motors. Murphy touched the heart of the problem: In a decade when the entire nation postponed the need to devise long-range solutions to its economic problems, the auto makers, too, postponed the obligation to develop the high-quality, fuel-efficient vehicles their market would want. "The auto industry," says Donald W. Mitchell, managing director of Mitchell & Co., consultants in Cambridge, Mass., "is the perfect example of short-term strategic planning."

But the auto executives are not alone. An air of disappointed perplexity has settled on managers of a wide spectrum of companies. Their industries grew in tandem with rising U.S. population and affluence in the 1950s and 1960s, and hence they often needed no broader business plans than to increase production capacity at the right times and in the right places. Now the same businessmen face a stable population and a redistribution of wealth in the world that has fostered new competition between domestic companies and between U.S. and foreign companies. Strategic planning specialists say U.S. corporations must now redefine their long-range goals and implement plans to reach them, even if heavy investment in research, retooling, and marketing programs hurt profits in the short run. But this challenge faces a business community that has grown up without a real need for visionary strategies and that is under pressure, especially in equity markets, to increase earnings each quarter by cutting investment (page 74).

Penalties in billions

Some of the economic penalties of short-term corporate strategies are apparent. The imports' share of the auto market is now worth more than $5 billion annually. The steel industry has clearly lost billions by postponing over decades the need to shift production away from outmoded facilities. It now lacks the capital to do so, let alone to launch the kind of foreign marketing drives so successful for the Japanese.

The rubber industry, meanwhile, hewed to the simple road of increasing tire production along with the rise in U.S. vehicle population in the 1960s. Now the entire industry is in its seventh consecutive year of financial difficulty because of its heavy dependence on tires at a time when the domestic auto market is declining and the use of long-lasting radial tires has been spreading. The top five rubber companies, at their historic profit-to-sales margins of 4% to 5%, should have earned about $1 billion in 1979. Actual profits were $268 million.

A single figure for the nationwide cost penalty of corporate short-term thinking is impossible to reach, but it is undoubtedly enormous. "The economic cost just of the auto collapse is incalculable," notes Richard Morgan, vice-president of Princeton Strategy Group Inc., a division of the big consulting outfit, Kepner-Tregoe Co. "It is extraordinarily dangerous [for short-term planning] to continue."

Of course, the U.S. business establishment is dotted with companies that have done much better. Corporations such as General Electric, Procter & Gamble, and Standard Oil (Ohio) have made huge investments in products and resources with no promise of quick returns but in order to position themselves for the future. Sohio is now flooded with profit (it earned $1.2 billion on sales of $7.9 billion in 1979) because of Alaskan oil investments that created threatening debts for a decade earlier.

But short-term plans seem more prevalent. In consumer products alone, recent campaigns by Colgate-Palmolive and Genesco to divest operations they acquired only a few years ago bespeak a lack of foresight in the 1970s. In some cases, as with machine tool producers who are now enjoying a cyclical boom but have not expanded capacity enough to prevent foreign market intrusions, the pain is yet to be felt.

It is not "stupidity or laziness," contends consultant Morgan, that has prevented companies from doing strategic planning, but a combination of pressures and simple inertia. Donald W. Fuller, chief executive of Microdata Corp., says his company was virtually forced to neglect long-term planning, causing eventual merger talks that resulted in the acquisition of Microdata by McDonnell Douglas Corp. last fall.

Fuller's story is that Microdata, founded in 1968, was forced onto a short-term strategy merry-go-round. He says he needed equity capital for growth in the company's minicomputer business, but that stock prices would respond only to growth at a torrid pace. From 1972 to 1977, Microdata did achieve fast growth—from $6.2 million in sales to $38 million—but only by sacrificing the future. Fuller concedes he used such techniques as bypassing the establishment of a direct sales force to hype earnings, and that he announced at least one new computer model long before it was commercially ready in order to make an additional impact on Wall Street.

Survival pressures

Eventually, these policies took a toll. To Fuller's consternation, his stock price fell anyway to $7 a share from $28. By last summer, Microdata had also used up $25 million in bank credit, and the company had lost all hope of garnering new funds. "When you are down, you can't sell future performance worth a damn on Wall Street," Fuller grouses today. "Chief executives of medium-sized companies too often get trapped into a bunch of short-term strategies."

Others, too, argue that many companies have no choice but to maximize profits now, and they see little hope for change in the near future. "I think the No. 1 issue of the 1980s will be survival, so there is going to be an inordinate pressure on the short term," says James F. Bere, chairman and chief executive of Borg-Warner Corp. Bere says he perceives his central mandate to be "the perpetuation of the company."

Bere and others thus suggest that economic dangers—inflation and new competition among them—are already so serious as to make reactive, short-term business planning irreversible for now at many corporations. But while no one would dispute the need for sheer survival, others criticize any lesser motivations for postponing investments clearly needed for future viability.

"The job of management is to balance pressures for the short-term mentality

The Concept of Strategy and Policy / 25

with the need for long-range planning," says Gary E. MacDougal, chairman of Mark Controls Corp., an industrial valve and control manufacturer in Evanston, Ill. MacDougal envisions his company, which had earnings of only $5.5 million on sales of $233 million in 1979, as a supplier of control products to industries on the upswing. Thus, Mark took a $1.3 million aftertax penalty last year, largely to develop a butterfly valve whose market may reach $400 million, particularly because the valve is ideal for tertiary oil recovery systems.

Survival reasoning also fails to explain short-term planning done simply because it has been successful in the past. Wendy's International Inc., for example, experienced phenomenal growth from its founding in 1969 to its rise to a current third rank in fast-food hamburger chains.

But now, R. David Thomas, Wendy's founder and chairman, and Robert L. Barney, its president, have run into a wall. In the late 1970s, other fast food chains turned from a simple growth-orientation to diversification of their menus, reducing dependence on beef. And, the others opened for breakfast. In 1979, Wendy's, which apparently missed the need to change course, saw earnings drop 5.7% to $23.1 million, while sales volume per restaurant dropped 10% to $620,000, far below McDonald's $1 million. Wendy's is only now struggling to catch up with new food offerings. "Maybe we got trapped by the fact that everything was working so well, we were afraid to tamper," says William C. Leiter, vice-president for finance.

Opportunities lost

Wendy's is just one example of missed opportunity in the food industry. Outside of agricultural commodity sales, and the activities of a handful of processors such as Coca-Cola Co., food companies have often ignored foreign markets. Domestically, others appear stuck in tradition. Kellogg Co., which boasts of its long commitment to breakfast cereals, has maintained a heady 42% share of that market. But because of conservative bids, it failed three times to broaden its activity in breakfast foods by acquiring Tropicana Products Inc. Says L. Craig Carver, director of research at the Piper, Jaffray & Hopwood Inc. brokerage in Minneapolis: "Kellogg knows it can't sustain its growth without acquisition."

Machine tools may be the clearest example of short-term planning done under pressure, but also because of tradition. Cyclical downturns have long prevented machine tool company executives from gambling in times of prosperity with construction of significant new capacity. Thus, when a boom that began in 1978 was heightened by tool orders from Detroit, which was desperately seeking to downsize its cars, U. S. toolmakers were caught short. Lead times now stretch as much as two years for some tools.

To fill the gap, Japanese, German, and other foreign manufacturers have stepped in and now hold an estimated 25% of the U. S. market. Frets James A. Gray, president of the National Machine Tool Builders' Assn.: "It is going to get worse, a hell of a lot worse." ∎

A NEW SOCIAL CONTRACT

How companies can lengthen their sights

Any new social contract aimed at speeding growth imposes "old-fashioned" requirements on business leaders. During the 1950s and 1960s, when the U.S. was perceived as an affluent society, "socially responsible" business behavior was aimed at social values. But the new social contract requires that management again focus on production values as its primary concern.

Management for growth is possible, for despite corporate America's protestations to the contrary, many—maybe most—of the typical company's problems have been internally generated. And they can be internally solved. Companies can change the signals that push their own people away from long-term vision into short-term myopia. They can reaffirm the need for basic research, for taking risks, for planning for the long haul. And they can create a climate in which educated risk-takers feel that their jobs are secure and that their willingness to take risks is appreciated.

'Decade of Determination'

Clearly, the message has to come from the very top of the organization. "We tell our guys they're supposed to take care of short-term profits with their left hand and long-term performance with their right," insists Thomas V. Jones, chairman and chief executive officer of Northrop Corp., a company with a good long-term track record. Chairman Ruben F. Mettler of TRW Inc. has been making the management-meeting rounds at his company, stressing that there should be no cuts in research and development and telling managers, "While we are in a recession and short-term actions are necessary, we don't want to take our eye off the long-term goal." And at Westinghouse Electric Corp., not known for its visionary strategies in the past, Chairman Robert E. Kirby chose "Decade of Determination" as the theme for this year's annual meeting of 225 key operational managers.

But verbal messages must be backed up with new policies, plans, and procedures that continually drive home to staff members that they must be more than caretakers of the bottom line. And perhaps the easiest, yet most critical, fix needed in most corporations is in incentive compensation programs. Because long-range plans are worthless if there is no money to carry them out, it would probably be foolish to abolish bonuses based on short-term profit performance. But there should be a way to reward savvy decisions that do not result in immediate payouts.

Of course, some purists say there should be no incentive compensation whatsoever. Management theorist Peter F. Drucker says that no truly successful company should even have a stock option plan. "Management should act along the old lines of trustees not having a stake," he says. "If you must give prestige, give the chairman two cars."

But the reality is that salary allocations have become so routine and automatic that bonuses are among the few methods management has to link performance with reward. The task is making sure that bonuses do not reward the status quo. One possible way, suggests Donald G. Carlson, a vice-president at Booz Allen & Hamilton Inc., is to "leverage" bonuses. In his plan, if under the conventional percentage-of-salary system a top executive would get $100,000, the company would give him $50,000, promise him the other $50,000 if he meets short-range goals, and dangle an additional $30,000 if he takes a risk that pans out. "That way he loses nothing and has a lot to gain," Carlson says.

A few companies have already implemented their own variations on that theme. Johnson & Johnson awards executives in the $70,000-and-up range shares of "phantom stock"—credits whose value are based on an internal formula that is tied to book value and profits. The executives get annual "dividends" on the shares for short-term performance, but they can cash them in only on leaving the company. Thus, they can collect later on long-term decisions made now.

For lower-level executives, J&J and Du Pont Co. have discretionary bonus systems that allow bosses to allocate moneys for outstanding contributions—presumably including smart risks. Du Pont also has a second set of bonuses for "achievements above and beyond the call of duty," awarded by a special compensation committee headed by the company's president. One R&D manager was rewarded for suggesting a more expensive but safer manufacturing process. "It cost a bundle to put in, but he got a bundle," recalls Senior Vice-President William G. Simeral.

Rewards for attitude

Some companies even try to reward attitude. International Harvester Corp. provides bonuses for employees who join professional societies and for those publishing scientific papers. It has changed the $10 award the company had been granting for scientists who received patents to a sliding scale of recognition and cash that increases if the product winds up profitable.

All these compensation systems signal staffers that immediate bottom-line results are not the end-all and be-all. The message can be reinforced by the types of reports managers are expected to make and by the criteria used for promotions. "The key is to tie the profile for promotion as well as for compensation to the long range," says management consultant John Diebold.

Few companies go that far, but sever-

A shift of focus: Management must avoid short-term myopia...

al are making changes. Westinghouse, which recently reorganized 130 separate units into 38 divisions, has switched from what used to be a voluminous financial reporting requirement to asking the 38 divisional presidents for a single page of numbers projecting cash flow rather than profits and losses. But the presidents must submit biannual plans projecting five years out, and they must submit them orally as well as in written form so that they can be questioned. J&J asks for similar reports—and purposely asks for them before annual operating and budget planning sessions so that managers do not use their strategic plan to justify their budgets.

Significantly, neither J&J nor TRW Inc. nor 3M Co.—all regarded as forward-thinking—has anyone on board called a corporate planner. Which is as it should be, maintains Frederick W. Gluck, head of McKinsey & Co.'s strategic practice. "I don't believe in strategic planning as being different from management," he says, adding that planning must be part of every manager's job.

But the glaring reality is that not everyone is good at planning. Different people have different skills and must be placed in the organization accordingly. General Electric, Chase Manhattan, Corning Glass Works, and a handful of others are already screening their staffs for such things as entrepreneurial flair, cost-cutting ability, and similar talents (BW—Feb. 25).

However, most are still following rigidly structured lines of promotion—letting the controller, for example, automatically move into the divisional manager's slot, or turning salesmen and researchers into managers.

What is needed is a dual ladder, a method by which skilled people who do not want to move into management do not find their careers stymied. Analog Devices Corp. has one, as does 3M. Titles such as "senior fellow" garner prestige and money at Analog. 3M has a system of honor societies to convey status for scientific achievement.

Few companies have extended the dual ladder up to the rarefied atmosphere of the executive suite. Robert W. Lear, Columbia University's executive in residence, only half-jests when he says that companies should appoint a "vice-president in charge of hope." James B. Farley, chairman of Booz Allen & Hamilton, envisions high-level corporate types whose main role is to think. "If they're considered a third elbow, then the CEO has to say, 'O. K., we're an animal with three elbows,'" Farley says.

The need for clout

But, to work, the think tank must have corporate clout. Some form of matrix management—a system whereby most employees have two bosses—is probably needed. Employees wind up accountable to a conventional manager for financial results, day-to-day operations, and the like, and to the thought leaders for concepts, ideas, and research. General Electric Co. and Union Carbide Corp. have had luck with matrixes. Hewlett-Packard Co. recently put in one in which many managers have dotted-line reporting arrangements to their own peers. "A manager may be asked to report to quite a few others to share information and increase communications," explains Friederich W. Schroeder, director of corporate development. More common is the setup at TRW Electronics, a division of TRW Inc., where groups developing new products report to the head of new ventures during the "incubation phase" of development.

A few other companies have moved at least slightly in this direction, hiring high-level people to spot ways to apply high technology to conventional products. International Harvester recently appointed Robert J. Potter, a former Xerox executive, to the new post of senior vice-president and chief technical officer, and gave him the mandate of scouting out technological improvements for IH's businesses. General Electric has a new corporate production and operating services unit under a senior vice-president whose charter is to "look at opportunities to infuse our manufacturing organizations with all the latest technical developments," says Reginald H. Jones, chairman and CEO.

Such people and their departments must be protected from the budgetary ax even in a rough economy. And the best way is to have sacrosanct research budgets that cannot be touched by operating people. At Control Data Corp., William C. Norris, chairman and CEO, has a "chairman's budget" used entirely for following up new ideas. "If that were in the operating budget, it would have been cut," he says.

Similarly, Texas Instruments Inc. maintains separate operating and strategic budgets—a setup that enabled it to continue research into minicomputers during the last recession. Today TI is the fourth-largest minicomputer manufacturer in the country. "To try to get managers to cut more heavily into operating areas while holding together the strategic area is kind of counterintuitive, but that's what we attempt to do," says Charles H. Phipps, TI's manager of strategic planning.

Separate funding

Within the strategic research budget itself, it is a good idea to keep specific funds for "pure" research. Joseph W. Davison, vice-president for research and development at Phillips Petroleum Co., sets aside 3% to 5% of his annual budget for "blue sky" ideas. "There are a great many short-range opportunities that are very high priority now, but the long-range and blue-sky categories are the areas from which our future business is built," he insists.

Separate funding for basic research also prevents operating departments from cannibalizing R&D budgets. That is

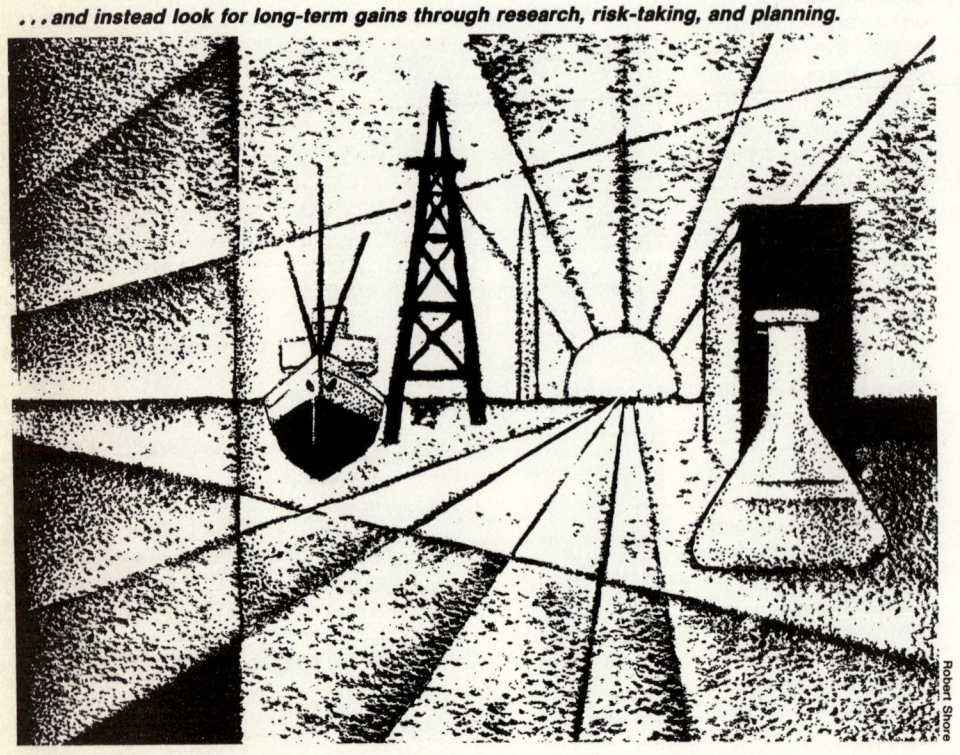

...and instead look for long-term gains through research, risk-taking, and planning.

A NEW SOCIAL CONTRACT

a problem that irks Walter L. Abel, vice-president of R&D at Emhart Corp. Abel cites a study that shows that about 75% of what companies define as R&D costs actually went for efforts that were just product improvements or line extensions. "If marketing goes to R&D for customer help, it should be charged to marketing, and if manufacturing needs a little help with a process, R&D's time should be charged to them," he says.

The best answer, however, is to move basic R&D away from the pesterings of operating departments. "We must have outposts of basic research with real channels of application," insists Herbert Simon, Nobel laureate at Carnegie-Mellon University. "Bell Labs and GE are good at this, but few other companies are. You need small clusters of basic scientists working within industrial corporations, but without pressure for immediate commercial applications."

Using the universities

Realistically, not many companies can afford to maintain staffed and equipped scientific think tanks. But they can certainly make better use of universities. Universities can also provide a neutral ground where competitors can jointly sponsor and use research. The fruits of such cooperation were exemplified in 1977, when the Georgia Institute of Technology, the National Science Foundation, the University of Missouri, the Illinois Research Institute, and various companies from Georgia's granite industry joined forces to see if the noise from plasma jets used to cut granite could be reduced to a level acceptable to the Occupational Safety & Health Administration. The result was a process using high-pressure water jets. The granite companies are now forming a consortium to manufacture and distribute the new OSHA-acceptable cutting tools.

At least one CEO agrees that cooperation is essential. "I believe executives should be looking around to see what other companies they can work with on R&D," says Control Data's Norris, who has spearheaded joint ventures with Honeywell, NCR, and others to produce computer tape drives, disks, and tapes. Norris has also set up small-business resource centers across the country to help incubate new small ventures.

Norris is not the typical CEO, either in attitude or in background. He not only heads CDC but also founded it. Under Norris, CDC has invested $150 million in Plato, a computer-based education system, and has still not broken even, yet he insists on continuing full funding. He knows his business inside out and has a clout with the board of directors that most professional managers never get. Yet Norris' attitudes—his willingness to back money-losing projects because he believes in them, his fearlessness of Wall Street, his willingness to cooperate with other companies and other researchers—are exactly what are needed in the next generation of managers.

And that raises a frightening question: What is to prevent the next generation of managers from falling prey to the same stockholder pressures, specialized orientations, and tunnel vision that characterize the majority of today's managers? The current crop of executive vice-presidents, vice-chairmen, divisional presidents—the people who seem targeted for tomorrow's top jobs—are cut from the same mold as their CEOs. Otherwise, they would not have attained the positions they now hold.

The problem may simply be one of age. The few companies that have young managements are simply more willing to take risks. Gary E. MacDougal, 43, chairman and CEO of Mark Controls Corp., a $233 million-a-year manufacturer of industrial valves, did not particularly care when Mark's earnings were recently penalized 50¢ a share because the company had pumped money into a new valve that will not be profitable for several years. "Maybe it's because our management is in its 40s that we can look at this longer-term," he surmises. Even Seatrain Lines Inc., which has sailed exceedingly rough financial seas for the last five years or so, has had a vice-president of industrial relations take 37 trips to Alaska because he believed that there was money to be made in cooperating with native Alaskan corporations for carrying crude—a belief that turned out to be correct—and has had numerous other managers push ahead with projects not specifically in their domains. "At 49 I'm the old man of the company—our president is 40, the president of our Atlantic Div. is 38, and they're just all entrepreneurial," says Robert Brown, executive vice-president.

The '32-year-old tiger'

Booz Allen's Farley suggests that companies skip a couple of generations and reach for the "32-year-old tiger" as the next potential head. This would bring a fresh approach to the executive suite and would give the top manager impetus to take risks, since he might still be around when they paid off.

But fresh blood is not enough. Attitude and forward thinking are not linked to age alone. Armand Hammer at 82 still supplies the imagination and vision for Occidental Petroleum Corp. in a way that none of his younger executives can match. Thus, corporations must also make sure that the younger managers are not allowed to specialize too quickly or too extremely. Both the internal and the external educational systems must change. Job rotations—not uncommon years ago but not used as frequently today—must be reinstated so that managers get a feel for several disciplines and for all the businesses. At J&J, Chairman James E. Burke says, top management plays a "chess game" with people to broaden them. Most inside members of the company's board have worked in at least two of J&J's four market segments. President David R. Clare has manufacturing and marketing experience from several of J&J's operating companies. This sort of broadening should spread to other companies.

Ethics and global thinking

Although nothing replaces good hands-on job experience, new types of educational seminars would certainly not hurt. But they should not be technique-oriented. They should teach ethics and global thinking—maybe even philosophy and English literature, if for no other reason than to teach managers to think and to ask questions. Money spent on such mind-broadening experiences as the Aspen Institute or the Dartmouth Institute is rarely wasted.

It may be time for a resurgence of the old liberal arts major as an acceptable entry into business. Business schools will not start stressing long-range thinking until companies stop recruiting MBAs with calculators permanently attached to their right arms. The mathematical techniques of management may have made an important contribution to the growth of American corporations, but it is time for the pendulum to swing back to visionary, insightful managers who place emphasis on gut feel and on a broad understanding of the total business picture.

Of course, they must understand the profit motive—but they must also understand the difference between maximized short-term profits and optimized long-term profits. As the itinerant philosopher who writes in Koppers Co.'s annual report put it: "For those of you who may not understand the difference between optimum and maximum, let me put it this way: Optimum body temperature runs about 98.6F. Maximum body temperature is likely to kill you." ∎

Five years ago the chief executives of two major oil companies determined that they would have to diversify out of oil because their current business could not support long-term growth and it faced serious political threats. Not only did they announce their new long-range strategies to employees and the public, but they established elaborate plans to implement them. Today, after several years of floundering in attempts to acquire and build new businesses, both companies are firmly back in oil, and the two CEOs have been replaced.

Each of the CEOs had been unable to implement his strategy, not because it was theoretically wrong or bad but because neither had understood that his company's culture was so entrenched in the traditions and values of doing business as oilmen that employees resisted—and sabotaged—the radical changes that the CEOs tried to impose. Oil operations require long-term investments for long-term rewards; but the new businesses needed short-term views and an emphasis on current returns. Successes had come from hitting it big in wildcatting; but the new success was to be based on such abstractions as market share or numbers growth—all seemingly nebulous concepts to them. Too late did the CEOs realize that strategies can only be implemented with the wholehearted effort and belief of everyone involved. If implementing them violates employees' basic beliefs about their roles in the company, or the traditions that underlie the corporation's culture, they are doomed to fail.

Culture implies values, such as aggressiveness, defensiveness, or nimbleness, that set a pattern for a company's activities, opinions, and actions. That pattern is instilled in employees by managers' example and passed down to succeeding generations of workers. The CEO's words alone do not produce culture; rather, his actions and those of his managers do.

A corporation's culture can be its major strength when it is consistent with its strategies. Some of the most successful companies have clearly demonstrated that fact, including:

■ International Business Machines Corp., where marketing drives a service philosophy that is almost unparalleled. The company keeps a hot line open 24 hours a day, seven days a week, to service IBM products.

■ International Telephone & Telegraph Corp., where financial discipline demands total dedication. To beat out the competition in a merger, an executive once called former Chairman Harold S. Geneen at 3 a.m. to get his approval.

■ Digital Equipment Corp., where an emphasis on innovation creates freedom with responsibility. Employees can set their own hours and working style, but they are expected to articulate and support their activities with evidence of progress.

■ Delta Air Lines Inc., where a focus on customer service produces a high degree of teamwork. Employees will substitute in other jobs to keep planes flying and baggage moving.

■ Atlantic Richfield Co., where an emphasis on entrepreneurship encourages action. Operating men have the autonomy to bid on promising fields without hierarchical approval.

But a culture that prevents a company from meeting competitive threats, or from adapting to changing economic or social environments, can lead to the company's stagnation and ultimate demise unless it makes a conscious effort to change. One that did make this effort is PepsiCo Inc., where the cultural emphasis has been systematically changed over the past two decades from passivity to aggressiveness.

Once the company was content in its No. 2 spot, offering Pepsi as a cheaper alternative to Coca-Cola. But today, a new employee at PepsiCo quickly learns that beating the competition, whether outside or inside the company, is the surest path to success. In its soft-drink operation, for example, Pepsi's marketers now take on Coke directly, asking consumers to compare the taste of the two colas. That direct confrontation is reflected inside the company as well. Managers are pitted against each other to grab more market share, to work harder, and to wring more profits out of their businesses. Because winning is the key value at Pepsi, losing has its penalties. Consistent runners-up find their jobs gone. Employees know they must win merely to stay in place—and must devastate the competition to get ahead.

But the aggressive competitor who succeeds at Pepsi would be sorely out of place at J. C. Penney Co., where a quick victory is far less important than building long-term loyalty. Indeed, a Penney store manager once was severely rebuked by the company's president for making too much profit. That was considered unfair to customers, whose trust Penney seeks to win. The business style set by the company's founder—which one competitor describes as avoiding "taking unfair advantage of anyone the company did business with"—still prevails today. Customers know they can return merchandise with no questions asked; suppliers know that Penney will not haggle over terms; and employees are comfortable in their jobs, knowing that Penney will avoid layoffs at all costs and will find easier jobs for those who cannot handle more demanding ones. Not surprisingly, Penney's average executive tenure is 33 years while Pepsi's is 10.

These vastly different methods of doing business are but two examples of corporate culture. People who work at Pepsi and Penney sense that the corporate values are the yardstick by which they will be measured. Just as tribal cultures have totems and taboos that dictate how each member will act toward fellow members and outsiders, so does a corporation's culture influence employees' actions toward customers, competitors, suppliers, and one another. Some-

CORPORATE CULTURE

The hard-to-change values that spell success or failure

times the rules are written out. More often they are tacit. Most often, they are laid down by a strong founder and hardened by success into custom.

"Culture gives people a sense of how to behave and what they ought to be doing," explains Howard M. Schwartz, vice-president of Management Analysis Center Inc., a Cambridge (Mass.) consulting firm that just completed a study of corporate culture. Indeed, so firmly are certain values entrenched in a company's behavior that predictable responses can be counted on not only by its employees but by its competitors. "How will our competitors behave?" is a stock question that strategic planners ask when contemplating a new move. The answers come from assessing competitors' time-honored priorities, their reactions to competition, and their ability to change course.

Because a company's culture is so pervasive, changing it becomes one of the most difficult tasks that any chief executive can undertake. Just as a primitive tribe's survival depended on its ability to react to danger, and to alter its way of life when necessary, so must corporations, faced with changing economic, social, and political climates, sometimes radically change their methods of operating. What stands in the way is not only the "relative immutability of culture," as the MAC study points out, but also the fact that few executives consciously recognize what their company's culture is and how it manifests itself. The concept of culture, says Stanley M. Davis, professor of organization behavior at Boston University and a co-author of the MAC study, is hard to understand. "It's like putting your hand in a cloud" he says.

Thomas J. Peters, a principal in McKinsey & Co., cites a client who believed it was imperative to his company's survival to add a marketing effort to his manufacturing-oriented organization. Because the company had no experts in marketing, it wanted to hire some. Consultants pointed out that this strategy would fail because all of the issues raised at company meetings concerned cost-cutting and production—never competition or customers. Rewards were built into achieving efficiencies in the first category, while none were built into understanding the second. Ultimately, the CEO recognized that he had to educate himself and his staff so thoroughly in marketing that he could build his own in-house team.

Similarly, American Telephone & Telegraph Co. is now trying to alter its service-oriented operation to give equal weight to marketing. Past attempts to do so ignored the culture and failed. For example, in 1961, AT&T set up a school to teach managers to coordinate the design and manufacture of data products for customized sales. But when managers completed the course, they found that the traditional way of operating—making noncustomized mass sales—were what counted in the company. They were given neither the time to analyze individual customers' needs nor rewards commensurate with such efforts. The result was that 85% of the graduates quit, and AT&T disbanded the school.

AT&T prides itself on its service operation, and with good reason. It provides the most efficient and broadest telephone system in the world, and it reacts to disaster with a speed unknown anywhere else. In 1975, for example, a fire

PepsiCo: From passivity to aggressiveness

Chairman Kendall: The effort to instill competitive spirit extends to interdepartmental team games at headquarters.

The Concept of Strategy and Policy / 31

swept through a switching center in lower Manhattan, knocking out service to 170,000 telephones. AT&T rallied 4,000 employees and shipped in 3,000 tons of equipment to restore full service in just 22 days—a task that could have taken a lesser company more than a year.

But costs for AT&T's service had been readily passed to customers through rate increases granted by public service commissions. Keeping costs down was thus never a major consideration. Now, however, since the Federal Communications Commission has decided to allow other companies to sell products in AT&T's once-captive markets, AT&T must change the orientation of its 1 million employees. In numbers alone, such a change is unprecedented in corporate history. Still, to survive in its new environment, Bell must alter its plans, strategies, and employee expectations of what the company wants from them, as well as their belief in the security of their jobs and old way of doing business.

To make the changes, Bell has analyzed its new requirements in exquisite detail that fills thousands of pages. It acknowledges its lack of skills in certain crucial areas: marketing, cost control, and administrative ability to deal with change. The company had rewarded managers who administered set policies by the book; today it is promoting innovators with advanced degrees in business administration. Once it measured service representatives by the speed with which they responded to calls; today they are measured by the number of problems they solve.

AT&T's new role model

Instead of its traditional policy of promoting from within, some new role models were hired from outside the company. Archie J. McGill, a former executive of International Business Machines Corp., was made vice-president of business marketing, for example. McGill is described by associates as an innovator who is the antithesis of the traditional "Bell-shaped man" because of his "combative, adversarial style." Just as IBM's slogan, "Think," encouraged its employees to be problem-solvers, McGill is hammering a new slogan, "I make the difference," into each of his marketers, encouraging them to become entrepreneurs. That idea is reinforced by incentives that pit salespeople against each other for bonuses, a system unknown at Bell before.

Even so, the changes are slow. Learning to become solution-sellers has produced "a tremendous amount of confusion" among Bell marketing people, reports one large corporate customer. For example, AT&T is "absolutely trapped" if a customer requests an extra editing part for its standard teletype system, he says. "If you want something they don't have, they tend to solve the problem by saying, 'Let's go out for a drink'."

Even McGill concedes that "anytime you have an orientation toward consulting [past practices] as opposed to being adaptive to a situation, change doesn't happen overnight." Bell's director of planning, W. Brooke Tunstall, estimates that it will take another three to five years to attain an 85% change in the company's orientation. Still, he insists, there has already been "a definite change in mindset at the upper levels." The arguments heard around the company now concern the pace of change rather than its scope. Says Tunstall, "I haven't run into anyone who doesn't understand why the changes are needed."

The AT&T example clearly demonstrates the need for a company to examine its existing culture in depth and to acknowledge the reasons for revolutionary change, if changes must be made. As AT&T learned from its earlier attempt to sell specialized services, change cannot be implemented merely by sending people to school. Nor can it be made by hiring new staff, by acquiring new businesses, by changing the name of the company, or by redefining its business. Even exhortations by the chief executive to operate differently will not succeed unless they are backed up by a changed structure, new role models, new incentive systems, and new rewards and punishments built into operations.

A chief executive, for example, who demands innovative new products from his staff, but who leaves in place a hierarchy that can smother a good new idea at its first airing, is unlikely to get what he wants. In contrast, an unwritten rule at 3M Co., says one manager, is, "Never be responsible for killing an idea." Similarly, if a CEO's staff knows that his first priority is consistent earnings growth, it will be unlikely to present him with any new product or service idea, no matter how great its potential, if it requires a long incubation period and a drag on earnings before it reaches fruition. At Pillsbury Co., for example, managers are afraid to suggest ideas for products that might require considerable research and development because they know that Chairman William H. Spoor is obsessed with improving short-term financial results, sources say.

The real priorities

One element is certain: Employees cannot be fooled. They understand the real priorities in the corporation. At the first inconsistency they will become confused, then reluctant to change, and finally intransigent. Indeed, consistency in every aspect of a culture is essential to its success, as PepsiCo's transformation into an archrival of Coke shows.

For decades, Coke's unchallenged position in the market was so complete that the brand name Coke became synonymous with cola drinks. It attained this distinction under Robert W. Woodruff, who served as chief executive for 32 years and is still chairman of the company's finance committee at age 90. Woodruff had an "almost messianic drive to get Coca-Cola [drunk] all over the world," says Harvey Z. Yazijian, co-author of the forthcoming book, *The Cola Wars*. So successful was Coke in accomplishing this under Woodruff—and later, J. Paul Austin, who will retire in March as CEO—that Coca-Cola became known as "America's second State Dept." Its trademark became a symbol of American life itself.

"A real problem in the past," says Yazijian, "was that they had a lot of deadwood" among employees. Nevertheless, Coke's marketing and advertising were extremely effective in expanding consumption of the product. But the lack of serious competition and the company's relative isolation in its home town of Atlanta allowed it to become "fat, dumb, and happy," according to one consultant. Coke executives are known to be extremely loyal to the company and circumspect to the point of secrecy in their dealings with the outside world.

In the mid-1950s, Pepsi, once a sleepy New York-based bottler with a lame slogan, "Twice as much for a nickel, too," began to develop into a serious threat under the leadership of Chairman Alfred N. Steele. The movement gathered momentum, and by the early 1970s the company had become a ferocious competitor under Chairman Donald M. Kendall and President Andrall E. Pearson, a former director of McKinsey. The culture that these two executives determined to create was based on the goal of becoming the No. 1 marketer of soft drinks.

Severe pressure was put on managers to show continual improvement in market share, product volume, and profits. "Careers ride on tenths of a market share point," says John Sculley, vice-president and head of domestic beverage operations. This atmosphere pervades the company's nonbeverage units as well. "Everyone knows that if the results aren't there, you had better have your resume up to date," says a former snack food manager.

To keep everyone on their toes, a "creative tension" is continually nurtured among departments at Pepsi, says another former executive. The staff is kept lean and managers are moved to new jobs constantly, which results in people working long hours and engaging in political maneuvering "just to keep their jobs from being reorganized out from under them," says a headhunter.

Kendall himself sets a constant example. He once resorted to using a snowmobile to get to work in a blizzard, demonstrating the ingenuity and dedication to work he expects from his staff. This type of pressure has pushed many managers out. But a recent company survey shows that others thrive under such conditions. "Most of our guys are having fun," Pearson insists. They are the kind of people, elaborates Sculley, who "would rather be in the Marines than in the Army."

Like Marines, Pepsi executives are expected to be physically fit as well as mentally alert: Pepsi employs four physical-fitness instructors at its headquarters, and a former executive says it is an unwritten rule that to get ahead in the company a manager must stay in shape. The company encourages one-on-one sports as well as interdepartmental competition in such games as soccer and basketball. In company team contests or business dealings, says Sculley, "the more competitive it becomes, the more we enjoy it." In such a culture, less competitive managers are deliberately weeded out. Even suppliers notice a difference today. "They are smart, sharp negotiators who take advantage of all opportunities," says one.

While Pepsi steadily gained market share in the 1970s, Coke was reluctant to admit that a threat existed, Yazijian says. Pepsi now has bested Coke in the domestic take-home market, and it is mounting a challenge overseas. At the moment, the odds are in favor of Coke, which sells one-third of the world's soft drinks and has had Western Europe locked up for years. But Pepsi has been making inroads: Besides monopolizing the Soviet market, it has dominated the Arab Middle East ever since Coke was ousted in 1967, when it granted a bottling franchise in Israel. Still, Coke showed that it was not giving up. It cornered a potentially vast new market—China.

With Pepsi gaining domestic market share faster than Coke—last year it gained 7.5% vs. Coke's 5%—observers believe that Coke will turn more to foreign sales or food sales for growth. Roberto C. Goizueta, who will be Coke's next chairman, will not reveal Coke's strategy. But one tactic the company has already used is hiring away some of Pepsi's "tigers." Coke has lured Donald Breen Jr., who played a major role in developing the "Pepsi Challenge"—the consumer taste test—as well as five other marketing and sales executives associated with Pepsi. Pepsi won its court battle to prevent Breen from revealing confidential information over the next 12 months. But the company's current culture is unlikely to build loyalty. Pepsi may well have to examine the dangers of cultivating ruthlessness in its managers, say former executives.

Quite a different problem faces J. C. Penney today. Its well-entrenched culture, laid down by founder James Cash Penney in a seven-point codification of the company's guiding principles, called "The Penney Idea," has brought it tremendous loyalty from its staff but lower profits recently. Its introduction of fashionable apparel has been only partially successful, because customers identify it with nonfashionable staples, such as children's clothes, work clothes, and hardware. It has also been outpaced in the low end of the market by aggressive discounters, such as K mart Corp., which knocked Penney out of the No. 2 retailer's spot in 1976 and which has been gaining market share at Penney's expense ever since.

Penney's is proud that two national magazines cited it as one of the 10 best places to work in the nation, a claim that is borne out by employees. "Everyone is treated as an individual," notes one former executive. Another praises the company's "bona fide participative" decision-making process, and adds that Penney has "an openness in the organization that many large companies don't seem to achieve."

But Penney's paternalistic attitude toward its work force has meant that it always tries to find new jobs for marginally competent employees rather than firing them, says Stephen Temlock, manager of human resource strategy development. He concedes that some workers "expect us to be papa and mama, and aren't motivated enough to help themselves." The corollary of that, he admits, is that the company sometimes fails to reward outstanding performers enough.

Penney's entrenched culture makes any change slow, Temlock adds, but he insists that this solidity helps to maintain a balance between "an out-and-out aggressive environment and a human environment." Penney Chairman Donald V. Seibert believes that the company's problems have more to do with the retailing industry's endemic cyclicality than with company culture. Although he admits that he worries sometimes that the company is too inbred, he notes that it has brought in different types of people in the last several years as it entered new businesses, such as catalog sales and insurance.

Seibert adds that the company firmly believes that the principles of "The Penney Idea" will be relevant no matter how much the economic environment changes. "You can't say that there's a good way to modernize integrity," he emphasizes.

Seibert may be right. One competitor notes that the aggressive newcomers in retailing have profited from older retailers' mistakes, and thus have found shortcuts to growth. But, says this source, "the shortcuts are limited, and the newcomers' staying power has yet to be proven." Still, if the new threat continues, Penney's pace must speed up, and it must soon act more flexibly to protect itself; it may even have to abandon some of the customs that have grown up around its humanistic principles.

Another gentlemanly company found that it had to do just that to regain its leading position in banking. Chase Manhattan Bank had cruised along comfortably for years, leaning on the aristocratic image of its chairman, David Rockefeller. In the mid-1970s, however, Chase was jolted out of its lethargy by a sharp skid in earnings and a return on assets that plunged as low as 0.24% in 1976. Its real estate portfolio was loaded with questionable and sour loans, and its commercial lending department's reputation had been severely tarnished because high turnover of its lending officers and the resulting inexperience of those who replaced them made the bank less responsive to customers. Some embarrassing questions about Chase's basic management practices began to be raised.

Rockefeller and a group of top executives, including Willard C. Butcher, now chief executive and chairman-elect, decided that the fault lay with a culture that rewarded people more for appearance than performance and that produced inbreeding and a smugness that made the bank loath to grapple with competitors. The typical Chase executive in those days was a well-groomed functionary who did not drive himself hard or set high standards for his own performance, banking analysts remember.

The first step toward change, Chase executives felt, was for the bank to define what it wanted to be. Early in 1977 it drew up a three-page mission statement that outlined the company's business mix. "We will only do those things we can do extremely well and with the highest level of integrity," the statement said. For Chase, this meant taking a hard look at some unprofitable parts of its business. Subsequently, it closed some 50 low-volume domestic branches in New York, and it began to turn away questionable loan business that it had accepted before.

The mission statement also spelled out specific targets for financial goals, such as return on equity and assets and debt-to-capital ratio. At the start, employees doubted that the company could meet these goals; one, for example, was a return on assets of 0.55% to 0.65%, more than double the 1976 figure.

Chase began a major effort to step up communications between top management and the rest of the staff. This was a departure from the old days, when

The Concept of Strategy and Policy / 33

decisions were simply handed down from the 17th-floor executive suite, says one former manager. The participation of all employees created a sense of "ownership" of the program by all, something consultant Robert F. Allen, president of the Human Resources Institute in Morristown, N. J., believes is essential to any long-lasting change.

Like AT&T, Chase promoted new role models, such as Richard J. Boyle, now a senior vice-president, who took over the bank's troubled real estate operations at age 32. Boyle, described as a "workaholic" with strong opinions and a willingness to make hard decisions, such as writing off floundering projects rather than carrying them on the company's books, is the antithesis of the old-style Chase banker, analysts say. To run commercial lending, the bank lured back James H. Carey, who had left Chase for Hambros Bank. "They put absolutely brilliant people in problem areas," remarks John J. Mason, banking analyst at Shearson Loeb Rhoades Inc.

Rewards for performers

But tradition suffered: One-third of the bank's top executives were replaced by outsiders. Salaries and incentive payments were overhauled to provide greater rewards for top performers. And an advanced management course was started for promising young managers. The culture has been altered from its emphasis on style to a focus on performance. And now that employees' expectations of the company have changed, the new order is likely to prevail. But even Butcher, although pleased with the improvement, warns, "The danger is always that you become complacent."

Chase was able to effect the change in its culture under the aegis of its reigning leaders, Rockefeller and Butcher. But some companies find that the only way to solve problems is to bring in a new chief who can implement sweeping change. Yet even a new strongman can run up against a wall unless he understands the company's existing culture.

Dennis C. Stanfill, a corporate finance specialist, ran into just such problems when he took over as chief executive in 1971 at Twentieth Century-Fox Film Corp. Stanfill's aim was to balance the risks of the motion picture business with steady earnings from other leisure-time businesses, which he began acquiring. But he also insisted on running all of Fox's businesses, including the film operation, on an equal basis by keeping the corporate purse strings pulled tight—and in his hands.

What Stanfill overlooked was that creative people require a different kind of managing than do typical business employees. While the latter group can usually be motivated by using the carrot-and-stick approach, creative people are self-motivated. They will work as hard as needed to perform as perfectly as they can, because they identify their work not with the company but with themselves. What they want from their patron-managers, however, is applause and rewards for a good job, and protection when they bomb.

Stanfill violated those expectations when he refused to give Alan Ladd Jr., president of the film group, control over bonuses for his staff, which had produced such hits as *Star Wars*. From Stanfill's point of view, the decision was sound: In just three years he had erased a $125 million bank debt and brought the company into the black after it had been in default on its loans. He believed the traditional extravagances of the film company would keep the corporation on a shaky foundation. Indeed, he says, he wants "to keep the balance between show and business."

Not a 'brokerage'

But the film company's response was predictable. Ladd quit to start his own operation, taking several key people with him. "In my opinion, Stanfill doesn't understand what motivates creative people," says Ladd. "You don't run a film business like a brokerage house."

Fox's directors quickly stepped in and demanded that Stanfill find a "name" replacement for Ladd. Stanfill has since picked Alan J. Hirschfield, who had been laid off by Columbia Pictures Industries Inc. and who has been praised by the industry for adding a creative spark to Fox this past year. But Stanfill now must make financial decisions jointly with Hirschfield.

Whether Stanfill will ever be comfortable in such a high-risk business remains questionable. One film industry analyst thinks not. He says: "Stanfill has never felt confortable running an entertainment company. He is downside-risk-oriented on motion pictures, and didn't know why Ladd was so successful." If that is true, Stanfill could be on a collision course with Fox's implicit culture.

Stanfill may have recognized that the strategy he was imposing on Fox's film business, which produces 63% of the corporation's pretax operating earnings, violated its culture. But he obviously believed that it was necessary for the company's survival. He has not, however, changed Fox's culture. As more and more chief executives recognize the need for long-range strategies, they will have to consider the effects of these strategies on their companies. It may well be that CEOs must then decide whether their strategies must change to fit their companies' culture or the cultures must change to assure survival. ∎

QUESTIONS

Texas Instruments Shows U.S. Business How to Survive in the 1980s:

1. Identify and discuss the major aspects of the Texas Instruments strategy.

2. How has each component of the overall strategy contributed to the company's evolution and growth since its inception in 1949?

Wanted: A Manager to Fit Each Strategy:

1. Based upon this article, what are the major advantages and disadvantages associated with attempting to match managerial personality types with specific corporate objectives?

2. A manager's personality traits have a strong impact on the successful achievement of corporate objectives. Discuss. Prepare an argument either for or against this statement.

Sun and Arco: How Contrasting Strategies Made Different Companies:

1. Discuss the major differences in the strategies of Sun Co. and Arco.

2. The primary factors contributing to the different industry positions of Sun Co. and Arco are the operating and management philosophies of their respective chairmen. Discuss. Prepare an argument either for or against this statement.

Trans World Corp.: The Strategy Squeeze on the Airline:

1. Why did TWA's diversification strategy fail to live up to expectations? Mention the goal(s) it was supposed to accomplish.

2. Describe the internal and external environments in which TWA now must operate. What impact do they have on strategy development?

What Caused the Decline: The Penalties of Short-Term Corporate Strategies:

1. Discuss some of the benefits that can be realized through long-term strategic planning. Mention the environmental factors that favor such a long-run focus.

2. What are the major reasons that many firms continue to focus on the short run? Discuss the associated costs of continuing to do so.

A New Social Contract: How Companies Can Lengthen Their Sights:

1. What are some of the key techniques that are being applied to encourage employees and managers to focus on the long term?

2. What can be done to instill a long-run orientation into managers of the future?

Corporate Culture: The Hard-to-Change Values That Spell Success or Failure:

1. The culture or values of a company permeate every aspect of the firm's operations. As a result, whenever a "cultural" change is called for, it requires a complete restructuring of the organization. Discuss how such a change can be effectively accomplished.

2. The culture of an organization can be either a primary strength or an overwhelming weakness for the company. Discuss whether the culture was (is) a positive or negative factor in one of the following companies: Pepsico Inc., J. C. Penney Co., AT&T, Chase Manhattan Bank.

Two.

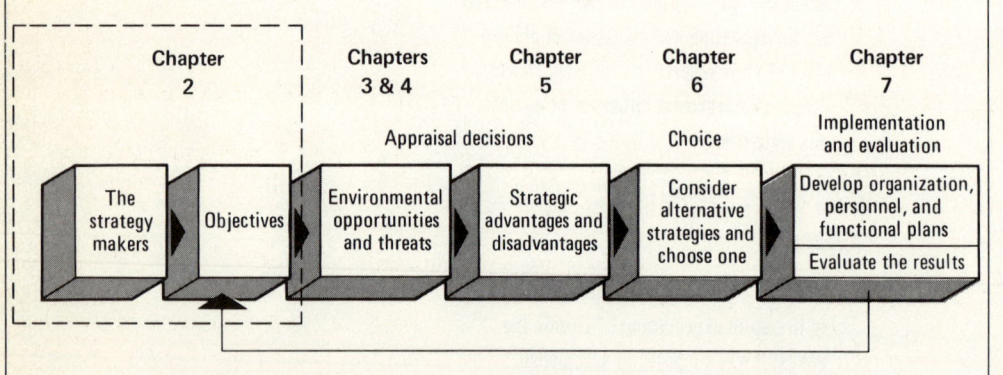

Table 2-1 A MODEL OF THE BUSINESS POLICY AND STRATEGIC MANAGEMENT PROCESS.

Chapter 2	Chapters 3 & 4	Chapter 5	Chapter 6	Chapter 7
	Appraisal decisions		Choice	Implementation and evaluation
The strategy makers → Objectives	Environmental opportunities and threats	Strategic advantages and disadvantages	Consider alternative strategies and choose one	Develop organization, personnel, and functional plans / Evaluate the results

In Chapter 1, the concept of strategy and policy was illustrated with examples of firms engaged in the business policy and strategic management process. Chapter 2 focuses attention on the strategy makers—those persons who formulate the objectives the firm will seek to achieve and who determine the way in which those objectives will be pursued.

Strategy makers do not have the freedom to choose a strategy arbitrarily without regard for internal and external constraints on the firm. The external environment offers both opportunities and threats. Strategy makers must avoid environmental threats while pursuing opportunities, but the firm's internal strengths and weaknesses will restrict the number of opportunities the firm can take advantage of. For example, if the strategy makers find an investment opportunity for which they need $10 million in capital and if they can raise only $5 million, then that investment opportunity is not a feasible alternative for the firm. Along a different vein, the values prevailing in the firm act as constraints on what the strategy makers can do. This point is made extremely well by the *Business Week* article in Chapter 1 entitled "Corporate Culture: The Hard-to-Change Values That Spell Success or Failure."

There are many factors which constrain what strategy makers can do, but it is not the purpose of this chapter to identify all these constraints. The purpose of Chapter 2 is to illustrate with *Business Week* articles how strategists influence and make business policy and strategic management decisions. So, who are the strategy makers? An examination of Ex-

The Strategy Makers

36 / Readings from *Business Week*

hibit 2-1 shows how important this question is. The strategy makers are central to the business policy and strategic management decisions such as analysis, choice, implementation, and evaluation. The answer to the question is not simple and straightforward. For the entrepreneurial firm, the answer is likely to be the entrepreneur and his or her backers. For the family business, the traditional answer has been the family and the top managers. For the large, publicly held corporation, the strategy makers include the top managers, the board of directors, and the corporate planning staff. The *Business Week* articles in Chapter 2 focus on strategy makers in large, publicly held corporations because these firms are so vital to the economy of the United States and the world.

The following *Business Week* articles describe two special problems with which some strategy makers must deal:

- "Following the Corporate Legend"

- "Managers Who Are No Longer Entrepreneurs"

Furthermore, several *Business Week* articles describe strategy makers attempting to implement particular strategies. Examples follow.

Retrenchment Strategies

- "ITT: Groping for a New Strategy"

- "The Pains of Turning Firestone Around"

- "Richard J. Ferris: Flying a Risky New Route for United"

Growth Strategy

- "After Years of Hoarding Cash Hearst Is Spending Big"

Merger Strategy

- "The Man Behind Kraft's Merger"

Turnaround Strategy

- "How a New Chief Is Turning Interbank Inside Out"

- "Trautman: A Goal Eludes a Willful Manager"

All the *Business Week* articles in this chapter are designed to help the reader understand how the strategist can strongly influence the direction of a company. However, the last article in this chapter focuses on the dramatic effect a strategy maker can have on the climate in his or her organization.

- "First of Chicago: New Management to Bring Back the Past"

FOLLOWING THE CORPORATE LEGEND

Anyone making the case that succeeding the company's founder or family manager is tough is not likely to get an argument from Lee A. Iacocca, who ended up trying to save a dying Chrysler Corp. after a run-in with the founder's grandson at Ford Motor Co. Nor is the point likely to be disputed by Lyman C. Hamilton Jr., who was recently ousted as chief executive of International Telephone & Telegraph Corp. by its entrepreneurial tyrant, Harold S. Geneen, who built ITT to its present size. Nor would an argument come from Arthur Taylor, the former president at CBS Inc., who, not long after inheriting that position from William S. Paley, soon also began inheriting the founder's wrath.

Clearly, the job of succeeding an entrepreneur—or any dictatorial CEO who has become a company legend—can be a no-win proposition. The problem dates from the dawn of the corporate era, but it seems to be getting worse, if only because transitions from entrepreneur to professional manager appear to be more prevalent. Fewer offspring now believe that following the footsteps of entrepreneurial parents is their destiny. Even when they would like to become successors, the company they would inherit may have grown too large and complex for family management. And in publicly held companies, increasingly active directors are insisting that nepotism should not be the sole qualification for a chief executive's appointment.

A family's mistakes

But if the shift to nonfamily management solves old problems, it creates a raft of new ones, rooted in actual or perceived differences between the owner-entrepreneur and the salaried professional. Successful entrepreneurs are often flamboyant and autocratic, and even after retirement their image looms larger than life to directors and employees. While the professional manager may be more inclined to delegate authority than the founder he replaces, he may also irritate subordinates by placing more emphasis on performance than on loyalty. "Whenever the new man makes the slightest misstep," observes one corporate psychologist, "employees keep thinking, 'if the old man were here, we wouldn't have these problems.'"

Indeed, any operating problems that crop up can expose the new manager's real vulnerabilities. Eugene B. Peters was a favorite of the late Robert A. Uihlein Jr., the former chairman of Jos. Schlitz Brewing Co. and the patriarch of the family that owns 75% of the Milwaukee brewer. With Uihlein's support, Peters rocketed to the No. 2 spot at Schlitz by 1974, only five years after joining the company as a vice-president. When Uihlein died unexpectedly two years later, the family-dominated board understandably chose Peters as CEO.

But at the same time, fierce competition caused Schlitz beer sales to drop. Without the patriarch, the Uihlein family began squabbling over solutions, making a spectacle out of the next annual meeting. Yet the family apparently agreed on one thing: Peters, only a year after assuming the top post, left the company, while Daniel F. McKeithan, a family member, replaced him.

A more recent case of the family reasserting its power when trouble develops is that of Firestone Tire & Rubber Co., still about 25% owned by the Firestone family. Ever since the recall of the Radial 500 in 1978, which helped produce a $148.3 million loss, the family has tried to reexert its influence. Leonard K. Firestone, who resigned from the board in 1974, is expected to resume a directorship this month. For now, his son, Kimball C., the only family member on the board, admits that "the others are frustrated, standing on the sidelines, and unity is difficult to get from them."

The one time they moved off the sidelines, it cost them close to $100 million. Family members urged that Firestone be merged with Borg-Warner Corp. in late 1978, then abruptly decided that they wanted more than the $16 a share Borg-Warner was offering. The family was fooled by Firestone's momentary comeback in earnings early in 1979. By October, Firestone stock plunged below $9 a share. Although Mario A. Di Federico, the company's president, actually had little to do with the collapse of the

GROOMING THE SUCCESSOR

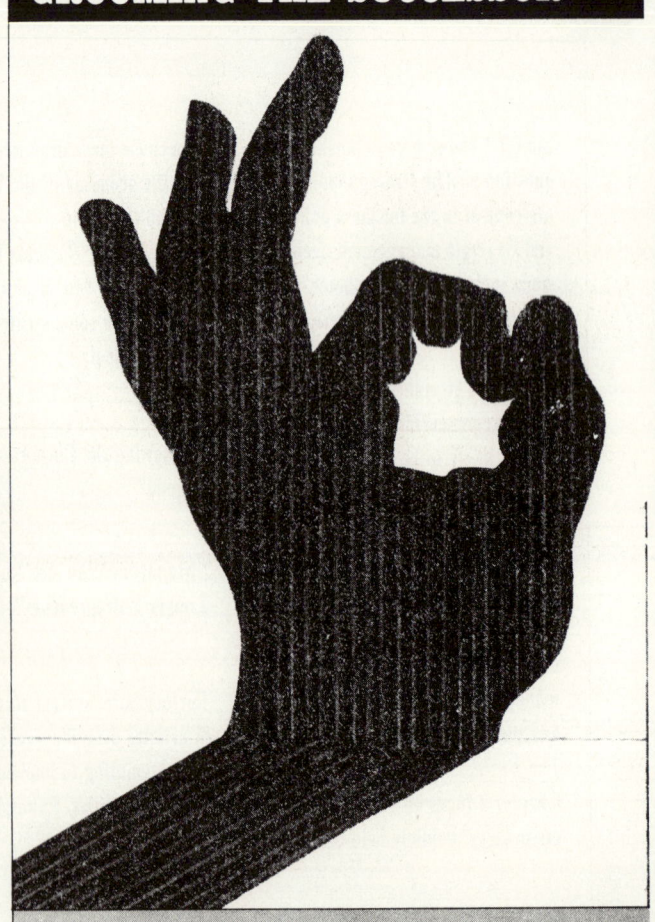

Edward W. Carter, who built Broadway Hale Stores into the nation's seventh largest department store chain, spent years grooming Philip M. Hawley as his successor by giving him broad experience as well as advanced management educa-

Illustrations by Paul Richer

38 / Readings from *Business Week*

High risk for the professional manager who succeeds a strong man

merger, no one was surprised when he found himself out of a job. Though Di Federico was only one part of the two-man professional management team that ultimately succeeded Raymond C. Firestone two years ago (Richard A. Riley has remained as chairman), he was the executive most responsible for the troubled tire operations.

Not surprisingly, executive recruiters say that those professional managers who are willing to run family-owned companies expect hazardous duty pay. "Candidates ask for much lengthier contracts and for more upfront money," says J. Gerald Simmons, president of Handy Associates, who says the added tab can run 50% more than the normal compensation package expected by people joining nonentrepreneurial corporations. Closing the deal is still rough because founders normally place far greater emphasis on chemistry between themselves and their successor. Observes René Plessner, president of René Plessner Associates Inc.: "Sometimes entrepreneurs surround themselves with clones, but too often they're really looking for slaves they can push around."

Such traps are avoidable, however. In fact, an examination of case histories during the last decade shows some rather striking patterns of where succession to professional management is likely to work and where it is likely to fail. It is much more likely to succeed, for example, when the founder has carefully groomed a successor and taken steps to protect his choice from internal attack. But the manager chosen for succession can help his own chances by respecting the wishes and massaging the ego of the owner-entrepreneur who steps down. However, when a family company gets into trouble and calls on a professional manager to rescue it, the successor's managerial skills, much more than diplomacy, will determine his tenure.

Still, many talented executives have failed in succeeding the founder because they did not consider his needs. Harry Levinson, head of the Levinson Institute, a psychological consulting firm, blames the Zeigarnik effect, which states that the closer the goal, the greater the intensity in pursuing it. "If the new man doesn't have patience and sensitivity [to the founder], he'll get into trouble," Levinson states. "Too often, [the new chief believes] he literally has overthrown the boss, and gets into an 'I'm in charge, I'll do it my way' type of narcissism."

Corporate annals abound with horror stories in which this tendency probably played a key role. Auto industry mavens often observe that a major factor behind Iacocca's fall at Ford Motor was Henry Ford II's dislike of sharing the limelight with such a strong-willed and visible executive. Similarly, Geneen virtually handpicked Lyman Hamilton to succeed him as CEO at ITT, in January, 1978, yet was the moving force behind Hamilton's ouster less than two years later. Geneen, insiders say, is a classic entrepreneur—a high-strung, energetic, fast-talking manager—and Hamilton's low-keyed, unharried, friendlier demeanor got under Geneen's skin when he saw it in action at meetings and in other arenas that had been his forte. Even more important, sources say, Hamilton's sin was moving too quickly to undo some of Geneen's legacy. The new chief, for example, shortened monthly management meetings and divested some food companies Geneen had acquired.

Second-successor syndrome

Arthur Taylor's quick rise and fall at CBS was also a classic power play between a founder who would not let go and a young comer who did not have the patience to deal with slow and steady change. Taylor, who was wooed from International Paper Co. to become CBS' president in 1973, was Paley's personal choice as heir apparent. At the time of Taylor's forced resignation in 1976, CBS had just reported a quarterly earnings increase of 40%. But sources close to the company note that Paley was incensed at the number of CBS executives who resigned during Taylor's tenure, apparently because of his heavy-handed style. And they say that Paley's prized reputation as a "show business person" was jeopardized when Taylor almost immediately divested the money-losing but prestigious New York Yankees and when

...tion. When Carter gave the reins to Hawley, he even changed the corporate name to Carter Hawley Hale. Says Hawley of Carter: "He did a textbook job" of stepping down. Under Hawley, CHH has become the country's fourth largest chain.

CBS' Nielsen ratings fell in 1976. Still chairman and CEO, Paley decided in late 1976 that it was time for Taylor to resign. His replacement as president, John Backe, successfully assumed the CEO title from an approving Paley in 1977.

Though Hamilton and Taylor may have been the wrong men for the jobs, the first professional manager to replace an entrepreneurial founder so often fails to pull it off that it has created a second-man-is-better syndrome: In many and perhaps even most cases, the second executive who tries to fill the shoes of the founder seems to have greater staying power. Among other things, by the time the second professional takes his shot, the entrepreneur may have at last accepted the fact that he must step down in order to preserve the corporation he built. Then, too, the second successor has the benefit of learning from the mistakes of the first.

Few cases better illustrate the syndrome than the succession to Nathan Cummings, who built Chicago-based Consolidated Foods Corp. into the nation's fifth largest food processor. William A. Buzick Jr., a veteran with the company, became chairman in 1970. Though Buzick continued Cummings' strategy of aggressively diversifying Consolidated into nonfood areas by making dozens of small acquisitions in such industries as apparel and furniture, Cummings—still the honorary chairman of Consolidated and its largest shareholder, with 3.6% of the stock—demanded Buzick's resignation in 1974. That year's recession produced Consolidated's first earnings decline in 19 years, and Buzick believes he became the scapegoat for that. "Nate wanted to retire, but he just couldn't do so," recalls Buzick, now an independent management consultant. "Nate Cummings is a man of great pride. For the first time in 19 years we couldn't increase dividends, so Nate's inclination was to lash out."

John H. Bryan Jr., 43, immediately became the new CEO, and one year later he even assumed the chairman's post. Cummings, 83, remains honorary chairman. Surprisingly, Bryan successfully replaced Cummings even though his approach to managing Consolidated is considerably different. He received little grief when he sold off 49 small, mostly nonfood operations that had been purchased under Cummings and Buzick. He then acquired control of two giants—Hanes Corp. and Douwe Egberts, a Dutch coffee company.

To be sure, Bryan's staying power has much to do with the company's successful performance during his tenure. Still, he may well have benefited from the second-successor syndrome. For one thing, Cummings' advancing age, observers suggest, made him less resistant to relinquishing his control.

Bryan also may have learned from Buzick's diplomatic miscues. One of his first moves after becoming the CEO was to raise Cummings' consulting fee from $50,000 to $75,000, a move Buzick had opposed. "It was the smart thing to do politically," Buzick now admits. A longtime associate of Bryan's explains that such political acumen is typical of him. "When Bryan was president of his family's specialty meat business, he would check with his father before putting a new sidewalk in front of the plant," says the associate. "This same deferential attitude carried over to his dealings with Cummings, but don't think it was out of respect for his elders."

Public image

Clearly, stroking the founder's ego is a key ingredient to an entrepreneurial succession that works. It probably has a lot to do with the success of Derick J. Daniels, the professional manager recruited from Knight-Ridder Newspapers Inc. in 1976 to assume the presidency of then-troubled Playboy Enterprises Inc. While Hugh Hefner remained the company's chairman and CEO, the founder and 71% owner of Playboy was, as one former executive of the company puts it, "so desperate for someone to take over [that] he gave Daniels a very free rein. He came in with the aura of being the chosen one and had a very well-constructed contract that protected him."

While Daniels was given nearly unlimited freedom as chief operating officer, he has been careful to give the requisite deference to the entrepreneur. Although he admits Playboy "had simply outgrown its management and had to be brought from the horse and buggy era to the jet age," Daniels lets Hefner be the company's sole outside representative.

In public, Daniels can be self-effacing to a fault, crediting Hefner with turning the company around, even though the Playboy founder headed the management structure Daniels says the company had outgrown. "Hefner is the creative leader, and it was Hefner who recognized the need for financial controls," Daniels says. "The key to my success here is that he has backed me 100% at every critical event."

Nevertheless, Daniels has apparently been wise enough to enlist that backing. Insiders say he calls the shots at Playboy now, but not without first seeking Hefner's approval on big moves, such as the 1977 firings that reduced Playboy's corporate staff by more than 10%, the retreat from the record and movie business, the expansion of publishing and casino ventures, and the creation of an internal auditing department. Such moves have boosted Playboy's earnings from $1 million in 1975 to $9 million last

WHEN SECOND IS BEST

Like some first-round successors to the entrepreneur, William A. Buzick Jr. may have been destined to fall after taking over from Nathan Cummings, who built Consolidated Foods. While his management style mirrored that of Cummings, Buzick lost his post because, he says, "Nate wanted to retire but just couldn't." When John H. Bryan Jr. became the second-round successor, an aging Cummings seemed less inclined to resist, despite Bryan's management differences.

40 / Readings from *Business Week*

year, but Daniels still is cautious of stepping on Hefner's toes. The one time he apparently went too far was when he fired Daniel B. Stone, a friend of Christie Hefner (Hugh's daughter) and the fair-haired boy of Victor A. Lownes, a high-powered senior vice-president. When objections were raised, say close observers, Daniels diplomatically retreated, and rehired Stone at a lower salary. "Daniels has a refined, diplomatic exterior, but inside he's a steel trap," says Lee Gottlieb, now with a public relations agency and one of a number of longtime Playboy executives and Hefner associates to fall victim to Daniels' ax.

Of course, the chances for a successful transition from entrepreneur to professional are always greater if the founder takes himself out of the picture entirely. "The board has to say, 'You did a great job, now take a vacation,'" insists William Zucker, co-director of the Wharton School's Entrepreneurial Center. The underlying problem, he says, is that although growing companies cry out for more structure and less personalized management, most founders "want to maintain the company as an informal, flexible, entrepreneurial group."

Letting go

As a result, most founders do not seek to avoid succession problems by strictly following a hands-off policy when they step down. Yet there are notable exceptions. Alonzo G. Decker Jr., 72, retired as chairman of Black & Decker Inc. last year, leaving the company to Francis P. Lucier, the CEO. Upon retirement, Decker explained: "Corporations have to be progressive and innovating, yet there's a tendency for older people to keep things the way they were." Thomas Watson Sr. retired when he turned over International Business Machines Corp. to his son, and Watson Jr. became U.S. Ambassador to the Soviet Union when he relinquished the company to Frank Cary. And possibly most dramatic of all, Royal Little, founder of Textron Inc., has kept his hands off his brainchild since he resigned from the board in 1962 at the age of 66. "I knew I wouldn't be able to sit there and shut up; I'd be a pain in the neck," Little explains. "It's a great mistake for the founder to stay on the board. It just creates confusion."

While few entrepreneurs can bring themselves to let go totally, many have recognized that they must channel their protective instincts for their company into making sure that their chosen successors work out. Often, they make some dramatic gesture to show that the new corporate head is there with the entrepreneur's blessing. Trammel Crow, the rich Dallas-based real estate developer, did it by starting five new wholly owned companies earmarked for his six children to manage, while at the same time reducing to 33% the family ownership of Trammel Crow Partners Ltd., which is the parent company for Trammel Crow Co., the nation's largest developer. In 1976, Crow sold two-thirds of the stock of that company to 15 of its executives, making them partners in the firm. At the same time, the company adopted an antinepotism rule: No close relatives of any of the partners can join the company or inherit voting stock. J. McDonald Williams, the professional manager who succeeded Crow as managing partner of Trammell Crow Co. in that year, says the intent of the 1976 move was to provide "the transition from an organization that had been dominated by one man to a company that will be here for the long pull." Williams says Crow has successfully made the psychological transition from autocratic ruler to one man among equals, and Crow insists that "Don Williams is the man to run this company."

The founders of Saga Corp. are trying to give Charles A. Lynch, whom they hired as CEO last year, a similar feeling of authority. Their dramatic gesture was to set up yet another nonfamily manager as a buffer between them and the CEO. Twice in the last decade the three cofounders—Harry W. Anderson, William F. Scandling, and W. Price Laughlin—have promoted general managers to head the food-service company, only to force them to resign shortly thereafter. "It was difficult to keep our hands off," Scandling admitted to BUSINESS WEEK (BW—Nov. 20, 1978). This time the three, who are still company directors and hold 36% of Saga's common stock, hired Ernest C. Arbuckle, the 67-year-old retired chairman of Wells Fargo & Co., as chairman of the board. Arbuckle, in turn, recruited Lynch from W. R. Grace & Co., and it is to Arbuckle—not the founders—that Lynch reports. Lynch says that using Arbuckle as a buffer seems to have worked. "I know of no instance where the founders have injected themselves into a situation to the embarrassment of any manager, me

STROKING THE FOUNDER

As the newly recruited president of Playboy Enterprises, Derick J. Daniels took bold initiatives in solving the company's troubles by closing down losing operations and axing more than 10% of the corporate staff, sparing founder Hugh M. Hefner the unpleasantness of performing a necessary task. Yet Daniels was careful not to move without Hefner's consent. While Daniels calls most of the shots at Playboy, he deferentially refers to Hefner as the company's "creative leader."

included," he says. For example, the founders went over every name on a list of about 125 employees Lynch either fired or shifted to new positions within the company, and yet they did not change Lynch's decision on any.

Perhaps the best example of an entrepreneur supporting his successor took place at Carter Hawley Hale Stores Inc., the Los Angeles-based chain that is a direct descendant of Broadway Department Stores Inc., founded in Los Angeles in 1896. Although Edward W. Carter was the first professional manager to take over the operation of the store from the founding Letts family, he is recognized as the founder of today's retailing giant. During his 31 years as chief exec-

The Strategy Makers / 41

utive, Carter built the store from a three-unit retailer into the country's No. 7 department store chain. Two years ago, Carter, who remains chairman, was succeeded as CEO by the man he had so carefully groomed for that role—Philip M. Hawley, who has taken the chain to its current No. 4 ranking.

Carter hired Hawley, now 54, 20 years ago, when the younger man was a buyer at another store. Carter says he noticed almost immediately that "every job I gave him, he did well." He transferred Hawley among divisions and encouraged him to get an advanced management degree, which the company funded. In 1972, Hawley became president—and two years later, when the store name changed from Broadway Hale Stores, the board, with Carter's blessing, put Hawley's name up there with his.

Although there are slight but significant discrepancies in the two men's perceptions of the succession process (Carter states that "I made him the boss," while Hawley consistently refers to the time "when the board voted me in . . ."), Hawley does say that "Carter did a textbook job when he stepped down, because he totally relinquished the reins."

Even when the retiring entrepreneur does not do anything as tangible as hire a buffer or change the company's name, he can smooth the path by simply ensuring that his chosen successor is well-groomed. When Leif J. Sverdrup, founder of Sverdrup Corp., the privately held construction company in St. Louis, died of a heart attack in 1976, Robert C. West took over as chairman with almost no ripple. West says that Sverdrup had slowly brought him into corporate long-range planning before he died and generally "made it clear that I was to succeed him." Apparently the message was clearly heard by the company's executive committee—it met right after Sverdrup died and elected West chairman.

Without such careful grooming, even handpicked successors may be destined to fail. When David Packard and William R. Hewlett tried to hand over daily operations to inside managers in the early 1970s, they quickly discovered that their good intentions to avoid interference were not enough to assure a smooth transition. "Our managers were putting products on the market before they were fully developed," Packard says. "We were not doing a good enough job of educating people."

Rather than replace those managers, Hewlett and Packard took back control over operations but immediately instituted an extensive management training program that stressed the founders' conservative approach to product development and pricing. The two founders slowly introduced John A. Young, a 20-year veteran of the company's test instrument business, into the strategic planning process, and over three years gave him experience in all phases of the company's operations. In 1977, Young took over the presidency, and the sales of Hewlett-Packard Co. have since increased 74%, to $2.4 billion, while earnings have climbed 68%, to $203 million.

Often, though, the entrepreneur has set a pattern of making all the major decisions himself, leaving him with a second-tier management group that is highly capable of implementing his plans but virtually incapable of drawing up plans of their own. Beyond that, explains Herbert Mines, a New York executive recruiter, an entrepreneurial company's brightest executives—those capable of major decision-making—often leave the operation long before it reaches the point of succession because they feel at a dead end. This is particularly true, he says, when family members are waiting in the wings. "People recognize that they are unlikely ever to be president, and strong managers simply do not stay," says Mines.

In such cases, the only route to successful transition from entrepreneurial to professional management may well be recruitment from the outside. Thus, when Charles Revson's sons did not work out at Revlon Inc., the autocratic founder recognized that he had to initiate an outside search. In 1974, Michele Bergerac was recruited from his post as an ITT executive vice-president to become Revlon's CEO.

When status helps

Recruitment of outside professionals is no panacea for the problem of succession. But it seems more likely to work when the incoming manager has enough of a professional reputation in his own right that employees—and even the retiring entrepreneur—are predisposed to view him with respect. For example, Michael Blumenthal's status served him in good stead when he joined Bendix Corp. in 1967 and became its head in 1972. His predecessor, A. P. Fontaine, resigned from the board in 1975 after a decade as chairman and CEO. Blumenthal had already become noted as a tough negotiator during his tenure as chairman of the U. S. delegation to the Kennedy Round of trade negotiations in Geneva from 1963 to 1967. He had also been Deputy Assistant Secretary of State for economic affairs, as well as U. S. representative to the U. N.'s Commission on International Commodity Trade. Blumenthal readily admits he treaded with anything but a light foot. "I undid some of the things Fontaine did, and I fired some people he wouldn't have fired, and I promoted some people he wouldn't have promoted," Blumenthal recalls. He admits that the power of his professional reputation, combined

REPAIRING A FAMILY COMPANY

When Peter G. Scotese succeeded family management at Spring Mills, the textile company was suffering the ill effects of rapid expansion. Scotese applied professional management methods—setting up profit centers and holding managers more accountable. While he was sensitive to family concerns, his record helps explain why his succession worked: Since Scotese took the helm in 1969, Spring Mills's profits have grown from $1.9 million to nearly $35 million last year.

with his forceful personality, enabled him to make his changes unscathed. Presumably, Blumenthal's stint as Treasury Secretary enhances his power as Burroughs Corp.'s new chief.

For less noted entrepreneurial successors, perhaps the only situations truly skewed in their favor are companies that are foundering when they take over. Then, the new manager gets a chance to establish himself as a hero from the onset and to make changes with no compunction to move slowly.

E. Russell Eggers, for one, started taking over Loctite Corp. from Robert H. Krieble, the founder's son, in 1975 at a time when the corporation's initial patents on its industrial adhesives were expiring and much bigger competitors, such as 3M Corp. and Eastman Kodak Co., were threatening to make inroads into markets Loctite dominated. Eggers created a five-man office of the chief executive, hired 20 new executives, promoted 40 others, doubled the sales force to 375 over two years, slashed the European staff from 155 to 30, and introduced formal strategic planning. Under his rein several Loctite divisions have been combined, and the company has started doing extensive premarket testing for new products. So far the strategy seems to be working—profits have increased fivefold over the last four years. "Loctite needed a management style befitting the passage from a $100 million company to, say, a $500 million company," Krieble admits.

Profits over volume

Krieble, who claims that he does not miss running his company, has only kudos for Eggers. Still, Eggers recognizes that Krieble, despite his publicly stiff upper lip, has occasional twinges. "Even though he would never say it, the change in style probably gives Krieble the most pain," Eggers says.

At Spring Mills Inc., Chairman H. William Close, a member of the founding family, is probably suffering less from CEO Peter G. Scotese's management style because the two are separated. Close is in South Carolina, Scotese in New York. But even without the distance, Scotese would probably have been successful. "The need [to bolster the company's earnings through new management] was sensed before Scotese came in 1969," explains James B. Lasley, the company's executive vice-president of engineering and corporate development. Close concedes that he "just was not doing a satisfactory job."

Scotese has certainly turned Spring Mills around. When Close became president in 1959, on the death of his father-in-law, he embarked on a rapid expansion program, almost tripling the number of plants in eight years and moving the company away from its mainstay lines of sheets and apparel fabrics into a variety of home furnishing items and fiber blends. He took the company public in 1966. But the expansions were coming at the expense of profits, which slipped steadily from $17.9 million in 1966 to $6.8 million in 1967 and to a low of $1.9 million in 1968.

Scotese, who was chairman of a Federated Department Stores division, was recruited to rescue the company in 1969. He strongly emphasized profitability rather than volume. He upgraded product lines and quickly sold off losers. What is more, he streamlined the company into profit centers headed by strong marketing executives. The result has been that sales soared from $293 million in 1969 to more than $800 million now, and profits have grown at a compounded annual rate of 20% to nearly $35 million last year.

'Immersed in detail'

Scotese changed the company's entire managerial atmosphere. One veteran Spring Mills executive recalls that Close rarely delegated responsibility and got "immersed in detail to the point that sometimes the journey rather than the destination became the objective." Scotese delegated both responsibility and authority and has gone on record saying he has no reservations about replacing any executive who does not perform well. "He made me so mad the first year I could eat nails," says another longtime executive, who admits that although being held closely accountable for performance was an irritant, he now has strong admiration for Scotese.

The question remains open, of course, whether these successful transitions will hold up if corporate fortunes suffer unexpected reversals. At Loctite, for one, the Krieble family still holds more than one-third of the stock, and at least one source familiar with the company says that the clout of that stock will be used if Eggers slips. Similarly, Hefner controls 71% of Playboy and what would happen to Daniels if he did tread on the wrong toes is anyone's guess.

Of course, longevity in the job eventually bestows on the successors to founders about the same type of job security other professional managers are accustomed to. Yet even hand-picked successors seldom gain any special security and almost never attain the unquestioned authority that the founder himself possessed. As one former IBM executive notes about Frank Cary's rein: "The Watsons were worshipped. They were the anointed, not the elected. With Cary, we've moved from the king to a prime minister, and we view him as such." ∎

MANAGERS WHO ARE NO LONGER ENTREPRENEURS

Item: Harry J. Gray, 60, chairman and chief executive officer of United Technologies Corp., points with pride to the "Spirit," his company's new commercial helicopter, as a true innovation. Although it drained profits for several years, he insists its potential made the losses worthwhile. Yet he also says that UT will now only make investments with a potential 20% annual return.

Item: H. Jack Meany, 57, president and CEO of Norris Industries Inc., says that over the last decade Norris has spent "more on new facilities than the market value or net worth of the company," even when it has meant settling for 10-year paybacks. Yet Norris managers have their bonuses based on annual financial performance.

Item: Fletcher L. Byrom, 61, chairman of Koppers Co., describes himself as an "enabler"—someone who encourages managers to take risks. Yet Byrom insists on a nonwaivable rule that new investments produce an average 25% return before taxes and interest during the first five years, as well as a maximum five-year payback.

There is a schizophrenia pervading U. S. business today. It is a rare CEO who has not publicly expounded on the need for focusing on the future—usually couched within a speech castigating government or labor unions for their short-term policies. Yet the compensation systems in their companies, the financial requirements for investment projects, the criteria for management-by-objectives goals and for performance appraisal, all point to an exceedingly short-term orientation.

Consultants, academics, and even some politicians have been sounding a red alert for some time. "The measure of achievement and the goals to be reached are as short-term as a politician's next election," Senator Lloyd Bentsen (D-Tex.) told businessmen participating in a conference on U. S. competitiveness last April. "When you want to make this year's annual report look as good as possible, why engage in market-entry pricing in East Asia? Why accept losses for two or three years to build volume and brand recognition?" he asked.

When pressed, most corporate chiefs will admit that Bentsen's rhetorically scathing questioning is fair. Even Koppers' Byrom wistfully admits that he does not know "how many potentially good investments never got [presented to me] because they didn't show a 25% return." But buck-passing for short-sightedness is rampant. Most corporate leaders blame pressure from Wall Street and from their own boards. "Stock analysts don't begin to spend the time researching key management structure and ability in the same manner they research the numbers," complains Peter G. Scotese, vice-chairman and CEO of Springs Mills Inc. Edson W. Spencer, chairman at Honeywell Inc., adds: "No matter how much I say about building the company longer-term, short-term performance is the issue that seems to take on most importance."

To be sure, the complaints are valid. But significantly, they are not universal. Thomas V. Jones, chairman and CEO of Northrop Corp., insists that "Wall Street can understand [investment in the future]. Investors who are interested only in the short-term shouldn't be our stockholders, and analysts' reports on our company reflect this." In fact, the fat profits that Northrop is today booking on its 747 business with Boeing Co. stem from a $62 million investment the company started making in 1966. Although it was a drain on profits for a number of years, Jones states that "if we hadn't dared [to make] the investment, we wouldn't have the profits today." Similarly, James E. Burke, chairman and CEO of Johnson & Johnson, insists that one of J&J's tenets is "not to be too fearful of failure." In the 1950s, he recalls, J&J took a $9 million loss on an abortive attempt to use collagen to replace catgut as a suture material—yet that research has led to a lucrative business in using the collagen for sausage

44 / Readings from *Business Week*

casing. Currently, the company is suffering heavy losses on its acquisition of Technicare Corp., a maker of high-technology diagnostic imaging devices, but Burke is not fearful. "Diagnostic imaging is going to be important," he states simply.

Why are so few business leaders unwilling to buck Wall Street by taking similar risks? The reasons are multifold. Some stem from a society that has stressed immediate gratification to a fault. Many stem from the structure of the typical company. But most stem from the managers themselves.

The tunnel vision pervading executive suites comes from a combination of psychological, cultural, and structural reasons. Corporate chiefs grew up in the same shortsighted culture as their directors and shareholders. And they have shaped the cultures of their companies. Not surprisingly, it is the people who work for companies that have remained entrepreneurial who are most willing to agree with that premise. "The nonentrepreneurial background of top managers attracts similarly minded people whose outlook is to make the fast buck and not plan for the future," says Friedrich W. Schroeder, director of corporate development at Hewlett-Packard Co., which is known for fairly innovative management. The occasional maverick who bucks the system rarely makes it to the top, adds Peter R. Sugges, professor of management at Temple University. "You can only become a manager if you adopt the mores and strictures of managers," he says. "The only way to change any company is to change the way people at the top think about the way business should be operated."

Ironically, the change that is needed probably would involve turning the clock back about 30 years. Before the merger craze of the 1960s, corporate leaders were, for the most part, autocratic, entrepreneurial types who were ready to take risks for ideas they felt in their guts would pan out. David Sarnoff took RCA Corp. into space-age technology. Thomas Watson Sr. and Thomas Watson Jr. plunged International Business Machines Corp. into computers when they were still in the realm of science fiction. Edwin H. Land would have grimaced at the idea of doing a discounted cash flow on research for the Polaroid camera.

But for the most part, today's corporate leaders are "professional managers"—business mercenaries who ply their skills for a salary and bonus but rarely for a vision. And those skills are generally narrow and specialized. Just as the general practitioner who made house calls is a dim memory, so is the hands-on corporate leader who rose through the ranks, learning every aspect of the business before managing it. Today's managers are known as great marketers, savvy lawyers, or hard-nosed financial men. Lacking a gut feeling for the *gestalt*

Robert Shore

Nonentrepreneurial managers look to the fast buck and not the long term.

of their businesses, they see managing by the numbers as their only recourse. What is more, they do not seem to generate those numbers through internal growth. All too often they see themselves as managers of a portfolio of companies, much like a portfolio of stocks. They become more concerned with buying and selling companies than with selling improved products to customers. According to Robert H. Hayes, a professor at Harvard Business School, more than $40 billion was spent on acquisitions in 1979 alone—more than was spent on research and development and none of which created new value. James B. Farley, chairman of Booz, Allen & Hamilton Inc., notes that as often as not the acquisitions add nothing to either party. "People used to talk about synergy, but they no longer do," he says. "There really is no synergy in most acquisitions."

Worse, there really is little synergy created between departments and divisions at most companies. And the blame can generally be laid at the top manager's doorstep. Theodore Barry & Associates, a West Coast consulting firm, recently studied 50 companies and, according to James B. Ayers, a company principal, concluded that "most executives have never participated in the line management process, so there is no sensitivity to the problems in this area."

Ayers warns that we will "have to see a shift in the background of top executives to technical and operating skills because [now their] attention never goes beyond financial reports."

It does not look as if that switch will happen immediately. Korn/Ferry International, an executive search firm, recently queried more than 1,700 corporate vice-presidents—the group from which future top managers are most likely to be drawn. About 47% began their careers in either marketing or finance, and nearly 64% say that those two areas of responsibility are the fastest track to the top. "Senior-level executives are geared to getting product out the door as opposed to being creative about it," explains John A. Sussman, Korn/Ferry's vice-president for research.

That type of bias filters down to all levels in the organization. Too often, chief executives send mixed signals to their staffs—on the one hand, they demand creativity, and on the other, they reward numbers. Anthony J. Marolda, vice-president of corporate development services at Arthur D. Little Inc., tells about a former client, a U.S. television manufacturer, that lost "bundles of money" by sticking with tube technology

The Strategy Makers / 45

while its competitors switched to solid state. "The president, who had a financial background, told his engineering staff, 'If you want the new technology you can have it—but keep in mind that your bonus is based on profits next year,'" Marolda recalls. "He told me later that he wasn't comfortable with the technology so he passed along technical decisions to others."

Not surprisingly, the easiest substitute for comfort with alien technological or marketing concepts is a technique to measure them. Not only has internal rate of return and discounted cash flow replaced educated instincts for deciding on new projects, but quantitative approaches—or, at best, formularized ones—have even pervaded human resource management. Top management has become insulated from its employees. The old days of motivating employees by example and by general day-to-day closeness to the field have given way to consultants' techniques such as behavior modification, climate and attitude surveys, and the like. Salary administration is almost totally depersonalized. Although the term "merit increase" still hangs on in business parlance, most salary programs have degenerated into automatic percentage allocations.

Because the link between payroll and performance has become so fuzzy, corporations have tried to develop incentive compensation systems. But, these too have been formularized into percentages of salary and percentages of profit, so that a manager's bonus is as much tied to the general economy or windfall sales as it is to his performance. Managers are well aware that the people making the bonus compilations often have had little chance to know them personally and that numbers will be their criteria.

For many corporations, the answer seems to be management by objectives or performance-appraisal systems based on goal-setting and review (BW—May 19). A few companies have made a point of including nonfinancial criteria in their management-by-objectives goals. But most still couch those goals in terms of increasing sales, profits, or productivity. Even the manager's personal goals are generally stated in quantifiable terms—for example, returning to school for an MBA. If there is a company that encourages managers to set a goal of, say, doing basic research that may or may not lead to an incredible product breakthrough, BUSINESS WEEK has certainly not run into it.

It is a frustrating situation for those managers who genuinely believe that basic research or other intangible costs are essential. Walter L. Abel, vice-president of R&D at Emhart Corp., notes that he had a very difficult time getting management to accept development costs for Emhart's microprocessor-controlled shoe-stitching machine, now one of the company's hottest sellers. Yet now management is pestering him to come up with another such success. "I say, 'Damn

Robert Shore

Business-school graduates have been educated to suit the corporations.

you, you won't put up money for three years of building up research knowledge, yet the stitching machine took seven years and that was a fast one,'" he says.

The problem rests as much in executive mobility as in executive myopia. Harvard's Hayes notes that job tenure is less than five years nowadays, half of what it was in the 1950s. Although a CEO is less likely than a middle manager to leave his job unless pushed, habits built up over a lifetime career are hard to break. Not surprisingly, it is psychologically difficult for the typical CEO, who is nearly 60, to make decisions that may depress current earnings but will prove lucrative for his successor.

And even if he wanted to, chances are excellent that he would have a difficult time within the organizational structure of the typical large corporation. Our major corporations have blossomed into multiproduct, multidivisional, multi-locational hydras. They became far too diverse for any one corporate leader to embrace. So one formerly monolithic company after another decentralized into such things as profit centers, strategic business units, and the like. Every profit center had to have a general manager or a divisional president. Corporate headquarters had to have new staff people to whom the divisional people would report. Layer upon layer of management jobs were added to the structure. This layering created numerous operating-level jobs, making executive job-hopping not only feasible but fashionable, claims Hayes.

And the would-be job-hoppers quickly learned that the best way to get on a fast track in their own companies—or raided by another company—was to turn out good quarterly numbers. That view became reinforced by bonus systems that rewarded those same good numbers. The worst-case example is the recent scandal at H. J. Heinz Co., where management at three subsidiaries allegedly tinkered with accounts payable and receivable in order to smooth out earnings pictures and have an easy crack at meeting each year's financial goals.

No one is saying that the move toward decentralization or incentive compensation or even scientific management techniques were not good ideas at the time. Even the merger movement made sense in that many companies had grown to the point where they needed the benefit of both professional management support and the kind of cash cushion only a

46 / Readings from *Business Week*

larger conglomerate could provide. But resistance to change seems to be endemic in corporate America.

"The greatest danger in turbulent times like ours is not the turbulence, but that you act rationally in terms of yesterday," says Peter Drucker in his new book, *Managing in Turbulent Times*.

No risk-taking

American B-schools have certainly not helped. Warns Arthur D. Little's Marolda, "Large corporations have been virtually overrun by a proliferation of profit-zealous MBAs who are turning every nut another half-turn to get a payoff." Indeed, MBAs are prepared to apply specific skills to entry-level jobs in specific specialties.

The unabashedly quantitative schools like Carnegie-Mellon University are at least honest about what they are doing—teaching students the mathematical and technique-oriented skills of management. But the qualitative schools do not encourage risk-taking or original thinking any more than do the quantitative schools. The managers steeped in case histories at Harvard rarely think of taking a potentially profitable plunge in a chancy market.

Some business-school deans admit the problem, but they claim their hands are as tied by corporate demands as the CEOs say theirs are by stockholders. "We find that most of the corporations who come to campus to interview our graduates are looking for students with specific skills and characteristics that will be applicable to an initial job," admits David H. Blake, associate dean of the University of Pittsburgh's Graduate School of Business. "My fear is that we've allowed our clientele to determine what it is we do to a great extent."

That clientele, of course, includes the students themselves, and many academics complain that today's youth is quick-buck oriented in a way that would make the flower children of the 1960s cringe. Robert W. Lear, Columbia University's executive in residence, has a set speech that he gives to most graduating classes at the school. "None of you want to be horses," he tells them. "You want to be jockeys, bookies, have the hay concession for the stables, be the jockey's agent, or best of all, the management consultant to the racetrack. That's why none of you will ever be CEO of a major corporation in the U.S."

The danger is that he is wrong, and that it is exactly these dollar-oriented specialists who will be the leaders of tomorrow. ∎

ITT: GROPING FOR A NEW STRATEGY

"People always ask me how we selected the things we acquired, and I can tell you exactly: What was available." This is how Harold S. Geneen, who was chief executive of International Telephone & Telegraph Corp. for 19 years, sums up his methods as the most vigorous acquirer of companies in recent corporate history. Relying on an array of investment bankers and his training in accountancy, and driven by a passion for fast growth, Geneen spread ITT from telecommunications businesses abroad to a mighty array of some 250 separate operations. With products ranging from industrial pumps to color television sets to Hostess cupcakes, ITT mushroomed into the ultimate conglomerate, by far the biggest and most diverse in the world.

But right now, ITT appears to be running in reverse. It has been less than three years since Geneen stepped down as chief and less than one year since his retirement as chairman. Yet the changes are remarkable. Just since January, 1979, the $24 billion (sales) giant, which cut its teeth on the stock swap and the big buy, has sold off or shut down no fewer than 33 of the companies and divisional operations Geneen had snapped up. Most of these have gone unannounced—a peculiar but entrenched company policy. Still, the combined revenues of the divested properties total more than $1 billion annually, and that figure will grow. Rand V. Araskog, Geneen's second successor as chief, says that as much as $1 billion in revenues of additional properties will be sold by the end of 1982.

Awesome risks

Two factors are driving these sell-offs. Sluggish profits for the past five years have pushed ITT to rid itself mainly of poor performers. But a second, less recognized factor weighs equally heavily. The future of ITT's main business, telecommunications equipment, is fraught with some awesome risks, partly because the company has been losing ground in a technological revolution. Both problems mean that ITT must trim itself to fight for improvement. How it will wage that fight when the pruning process is over is the primary question facing it today. The answer will determine the viability of its conglomerate concept.

For Geneen, the route was acquisition, mainly in the U. S. But in 1971, the pace of these acquisitions was slowed dramatically. To settle a Justice Dept. antitrust suit over ITT's purchase of Hartford Fire Insurance Co., ITT agreed not to acquire any U. S. company with assets of more than $100 million for 10 years.

Nevertheless, Geneen's immediate successor, Lyman C. Hamilton Jr., viewed the company as stretched too thin, and he favored massive divestitures followed by internal growth. But Hamilton lasted just 19 months before the board asked for his resignation—and Geneen, although 70 years old, appears to be more influential now than before.

Geneen remains a member of the executive committee of ITT's board and an ITT consultant. He also is a confidant of Araskog's. A tall, 49-year-old West

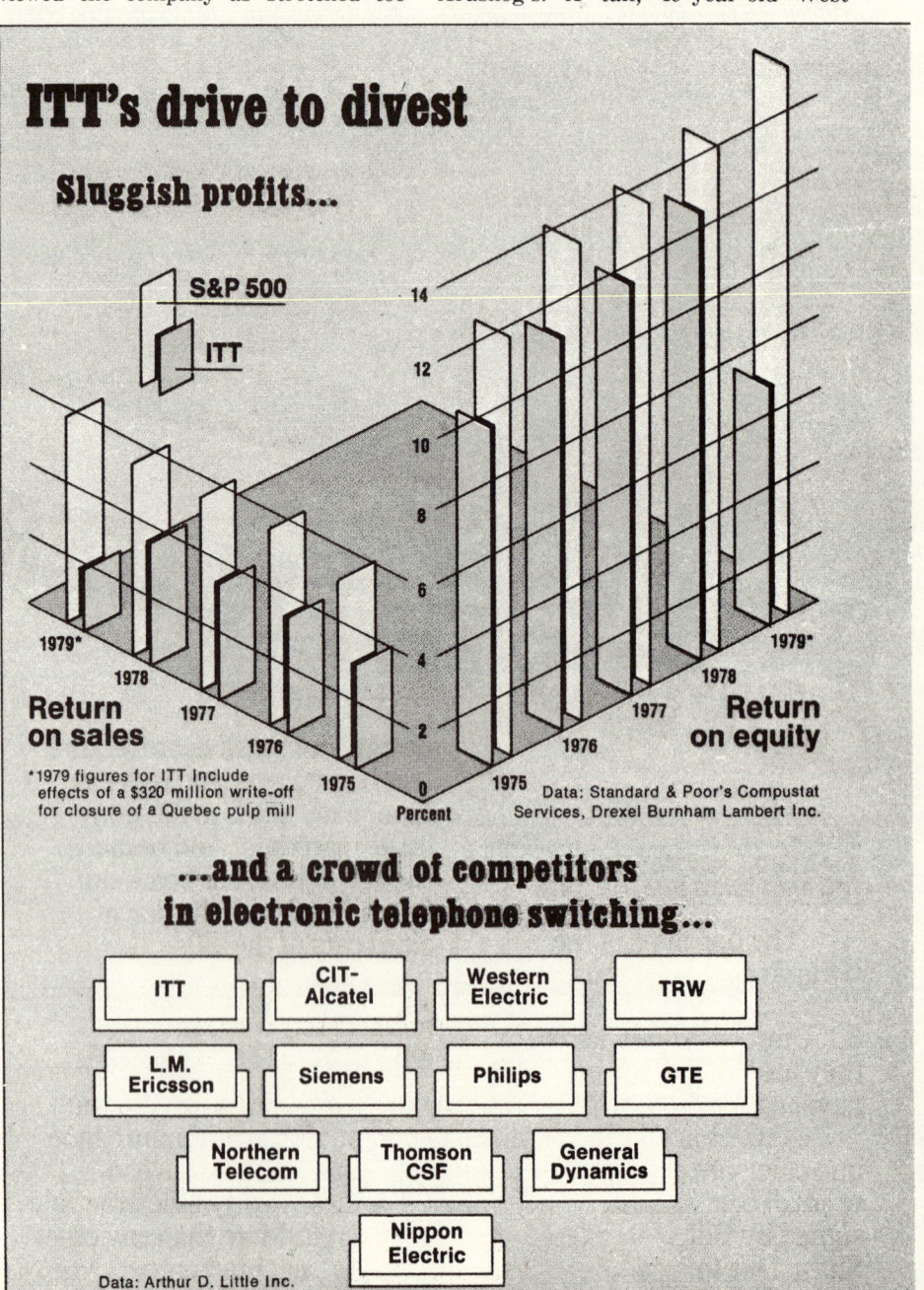

ITT's drive to divest

Sluggish profits...

Return on sales / *Return on equity* (1975–1979*)

*1979 figures for ITT include effects of a $320 million write-off for closure of a Quebec pulp mill

Data: Standard & Poor's Compustat Services, Drexel Burnham Lambert Inc.

...and a crowd of competitors in electronic telephone switching...

ITT | CIT-Alcatel | Western Electric | TRW
L.M. Ericsson | Siemens | Philips | GTE
Northern Telecom | Thomson CSF | General Dynamics
Nippon Electric

Data: Arthur D. Little Inc.

48 / Readings from *Business Week*

Point graduate brought quickly up the corporate ladder by Geneen, Araskog seems caught between the rival schools of thought. So far, he appears to be trying to work both strategies by following most of Hamilton's divestiture and internal growth planning while talking about acquisitions to come.

Araskog, who formerly headed the company's defense and avionics business in New Jersey, is ITT's first chief to come from operations. "The main part of our growth is clearly going to be internal," he says. But Araskog adds that he has no interest in seeing ITT reduce the number of industries in which it participates. Indeed, he says he recently considered two acquisitions of billion-dollar corporations that would have carried ITT into new industries. Although the company's high debt and low share price on Wall Street prevented him from moving, Araskog says that after the divestiture program is ended, ITT will again become a net acquirer of companies.

The risk is that following both growth plans may be impossible. The areas in which ITT wants most to grow internally—energy and electronic office equipment among them—would be major draws on cash. Making acquisitions at the same time would strain ITT's financial capability. If Araskog is led nonetheless into a Geneen-like acquisition program, it may be mainly because of the powerful imprint the former chief made during a generation in office. And with Geneen still active, Araskog must work out his goals for ITT under the scrutiny of a strong leader who still believes in his own original vision.

Big-name acquisitions

Geneen's scores of purchased companies manufactured rapid growth and in the process attached the ITT name to some of the country's best-known corporations, including Hartford, Sheraton hotels, and Continental Baking. Geneen was acclaimed for his ability to hold together what became the most complicated company in the U.S. He says he also is proud of the way the acquired companies were "operated after we got them."

But since the Hartford settlement, ITT's profitability in managing a less mercurial portfolio has been well under the average U.S. company's (chart, page 66). "If ITT was so well managed, how did it get so bad?" asks Carol P. Neves, a conglomerate analyst at Merrill Lynch, Pierce, Fenner & Smith Inc., referring to the company's below-average returns on equity, sales, and assets.

Outwardly, the divestiture program seems to offer a way to improve results. In the first nine months of 1980, ITT's profits have risen 10.3% to $609 million on sales of $17 billion—an improved performance, although it only keeps pace with price increases in today's inflationary environment. Because many of the companies sold had been in the red, improvements should continue as more losers are cut. These operations were kept on during Geneen's years because of his philosophical bent against making divestitures without first attempting a

...have forced sell-offs to gird for the battle ahead

Major ITT divestitures since Jan. 1, 1979

Name	Business	Terms of sale or closure
1979		**Millions of dollars**
European Food Div. (5 companies)	Food	$ 30
Yellow Cab of Washington	Taxi	1
Continental Snack Food	Food	1
Nesbitt	Heating and cooling systems	10
Pearson Candy	Confectioner	5
Rimmel	Cosmetics	25
Rayonier Quebec	Pulp mill	(320*)
SESA Rio	Telecommunications in Brazil (51% interest sold)	25
CSEA	Telecommunications in Argentina (25% interest sold)	10
STC	Telecommunications in Britain (15% interest sold)	50
1980		
Claude	Lighting	20
Canadian Wire & Cable	Wire products	10
Payot	Cosmetics	20
French distribution	Electrical parts distribution	(5*)
Steiner	Television sales and rentals	20
Canadian Lighting Fixtures	Lighting	5
Ashe Chemical	Drugs and related	20
Oceanique	Televisions and related	165 (50*)
U.S. Indoor Lighting Div.	Lighting	5
Courier	Printed circuit board plant only	25
Rayonier	U.S. timberlands	20
Rayonier British Columbia	Timber-cutting rights and production facilities	365
Allied Technologies Ltd.	South African telecommunications	39

Total annual revenues of companies sold or closed, 1979 and 1980: $1.2 billion

*Write-off

Data: First Manhattan Co., International Telephone & Telegraph Corp., BW estimates

The Strategy Makers / 49

So far Araskog is pushing internal growth—but he talks of future acquisitions. Telecommunications is fading as a cash cow

long resuscitation. Now even Geneen seems to be softening; he admits that some of his acquisitions were "damned errors, no question," and says he supports selling the businesses that cannot be repaired. "I don't feel any sensitivity to the idea that somebody should sell off a couple billion dollars' worth. That's probably 15% of [the total], so if all my errors added up to 15%, I think I was doing pretty damned good."

The trouble is, having rid itself of some consumer appliance companies in Europe, forest operations in Canada, cosmetics, food companies, and more, ITT still faces serious problems in its flagship industry, one that it can hardly leave—telecommunications. Steady and sizable earnings from telecommunications had handed Geneen a profitable base from which to expand. But as a cash cow, it has gone dry. Telecommunications has become much chancier because of hot competition and escalating research and development costs, both stemming from a technological revolution in which equipment is moving from electromechanical to fully electronic designs. As recently as 1978, this business accounted for 24% of ITT sales and 31% of operating income. Last year it accounted for the same portion of sales but just 24% of operating profit. Electronics, especially in ITT's biggest business, telephone switching equipment, also will make some ITT production plants obsolete and an increasing number of its employees redundant. The company's telecommunications margins thus may never be as healthy as they were.

Either join or get out

Araskog's challenge will be to pick a growth plan that will not count solely on telecommunications to supply financial power. Araskog says he recognizes this. "In the past, switching was the major profit producer as well as the most significant sales producer for the company," he declares. Although he agrees that the economics of electronic systems may not be so lucrative, Araskog contends the company's dependence on the business leaves only one set of alternatives—either to join the electronics race or "to get out of the business."

By staying in, ITT faces a tough struggle. The world's telephone operating companies, most of them government-controlled postal telephone and telegraph agencies (PTTs), have picked a clear technological path. Their new switching systems, which connect a caller with the number he dials, change voice waves into binary digits and reassemble them at the other end. But until about four years ago, ITT had argued against this form of technology. As a result, it now seems behind in the new system's development. For example, while France's CIT-Alcatel has installed 1.7 million lines of its digital switches and has lined up orders around the world for 5.9 million more lines, ITT's main digital product, the 1240, is still in development and at least nine months behind schedule. ITT has won orders for just 650,000 lines for the 1240, with delivery to begin at the end of 1981.

Other companies, such as Northern Telecom of Canada and L. M. Ericsson of Sweden, also are in production.

Ericsson, for example, has already installed 500,000 lines of its AXE electronic switching system, and the company has orders for 2 million additional lines from 25 countries. If the 1240 cannot be put into production soon, ITT may be in serious trouble.

"ITT is literally betting the company on the 1240," comments one former high-ranking executive, "and you don't do that at a big outfit very often." And even if the 1240 succeeds, he adds: "It cost us only $30 million to $40 million in 1963 to develop Pentaconta [ITT's older switching product], and it lasted for nearly 20 years. With electronic technological change, the 1240 will last just five to seven years. What will that do to margins?" According to Araskog, the 1240 has already sucked in $300 million to $500 million just in R&D costs.

Despite ITT's diversity, its telecommunications predicament is hard to overstate. The company has long been the world's second-largest equipment producer, behind American Telephone & Telegraph Co.'s Western Electric subsidiary. The original idea of ITT's founder, Sosthenes Behn, was to leave the U. S. market to AT&T and create a duplicate company, even with a similar name, for the rest of the world. Behn succeeded, and although ITT has since gotten out of most of its telephone operating businesses, it still claims a gigantic 35% market share for switching equipment outside the U. S. and Japan.

The disappearance of telecommunications as a prop for growth is far from Araskog's only problem. ITT's common stock is selling at just 5.4 times current annualized earnings. The company has relatively little cash on hand and modest borrowing power, with total debt currently at 45.9% of capitalization. This would appear to have frozen the company out of its acquisition mode of the past. Indeed, Araskog's own management team seems convinced that he will launch ITT's first great drive for growth almost strictly from internal product development. "I don't think of ITT as being a great acquisition company," flatly declares James V. Lester, a senior executive vice-president who functions as one of two chief operating officers. Adds Charles Herzfeld, director of R&D: "We really are in a transition from a mode of growth from acquisitions to a new phase where a large fraction has to be from internal growth."

In many ways, Araskog does seem headed in this direction. Herzfeld's research job itself is just one year old at the company, whose prior reputation for innovative products was modest. And staff and line executives are generating new ideas within ITT's 40 separate business strategies to launch internal ventures that will fall across a broad spectrum of industries. They hope to position the company solidly in electronic office equipment, add to reserves of oil, coal, timber, and clay, and roll some regional consumer products into national circulation, including O. M. Scott & Sons lawn fertilizer and C&C Cola.

But the final decisions about whether to spend on internal development or another round of acquisitions may depend on the relationship between Araskog and Geneen. The former chief is still very much officially associated with his company. This year he will earn $450,000 as a consultant under a contract that expires at the end of 1985. Geneen also remains an ITT director and sits on the executive committee of the board, whose members are an unusual mix of Geneen associates, the investment bankers Geneen had used, insiders, two outsiders who are chief executives of comparatively small U. S. companies, and a few others.

Although the board has set a mandatory retirement age of 72, it has agreed to make some exceptions, and Geneen says he hopes to be one of them. Most important, Geneen consults often with Araskog, while Hamilton was not interested in such conversations. "Some people will tell you that Geneen has no power anymore, but I say absolutely yes, he

50 / Readings from *Business Week*

wields power," maintains one former top-level executive.

'A good job of acquiring'

This makes Geneen's thinking still crucial to the overall strategy. And in many respects his ideas are little changed from the past. Although he has tempered some of his antipathy to divestitures, it is clear he still views acquisition as a solid means of growth for ITT, perhaps beginning very soon. "I think we did a good job of acquiring," says Geneen, looking back before the 10-year antitrust prohibition of 1971. He adds: "And we have been 10 years allowing everybody else to move. [Now] Rand has the privilege, starting next September," when the ban expires. Such remarks must come as a surprise to many Araskog staffers, who are expecting nothing of the sort. Lester, for example, declares: "As far as I'm concerned, it [the ban's end] is a nonevent." In charge of ITT's two most important businesses, telecommunications and electronics, and insurance and finance, Lester says he has no current plans for acquisitions in either.

Geneen also still appears satisfied with substantial debt financing and seems enamored with sheer corporate size. Chief Financial Officer M. Cabell Woodward Jr. portrays the company as striving for fiscal conservatism by using, for example, the full $365 million proceeds of its November sale of forest operations in Canada to reduce debt. ITT may thus approach a stated goal of trimming debt to 40% of capital by yearend, he says. Geneen says he approves of the Canadian sale, but he also declares that, because of inflation, "I have a funny feeling that the cheapest thing in the world is money, loans particularly, because you are going to pay them all off with 50¢ [on the dollar]."

And although ITT has been criticized because its annual sales grow only at or under the rate of inflation, Geneen is thrilled about the actual dollars that sales growth represents. "Don't forget this one point: $2.5 billion a year of internal growth," he says. "Now that's bigger than Campbell Soup or B. F. Goodrich or anyone else that's been in business for 50 years." Hyperbole aside (Goodrich sales exceed $2.5 billion), Geneen hammers away at the importance of ITT's size. "Go out and see how many other companies are doing this," he insists.

What bothers ITT-watchers about these ideas is that they do not address profitability, where ITT slipped so badly during Geneen's latter years. In 1973, ITT earned $521 million before extraordinary items on sales of $10.2 billion, providing a return on sales of 5.1% and return on shareholders' equity of 13.9%. By 1977, Geneen's last year, return on sales had dropped to 4.3% and return on equity to 11.5%. In its mix of businesses, ITT found itself bottled up with big ventures in many mature industries—auto parts and bread, for example—with only tiny entries in the decade's hottest industry, oil, and in the potentially lucrative coal industry. For these reasons, says Donald W. Mitchell, managing director of Mitchell & Co., consultants in Cambridge, Mass.: "ITT became almost the perfect case of all the things wrong with a conglomerate. It has not been an innovator."

Observers say the reason has much to do with Geneen's inflexibility in his demands on subordinates to show steady, quarter-by-quarter earnings increases, while he concentrated on buying companies. Geneen, says Comptroller Herbert C. Knortz, orchestrated management decisions like a "ringmaster at a circus," worked far into the night, and was the subject of such fear that executives would gather before the start of a Geneen-run meeting to get their stories straight. Araskog, he says, is much different. The new chief "listens and appears to hear" his managers, and has reduced working hours to the daytime. Incumbent executives also suggest that Araskog is more decisive than his immediate predecessor, Hamilton. Some former executives are more critical, contending that Araskog relies too much on a small coterie of aides, including financial chief Woodward and Richard E. Bennett, a senior executive vice-president and the man in charge of consumer products, natural resources, and engineered products. To be sure, after only 16 months in office, Araskog has not yet had a real chance to prove his merit, although he already has shown himself to be more politic than Hamilton.

In his brief reign, Hamilton proclaimed sweeping change, an obvious implied criticism of Geneen. He quickly declared that ITT's main objective had to be profitability rather than sheer growth. "Geneen wanted big, we wanted better," says one member of Hamilton's entourage. Although Geneen maintains he did not organize Hamilton's ouster—a subject about which he has been silent in the past—he now says he "agreed" with the decision, which he characterizes as a "courageous" move by the board. It came, he says, before Hamilton's stewardship caused "the roof to fall in."

Geneen may have sensed, but probably did not know, just how radical were some of the changes the Hamilton administration envisioned. Hamilton first organized ITT's business into five distinct groups, and one former insider says that the reorganization's real purpose was to spin off each one to ITT's shareholders by about 1990, putting an end to Geneen's creation. This idea was little discussed around ITT's politically charged offices at 320 Park Ave. in New York, yet Araskog says that he already has been approached by one outsider with a similar idea. Araskog turned it down as "silly."

Araskog also has removed from the divestiture list some properties that Hamilton placed on it, including some television manufacturing operations in Germany and Britain. The new CEO emphasizes his support of Geneen's notion that turnaround attempts should come before divestiture is considered. A number of companies "were on the list, and now they are off," Araskog confirms. Geneen clearly would like to see more of this. "I say this in front of Rand," Geneen told BUSINESS WEEK in an interview at which both men were present. "It always bothers me if I have to sell something at a loss that I feel I created as a bad product myself, or a bad division. I feel an obligation to try to build it back up and sell it for what it is worth, and I don't see anybody doing that." Araskog quickly reassured Geneen that he is trying to do just that.

Araskog confers regularly on the phone or in person with Geneen, and he strongly defends this as proper. "Harold Geneen to me is a very respected and friendly person," Araskog says. "He knows the company and the people in the company. I trust him completely about anything I want to talk to him about. I'll do that whenever I feel like it, and if somebody in the outside world wants to say that is decision-making, the hell with it." He adds pointedly: "On the other hand, this company is mine to run." Araskog says that contact between the two happens "very much on my initiative," although Geneen adds to that remark: "But if I have any ideas, I don't hesitate to call Rand."

Regardless of whose business philosophies will dominate the company, ITT will have to find growth in new areas, given the changing nature of its prime businesses. While telecommunications profits have already slumped under development costs for the 1240, ITT has relied on Sheraton and Hartford for cash flow. But it cannot do so forever.

When ITT bought Sheraton Corp., the latter owned most of its hotels and had assets of more than $800 million. Some of its hotels, however, were in poor condition, and ITT began a long series of sales of hotels and hotel franchises, paring assets back to about $400 million. Sheraton now owns outright just 15 of its 409 units. As ITT's holdings were pared back, the hotel sales pumped cash into ITT's coffers with some regularity. Now, however, ITT's Bennett says these sales are about finished, and Sheraton has begun taking equity interests again in new hotels.

The Hartford Insurance Group, meanwhile, has become a major source of profit, even though under ITT it has slipped from fourth- to seventh-largest among property-casualty insurers in the U.S. Investment income at Hartford and ITT's $518 million (sales) finance companies offset losses in underwriting and yielded operating income of $404 million in 1979 on revenues of $4.8 billion. Aftertax earnings of the group have more than tripled since 1975, and Hartford's management has restructured its portfolio away from personal insurance lines and toward commercial lines, where premium rates are less heavily regulated by state governments.

Even so, the ratio of Hartford's payouts on claims to its premium income is running at 104%, one to two points worse than the industry average, and the property-casualty business is just now entering the trough of a down cycle. Hartford's growth thus depends on its continuing ability to invest cash at high rates of interest—an uncertain factor should President-elect Ronald Reagan somehow succeed in reducing U.S. inflation. "If you depend totally on investment income, your risk is high," notes Joseph A. Branca, an analyst with Standard & Poor's Corp.

With hotels and finance less predictable in profit growth than telecommunications used to be, Araskog is hoping to turn his troubled original business around. Under serendipitous conditions, this could work. Prospects for future telecommunications equipment sales are lavish. Consultants at Arthur D. Little Inc. suggest that from 1980 to 1990 as much money will be spent on telephone equipment as was spent between the invention of the telephone and now. At the same time, there will be retrofitting orders as glass fiber replaces copper wire in cables, electronic systems replace huge chunks of electromechanical machinery in switching, and electronic private-branch-exchange systems proliferate in the world's office buildings.

ITT has an ideal position from which to take advantage of these changes internationally, and the company has even broken into the U.S. equipment market. Its manufacturing plants in foreign countries are big employers whose customers—local governments—are often concerned about unemployment. ITT thus has an automatic advantage in winning orders against imports. "They are part of the club, and that is a major strength," says one envious competitor.

In the U.S., ITT last February made what could be a major breakthrough in penetrating the Bell System. It settled an antitrust action against AT&T with an agreement mandating that Bell must buy up to $2 billion of telecommunications products and services from ITT over 10 years, and that it must help ITT convert its 1240 digital technology to the U.S. market, where technical construction and programming standards are vastly different from Europe. In 1977, ITT's purchase of small North Electric Co. from United Telecommunications Inc. also provided the company with at least one digital switching system that is in production. Finally, by integrating its technical knowledge of telecommunications systems with its current entries in electronic office equipment, including Courier video display terminals and Qume impact printers, executives such as Lester hope ITT will be a major producer of information processing devices.

But many obstacles block fulfillment of this perfect scenario. North Electric, which is believed to have had a $30 million to $35 million aftertax loss last year on sales of only $150 million, still does much of its business with its former parent, United. And even the Bell antitrust agreement may not be of substantial aid. Spread over 10 years, ITT's annual sales to AT&T boil down to just $200 million per year, and nothing in the agreement requires Bell to buy the 1240, which ITT must sell to defray development costs. A Bell spokesman notes that his company has made no commitment to the 1240.

And while ITT's digital switch is still in the laboratory, it is losing ground in the one market expected to grow faster than any. Quantum Science Corp. projects a 40.3% annual rate of growth in dollar volume for digital switching in the U.S. through 1983—much faster than any other major type of telephonic equipment. Some countries, including France, are moving to digitalize switching even faster. Orders have flooded in from the Middle East.

This bright market has drawn so many new competitors that most in the industry see a shake-out ahead. Among the newest entrants is Lynch Communication Systems Inc. of Reno, Nev., a $50 million (sales) maker of transmission equipment. Much bigger companies, such as TRW Inc. and Rockwell International Corp., have come into the switching field in recent years, and foreign companies, including Nippon Electric Co. and France's Alcatel, are establishing manufacturing plants in the U.S. "I have to believe that not everybody can survive," says a spokesman for Northern Telecom, which, along with others, is losing money right now in switching. He adds: "Quite frankly, we're wondering what they [the new entrants] know about the marketplace that we don't."

In the face of such competition, which may keep pricing down for years, ITT is not even scheduled to deliver its 1240 until the end of next year "ITT is definitely very much behind," snipes one competitor. One reason is that the 1240 is an attempt to show the world a relatively new technology in which the microprocessor virtually replaces most central computer control functions of typical electronic systems. Competitors say this fully distributed control invites extra difficulties in software development, which could take a long time to work out. Araskog concedes that the project is "certainly behind our original schedules," but he maintains that customers have been understanding. At the same time, Araskog agrees that an industry shake-out may be brewing and says, "The biggest problem is that this could go like semiconductors, with two or three people coming out of it with profits and the rest having their problems."

Such a picture is a far cry from the days when switching equipment producers typically reaped a fat 20% to 25% pretax margin from their products. For ITT, nearly half of whose telecommunications order backlog of about $6 billion is switching equipment, the situation is serious. Yet, in an entanglement that seems to have webs within webs, ITT also faces difficulties if it can succeed in digital switching. Prime among these is plant and employee obsolescence.

Electronic switches can be built in simpler factories and with several times fewer employees. ITT employs 70,000 of its 100,000 European telecommunications workers in the making of switches, and in Europe, government and union rules push costs to about $20,000 to terminate a single employee. In some countries, layoffs have become almost impossible. Araskog concedes that right now 3,000 out of some 15,000 ITT telecommunications employees in Spain are on the payroll but have no work.

One former ITT telecommunications executive suggests that for the company to change over all its switching plants, the redundancy cost may reach $1 billion in employee discharge expense alone. ITT's Lester maintains that this figure is overstated. But the company admits it is a problem; in 1979, ITT wrote off $150 million after taxes for "technological restructuring," and reportedly half of this cost was to cover employee redundancy now and in the near future.

As if this were not enough, ITT's foreign business, which accounted for 52% of its total sales last year, is plagued by an image problem. In Geneen's time, the company was wracked with scandals; the now-famous former ITT lobbyist Dita Beard allegedly had been involved in donating money to the Republican Party during Richard Nixon's Administration in exchange for favorable antitrust treatment of the Hartford acquisition. ITT also was accused of helping bring about the downfall of Chile's Marxist President, Salvador Allende.

An Austrian scandal

No illegalities were found in either case, but this year ITT is being investigated for alleged questionable payments in Austria. This scandal—Austria's biggest since World War II—involves bribes supposedly paid to government officials and others in exchange for contracts to supply a gigantic hospital complex in Vienna. Among others, three ITT officials so far have been jailed for "investigatory detention" in the affair.

ITT executives in New York claim that these incidents have never hurt business, but others disagree. In France, for example, ITT's telecommunications subsidiary, CGCT, has not yet succeeded in winning approval from the French PTT of the design of the 1240, a prerequisite to winning contracts. Others, including Alcatel and Thomson CSF, have won both. As recently as last year, vandals in France were still spray-painting "Remember Chile" slogans on ITT's buildings, says one former employee. And a financial analyst in Paris, looking at the government's hesitation to order ITT digital equipment, notes: "In electoral terms, ITT is the devil." Earlier this year, ITT's chief officer in Europe, John W. Guilfoyle, warned that without such orders, CGCT, which employs 9,000, may not survive beyond the end of 1981. In 1979 the subsidiary reportedly lost $24 million on sales of nearly $550 million.

The strong man tradition

The image problem simply adds another headache to managing a company so far-flung that it is probably the most complicated corporation to operate anywhere. Yet ITT's management style still is reminiscent of the Geneen era, in which a single strong man is expected to make all major decisions. Indeed, Araskog holds all three top positions—chairman, president, and chief executive—and says he has no plan to relinquish any of them soon. ITT lacks a head of strategic planning, which is done instead from the profit-center level on up, with Araskog and the board ultimately charged with approving or denying the plans that get past senior managers.

It is difficult, too, to see exactly where Araskog's priorities lie in funding internal growth, because the company declines to break out capital spending and R&D budget plans beyond 1980 in its five business segments. Certainly, Araskog's menu for capital allocation is huge. Telecommunications and electronics must be fed to keep up with changing technology and to expand in information processing. Meanwhile, ITT's Bennett, for example, wants to pump up to $200 million over five years into Continental Baking Co.—the only national bread producer in the U.S.—to remodel and modernize its ovens. And he sees major opportunities to add to subsidiary Eason Oil Co.'s 760,000 net acres of leaseholdings, and to timber acreage and clay production.

Araskog will need not only to fund such ventures but also to make certain they are managed carefully enough to fuel the telecommunications drive and give ITT's profitability a boost for the first time in years. "To establish confidence in the eyes of investors, ITT has to manage what it has right now," comments Brian R. Fernandez, an analyst at First Manhattan Co. Araskog may well believe he can do this and make acquisitions simultaneously, but it is apparent that to succeed he will have to do more than match Geneen's performance, and on a stage where the former chief is still a player. ∎

THE PAINS OF TURNING FIRESTONE AROUND

The appointment of John J. Nevin as Firestone Tire & Rubber Co.'s chief executive on Aug. 19 finally made official and public the mandate that Nevin has had since he took over the company's presidency in December: turn around Firestone's sagging fortunes, no matter how painful the process may be. And indeed, in the last six months, Nevin has left almost no facet of Firestone's business untouched. He has:

- Strengthened the company's cash position by omitting dividends at a saving of $35 million annually, cutting staff by 15%, and rescinding cost-of-living increases to salaried employees.
- Reorganized the company into four separate groups, each headed by a vice-president, and set up the sales and marketing of tires to stores and major dealers as a separate unit.
- Increased plant efficiency by paring tire-making capacity and slashing slower-moving tire lines.

To do so, he permanently closed six North American plants (BW—Mar. 31), cutting overall capacity by one-third and

A cut in tire inventories. Some doubts arise about retaining dealers

reducing capacity for bias-ply tires, which have been losing market to radials, by 55%. By lopping off nearly $300 million in sales to private-label customers who were buying the bias-ply or other unprofitable tires, Nevin was able to cut by 23%, to 2,093, the number of passenger car tire types Firestone makes.

The running theme behind Nevin's moves has been to cut tire inventories as far as possible, a reduction he says could save $24 million annually in finance charges. So far, the strategy is working: Between February and July, Firestone's North American tire inventories fell from 17.6 million to 13.5 million. Nevin is hoping to hit 10 million by Oct. 31.

Dealer discontent. Nevin's cost-cutting techniques are by no means winning him universal praise. "The jury is still out on whether they'll be able to retain the loyalty of Firestone-brand dealers," warns Saul H. Ludwig, an analyst with Roulston & Co. Indeed, some longtime Firestone customers who were buying tires Firestone has discontinued are already threatening to move their orders for radials to competitors who will meet all of their tire demands.

Observers also wonder whether Firestone may have quoted money-losing prices during recent negotiations with Detroit. The company asked for a price increase of only 10% over last year, rather than the roughly 16% that others in the industry had requested. One competitor howled: "They led the way in giving the shop away." And Harry W. Millis, an analyst with McDonald & Co., warns: "If the long-term strategy is to make money in the domestic tire business, I think [the price war] will come back to haunt Nevin."

For his part, Nevin insists that even with bare-bones pricing, Firestone will make "modest profits" on original-equipment sales to Detroit. He claims that even with the depressed market, it can operate at 85% of capacity—far above the industry's overall 57% rate in July—during the last three quarters of its 1981 fiscal year.

While Nevin does not lightly dismiss criticisms, he maintains that he had neither the "luxury to be charming" nor the time to concentrate on long-term goals during his first six months. "I'm not willing to apologize for short-term objectives," he says. "Most of the things we've done have been actions to cut risk."

Record losses. Clearly, Firestone needs to be on surer footing. In the quarter ended July 31 it suffered record after-tax operating losses of $33 million. Sales fell 12% from the same quarter last year, to $1.15 billion. In the last three years the company has dropped nearly $400 million in cash, and its long-term debt-to-equity ratio ballooned from 43% to 56% in the six months ending in April. Outstanding commercial paper climbed from nothing to $131 million during the last year, and its creditors informed Firestone they would permit no further increase. Sums up Nevin: "We were skating on thin ice."

Even in nonfinancial areas, Firestone has had more than its share of troubles. It has to live down the infamous radial 500 recall, a payoff scandal that saw its chief financial officer jailed, and management turnover that included the departure of former President Mario A. Di Federico. Even now, attorneys are preparing for an October trial involving alleged illegal gold trading.

Image. Nevin is trying the personal approach to burnish Firestone's image. He has met with Ralph Nader and Clarence M. Ditlow III of the Center for Auto Safety and has appeared on Nader's TV show. He is trying to ease relations with the National Highway Traffic Safety Administration by assigning technical people to work with them rather than lawyers, by voluntarily recalling up to another 5 million radical 500s, and by frequently calling Joan Claybrook, NHTSA'S administrator.

It is this personal touch more than anything else that is winning Nevin fans. Financially, Firestone's future is still chancy. Its heavy investment in truck tires remains an iffy proposition. The shutdown in late August of its remaining British plants has now pared its European presence to what one analyst calls "a skeleton operation." And much, of course, depends on whether the sickly tire market revives.

But in the meantime, Nevin is meeting with customers and critics to explain his moves. "He's really trying to resolve acrimony," Claybrook says. Perhaps Cincinnati Firestone dealer Patrick G. Brogan puts it best. After shooting the breeze with Nevin over a beer recently, he said with approval: "They're coming down to our level." ∎

Richard J. Ferris

FLYING A RISKY NEW ROUTE FOR UNITED

For the first six months of 1980, the U. S. trunk airline industry suffered an operating loss of $489.8 million, excluding results of hotel, food-service, and other nonaviation subsidiaries, in contrast with a $175.5 million operating profit for that period a year ago. Even though the third quarter is normally the strongest for most of the big 10 lines, July's traffic was down 9% from a year ago. All indications are that the last quarter of the year will be devastating because the losses will mount so fast. One thing is certain: There will be a lot fewer flights to choose from next fall.

United Airlines Inc., the wholly owned subsidiary of UAL Inc., is the nation's largest airline, and so far it has taken the most radical approach to the problem. It started eliminating money-losing flights in June. The approach, apparently, is working.

When President Richard J. Ferris of UAL peered at his company's modest second-quarter earnings and saw the $47 million loss for United, his reaction was surprisingly jubilant. "I think it's super, really nifty," he beamed. "We're starting to see the new route structure taking hold and things coming together. Now it's just a matter of waiting for the economy to improve." Ferris was encouraged because the airline's loss was $20 million less than in the first quarter and because, buoyed by aircraft sales and an income tax reduction, the parent had posted a $25 million profit after losing $40 million in the previous quarter.

But the latest results for UAL and United can be more accurately read as dramatic evidence of the enormous risk Ferris is taking in radically restructuring the airline in the face of plunging traffic. Because of the current recession, U. S. trunk airline traffic is down 1.2% for this year's first half after years of double-digit growth. Ferris is gambling, however, that he can build traffic on scores of new routes even though the market is soft. He is not moving as recklessly as Braniff Airways Inc., which has expanded willy-nilly and run itself into a deep financial hole. Instead, United has been careful to add routes from such points as Chicago and Denver, where it has inherent strength. But Ferris is clearly adopting a strategy that contrasts vividly with that of the rest of the industry.

Vulnerability

United has made so many changes—abandoning service between 123 pairs of cities and adding service between 80 other pairs—that it is highly vulnerable if the new routes fail. "We're giving up established positions in many markets because management wants to pursue better opportunities," says one skeptical United pilot. "I hope they guess right about where we can compete because we'll never be able to regain the business we've walked away from."

Ferris, a 43-year-old marketing whiz who came up through the management ranks of UAL's Western International Hotels Co., admits that his strategy for flying the deregulated skies is a long way from proving itself a big financial success. But he adamantly defends his decision in the mid-1970s to become the most visible industry champion of airline deregulation. That decision astonished many major competitors, who thought the big trunk carriers were better off under the protective wing of the Civil Aeronautics Board.

United, with almost 20% of the industry's capacity, clearly had the most to lose from deregulation. It is so big that it has long had a reputation for being ponderous. One purpose of deregulation was to permit fast-on-their-feet entrepreneurs with hustle and low overheads to enter the industry, slash fares, and carve market shares out of the hides of the grandfather carriers. Compounding the puzzlement over United's support of deregulation were the airline's sharply improving profits in the two years preceding President Carter's signing the Airline Deregulation Act in October, 1978.

Nevertheless, Ferris apparently foresaw opportunities as well as dangers in deregulation and favored it virtually from the beginning. Then, last year he decided that instead of gradually redrawing United's system map, he would institute all the changes immediately. He made that decision even though he knew the U. S. economy was probably headed downward and that United itself was undergoing a series of financial setbacks. In 1979 the airline was hit by a 58-day shutdown because of a strike by the International Association of Machinists & Aerospace Workers, a 38-day grounding of its 37 McDonnell Douglas Corp. DC-10s, and a 77% rise in jet fuel prices. The bottom line: a $99.6 million loss on revenues of $3.3 billion for the airline.

Amid all those difficulties, Ferris moved ahead with his bold changes to position United in more profitable markets for the 1980s. The strategy is to winnow out flights of 200 mi. and less that have lost money or been only marginally profitable and to divert resources to longer routes that will profitably support United's fleet of large aircraft and the company's huge overhead.

Cutbacks and buildups

Nowhere is this strategy demonstrated more dramatically than in Cleveland, where, in the mid-1970s, United had built one of its largest traffic hubs. In October, 1978, before deregulation, it operated 96 daily nonstop flights from Cleveland to 35 cities. By last June, when Ferris's plan went into effect, it operated 53 a day to 23 cities.

United also got completely out of Atlanta and New Orleans, where it felt hopelessly outgunned by more entrenched competitors. And it left Bakersfield, Calif., perhaps the most publicized city affected by airline deregulation (BW—Nov. 5).

At the same time, however, United is building new hubs in Memphis and Kansas City, Mo. And it has increased service between its traditional Midwestern and Eastern strongholds and Denver, Miami, Tampa, San Diego, and San Francisco. Typical of the new thrust to longer-haul markets, United will inaugurate nonstop flights this fall between Chicago and three markets—Houston,

The Strategy Makers / 55

How deregulation increased efficiency and reduced fares

This year has all the indications of being disastrous for the airline industry (page 78), and it may wind up as the worst in its history.

A logical conclusion would be that deregulation has been partly to blame, since it is a principal new element with which the industry must contend. In a small sense, this is true. Deregulation has enabled seven lines to fly nonstop now between New York and Los Angeles and San Francisco, charging fares so low that William T. Seawell, chairman of Pan American World Airways Inc., characterizes them as "crazy." Prior to deregulation in October, 1978, only three airlines flew coast-to-coast.

But the evidence is strong that the airlines would have been a lot worse off in this year of soaring fuel costs and falling traffic had they not been deregulated. "I'm not sure we could have handled it," says Neil M. Effman, vice-president for airline planning at Trans World Airlines Inc.

Senator Howard W. Cannon (D-Nev.), sponsor of the Airline Deregulation Act of 1978 and generally considered to be the father of deregulation, is particularly pleased about the impact of the new law. "The system as a whole has gotten more efficient because airlines can put their equipment where it can be used best. Efficiency is what deregulation is all about," he says.

The biggest problem confronting the airlines, of course, is the price of jet fuel. It now accounts for 30% of airline costs, having risen 71% from June, 1979, to June, 1980, industrywide, or to an average 91¢ a gal. from 53¢.

Higher efficiency. Had the airlines remained under regulation this year, they would have had to continue flying unsuitable planes in many unprofitable markets, and losses in all probability would have been even greater. Under the old rules, the Civil Aeronautics Board had an absolute say over where airlines flew and it did not often allow the lines to abandon markets.

"Deregulation gave us the opportunity to restructure the airline," says Charles L. Demoney, vice-president of market planning for Frontier Airlines Inc. "We're not locked into service and we can move our equipment around." Adds Anthony McKinnon, vice-president for marketing administration at Delta Air Lines Inc.: "Deregulation lets us pick and choose our markets." And Morton Ehrlich, senior vice-president for planning at Eastern Air Lines Inc., claims that "airlines have changed their product line. This has resulted in improved efficiency."

A typical example is a plane that Frontier used to fly from several points in Kansas to Chicago at an operating deficit of $500,000 a year. The line moved the plane to a more profitable part of the system and now, in fact, reviews its fleet use on a monthly basis.

Fares. In addition to moving equipment to profitable routes, airlines have adopted more discount pricing than ever. "The most efficient way to run an airline is with two tiers of fares," says TWA's Effman, citing the need for both full fares and traffic generating discounts. Such pricing existed before deregulation, but airlines now have virtual carte blanche to fill seats.

Robert H. Frank, director of the CAB's office of economic analysis, believes that the overall improved efficiency has tangible results. "If the airlines had kept doing what they were doing at the end of 1976," he says, "fares would have gone up 53% by the end of 1979. Instead, fares went up 27%." Concludes Marvin S. Cohen, chairman of the CAB: "The success of deregulation as a concept has been the increase in airline efficiency."

Phoenix, and Tucson—that it has never served. It will also soon announce additional transcontinental service, much to the surprise of the industry and its observers. Of the three traditional transcontinental airlines, United has invariably been No. 3, partly because its headquarters and power base are in Chicago. American Airlines Inc. has always been strong in New York, while Trans World Airlines Inc. has been strong in Los Angeles. Perhaps because he wants to knock out the newcomers on the transcontinental routes, Eastern Air Lines Inc. and Pan American World Airways Inc., before they can get a foothold, Ferris is adding a sixth daily flight between New York and Los Angeles and a fifth between New York and San Francisco on Aug. 8. In referring to United's commitment to fight its way into a bigger share of the transcontinental market, Ferris says: "If they [the competition] haven't got the message yet, maybe they will now."

Ferris claims that his new structuring will cut the airline's breakeven load factor by more than a couple of percentage points, and that this will make United more lucrative when the economy snaps back. The problems are that United's load factor has dropped more than that of most other lines this year because of the restructuring, and that the economy may take its time turning around. By Ferris's own estimate, domestic trunk airline traffic will dive 10% to 14% in the last half of 1980 from a year ago and will show no growth in 1981. Given that bleak scenario, the period of what Ferris calls "excess capacity, industry irrationality, and blood-letting for a couple of years following deregulation" may extend far longer.

Almost without exception, United's competitors and other industry observers believe United is correct in trying to bolster its long-haul business. But many are just as convinced that United is going about the repositioning in an extremely risky way. "The company has always preached to us the importance of our feeder flights in building the volume we need on the long hauls," explains another United pilot. "It's hard for me to believe we can suddenly cut back much of that feeder network without starving our longer flights." Even Howard D. Putnam, the former United marketing vice-president who is now president of Southwest Airlines Inc., a fast-growing regional carrier based in Dallas, expresses concern. "I think United management has done a good job of figuring out its strengths and playing to them," he says. "But they must wonder how they will feed themselves in some of their markets."

Old-friend competition

United may also find that the regional airlines that it is counting on as feeders will grow and contend for the long-haul traffic that United wants to keep. Such tactics are already emerging as such carriers as USAir, Frontier, and Texas International expand toward coast-to-coast service. And United's determination to fight it out in the transcontinental markets, where price competition is ferocious, surprises many. "You can't tell me it is better business to fly passengers from New York to Los Angeles for $129 than to charge a reasonable fare for a short route," declares one regional airline executive.

At United's headquarters in the Chicago suburb of Elk Grove Village, executives brush aside arguments that United should hold on to more short-haul routes. "Few companies have the resources or the cost structure to support profitable production of all kinds of products in all kinds of markets," declares Edward A. Beamish, UAL's senior vice-president for corporate planning. "United is placing emphasis on products and markets that match our capabilities, something that could not really be done under tight regulation."

Ferris argues that there is compelling logic for United's new direction. "We used to figure our loss on the short-haul trip was the price we paid for controlling the feed traffic to our long-haul flights where we could make a buck," explains Ferris. "But guess what. When we looked at what was actually going on, we found that we were paying a very high price for very little feed traffic." United computer studies brought United executives to the conclusion that from 70% to 90% of the passengers carried on short hops from small and medium-sized cities did not connect with any other United flight, let alone with a long-haul flight.

Because United took so much abuse for leaving Bakersfield, it is happy to reveal what the computer showed there. In June, 1978, United carried a daily average of 183 passengers from Bakersfield to Los Angeles and 171 passengers to San Francisco, and it lost money on every one for those legs of its trips. From the Bakersfield flights, it carried an average of only 19 passengers each

from Los Angeles and San Francisco to Denver and points east, five from Los Angeles to Honolulu, and two from San Francisco to Honolulu.

As an example of the kind of payoff Ferris expects throughout United's vast system, he likes to point to results in such cities as Grand Rapids, Mich., where United reduced daily departures to seven from 12 last May. That included a reduction of flights to Chicago from five to two and the addition of nonstops to Denver and Kansas City, Mo. Ferris says the new schedule has increased United's passenger miles per departure and its long-haul traffic west of Chicago by 40%. Similarly, he claims, by halving the 10 short hops from Fresno, Calif., to San Francisco and Los Angeles, the carrier has been able to add new flights from Fresno to Denver and Chicago, raising its long-haul volume east from Fresno by 20%. "United is still a hub-and-spoke airline," explains Ferris. "We still love our spokes from rim cities such as Cedar Rapids [Iowa], Moline [Ill.], and Norfolk [Va]. We're still building our strong hubs and we're developing our

smaller hubs. The difference between our new route structure and our old route structure is one thing: Our spokes are now longer."

Developing those longer spokes is sometimes easier said than done, particularly in a wobbly market. This fall, United will drop the new Chicago-Fresno nonstop because there is not enough traffic to justify it along with two Fresno-Denver trips.

But perhaps the biggest gamble of all for United is in Cleveland, and the whole industry is watching, utterly fascinated, to see what develops. For 10 years United had expanded service there, becoming dominant in the market. In part, the plan was to create a hub that would relieve pressure on Chicago's overcrowded O'Hare International Airport. But under the Ferris restructuring, a lot of the short-haul flights have disappeared. "We're now losing a lot of Cleveland long-haul traffic," says still another United pilot, whose base is in the Midwest. "The short-haul passengers are going to Pittsburgh or Detroit and con-

Top rival American sticks to its old ways

The most formidable competitor for United Airlines Inc. has always been the second largest U.S. airline, American Airlines Inc. Indeed, since deregulation it has become even more so. Even as United is gearing up to attack American in Houston, Phoenix, and Tucson, where American has long had strong identity, American is attacking United's turf in Seattle. In the big East Coast-to-Chicago and Chicago-to-West Coast markets, the two airlines have been knocking each other over the head for years.

By coincidence, Robert L. Crandall, who became American's president on July 16, is, like United's Richard J. Ferris, young (44), aggressive, opinionated, and marketing-oriented—but he is completely at odds with Ferris philosophically. He still thinks that airline deregulation was a mistake—and he is just about the last major airline executive who feels that way. "Airlines," Crandall says, "are spending a lot more, burning a lot more fuel, and charging higher prices than they would in a regulated environment."

Under the leadership of its chairman and chief executive officer, Albert V. Casey, American is getting into the oil business, where it is doing well. But in the operation of its airline it is not getting high marks. In the second quarter this year it suffered an operating loss of $45.3 million in contrast to an operating profit of $66.4 million a year ago, when American benefited hugely from United's problems. "American doesn't have a clue as to what it wants to do now that we have deregulation," says the president of a fast-growing regional airline. "They just have a bunch of planes they fly around. They don't seem to me to really have a long-range plan."
Unchanged goals. Crandall himself appears embarrassed by questions on what, if anything, American is doing differently because of deregulation. "That's not a question I can really answer," he says. "It's the environment that has changed, not the company. Our basic goals are still the same."

The key fact about American is that it has no intention of changing the way it operates its hub-and-spoke route system. Over the past two years it has been adding to the number of flights in and out of its two main hubs, Dallas-Fort Worth and Chicago. "Maintaining short-haul support for long-haul traffic is and will remain an important concept at American," Crandall says.

By far the biggest problem confronting American is its fleet of 59 Boeing 707s and 57 Boeing 727-100s. Both types of jets were designed and built when jet fuel cost about 11¢ a gallon, and today they are hopelessly uneconomic to operate. Partly because of this, Crandall

is planning to cut American's available seat miles this fall by 11%, a good deal more than its normal seasonal cutback. Unlike Ferris, he declines to tip his hand on where the cuts will be made, but it is a good bet that American will reduce the flight frequencies for these elderly jets.
A good buy. Crandall and American pulled off an extraordinary coup late in July. The company bought 15 of the newer, more fuel-efficient 727-200s from Braniff Airways Inc. to add to its fleet of 40. Now, while escaping the cost of training its pilots on a new airplane, American can ground many of its 100s and fly the 200s on its growing short-haul routes at a profit.

Analysts are looking to Crandall to provide a bold new strategy for American, but it is clear that, for a while anyway, he does not want to rock the boat, even if the boat does seem to be leaking a bit. Casey, who is 60, obviously will stay active in day-to-day management. For his part, Crandall, who had been senior vice-president for marketing, carefully refrains from criticizing any policy decisions made at American in recent years. Although widely considered a tough, demanding taskmaster, Crandall has announced goals for American that are surprisingly mild in contrast to what has been going on at United: "To return American to adequate profitability, to provide high-quality transportation, and to be a good place to work for our employees."

The Strategy Makers / 57

necting with other airlines for long-haul flights."

United claims it has so far held on to a fair amount of long-haul traffic at Cleveland by working closely with commuter carriers such as Freedom Airlines Inc. and Air Wisconsin Inc. that serve the city. But with commuter airlines taking over the feeder routes that United has abandoned, other trunk airlines have the same prerogative as United to adjust long-haul schedules to coincide with commuter schedules. That is precisely what American plans to do. "We will try to get as much business as we can away from them," vows Walter J. McKenna, acting general manager for American in the Cleveland-Akron area, who anticipates making such schedule moves later this year. "United spent a lot of money in Cleveland; it owned the Cleveland market," adds Jack Westman, district manager for Delta Air Lines Inc. "It doesn't any more."

One reason United has moved swiftly to restructure is that, with the recent rise in fuel prices, its older and larger jets suddenly need much longer flights to become economic. United has made $3 billion in commitments since 1976 to modernize its fleet, and the airline is making progress. When the program started, less than half of the 365-plane fleet was considered fuel efficient. Now about three-fourths make the grade.

In the next few years, however, United's upgrading of its fleet will slow markedly. The carrier has taken delivery of five DC-10s this year and will add five in 1981, providing modest improvement. But it had to cancel options to buy 22 Boeing 727-200s because last year's strike cost $350 million. United is now banking on 30 new-technology Boeing 767s to increase the percentage of efficient aircraft in its fleet to 85% by 1984. The 767, a wide-bodied, twin-engine jet, will carry 197 passengers and will be ideal for flights of from 500 mi. to 2,200 mi., where United will increasingly specialize. Unfortunately, United cannot take delivery of its first 767s until 1982, so it must delay retirement of its less efficient planes. The inefficient fleet and the slack economy have already prompted United to ground 44 jets this year and to plan a 7% reduction in available seat miles in the fall compared with last fall's schedule.

Boosters and critics

Executives of other airlines believe that United's fleet and other high operating costs have forced it to take the plunge with its new route structure more quickly than it would have liked. "It's risky to give up your feeder system like that," says President Glen L. Ryland, of Frontier Airlines Inc. "But United's high cost structure really gives it no choice." Adds C. Edward Acker, chairman of Air Florida Systems Inc. and a former president of Braniff: "Considering their aircraft, I think they are moving quite properly. They need to concentrate on long-haul markets, and they are also getting out of some of their bad weather spots [where the operating costs are exorbitant]. They may have to go through some tough times, but they're eventually going to end up with a highly profitable system."

One aspect of the restructuring that many observers feel has hurt United was a presentation by Ferris to security analysts in Boston last fall in which he laid out many route changes that would not be implemented until the following June and even next September. By doing that, Ferris gave his competitors an early look at his strategy and thus a chance to adjust their own plans accordingly. "In a deregulated environment, where you can quickly adjust prices to meet the competition, your long-term scheduling plans are about the only hole card left," says Julius Maldutis, airline analyst for Salomon Bros., who believes United would have been better off quietly and gradually testing longer spokes to its hubs. Ferris counters, however, that because he was the first and virtually only airline champion of deregulation, he feels deeply that United had a responsibility to warn communities of impending changes—particularly service cutbacks.

With the basic restructuring completed, Ferris does not expect very many future changes. "I'm very pleased with our new, longer spokes, but I cannot answer yet whether it's a 100% categorical success," he says. United management contends it has met every internal goal set for itself in terms of generating traffic, but that industry cutthroat fare wars have not allowed the traffic volume to be reflected on the bottom line. "We're carrying the numbers but not getting the yields," Ferris says. That is something he expects to start correcting in the next six months. "The harsh realities of the marketplace for those airlines that have not made rational moves will bring about discipline very rapidly," he says. "By this fall or early next year, the red ink is going to be flowing so badly that they will have no choice." ∎

After years of hoarding cash
HEARST IS SPENDING BIG

Ever since the death in 1951 of its flamboyant, profligate founder, William Randolph Hearst, Hearst Corp. has been one of the best-kept secrets in publishing. Some observers see the private company as well-run and conservative but far from fulfilling its potential. To others it is an enigma. One analyst, who follows publishing companies, when asked recently about Hearst, said: "Their resources don't amount to a hill of beans. There is no forward planning, and they are not involved in acquisitions." He is wrong on all counts. Hearst's assets are impressive, it has long-range goals, and it is spending millions on acquisitions.

In a rare series of interviews, Frank A. Bennack Jr., president and chief executive officer, outlined for BUSINESS WEEK the company's ambitious plan for the 1980s. A lifelong Hearst employee, Bennack, 47, speaks with the quiet confidence of a man who knows where he is headed and has the money to get there. Determined to make Hearst a profitable, well-managed, and respected multimedia company, he says: "Hearst, by the nature of its founder, is the best-known name in publishing. My goal is to make it the best-regarded."

Every division at Hearst is being strengthened and expanded. After 20 years of hoarding cash, the company is now spending it. In the past 20 months, Hearst has gone on a $154 million splurge, buying five daily newspapers, one TV station, a hardcover publisher, a technical publishing house, and other properties.

At the same time, the company has spent $50 million to improve what it already owns. Bennack has lured to Hearst more than a dozen top-flight executives and editors to spearhead new ventures. While Bennack will not say how much cash is left in the company's coffers, he confirms that there is enough for more acquisitions. "We bought a lot of properties, and we don't owe a nickel," says Vice-Chairman John R. Miller.

In addition to cash, Hearst's assets include vast information resources that will be the foundation for future projects. Already, three new magazines—*Country Living, Cosmopolitan Living,* and a revised *Science Digest*—have been spun off existing publications. The company makes a tidy sum by licensing the rights to 30 of its magazine titles to publishers in 14 countries. Its King Features Syndicate, which owns three of the top comic strips in the country, has licensed the movie rights for *Popeye* to Paramount Pictures Corp. and for *Flash Gordon* to Dino de Laurentis, and stands to gain from box office receipts and merchandise sales. The company expects to expand its book publishing and, through acquisition, to begin publishing business and technical magazines. Hearst TV and radio stations are big contributors to corporate profits, and the company plans to buy more.

But probably most important from the company's point of view, Hearst is moving into the one medium it has thus far neglected—cable TV systems. In the next few months, Bennack says, Hearst will purchase a multiple system operator that will serve as a base for acquiring other cable TV franchises. Also, with its immense store of print information and films, Hearst is gearing up to produce software for cable TV, videocassettes, and videodiscs (page 94).

But Hearst's expansion plans do not stop with its media holdings. Although William Randolph Hearst's castle at San Simeon was given to California in 1958, the company owns 77,000 acres nearby on which it raises cattle and grows crops. The Sunical Div., which is the company's real estate holding company, would like to use part of that property to build hotels, motels, and a golf course for the estimated 900,000 tourists who visit the castle each year. In addition, Sunical is seeking to acquire more land.

All of this expansion will present new opportunities to a company that was already prospering. As a private company, Hearst guards its figures closely. But one observer estimates that in 1977, Hearst had sales of $591 million and profits of $70 million. This year the company's sales could reach $1 billion.

Bennack does say that since 1975 the company's revenues have doubled. That tremendous growth excludes revenues from any of the company's recent acquisitions. "We are just now feeling the effects of growth that come from those," says Bennack.

Many of Hearst's competitors believe that the company is merely playing catch-up. "They have been sleepy for quite a while," says the head of one large media company. Another, when asked to comment on Hearst's strategy for moving into cable, quipped: "How can I disagree with it? They're doing what we're doing." J. Kendrick Noble Jr., a vice-president at Paine Webber Mitchell Hutchins Inc., agrees. "Their pattern is more or less the pattern for all media companies today," he says. "Ten years ago, it would have been unique."

Observers feel that now in its desire to expand quickly, Hearst may be paying too much for some properties it is acquiring. For instance, Hearst recently agreed to pay $26 million to buy Cox Broadcasting Corp.'s United Technical Publications, which had revenues of only $22.4 million last year.

Bennack concedes that Hearst may not have kept pace with its competitors. "I would like our position better if we were doing in 1965 what we're doing today," he admits. "But there's nothing we can do about past strategy."

The one criticism that Bennack cannot accept, however, is that Hearst may be spending its money carelessly. The price that Hearst has paid for each acquisition, Bennack claims, "has been in the ball park." In several cases, he notes, Hearst passed up an acquisition rather than raise its bid. He adds, "Never has an acquisition been made that the unsuccessful suitor didn't say that the winner paid too much."

It wasn't until fairly recently that changes occurred within Hearst's executive offices to allow this new direction. Richard E. Berlin, who served as president from 1949 until retiring in 1972, was credited for turning the company around financially, but many felt that he became too conservative. "After having

The Strategy Makers / 59

THE BIG-CITY DRAIN ON HEARST PAPERS

When people think of Hearst Corp., they think of newspapers. Ironically, it is that division that is giving the company most of its headaches.

At its peak, the Hearst newspaper chain consisted of 33 papers, most in large metropolitan areas where William Randolph Hearst felt they could do him the most good politically. But now, buffeted by labor problems and the exodus of urban dwellers to suburbs, many big-city newspapers have fallen on hard times. Hearst still owns five—the *Los Angeles Herald Examiner*, the *Boston Herald American*, Baltimore's *News American*, the *San Francisco Examiner*, and the *Seattle Post-Intelligencer*.

Although Hearst officials claim that the newspaper group as a whole is profitable, at least three of the company's big-city papers, in Boston, Los Angeles, and Seattle, are losing money. Most of the $50 million that Hearst has spent in the last three years on capital improvements has gone into its newspapers. Robert J. Danzig, a vice-president and general manager of the newspaper group, says that all Hearst papers now are made up by photo composition processes and all but Boston use computers and terminals rather than typewriters. But many still feel that the papers are woefully underfunded. Says one former editor, "You can tell by looking at those papers that they're not putting much money into them."

Perhaps in the worst shape is the Boston paper, which, with a daily circulation of about 240,000, has half the circulation of *The Boston Globe*. Although the paper was in the black during 1976 and 1977, informed sources say that it had been consistently in the red for at least a dozen years before that and is now piling up losses in the neighborhood of $10 million to $15 million yearly. "Obviously, they're in trouble," says Robert Bergenheim, the former publisher, who now is vice-president of labor and public relations at Boston University. Many believe that Hearst intends to sell the Boston newspaper, but such rumors are vigorously denied by Hearst management.

A fall from No. 1. Also in trouble is the *Los Angeles Herald Examiner*. While it is attracting more advertising and a more affluent reader than it was three years ago, circulation continues to fall. The major blow to the paper occurred from 1967 through 1977, when it was involved in a sometimes bloody strike by its 13 craft unions. The paper fell from its position as the No. 1 afternoon daily in the U.S., with a 730,000 circulation, to less than half that. After the strike, Hearst began a vigorous campaign to recoup what it had lost to the *Los Angeles Times*. It brought in a new publisher, Francis L. Dale, who had made *The Cincinnati Enquirer* the ad leader in its market, and a new editor, James G. Bellows, who had scored small gains in reviving *The Washington Star*.

Bellows is working hard to upgrade the editorial quality of the paper and claims to be unworried that the paper's circulation has not increased. "It didn't get into trouble in two and a half years and it won't get out in two and a half years," he says. Danzig also appears pleased with the paper's progress so far, stressing that the Los Angeles franchise is the second largest in the U.S. and the possibilities for growth are enormous.

The San Francisco paper was losing money until 1965, when it entered into a joint operating agency with the *San Francisco Chronicle*. Under the agreement, the two papers combine advertising sales, printing, and distribution while maintaining separate editorial staffs. The operating agreement has come under legal attack on the grounds that it makes it harder for smaller papers in the suburbs to compete. In the latest legal challenge, brought by a Marin County weekly, a jury in January failed to reach a verdict. A retrial has been scheduled for next year.

Lagging. A slump in the housing market has damaged the economy of the lumber-producing Northwest, and has added to the woes of the *Seattle Post-Intelligencer*. That newspaper, with about 200,000 in circulation, lags behind *The Seattle Times*, owned by Knight-Ridder Newspapers Inc., with about 258,000. The Baltimore *News American* is trying to wrest readers away from *The Sun* by emphasizing local news. While observers give the Hearst paper high marks for its local stories, some claim that the strategy has resulted in light coverage of hard news.

Hearst's hopes for its newspapers lie with the ones that are located in smaller cities and towns. Even though Rupert Murdoch bought the *San Antonio Light's* competition, the *Express-News*, the Hearst paper is still first in circulation. Hearst's two newspapers in Albany, N.Y., the *Times-Union* and the *Knickerbocker News*, have always been profitable. Danzig says that the papers have been further improved since Harry M. Rosenfeld, formerly of *The Washington Post*, became editor.

Hearst executives are optimistic about the five newspapers they have recently purchased, in particular the *Midland Reporter-Telegram* in Texas. Some analysts believe that the $32 million Hearst paid was too high for a newspaper whose yearly revenues are only about $7 million. Others feel that the paper is a gold mine. It is the only paper in Midland, in the energy production heart of Texas, which is ranked in the top 10 U.S. cities in income per family. Hearst also is proud of its other purchases: the *Plainview Daily Herald*, also in Texas, the *Daily News* in Midland, Mich., *The Huron Daily Tribune* in Bad Axe, Mich., and the *Intelligencer* in Edwardsville, Ill. Danzig says that Hearst is looking at other newspapers, preferably in the West or the Sunbelt, and says they will be similar to the five already bought.

---

been through that terrible period when the sheriff knocked on the door in the middle of the night, he wanted to look at the balance sheet rather than look ahead," says Richard E. Deems, a former president of Hearst Magazines Div., who now serves as a consultant.

In 1975, Miller, who had started working for Hearst Corp. in 1934 as a clerk in the circulation department, was promoted from vice-president to president. Nearing retirement, he began to plan for Hearst's future and tapped Bennack as his successor. "I think it's a moral obligation of the CEO that when he goes, things go on," explains Miller.

Bennack, who is the youngest person ever to serve as Hearst president, began as an advertising salesman for the *San Antonio Light*. Early in his career, the soft-spoken Texan attracted the attention of Berlin and other top corporate executives in New York. By 1967 he was made editor and publisher of the *Light*. "In a tough competitive market, we were the No. 1 paper," says Miller.

In late 1974, Bennack was made general manager of the Hearst newspaper group. He lost no time in hiring top editors to revive some of the flagging papers. Bennack was instrumental in bringing to Hearst many of its media stars. J. Reg Murphy of the Atlanta *Constitution* was brought to the *San Francisco Examiner*, James G. Bellows of *The Washington Star* to the *Los Angeles Herald Examiner*, and Harry M. Rosenfeld of *The Washington Post* to the *Times-Union* and *Knickerbocker News* in Albany, N.Y. Part of Bennack's plan was to rid the newspapers of the last vestiges of their "yellow journalism" image by upgrading the editorial quality. "I think the fact that I'm with Hearst is my own vote that it has changed," says Rosenfeld.

By late 1975, Bennack had been made executive vice-president and began working closely with Miller to map out the company's expansion. Miller retired in January, 1979, and Bennack took over. However, Bennack soon persuaded Miller to stay on as vice-chairman. The two men work together so closely that many employees say that talking to one of them is like talking to both. "Bennack is the architect of change," says John Mack Carter, editor of *Good Housekeeping* magazine. "But Miller was the one who said, 'Let there be change,' and made it possible because of his knowledge of the company, relations with the Hearst family, and the respect he had from outside financial institutions."

Miller's confidence in Bennack, Hearst observers believe, has not been misplaced. "Frank is very anxious to build solidly on the foundation that Hearst has and take the company into the 1980s in a big way," says Deems. Officials from all divisions praise Bennack's knowledge and judgment in their area. "He can shift directions almost immediately," says one. And he gets high marks for his business acumen and negotiating skills. "Frank is a good deal maker," says Gordon L. Jones Jr., a Hearst vice-president. "He could easily run a Salomon Bros. or a Lazard Frères."

Even though members of the Hearst family are involved in the company, they are content to let outsiders run the show. Randolph A. Hearst, one of William Randolph Hearst's sons, is chairman, but does not take an active role in the day-to-day operations and credits Miller and Bennack with the company's success. "The two of them have used our people a lot better and have given the company a sense of direction it hadn't had in a while," he says. William R. Hearst Jr., another son who serves as editor-in-chief of the newspapers and writes a column, reflects that he and his brothers were never given the necessary business training that would have prepared them to take over the company. "We didn't have the responsibility that people have when they rise to the top," he says. "If we didn't perform, Pops didn't fire us, although he would let us know he wasn't pleased."

It is apparent that things will be different for the newest generation of Hearsts. Those that are employed by the company have been given lower-level jobs that will give them valuable experience. Still, Miller stresses that a Hearst would be chosen to head the company only if that family member demonstrated that he or she had the necessary talents. "There's a lot at stake here, a lot of people's jobs," says Miller.

Members of the Hearst family still benefit from the financial well-being of the company. The corporation's preferred and common stock is held in a family trust that is divided equally among Hearst's five sons or their survivors. No matter how many heirs one of the sons may have, they collectively still have claim to only 20% of the trust. The trust is overseen by 13 trustees, including five family members, who, with seven others, make up the 20-member board of directors. The trust receives dividends declared by the corporation and redistributes them to family members.

Being a private company, Bennack feels, is an advantage. Without outside stockholders to answer to, he says, the company is not tied to quarterly earnings. Hearst therefore can make long-range plans without worrying about short-term effects. "As long as a company through its own cash generation and through borrowings can make the acquisitions and investments and grow in an orderly fashion, there is not much benefit in being public," says Bennack.

Opening up to outsiders

Still, being private sometimes has its drawbacks. Hearst must pay its executives larger salaries than a public media company to make up for the lack of stock options and other benefits. Sometimes, even those larger salaries are not enough. Roger Barnett, who was head of Hearst's special publications, recently left to become associate publisher of *The Saturday Evening Post* and president of *Country Gentleman* at Curtis Publishing Co. While Barnett has words of praise for Hearst and its management, he notes that at Curtis he will receive equity in *Country Gentleman*. "I'm making more money than I ever made at Hearst," Barnett says.

In addition, Hearst's desire to keep its name out of the press—and the distorted public image that has resulted—can only hinder the company in its acquisition and hiring attempts. Perhaps because of that, Bennack is working to open up the company to outsiders. Those within the Hearst family and corporation have granted interviews to Lindsay Chaney and Michael Cieply whose book, *The Hearsts: Family and Empire*, which follows the company and descendants of Hearst from 1951 until the present, will be published by Simon & Schuster in January. Press releases, often announcing an acquisition or promotion, are more frequent, and there have been more interviews with the trade press.

Bennack would like to change the public's perception of Hearst as a newspaper chain by publicizing other areas of the company.

Actually, the company's magazine division is its most profitable, accounting for about one-third of Hearst's total earnings. Gilbert C. Maurer, president of the division, says that magazine revenues this year will be about $200 million, an increase of 142% since 1975. *Cosmopolitan* and *Good Housekeeping* account for the biggest share of that revenue, and, in fact, the greatest single portion of Hearst's profits.

The current success of these two magazines is attributed almost completely to the talents of their editors, Helen Gurley Brown and John Mack Carter. Brown took over the now 94-year-old *Cosmopolitan* in 1965, shortly after she wrote *Sex and the Single Girl*. From the first issue that Brown edited, the magazine took off, finding its audience among young women who wanted her advice. Its current circulation hovers around 3 million. Brown's method for running *Cosmopolitan* is typical of Hearst management philosophy and one reason for the company's high profit margin. "I hire a few people, pay them well, and give them a great deal to do," she says.

What the public wants

Brown is a ruthless editor—often asking well-known authors to rewrite their pieces two or three times—who still works 14-hour days. "From an advertising person's point of view, I so admire the direction and single-mindedness that Helen has established," says Alvin Hampel, president of the Chicago office of Wells, Rich, Greene Inc. "I consider it a model for people in this business to study." Her success is underlined each month by the ad pages garnered by *Cosmopolitan*. For 1980, *Cosmopolitan*, with about 2,400 ad pages, leads the other women's service magazines.

John Mack Carter arrived at *Good Housekeeping* after stints with *Ladies Home Journal* and *American Home*. Even though *Good Housekeeping* with a circulation around 5 million was making money, its profits were decreasing, and Carter was called in to stop the decline. Maurer claims that since Carter came on board, the magazine's profitable newsstand sales have increased 13½%. Carter's major changes in the magazine stemmed from his recognition that more women are working outside the home.

Carter's ability to anticipate the needs of *Good Housekeeping* readers so impressed Hearst executives that he was selected to develop new magazines. Hearst would like to add other magazines to its roster, either through acquisition or by spinoffs. In addition to *Cosmopolitan* and *Good Housekeeping*, its magazines include *American Druggist, Colonial Homes, Cosmopolitan Living, Country Living, Harper's Bazaar, House Beautiful, Motor, Motor Boating & Sailing, Popular Mechanics, Science Digest, Sports Afield,* and *Town & Country*. "I don't feel that we're more

DRAWING ON THE PAST FOR FUTURE SOFTWARE

Hearst Corp. officials are enthusiastic about producing software for cable TV, videodiscs, and videocassettes. Their reason: Hearst's film resources include more than 25 million ft. of Hearst Metrotone newsreels—covering national news, sports milestones, Hollywood's golden era, and *Popeye, Krazy Kat,* and *Beetle Bailey* cartoons.

Besides its films, Hearst believes that its print resources will provide valuable material for programs aimed at a narrow audience. For instance, Hearst could use information from *Good Housekeeping, House Beautiful,* and *Harper's Bazaar* to write programs that cover cooking, home decorating, and fashion. And Hearst's 13 newspapers could be used in any form of electronic news. "The deeper the resources of ideas and useful information that you have, the greater you will be able to use these new media," says Frank A. Bennack Jr., Hearst Corp.'s president and chief executive officer.

An uncertain course. But while Hearst's resources are impressive, its success as a programming supplier is by no means assured. The company is likely to discover the difficulties involved in adapting magazines to the screen. Even Helen Gurley Brown, editor of *Cosmopolitan,* notes that in the past she has rejected proposals to develop a TV version of her magazine. Brown does not believe that *Cosmopolitan's* self-help features can be effective on the air.

And Hearst's slowness in recognizing cable TV and other video technologies as possible outlets for its resources has caused it to fall behind more aggressive companies. Units of New York Times Co. and Time Inc. are far ahead of Hearst in producing and marketing films.

Bennack, who took over as president in 1979, realizes that he must move quickly to establish Hearst as a force in these new areas. He has brought on board Raymond E. Joslin, who built from scratch two of Continental Cablevision Inc.'s systems in Ohio. Hearst also wants to own cable TV systems, and Joslin will have to identify which multiple system operator Hearst should purchase. As soon as Hearst makes an acquisition—which Bennack claims will occur before the end of the year—it plans to bid for other cable franchises.

Recently Hearst had studied Cablecom-General Inc., which was sold by General Tire & Rubber Co. to Capital Cities Communications Inc. for $139.2 million. Joslin says that Cablecom, which operates 43 cable TV systems in 12 states, would have been a "pretty big bite" for Hearst and that the company is interested in an investment about half the size.

---

than 60% toward fulfilling our potential in magazines," says Bennack.

Hearst's method for starting new magazines from existing ones has struck some observers as unorthodox. The new magazine is given little or no promotion and is thrown on the newsstand to see if it will sell. Maurer explains that Hearst hopes to avoid the "first-issue syndrome," where a magazine sells well in the beginning in response to promotions. *Colonial Homes,* a *House Beautiful* spinoff, was the first magazine launched in this manner. "It disappeared so quickly, we were not sure it had hit the newsstand," says Maurer. *Colonial Homes,* which began as an annual, now comes out six times a year and has a circulation of nearly half a million.

Although Hearst says it is interested in buying new magazines, it has passed up several chances recently. One observer believes that Hearst erred in not purchasing *US* magazine from New York Times Co. Hearst apparently felt that the magazine did not have enough of a track record. "Hearst still likes to operate within its comfort level," the observer says. In addition, Hearst did not stand in line for *Harper's* magazine, eventually purchased by two foundations and turned into a nonprofit enterprise. "We are not in that business—magazines published for ego or the business of intellectual thought," explains Carter.

Hearst is eager to get into technical publishing. In August, Hearst purchased Cox Broadcasting's United Technical Publications, whose catalogs, looseleaf services, buyers guides, and newsletters serve the electronics, office equipment, metalworking industries, and others. The publishing group will report to Gordon Jones, who was brought to Hearst after his nearly 27 years at McGraw-Hill Inc., a major publisher of books and technical and business magazines, including BUSINESS WEEK.

Jones also supervises Hearst Books, Avon Books, a paperback publisher, and Arbor House, the hardcover book publisher bought by Hearst in December, 1978. At Hearst Books, the emphasis is on how-to-do-it books, which are updated periodically and have long life cycles, Jones says. Although Jones claims that books make only a "tiny contribution" to Hearst's income, sources say that Avon, which currently has three books on the *Publisher's Weekly* paperback best-selling list, does quite well.

Airwaves and acreage

According to Jones, popular novelist Irwin Shaw signed a $3.8 million contract with both Arbor House and Avon. Shaw, author of the best-selling *Rich Man, Poor Man,* is to write three books that will be published in hardback by Arbor and in paperback by Avon. Jones claims that the two book divisions will be signing more joint agreements to avoid bidding at auctions for paperback publishing rights. The increasing competition for paperback rights escalates the bids. The high bid for paperback rights is the $3.2 million paid by Bantam Books for Judith Krantz's *Princess Daisy.*

Hearst's expansion strategy for its TV and radio stations differs from the strategy for its newspapers. The company prefers to buy newspapers in smaller cities and towns. But because the Federal Communications Commission limits the number of stations any one company can own, Hearst is aiming for larger markets. Under FCC rules, Hearst could purchase three more TV stations and seven more radio stations.

Recently, Hearst paid an estimated $50 million for WDTN in Dayton, located in the 44th largest market. In addition to WDTN, two of Hearst's other TV stations, in Pittsburgh and Milwaukee, are ABC affiliates. Each one is first in its market and a big moneymaker. Hearst's fourth station, in Baltimore, is an NBC affiliate and has not fared as well. As for the radio stations, Franklin C. Snyder, head of the broadcast group, notes that they have always been profitable.

Although William Randolph Hearst's father, George, originally made his fortune in gold, silver, and copper mines, the company no longer is involved in mining. It had a 49% ownership, split among various family members and the corporation, in a Mexican mine, but sold that stake last year. The company does own 337,000 acres of land, which include two cattle ranches, timberlands, and urban real estate in just about every city in which Hearst operates. Hearst's Sunical

Div. manages the company's real estate and cattle in San Simeon, Cholame, and McCloud, Calif., and timberlands in Northern California. Its Pejepscot Div. manages the timberlands in Maine and Canada and produces specialty papers.

Sunical's vice-president and general manager, Amory J. Cooke, says that Bennack has encouraged Sunical to look at land acquisitions, and he notes that if the company "is fortunate," total Sunical acreage could increase 30% in five years. While Cooke says Sunical is too small to make a large contribution to corporate profits, he suggests that if it were independent, "it would be a pretty nice farming company."

Hearst's timberlands consist of 65,000 acres in Northern California and 130,000 acres in Maine and across the border in Canada. Most of the wood is sold to other paper manufacturers, except for a modest portion that goes to a Hearst paper mill in Maine. Although most of its output is lower-quality construction paper, it can turn out magazine-quality paper in a pinch. "It's a little bit of an insurance policy for the magazines in tight-paper times," says George R. Hearst Jr., a Hearst vice-president and a grandson of William Randolph Hearst.

Also an insurance policy against paper shortages is Hearst's relationship with and investment in Southwest Forest Industries Inc. Hearst currently owns 20% of the company's stock, and three Hearst executives sit on Southwest's board. Bennack denies the possibility of a takeover, saying that it is merely an investment in a company with which Hearst has had a long association.

Although the many Hearst divisions are united in the new strategy, most are run as separate entities. Hearst is not as centralized as Time Inc., for example. There is little contact among the staffs of the various Hearst publications. While one senior official observes that such an approach may not be a conscious effort by Hearst management, he notes that the advantages are surely evident. "It's a benefit in that it keeps the editors from ever forming any kind of a coalition about pay scales, employee problems, or other things." This official notes that Hearst has never published an employee booklet, and adds, "Isn't it interesting that there isn't one?"

According to Bennack, Hearst has deliberately chosen to stress the individual identity of its publications and properties, rather than play up the corporate image. But Bennack has already begun to modify that policy. Increasingly, advertisements for the company's books and magazines include the statement that they are Hearst publications. And Bennack confirms that Hearst is developing a booklet that will describe the company to its employees. Bennack says that he recalls wanting to know more about Hearst when he began his own career in San Antonio. "We have so many more strengths than downsides that we can share with our employees," he observes. Bennack also has not overlooked the positive effects that such a policy could have on recruitment and acquisition activities.

Making up lost ground

While the legend of William Randolph Hearst remains a part of the Hearst organization, there is little of his flamboyant style and heavy-handed management techniques evident in Bennack. Hearst made a career of second-guessing his editors. Bennack leaves his editors and other top managers alone. Hearst used his publications to promote his own political causes. Bennack is more concerned about profits. Although Hearst was a millionaire many times over, he often had no cash in his pockets, failed to pay his bills on time, and usually spent more than he made. In contrast, under Bennack, Hearst is a well-run, profitable company. Hearst succeeded in his goal to make his newspapers a powerful media force in America. Bennack's goal is basically the same.

There is no doubt, however, that while Hearst was ahead of his time, Bennack will have to make up lost ground. Some feel that the company may be 20 years too late in its efforts to buy more TV stations and 10 years too late in establishing a presence in cable TV. Bennack will have to continue the momentum—selecting the best new properties for Hearst's purposes while pushing to improve what the company owns. There are many who believe that he can do it. Observes *Good Housekeeping's* Carter: "For the first time, the corporation has become the acquisition-minded company that William Randolph Hearst established." ■

THE MAN BEHIND KRAFT'S MERGER

Persuading a strong-willed entrepreneur to merge his fast-growing conglomerate with a conservative, stodgy company requires the skill of a diplomat and the long view of a historian. John M. Richman, chairman and chief executive of Kraft Inc., displayed both qualities last spring when he engineered the deal that seasoned merger experts said could not be done—the marriage of Dart Industries Inc., the $2.4 billion consumer products manufacturer, with the nation's largest food processor. By carefully anticipating Justin Dart's potential objections and by laying out the long-range synergies of the two companies, Richman convinced Dart's chairman and chief executive, who founded his company in 1963, that the two companies would make an unbeatable combination.

Although Richman, 52, admits to some trepidation before he presented the plan to Dart, who is 73, he says his fear evaporated after 30 minutes with the reputedly tough Californian. "I thought about rejection," recalls Richman, "but I figured I might as well take my fling. In about a half-hour, Justin looked up and said, 'You've got a hell of an idea.'"

The deal itself is surprisingly simple. A straightforward merger, it calls for a cash-free, share-for-share exchange that will give Dart shareholders about 47% of the new entity. Even so, Dart's name will get top billing in the new enterprise. And although Dart will have only 10 of the 23 seats on the enlarged board, Justin Dart will head its powerful executive committee. Moreover, there will be equal participation at the planning level. Richman proposed a four-person policy committee to be staffed by him, Justin Dart, Dart's new president (soon to be named), and Kraft's former chairman and chief executive, William O. Beers. When Dart executives balked at moving to Kraft's hometown, Richman assured them that they would continue to operate their businesses out of Dart's California offices, with corporate headquarters remaining in Glenview, Ill.

Can Dart let go? Says one acquisition specialist who knows Dart well: "I couldn't imagine [Justin Dart] going along with being acquired. But Richman came up with a brilliant approach." Nonetheless, skeptics maintain that Dart will be unable to adapt to his new role. He owns only 1% of the company's stock but has always been its undisputed leader. But Dart says he will be able to let go. He claims that being an adviser to Ronald Reagan in the past two years has left him as "more of an adviser" to his own business than an operator. Still, Richman is taking no chances. He has designated Beers to serve, in effect, as a mediator between him and Dart should conflict arise.

The deal was particularly attractive to Dart because the stability of Kraft's food business could smooth Dart's more volatile earnings pattern. Moreover, Kraft's AAA credit rating (Dart's rating is A) would give the new company in excess of $1 billion of unused borrowing capacity. That, combined with more than $250 million in cash on hand, would allow quick and substantial acquisitions to be made—another enticement to the entrepreneurial Dart.

From Kraft's viewpoint, the deal was equally sound. Former Chairman Beers's often talked-about goal was to diversify Kraft and spur faster growth through a big acquisition. Through the years, that goal had eluded him, even though he turned Kraft from a holding company for a gaggle of food and dairy companies into an operating company organized along market lines. As CEO from 1972 to 1979, Beers was a hands-on executive who centralized decision-making in the chairman's office. Kraft last year made $188 million on sales of $6.4 billion.

'A good listener.' Beers looked to his successor to take the company further. He stunned the business community last year when he bypassed more seasoned operations executives and tapped the soft-spoken, pipe-puffing lawyer for Kraft's top job. "Richman's not the effusive sort of fellow that Beers is," says one outside director, "but he's shown he's a doer."

Richman, formerly Kraft's general counsel, wasted no time in putting his stamp on the company. His more open management style was a distinct departure from tradition for Kraft executives, who were previously reluctant to speak up at meetings. That changed dramatically at Richman's first major planning session. "It took a whole day to get the managers to open up and really realize that John wanted to listen," recalls William E. Reidy, Kraft's senior vice-president for corporate strategy and development. Adds John L. Weinberg, a Goldman Sachs senior partner and a Kraft director since 1962: "John is a very good listener. He's also firm, once he's relying on his judgment."

A surprise move. Nowhere has Richman's determination been more evident than in the month of negotiations leading up to the deal with Dart, which, he proudly notes, will bring "diversification in one fell swoop to Kraft. This is probably the alternative to a 10-year acquisition program." Dart's basket of products includes Tupperware containers, Duracell batteries, and West Bend appliances. Last year it earned $172 million—only $16 million less than Kraft—on sales of fully $4 billion less than its prospective merger mate.

"I guess you could say [I made] a big move that caught everyone by surprise," says Richman with characteristic understatement. Much of the surprise stems from Kraft's history as a staid—albeit solidly profitable—cheese and dairy products company that slowly branched out into other processed foods. The merger proposal, in fact, astonished even Kraft's directors, who were unaccustomed to such innovative thinking from former managements.

Richman will finally be moving Kraft away from the safe harbor of the slow-growing retail food business, which accounts for 80% of its sales and profits. Kraft previously has dipped its toes into nonfood operations, but not successfully. One of Richman's first moves as CEO, in fact, was to take a $23.3 million write-off for anticipated losses from the sale or closing of most of those operations—glass bottles, bulk chemicals, and aluminum specialty products.

Dart Industries also has been cleaning house. It completed the $252 million acquisition of P. R. Mallory & Co. (now called Duracell International) last January and sold operations peripheral to that company's high-growth battery business. Dart this year also bought two small specialty chemical makers and sold its share in joint ventures in heavy chemicals and plastic films.

The new Dart & Kraft will be a true corporate hybrid. The two companies' combined sales last year were nearly $9 billion, which would have ranked the combination No. 27 among U.S. industrial companies and second only to Procter & Gamble Co. in consumer products. Kraft's stable food business should smooth Dart's more volatile earnings pattern. Richman, in turn, is looking to the fast-growth mentality of Dart's managers to rub off on Kraft's more conservative executives.

Richman will rely heavily on Justin

Dart's sharp eye for acquisition opportunities in plotting the company's course. In fact, it may be that Kraft's real coup in hooking up with Dart will be access to

Richman had 'a brilliant approach' to the Dart merger, says an observer

its acquisition-wise management, led by Justin Dart. In the past 35 years, Dart has started, bought, or sold more than 50 companies. Its knack for making lucrative acquisitions and weeding out its lemons has produced a compound earnings growth rate of 20.7% over the past five years, compared with Kraft's unspectacular 14.5%, and, not surprisingly, given Dart a large following on Wall Street.

'Action-oriented.' Much of that following is dismayed by the merger. Analysts claim that Dart's shareholders could have reaped a hefty profit if the company had been bought out and that it will not be able to sustain its heady growth as part of a larger entity. Richman is bothered by that kind of thinking.

"I don't think that some in the investment community are using their imaginations to realize the advantages of putting two companies together, as opposed to one acquiring the other and stripping itself of its cash and credit," he maintains.

Thinking in such financial terms was not Richman's original inclination. The stepson of a career naval officer who billeted the family "at every base up and down the East Coast," Richman majored in history at Yale and intended to become a history professor. But he abandoned history for the law, figuring he could develop his growing interest in business and "be more action-oriented. I have a pragmatic sense that likes to accomplish things and see results," he says.

After graduation from Harvard Law School in 1952, Richman practiced corporate law in New York for two years before joining Kraft. During the next 12 years he worked up to the position of general counsel of the Sealtest Foods Div., where he caught the eye of Beers, then a Kraft subsidiary president.

Recalls Beers: "John wasn't the stereotyped Harvard lawyer in a pinstriped suit who doesn't know one end of a supermarket from another. What he didn't know, he was willing to listen and learn. He won the respect of the operating people. And unlike many, pride of

Justin Dart's sharp eye for acquisition opportunities is not lost on Richman

ownership [of an idea] wasn't the most important thing for him. He cared more about getting things done."

Beers never designated Richman as heir apparent—Arthur W. Woelfle, 60, Kraft's president and chief operating officer, was thought to be the frontrunner. But throughout the 1970s Beers groomed the lawyer for the top spot by giving him a series of special assignments. One key task was the delicate job of chairing the committee that reorganized Kraft from a holding company into an operating company in 1976.

Richman's first task as chairman of Dart & Kraft (shareholders will vote on the proposed merger next month) will be another delicate one: selecting a new president for the Dart division. Thomas P. Mullaney, Dart's ambitious 47-year-old president, announced his resignation from that job on July 23. Justin Dart's continuing support for the merger despite his protege's dissatisfaction underscores his faith in Richman's ability to lead the new company. Mullaney's departure, however, underlines analysts' doubts about the pace of Dart's continued growth.

Richman is now under pressure to prove the deal is a good one. Obvious synergies can be achieved by pushing Duracell and other Dart products through Kraft's vast supermarket distribution network and by distributing coupons for Kraft products with Tupperware and West Bend items. But what Wall Street really is looking for is a major acquisition. Sources at both Kraft and Dart admit to some interest in specialty chemicals. Richman will not elaborate. But as if to put to rest forever Kraft's reputation as a slow-moving company that can study a proposal to death, he promises: "We're not going to take too long doing it. There comes a time when you've got to stop studying and get on your horse and ride." ∎

The Strategy Makers / 65

HOW A NEW CHIEF IS TURNING INTERBANK INSIDE OUT

When a company's market share erodes so that it loses its No. 1 spot in its industry, it is usually time for a new chief with a new approach to take over. But the new head has to walk a veritable mine field in trying to regain the company's original momentum. If he changes things slowly, he can be left with a management team that is uncertain about its future and unwilling to act until it receives clear and unequivocal direction. If he shakes things up quickly, morale can be devastated.

Those were the options facing Russell E. Hogg when he assumed the presidency of Interbank Card Assn. last February. In 1979, Interbank, the umbrella organization for MasterCard, fell into second place behind Visa both in dollar volume and number of cardholders, and Interbank's board was clearly pushing for some changes. But Hogg (pronounced Hoag) has made his changes with such speed that people both within and outside Interbank are wondering what hit them. His method: get unwanted executives out as quickly as possible, get a new team on board almost simultaneously, and then institute so many sweeping changes that people are too busy reorienting themselves to get depressed. As he puts it, "The alternative of dropping one shoe today and another tomorrow did not make sense."

The moves. In the last four months, Hogg, a former Macmillan Inc. executive who also has eight years' experience with American Express Co.'s Card Div., has turned Interbank inside out. He has:

■ Redrawn the organizational chart, inserting horizontal reporting lines into what had been a classic vertical hierarchy. The aim is to encourage communication, particularly about international affairs.

■ Moved several of the support divisions to St. Louis, where they are being consolidated under Lawrence J. Szambelan, a newly hired senior vice-president for operations.

■ Abolished all high-level positions involved with international affairs, making international responsibility part of each department's job.

■ Eliminated all people involved with drumming up new U. S. members. Hogg believes the domestic credit card market is already saturated.

■ Summarily fired eight high-level officers of the company, giving them just enough time to pack their things and contact the outplacement firm he retained for them.

Now, Hogg's new executive team is in place. But even with a new team and new directions, it will be no easy task to turn MasterCard back into the front-runner. The vast majority of card-issuing banks in the U. S. already issue both MasterCard and Visa, but Visa appears to have a clear lead in forging a cohesive international identity. Before National

For Interbank's Hogg, the challenge is to best an aggressive Visa.

BankAmericard Inc. changed its name to Visa in 1977, it had been issued under 22 names around the world. Now its image is consolidated under the Visa logo. MasterCard, by contrast, is not only suffering from a fragmented identity among affiliates and joint ventures in Europe and Asia, but it is still struggling with ways to persuade its U. S. members that the name-change from Master Charge implies broadened usage for the card above and beyond credit.

Interbank is also trailing in the new-product area. When it tried to enter the traveler's check market a few years ago, it was immediately slapped with a suit from Citibank, charging that it was infringing on its own members' turf. Visa, which avoided similar suits or disaffection from members by issuing its checks through its member banks, has had a relatively smooth entry into that market. Although Citibank recently dropped its suit, clearing the way for Interbank again to pursue traveler's check revenues, the MasterCard agency has a lot of catching up to do.

The same holds true for Interbank's attempt to move MasterCard away from being exclusively a credit instrument. Hogg says he is giving top priority to developing a "debit" card that allows fund transfers and payments rather than credit. But the Visa card has been doing double duty in this area for some time. In fact, Dee W. Hock, Visa president, seems singularly unperturbed about the threat of competition from the "new" MasterCard. "Nobody has reached a stage to be able to compete with Visa on a worldwide payment system," Hock states. And even Hogg reluctantly admits that "Visa developed sophisticated products and knew how to sell them."

Consultants. Clearly, Hogg felt that the only way he could infuse such knowledge at Interbank was by making a clean sweep of the talent in place. Although the firings were sudden for the released executives, none of whom could be reached by BUSINESS WEEK, they were by no means impulsive moves on the new chief's part. Shortly after joining Interbank, Hogg called in consultants from Coopers & Lybrand Inc. to evaluate the existing staff to see whether it could fulfill his requirements for strong international marketing and new-product development skills. Apparently, as soon as the eight executives got the thumbs-down sign from C&L, Hogg began searching for their replacements. The result: Scarcely three weeks after he lowered the boom, a new executive team had been formed.

Brian W. Smith, senior vice-president for legal affairs, remains one of the few familiar faces. F. David Brangaccio, formerly a Coopers & Lybrand consultant who did work for Interbank, has already come on board as senior vice-president of planning and administration. And

66 / Readings from *Business Week*

within a few weeks, George J. Fesus, now a senior vice-president at American Express' Card Div., will assume the post of senior vice-president of marketing.

Hogg makes no bones about wanting to institute a higher degree of "professionalism" into the running of Interbank. In fact, he is borrowing a page from classic business textbooks in his new setup. The four senior vice-presidents have been formed into an executive council that will meet regularly with him for planning and continuity.

But apparently he is also hedging his bets. Despite the implied slap at himself and his new team, Hogg readily admits that people who see association work as a lifetime career may not be the shakers and movers that a floundering association needs. And he is currently scouring the employment market for a rotating cadre of at least four young MBAs who would come in as short-term semi-turnaround artists. "I want people who will stay no less than 18 months but no more than three years, who want exposure to strategic planning and international marketing, who want to work with banks," Hogg says. "These are the people whose career objectives go far beyond the presidency of an association."

The new organization has the clear support of Interbank's 27-member board, all of whom seem to believe such changes were long overdue. Hogg's predecessor, John J. Reynolds, did not step down by choice. Now 57, he candidly admits that he intended to stay until he was 60. Instead, he is now serving out a three-year contract as a consultant to Interbank. "This is the era when heads of companies are fired whenever something goes wrong," he says bitterly. Reynolds describes himself as a "people-oriented" manager, and says Hogg relies heavily on "management techniques."

In Hogg's reorganization, eight top executives were summarily dismissed

Not surprisingly, Reynolds believes the massive executive firings in June were as unnecessary as his own dismissal. "Some of the people who are now not there were excellent employees, and I think they'll be missed," he says.

But board members and outsiders who have been close to Interbank disagree. Robert F. Martin, head of Coopers & Lybrand's search division and the man who found Hogg for Interbank, recalls that at the time of instituting the search board members told him they "weren't certain of the quality level of the people at Interbank," and that it was clear they expected a new man to clean shop. "When Russ fired those people, rumors took off that he was ruthless, but he did it in the most humane way he could," Martin insists.

Upgrading. Evan H. Housworth, who until February was chairman of the board, confirms that "we obviously hired a new president to review Interbank and see if staff changes were needed, since we felt there would be areas of the staff that needed upgrading." And J. Donald Saul, the current chairman, says: "We wanted someone heading our organization who would solidify our market in the world. Whenever there's a change at the top there is a change in lower echelons. You have to start riding new horses."

As far as Hogg is concerned, talk of whether he should or should not have fired people is just so much wheel-spinning. He says he called together nearly all of Interbank's 200-or-so employees, explained the reorganization to them, and now is ready to move on with the business at hand. "The reorganization was done on a clinical, not an emotional, basis," he says. "My first and foremost priority is ensuring that we get back into the competitive market." ■

Steering Greyhound Corp. onto a smoother road before he retires has been the consuming ambition of Gerald H. Trautman, its 68-year-old chairman. But Trautman's goal is proving elusive. Having completed a two-year effort to revive Greyhound's ailing bus line, he now faces a new and possibly tougher struggle: salvaging the company's biggest operation, meatpacker Armour & Co., from a poorly executed switch in strategy that has left the subsidiary a shambles. To make matters worse, Trautman must hunt for a new successor. Robert K. Swanson, who joined Greyhound as president and heir apparent in February, left on Oct. 7 after losing a rancorous power struggle with Greyhound's board of directors.

TRAUTMAN: A Goal Eludes a Willful Manager

Greyhound watchers figured Swanson left because Trautman, a willful manager, refused to relinquish authority. Insists one former executive: "He's like Armand Hammer, challenging an heir apparent to push him off the mountain"—a reference to the tenacious, 82-year-old chairman of Occidental Petroleum Corp. Last July, without even consulting Swanson, Trautman went so far as to decree an about-face in Armour's strategy, moving it back to commodity meat production from a short-lived focus on marketing brand-name products.

But the fact is that by July, Swanson's departure was already sealed. Far from lacking power, he had tried to wield it too quickly. Despite opposition from Greyhound's board, Swanson attempted to bring in his own appointees to replace top managers at successful Greyhound subsidiaries, including the bus line and financial services units. Friction over these maneuvers made Swanson's split with the board irreparable, and his resignation a matter of time.

Strongman. This has left Trautman more entrenched than ever as Greyhound's strongman. A former San Francisco attorney who for a time managed Greyhound's legal affairs, Trautman became president in 1966, with the intention of turning the bus company into a diversified giant. He acquired Armour in 1970 and has moved since then into profitable equipment leasing, insurance, and other financial services. Trautman stayed on despite his age because the bus operation fell on hard times after the diversification was achieved. Trautman felt that only he could set it back on course, and he feels the same way now about Armour.

He intends to pick a new president for Greyhound by the end of November—probably an insider this time (Swanson came from General Mills Inc.). A clear front-runner is Ralph C. Batastini, the company's vice-chairman and chief financial officer. Trautman vows he will "definitely" retire when his management contract expires in 1982. But the mess at Armour, like earlier problems with buses, seems to have drawn Trautman into more hands-on involvement than ever. Just last February, he named himself chairman of the meat and personal care products operations.

Armour is a conservative, 113-year-old meatpacker whose food business last year accounted for 52% of Greyhound's sales of $5 billion but only 12.5% of its profits of $123 million. In 1978 the company devised a plan to revive itself. Trautman hired consultants Booz, Allen & Hamilton Inc., which mapped a change from production-oriented slaughtering to a marketing plan that would focus on processed meat with higher value added. The tactics were to drop low-profit, private-label production sold in food retailing chains, develop new products, and advertise heavily to promote the Armour Star brand as a quality product, which would carry a high price.

These moves seemed logical enough, and Trautman had his staff put them into practice. Like other old-line packers, Armour has long envied the 3% profit margin that bacon-and-salami king Oscar Mayer & Co. achieves (vs. less than 1% for Armour). Oscar Mayer, which has built a quality brand image, sells bacon for 30¢ to 40¢ more per lb. than Armour. Moreover, the old packing houses have had to cope with high labor costs in fresh meat compared with newer, nonunion competitors. Another problem for Armour: The biggest newcomer in beef, Iowa Beef Processors Inc., has announced plans to expand into pork, Armour's primary market.

New blood. Trautman hired new marketing men from outside the company and moved in personnel from Armour's Dial

At 68, a new struggle to shore up Greyhound's Armour subsidiary

soap business, because they had more expertise in branded consumer products. The new team boosted advertising to $23 million this year from $16 million in 1978, and developed new items such as frozen dinners and breakfasts.

But the plan has not succeeded, despite Trautman's hopes that it quickly would. Sales of processed meat products slumped 11% by tonnage in 1979, and they are off another 11% so far this year. Normally profitable in the past, processed meat lost $750,000 last year and $11.6 million after taxes in the first eight months of 1980. Oscar Mayer has pushed Armour out of first place in bacon sales volume. Trautman, completely disillusioned, now talks about the "Booz Allen fiasco," despite his own early enthusiasm. But he also blames himself and Armour management. "We did it to ourselves," he says.

New strategy. In July, Trautman tossed the entire strategy out the window, although the move has received little attention outside the industry. In what some describe as typical Trautman style, he simply told Armour President Donald J. Shaughnessy on July 18 that Armour was to be restructured and would return to cranking out pork roasts and other commodity meats. Plans to distribute new frozen meals nationally have been canceled. According to Trautman, Shaughnessy listened, resigned, and cleaned out his desk the next day. Two other Armour executives left because of the change, which Trautman put in place even though the consultants, in a second look at the operation, advised him to wait and have faith in the marketing-oriented approach.

Trautman has named Wallace L. Tunnell, a veteran Armour fresh meat manager, to run the processed meats operation as well. Tunnell is cutting his expanded marketing force and headquarters staff from 201 people to 119 and has returned sales and pricing authority to field managers. Former Armour executives, however, say they do not understand how a reversion to the old strategy, already disproved, can work. "I see a slow bleeding to death," says one. "Trautman is very sharp, but he doesn't understand meat or consumer marketing. It takes time and money to build a brand's image." Industry sources note that it will be especially hard to return to private-label meat production, because prior customers already have new suppliers.

But Tunnell is predicting a return to the black in processed meat in six months, and with fresh meat still profitable, he foresees net earnings in the total meat operation in 1981 of about $7 million, compared with an expected $8 million aftertax loss for all of 1980. Part of his strategy is to seek reduced labor costs through union concessions. Armour won one such concession in April, when the union at a small beef slaughtering operation pledged itself to a 15% productivity increase when threatened with plant closures.

On the way out? Some industry observers, however, suspect Trautman's real plan is to fatten Armour as quickly as possible for the kill. Trautman acknowledges he has had "offers" from Japanese and British companies to buy the meat-packing subsidiary. Competitor Esmark Inc. is moving out of fresh meat by selling or closing some of its Swift Div.

A sudden switch away from emphasis on brand-name meat products

plants (BW—July 14). Another possibility is that Armour could enter a joint venture with a more efficient packer, such as Iowa Beef, and limit itself to marketing. Trautman says he is "very intrigued" with this idea.

But the Greyhound chairman's "first preference" is to do with Armour what he has done with buses—revive the operation and hold onto it. For Trautman, this is a matter of pride—some say obstinacy—because he engineered Greyhound's purchase of the meat company. "I don't like to think I can't turn any company around," declares Trautman. "I don't like to lose." ∎

First of Chicago
NEW MANAGEMENT TO BRING BACK THE PAST

Barry F. Sullivan could well credit his style with giving him "the best job in banking today." That job—chairman and chief executive of First Chicago Corp., the holding company for First National Bank of Chicago—which Sullivan assumes on July 28, distinctly needed a change of style from that of Sullivan's predecessor, A. Robert Abboud. Three months ago, when the bank's board fired Abboud after his five-year reign, the reasons centered on the domineering and abrasive style that made Abboud banking's most controversial executive and that produced endless management turmoil and turnover. Sullivan, a well-liked executive vice-president of Chase Manhattan Corp., has been deemed to have the "people skills" that Abboud lacked.

But the fascination with Abboud's battles with his managers masks the bank's seriously flawed corporate strategy, according to a growing number of former officers and customers of First Chicago, the nation's ninth-largest bank. Abboud, they say, was so preoccupied with curbing the loan excesses of previous management that he turned off a lot of corporate customers and never prepared the bank to go after new business once the old problems were solved. To be sure, the catalyst for Abboud's ouster was his falling out with Harvey Kapnick, the former chairman of Arthur Andersen & Co. who was chosen by Abboud last December to be the bank's deputy chairman. But it was Abboud's defensive strategy that better explains First Chicago's dismal profit performance and now defines Sullivan's real challenge.

Long-term challenges

In the last five years, First Chicago's per-share earnings grew at a meager 3.7% annual average—the lowest among the top 10 money center banks. And last year the bank's 10% return on equity also was the lowest among the money centers, one-third below the average return of the 25 biggest banks.

Just how weak the bank's competitive position is became even clearer one week before Sullivan took office, when the bank reported its fifth consecutive quarterly earnings decline and a 37% profit drop for the first half of 1980. By contrast, other money center banks were reporting major profit gains because of record spreads between their prime rates and their costs for short-term funds.

Most of First Chicago's poor results can be attributed directly to Abboud's conservative tactics, which first lost the bank both customers and momentum in growth and later led to risk-taking. Now, when banking is on the eve of a revolution, with new competition from electronic funds transfer and profits to be made from such new services as cash management and data processing, First Chicago must repair its basic banking business by wooing back corporate customers and shoring up its position in commercial real estate lending.

This is why Sullivan might well have been chosen chairman even if he lacked his good-guy image. His 23-year tenure at Chase made him one of the most broadly experienced executives in banking: Aside from the treasury function, notes Chase Vice-Chairman George A. Roeder Jr., "it's hard to find a key area in this bank that he hasn't had reporting to him." More important, Sullivan was part of the team that directed the kind of resurgence at Chase that the First Chicago now needs. He played a key role in drafting a comprehensive strategic plan that Chase recently adopted. "Bar-

How First Chicago slipped from first to second

It fell far behind in commercial loans...

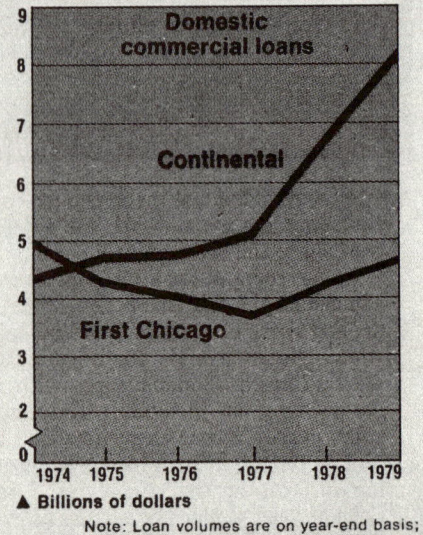

Data: First Chicago Corp., Continental Illinois Corp. ▲ Billions of dollars. Note: Loan volumes are on year-end basis;

70 / Readings from *Business Week*

ry Sullivan functions with strategies, and that's one reason he was chosen," observes Ben W. Heineman, president of Northwest Industries Inc. and the bank director who supervised the transition in top management. "This bank is going to have a strategy three years from now," he adds.

If Sullivan has his way, the timetable will be closer to three months. Even before officially taking over, Sullivan seized upon a nascent planning effort begun at First Chicago in February. And he has already ordered it broadened and expedited so that by October he can present the board with a comprehensive five-year corporate plan, something never developed under Abboud. By yearend, Sullivan intends to make any management and organizational changes that are needed to implement the plan. Says Sullivan: "The challenges are long-term ones." Clearly, he will not seek quick fixes at the First. What intrigues him now is the impact he can make in changing the bank's course through the 1980s. That is why he claims to have the best job in banking today.

Even without a formal plan in place, Sullivan is already suggesting that his highest priority will be developing a sustained marketing drive to rebuild the bank's once strong, but now shattered, position in corporate lending. Many close observers insist that is precisely what First Chicago needs to counteract what they believe was Abboud's balance-sheet myopia, an obsession with avoiding leverage and with upgrading asset quality that destroyed much of the bank's marketing punch, particularly in the commercial sector.

When Abboud took over at the bank in 1975, he had no choice but to rein in a bank whose fast-paced expansion—under his predecessor, Gaylord Freeman—had left it with more than its share of bad real estate loans. Despite First Chicago's controversial loans to Bert Lance and to the Hunt family in connection with their silver futures caper, Abboud earned a reputation as one of America's most conservative bankers by strictly controlling credit approvals, demanding higher margins on corporate loans, centralizing management decisions, and generally bringing an abrupt end to First Chicago's go-go era.

Speculative earnings

His limited push in marketing centered on retail banking, and First Chicago's consumer lending doubled in five years. That emphasis is curious, because Illinois has some of the harshest strictures against branching of any of the states. Former associates ascribe that focus to Abboud's populism. One of the country's rare Democratic big bankers (he is considered an informal adviser to the Carter Administration), Abboud is said to possess a flare for consumer business while displaying discomfiture in dealing with the corporate establishment. In any case, Abboud's stringent conservatism on credit hit the bank's corporate customers hardest—and corporate lending accounts for about half of First Chicago's total U.S. loan volume. As a result, that segment has remained virtually flat throughout Abboud's five-year term.

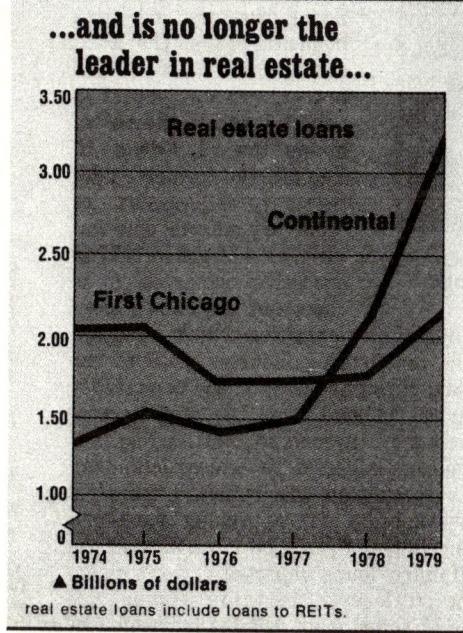

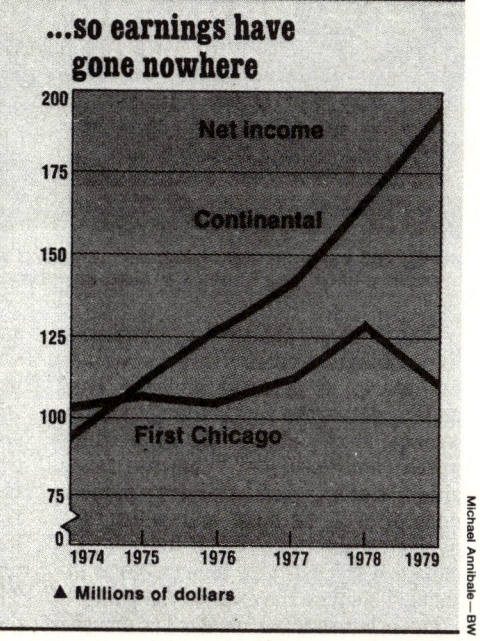

To be sure, First Chicago began winning the battle of the balance sheet, but it also began losing important corporate business from such accounts as Gould Inc., Inland Steel Co., and Chicago's powerful Pritzker family, reportedly once the bank's largest commercial customer. Much of that business apparently was lost because Abboud's crisis management lasted long after the crisis was over and because managers failed to respond to competitive moves that others began after they had adjusted for their own mid-1970s' excesses.

More than anything else, First Chicago left its corporate customer base wide open to an assault by archrival Continental Illinois Corp., seventh among U.S. banks. Boasting a planning staff that now numbers 25 professionals, Continental, in 1976, began to implement a bold five-year plan to increase its national position in commercial lending to third place from a tie for fourth place with First Chicago. It achieved that goal in 1980's first quarter while the First has slipped to seventh. First Chicago set no similar marketing goal, and its planning staff under Abboud never consisted of more than three persons.

Predictably, Continental steamrolled First Chicago. In 1975 the two were amazingly similar in size and makeup. Both were wholesale banks, heavily dependent on commercial loans for volume and on money markets for funding. By the end of last year, however, Continental's total loan volume had grown to $23 billion, nearly 50% larger than First Chicago's. The biggest reason for the difference is that commercial loan volume at the First actually shrank by 6% in five years, while Continental's corporate business almost doubled. As a result, Continental's earnings grew 73% from 1975 to $196 million last year, while First Chicago's profits grew only 4% to $112 million.

"The bank's strategy seems to have been to obtain the best balance-sheet ratios in the country, but in order to get there it lost relationships with customers," notes Robert K. Wilmouth, president of the Chicago Board of Trade and a former executive vice-president of First Chicago who lost out to Abboud in the race for chairmanship. Adds the former director of First Chicago's Energy Lending Div., who left the bank early this year. "Bob slammed on the brakes and put in severe controls, but he never developed initiatives to get business so that we could also improve the balance sheet through better earnings."

By last year, Abboud was pointing with pride to a 22-to-1 ratio of assets (loans and other investments) to equity, making the bank second only to J. P. Morgan & Co. in low leveraging. By then, however, the balance sheet became an apologia for the bank's inability to ride the steep upward slope on the national loan demand curve. For three years, former officers insist, the bank—despite a growing desire to lend—simply could not attract the commercial business that other banks were pulling in.

That is when extreme conservatism at First Chicago apparently gave way to risk-taking, as Abboud and the bank made a desperate reach for speculative earnings in two areas. One involved aggressive marketing of fixed-rate loans, which during inflationary periods amount to a discount and which also involve considerable risk if many of the loans are funded with shorter-term deposits. This was the case at the First.

The other gamble involved a massive arbitrage play that put the bank in a Eurodollar position that would bring it profits if interest rates fell. When interest rates soared in late 1979 and early 1980, both moves backfired. Aside from the underlying problem of loan demand, both misplays explain the bank's recent earnings tumble.

"Abboud realized in 1978 that the bank had no steady ground game, and so he threw the football," observes a former executive of the bank. "Our conservative banker became a plunger."

The major push for fixed-rate loans began in 1977, when First Chicago's percentage of fixed-rate to total loans jumped in one year from 27% to 33% — a level it maintained for the rest of the decade. The loans, many of which ran five years or so, were initially funded by certificates of deposit with matching maturities. But in 1978 fixed-rate lending began to exceed the bank's ability to find matching funds, partly because of the sheer volume of the loans and partly because of excessive delays by loan officers in reporting their commitments.

Thus, by mid-1979, when the economy was on the brink of the steepest interest rate climb in its history, First Chicago found itself with $1 billion of fixed-rate loans being funded by short-term money, the cost of which was escalating rapidly above the yields on the loans. Some directors and bank insiders suggest the loans could have been funded better, which points a none-too-subtle finger of blame toward Edwin H. Yeo III, the former Under Secretary of Treasury for Monetary Affairs, who was hired by Abboud in 1977 as executive vice-president in charge of the bank's asset and liability committee, which is responsible for funding. Sources close to the matter argue that Yeo repeatedly warned Abboud about the bank's excessive fixed-rate lending. But lending officers complained of Yeo's obstructionism. His committee was removed from its responsibility for approving fixed-rate loans during the period when most of the unfunded loans reportedly were made. The battle over fixed-rate lending was one of the stormy debates between Abboud and Yeo that finally led to Yeo's resignation last January.

While fixed-rate lending probably had a bigger impact on earnings, the Eurodollar play better illustrates the new risks the bank was willing to take last year to compensate for lackluster loan volume. All money center banks operate large Eurodollar deposit books, partly to tap European banks for funding, but also to generate arbitrage profits. If rates are correctly forecast as rising, a profit can be made by accepting long-term Eurodollar deposits and investing them in short-term deposits that roll over at higher rates. To profit from a decline in rates, the opposite is done.

While money center banks generally increased their Eurodollar books last year, none came close to First Chicago's expansion. It moved from $3.1 billion at the end of 1978 to $6.7 billion a year later. It is obvious that the bank was reaching for earnings because it had mismatched maturities so much on its overseas book.

But once the Federal Reserve began its tightening act last fall, First Chicago found itself funding its Eurodollar placements with higher-cost deposits. It is not clear why the mistake was made, since the bank's official forecast called for interest rates to rise, but that was no comfort to those directors and officers who were upset that so large an arbitrage was even attempted. One former vice-president angrily cites it as one of his reasons for quitting the banking early this year. "It was rank speculation on a massive scale."

Because of falling rates, the ill effects of the arbitrage gamble and the foray into fixed-rate lending are now behind First Chicago, and Sullivan will turn the bank's attention to winning back corporate customers. He explains, "We're going to find out from them what the impediments are in doing more business, and then we're going to eliminate [those impediments]."

Sullivan plans to improve the bank's coverage of corporate accounts by hiring away from other banks some 75 experienced officers primarily to expand his 300-person corporate lending staff.

Eliminating the impediments, he says, might also involve pricing more competitively and cutting down response time to corporate loan requests, partly by increasing the lending officer's authority to make loans without getting a lengthy list of approvals. Such a move would reverse Abboud's policies of centralization. Since concepts such as decentralized lending are considered responsible for some of Continental's success, Sullivan is obviously signaling his intention not to give any more business away. "Continental Illinois has done an extremely effective job," he says, "and the only way to assure that their management stays sharp is for us to be more aggressive marketers."

Nevertheless, the apparent damage done to the bank's corporate lending base seems so great that it could take many years for First Chicago to regain its lost market share. The reason lies in an analysis of how Abboud changed the bank's lending policies and how those alterations affected corporate customers.

Since the days of Edward Eagle Brown, the legendary chairman of First Chicago from 1945 to 1959 who pioneered the development of highly specialized industrial lending divisions, corporate customers viewed First Chicago as a bank that responded quickly and innovatively to their financing needs. The bank's specialists were among the most expert in banking, and the industrial lending divisions became powerful entities within the bank, each capable of committing the bank to its legal lending limit.

That responsive lending style ultimately led to horrendous problems after Freeman took the helm in 1969. He more than doubled the bank's size in just five years. First Chicago became known as one of the most aggressive recruiters of top MBA graduates, who were quickly promoted to positions that had considerable lending authority.

By the time Abboud became chairman, Freeman's expansionism had produced one of the worst loan portfolios in the industry. According to a study by Keefe, Bruyette & Woods Inc., the bank's percentage of nonperforming loans (loans foreclosed, restructured at lower rates, or otherwise considered doubtful) reached a peak of 11% in 1976, slightly more than double the national average. By the end of the decade, Abboud had reduced that to 5%, still double the current average.

Even his virulent critics concede that Abboud's response was initially correct. Committees scrutinized loans much more cautiously, and the amounts that individual division heads could lend without senior officer approval were slashed by as much as 90%. The legal department was also inserted into the loan approval process, and Abboud involved himself much more than his predecessor did in the approval of loans.

According to former lending officers, such controls tended to double the time it took First Chicago to approve loans, but they also created a new uncertainty among established customers about whether they would get approvals. "The bank became less sensitive to the needs of its commercial customers," says Joseph G. Migely, a commercial loan vice-president who quit the bank last year after a 20-year career there. "Customers perceived that it was no longer a steady source of borrowed funds."

Initially, that insensitivity took the form of higher pricing and tougher loan requirements. Among other things, Abboud began requiring corporate customers to maintain compensating balances on 15% of an unexercised credit line instead of competitors' 10%. But such noncompetitive terms were applied across the board, and they drove away some good commercial customers.

In the mid-1970s, when Inland Steel was looking to renew a $125 million credit line with a group of banks led by First Chicago, it avoided the First altogether and restructured the line with Continental as lead bank. Although Inland Chairman Frederick G. Jaicks, a director at First Chicago, is reportedly miffed by inquiries about his company's shift in banks, the company confirms that Inland's existing bank lines—now expanded to $200 million—retain Continental as lead bank. Although the First has been restored to the line, its portion is smaller than it once was.

Inland's move is not the only example of an embarrassing shift of business from the First by one of its own directors. Early this month, Field Enterprises Inc., owner of Chicago's *Sun-Times* and other communications properties, paid off a $35 million loan at the bank three years early because First Chicago tried to exercise a clause in the agreement allowing it to reprice the loan if the company bought or sold properties without the First's approval. Since Field's move involved the sale of a coal mine for an amount about equal to its investment in the asset, it was easy for that company to conclude that the bank was merely invoking the clause to increase the rate on the loan. "They were technically within their rights, but not within the spirit of the loan covenants," huffs Marshall Field, chairman of Field Enterprises and a director at the First. Now Field will replace that loan with one from another bank, possibly Continental. "The biggest weakness the First has is bad customer relationships," says Field. "I thought this was the best way I could get my message across."

Insensitivity toward customers, however, went well beyond pricing. While many longtime corporate customers of the bank such as Hertz Corp. and Colonel Henry Crown's Material Service Corp. still commend the First for its service, other traditional customers chafed under the bank's more rigid style. One such account apparently was the Pritzker family, whose corporate empire includes Hyatt Corp. and the $2-billion-a-year Marmon Group.

These entities had loans at the First estimated at about $200 million. According to sources close to both sides, First Chicago's directors wanted the bank to diversify risks by reducing the exposure it had on such large family accounts as the Pritzkers. But because of its intransigent attitude, the bank probably got more diversity than it bargained for. More than half of the once-exclusive Pritzker account has been shifted to Continental in the last two years, and the First's position on getting future Pritzker business has been seriously jeopardized.

Sources say that the key dispute between Abboud and the Pritzkers centered on the sale, two years ago, of Great Adventure, a New Jersey theme park. The bank had financed the development of the park, but wound up owning it when the loan turned sour. Later, a half interest in the park was obtained by the Pritzkers, who had come to the aid of the bank by pumping in some $25 million as part of a refinancing package.

By 1978 the bank wanted to unload the park. But the Pritzkers were reportedly angered when Abboud tried to encourage them to accept terms in one proposed sale that would have stuck them with a potentially large tax liability. A new deal was later arranged in which the Pritzkers avoided the tax burden. But the incident plainly strained the bank's relationship with one of its most important customers. Other close observers believe the bank reduced its exposure to Pritzker business in a cavalier fashion. Instead of merely requesting that the family reduce its deposits at the First, says one source, "they should have gotten the Pritzkers to shift some of their business to a New York bank, making it clear that it would play a subservient role. They should never have let the business go to the Continental, where it's too easy to have lunch, play tennis, and take away future business."

What may have caused First Chicago's greatest loss of market share, however, was its simple failure to develop further the very industrial specialization it was known for. In two major areas particularly—energy and commercial real estate—the bank, during the last half of the 1970s, allowed Continental to become far more proficient. About a decade ago, both banks were considered equal competitors in lending to the energy and mining industries, but after the Arab oil embargo in 1971, Continental began increasing its energy and mining loan staff at more than twice the pace of First Chicago's expansion. As a result, Continental now is considered by many to be the nation's leading energy bank. Not surprisingly, its energy-related lending is estimated to be at least double that of First Chicago's.

But nowhere are the differences in marketing more noticeable than in commercial real estate. Five years ago, both banks directed most of the efforts of their real estate staff to working out bad loans rather than making new ones. But First Chicago remained gun-shy on real estate lending long after Continen-

The Strategy Makers / 73

tal decided that the area was safe for reentry.

The key to Continental's optimism was James D. Harper Jr., a real estate specialist who headed an REIT management company purchased by the bank in 1973. By 1977, he was pushing the bank into another major move to real estate lending. "A lot of banks were still retrenching in real estate, but we went ahead because we saw opportunities and decided we had the right players," recalls Continental President John H. Perkins.

The renewed emphasis was well timed. With the resurgence in Chicago's commercial real estate in the late 1970s, Continental today holds construction financing on 7 of 12 high-rise projects now under way in the area of the downtown Loop. Having lured a number of major Chicago developers away from long-standing relationships with First Chicago, Continental's total real estate portfolio has swung in five years from being 25% smaller to 50% larger than that of its rival. Says Louis S. Kahnweiler, a Chicago-based office and industrial park developer who has recently been shifting his business to Continental after 15 years at the First: "When you just couldn't make a dent at the First, Continental was out wooing developers."

Given Sullivan's marketing priorities, First Chicago still will be unable to recapture its lost market share until the new chairman rebuilds the bank's demoralized and depleted management ranks. In certain areas, First Chicago's turnover has been so massive that some customers believe that this is largely responsible for lost corporate business. A chairman of a Chicago-based manufacturer declares that he recently reduced his company's business at the First because the bank had assigned five different loan officers to the account in three years.

Although a number of former officers prefer to attribute all the executive turnover to Abboud's interference, the initial departures more likely came from the four-man race for the chairmanship that was set up intentionally by Freeman in 1972, when he appointed Abboud and three other youthful managers as executive vice-presidents. When Abboud won out, no one was surprised that two of his rivals—Wilmouth and Chauncey E. Schmidt (now chairman of Bancal Tri-State Corp.)—left and took many of their loyalists with them.

But the turnover problems persisted, and these are more easily pinned on Abboud's widely publicized tendency to insert himself in even mundane operations of the bank. Former associates note that the day-to-day concerns kept Abboud from developing a long-term strategy. In fact, some recent departures from the bank had been named to their posts by Abboud, including Yeo, Homer J. Livingston Jr. (son of a former First Chicago chairman), James E. Smith (a former Comptroller of the Currency who was hired by Abboud as an executive vice-president in 1976), and James M. Shipton (a department store executive Abboud recruited in 1977 to head the bank's personnel department). Kapnick was ousted at the same time as Abboud.

Throughout the bank there are now talented executives in the wrong jobs

The question for Sullivan: Is a top management shake-up in order?

simply because the bank was so desperate to fill key slots. The new head of the energy lending group is a specialist in communications. The personnel director is one of the bank's top international bankers, and the replacement for Livingston, the former corporate lending chief, came from another department.

Still other mismatches resulted from Abboud's penchant for making apparently political appointments. One is Neil F. Hartigan, whose background as a municipal lawyer and an Illinois lieutenant governor may not have prepared him for his present post at the bank—senior vice-president in charge of the Western Hemisphere in the bank's international department.

Sullivan believes that many of these management gaps can be eliminated with some adroit internal shuffling to place executives in the types of jobs for which they have the most experience. The rest of the gaps in middle management will be filled by the recruiting effort the bank will undertake to hire experienced lending officers away from other banks.

Sullivan also plans to revitalize an MBA recruiting program that became nearly moribund under Abboud. Since 1975, Continental has hired nearly four times as many MBAs as the First. Now Sullivan plans to accelerate that pace, and he intends to head the recruitment team that visits the business schools.

A more crucial issue facing Sullivan is whether a top management shake-up is in order. Some close observers of the bank predict that it is. They suggest this could include reassigning or replacing such executives as President Richard L. Thomas or Vice-Chairman Neil McKay. "The top guys who went along with Abboud were like weather vanes, and they don't have the respect of middle management," says one former officer, echoing a common refrain among First Chicago alumni. "My concern is that the board has told Sullivan, 'Please, no more shakeups.'"

Sullivan insists he is under no such constraints, but he also says that his initial impression of the bank's top managers is favorable. Still, by yearend he will decide if any major changes are needed. While he tactfully avoids any hint that such changes may be in the works, he rejects the notion heard in some quarters that he may be too personable an executive to conduct a top management overhaul. "Sure, I'm a nice guy," says Sullivan, "but I can make the tough people decisions." ∎

QUESTIONS

Following the Corporate Legend:

1. The influence of a retiring entrepreneur (founder) is the key determinant of whether his successor will succeed or fail. Discuss.

2. What factors (in addition to this influence of the retiring founder) have an impact on the success of the new corporate leader?

Managers Who Are No Longer Entrepreneurs:

1. Contrast the entrepreneurial style of management with the management style commonly found in large corporations. Discuss the effects each has on a business.

2. What factors tend to perpetuate the latter style in many organizations today?

ITT: Groping for a New Strategy:

1. Should ITT switch from its strategy of growth by acquisition to one of internal growth? Include a discussion of the primary internal and external factors that affect the decision.

2. Discuss how the philosophies of former CEO Geneen continue to influence the strategy-making processes at ITT today.

The Pains of Turning Firestone Around:

1. What are the major objectives CEO John Nevin has established for Firestone Tire and Rubber Co.?

2. Through what means does he hope to achieve these objectives?

Richard J. Ferris: Flying a Risky New Route for United:

1. Given the current position of United Airlines Inc., was the strategy chosen by President Richard J. Ferris a sound one? Explain.

2. Are there any uncontrollable factors that have a direct bearing on whether or not Ferris' strategy will prove to be viable? Discuss.

After Years of Hoarding Cash Hearst Is Spending Big:

1. Outline the plan of President and CEO Frank Bennack, Jr., to make Hearst Corp. "the best regarded" firm in publishing.

2. How do the private status of the corporation and the relations among the owners and managers affect the operations at Hearst Corp.? Discuss.

The Man behind Kraft's Merger:

1. What are the primary benefits to be derived from the Dart-Kraft merger?

2. Discuss the characteristics of Justin Dart and John Richman, and how these traits will help the newly merged company to meet its goals.

How a New Chief Is Turning Interbank Inside Out:

1. Who are the strategy makers at Interbank, and what are the major goals and objectives they are trying to achieve?

2. What was the position of the company at the time Hogg took over, and what major changes did he make?

Trautman: A Goal Eludes a Willful Manager:

1. How has Greyhound's Chairman Gerald H. Trautman influenced the strategic choices of the firm?

2. What impact have his management style and personality had on the overall performance of the company?

First of Chicago: New Management to Bring Back the Past:

1. Contrast the management styles of Abboud and Sullivan, and discuss the impact each had or will have on First National Bank of Chicago.

2. Discuss the present position of First National Bank of Chicago and the major objectives Sullivan has established to turn the bank around.

The Strategy Makers / 75

Three.

Chapter 1 focused on the concept of strategy and policy, and Chapter 2 investigated the strategy makers. As Exhibit 3-1 shows, the next step in our model considers appraisal decisions which consist of two parts: appraisal of opportunities and threats emerging from the firm's external environment, and appraisal of the firm's internal strategic advantages and disadvantages (or strengths and weaknesses). In Chapters 3 and 4, we will examine the first part of the appraisal decision—appraisal of the external environment.

Three sectors of the environment produce changes which strategy makers must monitor if their firms are to be successful in the long run. These are the general environment, the market, and the supply sector.

THE GENERAL ENVIRONMENT

The general environment includes the following forces affecting or potentially affecting the firm: the government, the economy, consumer pressures and attitudes, and population and wealth changes.

The Government

The government—federal, state or provincial, or local—can change its structure, pass laws, issue regulations, and become or cease to become a major customer or competitor of the firm. Government action or inaction is very important to business, and most knowledgeable people agree that the government sector will increase in importance to business over the next decade. Chapter 4 in this book will devote a great deal of attention to the government sector.

The Economy

The economy affects firms in many ways, including the following:

- Unemployment rates may affect the demand for the firm's product or services; they also affect the availability of labor.
- Inflation rates affect the pricing of the firm's product or service.
- The money supply policy can affect the availability of capital and the cost of capital.

The general status of the economy, which is a consequence of government policy, consumer decisions, and managerial decisions, affects different firms differently. Some products or services tend to hold up better in economic downturns than others.

Consumer Pressures and Attitudes

Consumer attitudes and values toward various products and services change over time. For example, some consumer attitudes toward cigarettes, liquor, drugs, gambling casinos, massage parlors, X-rated movies, bingo, and other products and services are frequently strongly held. If the firm is involved in these businesses, it is likely to be affected by changing values toward its offerings to the public. Consider the changes in consumer attitudes toward the following over the past few years:

- Oil companies before and after the energy crisis.
- Oil company profits before and after deregulation.
- Small cars before and after the energy crisis.

Population and Wealth Changes

Changes in the characteristics of the population affect most firms. For example,

- Gerber Baby Food executives are quite concerned about the drop in the birthrate from 1957 to 1980. So are most college presidents.
- Coca-Cola Company executives are concerned about the

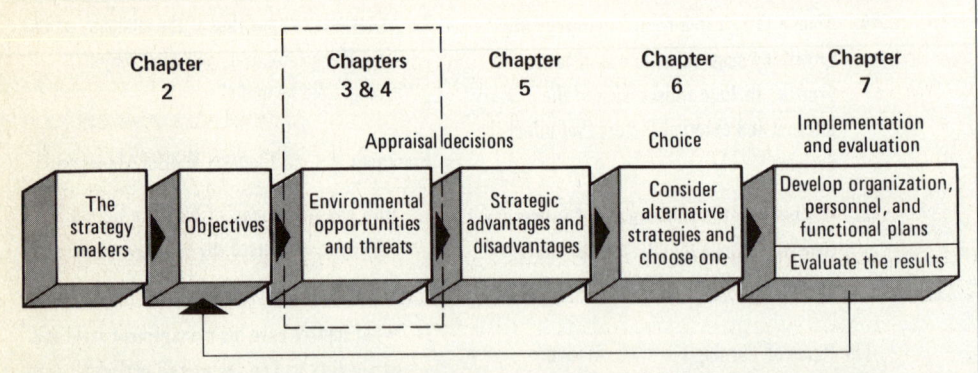

Exhibit 3-1: A MODEL OF THE BUSINESS POLICY AND STRATEGIC MANAGEMENT PROCESS.

Environmental Opportunities and Threats to Enterprise Strategy

76 / Readings from *Business Week*

population getting older and drinking fewer soft drinks.
- Government executives are concerned about the population getting older and not producing enough tax revenue to fund their programs.

THE MARKET

The second factor most executives watch closely is the marketplace in which they compete to distribute their goods or provide their services. Some of the aspects of the market that the executives must analyze if they are to be effective strategists include

- Major new products and services introduced in the industry.
- Major shifts in the pricing structure of the products or services.
- Major shifts in the demand for the products and services.
- Major shifts in consumer preferences affecting the firm's products and services.
- Major competitors entering or leaving the industry.

Most studies show that strategists examine the market environment most closely. In many industries, it is the most important factor. In others, governmental factors or shifts in the economy are more important.

THE SUPPLY SECTOR

The final sector is the supply sector. This sector provides the raw materials, money, and equipment needed by the firm to offer its service or produce its product. Some aspects of the supply sector include

- Changes in the availability of major raw materials, subassemblies, and so on.
- Changes in the prices of raw materials, subassemblies, and so on.
- Entry or exit of major suppliers, raw material producers, and so on.
- Technological breakthroughs on the supply side.

Executives analyze these factors after receiving information or data from

- Formal forecasts (rarely).
- Spying (very rarely).
- Information gathering.

Information gathering usually involves the executives' phoning or talking with knowledgeable people such as subordinates, bankers, industry analysts, and other executives in the industry. How intensely they seek information and on what factors depends on the executives and the industry. For example,

- If the company is clearly the most powerful firm (for example, General Motors, Xerox, IBM) in the industry, it may be somewhat less concerned with competitors' moves than if it is the smallest, weakest firm.
- If the firm has millions of customers (General Foods, Goodyear) rather than a very few customers (McDonnell Douglas), the former type of firm may pay less attention to each customer than the latter.
- If the firm is dependent on a few suppliers (for example, firms using copper), it may pay close attention to the supply factor.

Executives tend to focus their environmental analysis on forces they are most vulnerable to in the short run. Further, firms employing a systematic business policy/strategic management process prepare a profile of their firm and its opportunities and threats to help develop their strategies. This chapter of the book provides a series of examples from *Business Week* describing how the environment can provide opportunities, threats, or both to a firm.

Strategy makers must constantly be on the alert for changes in the environment which represent opportunities their firms can exploit. These changes can emerge in any environmental sector. The following *Business Week* articles describe environmental changes which spell opportunity for firms with the appropriate resources and insights:

- "Magazines Targeted at the Working Woman"
- "The Investor Excitement over New City Hotels"
- "The Microchip Revolution: Piecing Together a New Society"

At any time, a firm faces a multitude of environmental forces simultaneously. Some of these forces represent threats to the future progress of the firm. The following *Business Week* articles are included to describe forces which pose significant threats with which firms must come to grips:

- "The Shrinking Standard of Living"
- "Southeast Banks: Set for a Slump"
- "Antibusiness Forces Aim at Corporations"
- "A UN Space Treaty That Could Zap Industry"
- "U.S. Autos: Losing a Big Segment of the Market—Forever?"
- "Luxury Car Sales Skid to New Lows"
- "Detroit's High-Price Strategy Could Backfire"
- "Tight Credit Slams Car Dealers Two Ways"
- "What Caused the Decline: Inflation Skews the Profit Incentive"
- "What Caused the Decline: Expectations That Can No Longer Be Met"
- "Maine's Nuclear Vote Has Industry Jumpy"

An old adage states that "every cloud has a silver lining." The same holds true for environmental threats. Change in the environment represents threats for some firms and opportunities for others. Several *Business Week* articles in this chapter describe environmental changes which some firms are positioned to exploit as opportunities and others perceive as threats:

- "A Skewed Recession Has Hidden Strengths"
- "Cable TV: The Race to Plug In"
- "The Implications of Oil Company Profits"
- "Videodiscs: A Three-Way Race for a Billion-Dollar Jackpot"
- "U.S. Home: Defying a Slowdown by Continuing to Expand"

MAGAZINES TARGETED AT THE WORKING WOMAN

A new class of magazines is emerging to serve the nearly 44 million U.S. women who work for pay, a group that constitutes almost half the country's labor force. The new publications do not yet challenge such long-established women's magazines as the mass-circulation *Family Circle*, *Woman's Day*, and *Ladies' Home Journal* for supremacy among female readers. But they make up in novelty of approach—and potential influence—what they lack, so far, in commercial success.

The three-year-old *Working Woman*, the first magazine to respond specifically to the new market, gives its 350,000 readers everything from female success stories to recipes. Eight-year-old *MS Magazine*, its ideologically oriented predecessor, feeds the fervor for equal rights. *Self* and *New Woman* boost the psyche. Other newcomers include *McCall's Working Mothers*, *Women Who Work*, and a few regional magazines such as *Texas Woman*. Even old-line publications have caught the bug: Veterans such as *Mademoiselle* have begun to feature articles for working women.

Two for the managers. Now two new monthly magazines—both first published in New York City in November—have appeared to serve a particular kind of working woman: the manager, professional or entrepreneur. The two, *Savvy*, and *Enterprising Women*, face even stiffer odds than the 10-to-1 chance of success estimated for all new magazines.

Like any publication that tries to be both women-minded and business-minded, they must compete with traditional business publications that provide more business information and with traditional women's magazines that offer more fashion and lifestyle material. In effect, they are gambling on the possibility that women achievers want different business and lifestyle information than is available in old-line publications or, at least, want it in magazines they can regard as their own. At the same time the traditional business press has begun to make a conscious pitch for women readers—in some cases, advertising in the new magazines.

Until recently, no magazine has aimed directly at the woman committed to a business career and doing well at it. "*Working Woman* is a great magazine for women who have reentered the work force or are in the early work stages," says Wendy Rue, president of the National Association for Female Executives (NAFE). It is not particularly useful to those higher up, she says—an assessment possibly affected by the six issues of *The Executive Female* she publishes annually for NAFE's 40,000 members. Among commercial publications, only newsletters have aimed at the businesswoman over 30 who earns more than $25,000 a year. Now, with market studies showing that a third of all working women are embarked on careers and that they are the heaviest users of magazines in the country, *Savvy*, with a circulation of 125,000, and *Enterprising Women*, with 50,000, seek to capture this market of managers and entrepreneurs.

Competing with tradition. The market studies are underscored by figures showing that women are accounting for an increasing percentage of the circulation of most business magazines—up from 3% in 1967 to 6% in 1978 for *Fortune*, from 3% in 1976 to 8.8% in 1979 for BUSINESS WEEK, and from 2.4% in 1968 to 3.6% in 1979 for *Forbes*. The increases would be larger, says Kate Rand Lloyd, editor-in-chief of *Working Woman*, were it not that the business magazines "are a very discouraging group of publications. The sense that women aren't represented is pervasive."

Despite Lloyd's gibe, most business magazines have begun to pay attention to women managers and entrepreneurs, both as subjects and readers. *Fortune* devoted eight pages to the woman MBA phenomenon in its August, 1978 issue, and BUSINESS WEEK's Corporate woman department marked its fourth anniversary last November. BW's manager of direct marketing, Lee M. Stein, says the magazine actively seeks women readers through direct mail and is taking advantage of discount advertising rates in *Working Woman* and *Savvy*.

Elusive quarry. The new for-working-women-only press is finding its readers an elusive quarry. Begun in November, 1976, *Working Woman* fell into bankruptcy in December 1977—partly, says current publisher James B. Horton, because of bad management, and partly, says current editor Lloyd, because the magazine misidentified its readers. Originally intended for all working women, the magazine actually was being read by professional, managerial, and technical workers "whose mindset was moving very fast," says Lloyd.

At first, the reorganized magazine dealt with what Lloyd perceived as the readers' guilt about being in the labor force. Now the readers recognize "that women are in the labor force for keeps, and they want all the tools they can get hold of to perform at the top of their ability," Lloyd says.

In addition to a new editorial direction, *Working Woman* received a substantial sum for promotion when Horton took over in 1977. Revenues have doubled in the past year, to a claimed $3.5 million, though Horton admits that the magazine is not yet profitable. Circulation has increased from 100,000 in 1978 to 350,000 in 1979, and 1980's goal is 450,000, with gross sales of $6.5 million.

Inroads. Although the new magazines are far from the big time (*Working Woman* ranks 378 in gross sales on a list of 400 magazines rated by *Folio*, a trade publication), they may be making inroads on some traditional women's magazines. According to the Audit Bureau of Circulation, *Woman's Day* has dropped 7.2% in circulation during the past three years; *Family Circle*, 5.9%; *Redbook*,

3.3%; and *Ladies Home Journal* 3.8%. *Woman's Day* attributes the declines to inflation and the growing specialization of women's magazines.

Ava Stern, publisher of *Enterprising Women*, believes that her magazine for women entrepreneurs can achieve 100,000 subscribers by the end of 1980 and turn a profit in less than two years.

The new women's magazines are small but fast-growing

She bases her confidence on an estimated market of more than 1 million U.S. women business owners and on her experience with a five-year-old newsletter also called *Enterprising Women*. The newsletter, which attracts 10,000 subscribers with information about how to run a business, broke even in three years on an annual subscription cost of $28, Stern says. The profits since then have been pumped into the magazine.

Savvy, which calls itself "the magazine for executive women," aims at readers who are more varied than the entrepreneurs of *Enterprising Women* and earn more money than the readers of *Working Woman*. "There is a real gap in the market for the higher-income, higher-job-level woman," says Editor Judith Daniels. *Savvy* apparently assumes that this woman has wide-ranging concerns and a keen interest in upward mobility. *Savvy*'s first issue ran articles about handsome men, women's networks, and the business press. Its promotion invites readers "to see how other women live, to identify at a high career level with them." Daniels predicts a subscription list of 250,000 by the end of 1980 and expects to break even in three years.

Advertising acumen. Getting advertising is a hard job for the new magazines, as it is for all fledgling publications, because, Stern says, "advertisers have seen so many magazines fold." *Enterprising Women* seeks such advertising as financial services and technical equipment, ads relevant to its readers, Stern says. The magazine offers a discount to women-owned businesses. "Our approach is going to have to be as specialized as our market and our product," says Stern.

Savvy's advertising covers a wider field—from financial services to such conventional women's products as cosmetics. "Two years ago ads would have been an uphill fight, but now advertisers have done their own studies and discovered a whole market they haven't reached," says Publisher Alan Bennett. Market studies have shown that affluent, successful women do not merely read about investments, he says, but also spend lavishly on grooming and fashion. So getting ads now "tends to be a self-selecting process," he contends. ∎

THE INVESTOR EXCITEMENT OVER NEW CITY HOTELS

Almost everywhere you look in city business districts these days, new hotels are sprouting up. Houston has 12 under way or announced, Dallas has 6, New York has 5, Boston has 3; BUSINESS WEEK has counted at least 56 hotels under construction or about to begin in 18 cities.

In part, of course, the surge of new construction reflects increased demand for hotel space. During the past five years—as the glut of hotel rooms of the mid-1970s turned into today's tight supply—occupancy rates nationally have climbed from 62% to 73%, according to Laventhol & Horwath, a Philadelphia firm that monitors the hotel industry.

But the rush to build also reflects the conviction of a wide range of real estate investors—insurance companies, pension funds, syndicates of wealthy individuals and foreign sources—that downtown hotels are a good place to put their money. "The central-city hotel in the major metropolitan areas will be an outstanding investment" this year, says John R. White, president of Landauer Associates Inc., New York real estate consultants. This new investor appetite for hotels, in fact, makes possible the continuing shift of emphasis by the big hotel chains from owning their own hotels to managing those built by independent developers.

Inflation responsive. Today's record-high interest rates are, of course, substantially slowing down the pace of new projects, and most of the hotels now under way were planned and financed a year to 18 months ago. But long term, the outlook for new construction is promising. "There are high occupancy rates, and the supply-demand characteristics of the industry look good," says John V. Giovenco, senior vice-president of Hilton Hotels Corp. Victor J. Raskin, a first vice-president of Dean Witter Reynolds Inc., estimates that 50,000 new hotel rooms will be built annually during the next five years.

There is little doubt that investor attitudes toward hotels have changed, especially as office buildings and shopping centers approach saturation in many markets. "Traditional thinking has been that hotels are riskier types of investments in which you limit your portfolios," says George R. Puskar, vice-president for property acquisition at Equitable Life Assurance Society. In 1973, Equitable had no hotels. Today it owns 23 and has a $159 million deal to buy six more from Marriott Corp.

A key reason for the new investor interest is inflation. "Over the past 10 years," says James Richmond, vice-president for real estate investment at Aetna Life & Casualty Co., "hotels have shown a better-than-average ability to respond to inflation."

Harry B. Helmsley, one of Manhattan's biggest real estate developers and owners, concurs. "You can adjust yourself to inflation daily" by raising room rents, he points out. Helmsley, who owns five Manhattan hotels (and 28 nationally), is building two more, including the super-luxury, $100 million Palace, scheduled to open in July before the Democratic national convention. "In a period of inflation, your investment has to become more valuable," says Helmsley.

High yields. Some big institutions agree. Prudential Insurance Co., for example, has $400 million of equity in 103 hotels, 21 of which it owns outright. On the lending side, Prudential has $900 million committed to 300 hotel mortgages. John Hancock Mutual Life Insurance Co. has $307 million in hotel loans in its mortgage portfolio, compared with $189 million in 1976. And hotels account for 27% of the $600 million that Connecticut General Insurance Corp. put into new mortgages last year. Notes Harvey G. Moger, real estate vice-president at Connecticut General: "Your flexibility is tremendous. You are not tied up with multiple leases as you are in so many other types of real estate."

A key reason for the investor interest is that hotels can produce yields that compensate for the risks, especially at a time when the selling prices for, say, good shopping centers are pushing returns down to the 6% to 5% level and below. Financing for Helmsley's Palace

Hedge: Pension funds and insurance companies put hotels in their portfolios

hotel, for example, includes—in addition to a $50 million mortgage from Metropolitan Life Insurance Co. and Massachusetts Mutual Life Insurance Co.—$23 million in equity from 23 limited partners (Helmsley himself has $5 million invested as a limited partner), plus an additional $5 million from Helmsley as the general partner. Helmsley says he expects the return to investors will be "substantially better than 10%, and a good part of that will be tax-sheltered through depreciation."

Investor interest in hotels is changing the way the hotel industry operates. Most large U.S. hotel chains, for example, are planning major expansions. But most of the expansion by Sheraton Corp., Hilton Hotels, Marriott, and Stouffer Corp.'s Hotels Div. will come from signing management contracts to run hotels built by independent developers, rather than building and owning new hotels themselves. "The primary reason you see most of the major chains doing a lot of management contracts is the availability of equity," observes Sam D. Haigh, vice-president for operations at Stouffer, which expects to grow from 21 hotels to 50 by 1990.

Marriott plans to more than double, to 50,000 rooms, by the mid-1980s. Until the mid-1970s, recalls Senior Vice-President Thomas E. Burke, "our policy was to own all our hotels and take all the profits right to the bottom line." But Marriott found itself borrowing heavily to pay for hotels, plus expensive new amusement parks; by 1975, debt had risen to 55% of equity. To solve the problem the company sold off marginal nonhotel assets and turned more to managing, rather than owning, hotels.

More rooms faster. As managers, Marriott makes less on each hotel than it did as owners, since it gets only a percentage of the unit's gross operating profit. But because it relies less on its own financing, Marriott has been able to expand its number of rooms more rapidly. Thus the total pie—and Marriott's income—is larger. Earnings gains have been averaging 20% a year, and return on equity is up from 9.7% in 1975 to 17.1% last year.

Investors are also putting money into chains that have many properties abroad but that are just starting to crack the U.S. market. Meridien Hotels, a subsidiary of Air France, will start managing its first two U.S. hotels this year, in New York and Houston, both owned by independent investors.

Likewise, Hilton International Co., a subsidiary of Trans World Corp., which operates 78 hotels worldwide, will open its second U.S. hotel in July, the 825-

room Vista International, in New York's World Trade Center. It will also operate new hotels in Washington and Kansas City, Mo. Intercontinental Hotels Corp., owned by Pan American World Airways Inc., is also readying a push into the U.S., initially in Houston, Boston, Dallas, and New Orleans.

Hotels, of course, entail substantial risks. Clyde C. Jackson Jr., of Wynne Jackson Inc., developers of the 442-room Plaza of the Americas Hotel in Dallas, points out that "hotels are involved with high labor levels and food and beverage services, all of which are very susceptible

Promising forecast: 50,000 new hotel rooms each year for the next five years

to inflation. This means they need a strong operator."

A striking example of what can go wrong is Detroit's Radisson Cadillac Hotel, where occupancy averaged an abysmal 38% last year. Its former owner, Bank of the Commonwealth, has lost $2.5 million since it bought the property in 1976 and would have shut down the hotel if it were not for a $300,000 emergency loan from a local business group, Detroit's Economic Growth Corp. (EGC). In mid-February, EGC took the hotel off the bank's hands for a dollar, and it intends to pour $2.5 million into the property and resell it in a year or two.

Another worry for hotel investors and builders is the increasingly high cost of construction. Some are seeking to recover those escalating costs by building luxury hotels that command top rates.

Big slowdown? Not every city, however, can support several luxury hotels. So some investors and developers are combating inflation by taking the cheaper alternative of renovating older downtown properties. Some examples: Renovation began Mar. 1 on the 50-year-old Curtis Hotel in Minneapolis; in Louisville, the 75-year-old Seelbach Hotel, a beaux arts jewel, is undergoing a $17.5 million overhaul; and in October, Seattle's Olympic Hotel will close for a $38 million renovation.

Rehabilitation can be 25% to 30% cheaper than building from scratch, says J. Patrick Foley, president of Hyatt Hotels Corp., which has three big renovation projects under way in New York, Chicago, and Fort Worth. "I suspect you will see more and more of this activity," says Foley.

While hotel construction is expected to continue apace at least through the mid-1980s, a pause may be on the horizon. Last year, Hyatt saw eight projects in which it was involved as manager fall through. And Sheraton says many franchises have been delayed because of high-cost money. "Many lenders are no longer making loans," points out Hyatt's Foley.

But most investors are ready to ride out a downturn. "I have to take the long-range view," says New York's Helmsley. "When you build a hotel, you're investing for the next 50 years." ∎

The microchip revolution: Piecing together a new society

In little more than a decade, microelectronics technology has blossomed from an expensive space-age curiosity into an irresistible force that is rapidly transforming society. Even the most cursory comparison of the artifacts of society in the late 1960s with those of today reveals sweeping changes, down to such trivia as the wristwatches people wear and the toys children use. Yet the progress to date is merely a beginning.

Microelectronics has spawned myriad tiny components, epitomized by the microprocessor and the computer on a chip, that are working their way into an ever-increasing array of manufactured goods. Because of the technology's singular characteristic of continually developing new semiconductor components that are more powerful and cheaper, the trend toward digital, solid-state products is certain to gather momentum through the remainder of this century. Notes Isaac Asimov: "We can't stop the world from becoming digitalized."

The big changes. Along the way, there will be plenty of opportunities for investors. For example, the first offering of Apple Computer Inc., a leading producer of personal computers, is due to hit the market soon and has stirred up almost as much excitement as greeted Genentech Inc. Magnuson Computer Systems Inc., which started making mainframe computers only two years ago, went public last summer, offering 1.1 million

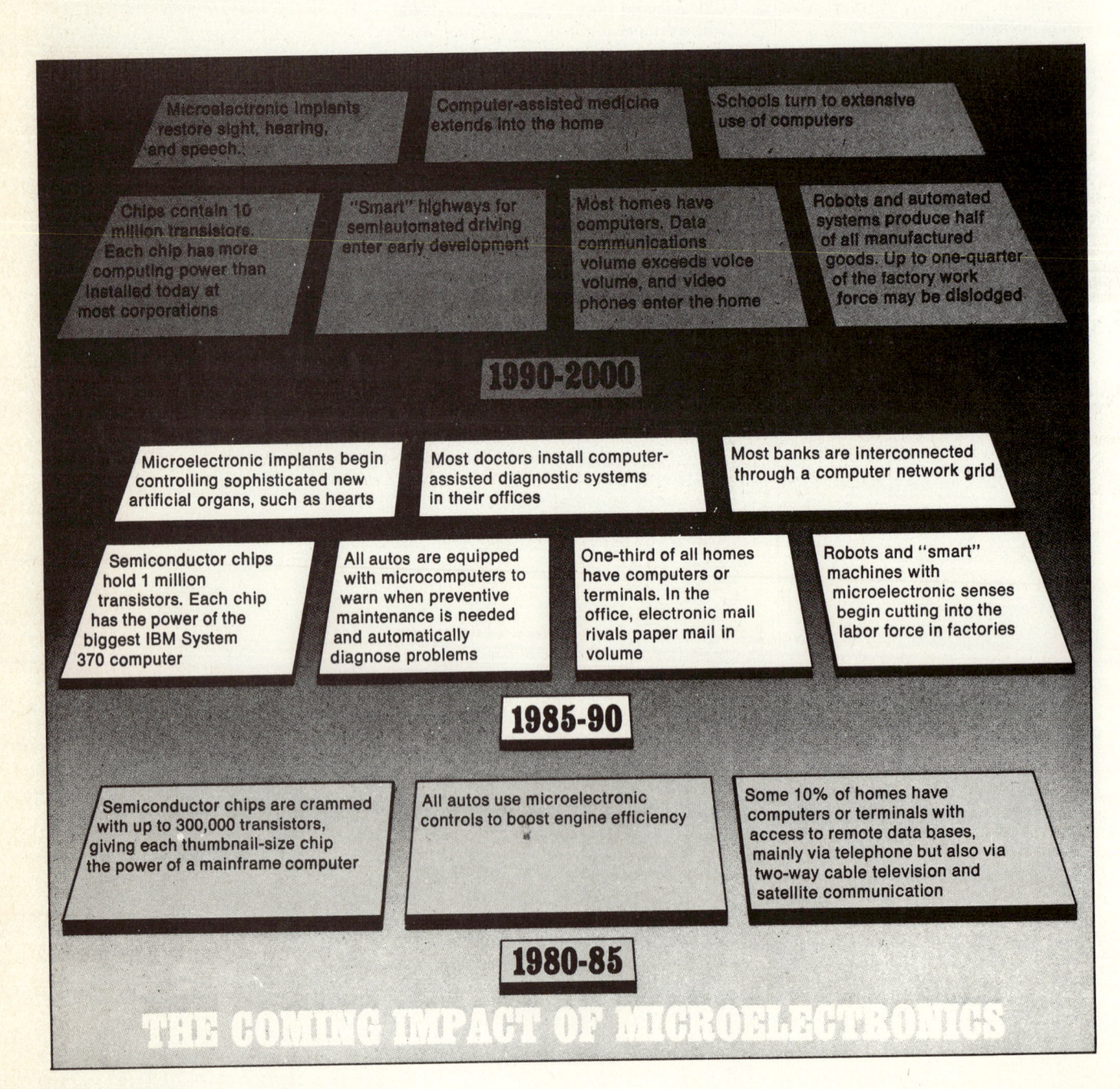

THE COMING IMPACT OF MICROELECTRONICS

1990-2000

- Microelectronic implants restore sight, hearing, and speech.
- Computer-assisted medicine extends into the home
- Schools turn to extensive use of computers
- Chips contain 10 million transistors. Each chip has more computing power than installed today at most corporations
- "Smart" highways for semiautomated driving enter early development
- Most homes have computers. Data communications volume exceeds voice volume, and video phones enter the home
- Robots and automated systems produce half of all manufactured goods. Up to one-quarter of the factory work force may be dislodged

1985-90

- Microelectronic implants begin controlling sophisticated new artificial organs, such as hearts
- Most doctors install computer-assisted diagnostic systems in their offices
- Most banks are interconnected through a computer network grid
- Semiconductor chips hold 1 million transistors. Each chip has the power of the biggest IBM System 370 computer
- All autos are equipped with microcomputers to warn when preventive maintenance is needed and automatically diagnose problems
- One-third of all homes have computers or terminals. In the office, electronic mail rivals paper mail in volume
- Robots and "smart" machines with microelectronic senses begin cutting into the labor force in factories

1980-85

- Semiconductor chips are crammed with up to 300,000 transistors, giving each thumbnail-size chip the power of a mainframe computer
- All autos use microelectronic controls to boost engine efficiency
- Some 10% of homes have computers or terminals with access to remote data bases, mainly via telephone but also via two-way cable television and satellite communication

shares that by October had climbed to nearly double the original $20 price.

Even in the underlying semiconductor industry, new opportunities continue to attract investors who remember what happened to Intel Corp. That semiconductor company went public in 1971 with $9 million in sales; two years later, after Intel invented the microprocessor, its stock jumped to $40 from $14, and the company is today an industry leader with 1979 revenues topping $660 million. Thus, when Nitron Inc., a fledgling semiconductor company, went public in late May, its stock soon tripled to $15.

One attraction of semiconductor stocks is the pervasive promise of this technology. The companies that turn out chips seem almost contemptuous of the gears, cams, limit switches, and other mechanical doodads that are the guts of pre-electronic products. Electronic engineers relish the job of reducing such mechanical functions to digital circuits on a cornflake-size silicon chip. And once that has been done for a given type of product, chances are good that the mechanical predecessor will be at a cost and performance disadvantage—as many former makers of mechanical adding machines and watches can testify.

The chip has thus become a symbol of technological liberation. Using the latest chips, a small company can develop a superior product that can cut into the business of a corporate giant. But there also is an analog: The products of any company—or country—without microelectronics expertise become increasingly vulnerable as each new generation of chips comes along. The computing power of chips continues to double every two to three years, making it possible to build solid-state versions of products whose complexity had defied digitization just a short time earlier. The company or country that makes the best chips thus sets the technological pace for a host of user industries. That realization is behind the urgent drive in Japan and Europe to develop indigenous semiconductor industries that can challenge the U. S. lead in microelectronics.

This process of continual innovation places a premium on research—and being the first to market. After a year or perhaps two, imitators and so-called second sources enter the market, and prices and margins drop rapidly. Intel and other major semiconductor companies have maintained their lead by reinvesting an unusually high portion of earnings in research, and most of them have yet to pay their first dividend.

Potential. Because of the strategic importance of the new technology, executives in California's Silicon Valley are fond of referring to semiconductors as the crude oil of the 1980s. But Peter Schwartz, director of the strategic environment center at SRI International, a Palo Alto (Calif.) research organization, believes that the simile needs elaboration: In microelectronics, he says, "we're about where oil was in 1870—trying to use petroleum as a substitute for whale oil." Instead, he asserts: "It's the fuel for a new, information economy."

Some people, including a few semiconductor experts, worry about where that information economy will head once it really takes off. In particular, the prospect of the factory work force shrinking because of incursions by robots and automated systems disturbs both labor leaders and businessmen.

Still, Martin Cooper, vice-president for research and development at Motorola Inc., believes there is no turning back. "With electronics, we already have the ability to sense beyond human hearing and vision, and the strength and precision of machines is better than humans," he notes. "So robots can make things better than people."

Social changes. There will be equally profound long-range impacts in communications, medicine, transportation, education, and most other areas of daily life. "Home computers," notes George H. Heilmeier, a Texas Instruments Inc. vice-president, "are going to be an integral part of new housing—for energy management, if nothing else."

Ticking off lists of accomplishments is a far cry from assessing their social implications, which have yet to be systematically addressed. Says one concerned observer: "We're flying blind—in a plane that keeps going faster and faster." But Walter S. Baer, a Rand Corp. executive who follows high technology, points out that the current situation parallels the concern felt in many quarters in the late 1950s and early 1960s when computers appeared on the commercial scene. A federal commission looked into the matter then and concluded that while automation might well involve major dislocations, society as a whole would be better off. Baer believes that that conclusion also applies to microelectronics—with one caveat. Today, the U. S. is much less insulated from the world economy than it was in 1960. "The result," he says, "may well be to displace blue-collar jobs in the U. S. to other nations. But it's unclear whether we will be compensated with a long-term gain." ∎

INFLATION'S LONG-TERM TOLL ON THE U.S. ECONOMY

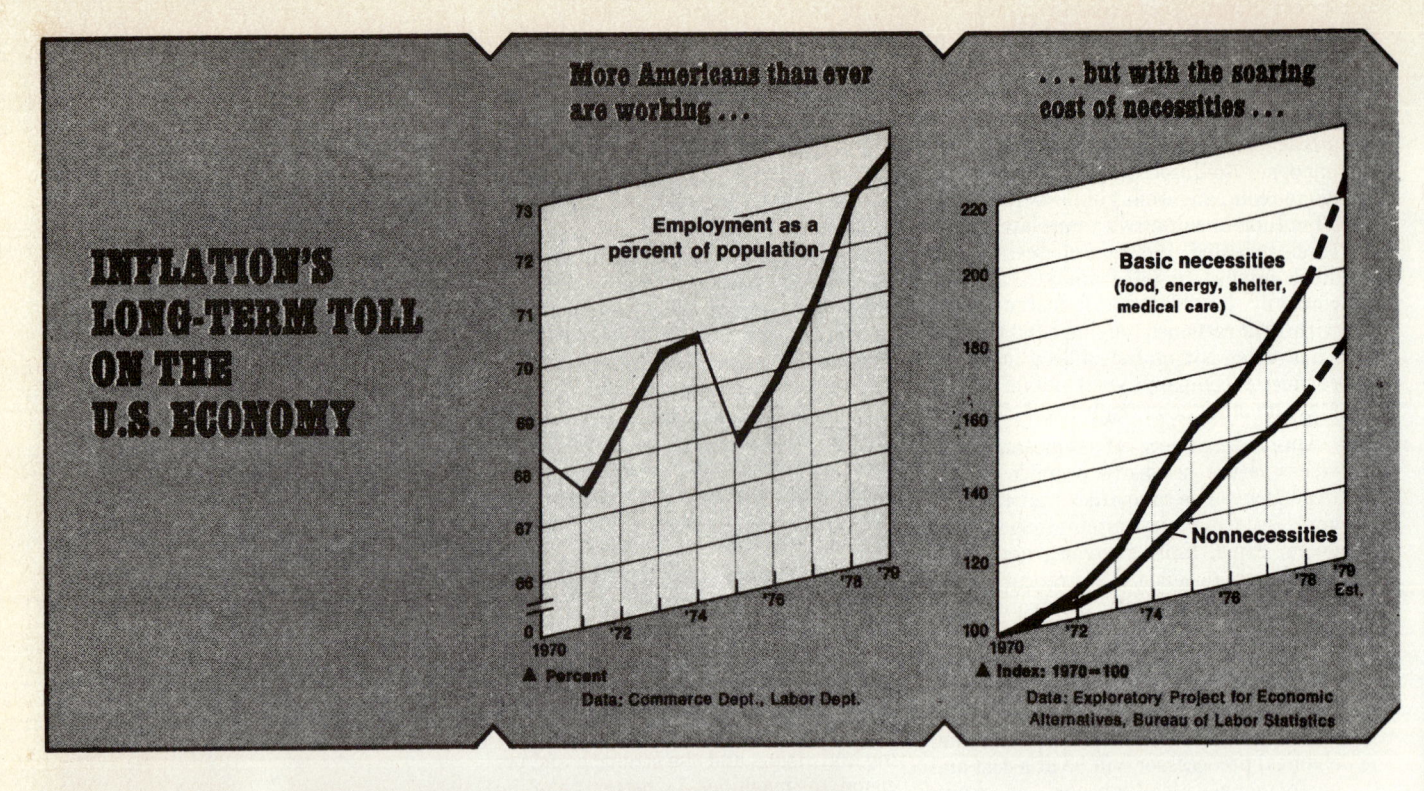

More Americans than ever are working...
Employment as a percent of population
Data: Commerce Dept., Labor Dept.

...but with the soaring cost of necessities...
Basic necessities (food, energy, shelter, medical care)
Nonnecessities
Index: 1970=100
Data: Exploratory Project for Economic Alternatives, Bureau of Labor Statistics

THE SHRINKING STANDARD OF LIVING

"A chicken in every pot, a car in every garage."
—1928 Republican campaign slogan

The American people had to endure a great depression and fight a great war before this promise of affluence could be realized—and then spectacularly transcended. For three decades after the end of World War II, Americans enjoyed an ever-rising standard of living: Each successive year, with few exceptions, found people working less and earning more. It became not only two chickens in every pot, but two cars in every garage for most Americans, not to mention the radios, TV sets, hi-fis, blenders, wall ovens, and trash compactors. The appetite of the U. S. consumer for more and more goods made this country's factories hum, as well as those of Europe, Japan, and the Third World, creating more than a quarter-century of unprecedented economic growth.

But the golden age of the consumer is over. The U. S. standard of living is shrinking. Even before the onset of recession this year, living standards were being battered by the combination of sagging productivity, rip-roaring inflation, and the transfer of more than $60 billion of income a year from the pockets of U. S. consumers to the oil-exporting countries. On top of this comes yet another jolt: the burden of increased defense spending—a consequence of Afghanistan—which will put the federal budget deeper in the red, push inflation even higher, and doom any chance that Americans will get a tax break. In the wake of these blows, the American credo that each generation can look forward to a more comfortable life than its predecessor has been shattered.

Shattered, too, is the optimism about the future that uniquely characterized the U. S. economy. Not only did parents believe that their children would have more opportunities than they did, but they were convinced that they themselves would be better off this year than last. It is this optimism, perhaps more than any other factor, that sparked the American family to spend and spend. Says David L. Littmann, vice-president and senior economist at Detroit's Manufacturers National Bank: "The country is festering in a quagmire of gradually declining living standards and national wealth the way England is," he says. "But the U. S. doesn't have the stiff upper lip of the English. There's no tradition of doing with less."

Indeed, so deeply ingrained is the American promise of "more" that many economists and businessmen refuse to accept the idea of a shrinking standard of living, much less recognize the dire implications for the U. S. economy:

MORE INFLATION. A shrinking standard of living means that the battle over income shares will intensify. This will generate even more inflation on top of the current double-digit rate.

INCREASED SOCIAL AND POLITICAL TENSIONS. The fight over a smaller economic pie is already straining traditional alliances, such as those between blacks and Jews. Unions may launch organizing drives, which could lead to increased confrontation between labor and management. The shrinking pie may spur conflict between workers and the greatly growing number of retirees. And there may be heated political battles over funding such social initiatives as national health insurance and a federalized welfare system, especially in light of the new thrust to defense spending.

WEAK CONSUMER SPENDING AND DIMINISHED ECONOMIC GROWTH. With less real disposable income available for discretionary purchases, consumers will be directing

84 / Readings from *Business Week*

...especially imported oil...

U.S. petroleum imports

▲ Billions of dollars
Data: Commerce Dept., BW estimate

...discretionary income is sagging both in total...

Real discretionary income*

▲ Billions of 1967 dollars
Data: Chase Econometric Associates Inc.

...and in terms of income per worker

Real discretionary income per worker*

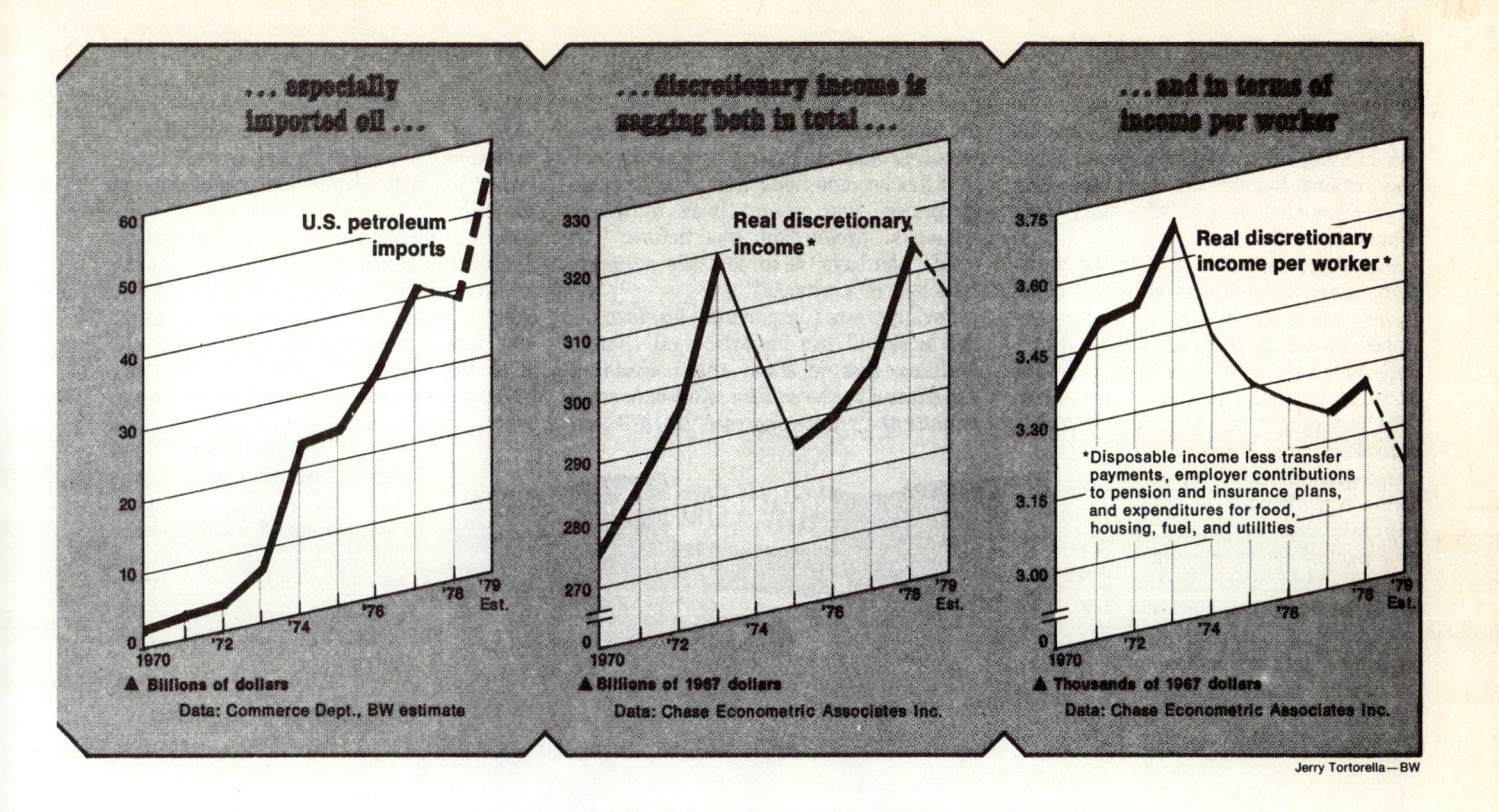

*Disposable income less transfer payments, employer contributions to pension and insurance plans, and expenditures for food, housing, fuel, and utilities

▲ Thousands of 1967 dollars
Data: Chase Econometric Associates Inc.

Jerry Tortorella—BW

'More and better' is no longer automatic, and consumer spending and growth will suffer

their dollars toward fewer but longer-lasting goods. Big-ticket items will be especially hurt. This will mean less capital investment by business and dampened economic growth.

By some measures, the economic wellbeing of Americans appears to have improved in the 1970s, although not at the heady rates it did in the 1960s. For example, the nation's disposable income, adjusted for population and changes in the consumer price index, rose 20% in the past decade, compared with 30% in the 1960s.

But this is an illusion, an illusion born of that streak of optimism in the American psyche that colors the future brighter than the past. It fails to consider that the world was changed drastically in 1974. The Organization of Petroleum Exporting Countries, by quadrupling oil prices, delivered the first in a series of body blows to the world economy. And only by separating the data into pre-OPEC and post-OPEC periods can the extent of the damage to the U.S. standard of living be assessed.

Between 1967 and 1973, real disposable income per person increased by 17.5%; over the next six years the gain fell to a meager 5.5%. And beginning in 1979 the numbers actually turned negative. "The two-earner family has about peaked, average real weekly earnings are falling, and now you are going to have to put teenagers to work just to keep real income stable," says Lacy H. Hunt, chief economist for Fidelity Bank in Philadelphia.

The story is more dismal when looking at what is left over from income after taking into account spending on basic necessities, such as food and shelter. Unlike the 1950s and 1960s, in recent years the prices of essentials have skyrocketed (chart). So the nation's real discretionary income in 1979 actually fell 4.6% below the level reached in 1973.

In fact, adjusting income for the huge recent increases in employment, to reflect the sweat that goes into producing that income, shows that discretionary income per worker over the past six years declined by 16%, compared with a 7% increase in the previous six years. "People are trading down on food, cutting back on the quality of consumption—they are simply less well off," says Carol Brock Kenney, economist at Shearson, Loeb Rhoades Inc. Says Leonard A. Rapping, a University of Massachusetts economist: "Everybody is working harder to maintain their standard of living, but they are not making it."

To be sure, unionized workers are continuing to outpace all other employee groups in terms of wage increases. Members of most unions achieved wage and fringe benefit increases last year of somewhat more than 8%, while nonunion workers came in considerably below that, according to Daniel J. B. Mitchell, director of the Institute of Industrial Relations at the University of California at Los Angeles. And public-sector employees throughout the nation are doing much worse, with most raises at 7% or below for 1979. With the consumer price index rising at 13%, "no one is keeping up against the CPI," Mitchell says.

'A stick with two short ends'

The soaring prices for essentials are putting a double whammy on consumers. Of the seven major groups that make up the consumer price index, food increased most sharply in 1978—12.8%—followed by housing at almost 11%, well above the average of 7.6% for all the groups. This means that not only were lower-income families hit hard but so was the

Environmental Opportunities/Enterprise Threats / 85

average middle-class family, which spends about one-third of its budget on food and one-quarter on housing. And the 70% increase in the price of gasoline and heating oil in 1979 clobbered those who depend heavily on the automobile for transportation and who heat their homes with oil.

Moreover, as a result of rising mortgage interest rates and climbing home prices, the average yearly income required by banks to qualify for a mortgage on a new home has increased 74% from November, 1978, to November, 1979, jumping from $15,500 to $26,400, according to Townsend-Greenspan & Co., the economic consulting firm. This dramatic rise is pricing a good part of the middle class out of housing, especially the young new families that are just starting out. But few have been left unscathed in the current bout of inflation. Says Arthur M. Okun of the Brookings Institution: "Almost everybody thinks he has the short end of the stick and is sure that someone else has the longer end. But when you look at the data, it becomes clear that the great new product of this era is a stick with two short ends."

High-priced oil lies at the heart of the shrinking U.S. standard of living. For one thing, the huge increase in energy prices since OPEC began flexing its muscles is forcing industrial companies to try to reduce the energy-intensity of production. Because energy and capital equipment go hand in hand in the production process, the result has been to decrease capital-intensive production and lift labor-intensive output. Because labor has relatively fewer capital goods to work with, labor productivity stagnates and so does economic growth. Indeed, since 1973, output per worker has increased only 0.7% per year vs. a 2.1% rate over the previous six years. It is little wonder that real hourly earnings in 1979 were 3.6% below the 1973 level.

One indirect, but no less disturbing, impact of the high prices that Americans must now pay for oil, says economist Anne P. Carter of Brandeis University, is that a great deal of domestic research and development is being diverted into making the nation's transportation systems, heating units, and industrial plants and equipment less energy-intensive. Thus, precious R&D resources are being taken out of more productive uses, such as creating new products, and are being transferred into retooling and reshaping a capital stock that has become inefficient at high energy prices—just to get back to where industrial production was before. The result, she says, is to deal the economy "one hell of a whack."

Perhaps most important, however, is the huge bill for importing oil that is draining income from the pockets of Americans to the coffers of oil-exporting nations at an alarming rate. In 1978 that drainage amounted to $39 billion. It rose to $60 billion in 1979 and is expected to hit $75 billion in 1980. In 1973 the U.S. had to produce less than 1 bu. of wheat to get 1 bbl. of oil from abroad. Today the nation surrenders 7 bu. of wheat for that same barrel of oil. "We are poorer," says Rapping, "because of lower productivity and because oil imports are so much more expensive in terms of U.S. exports."

The 1979 increase in OPEC oil from $12.75 a bbl. to almost double that by yearend helped to push the inflation rate from 7.6% in 1978 to 13% last year. And with $30-a-bbl. oil this year, the 1980 inflation rate will slacken little. But inflation per se does not reduce the standard of living. Generally, although someone is paying higher prices that lower his real income, someone else gets the higher prices and his real income goes up. There may be some distribution problems among different income groups, of course, with some losing while others gain, but on average, inflation will have a zero impact on the standard of living. This holds true only when the inflation is internally generated, however. "Just as there are losers, there are lots of winners," says Sandra Shaber of Chase Econometric Associates Inc. "People spend more dollars, but there is someone on the receiving end. In this inflation, the people on the receiving end are the Arab sheiks."

Consumer spending

That most people will continue to be losers when it comes to their standard of living means that consumer markets in the 1980s will be shrinking. Given the stellar performance of consumer spending over the last 30 years, this may be an idea difficult to accept. Indeed, the American consumer has been fighting tooth and nail to maintain his spending. The saving rate has fallen to about 3% of disposable income, the lowest level in 30 years, and installment debt as a percent of disposable income has risen to an unprecedented 18.4%. Moreover, in an environment where prices are rising, taking on more debt appears to be the rational thing to do. That explains the buy-in-advance psychology that has been evident since mid-1977. "It is still there," says F. Thomas Juster, director of the Institute for Social Research at the University of Michigan, "but it has been greatly diminished because, unlike 1977 and 1978, there have been no real income gains to support it. The desire may be there, but there's a constraint of shrinking real income."

The squeeze on real income, in Juster's view, will have a profound effect on consumer psychology and spending. "There's been a shift in long-run expectations that real incomes will rise and bail people out of some tough financial decisions," says he. "This could mean a move toward caution in family financial management." Sanford C. Sigoloff, recently appointed vice-chairman and chief operating officer at homebuilder Kaufman & Broad Inc., shares Juster's concern. "The postwar buying spree has slowed down, and I'm not so sure it will pick up once we're through the recession," says Sigoloff. "I expect consumers to recover from this recession with greater caution than ever before. Spending in the 1980s will be more conservative." Adds Alan Greenspan, president of Townsend-Greenspan and a former chairman of the Council of Economic Advisers: "The big surges in consumer markets are over." And Chase Econometric is forecasting a weak recovery from the expected 1980 recession precisely because of lackluster consumer spending. "Weakness in real income growth will translate into an anemic consumer sector," says Chase's Shaber.

Not only should total consumer spending be anemic, but the consumer will be shifting his dollars around. Ellen I. Metcalf, a senior consultant in the consumer section at Arthur D. Little Inc., expects to see more purchases of higher-quality products and a sharp cutback in the purchasing of lower-quality ones. "I see

> 'In this inflation, the people on the receiving end are the Arab sheiks'

a toning down in the volume of purchases from the last decade," she says. "We have realized for the first time that there is a limit to our standard of living growth rate." This, in turn, she maintains, is forcing consumers to get their money's worth from their discretionary income. For example, consumers are paying more attention these days to the total cost of an auto purchase, says Metcalf. "It's not just the purchase price that counts. It's the operating costs, trade-in value, and the opportunity costs—that is, the cost of forgoing other purchases."

Big-ticket purchases will be particularly hard hit in the new era of the income-constrained consumer. Greenspan notes that in the past, many consumers have been helped by taking realized capital gains on their homes and spending on such items as vans, campers, and big vacations. With these gains harder to come by now, and with real incomes being squeezed, outlays on such purchases should nosedive. Littmann of Detroit's Manufacturers National Bank also sees cutbacks in the buying of big-ticket durables and expensive vacations, and he views the outlook for Detroit as particularly grim. "The auto companies depend on 3% growth in real personal income to assure a good auto year," he says. "And Chrysler needs back-to-back good years to survive as a full-line car producer." Littmann believes that short of nationalization, Chrysler Corp.'s doom is sealed, even with massive government aid.

The shrinking standard of living will also affect the nation's No. 1 industry—homebuilding. "We've seen a gradually growing willingness among homebuyers to settle for less than the single-family house on a large lot surrounded by a picket fence," says Merrill Butler, president-elect of the National Association of Home Builders and president of Butler Housing Corp., a $75 million-a-year

The bleak outlook for living standards abroad

The sharp blows to the standard of living in Europe and Japan from ever-rising oil prices have been softened by such factors as a strong increase in labor productivity and generous social welfare programs and unemployment insurance. Then, too, crude-oil prices are quoted in dollars, and the sinking U.S. dollar relative to other currencies held down the real cost of oil.

But these supports of the standard of living abroad are fast being eroded. The outlook for the major allies of the U.S. therefore is bleak, and the struggle over income shares could be more heated than in the U.S.

Most economists expect the dollar to perform a lot better over the next few years than it has over the past few, and it could recover some lost ground. This means that the doubling of OPEC prices in 1979 will really start to hit the other industrial countries hard in 1980.

A sharp slowing. Productivity gains will be harder to come by, even in such countries as Germany, while economic growth there and in the major industrial nations will slow sharply. German productivity has benefited from strong investment growth. "German industry is used to having to make do with fewer workers and putting more into investment," says Norbert Walter of the Kiel Institute. Walter notes, however, that with a sharp rise in young, less experienced workers coming into the labor markets, a result of the baby boom of the 1960s, these investments will yield less in productivity growth in the future. This will put pressure on real wages.

The increase in social welfare programs abroad has sharply boosted government spending. In the European Community, such spending jumped from 41% of gross domestic product in 1973 to 47% in 1979. This brought sharp increases in taxes that hit the vocal middle class especially hard, making it likely that expected rises in unemployment will not be accompanied by greater welfare benefits.

But labor, too, is unhappy about government economic policy. In Germany, for example, unions accepted wage gains of around 4% last year, because they were promised that inflation would not exceed 3%. But with inflation running at 6%, real incomes are being squeezed and Germany had its first major steel strike in 51 years.

The tax bite. In France last year, prices rose 11%, while wages and salaries increased less than 10%. In addition, taxes, including huge jumps in social security taxes, are taking an increasing bite out of income. "Short of trying to earn more from the black economy [where there are no taxes] there is little consumers can do," says Otto von Fieandt, economic adviser to the Eurofinance Consulting Group.

Even in Britain, which is fast becoming self-sufficient in oil, living standards are shrinking. After showing solid increases in 1977 and 1978, real income growth is stagnating once again. Average earnings in 1979 increased by an estimated 16% but prices rose 17%. And the London-based National Institute of Economic & Social Research is forecasting a 1.6% decline in real personal disposable income between the fourth quarter of 1979 and the fourth quarter of 1980. According to some economists, the turn toward income stagnation in Britain is already giving rise to increased militancy. "The latest group to become militant," says one economist, "is the civil servants."

In usually fast-growing but oil-poor Japan, the rise in real income is headed for a sharp slowdown in 1980—an estimated 2% rate of gain, compared with 4.8% in 1979. Says Takayuki Hazumi, senior economist at Sumitomo Bank Ltd.: "The government doesn't publicize the dangers of the oil crisis on Japan's lifestyle, so people don't get too pessimistic or panicky. But as time passes and reality becomes clear, spending behavior may change."

Environmental Opportunities/Enterprise Threats / 87

homebuilder based in Irvine, Calif. For instance, there is the continually rising acceptance of townhouses, which run 15% to 25% less for comparable housing features. And Butler indicates that even before escalating interest rates, consumers were beginning to settle for less.

In retailing, the industry has already seen signs of a decline in discretionary spending by families with incomes of less than $25,000 a year. Such chains as Sears, Roebuck & Co. and Montgomery Ward & Co. have been especially affected—their sales, adjusted for inflation, declined in 1979. Walter Levy, a New York retailing consultant, predicts that the discounting of department-store-quality merchandise will accelerate in the future as shrinking income begins to dent the spending of higher-income households.

"What turns out to be bad news for consumer spending will ultimately turn out to be bad news for capital investment," says Okun of Brookings. A shift from consumption and toward more saving, he explains, might well be desirable to provide the wherewithal for capital investment. But that is only the case when total real income is rising, not when that shift is brought about simply from less growth in disposable income. "There's still one law in economics that holds true," says Okun. "Businessmen don't invest for a market that's not there."

Can tax policy help?

To be sure, tax policy can be employed to offset, in part, this adverse effect on investment. But at the very time that the nation needs investment to break the vicious cycle of economic stagnation, the squeeze on the standard of living could prevent the enactment of favorable tax breaks to spur investment. "The fight over income shares heats up when the pie stops growing, and that could mean that we don't get the necessary tax measures, such as cuts in capital gains taxes and bigger investment-tax credits," says Gary M. Wenglowski, chief economist for Goldman, Sachs & Co. "In the long run, they benefit the whole society, but in the short run the effects are to benefit the upper-income groups."

Rudolph G. Penner, director of tax studies at the American Enterprise Institute, notes that giving tax breaks to capital investment and increasing defense spending will mean that someone's taxes will have to go up, and "one way or another it will be the wage earner." This will be done, says he, "by letting the income tax drift up as inflation continues to push taxpayers into higher brackets. It's hard to believe that people will sit back and accept all this."

Indeed, the fight over income shares may well exacerbate inflation. As the University of Massachusetts' Rapping puts it: "OPEC grabs its piece of America and starts a roaring inflation. Then the doctors and dentists and the corporations and the strong unions start grabbing, and off prices go." As economic growth sags and the standard of living keeps falling, he maintains, the inflation rate could keep rising, because different groups will try desperately to hold on to their real income share.

However, it is virtually impossible for most groups to maintain their real income, and all they succeed in doing is raising their nominal income, which is more than offset by the increase in prices. Only those in powerful bargaining positions, such as the stronger unions, seem able to stay even with inflation, and now they, too, are beginning to fall behind. Generally, companies have fared not much better. Corporate profits in 1979, adjusted for inflation and inventory gains—even including bloated oil company profits—were only 6% higher than in 1973 and actually below the 1965 level. "Whether you argue that the oil cartel is all to blame or whether it's also that the earth's crust is yielding less oil, the effect is the same: The battle over income between the owners of capital and the workers intensifies," says Rapping.

And no one is sure how that battle will end. Although labor experts believe the declining standard of living will have a profound impact on labor-management relations, it is unclear whether unions will emerge stronger or weaker. In the short run, the first and most dramatic impact may well be a cut in contract gains as even major employers—such as the auto and steel industries—try to slash costs to maintain their profitability. Until 1979, such unions as the United Auto Workers, United Steelworkers, and International Brotherhood of Teamsters kept their members about even with inflation or even slightly ahead. But "members have got to understand that maybe it can't happen over the long haul—that they may not get real wage increases in perpetuity," says Douglas Fraser, president of the UAW.

This does not mean that the UAW will become any less militant; rather, it exemplifies a growing recognition in union circles that real income growth is slowing sharply. Indeed, collective bargaining will get tougher and more antagonistic, as labor and management fight over the declining shares. But whether this will cause major disruptions through more strikes will depend on the industry and union involved.

The growth of social conflict

The inability to bargain for real wage increases because the growth in the nation's real income is being squeezed will also cause unions to adopt other strategies. Arnold R. Weber, a labor expert who will become president of the University of Colorado on Feb. 1, believes that the politically conservative, pro-capitalistic U.S. labor movement is likely to move to the left toward "a commitment to a program to significantly modify capitalism." Unlike labor in Western Europe, American unions cannot capture a political party and spread a leftist ideology in U.S. politics. But the unions may be moving toward what is called democratization of capital in Europe.

Unions will gain a voice in decisions on plant closings, pension fund investment, and perhaps on capital spending. This will be accompanied, Weber believes, by the election of union officials to corporate boards, just as the UAW's Fraser will become a director of Chrysler. Unions will also try to strengthen themselves in traditional ways, primarily by stepping up organizing of predominantly nonunion white-collar and service workers. And they could be extremely successful if nonunion employers try to make their workers bear the brunt of lower economic growth. The Conference Board's labor economist, Audrey Freedman, says tighter management that is provoked by falling profits could spur white-collar workers to organize. This could trigger bitter confrontations between labor and nonunion employers.

The declining standard of living and the drying up of economic opportunities are responsible, at least in part, for the worsening of relations between such traditionally allied groups as blacks and Jews, and minorities and the labor movement, according to Robert Lekachman, of the City University of New York. "The way unions see it, with growth shrinking, affirmative action goes by the board," he says. The unions, however, say that to end seniority systems would create other disruptions.

The U. S. wage earner, union or nonunion, is being hit with a steeper and steeper tax bill for services to the poor, the elderly, and the unemployed. "We are really committed as a nation," says Brandeis' Carter, "to not allowing the very poor to take the entire brunt [of the declining standard of living]." Thus, workers must continue to support the nonworking population at sharply higher prices. And because of demographic changes, the number of retirees per worker will be rising sharply, reaching one for every two workers by the turn of the century, up from the current one for every three. At some point this ratio generates a strong domestic backlash, as in the case of California's Proposition 13.

"It's part of a 'that's as far as we're going to go' attitude," says Carter.

'Not much to give'

Indeed, the shrinking economic pie is bound to drive all vested interests—the consumer, the government, the military—into wider conflict, asserts Gary Fromm, director of economic research at SRI International. And it will make it a lot harder to enact social reforms, such as national health insurance and a federalized welfare system, especially because the Soviet threat has heated up and defense spending will take priority. Says Fromm: "People are trying to preserve their real assets and income by putting a lid on all kinds of government services—not just welfare." And the AEI's Penner notes that in prior years the U. S. had financed nondefense spending with cuts in real outlays for defense, but "that source of funds is no longer available."

When the nation's economic pie was growing faster, it was easy to give up some helpings for defense, foreign aid, welfare, and care of the elderly. The great squeeze on income will mean wider conflict. In the past era of faster growth, says Lekachman, the nation handled conflict by giving a little bit to each contender. "Even the losers got consolation prizes," he says. "Now there's not much to give." ∎

MONEY & BANKING

SOUTHEAST BANKS: Set For a Slump

Although banks throughout the nation took a pounding during the recession of 1974, no group was harder hit than the major regionals in the Southeast. Indeed, a reckless real estate lending binge caused such go-go banks as North Carolina National, Atlanta's Citizens & Southern, and Florida's Flagship Banks to write off millions of dollars when the economy softened and developers went bankrupt in droves.

Despite the debacle, Southeastern bankers today seem almost eager for the next recession, which most economists agree is now beginning. According to Thomas I. Storrs, chairman of NCNB Corp., the last recession was "our education." He adds: "It is not much of an exaggeration to say we have been preparing for another for the past five years."

Turnaround. None has prepared more than C&S, which took a severe beating, primarily on sour real estate loans that were piled on before Atlanta's overheated economy collapsed in 1974. Hoping for a quick recovery, the bank did not complete its write-down until 1977, when C&S posted a $7.8 million loss. The loss forced C&S to do something that all corporations strive to avoid—eliminate its dividend.

The turnaround began in February, 1978, when Bennett A. Brown, who had been assistant president, took over as chief executive. Since then, says Brown, "our loans have been flat. Our growth in the past two years has been in core deposits. We are running a conservative company."

Indeed, loans have held steady at $1.9 billion, while core deposits have surged by 14% to $2.5 billion. At the same time, nonperforming assets—loans that either have been foreclosed, are earning no interest, or for which the interest rate has been reduced— have been chopped almost in half, to $113 million from $207 million.

Most important is the recovery in earnings that enabled the bank to restore its dividend in October, 1979. Earnings were boosted largely because C&S's new conservatism has allowed the bank to cut its loan-loss provision dramatically.

In short, C&S has done nothing less than a complete about-face in its banking philosophy. What is remarkable is that virtually all major banks in the region—acting independently—have done the same thing.

By far, the most important step was to shrink balance sheets faster than other banks. This was done by unloading bad assets, or loans that had gone sour. The banks also sold marginally profitable assets and eliminated high-risk loans to companies outside the South. Moreover, Southeastern banks also implemented stringent credit policies that have curtailed asset growth.

Most of the region's banks have also increased liquidity substantially. They have done so through massive marketing campaigns for low-cost consumer deposits, such as passbook savings accounts, as well as higher-cost savings certificates that have locked up floating rate money from six months to eight years.

In the go-go days of the 1970s, by contrast, those banks gleefully lent millions, particularly in risky real estate deals, with few internal credit controls. Growth at any cost was the policy as loan officers had faith that inflated asset values would paper over mistakes.

Rebound. In 1973, by contrast, NCNB, which had long been a Wall Street favorite because of its emulation of aggressive money center banks, made the mistake of forecasting that interest rates would fall. Consequently, it loaded up on fixed-rate loans in the belief that they would soon be financed by cheap money market funds. Instead, interest rates soared, and NCNB had to fund these loans with money that cost more to buy than the loans yielded. Another problem for NCNB was a portfolio that was stuffed with sour real estate credits.

Overall, earnings plummeted 35% to $17.6 million, and return on assets fell 39% to 0.56%. NCNB did not fully recover until 1978, when earnings hit a record $35.6 million and return on assets rose to a comfortable 0.73%. That strong rebound has continued this year as NCNB posted earnings of $44.5 million, while return on assets rose to about 0.82%.

NCNB Chairman Storrs adds that he has his balance sheet under firm control. Moreover, Storrs is confident that NCNB's forecasting ability is far better than it was five years ago. But as a hedge, he says "we don't put too many chips on it. Even if our forecast [on interest rates a year ago] had been completely wrong, I don't think we would have been damaged materially."

The 1974 recession hit the area so hard that even banks that performed relatively well, such as Southeast Banking Corp. of Miami, continued to struggle until recently. Indeed, earnings did not rebound past 1977's record until 1978. And despite a booming real estate market, Southeast's construction lending over the past five years has decreased from 9% of loans to just 5%. "We have basically gotten out of the construction business," says Thomas B. Walker, Southeast vice-president and treasurer.

Worrisome consumer debt. Southeast's neighbor, Flagship Banks Inc., was one of the most badly burned by its excessive real estate lending, and overall the bank lost $14.7 million in 1975 and 1976. Flagship now makes almost no loans for multiunit projects or for land development, which in 1975 accounted for the bulk of nonperforming assets of $63.9 million, or 7.9% of its loan portfolio. "Most of those loans should not have been made," concedes Flagship Chairman Philip F. Searle, a strong executive who took over in 1975.

Both Searle and Walker contend that their institutions will suffer much less during the new recession, both because of caution in real estate lending and the fact that Florida's economy is more diversified than it was five years ago. And bank analyst Richard A. Leech of Keefe, Bruyette & Woods agrees: "They know what their vulnerability can be, and they have positioned themselves accordingly."

Even so, problems remain—in the Southeast and elsewhere. At the moment, the big worry involves consumer debt, which is at an all-time high. Indeed, some observers fear that consumer debt will do to banks precisely what construction lending did in 1974-75. But even here Southeastern banks may be comparatively well off. Says John P. Dulin, president of First Tennessee National Corp. in Memphis: "We're going to see some softness. But our delinquencies and our losses in the [consumer] portfolio are at an all-time low, and we really have strengthened it going into this recession."

Dulin is confident that there will not be a repeat of 1974-75. "At that time, there was a lot of talk that no matter what you did inflation would bail you out," he says. "One of the lessons we've learned in this period of high inflation is that this will not happen."

One exception. Inflation certainly did not bail out National Bank of Georgia, which was headed by Bert Lance in 1975-76 and then plunged $2.2 million into the red in 1977, after Lance left to become U. S. Budget Director. Lance had begun an aggressive expansion program at a time when most Southern banks were trying to curb asset growth.

Although Lance's successor, Robert P. Guyton, reversed NBG's fortunes—the bank earned $1.3 million in 1978—he was ousted last December. NBG's 70%-owner, Saudi Arabian businessman Ghaith R. Pharaon, reportedly felt the bank had recovered sufficiently to resume its aggressive growth.

But National Bank of Georgia is an exception. Most major Southeastern banks today want to pattern themselves after North Carolina's Wachovia Corp., which managed to avoid the excesses of its counterparts five years ago. Wachovia was heavily criticized in the early 1970s for being too stodgy. But it came through the recession relatively unscathed largely because of the conservative philosophy of John F. Watlington, its longtime president.

Watlington, since retired, explained that he was old enough to remember the devastation done to real estate lenders during the Depression. Says Buck Jones, a bank analyst with J. C. Bradford & Co. in Nashville: "Wachovia is the banking organization which others in the Southeast emulate." ∎

ANTIBUSINESS FORCES AIM AT CORPORATIONS

"It's a challenge they won't be able to turn down," says Ralph Nader in referring to a letter some 500 chief executive officers will receive shortly inviting them to take part in a series of teach-ins on the role of the corporation in America, to be held in Washington and about 100 other cities on Apr. 17. Building on the concept of the 1970 Earth Day demonstrations, a coalition of labor, consumer, environmental, and religious groups has chosen that date to stage Big Business Day to help dramatize what consumer advocate Nader calls the "corporate crime epidemic that is sweeping America" and to kick off a decade-long campaign aimed at curbing "corporate abuse."

The coalition, calling itself Americans Concerned About Corporate Power, has only just begun soliciting contributions and lining up individuals and groups sympathetic to its cause. But a number of large corporations have already bought, at $10 each, copies of the coalition's proposed Corporate Democracy Act of 1980, centerpiece of the campaign. General Motors Corp., for example, ordered 13 copies.

Provisions. A draft bill has not yet been introduced in Congress, but Nader and other coalition leaders are working on several potential sponsors. Among other things, the draft's provisions would: enhance corporate accountability by requiring boards to be made up of a majority of independent directors and to have some of the directors responsible for such things as employee well-being and consumer relations; require 24-month notification of plant relocations and closedowns; prohibit discrimination against employees for "whistle-blowing"; prohibit anyone from simultaneously serving as a director of more than two companies; and provide stiff penalties for violations of environmental and other laws, restitution to victims of chemical spills and the like, and disqualification of convicted executives. The coalition likens the bill to the 1959 Landrum-Griffin Act.

Legislative support. According to Michael Schippani, national coordinator of Big Business Day, the proposed bill has tentative support from Senator Howard M. Metzenbaum (D-Ohio), chairman of the antitrust and monopoly subcommittee; Representative Benjamin S. Rosenthal (D-N.Y.), chairman of the subcommittee on commerce, consumer and monetary affairs; and Representative Frank Thompson Jr. (D-N.J.), chairman of the labor-management relations subcommittee. Schippani was one of the coordinators of the Amalgamated Clothing Workers' battle over unionizing J. P. Stevens & Co.

Besides Nader, the coalition's sponsors and advisers include such people as John Kenneth Galbraith, United Auto Workers President Douglas A. Fraser, Julian Bond, Cesar Chavez, Barry Commoner, former Federal Trade Commissioner Mary Gardiner Jones, and Arthur Schlesinger Jr. "This is not a fringe group," says Nader, adding: "The support is America."

A U.N. SPACE TREATY THAT COULD ZAP INDUSTRY

It still sounds like science fiction, but a "moon treaty" that would grant all nations equal rights to resources and products developed from space exploration is ready for signing. In fact, the exploitation of space seemed so far off that U.S. industry ignored the treaty during a decade of negotiations at the U.N.

But now companies interested in exploiting the earth's oceans are voicing last-minute opposition. They want the Administration to withdraw its support of the agreement because it would set a precedent that would jeopardize their plans to tap oil and gas reserves beyond the continental shelf and to mine the ocean floor.

Officially called "The Agreement Governing the Activities of States on the Moon and Other Celestial Bodies," the moon treaty would declare the fruits of space exploitation as "the common heritage of mankind." That same principle has long stymied the Law of the Sea Conference, which reconvened late in February in New York.

'**Patchwork response.**' Pushing the "common heritage" theme in the space treaty could weaken the U.S. negotiating position on the law of the sea, according to some State Dept. officials, as well as officials of the ocean-mining companies. "This is an end run around us," declares Northcutt Ely, an attorney for Ocean Mining Associates, a consortium of U.S. Steel, Sun Co. Inc., and Belgium's Union Minière. "It is a vital concern if that moon treaty is endorsed," Ely says, "because it becomes a precedent."

Ironically, both the State Dept. and the National Aeronautics & Space Administration have backed the space agreement since it was first proposed in 1970. The treaty calls for an indefinite moratorium on commercial development

Nations with the expertise to exploit space would have to share their technology

in space so that an international organization could be set up to control it. That would require those nations with the ability to exploit space to share their technology and its benefits with other countries. "The treaty is an ad hoc, patchwork response reflecting the lack of national policy of the Carter, Ford, Nixon, and Johnson Administrations," declares George S. Robinson, a former NASA attorney specializing in space law.

The treaty's most visible foe is Leigh S. Ratiner, a Washington lawyer who formerly represented companies interested in mining manganese nodules from the ocean floor. Ratiner now represents the L-5 Society, an organization of 4,000 scientists and futurists advocating space development.

Support from the aerospace industry was slow in coming. United Technologies Corp. in February became the first company to denounce the treaty when it inserted advertisements in *The Washington Post* and several New England newspapers. Under the headline, "Stranglehold on the Moon," the company called for an effort to "head off this Third World drive to frustrate America's hard-won technological supremacy."

'**A snowball's chance.**' Last fall, Senator Frank Church (D-Idaho), chairman of the Foreign Relations Committee, and Senator Jacob Javits (R-N.Y.) urged Secretary of State Cyrus Vance to reconsider the U.S. position. But it took the current flurry of opposition to persuade Vance to advise the U.S. Mission to the U.N. to hold off endorsing the treaty. Vance also requested an interagency review that should reach President Carter by the end of May. And the Senate Committee on Commerce, Science & Transportation has requested four studies of the treaty.

For the treaty to be binding on the U.S., President Carter will have to sign it and the Senate will have to ratify it. While it may be difficult for President Carter to reject 10 years of support by the U.S. for the agreement, one Senate staffer says it "hasn't a snowball's chance in hell of passing the Senate." Since it only takes the approval of five nations for the treaty to be adopted, and Chile and France have already signed, the U.S. will have to ignore the treaty if it wants to support commercial exploitation of space. ■

U.S. autos
LOSING A BIG SEGMENT OF THE MARKET—FOREVER?

Through the first 10 days of March this year, automobile sales have been surprisingly strong, but only because imports are racking up record sales. Few car buyers want Detroit's big models—the kind Detroit still predominantly makes—and despite rebates of $500 or more, sales of U.S.-made cars are slipping badly. Through the first days of March they were running at an abysmal annual rate of 7.7 million units, down 14% from a year ago. And in February, imports grabbed a record 27% share of the market.

Incredible as it now seems, just a year ago the U.S. auto industry was scrambling to meet a surging demand for big cars. While imported-car dealers were drowning in record inventories of unsold small cars, General Motors Corp. was toying with the idea of converting a compact-car plant to build full-size Oldsmobiles. Chrysler Corp. worried that the botched introduction of its slimmed-down New Yorker would leave it behind in the new big-car battle. Ford Motor Co. rationed V-8 engines because it could barely keep ahead of demand. How, Detroit executives fretted, would they sell the millions of smaller cars on which they had spent billions in new tooling? Recalls Ford President Philip Caldwell: "We all faced the specter of forcing the American people to buy something they hadn't indicated they wanted to buy in large quantities."

That fear has disappeared, of course. Now, a much more ominous specter is haunting Detroit. The sudden death of big cars—on which the industry earned the bulk of its profits—will seriously hamper its ability to finance the shift to small cars, a change that must now come much faster than Detroit had planned. And if it is unable to supply enough of the small cars Americans want today, the U.S. industry could permanently and perhaps disastrously lose a huge share of its home market to overseas producers. No one is seriously suggesting that Detroit will go the way of U.S. radio manufacturers—yet—but for the next several years, the U.S. automobile industry will be virtually impotent in the face of an onslaught of foreign cars. "We've accelerated our programs [for small cars] down the road," says GM President Elliott M. Estes, "but we can't do anything about the short term."

Estes is not exaggerating. It will take U.S. auto makers until 1985, at least, just to expand their four-cylinder-engine capacity to 40% of output (chart, page 81). Nearly all imports are now powered by fours. With waiting lists for small cars running as long as six months, imports, which captured a record 22% share of the U.S. car market last year, now seem almost certain to coast to an easy 30% share in 1980.

More than humiliation

To be sure, Detroit will be rolling out a new crop of small cars this fall. But they will be too few to turn around the situation rapidly. Detroit, once again, is simply out of step with the market. "We thought—rightly or wrongly—that we had to move down in an evolutionary way to better fuel economy," says Estes.

The revolution in Iran and the subsequent spiral in gasoline prices made that choice utterly wrong. While future gasoline price increases may moderate, U.S. auto makers cannot hope for the flattening of prices that gave them breathing room in the years following the Arab oil embargo. Even the most optimistic sce-

94 / Readings from *Business Week*

Illustration by Gary Viskupic

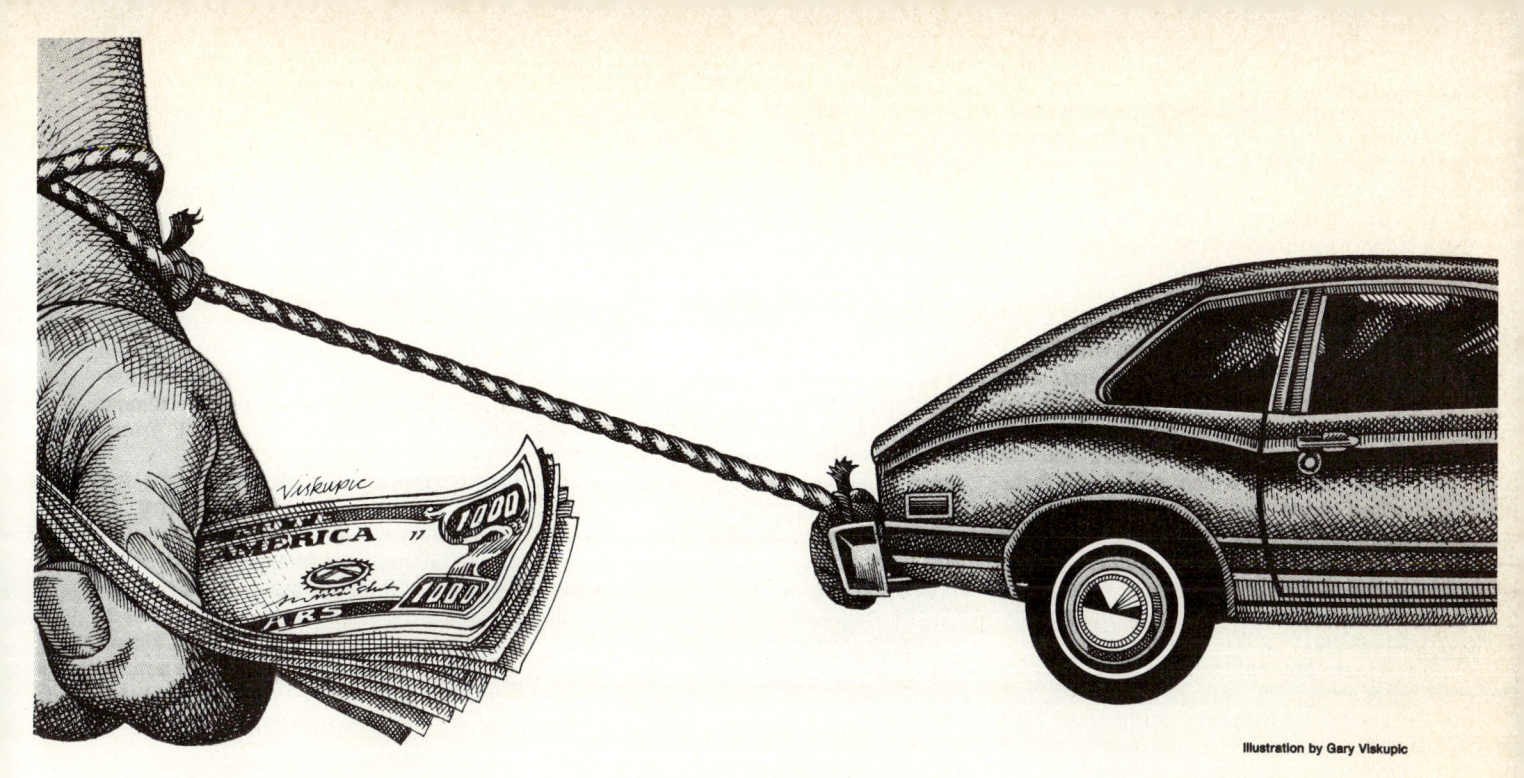

narios project that gasoline will rise from $1.25 per gal. today to more than $2 per gal. by the end of 1982. That in itself practically guarantees that the import share will remain at least at 30% through 1985 unless foreign exchange rates change radically.

For an industry that has always prided itself most on its marketing skills, nothing could be more humiliating than the prospect that it may have to cede nearly a third of its home market. But much more than Detroit's wounded pride is at stake. Indeed, what may be at stake is Detroit itself—at least in its present form. Already, there is ample cause for alarm:

- Since the beginning of the year, 210,000 workers have been idled, many indefinitely, and six plants have been closed as Detroit begins to board up big-car assembly and parts facilities.
- The big-car sales slump has vastly increased the chances of a Chrysler bankruptcy, has seriously weakened Ford, which lost $1 billion last year on its North American operations, and has reduced GM's earnings 18%, all at a time when Detroit must make huge new investments to improve its product.
- The poor earnings outlook will probably force auto makers to slash dividends even as they must seek record amounts of outside financing in markets that are in terrible turmoil.

Detroit's malaise will probably lead to increased manufacturing in the U. S. by foreign-owned automobile makers. Some will make the move because U. S. manufacture is cheaper. Others, particularly the Japanese, are likely to manufacture here only if there is a possibility of import restrictions being placed on their cars.

In February, Volkswagen announced that it would open a plant in Michigan, its second in the U. S. By 1984, vw will be cranking out 200,000 Rabbits a year at its new plant, in addition to some 225,000 at its Westmoreland (Pa.) plant. Renault, a leading importer in the late 1950s, plans to make another large-scale assault on the U. S. market by having 100,000 cars a year made by American Motors Corp. at its Kenosha (Wis.) plant.

The Japanese, with lower labor costs and spare capacity at home, are reluctant to start U. S. production. But they, too, are moving to manufacture in the U. S. Honda will produce up to 10% of its cars in a new facility alongside its motorcycle plant in Marysville, Ohio. Toyota and Nissan both say that they are exploring the possibility of some U. S. manufacture. Their decision will probably be determined by how much anti-import pressure can be generated by the United Auto Workers (page 88).

A devastated profit structure

An increase in foreign-car manufacture in the U. S. would further cut Detroit's market share, although the cars would be counted as U. S.-made. But the predicament of the Big Three goes much deeper than lost market share. The collapse of big-car sales has devastated the industry's profit structure. Industry observers estimate that GM, for example, makes as much as $1,000 on a large car and only $200 to $300 on a small car. In the last year the market share of big cars—so-called full-size and intermediate models—has plummeted from 42% to 33%. Unless there is a miraculous recovery of large-car sales, Detroit's profits will be wretched, to say the least. For example, even though GM is selling a record 63% share of U. S.-built cars this year, it is expected to earn only $6.25 a share, half of 1978 earnings. Between them, Ford and Chrysler will probably lose $2 billion in the U. S. Sums up one industry analyst: "Detroit's dilemma is that it must sell cars that no one wants to get the cash to make the cars that people will buy."

To make that task even rougher, the outlook for car sales generally—big cars or small—is becoming increasingly gloomy. Rising fuel prices may push some buyers into small cars, but others, recognizing that they can rarely recover the cost of a new car in fuel savings, may simply not buy for as long as possible. Other consumers, aware that Detroit must make more fuel-efficient cars in the next few years, may also hold on to their cars. Such balking by consumers was responsible for the 1974-76 slump in auto sales. It could easily occur again. "We're tremendously overautomobiled in the U. S.," says a Ford executive. "We'd be able to drive for years without buying another car."

No such apocalypse is yet at hand, but the economic factors confronting Detroit are enough to make even the brashest auto salesman fidget nervously. The most serious is the runaway economy itself. The choices for next year, most economists believe, are continued outlandish interest rates and inflation—or recession. Whichever occurs, Detroit will not benefit. Interest rates, as high as 18% on auto loans, are scaring away all but the most determined buyers. And they are badly pinching dealers, who cannot afford to pay 18% to 20% to finance an adequate level of inventories.

Prospective car buyers also face declining real income because of the high inflation rate. Even worse from Detroit's standpoint, disposable household income, one of the best indicators of future car purchases, is falling after rising for four years.

About the only bright spot in this gloomy picture is the series of new small cars that Detroit will introduce next fall. Chrysler is hoping it can sell as many as 600,000 of its new front-wheel-drive compact, code-named the K-car. Ford will replace the hoary Pinto and the Lincoln-Mercury Div.'s version of the car, the Bobcat, with the Escort and the Lynx, both of which will have front-wheel drive. GM, which introduced its first U.S.-made front-wheel-drive car last year, is planning another, the so-called J-car. It will give Chevrolet and Pontiac each a subcompact to go with the hot-selling Citation and Phoenix compacts.

These cars could help Detroit out of its sales slump. But because of the long lead times in the industry—all of these cars were designed in 1976—there is no possibility that it can shrink its big cars until at least 1983. Detroit made the error of relying too long on its time-tested formula of wringing out the bulk of its profits on large cars. As recently as nine months ago, the auto makers were pleading with the government to relax the standards that require every auto maker's fleet to average 27.5 mpg by 1985. Now the demands of the market have outstripped the regulators, and suddenly there is no end in sight to the quest for better fuel economy. Analysts say the market will want the mandated average of 27.5 mpg as early as 1982, and will want 40 mpg by 1990.

There is no way that Detroit can move up to 27.5 mpg by 1982, and even meeting the mandated 1985 goal will still require a desperate effort. The first forced change—after the Arab oil embargo—resulted in a weight reduction of 800 lb. in large cars. That helped to boost the fuel economy of domestic cars by 6 mpg to the present 20 mpg. The slim-down, minimal as it was, cost the industry $30 billion. Now the auto makers must spend at least as much again within four years. Merely reducing the weight of a traditionally designed big car will not work. To preserve maximum passenger room at the same time, auto makers must scrap their front engine-rear drive designs and switch almost entirely to the more efficient front-wheel-drive configurations.

The imperatives of economy

The costs will be astronomical. Auto "facelifts" that cost $500 million are giving way to $3 billion-a-model overhauls. The industry must spend $75 billion on new plants and products to reach a mileage goal that imports nearly match today (chart, below). And pushing to 40 mpg by 1990 would double the cost,

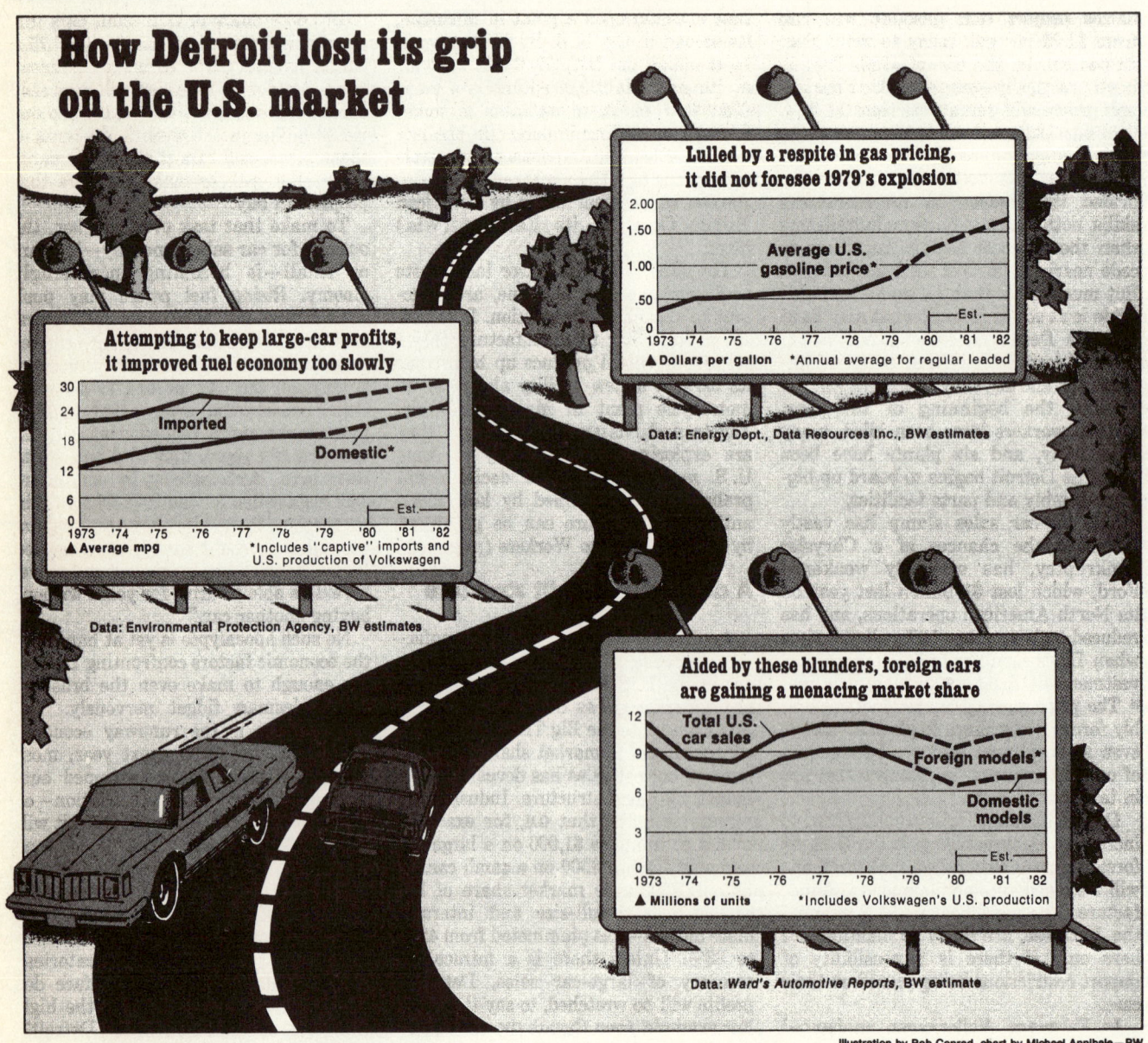

How Detroit lost its grip on the U.S. market

Attempting to keep large-car profits, it improved fuel economy too slowly
▲ Average mpg *Includes "captive" imports and U.S. production of Volkswagen
Data: Environmental Protection Agency, BW estimates

Lulled by a respite in gas pricing, it did not foresee 1979's explosion
Average U.S. gasoline price*
▲ Dollars per gallon *Annual average for regular leaded
Data: Energy Dept., Data Resources Inc., BW estimates

Aided by these blunders, foreign cars are gaining a menacing market share
Total U.S. car sales
Foreign models*
Domestic models
▲ Millions of units *Includes Volkswagen's U.S. production
Data: Ward's Automotive Reports, BW estimate

Illustration by Bob Conrad, chart by Michael Annibale—BW

96 / Readings from *Business Week*

according to a study by Rath & Strong Inc., a Lexington (Mass.) capital-goods consulting firm.

Wall Street analysts calculate that the cash crunch will force Detroit to borrow at least $5 billion by 1985, doubling the industry's long-term debt. And during the latter half of the decade the auto makers may have to borrow another $5 billion or more. But until auto sales reverse their current decline, lenders may be tough to find. "There will be a need for tremendous outside capital," warns auto analyst Maryann Keller of Paine Webber Mitchell Hutchins Inc., "and I don't think it will be available."

Officially, auto executives downplay the problems of financing what is sure to amount to a $150 billion capital spending program over perhaps 15 years, even though that figure amounts to nearly two years' domestic sales for GM and Ford combined. Detroit hopes that sales will rebound by the end of 1980, returning profit margins from their current level of near-zero or worse to a more traditional 6% to 7%. But even such profits, coupled with non-cash allowances for depreciation and tool amortization, will not be enough (chart, page 84). Concedes Ford's Caldwell: "We'll probably have to go to the money markets to get through this gap."

But getting loans may be difficult, particularly if Detroit's profit margins continue to suffer. Some analysts speculate that the federal government could find itself bailing out the industry, much as it has propped up Chrysler with $1.5 billion in proffered loan guarantees. As part of the Chrysler loan legislation, Transportation Secretary Neil E. Goldschmidt was ordered to undertake a wide-ranging review of the capabilities of the nation's most basic industries—including autos—to finance their own rejuvenation. "I wouldn't say auto companies are necessarily headed down the road to direct federal assistance," insists Charles Swinburn, Transportation's Acting Assistant Secretary for policy, "but [survival] will require a combination of private financing, selling more cars, and plowing back every penny."

Billions needed now

The automotive borrowing binge begins this year with a bang, despite a prime interest rate of 17% and more. Chrysler, which reported a $1.1 billion loss on $12 billion in sales last year, will need $2 billion in 1980 from various sources—including those covered by government loan guarantees—to pay for its new-car programs and to cover another $500 million to $600 million loss for the year. Analysts say Ford will need roughly $1 billion to recoup the decline in working capital suffered in last year's billion-dollar loss on North American operations. In addition, Ford must seek outside financing for part of the $3.5 billion in capital spending in 1980 needed to revamp its cars and trucks.

Even GM may be a heavy borrower in 1980, for the first time in five years. That is partly because of the company's decision last August to accelerate its conversion to front-wheel-drive cars by about two years, from 1985 to 1983. As a result, GM's predicted outlays of about $6 billion per year worldwide have now risen to about $7 billion annually. "GM can live off its balance sheet for a while,"

Detroit's increasing use of small auto engines

[Chart showing percentages of 4-Cylinder, 6-Cylinder, and 8-Cylinder engines in 1975, 1980, 1985 Est., and 1990 Est.]

Data: Ward's Automotive Reports, Rath & Strong Inc.

says auto analyst David Healy of Drexel Burnham Lambert Inc. "But if they keep their dividend of $4.60 a share, their working capital will decline about $2 billion this year."

Ironically, in many cases, Detroit will be borrowing money to finish production lines for components that are already obsolete. The three-year lead time on tooling orders means that the auto companies are still locked into spending plans for engine, transmission, and other parts that were ordered in the late 1970s to preserve full-size cars. But interest in full-size autos is dead. Their share of total U.S. sales has fallen from 30% in 1977 to only 14% today.

That spells trouble for some major facilities. It will have a severe impact on Detroit's 11 V-8 engine lines that three years ago were running full-tilt to equip 76% of U.S. cars sold. It could mean premature write-offs for the V-8 diesel capacity that GM has built up in the past two years for its large cars, because front-wheel drive versions due in 1983 and 1984 will require smaller powerplants. And it promises disaster for Ford's one-year-old, $313 million lockup automatic transmission, built in Livonia, Mich., which was designed solely to extend the market life of Ford V-8 engines. That line will probably have to be shut down and written off within several years.

LeRoy H. Lindgren, a vice-president with Rath & Strong, estimates that the Big Three must write off undepreciated capital goods totaling at least $8 billion between now and 1990 because of the premature obsolescence of its big-car plants. "Basically," he says, "anything spent on rear-wheel drive in the past two years is a write-off."

There could be a bright side to these capital investments: improved productivity. Auto industry managers are hoping that the steps required to revamp their product lines will also let them beat the now-lower production costs of foreign rivals by incorporating the latest technology, set in new or completely remodeled factories. "In the next three years," declares Robert C. Stempel, general manager of GM's Pontiac Motor Div., "we're going back to a 3% gain in productivity per year."

Production planning

Smaller cars and more automation invariably mean higher assembly-line speeds as older plants are converted or new ones built. GM, for example, plans to build two brand-new assembly plants that together will be able to produce 150 cars per hour with no more manpower than it took to build 115 per hour at the 60-year-old plants they will replace at St. Louis and Pontiac, Mich. Ford's venerable Dearborn (Mich.) engine plant—converted at a cost of $650 million—will turn out 250 four-cylinder engines per hour compared to 200 per hour at the best of its V-8 engine plants.

To squeeze out better fuel efficiency, cars of the future will be more complex. But the productivity penalties from more sophisticated assembly work are being offset by a sharp reduction in the variety of model sizes, engines, and other mechanical options. Those parts of the car not outwardly visible will become increasingly standardized and interchangeable. Product differentiation—the cornerstone of Detroit's marketing philosophy—will be preserved through a wider array of highly visible buyer options, such as interior finishes. The goal of the production planners is to build a wider variety of cars on each assembly line without creating a parts-flow nightmare. GM, moreover, is designing plants that could shift quickly from one car size to another to gain higher utilization rates than in the past and to respond to the increasingly volatile swings in consumer preferences. Three-shift operations will become the norm at capital-intensive engine and transmission plants. And analysts predict that a larger share of the Big Three's parts needs will be farmed out to suppliers, rather than made in-house.

The reason is that the cost of capacity has soared (chart, below). The longtime GM policy of building enough plants to meet peak demand without requiring heavy overtime may no longer be affordable. "After being burned twice [in 1974-75 and again in 1979-80]," says Robert J. Orsini, automotive consultant with A. T. Kearny & Co., "they won't let it happen again."

Eventually as many as 7 of the 46 car and truck assembly plants operated by the Big Three last year may simply be closed rather than converted or replaced. The first signs of this came in February with the permanent closings of Chrysler's huge Hamtramck (Mich.) assembly plant and Ford's suburban Los Angeles assembly plant. Higher efficiency at the remaining plants, converted to build smaller cars, could probably handle current levels of demand plus modest growth. "Over the next three years there undoubtedly will be extra capacity," acknowledges James K. Bakken, Ford's vice-president of operations support staffs.

That could be an understatement. For there is no guarantee that Detroit will win back a substantial portion of the market it has lost. Many Detroit executives fear that the industry will simply not be able to make small cars whose quality, price, and performance will prevent further erosion of U. S. market share. It is a concern rarely voiced in Detroit. But Lee A. Iacocca, Chrysler's outspoken chairman, concedes that imports' reputation for superior quality, at least, is not undeserved. "They earned it," he says. "In fits and finishes, they've done better."

What does the market want?

And car buyers' perceptions go a lot further than that. When the Motor & Equipment Manufacturers Assn. canvassed 10,000 American households in 1978 and 1979, it found that imports strongly outranked U. S. small cars in perceived fuel economy, engineering, and even durability. "It's a deep-seated conviction," says James A. Lang, the association's director of marketing and research, "and it's going to be very, very difficult for Detroit to dislodge that feeling just by making its cars smaller."

In fact, every time that Detroit has brought out a so-called import fighter, such as the Chevrolet Vega, it has failed. Part of the reason is that while foreign car manufacturers were forced to engineer cars for very high fuel prices, U. S. manufacturers were pursuing their "bigger is better" style of marketing, happily loading up their cars with profitable but gas-guzzling features, such as automatic transmissions, power brakes, and power steering. The average fuel economy of U. S.-built cars declined from 15.4 mpg in 1936 to only 13.5 mpg in 1972.

But when it comes to small-car technology, Detroit has lagged. For years it resisted front-wheel drive. Chevrolet's rear-wheel-drive Chevette, for example, which was introduced in the U. S. in 1975, was a design unchanged from the same car produced elsewhere in the world by GM for three years before that. Chrysler's popular four-door Omni and Horizon subcompacts—both front-wheel-drive—are virtual copies of Volkswagen's five-year-old Rabbit.

Detroit's inability or unwillingness to develop small-car technology could very well mean that once buyers turn to foreign cars, wooing them back to U. S. makes is very difficult. GM's X-car—the Chevrolet's Citation is one—has been wildly successful: 390,000 Citations were sold in the first year. But the Citation has flopped as an import fighter. GM concedes that the car is appealing largely to former big-car buyers. Very few foreign-car owners have switched. No one in Detroit knows what these new small-car buyers want. "We are dealing, or about to deal, with a generation that is inherently anti-big," says Bennett E. Bidwell, vice-president of Ford and head of its Car & Truck Group. "We still don't know what compromise in vehicle size this younger generation will accept."

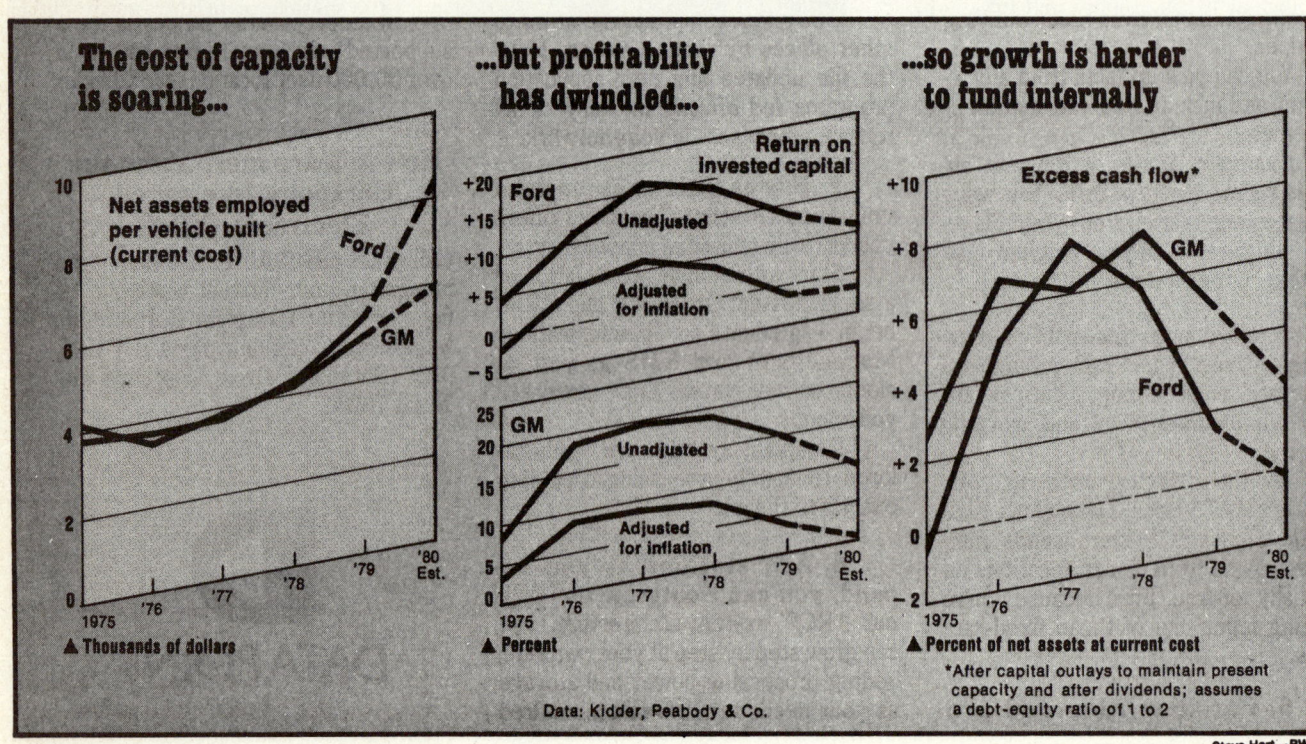

That means that Detroit's investments have suddenly grown riskier. The industry is dealing with a market that it does not understand. At this point, it feels it cannot simply abandon its full-size and intermediate cars. But it could spend billions to improve them only to find buyers turning up their noses.

This heightened risk has not been lost on the government. The Transportation Dept., for example, has delayed proposing fuel economy standards for cars built after 1985. Says Transportation Secretary Goldschmidt: "We will not make a move until we have a lot better feel for the difficulties and problems of the industry." The hitch, says Goldschmidt, is that in the past it could make huge investments—in engines, for example—and expect to get a return on that capital for as long as 20 years. Now, he says, "they are confronted with the prospect that today's entire retooling effort might have to be done again in some significant fashion after 1985."

Whether the market or the government demands it, that would be a horrifying prospect for Detroit. But if the industry must lay out $75 billion in new investment between now and 1985 only to be forced to do it again, it will have only itself to blame. It shortsightedly tried to prop up the big car, a dinosaur that relied on cheap energy. Cheap energy is now gone for good, and with it the big car. "After the oil embargo in 1974, we went back to big cars as if nothing had happened," admits a chastened Caldwell. "I think the elasticity is out of the rubber band now. A permanent set has taken place." ∎

LUXURY CAR SALES SKID TO NEW LOWS

If the decision of General Motors Corp.'s board to cut the auto giant's second-quarter dividend to 60¢ from $1.15 were not enough to destroy any lingering hopes for a spring recovery in the auto market, plummeting April sales finished the job. In a decline spread across the board, April sales were 31% below a year ago. Small cars as well as big ones were hit; imported car sales also were off more than 9% but retained their record 27% market share. Even if interest rates continue to fall (page 31), the gloom of recession is likely to keep car sales in low gear throughout the summer. Thus, Detroit's carmakers are making sharp production cuts to cope with a slump now seen as deeper and longer than the 1974-75 automotive downturn.

The impact of the disaster is sharpest in the luxury market, in which auto makers are said to make six times the $700 to $800 profit per car (before fixed costs) that they make on a subcompact. This premium-priced realm, where cars cost $12,000 and up, has traditionally been immune to economic cycles, high interest rates, and gasoline prices. But April deliveries of such prestigious U. S. nameplates as Cadillac's Eldorado and Lincoln's Mark VI fell a startling 53% below deliveries last year.

For the first time since the 1940s, General Motors Corp. has dropped the second shift at its main Cadillac plant in Detroit. Ford Motor Co. has made similar production cuts on Lincoln models, and there is growing fear that this market segment is in for basic change. Says a suburban Detroit Cadillac dealer: "Cadillac knows they'll never again sell as many cars as the 351,000 in 1978."

Even well-heeled buyers are feeling the pinch of luxury car prices, which in the case of Cadillac's restyled, $21,000 Seville are up 26% from a year ago. In past years, the trade-in value on a year-old "Caddy" or "Mark" covered most of the cost of a new model. But in recent months that "cost of trade" has ballooned from $2,000 to $4,500 on a typical luxury car because of problems in reselling the big, older models taken in trade.

Marginal buyers are out. A related problem is that both Cadillac and Lincoln increased their sales to record levels in the late 1970s by enticing Oldsmobile, Buick, and Ford buyers to trade up. That helped push up the luxury share of the total car market from its traditional 5.5% range to around 7%. Now it has fallen into the 4% range. "The marginal buyer is out of the market," says Edward C. Kennard, general manager of GM's Cadillac Motor Car Div., "and the guy who's got money says, 'I've got a good set of wheels, so I'll tread water rather than trade.'"

Price is only part of the problem. The other part is the way potential owners perceive luxury cars. "Our customers feel like they're being greedy," laments Jacques J. Moore, president of Moore Cadillac Co., of Alexandria, Va., and also chairman of the Cadillac Dealer Council. Even though a new diesel-driven Cadillac might get 31 mpg on the highway, he says, "people think it looks like the most selfish car of our time."

The result has been some defection to smaller luxury imports such as Mercedes, BMW, Volvo, and Audi. These imports have been hard hit by the closing of car-loan windows by banks because they lack the in-house credit arms of GM, Ford, and Chrysler Corp. But even though they continue to lag behind the import penetration of the total U. S. market, the luxury imports have boosted their share of the market dramatically in the past year to more than 14% from barely 10%. "Now that we've got that customer," says J. Gordon Bingham, marketing vice-president of BMW of North America Inc., "we'll be working hard to keep him."

Stopgap measure. GM and Ford are locked into their present luxury car sizes for at least the next two years and possibly longer. With heroic optimism, Chrysler this fall will reenter this market with its Imperial line, after a five-year absence. GM will benefit from increasing use of energy-efficient diesel and V-6 engines and front-wheel drive. But Ford and Chrysler are likely to depend on V-8 engines and rear-wheel drive, which can only deliver about 20 mpg.

As a stopgap measure, sources say GM will offer Cadillac dealers in 1982 a deluxe version of its compact "J-car" replacement for the Chevrolet Monza. But there are doubts it will be called a Cadillac, for fear of hurting the division's quality image. ■

DETROIT'S HIGH-PRICE STRATEGY COULD BACKFIRE

Auto makers may lose a big chance to recoup dwindling market share

Battered by surging imports, slumping sales, and record losses, the U. S. auto industry is attempting to reverse its fortunes by introducing new lines of smaller, fuel-efficient cars. Detroit has priced these cars relatively high to replenish its depleted coffers as quickly as possible. It is gambling that demand is so great that consumers will buy the cars even at much higher prices. And the fast pace at which the 1981 fuel-efficient models sold in October indicates that the gamble may pay off—for a while.

Over the longer run, however, many economists maintain that this pricing strategy could backfire and that Detroit may be missing a great opportunity to recapture much of the market share lost to imports in recent years (chart). They argue that automobile demand, even for smaller, fuel-efficient cars, may not hold up in an economy emerging tentatively from a recession and expected to grow only very slowly for the next several years. And even if demand does remain strong, foreign competitors will be flooding the U. S. market with lower-price imports. This is particularly true since the International Trade Commission's decision on Nov. 10 not to recommend curbing the influx of Japanese cars means that the government will not even begin to consider any actions to stem imports until well into 1981, if then. Moreover, Detroit is still not producing cars that are fully competitive in terms of fuel efficiency and other qualitative features, according to many observers.

Risky assumptions? "I'm a little confused by Detroit's strategy," says Saul H. Hymans, chairman of the economics department at the University of Michigan. "I would have thought that at this time it would be risky to assume that demand would remain strong or that you are still not producing pink elephants when the market is looking for black panthers." Hymans and others point out that a similar pricing policy following the 1974-75 recession was a disaster and that to attract customers the industry quickly had to begin to discount cars through rebates.

Implicit in the pricing strategy of U. S. manufacturers is the idea that the demand for automobiles is highly "inelastic." That means that demand is relatively insensitive to price changes and that even a sharp increase in prices, such as occurred over the past year, will not depress sales much, if at all, and will result in a substantial increase in revenues. "I don't know why Detroit believes that demand is so inelastic," says Hymans. "This strategy is partly one of desperation, since profits are down and cash flow is abominable."

Detroit planners, however, believe that automobile demand has changed fundamentally since the Iranian revolution. Over the past 18 months, gasoline prices have about doubled. And the consumer's desire to shift to more economical, fuel-efficient cars is so great, they say, that it overshadows more traditional factors shaping demand, such as price and the growth of the economy. "If there is another round of [higher] gasoline prices or more problems in obtaining gasoline, the demand for smaller, fuel-efficient cars could rise even more," says Paul Root, director of economic studies for General Motors Corp. Adds Gar Laux, vice-chairman of marketing and sales for Chrysler Corp.: "There's no doubt that, during the next couple of years, the U. S. auto industry is not fully prepared to meet the demand."

A question of myopia. No one disputes that Detroit must increase its cash flow, especially to help finance the estimated $60 billion needed to retool the industry in order to downsize cars and shift to the more fuel-efficient front-wheel drive. But many economists question whether Detroit is recouping short-term losses at the expense of longer-term gains of market share. "Detroit's strategy is myopic," says Robert Gough, vice-president at Data Resources Inc. "Unlike the Japanese, who price aggressively in order to secure markets and do not worry about a few negative numbers, Detroit is primarily concerned about short-term profits."

To reverse the sharp rise in imports in recent years, Detroit must offer a smaller, fuel-efficient car that competes in both price and performance, say economists. On both counts the industry may be missing the mark. "Imports tend to score better on both price and fuel economy across the board," says Ratnam Chitturi, vice-president of the Auto Div. at Chase Econometrics.

Unless the market share for imports is reduced substantially, the future of Chrysler, or even Ford's U. S. operation, will be in jeopardy. The difference in revenues for U. S. manufacturers between imports at 20% of the market and at 25% is about $3 billion in a 10 million-car year. Ford posted a loss of $595 million in the third quarter, GM $567 million, and Chrysler $490 million, and that kind of revenue will be essential to help offset the red ink.

Publicly, Detroit appears confident that it can slash the market share for imports in the next two to three years. But privately the manufacturers worry that once consumers have changed to foreign cars it could be difficult to lure them back. "It is important to try to gain acceptance in the market quickly,

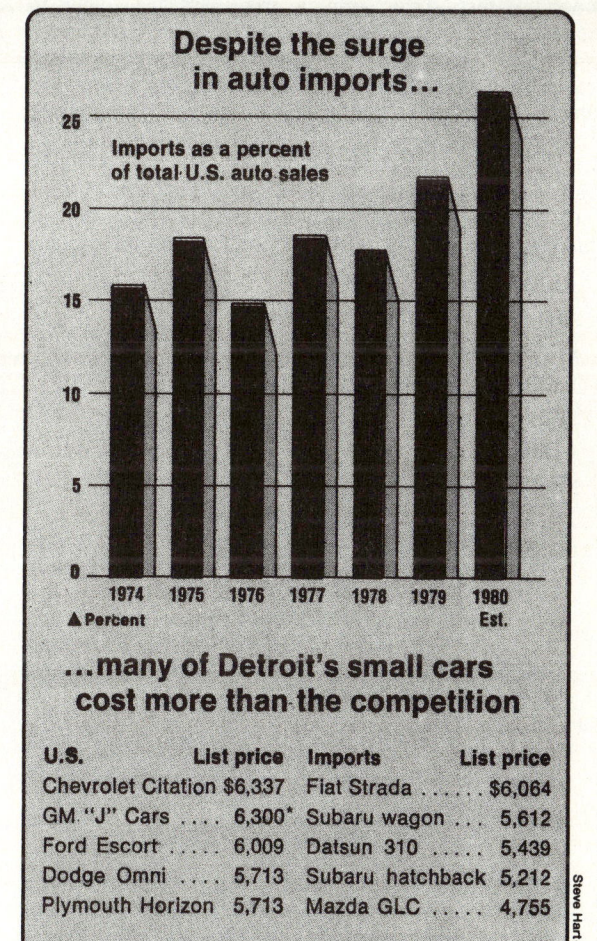

Despite the surge in auto imports...

Imports as a percent of total U.S. auto sales

Year	Percent
1974	~16
1975	~18
1976	~15
1977	~18
1978	~17
1979	~22
1980 Est.	~27

...many of Detroit's small cars cost more than the competition

U.S.	List price	Imports	List price
Chevrolet Citation	$6,337	Fiat Strada	$6,064
GM "J" Cars	6,300*	Subaru wagon	5,612
Ford Escort	6,009	Datsun 310	5,439
Dodge Omni	5,713	Subaru hatchback	5,212
Plymouth Horizon	5,713	Mazda GLC	4,755

Data: Data Resources Inc., BW *Estimate

Environmental Opportunities/Enterprise Threats

since the imports have such a headstart and are becoming established," says Gough.

Complications. No one outside the industry knows for sure how much Detroit is making on its high-priced, smaller cars. But Gough and other economists argue that by pricing more competitively, the U.S. auto industry could increase its market share and lower unit production costs, which would enable it to maintain healthy profit margins.

From Detroit's point of view, however, any effort to regain market share for the next few years will be greatly complicated by its higher production costs and shortage of capacity to build smaller cars. "The basic problem is labor costs," says Chitturi. "Unit labor costs in the U.S. have risen 40% since 1975, while remaining constant in Japan during the same period." Also, U.S. auto makers say costs are boosted considerably by environmental and safety regulations.

U.S. manufacturers are counting on rising costs abroad to help narrow the cost gap, particularly in Japan, which produces an estimated 80% of all imports. Many Detroit industry officials believe it is only a matter of a few years before Japan goes the way of Europe, where high labor costs are making price competition increasingly difficult. High labor costs in Germany are a major reason Volkswagen decided to build a plant in the U.S. "The imports are under the same cost pressures as we are," says Emmett P. Feeley, director of marketing at the Chevrolet Motor Div. of GM.

The cost gap could be closed further as Detroit continues to install new capacity to produce smaller, fuel-efficient cars. Retooling and installing new capacity means putting in place new plant and equipment, which will be more productive and help reduce labor costs.

The foreign push. The problem is that even though in the past year Detroit has boosted its capacity to produce more competitive cars, such as those with front-wheel drive, to 2.9 million from 1.6 million, it will take until 1985 by most calculations to expand capacity enough to meet domestic demand. In the meantime, foreign producers are likely to push harder.

Most European industrialized countries are now in or heading into recession, and they probably will try to export more to the U.S. in order to offset the slump in their domestic sales. And the Japanese have already expanded capacity to 11 million vehicles from 10 million in the past year and have projects in the works that could boost it to 12.8 million by 1982.

U.S. industry officials are confident their lineup of cars will stave off imports and even cut into their market share quickly. They point out that the introduction of new cars such the Chrysler K-cars were largely responsible for the drop in import share to 22% in October—the first month they were launched—from 27.5% a month earlier. "By 1983, we'll have [imports] back to 15% of the market," predicts Robert D.

U.S. auto makers may be wrong in assuming that demand is 'inelastic'

Lund, general manager of Chevrolet.

Many economists, however, think that unless Detroit changes its pricing strategy soon, such predictions will prove far too optimistic. Prices for K-cars, such as the Dodge Aries and Plymouth Reliant, on which Chrysler is depending for its survival, are $800 to $1,600 higher than many imports. And it is not only a question of price. Says Chase's Chitturi: "It will take a long time to improve the public's perception of the quality of the new smaller cars, given the record of the small cars that came out of Detroit." ■

TIGHT CREDIT SLAMS CAR DEALERS TWO WAYS

However grim the numbers coming out of Detroit have been, sluggish new car sales are not the U.S. auto industry's only problem. Soaring interest rates are loading dealers with staggering inventory costs and are sending an increasing number of them to the wall, while discouraging would-be buyers by making it tough to get consumer auto loans.

Signs of trouble were apparent in mid-March, when sales by Detroit auto makers dropped 11% behind year-ago levels. Ford Motor Co. and Chrysler Corp. have led the decline, each with 25% sales slumps for the year. The domestic industry's only sales winners were American Motors Corp., up 32%, and Volkswagen of America Inc., up 20%, manufacturers who are staking their future on small cars (page 80).

The credit crunch is pressing auto makers from both the wholesale and retail side of their sales fence. Car dealers, who are paying nearly 21% in interest to finance the cars they keep in stock, are trying to cut costs by trimming their inventories and reducing further purchases from the factory. And tightening bank credit is beginning to squeeze the spirit out of the dwindling number of consumers still eager to buy a new car. Warns auto analyst Richard L. Haydon, of Goldman, Sachs & Co. in New York: "It's forcing out the marginal dealer and the marginal buyer."

Postponed purchases. The dealer shakeout, in fact, began last year when a market shift toward smaller cars left many domestic sellers stuck with trucks and large cars. Some 600 dealers folded in 1979—four times the number in the previous year. And George S. Irvin, president of the National Automobile Dealers Assn., says 200 more of the nation's 28,000 car and truck dealers closed in the first two months of 1980. He estimates that the average new car is now languishing on a dealer lot for 75 days, compared with 50 days last year. Irvin figures that inventory costs for the average dealer are now $150,000 a year—triple what they were in 1978.

A perk-up in sales would help dealers clear out their stock, of course. But willing buyers are finding the going rougher every day, as more and more banks and credit unions back away from consumer lending.

While auto loans, along with home mortgages, were exempted from the Federal Reserve Board's Mar. 14 credit restrictions, many lenders are still refusing to make new car loans. Some are

Dealers are paying almost 21% in interest to finance the new cars on their lots

reacting to usury ceilings in 19 states that limit annual interest rates for such credit to 13% or less. Yet even banks that are able to lend at higher rates report that many would-be car buyers, shocked by interest rates, simply decide to forgo purchases. BancOhio National Bank in Columbus, for example, says its auto-installment-loan business has dropped by 50% since last year.

Captive auto credit subsidiaries are trying to take up the slack in loan sources. General Motors Acceptance Corp. (GMAC), and its counterparts at Ford and Chrysler, provided 31% of the $7.8 billion in new-car financing in January (the latest month calculated), compared with 21.5% a year before.

The auto finance subsidiaries are holding their own in loans to dealers for wholesale purchases, since they typically underprice banks by adding just ¾ of 1% to the prime rate, now 20%. But the formula for retail business, particularly in markets where banks are refusing to make auto loans at all, is a losing proposition. Ford Motor Credit, for example, has assumed 50% of new-car financing in Arkansas, where usury laws limit interest to 10%—a loss to the company of at least 6% on a loan. Concedes Chairman James W. Ford: "This is not our best profit year."

The finance units, in fact, are a net cash drain on their parents even though, as in 1979, they all reported profits. The reason is that they can assure their position in the commercial paper market only through commitments to make sure their own interest charges are well covered. Last year those commitments prompted GM to funnel $500 million into GMAC, while Ford paid in $200 million to Ford Motor Credit. Even cash-strapped Chrysler pumped $52 million into Chrysler Financial Corp.

Imported-car dealers, however, are at a handicap in this market, because most must rely on high-cost bank credit for both their wholesale and retail credit. Howard J. Cooper, owner of a Volkswagen dealership in Ann Arbor, Mich., and chairman of VW's national dealer advisory council, notes that local banks are taking only one-third of the car loan customers he currently generates, down from almost 90% at the beginning of the year. But Cooper says the boom in small-car sales helps offset banker resistance by providing stronger collateral than many big Detroit models whose resale values are faltering. ∎

WHAT CAUSED THE DECLINE: INFLATION SKEWS THE PROFIT INCENTIVE

The stagnation of U.S. industry has been largely camouflaged—particularly during the past decade—because inflation has made a shambles of the key corporate performance measure: reported profits. Traditional financial accounting has been providing disturbingly misleading signals about the growth and health of company earnings. Year after year, the flossy annual reports from corporate America boast of record sales and earnings, while in real terms profits are flat or even eroding.

What this means, baldly, is that the ability to develop and market new products, finance essential investment in new plant and equipment, and, at the same time, pay handsome dividends to shareholders simply is not there, even though traditional accounting methods say that it is. For example, in its most recent financial report, a company's sales are stated in 1979 dollars because that is the year in which it actually gets most of its money for the products it sells. But to arrive at a profit figure, it has to deduct from these 1979 revenues the cost of raw materials that may have been bought at 1977 or 1978 prices. In addition, the company must make a charge for the depreciation of its fixed assets, based on costs that may date back 20 years or more. Yet when the company replenishes its inventories and replaces its plant and equipment, it has to do so at far higher current or future prices. For this reason, many business analysts argue that such earnings reports are overstated and illusory.

Noted management consultant Peter F. Drucker puts it succinctly: During inflation "the figures lie." And what bothers him most is that even the most knowledgeable executive becomes victim to such illusions. "He may know that the figures he gets are grossly misleading," Drucker asserts, "but as long as these are the figures he has in front of him, he will act on them rather than on his own better knowledge. And he will act foolishly, wrongly, irresponsibly."

According to Commerce Dept. calculations, aftertax corporate profits based on traditional accounting measures rose 485% during the three decades from 1950 to 1979—a linear compound annual growth rate of 13.1%. But if earnings are calculated on a current-cost basis in each of the 30 years by making adjustments for underdepreciation and the higher replacement costs of inventories, annual profit growth is only 7.4%.

Even so, the current-cost earnings numbers fail to tell the whole story of inflation's toll. While 1955 profits may reflect 1955 costs and revenues, and 1970 profits are in 1970 dollars, the current-cost measure fails to take into consideration what has happened to the purchasing power of the dollar during the three decades. If each year's current-cost profits are translated into a common monetary measure—say, in 1950 dollars through use of the gross national product deflator for nonfinancial corporations—the earnings picture is sobering. It indicates that such "real" profits barely doubled over the three decades, a minuscule annual growth rate of 2.6%, that contrasts sharply with reported corporate earnings growth of 13.1% a year.

As long as inflation remains relatively low or uniform, the gap between reported and "real" profits is not particularly worrisome. But once inflation begins to accelerate, as it did during the

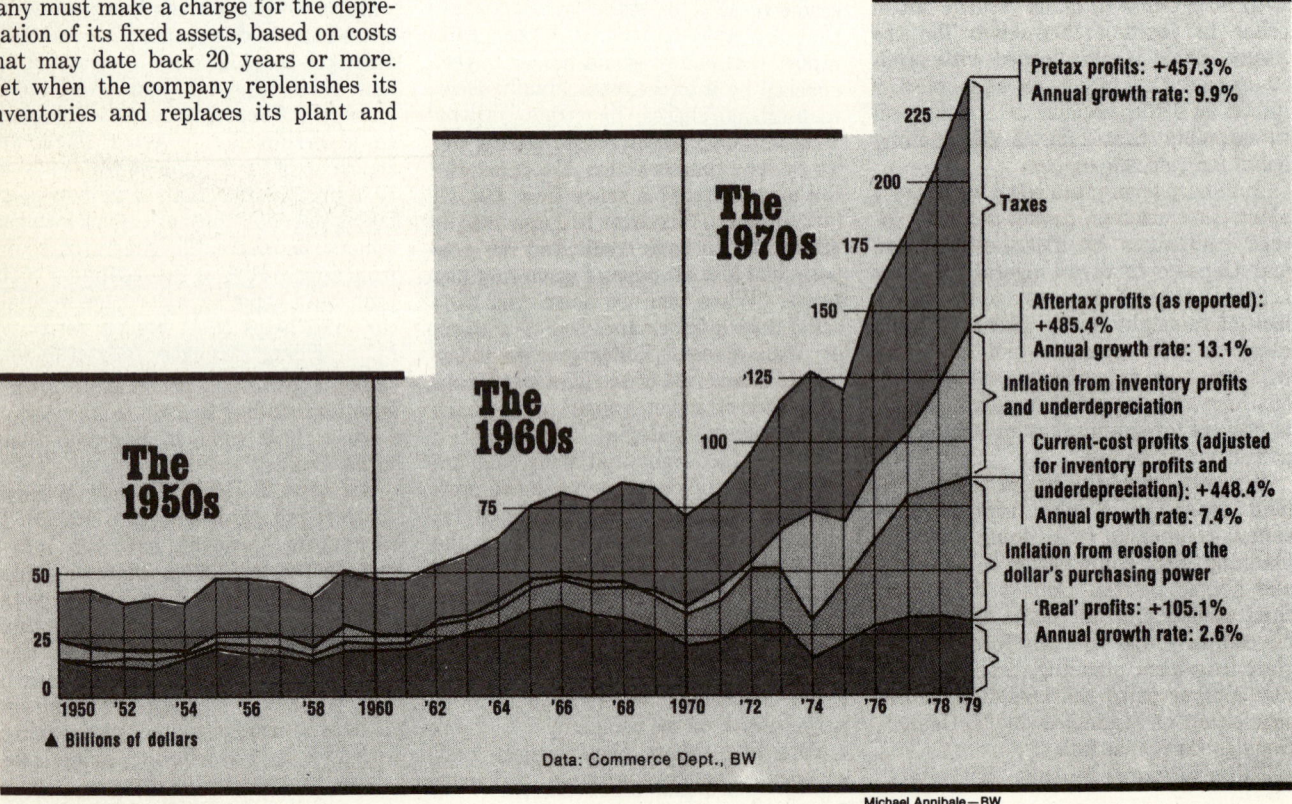

104 / Readings from *Business Week*

1970s, the performance measures become grossly misleading (chart).

During the 1950s, for example, when inflation was low, both reported and real earnings averaged about 2.5%. In the following decade, traditional aftertax profits showed a 7.5% annual growth rate—6.1% in real terms. But during the 1970s, although reported profits appeared to soar 17.3% a year, real growth came to only 3.7%.

Meaningful tax relief

This anomaly in accounting for corporate profits also generates another illusion: the measurement of effective corporate tax rates. Companies have the option of adopting last-in, first-out (LIFO) accounting for inventories, which has the advantage of reflecting costs—and thus reported profits—at more nearly current price levels. LIFO also reduces a corporation's current tax burden. But as experts quickly point out, companies have no LIFO option for plant and equipment. Without that option as inflation soars, companies fall further and further behind in their ability to replace capital facilities.

Many corporate executives say that meaningful corporate tax relief and investment incentives can only come through a current-cost or inflation-indexed depreciation deduction. Such an innovation faces major battles. Among other things, the mating of traditional accounting and rampant inflation has produced the unfortunate illusion of "obscene profits" in the public eye. Although difficult to do, that commonly accepted notion must be revised. ∎

WHAT CAUSED THE DECLINE: Expectations That Can No Longer Be Met

The decline of U.S. competitiveness is rooted in more than the policies and practices of management, labor, and government. It is rooted also in the emergence of new attitudes toward work, government, and what citizens have a right to expect from institutions. These attitudes challenge older beliefs concerning the need to save and invest as well as the notion that rewards should be based on effort and achievement. Put simply, says public opinion expert Daniel Yankelovich, chairman of Yankelovich, Skelly & White Inc., sometime in the mid-1970s a psychology of affluence began to replace the psychology of scarcity inherited from the Great Depression. Unfortunately, this happened just about the time that the enormous production capacity of the U.S. economic system—which engendered this psychology of affluence—began to falter.

In the decades following World War II, memories of the depression began to fade. What took hold was an often-unexpressed idea that the U.S. economy was limitless and invulnerable. It could, it was believed, support an ever-rising standard of living; create endless jobs; provide education, medical care, and housing for everyone; abolish poverty; rebuild the cities; restore the environment; and satisfy the demands of blacks, Hispanics, women, and other groups. Unbroken growth was taken for granted.

Social betterment in the U.S. has always depended on constantly expanding economic growth, following the principle that a rising tide lifts all boats. The underlying conviction that the American system could do everything, though, engendered some subsidiary attitudes that helped undermine growth. These included the notion of entitlement, a new definition of equality that called on government to level economic and social disparities, an adversary stance toward government and business, and changed motivations toward work.

Throughout the late 1960s and early 1970s, groups struggling for more jobs, more federal assistance, and a cleaner environment began to feel that these were rights to which they were entitled. Further, they felt they were entitled to all of them: Tradeoffs and compromises were out. The system, in this view, can do everything—and it should.

Creating wealth

A second attitude supported the entitlement concept. Equality of opportunity was no longer viewed as sufficient. Since people are manifestly unequal in ability and condition, this view argued that it was the obligation of government to make them equal. Society, Harvard philosopher John Rawls argued, should follow a "principle of redress" in dealing with disadvantaged citizens. This principle, together with the notion of entitlement, helped spawn an enormous expansion in government programs aimed at correcting inequities.

In the context of a belief in limitless resources, a logical consequence of the attitude that one is entitled to become equal in every respect was the emergence of a fierce, adversary posture toward societal institutions. If government and business failed to meet every demand, ran this thinking, then the reason was their bad faith. And aggrieved citizens were justified in forcing them to comply. Nonnegotiable demands, demonstrations, boycotts, takeovers of buildings, "trashing" or destruction of property became commonplace tactics.

Finally, the belief in permanent affluence, coupled with new beliefs generated by the social upheavals of the 1960s and early 1970s, produced changed attitudes toward work. Some businessmen believe this involved the destruction of the older work ethic, but most experts on worker attitudes feel what happened was that incentives needed to motivate people changed. Raymond Katzell, a professor of psychology at New York University who has studied worker attitudes, says: "The affluent society hasn't made people lazy, but it takes something different to turn them on than it does impoverished people."

Experts say that today people are looking for something more than material rewards. Labor economist Clark Kerr explains: "The work ethic has not disappeared. People today are willing to work hard on 'good' jobs, providing they have the freedom to influence the nature of their jobs and to pursue their own lifestyles."

To identify these changed attitudes is not to say that they are all wrong or misguided. Redressing legitimate social grievances is necessary for any healthy society. Changed worker attitudes challenge management to find new ways to motivate people.

But it is fair to say, too, that to the extent these new attitudes, especially their extreme manifestations, focus attention and resources on how the economic pie is divided, they divert attention and resources away from how to make the pie bigger. Says Reginald H. Jones, chairman of General Electric Co.: "We have become so concerned with problems of redistributing wealth that we've forgotten all about creation of wealth."

Shifting the emphasis back to making the U.S. economy more productive and competitive will involve a major national effort, one that must include attitudes that recognize new realities. And one reality is that limitless growth can no longer be taken for granted: It must be worked for. ∎

MAINE'S NUCLEAR VOTE HAS THE INDUSTRY JUMPY

Hoping to capitalize on the public fears stirred up by last year's accident at Three Mile Island, Pa., opponents of nuclear power are once again taking their cause to the ballot box. In at least three states this fall—starting with Maine on Sept. 23—voters will decide the future of nuclear power in their states. While the nuclear industry has been largely successful at the polls in the past, industry officials are not taking the new challenge lightly. As one utility official puts it: "It's a battle we can't afford to lose."

Beyond their direct impact, the upcoming referendums could have a profound effect on "the public perception of where nuclear power is going," says Carl Walske, president of Atomic Industrial Forum, an industry trade association. Of greatest concern to the industry is the vote in Maine. Unlike any previous initiative, the referendum there calls for shutting down an operating plant. Passage would cast an ominous shadow over the 69 nuclear plants in commercial operation in the U.S., as well as over the 87 plants under construction.

"Everyone is worried about the domino effect," says Elwin W. Thurlow, chief executive at Central Maine Power Co., which owns 38% of Maine's sole nuclear plant. Utilities and nuclear-equipment suppliers from across the country are pouring money into Maine in an effort to mow down the grass-roots movement. Observers estimate that the campaign to defeat the referendum has already raised nearly $1 million—nearly 10 times as much as the pro-referendum forces. Among the contributors, Westinghouse Electric Corp., a leading nuclear vendor, chipped in $50,000, and General Electric Co. added $30,000.

State campaigns. The Maine initiative is only the second antinuclear referendum to reach voters since 1976. In that year, referendums appeared on seven state ballots, and all went down to defeat, most by large margins. Since then the only public vote on nuclear power has come in Montana, where voters in 1978 backed a plan to restrict future nuclear-plant construction within the state.

Now the antinuclear activists are making another push. Six weeks after the Maine vote, residents of Oregon and South Dakota will decide whether to restrict future nuclear construction. The question may also be on the ballot in Missouri, if supporters of an initiative gather enough signatures. At the same time, residents of Washington and Montana will vote on restricting nuclear waste disposal within their borders.

Of all the referendums, the effort to close down the 830-Mw Maine Yankee plant in Wiscasset is the most drastic. The $275 million plant, operating since

The first referendum to call for the shutdown of an operating plant

1972, generates one-third of Maine's electricity. If the plant closes, utility officials in Maine claim that more imported oil would be needed to fill the gap, increasing electricity bills in the state by a huge $140 million, or 33%, a year.

A bad gamble. In their aggressive media campaign, pro-nuclear groups argue that these increases would wreak havoc with Maine's economy. Already, a number of companies have warned that passage of the referendum could mean significant job losses in the state. Bath Iron Works Corp., a shipbuilding subsidiary of Congoleum Corp., estimates that its annual electricity bill could jump as much as 60%, or an additional $1 million. "That's bound to make us less competitive," says John F. Sullivan Jr., president.

Proponents of the nuclear shutdown dispute many of these claims. According to Raymond G. Shadis, a North Edgecomb (Me.) artist who heads the pro-referendum effort, all the lost capacity could be replaced by a three-point program consisting of conservation, co-generation, and hydro-electric power. "We do not feel that the state would suffer if the plant closed," says Shadis. By keeping the plant running, he argues, "we place the entire state on the gambling table for a dubious return."

Despite all the money and arguing going into the campaigns in Maine and elsewhere, some observers believe that the upcoming referendums, even if successful, will mark just the beginning, not the end, of the battle. Already the nuclear industry is questioning the legality of the initiatives, arguing that the federal government has exclusive control over nuclear power. Indeed, a federal district court ruling in California last spring invalidated state regulations for nuclear power. Nevertheless, industry officials would prefer to resolve the matter before it gets to the courts. "If we lose, we'll resort to the courts," says Thurlow of Central Maine Power. "But who knows what would happen there?" ∎

Environmental Opportunities/Enterprise Threats

Economic trend

By Seymour Zucker

A skewed recession has hidden strengths

With the prime rate soaring 450 basis points to 18½% in just five weeks, with automobile sales—even for Detroit's new fuel-efficient models—slumping badly in November, and with October housing permits declining 15%, economists are beginning to revise their forecasts downward. Indeed, many are saying that the economy, which only a few months ago appeared to be making a brisk recovery from the sharp downturn in the second quarter, could once again be heading into a severe decline.

But the forecasters, who look mainly at economywide numbers, may be missing a crucial feature of the recession of 1980 and one that could shape economic policy: The recession has been skewed in its impact on industries and regions. "It's an unbalanced economy," says 1980 Nobel Laureate Lawrence R. Klein, "and this means that the economy has more strength than the overall numbers suggest."

Industries such as autos, tires, and steel have been in the throes of what comes close to a depression. Employment in the auto industry is down 15% from the comparable period last year. In the second quarter, steel production fell from 88% of capacity to 53% in just a few months. And although steel has recovered to about 72%, the rate could slump again because auto sales simply are not recovering. Unemployment in Michigan stands at 13.4% and will no doubt move higher as layoffs spread in the auto and related industries. And in Illinois, with its concentration of basic manufacturing, the jobless rate is 9.2%.

Yet such industries as computers, information processing, oil drilling, and aircraft are booming. And high technology companies worry how to get workers to fill new jobs. It is little wonder that areas where such industries are centered—the Sunbelt, Silicon Valley in California, and in parts of New England—are experiencing low rates of unemployment.

Supply-side growth. Despite bone-crunching interest rates induced by the Federal Reserve Board, rapid output and employment growth in high technology industries are giving the economy some resilience. "Productivity growth is coming in computers and allied industries where there is technological progress and innovation," says Robert J. Gordon of Northwestern University. "Growth here is not coming from the demand side but from the supply side as breakthroughs are made." The strength in oil exploration, of course, is being generated by high prices set by the OPEC cartel.

Moreover, the boom industries are not involved in selling to the general public, where credit availability and interest rates play a key role in determining demand. It is precisely in industries that sell to the consumer, such as autos and housing, where demand had been clobbered in this recession by the Federal Reserve's tight credit.

Ironically, the unevenness of the recession's impact has been heightened by government policy adopted over the last few years to protect housing. Changes in federal regulations on money market instruments have allowed interest rates to reach dazzling heights before slowing home construction. Tight money used to hit housing quickly and hard. But now the housing market is being sheltered somewhat by the ability of thrift institutions to pay higher rates for money (page 29). "This means tight money overlaps into autos and other big-ticket durables," says Gordon. So while in previous recessions the impact of tight money was almost entirely on housing generally spread across the nation, it now affects the durable goods industries which are concentrated in the nation's industrial heartland.

New patterns. Indeed, the recessionary impact on employment in durable manufacturing this year was worse than it was in the far more severe 1974-75 recession. In that recession, employment in this sector fell from peak to trough at an annual rate of 7.8%, while in 1980 employment fell at an annual rate of 13.1%. The disparity between manufacturing employment and employment in services has widened this year. Jobs in service industries were increasing by 3.4%, at an annual rate, about the same rate of growth as in the previous recession. Since women are mostly engaged in the service industries, this is why, for the first time in a postwar recession, unemployment among adult women is below the rate of adult men.

The skewed recession holds important implications for policymakers. It suggests that policy concentrate on helping particular industries rather than using broad-based measures that affect the overall economy. The danger is that overall stimulus could exacerbate inflation, since major sectors of the U.S. are a lot more robust than the forecasters would have us believe.

Cable TV
THE RACE TO PLUG IN

Bidding for cable-TV franchises is at a fever pitch as companies put up millions to get a foothold in the industry. Spurring their frenetic activity is the realization that within a comparatively short time—one industry analyst estimates that it will take only two years—municipalities will have awarded whatever franchises remain. Large cable companies are fending off newcomers by working overtime to win the right to hook up as many homes as possible. And those who are not in the game are paying huge sums to enter.

In a deal that stunned Wall Street analysts, Westinghouse Electric Corp. recently agreed to pay $646 million for Teleprompter Corp., the nation's largest cable company, with 1.3 million subscribers among 112 systems in 32 states. The reason: Even a major corporation such as Westinghouse, which owns eight cable franchises in Florida and Georgia, had found itself outdistanced. "Unless you are a large, multiple system operator, it is difficult to get other franchises," explains Westinghouse Broadcasting Co. President Daniel L. Ritchie.

Capital Cities Communications Inc., owner of seven cable systems, saw the light sooner than Westinghouse and last July snatched up Cablecom-General Inc. with nearly 250,000 subscribers, for $139.2 million. New York Times Co., which has never been in cable, recently sewed up an $83 million deal that will give it a base from which to operate—55 cable franchises in New Jersey. Many more companies are poised on the sidelines seeking a chance to buy in, wishing that they had acted years ago when prices were lower.

Not everyone is cheering cable on. Theater owners are worried that the movie companies may be tempted to release their first-run films over pay-TV, cutting into box-office revenues. And the three major networks, barred by federal regulation from owning cable systems, are beginning to see some of their audience defect to cable and pay-cable channels. While the networks continue to argue that commercial TV will remain the dominant form of television entertainment, all are in some way involved in cable TV. CBS and ABC are developing cable programming, while NBC's parent, RCA, owns satellites.

The vast need for capital

As the competition gets rougher, even large, well-established multiple system operators (MSOs) are having to run to catch up. UA-Columbia Cablevision Inc., the 10th-largest cable operator, is exploring ways to increase its cash. "If we're going to go beyond where we are, we're going to need large amounts of capital to walk on a par with some of those big companies," observes Robert M. Rosencrans, president and chief executive officer. UA-Columbia, he says, is wrestling with the idea of letting a large corporation buy in, similar to the deal made a year ago when American Express Co. for $175 million bought into Warner Cable Corp. Warner Amex Cable Corp. now has 750,000 cable subscribers.

Despite the stampede, the cable industry still faces formidable obstacles. "All of cable could be blown into a cocked hat by a change in technology," worries William B. Strange Jr., vice-president for corporate development at Sammons Communications Inc. Looming on the horizon is direct satellite to home transmission, which would obviate the need to wire each TV set. Cable also faces competition from other pay-TV services—subscription television (STV), which is delivered via broadcast signals, and multipoint distribution service (MDS), which is delivered via microwaves.

But cable may well prove to be its own worst enemy. Because of the high cost of wiring each home, the cable industry will need huge amounts of capital. Many of the companies that are gambling millions on the industry's future may not be around to collect on their bets. "The investment is colossal, both in capital and ongoing expenses," says Alan P. Brigash, a communications consultant at International Resource Development Inc. "You will see small companies getting franchises and being unable to fulfill them."

Already it is clear that only the strong will survive. With so many giant corporations now participating and spending thousands of dollars on engineering studies, lawyers' fees, and elaborate presentations, the level of franchise bidding has risen to new plateaus. "Ten years ago you could have had a cable franchise for the asking," notes one industry official. Yet six companies, locked in a tense struggle, spent $500,000 each—before the franchise was awarded—in competi-

Westinghouse Electric pays a huge price for Teleprompter **$646 million**

Capital Cities moves firmly into cable TV by buying Cablecom-General **$139 million**

> The New York Times gobbles up 55 cable franchises in New Jersey
>
> $83 million

> Nine contenders gamble big to enter bidding on Connecticut franchise
>
> $250,000 each

> Six companies vie for chance to bid on Dallas franchise
>
> $500,000 each

charge and a monthly fee to have his TV set hooked up to cable. In addition to the basic cable service, the consumer may purchase for an extra monthly charge a premium service, such as Home Box Office or Showtime. Any such service that a subscriber receives through cable is considered pay-cable. Pay-TV services may also be provided by pay-cable's competitors, STV and MDS.

For anyone gambling that cable and pay-cable TV will win out, the statistics detailing the industry's growth provide considerable comfort. In 1968 about 2.8 million, or 5% of the nation's 56 million TV homes, had cable. Today that figure has climbed to 14 million, or 18.9% of the nation's 74 million homes. The most conservative industry observers predict that cable penetration could rise to 17 million homes by 1985, while those more bullish on the industry's growth, such as Paul F. Kagan, publisher of seven communications newsletters, expect 46.1 million cable and pay-cable subscribers by 1990.

In 1978 the cable TV industry's revenues exceeded $1.5 billion, a 25% increase from 1977 revenues. Pay-cable services yielded revenues of $192 million, or about 13% of the industry's total revenues. Kagan believes that by 1990, basic cable revenue will be $5.4 billion a year, and pay-cable revenue will reach $8.4 billion. Kagan's estimates exclude revenues that might come from advertising or from the sale of home-security systems that can be hooked up to cable.

Flowering after deregulation

Many observers believe that cable is now on solid ground, mainly because the Federal Communications Commission is

tion for the rights to wire 400,000 homes in Dallas, the largest single municipal chunk ever awarded. The Dallas franchise, because of the area's growth and upwardly mobile population, is considered such a plum that the runner-up, Sammons, has refused to quit. Contesting the city council's decision to give the franchise to Warner Amex, Sammons collected signatures on petitions to force a referendum.

There are battles elsewhere. In Cincinnati, where the franchise also went to Warner Amex, the corporate campaigns—each cable company criticizing its rivals—were played out each day in full-page newspaper advertisements. Nine companies have spent an estimated $250,000 each to fight for the right to bid on a franchise in the New York City bedroom communities of Greenwich, Darien, New Canaan, and Stamford, Conn. So extensive were some of the proposals handed in to Connecticut's Public Utilities Control Div. that one lawyer needed a hand truck to wheel in the required 15 copies of his client's proposal and supporting documents. Other cities that have yet to award franchises include Denver, Chicago, New Orleans, Boston, Fort Worth, and the New York City boroughs of Queens, Brooklyn, the Bronx, and Staten Island.

Cable television began in the late 1940s as a means of delivering television signals to areas unable to receive over-the-air TV channels because they were too far from the transmitters or cut off by mountains. Thus in its early days cable was viewed primarily as a utility, offering better reception of network TV. But aided by dish antennas that can pick up and relay services from satellites, cable now provides a wide spectrum of entertainment choices.

A consumer pays an installation

working hard to abolish the many regulations that have hampered cable's growth. "The flowering of cable is directly related to deregulation," states Gustave M. Hauser, president of Warner Amex. "We were bound hand and foot."

Currently the FCC is proposing to do away with two of its rules that have limited cable's use of broadcast signals. Under the rule changes, cable systems would be allowed to bring in as many distant TV stations as they like—thus increasing the number of program offerings available to viewers—and also would be allowed to add some network programming that was formerly reserved for local stations.

But the FCC's activities have infuriated the broadcasters, who have succeeded in holding up the rule changes—scheduled to take effect on Nov. 28—by persuading the U. S. Court of Appeals in New York to hear their arguments. The broadcasters believe that they are being forced to aid cable's development at the risk of losing their own viewers. "If cable wants to develop, let it develop on its own with its own programming," complains Leonard H. Goldenson, chairman and chief executive officer of American Broadcasting Cos.

Thomas E. Wheeler, president of the National Cable Television Assn., is pleased with the progress that the FCC has made so far and anticipates even fewer government restrictions under the new Administration. "I take Mr. Reagan at his word," Wheeler says. "He says he wants to get government out of the marketplace where consumer interests are not at stake."

Even though cable officials hope that the FCC will continue its activities, there is concern that it may go too far and allow two other players to get into the game: the television networks and the phone companies. In 1972 the FCC excluded ABC, CBS, and NBC from owning cable systems because it feared that the networks would attempt to retard the industry's growth to protect their broadcasting interests.

Current FCC rules prohibit phone companies from owning cable systems in areas where they also operate phone service. General Telephone & Electronics Corp. had been the 20th-largest MSO, but because of the FCC rule, it was forced to divest itself of 50 franchises in 10 states. "We would welcome a change in the environment and a chance to reconsider what the cable business could mean to GT&E," says Sam F. Shawhan, assistant vice-president for regulatory affairs.

But cable operators view ownership by phone companies—whose wires run into 98% of U. S. homes—as a possibility, with American Telephone & Telegraph Co., the industry leader, as the greatest threat. While AT&T officials publicly state they are not interested in cable, Wheeler and others remain unconvinced. "We will fight telephone company ownership to the death," vows Wheeler.

Cable faces competition from other pay-TV services. Subscription TV now has 750,000 customers, and multipoint distribution service has 350,000. STV officials claim that ultimately cable will reach only 40% of U. S. homes. "The wired country is a fallacy," says H. Brian Thompson, president of Subscription Television of America. He notes that unlike STV, cable is capital-intensive and slow to return money to its investors. "With STV, the minute you throw the switch, you cover the market," he says. Cable officials are quick to point out that STV and MDS also have serious technological problems. STV, for example, can deliver into the home only one channel at a time.

"I don't think that people will settle for one channel if cable offers 35 or 40 channels," says Arno W. Mueller, president of Storer Broadcasting Co.'s Cable Communications Div. MDS's signal has a range of only 25 mi. and requires the receiver to be in the line of sight of the transmitter. "We haven't gone to the FCC to try to stop subscription television or multipoint distribution, and we aren't going to," declares Wheeler. "We are going to fight this out in the marketplace." Many suspect that cable operators would ask the FCC for protection against direct broadcast satellites. But at present that technology remains a futuristic approach, since each home would have to install its own costly receiving dish.

Consumers want cable

Right now the marketplace is a cable operator's dream. "A couple of years ago people would ask me what field I'm in. I'd say cable, and they'd say: 'What's that?'" recalls Bill Daniels, head of the Denver-based Daniels & Associates, a multiple system operator that also offers brokerage, management, and financial services to the industry. "But now people want cable service." Daniels notes that every sizable U. S. city has already made, or is about to make, a decision on cable. Monroe M. Rifkin, president of American Television & Communications Corp., a Time Inc. subsidiary, agrees: "For every franchise that is granted, we have one less area left open," he says. As a result, he notes, "the competition for franchises is very intense, very difficult."

With all the competition, the cable companies seem determined to avoid any charge of impropriety. The industry has had a tough time achieving respectability after a highly publicized 1971 bribery scandal in Johnstown, Pa., involving a franchise award. During the recent bidding in Dallas, Warner Amex officials helped the police apprehend someone who had offered to sell the company information that would guarantee it the franchise. Says Storer's Mueller: "I don't think there is any company of any substance engaged in illegal activities."

But the politicking—currying favor with powerful local citizens, promising profits to local charities, and taking out advertisements in local newspapers—continues. Cable operators point out that this is an inherent part of the process, because city councils, usually responsible for deciding which company gets the award, are made up of politicians. "This may be the most political thing going in America today," says John M. Lewis, president of the cable communications division of Wometco Enterprises Inc.

Many of those politicians, notes Warner Amex's Hauser, are susceptible to pressures from affluent local citizens often aligned with a cable company. "How do you say no to someone who financed your whole campaign?" asks Hauser. Some officials fear, however, that in the heat of battle many cable companies are overbidding by making promises that will be impossible to keep. These include guaranteed low subscriber fees, early startup of the system, numerous channels and services, and extensive local programming. "They'll promise them anything," says Leonard Tow, president of Century Communications Corp., a cable operator with 135,000 subscribers.

But some cable companies blame city officials for pushing companies to make wild promises. "Many communities are insisting on more channel capacity than they will need in the future," says Russell Karp, president of Teleprompter. "That will require capital investment that is not necessary."

While some communities may have been overwhelmed at the corporate desire to please, others are taking advantage of it. In Newton, Mass., for instance, the eight cable companies competing for the franchise were asked to benefit the city in some way in their

Top ten cable companies

Company	Systems	Subscribers	Revenues 1979	Revenues 1980*	Income 1979	Income 1980*
			Millions of dollars			
1. Teleprompter	112	1,300,000	$174.6	$143	$14.3	$18.2
2. American TV & Communications (Time Inc. subsidiary)	124	1,250,000	$113.7	NA	$19.7	NA
3. Tele-Communications	150	1,034,519	$92.1	$57.6†	$28.9	$2.8†
4. Cox Cable Communications	59	842,000	$90.9	$89.9	$21.9	$16.1
5. Warner Amex Cable	149	750,000	$84.0	NA	$4.5	NA
6. Times Mirror††	53	549,000	$86.2	$96.6	$32.2	$31.2
7. Storer Broadcasting	300	500,000	$40.3	$46.7	$7.3	$4.7
8. Viacom International	101	450,000	$107.4	$112.8	$11.9	$10.9
9. Sammons Communications (Sammons Enterprises Inc. (subsidiary)	45	403,000	$38.9	$36.4	$4.1	$1.3
10. UA-Columbia Cablevision**	21	380,000	$40.0	$54.9	$4.2	$4.79

* Figures for first 9 mos.
** Fiscal year from Oct. 1 through Sept. 30
† Figures for first 6 mos. only
†† Figures include broadcast properties
NA = Not available

Environmental Opportunities/Enterprise Threats / 111

THE PAY-TV DIET THE PUBLIC WILL PAY FOR

What people want most on pay-cable is movies. Subscribers also like the way they see those movies—"uncut, uninterrupted, uncensored"—according to an official from Time Inc.'s Home Box Office. "There just doesn't seem to be any barrier to what people will pay for what they want," adds John M. Lewis, president of the cable communications division of Miami-based Wometco Enterprises Inc. "Some people are paying as much as $28 a month for service, and some bills run over $40 a month."

The pay-movie market is a godsend for Hollywood, where a $15 million film now must gross $32 million at the box office just to break even. While costs escalate, the movie-going population of 12-to-29-year-olds is expected to shrink as a percentage of the population—from 32.5% now to 26.5% in 1990. "We clearly must succeed in these new markets if we are going to sustain the viability of the theatrical motion picture business," says Alan J. Hirschfield, vice-chairman of Twentieth Century-Fox Film Corp.

Theater venture. Pay-movie services could revolutionize Hollywood's distribution system. "I see a day when there is a major investment in a film premiering in 20 million homes," says Frank E. Rosenfelt, chairman of Metro-Goldwyn-Mayer Film Co. His predictions have not been ignored by theater owners already concerned about declining box office attendance. Metropolitan Theater Corp., for instance, has formed a joint venture with Falcon Communications and has won two cable franchises in Southern California. "As long as this is going to be part of the industry, we should be part of it," explains Metropolitan Theater President Bruce Corwin.

But movie producers have been slow to realize what pay-cable could mean to their business. Middlemen such as Time's HBO and Showtime, jointly owned by Teleprompter Corp. and Viacom International Inc., have sewn up 85% of the pay-TV market, commanding 30% of the revenues and leaving unhappy Hollywood suppliers with about 20%. Cable operators usually get 50%.

Four movie companies—MCA-Universal, Paramount, Columbia, and Fox—have joined forces with Getty Oil Co. to launch their own pay-movie service called Premiere. The Justice Dept. has filed suit against the five companies, charging them with violating U. S. antitrust laws. However, Premiere executives say that HBO and Showtime are the culprits. "How can the pay-movie market be competitive when two people have 85% of the business?" asks Francis T. Vincent, president of Columbia Pictures Industries Inc.

The suit is expected to be tied up in court for some time. In the interim, Premiere executives are moving ahead with a $200 million investment—promoting Premiere in trade magazines, hiring employees, and lining up transmission space on satellites.

More movie channels. Whether HBO or Premiere dominates the pay-movie market, it appears that there will still be room for others. Cable operators have discovered that subscribers are willing to buy more than one pay-cable channel. Warner Communications' Movie Channel now has 600,000 subscribers. HBO is offering a second pay-movie service called Cinemax, designed to complement HBO's schedule. Rainbow Programming Service Corp., owned by four multiple system operators, is selling two services, Escapade, featuring R-rated movies, and bravo!, featuring cultural events. Galavision, the pay service in Spanish, shows movies from Latin America, as well as sports events such as soccer and bullfights. Other companies that have indicated they will soon begin pay-TV services include Times Mirror Co. and Falcon Communications.

In addition to pay-cable services, programming is being developed that will be provided to cable subscribers with basic cable service. Two channels already operating are Ted Turner's Cable News Network and Getty's Entertainment & Sports Network.

Making its debut in mid-1981 will be CBS Inc.'s cultural cable channel. CBS executives hope to popularize the dance, theater, and musical events that have made the Public Broadcasting System (PBS) such a hit among more sophisticated television viewers. One of the CBS channel's early offerings is expected to be the Joseph Papp production of *The Taming of the Shrew*, starring Meryl Streep and Raul Julia.

Networks join in. Robert E. Shay, CBS Cable's vice-president, says a cultural channel will be just the beginning of the network's involvement in cable programming. William S. Paley, chief executive officer of CBS, has plans for a second channel, Shay says.

CBS's cultural channel, like Turner's CNN and Getty's ESPN, will accept advertising. While these channels command smaller audiences than network TV, most advertisers believe that the narrow subject matter means that they will capture the right audiences for their products. Anheuser-Busch Inc., for instance, interested in reaching the beer-drinking sports fan, recently signed a $25 million five-year contract with ESPN.

Other pay-cable services, however, are afraid that they will lose viewers if they add commercials to their shows. "We are convinced that a consumer will pay more for a service without commercials than an advertiser would ever be willing to pay to reach those consumers," says Peter A. Gross, HBO's general counsel.

Many executives in the cable industry believe that the combination of subscriber fees and advertising revenues will let cable outbid the networks for blockbuster movies and sports events. In the not too distant future, predicts one cable official, viewers will pay to see the Olympics and the Super Bowl.

112 / Readings from *Business Week*

bids. Continental Cablevision, which ultimately won, offered to build an addition to the town's library to house a media center. In other areas, cities have asked the cable companies for help with budget deficits and water pollution problems.

The problems that both the companies and cities are having with the franchise process indicates to many that some guidelines are needed. The National League of Cities has formed a task force to develop fair franchising practices, beefing up the enforcement powers given to local governments. But now that the federal government is getting out of the cable regulation business, many cable operators would like to see local regulation end, too. "I feel that rate regulation is completely unwarranted," says Ralph M. Baruch, chairman and chief executive officer for Viacom International Inc. "The cable company wants the largest audience, and the only way to get it is by marketing it at a good rate."

'The funds are available'

Still, most cable company officials want the FCC to continue to enforce its rule holding the municipal share of cable revenues to 5%. "We are concerned that some cities would get greedy if the limits were lifted," says Ralph J. Swett, president of Times Mirror Cable Television Inc., the sixth-largest cable operator. Those revenues are important to the cable industry because it is apparent it will need all the cash it can get to finance its expansion. That task is proving to be gargantuan. Industry observer Kagan estimates that for the next 10 years, the cable industry will need $14 billion in capital to build new systems and rebuild old ones.

In many parts of the country, cable wiring can be strung up on existing telephone poles. In the past this was a lengthy and expensive process because of conflicts with the telephone companies. But in 1976, Congress passed a law

The new frontier: Talking back to your TV

In the last six months, every company bidding for a city's cable franchise has promised a system that will let viewers talk back to their TV sets. Suddenly, QUBE, Warner Amex Cable Corp.'s well-known, $20 million, Columbus (Ohio) experiment with two-way, or interactive, cable systems is no longer an anomaly. From Fort Lauderdale, Fla., to Portland, Ore., local governments are demanding that the franchises they award include such two-way services as opinion polling, fire protection, and news-wire stories.

Other cable companies, however, are annoyed at suggestions that two-way, or interactive, systems are Warner Amex's brainchild. In fact, Tocom Inc., a cable-equipment manufacturer based in Irving, Tex., is suing Warner Amex for patent infringement and unfair trade practices involving two-way cable. Although Warner Amex has won two large franchises—in Cincinnati and Dallas—on the strength of QUBE, other cable companies also are winning franchises because of their own two-way systems. Cox Cable Communications Inc., for instance, credits INDAX, its interactive system, for winning it the Omaha franchise.

The cable industry has yet to determine just what interactive service will attract consumers. "We are able technologically to do a lot more than our society is willing to accept," notes Donald J. Barhyte, vice-president of Multimedia Inc.

The industry faces a further obstacle to the development of interactive services. Much of the nation is wired with older, 12-channel cable systems that cannot accommodate two-way traffic. Other cable systems built after 1972 can handle this load, but not without additional parts. Less than 1% of the 4,150 cable systems in place today are interactive.
Costly rewiring. Michael R. Corboy, Tocom's president, estimates that companies will spend $1,000 to $1,500 per mi. to refurbish the older cable systems and $200 per mi. for those already built but not yet operable as two-way.

The challenge ahead is finding those two-way services that will be successful enough to justify this massive investment. Not every service will work. "Opinion polling did not prove to be a business," explains Corboy. "People got tired of it after a while and went back to watching *Mork and Mindy*."

Now, Tocom and Warner Amex are convinced that home security and information retrieval are the next ancillary cable services consumers will buy. Warner Amex added fire, burglar, and medical alert services to its QUBE offerings last year and already has signed up 2,500 of its 25,000 cable subscribers in Columbus.
Security demand. Home-security services may even overtake pay-TV in popularity. In the 30,000-acre, federally supported "new town" of Woodlands, Tex., just north of Houston, Tocom has found that 90% of the city's 3,000 homes take basic cable, 50% buy pay-TV, and 65% purchase its security system. And at $12 a month, the security system costs a little more than movie channels in Woodlands.

The next frontier, information retrieval services, has won the commitment of Warner Amex and Tocom. A company with $10 million in sales last year, Tocom recently went out and raised that amount through Rotan Mosle Inc. in Dallas and E. F. Hutton & Co. to finance what the company calls its Tocom 55 plus, a handheld, wireless terminal that can manage 55 channels of video and another 55 channels of data—a total of 110 cable channels. Not to be outdone, Warner Amex will introduce a comparable information retrieval service on the Columbus QUBE system in December.

Environmental Opportunities/Enterprise Threats / 113

setting cable-to-pole attachment rates. Increasingly, however, the construction is going underground, and the cost of building such systems can be prohibitive. In certain parts of San Francisco, for instance, Viacom will spend $100,000 per mile to relocate or get into underground ducts and to avoid the city's sewer system.

Because most cable companies are developing reputations as sound financial investments, industry officials are optimistic that the capital will be there. "The funds are available from lenders to help us construct our systems properly," says consultant Daniels. Business Development Services Inc., the venture capital subsidiary of General Electric Co.—which also is the parent company of General Electric Cablevision Inc.—is actively seeking equity in cable systems. President Pedro A. Castillo says the company has invested $2 million in a cable system being built in Arlington, Va., in exchange for a 49.9% equity position.

Kagan says that in addition to loans from banks and insurance companies, and from sales of stock, a great deal of capital will be generated by the industry itself. "A considerable amount can be internal because their cash flows are so high," Kagan says. "The industry won't have any difficulty funding its requirements over the next several years."

Gobbling each other up

Small cable companies without large cash resources are not expected to survive. Already these smaller systems are being gobbled up by the larger ones. Such a trend will mean a further consolidation of the cable industry. At present, 50 of the largest MSOs own 75% of the nation's cable systems. "I think we'll wind up like the utility industries, with only a few moms and pops," says Wometco's Lewis. "I can't even count the number of systems we've bought over the years."

Rifkin, of American Television & Communications, admits that the company is constantly looking for acquisitions. "We are now looking at a big one in Honolulu," he says. According to Dennis H. Leibowitz, an industry analyst with Donaldson, Lufkin & Jenrette Securities Corp., the value of cable systems has escalated so much in the past few years that smaller operators find it difficult not to sell out. "It's got to be tempting to them," he says.

When all the frantic bidding and expensive building is over, the companies that make it through the long drought—surmounting the problems of capital demand, competition, construction, and regulation—could reap a bountiful harvest. "You don't make money on day one," says Warner Amex's Hauser. "You have costs, depreciation, and not enough subscribers to pay for it all."

Such words of caution do not appear to be dampening anyone's enthusiasm. "The cable industry is on a high right now—it's taking off," declares Carl Pilnick, president of Telecommunications Management Corp. And more than one company, afraid of missing the gravy train, is jumping on board. ■

THE IMPLICATIONS OF OIL COMPANY PROFITS

In the 1970s, the world economy witnessed a major revolution as the Organization of Petroleum Exporting Countries raised the price of oil tenfold and brought about a massive international redistribution of income and wealth from oil consumers to oil producers. In the 1980s, the U. S. economy seems to be set for a revolution along similar lines as higher oil prices bring a large-scale redistribution of wealth and income from consumers and corporations to the oil industry. And just as the world economy faces a monumental job in recycling the enormous OPEC petrodollar surpluses during this decade, the U. S. economy is faced with the challenge of recycling the huge oil profits in order to ensure that other industries have the capital to invest in badly needed plant and equipment.

This redistribution of profits was sparked by the fourfold boost in oil prices by OPEC in 1974. Profits dipped over the next few years but then really exploded at the end of the decade when oil prices were again boosted sharply (chart). The magnitude of the oil industry's growth in the share of total corporate profits is mind-numbing. Oil companies now account for 40% of total profits of the manufacturing sector, in sharp contrast to 18% only two years ago and 15% in 1972. That this process is accelerating is evidenced by the BUSINESS WEEK Corporate Scoreboard (page 53), which shows that in the middle of one of the sharpest recessions on record oil companies increased their net aftertax earnings in the second quarter by some 32% over the year-ago figure, while the rest of U. S. industry was suffering a profit decline of 18%.

If this trend continues, and the evidence suggests that it will—despite the windfall profits tax—then the massive shift in corporate profits could have serious implications for the U. S. economy in the next decade. It could:
■ Lower the rate of economic growth as more and more companies find it increasingly difficult to acquire funds for capital investment either from internally generated sources or from financial markets.
■ Lead to a continued loss of economic efficiency within the corporate sector as oil company managements, with more money than they know what to do with, take on unfamiliar projects, while other companies have to abandon some ventures because of lack of funds.
■ Exacerbate inflation as companies seek to boost their declining profit margins by raising prices.

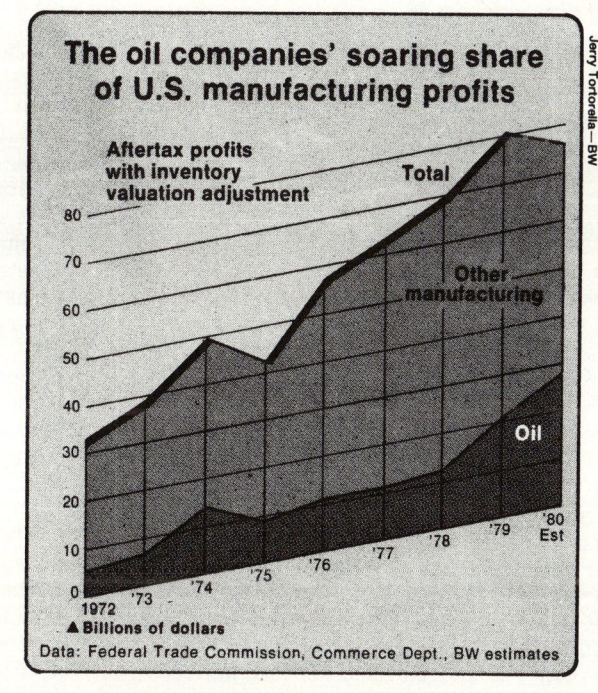

The oil companies' soaring share of U.S. manufacturing profits

Aftertax profits with inventory valuation adjustment

Billions of dollars
Data: Federal Trade Commission, Commerce Dept., BW estimates

The extent of the redistribution of profits to the oil industry and the implications it holds for the U. S. economy are not yet fully appreciated by most economists, in part because conventional economic statistics understate the problem.

The oil giants appear to have more money than they can invest efficiently

The figures published by the Commerce Dept. as part of the national income accounts, for example, exclude foreign earnings, which for the oil industry amount to about one-third of its reported profits.

The clearest picture of oil company profits relative to all other profits can be derived from the Federal Trade Commission's *Quarterly Financial Report*, which includes foreign earnings. Adjusting these numbers for the paper profits arising from gains in inventories shows that the oil industry accounted for nearly $2 of every $5 in total manufacturing profits in the first three months of 1980. And the situation is not expected to be much different for the year as a whole.

More important, the oil industry appears able to retain its huge share of profits. The existence of price controls on crude oil and natural gas was, of course, one of the major factors that kept oil profits relatively limited after their initial surge in 1974 and allowed the rest of the corporate sector to escape the full impact of the OPEC revolution. But the cost was an unsustainable increase in oil imports as domestic demand was encouraged and domestic production restrained. Thus decontrol, which will be complete for crude oil by October, 1981, and largely so for natural gas soon afterward, will represent a catching-up process that is likely to bring a new surge of oil company profits regardless of what happens with OPEC's pricing policy.

To be sure, the fall in profits for many oil companies between the first and second quarters of 1980 suggests to some observers that an erosion of profits similar to that of the mid-1970s may be under way. But a closer examination of the profit pattern shows that this dip is temporary. For one thing, operating profits were not really as low as they seemed, because the bottom line for most majors was penalized by foreign-exchange losses caused by the decline of the dollar. In contrast, there were sizable foreign exchange gains during the first period. But more important was the effect of the windfall profits tax, which became effective on Mar. 1 and caused a one-shot dip in profits from oil production. Now, however, production profits will be rising steeply once again as the process of decontrol picks up.

According to Warren M. Shimmerlik, an oil expert with Merrill Lynch, Pierce, Fenner & Smith Inc., pretax income for domestic oil and gas producers will just about double between 1979 and 1982 to about $50 billion. And the figure could be higher, since Shimmerlik does not take into account that the windfall profits tax will probably be less because it is indexed to the rate of inflation.

At others' expense. If higher oil company profits were simply added on top of normal earnings for the rest of the corporate sector, they would not pose much of a problem. But, says Gary M. Wenglowski, director of economic research for Goldman, Sachs & Co., "rather than increasing total corporate earnings, the high oil profits are coming at the expense of other industries."

What seems to be happening is some-

Environmental Opportunities/Enterprise Threats / 115

Last year's gain in the value of reserves far outstripped oil company profits

1979

	Net income	Gain in oil reserves' value
	Billions of dollars	
Exxon	$ 4.295	$ 9.819
Mobil	2,010	5,358
Standard Oil (Calif.)	1,785	3,570
Texaco	1,759	4,001
Standard Oil (Ind.)	1,507	4,896
Gulf	1,322	3,681
Standard Oil (Ohio)	1,186	6,787
Atlantic Richfield	1,166	4,300
Shell	1,126	2,150
Phillips	0,891	2,543
Conoco	0,815	2,254
Sun	0,700	1,272
Getty	0,604	3,550
Amerada Hess	0,507	1,051
Union Oil	0,501	2,171
Total	**$20.174**	**$57.403**

Data: Corporate 10-K reports.

thing like a zero-sum game in which the process that brings wealth to the oil companies takes it away from other sectors of the economy. Airlines and truckers, for example, do not seem to be able to recoup increased fuel expenses in the fiercely competitive markets they now face because of deregulation, while auto companies and their suppliers have suffered from the impact of higher gasoline prices on the demand for U. S.-made cars. And there is a more general cyclical phenomenon as oil-generated inflation has both reduced real consumer incomes and provoked monetary authorities into engineering a recession.

Investment lag. According to William Nordhaus of Yale University, the rate of return on plant and equipment for most of U. S. industry is now at the lowest level since the Great Depression. Nordhaus believes this clearly signals a continuation of the capital investment lag that has largely been responsible for the lack of major renovation by older industries and the dismal showing of productivity. The growing maldistribution of profits will exacerbate these problems and lead to slower economic growth as much of U. S. industry is unable to generate the earnings needed to finance investment.

"You have one sector—oil—that's vigorous, and essentially the rest of the economy that is more or less stagnant. This will change the entire pattern of investment," says Paul Davidson, of Rutgers University. The critical question of whether this will lead to less capital investment for the economy as a whole will depend, explains Davidson, on whether the capital markets are efficient in recycling the oil profits to other industries and whether other industries will be demanding those funds. "Even if the markets worked perfectly, the problem is that because profit prospects are poor for the rest of industry, the demand for investment funds will be falling short," argues Davidson.

Oil companies, meanwhile, appear to have more money than they can invest efficiently. For not only do higher oil prices mean greater current income but they also substantially increase the net worth of the oil companies and their borrowing power as the value of reserves soars. Some notion of the size of this increase comes from the new system of "reserve recognition accounting," which the Securities & Exchange Commission now requires oil companies to include with their annual 10-K reports. The unrealized capital gains that resulted from last year's runup in domestic prices for the 15 largest domestic oil producers came to $57 billion, nearly three times their reported profits. And since domestic oil prices, net of windfall profits taxes, are certain to rise by at least $8 a bbl. over the next 15 months, a boost of similar size is obviously in the works. This will add to the oil companies' considerable leverage in financial markets.

Much of the industry's profits and new borrowing power will continue to be invested in developing both oil and alternative sources of energy. But with a 40% increase in drilling activity over the past year and wild bidding contests that are inflating the price of even highly speculative leases, there is mounting evidence that the practical limits for domestic exploration and development may soon be reached unless major changes are made in federal landuse policies. Meanwhile, the synfuels program, which was once thought of as an attractive target for private investment, has been just about preempted in its opening stages by government funding from the proceeds of the windfall profits tax. Large-scale private investment is not now expected until the 1990s, when the results of current pilot projects are known.

Power concentration. There is a real possibility, therefore, of a wave of conglomerate mergers by oil companies seeking to employ idle resources. William A. Lovett, director of the energy policy center at Tulane University, estimates that the oil companies will have as much as $150 billion available for such enterprises over the next few years. "Tax laws, force of habit, and corporate management's desire to expand their own bureaucratic growth horizons make it likely that much of it will be used for that purpose," he says.

The prospect of giant oil companies spreading out in all directions is alarming to conventional antitrusters who see it threatening a dangerous concentration of economic power. But the real problem to most economists is that in the past the conglomerate movement has suffered from a lack of managerial expertise as executives in one industry proved unequal to the task of running enterprises that require a different set of skills. And there is nothing about the oil industry to suggest that their side ventures will be any more successful.

One way to reduce the possibility of misdirected mergers is to reduce the oil industry's cash hoard through additional taxation. But a far better solution, say economists, is to recycle oil profits back to the stockholders in the form of higher dividend payments. Since much of these dividends will probably be reinvested, this would allow the private capital markets, rather than the government, to determine where the oil profits could be most efficiently employed. Right now, oil companies pay out only 24% of their earnings in dividends, compared with 40% for other manufacturing industries.

Special tax credit. Encouraging bigger dividend payments by the oil companies, however, would probably require some change in the tax laws. Because dividends are now subject to double taxation, the integration of corporate and personal income taxes might encourage oil company stockholders to pressure managements for bigger payouts.

Other business tax measures may also be required. For example, energy intensive industries are contributing a disproportionate amount to oil company profits. In order to recycle those profits back to financially strapped industrial energy

Some economists suggest recycling oil profits in the form of higher dividends

users, some economists advocate that they be granted a special tax credit.

Aside from the recycling issue, however, there remains the problem of the effect on inflation of the maldistribution of profits. For as soon as the recovery gains strength, more and more companies will be tempted to repair depressed profit margins by sharp increases in prices. Just how successful these companies will be in raising prices will depend both on the strength of the demand for their products and on foreign competition. But the very scramble to raise prices initially could be inflationary, because unions will be tempted to increase wage demands. Moreover, bottlenecks created by lagging investment in energy-intensive basic industry, which is particularly affected by the profits shift, could exert further inflationary pressures.

The difficult adjustment that the U. S. economy faces over the next several years can be blamed in part on Washington's long procrastination in dealing with the full implications of the OPEC revolution. The massive adjustments that are required in the U. S. economy would have been far easier to make if government had decontrolled oil prices after the first surge in OPEC prices rather than waiting until last year's repeat performance. Likewise, it is better to make the adjustments now than to wait for the next OPEC price explosion. ∎

VIDEODISCS
A THREE-WAY RACE FOR A BILLION-DOLLAR JACKPOT

The world has spent more than a decade and nearly $1 billion arming for the coming battle over videodiscs. By the end of next year, three technologies and at least twice that many giant companies will be pitted against one another, each with the same goal: to win the lion's share of a lucrative new U.S. consumer market that promises to outstrip the $6.5 billion annual color-TV business.

The impact of videodiscs will go far beyond the consumer marketplace, however. Coupled with a little computer power, they promise to change the way that employees are trained, equipment is maintained, students are taught, and products are demonstrated and sold. As the companies perfect ways to write on discs as well as read from them, videodiscs are likely to find a niche in "the office of the future" by performing all the jobs done by today's photocopier, file cabinet, and facsimile machine. And, by storing digital data instead of images, they threaten to upset the current hierarchy of products that store computer data—magnetic tapes, discs, and cartridges (page 78).

The competition for such industrial applications will be keen, but the contenders have pretty much agreed on the videodisc technology to use. Not so the consumer companies, each of which is betting that it can sell enough discs and players to dominate the market and, that way, recapture a massive investment in proprietary technology.

Although their goal may be the same, the consumer companies' strategies are different and their technologies incompatible. The videodisc player is the visual equivalent of the phonograph; it plays discs prerecorded with television signals much as a turntable spins audio records. But of the three systems now proposed, none will play discs manufactured for the others. The resulting confusion will dampen consumer enthusiasm, just as incompatible formats stalled the early years of color TV and long-play records. Further, videodiscs face growing competition from other video media—pay television, for example, and videotape recorders, which can record TV signals as well as play them back.

The fight for the consumer dollar will be a struggle among giants, and those giants have already started forging powerful international alliances. RCA Corp., for example, has lined up archrivals Zenith Radio Corp. and CBS Inc. to make its version of players and discs. Early next year, that team will launch its products against the only videodisc system now on the market, a version developed by Philips, the $16.6 billion Dutch electronics giant, and MCA Inc., the Universal City (Calif.) entertainment conglomerate. MCA has drawn International Business Machines Corp. and Japan's Pioneer Electronic Corp. into a tangled web of joint ventures that sell players and discs to both the consumer and industrial markets.

Neither of those teams is discounting the Japanese entry, a latecomer proposed by Matsushita Electric Industrial Co., which, with its National, Panasonic, and Quasar brands, is the world's largest consumer electronics company. Matsushita has adopted a videodisc format developed by subsidiary Victor Co. of Japan (JVC) and has so far enlisted General Electric Co. in the U.S. and Britain's Thorn EMI Ltd. in a scramble to be ready for next year's Christmas market (BW—June 23).

Such an array of incompatible players "will slow the market down," contends Thomas R. Shepherd, senior vice-president at GTE Entertainment Products Group, "even though the consumer is not interested in the features of the player, but in the artist or performer he can get." The General Telephone & Electronics Corp. unit, known for its Sylvania and Philco television lines, is the only major U.S. setmaker that has not picked a videodisc system—a job that will be completed next month. The choice is a tricky one, Shepherd notes, because in 1985 "we'll still have three formats, since there are three powerful groups backing them."

Most observers agree that videodisc player sales can grow side-by-side with videotape recorders (VTRs). Although the prerecorded videotapes are more expensive than videodiscs, VTR machines enjoy a distinct competitive advantage over disc players: They can record video programs as well as play them back. Later in the decade, as video camera prices fall, VTRs will give conventional film cameras a run for the money in the home movie market.

For watching movies, premium cable-TV channels, such as Home Box Office, can offer the consumer a far greater range than videodiscs and at lower prices, reasons George K. Tucker, senior consultant at SRI International. "The question," he says, "is whether the disc industry can develop some sort of programming unique to the medium."

Most analysts agree, however, with RCA's forecast that annual disc player sales will pass 5 million by the end of the decade. Those sales, when coupled with prerecorded disc sales of 200 million to 250 million, would then total a $7.5 billion annual business. But some observers dispute RCA's view of how fast the market will build. Tucker, for one, estimates that only 600,000 videodisc players will be sold in 1985, while RCA alone is planning to hit an annual production rate of 500,000 by the end of next year.

It is clear that the battle will be waged first in the U.S. European announcements are lagging by a year or more, and the Japanese government wants manufacturers to agree on a single format before they enter their home market. In the U.S., RCA is the current favorite.

"The videodisc is RCA's Manhattan Project," declares RCA Executive Vice-President Roy H. Pollack. RCA figures that it has already spent more than the $138 million it took to bring color TV to market 25 years ago. In the 19 months since RCA Chairman Edgar H. Griffiths gave the go-ahead, the company's Indianapolis-based videodisc staff has ballooned tenfold to nearly 300.

The company's strategy is to distinguish its videodisc player from the more versatile videotape gear by price. When it reaches dealers' shelves early next February, the $500 SelectaVision videodisc player will be about half the price of RCA's cheapest VTR. An accompanying catalog will list 150 discs at $15 to $25

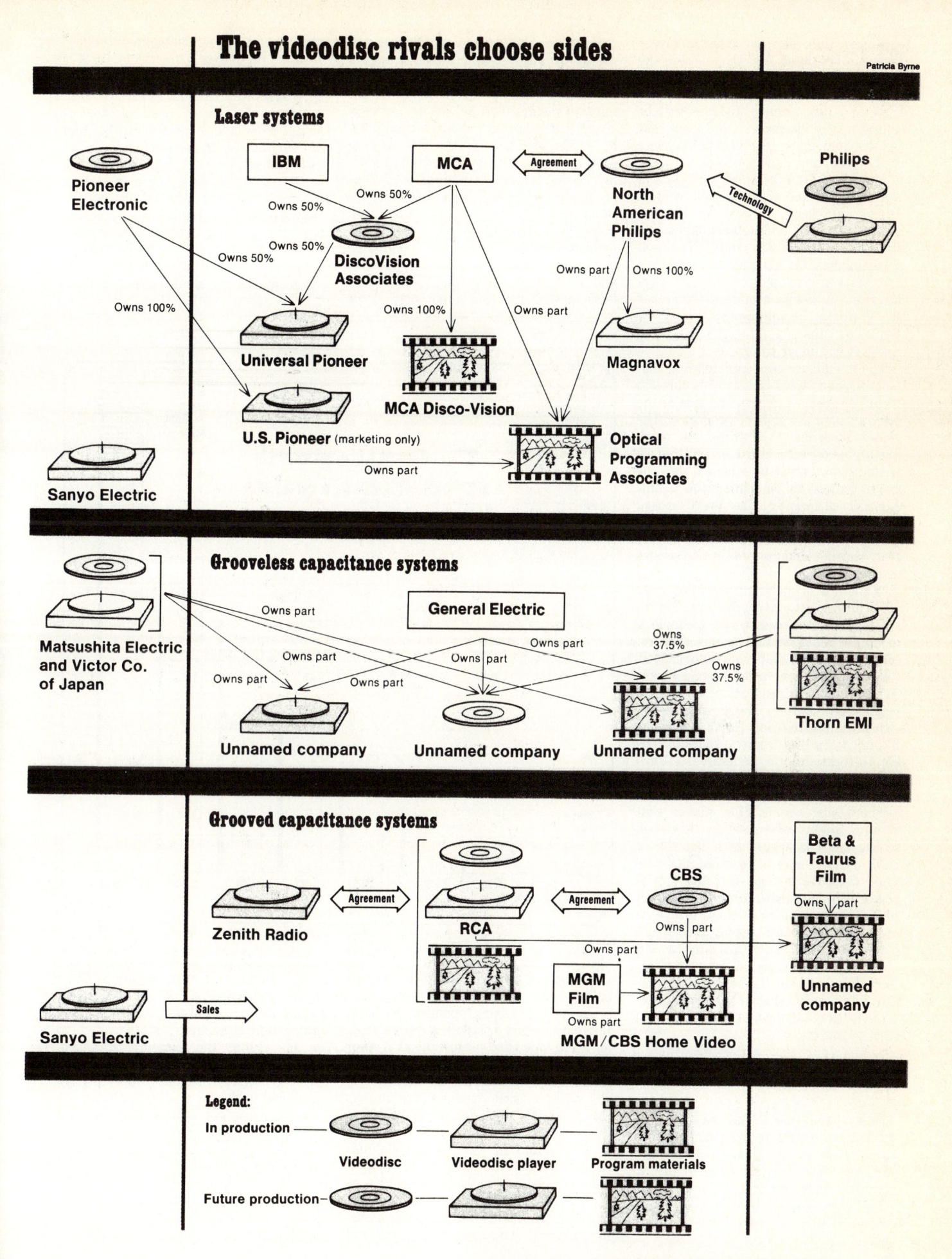

The videodisc rivals choose sides

Patricia Byrne

Laser systems

- Pioneer Electronic — Owns 100% → Universal Pioneer; → U.S. Pioneer (marketing only)
- IBM — Owns 50% → DiscoVision Associates
- MCA — Owns 50% → DiscoVision Associates
- DiscoVision Associates — Owns 50% → Universal Pioneer; Owns 50% → U.S. Pioneer
- MCA — Owns 100% → MCA Disco-Vision; Owns part → Optical Programming Associates
- MCA ↔ Agreement ↔ North American Philips
- Philips — Technology → North American Philips
- North American Philips — Owns part → Optical Programming Associates; Owns 100% → Magnavox
- U.S. Pioneer — Owns part → Optical Programming Associates
- Sanyo Electric

Grooveless capacitance systems

- Matsushita Electric and Victor Co. of Japan — Owns part → Unnamed company (player), Unnamed company (disc), Unnamed company (program)
- General Electric — Owns part → Unnamed company (player), Unnamed company (disc), Unnamed company (program)
- Thorn EMI — Owns 37.5% → Unnamed company (program); Owns 37.5% → (player)

Grooved capacitance systems

- Sanyo Electric — Sales → Zenith Radio
- Zenith Radio ↔ Agreement ↔ RCA
- RCA ↔ Agreement ↔ CBS
- RCA — Owns part → Unnamed company
- CBS — Owns part → MGM/CBS Home Video
- MGM Film — Owns part → MGM/CBS Home Video
- Beta & Taurus Film — Owns part → Unnamed company

Legend:

- In production — Videodisc, Videodisc player, Program materials
- Future production — Videodisc, Videodisc player, Program materials

Environmental Opportunities/Enterprise Threats

each, less than half the price of prerecorded videotapes. By the end of the year, Pollack hopes to have sold 200,000 players and more than 2 million discs.

By mid-1981, Zenith and CBS will be selling RCA-made players and discs, but CBS will turn on its own disc factory late in the year, and Zenith will switch over to players of its own design sometime in 1982. Zenith and RCA together control nearly half the U.S. color-TV market, and CBS claims a similar distribution strength for its records group. "You need a mechanism for getting the hardware and software to the consumer," says Raymond L. Boggs, a market researcher at Venture Development Corp., of Wellesley, Mass. "RCA has the marketing skills. It can move the goods."

The RCA player uses a microscopic diamond-tipped stylus that travels through 12 mi. of grooves to play one side of the disc, an hour's worth of programs. The glossy black disc is stamped out much like a phonograph record, except that 38 of its grooves must be squeezed into the space that a single audio groove fills. Another difference: The metal-backed stylus picks up electrical information from the conductive-plastic disc rather than sensing undulations in the groove mechanically.

While RCA is pushing its technology to get a low-priced player, the MCA/Philips strategy is to harness a new technology to obtain features that a videotape recorder—or RCA's player—cannot match. "We wanted a system that could live in the market for a generation, at least 25 years," says John C. Messerschmitt, the vice-president heading North American Philips Corp.'s videodisc program. The key to that long life, he figures, is Philips' optical technology and the advancements that it affords.

The result was a $775 player that Philips' Magnavox subsidiary has been selling since late 1978 in a handful of U.S. cities. Using a laser to read pits pressed into a silvery disc, the optical player can page through, one by one, all 54,000 frames on one side of a disc, or it can search for and display any single frame randomly. That opens up the potential for new types of programming: discs that combine slides, motion pictures, and music—discs that are not necessarily played straight through from start to finish.

A new capability

"Any new system that goes into the market has to lean on existing programming," Messerschmitt concedes. "But for the long term, our thrust is not just to provide programming that's available in other ways. We see the need for a new communications capability for the home."

But the same technology that is the source of Philips' and MCA's strengths has given the consortium a number of fits and starts. Without a stylus grinding into them, the MCA discs do not wear out. Neither do they require a rigid plastic caddy such as the one RCA uses to protect its disc from dust and fingerprints. But where RCA stamps both sides of its discs at once from a single shot of conductive plastic, the MCA discs are made from two three-layer disc sides bonded together. The process is undoubtedly more troublesome and expensive, and, indeed, MCA has had major problems perfecting continuous-play discs that can match RCA's hour-per-side.

The optical player's gas laser makes it bulkier and more expensive than the proposed RCA and Japanese versions. But, says Stuart J. Lipoff, a design engineer and videodisc consultant at Arthur D. Little Inc., "RCA is running at the limits at what mechanical technology can do, while optical systems are at the threshold of a steep descent in price."

The most immediate candidate for cost reduction is the player's helium-neon laser. A solid-state laser replacement, he says, "would be amenable to the bulk-process semiconductor technology that has made all other semiconductors cheap." Although Lipoff will not predict when such a change will be cost-effective, the player's makers figure it is still two to three years away. "Our strategy," says Ken T. Kai, executive vice-president of U.S. Pioneer Electronics Corp., "is to hold on to the market and wait for the second generation."

Pioneer on June 20 introduced its $750 version of the Philips player in Dallas, the first stop in a city-by-city rollout that will lead to national distribution sometime next year. Pioneer, the world's largest component hi-fi supplier, should bring the MCA/Philips team badly needed marketing clout as well as open up sales channels other than TV dealers.

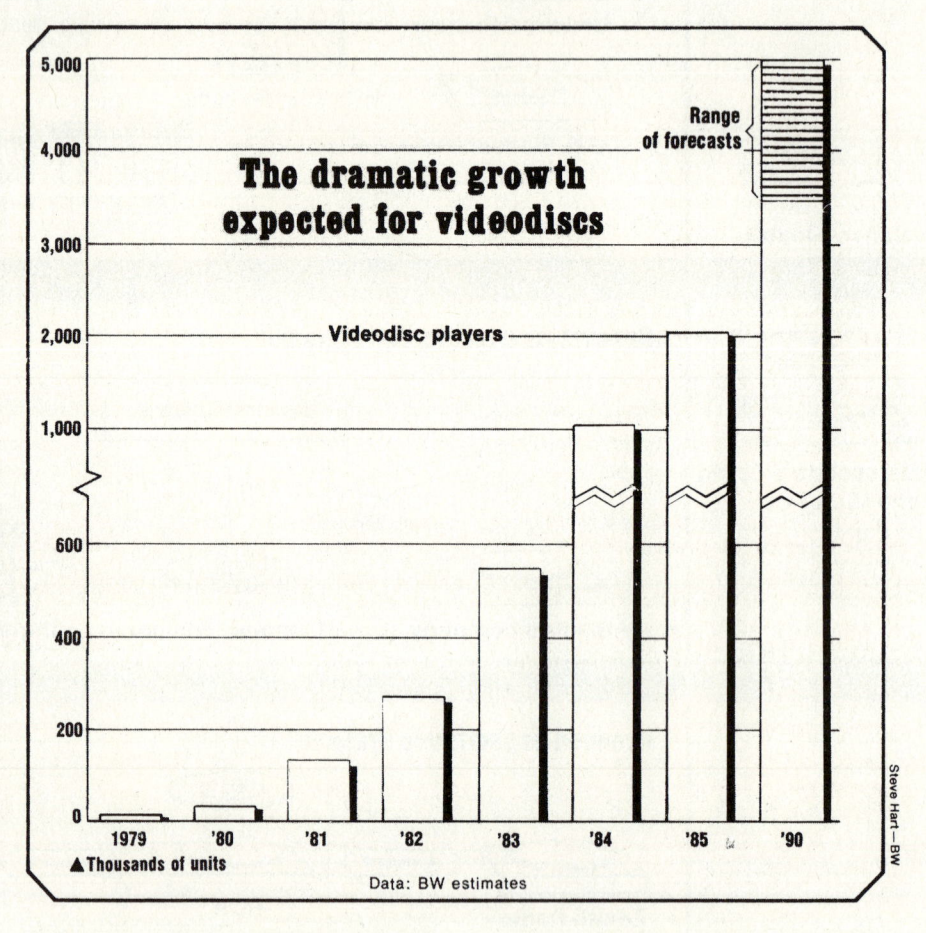

The dramatic growth expected for videodiscs

Videodisc players — Thousands of units
Range of forecasts shown for 1990.

1979: ~10
'80: ~30
'81: ~130
'82: ~270
'83: ~550
'84: ~1,000
'85: ~2,000
'90: ~4,000–5,000 (range of forecasts)

Data: BW estimates

Most Japanese manufacturers, however, have taken a wait-and-see attitude toward videodiscs, a posture encouraged by the Japanese government. But giant Matsushita is pushing for its system to be adopted as the Japanese standard. With partners GE and Thorn EMI, Matsushita and its JVC affiliate hope to have products ready for the 1981 Christmas rush, and the player will strike a compromise between the opposing camps. Matsushita claims that its price will be somewhere between RCA's and Philips', but it will incorporate the "freeze" frame and slow-motion features, for example, of the Philips technology.

"We've been able to go to school on

The rivalry to supply programs

Shortly after RCA Corp. decided that its videodisc player was finally ready to market, Herbert S. Schlosser, in charge of programming, called Roy H. Pollack, who runs the consumer electronics operation, to say that he had clinched the first deal for the company's disc catalog. "I told Roy we'd lined up *Jesus of Nazareth*," Schlosser recalls, "and he said, 'Great! We need all the help we can get.'"

The story may be apocryphal, but it underscores the point. The two RCA executive vice-presidents realized that the videodisc customer would not be interested in the player but only in the programs it will bring him. RCA's first catalog will list *Jesus of Nazareth*, a television special, along with 150 other titles.

Such software, as the industry calls the programs going onto videodiscs, is owned largely by the entertainment industry—the movie studios, the record companies, and the TV networks. Already, these companies have begun moving to tighten their grip on a market that they figure is rightfully theirs.

"We will license our product to no one," insists Stephen Roberts, president of Twentieth Century-Fox Film Corp.'s Telecommunications Div. "We will manufacture the discs ourselves, or cause them to be made." Fox and the other major studios want to control the disc product from back lot to consumer. Columbia Pictures Industries Inc., for example, will launch its first batch of videodiscs this summer.

Home screenings. Movies are likely to be the best sellers in the videodisc's early years. The studios have a ready supply in their film libraries, and the films are easily transferred to discs. Most player makers figure that most early customers will want discs in order to screen movies inexpensively at home.

In recent months, the major studios all formed divisions to handle the production, acquisition, licensing, and distribution of their software. But those divisions are aiming their products not only at the fledgling videodisc market, but also at buyers of videocassettes and at pay TV and cable TV as well. Such new markets will mean new revenues, and analysts estimate that software producers, by controlling distribution, would be able to collect 20% of a disc's retail price in addition to the 15% to 20% cut they would receive for producer royalties.

For the most part, the entertainment companies are likely to offer their products on the discs of all three rival systems. "Our loyalty is to our repertoire," explains Robert W. A. Hart, director of video development for EMI Music Ltd. But EMI's parent, Thorn EMI Ltd., will be making the player designed by Victor Co. of Japan (JVC). Adds Seymour Leslie, president of CBS Video Enterprises, which has committed a factory to RCA-type disc production: "We have the option to do others as well."

The studios, in fact, are stepping up movie production to satisfy the demand created by these ancillary markets. Fox, for example, plans to release more than 25 films a year in the early 1980s, one-third more than last year. Metro-Goldwyn-Mayer Inc., which has formed a joint marketing venture with CBS Inc.'s Records Group, will triple its output of films this year and will boost it again next year.

'Audio-plus.' But while movies may be the initial bait, many companies believe that musical programming will be the key to the long-term success of the videodisc. "Video will be to music as sound was to motion pictures," says Fox's Roberts. Adds CBS's Leslie: "Music will be the second most important category and, in some cases, will vie with commercial films."

These music discs will not be simply films of concerts. Instead, videodiscs will lead to a new art form, suggests Thomas R. Shepherd, senior vice-president of GTE Entertainment Products Group. He calls it "audio-plus." "There are all kinds of video that can be interrelated to audio," he says, citing animation, video graphics, and photography that reflects the theme of the music.

Pioneer Electronic Corp., in fact, is betting that it can turn its large base of audiophiles into videophiles. It started rolling out its optical players in June and recently set up a new subsidiary—Pioneer Artists—specifically to produce music for videodiscs.

An ample supply of television, movie, and music programming is crucial for the initial acceptance of videodisc players. But while RCA has spent millions of dollars in royalty guarantees to license other companies' films, North American Philips Corp. has left program acquisitions to its partner, entertainment conglomerate MCA Inc. Now, faced with the prospect of meeting the powerful RCA-CBS combine in head-to-head competition, Philips has decided to invest some of its own money in programming.

In May, along with DiscoVision Associates and US Pioneer, Philips set up a new venture to acquire programming that exploits the special features of its laser optical players—features not found on RCA's machines. The first disc from Optical Programming Associates, as the venture is called, will be this fall's *How to Watch Pro Football*, a disc explaining football strategy. The viewer can select the type of play to study, freeze the picture to inspect the play diagram, and then watch a complex play in slow motion. Two other discs likely to follow are guitar playing and tennis.

Specialized shows. One of the videodisc's major appeals, in fact, is its ability to offer such specialized programming for small audiences. The industry figures that, when disc production is in full swing, as few as 10,000 discs of one title need be sold to turn a profit. "You can really produce programming for particular interest groups, programming that won't work on broadcast, cable, or pay TV," says Bruce A. Barnet, senior vice-president of Time-Life Films Inc., who runs the nine-month-old video unit of the Time Inc. subsidiary. Besides rock concerts and movies, the Time group plans extensive programming that Barnet calls "video publishing": a health series, for example, and such topics as speed reading and reading efficiency.

American Broadcasting Cos. is also looking to the education market, both for home and schools. Its first disc will be released this summer as part of a joint project with the National Education Assn. Using material gathered by ABC News, the programs will teach such skills as "how to listen" and "how to come to a conclusion," says Herbert A. Granath, the vice-president in charge of ABC Video Enterprises. And ABC has begun a joint effort with the Shubert Organization and independent director Robert Altman to produce theatrical presentations, including ballet and opera, on videotape and discs.

Not all entertainment companies, of course, are as sanguine about the future of videodiscs. "There's just too many people selling too few customers," says Nathaniel T. Kwit Jr., vice-president for video and special markets for Transamerica Corp.'s United Artists Corp. Both United Artists and Gulf & Western Industries Inc.'s Paramount Pictures Corp. have elected not to distribute their own discs. "We think there's going to be a shake-out among the hardware and software distributors," Kwit says.

ABC's Granath agrees. "The potential is there for large growth, but the question is when," he says. "There's been a huge investment in hardware and software, and we're not talking an inexhaustible font of dollars." But no matter which companies succeed or fail, he adds, "the winner will be the viewer."

Environmental Opportunities/Enterprise Threats

A consumer's guide to videodisc players

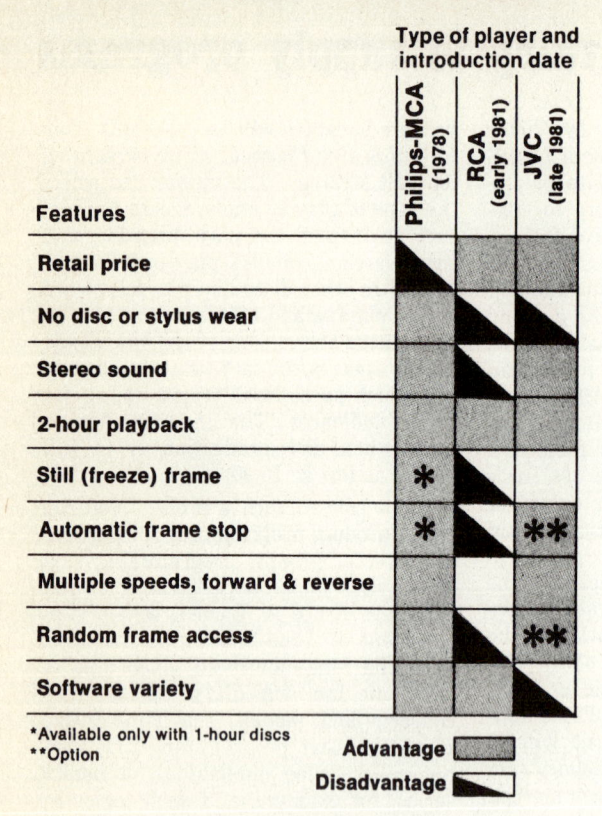

Features	Philips-MCA (1978)	RCA (early 1981)	JVC (late 1981)
Retail price	Disadvantage	Advantage	Advantage
No disc or stylus wear	Advantage	Disadvantage	Disadvantage
Stereo sound	Advantage	Disadvantage	Disadvantage
2-hour playback	Advantage	Advantage	Advantage
Still (freeze) frame	Advantage*	Disadvantage	Advantage
Automatic frame stop	Advantage*	Disadvantage	**
Multiple speeds, forward & reverse	Advantage	Disadvantage	Advantage
Random frame access	Advantage	Disadvantage	**
Software variety	Advantage	Advantage	Disadvantage

*Available only with 1-hour discs
**Option

Data: Manufacturers' specifications

our videotape recorder, so we know the kinds of features people want," says Richard F. O'Brion, executive vice-president of US JVC Corp. in Maspeth, N.Y. "We want to give the consumer as many features as we can in the beginning instead of dragging them out one at a time." Some of the more advanced features, such as random access to individually numbered frames and the ability to preprogram the player to read disc segments in any order, will be housed in a $150 companion unit.

Most of the features are possible because the JVC design does not trap the stylus in a groove. Like RCA's, the JVC-designed player picks up electrical capacitance signals pressed into the disc. But the disc has no grooves. Instead, a flat metal shoe rides the disc surface, guided by tracking signals from the disc. The system's proponents claim that the technique enhances the life of both the disc and the stylus.

"We wanted something easy to make, with indestructible discs," says Yasumasa Noda, general manager of JVC's video product sales. But analysts suggest that there are other reasons for Matsushita's choice of a third, incompatible videodisc format. They did it "to keep from being left behind," says SRI's Tucker. The Japanese build virtually all consumer videotape recorders, but the U.S. has leapfrogged the Japanese with the videodisc—which "the Japanese feel is a threat to their dominance in consumer electronics," he says. "It's the latest new product, and they want to have a proprietary version."

Sanyo Electric Co., too, is impatient with its industry's indecision. The Japanese company said in May that it will build optical players for the European and possibly the Japanese markets—"where quality is important," explains one Japanese competitor—and it will build RCA-type capacitance players for the U.S. Sanyo is the first company to endorse two disc formats.

Although the lack of product standardization may slow the early growth of the consumer videodiscs, it will not impede their use in commercial and industrial applications. For one thing, the programming is almost always commissioned by the machine's owner. For another, industrial users overwhelmingly prefer the advanced features of the optical format, and DiscoVision Associates, the IBM-MCA joint venture, has a healthy head start. It has been shipping its $3,000 industrial-grade player since late 1978.

But DiscoVision will soon face competition. Sony Corp. hopes to introduce its institutional optical disc player by the end of this year. Although the Sony machine will play the MCA discs, the Tokyo-based company will set up its own disc-manufacturing plant as well. And France's Thomson-CSF will put a similar optical player into production this fall. Unlike the Sony and DiscoVision versions, which use the Philips technology, Thomson's $3,500 player uses transparent discs. That way, discs need not be flipped over; the player's laser automatically refocuses to read the other side.

Early applications for industrial players include education and training, point-of-sale aids, and prerecorded communication. DiscoVision Associates has already lined up more than 100 customers for such uses. "We offer a whole new potential that other technologies are not able to address," says John J. Reilly, DiscoVision president. "We offer the features of slides, film, videotape, and sound all in one device, and all under the control of a computer or the viewer."

General Motors Corp. is the largest single user of videodiscs, with 10,200 players scattered among its 13,500 dealers. Initially installed to spur the sales of the Chevrolet Citation, they now also guide mechanics through complicated repairs. Nearly all the 28 one-hour discs that GM has so far issued to its dealer organization are interactive. They are programmed to stop and ask questions and continue when the viewer—mechanic or salesman—answers. A few discs, however, are designed to be played straight through. One recent example: Penn State University football coach Joe Paterno inspires dealers with a homily on the joys of dedication in the face of adversity.

"For the purposes we're talking about—bringing information to dealers—you can't improve on this method," says Edward E. Sullivan, GM's corporate merchandising manager. GM selected discs instead of film or videotape because of the system's almost instant access to any program segment. "You find the customer is always interested in the sixth subject," he explains, "and it takes four minutes on tape to go from front to back. You can whistle or tell stories, but you have to be good to get the customer to stay four minutes."

Ford Motor Co. will replace its videotape network with videodiscs in 1987 for many of the same reasons. "You have more flexibility in the kind of information you can store, the freeze frame is better, and the sound is better," says David M. Pohlod, Ford Div.'s manager for training and communications.

As industrial users learn how to harness videodiscs, they will almost certainly link videodisc players to computers. "Without a controlling computer, the problem of indexing and locating the information stored on discs is enormous," says Craig I. Fields, assistant director for cybernetics technology at the Defense Advanced Research Projects Agency (DARPA), the most sophisticated user of industrial videodiscs.

122 / Readings from *Business Week*

Training the military

DARPA is funding projects that use videodiscs in data-base-management systems, teleconferencing systems, and training simulators. The agency has produced an interactive training movie on karate—the same scene can be viewed from several different vantage points, for example—and it is considering other videodiscs on traversing minefields and defusing bombs. Last month DARPA filmed the San Francisco harbor for a videodisc, a technique that Fields says will be the key to improving conventionally made military maps.

Hughes Aircraft Co. has developed programs for maintaining industrial manufacturing equipment, and it recently packed a 6-ft. stack of maintenance manuals for the Army's M-60 tank onto a single videodisc. Its system, called TMIS for training and maintenance instruction system, weds a Hughes microcomputer to a Thomson-CSF disc player. For each step of a diagnostic procedure, TMIS uses words and pictures to tell a technician what to do. It then quizzes the technician and, based on his response, moves on to the next appropriate step.

Boeing Aerospace Co. is experimenting with discs in conjunction with voice recognition and touch recognition, in part because people do not like to use keyboards and because keyboards are error-prone. One scenario: The technician calls up a picture of a missile on the screen and touches, for example, the nose cone. That brings up a picture of the nose cone, which he can touch again to request more detailed information.

Such an elaborate computer-controlled system is not likely to win widespread use. But the National Science Foundation is funding work at the other end of the scale that could result in a product with far broader application. In a $387,000 project, Wicat Inc., of Orem, Utah, is developing a videodisc system for education that couples a microcomputer to a Magnavox consumer-model player. The system will be tested this fall in biology classes at Brigham Young University at nearby Provo and at Brookhaven College in Dallas.

The programming is a McGraw-Hill Inc. videodisc originally produced to overcome problems associated with the same material's presentation on film. At one point in *The Development of Living Things*, for example, 14 new ideas are introduced in a three-minute film segment. The videodisc uses the same film sequences, but introduces 650 still frames and commentary and gives the student control over how quickly he moves through the course.

"Videodiscs have an incredible opportunity as an instructional device," says one textbook publishing executive who created an experimental videodisc around the features of the Magnavox consumer player. "But it is the consumer market that will lead the way into schools. The analogy is the record player: not until it reached 60% of the homes did it get into the classroom."

The videodisc will revolutionize data storage

The same videodisc technology being developed for the consumer market will have a profound impact, as well, on the information processing business. Dozens of computer equipment manufacturers hope to piggyback on the high-volume consumer marketplace with a development of their own: optical disc products that use lasers not only to play back data but also to engrave the data on the plastic discs. This technology is emerging as the next candidate for the mass storage of images and data on computers.

"Optical discs will impact everything from word processors to large-scale computers," promises Michael Ettenberg, head of the optoelectronic research group at RCA Corp.'s Princeton (N.J.) laboratories. The first commercial products using optical disc memories are likely to be relatively simple, high-capacity storage devices that work with word- and data-processing systems in the office. Japan's Toshiba Corp. will bring a version of such an "electronic file cabinet" to market early next year.

Further off are the more complex systems designed for the computer room. They will make inroads into the magnetic-tape memory business as archival storage systems and as backup storage units for magnetic discs. Eventually, optical discs will take on some of the tasks now performed by microfilm, and they will seek out specialized niches—for example, replacing X-ray film.

Working much like optical-disc players for the consumer market, such systems will read data from a disc by reflecting laser light from the disc's tiny pits—each about 1/100th the diameter of a human hair. But the disc itself is different from its consumer cousin because data storage systems need to record information as well as play it back. While the pits on consumer discs are stamped at the factory, data recording discs are coated first with a thin metal alloy. That way, the recorder's laser can melt the pits—each representing a single "bit" of computer code—into the disc's metal layer. To read the data, the machine switches to lower laser power.

The technology is ready

The big advantages of the optical disc memory are its overwhelming capacity for data and its extremely low cost. It has been the dramatically declining cost of storing data, of course, that has provided the major impetus for the exploding use of computers over the past two decades. Now both North American Philips Corp. and RCA have demonstrated laboratory discs that could store 100 billion bits—roughly equal to the Encyclopaedia Britannica translated into digital form. Philips, meanwhile, has four working systems attached to computers that will record 10 billion bits on each side of a disc. That equals 2,500 megabytes (million characters), the capacity of 25 reels of magnetic tape.

"The technology is ready to go into product development," says Kenneth L. Hutchinson, vice-president, market planning at Magnavox Government & Industrial Electronics Co., a Philips subsidiary. But, adds George R. Sollman, vice-president of Xerox Memory Systems, "the digital disc depends a lot on the consumer world." If the consumer optical disc is a success, he says, it may well set the standard for the optical disc in industrial applications. "Every key component—lasers, lenses—will be very attractively priced. In a certain sense, we're all coming down the same learning curve," says Sollman.

Xerox in April announced that it had teamed up with France's Thomson-CSF to develop jointly an optical disc recorder for data processing and office automation systems; that recorder will be ready by 1982, according to Thomson-CSF Vice-President J. Edouard Guigonis. Philips and RCA both admit to seeking partners in the computer industry. Other companies working on optical storage systems include IBM, Control Data, Honeywell, and Exxon, as well as Japan's Toshiba and Hitachi.

Computer makers probably will not push the optical disc to the 2,500-megabyte capacity that many of them have demonstrated in their labs. "A 1,000-megabyte optical disc is readily doable," says one data processing industry executive. He figures that a recorder-player for such a product can be made for one-quarter of the cost of a similar-size—but magnetic disc—player. "That's a 4-to-1 improvement in the cost of on-line storage," he says. The improvement in off-line storage, calculated on the media cost alone, is even more dramatic. One thousand megabytes on a $100 optical disc would replace $1,000 worth of high-capacity magnetic disc packs.

The biggest market is likely to be for word-processing applications. "Each disc

How memory capacities compare	
Memory device	Storage capacity (millions of characters)
Human brain	125,000,000,000
National Archives	12,500,000,000
IBM 3850 magnetic cartridge	250,000,000
Encyclopedia Britannica	12,500,000
Optical disc memory	12,500,000
Magnetic (hard) disc	313
Floppy disc	2.5
Book	1.3

Data: RCA Corp. Advanced Technology Laboratories

could handle many offices' worth of work, both graphics and digital," says RCA's Ettenberg. He estimates that such storage devices are three to five years from commercialization, "but then there will be hundreds of thousands of them sold."

Another significant market will be in archival storage, replacing today's large vaults of computer magnetic tape. Besides the obvious space advantage—one disc replacing 25 reels of tape—the disc players will be able to retrieve any information from the disc in less than half a second, a dramatic improvement over the 45 seconds it now takes to run through a tape reel. Further, most researchers feel that an optical disc will retain data for far more than 10 years, while magnetic tape is generally limited to two or three. Yet another application: The data on fixed magnetic discs are typically "dumped" onto off-line tape once each day to protect them from disc or system failures, and usually they are never read. As potentially the cheapest form of data storage, optical discs would be ideal for this job.

A peek at the future

Toshiba will allow a peek at this future next year when it starts delivering its DF-2000 image recorder to U.S. and Japanese customers. The company has actually marketed the product in Japan since January, focusing initially on customers with big paper files, such as banks, insurance companies, and real estate firms. The $60,000 system includes a laser scanner, optical disc storage, and a plain paper copier, all hooked to a keyboard and display. It will store 10,000 documents per disc, and the discs, which cannot be erased once data are recorded, sell for $140 each.

Working much like a facsimile machine, the device scans and digitizes a page, and writes the data on the disc in less than four seconds. When the document's address is later typed into the keyboard, the page is retrieved and displayed within four seconds. It takes an additional 14 seconds to print a copy. Toshiba is now working on product improvements, says research and development Section Manager Naoto Nakayama, including better display resolution, an automatic disc exchanger, and the ability to communicate with other equipment, especially facsimile and computer networks.

"Word processing and data processing already are merging, and image processing will merge right along with them," says Edward S. Rothschild, the author of a study on optical image and data memories for Strategic Business Services Inc. of San Jose, Calif. "By the end of the decade, laser optical systems will replace facsimile machines and probably the more expensive photocopiers."

Replacing microfilm will be a more difficult job for optical discs. For one thing, film is cheaper than magnetic tapes and discs and, like optical discs, it is a permanent record. Moreover, microfilm images can be viewed on a $200 reader without requiring a high-resolution display or printer. Still, at least two business segments—computer-output-microfilm and active business records—are likely to feel the competition.

About one-quarter of the estimated 100 billion pages of computer output each year goes directly from computer to microfilm. "In time, computers will dump their data on videodiscs instead," says Robert B. Huff, executive vice-president of Bell & Howell Co. For storing active business records—one of the microfilm industry's hottest fields—optical disc memories begin to make sense, Huff says.

"But on balance, videodiscs aren't going to hurt our microfilm business very much," Huff maintains. Especially immune will be microfilm used for archival storage: No one will want to convert massive files of microfilmed blueprints, parts catalogs, magazines, or newspapers, Huff contends. Neither will optical discs affect the archival of documents that are not often consulted—bank checks, for example.

Hurdles to overcome

Both Thomson-CSF and RCA have demonstrated optical disc recorders for the TV industry—for broadcasting, where it takes too long to access videotape, and for production editing, where manipulation of the tape is a problem. RCA is also developing a storage technique for X-rays, prompted by the rising cost of silver-halide film and the advantages of digital X-rays. "If you digitize the image, you can process the image," says RCA's Ettenberg, "so you can get more information out of the X-ray." Physicians already are getting accustomed to the digital pictures produced by the computerized axial tomography of the so-called CAT scanners. Since images and data can be mixed on the disc, Ettenberg foresees optical discs carrying a patient's complete medical history, including X-rays.

There are still hurdles to overcome before optical discs can be widely used for digital data storage. For one thing, the computer industry will not be comfortable adopting discs until their error rates can match those of magnetic storage techniques. Magnetic discs miss one bit out of every trillion. That kind of accuracy is not critical in image storage—in Toshiba's office system, for example, an error shows up as a black fleck on a page—but for digitally encoded data, an error will produce the wrong letter or number.

Moreover, the discs cannot now be erased. This "write-once, read-only" characteristic, as the industry calls it, will impede the replacement of magnetic discs and tapes in on-line systems. But, says consultant Rothschild, "the feeling is that the storage potential of optical discs is so huge that you can just write the new information somewhere else on the disc." ∎

U.S. HOME: Defying a Slowdown By Continuing to Expand

One lesson the housing industry learned from its 1974-75 recession was that some of the most ambitious builders—those that had grown too fast or strayed too far from home base—took the biggest lumps. But as the current downswing gets under way, Guy R. Odom, chairman of U. S. Home Corp., now the country's biggest homebuilder, is paying no attention whatever to that lesson.

In his three years in charge, Odom has taken a disorganized company and expanded it: It is building in five new states and has plans to start construction in at least six more in the next two years, with possible moves into Canada and Mexico as well. In fact, Houston-based U. S. Home has just entered California by buying a Bakersfield homebuilder, raising to 15 the number of states in which the company operates.

Such expansion is one reason why Odom says U. S. Home will increase its sales, earnings, and market share during the next two years despite a housing downswing. Another reason is the set of management, marketing, and financial changes Odom has introduced, especially a controversial management recruitment and training program about which the chairman is a near-fanatic.

Rewriting the rules. Odom's confidence naturally arouses some skepticism now. With mortgage rates at 13% and heading upward, most builders are making a frantic retreat, fearful of a repeat of the 1974 debacle in housing. U. S. Home, by contrast, continues to build on speculation, hold a large inventory of lots, and construct multifamily projects.

In doing so, the company is aiming to become the first truly national homebuilder in an industry that remains essentially localized—divided into tiny pieces by as many as 60,000 competitors. That ambition, of course, is not new, and it was pursued vigorously by Levitt & Sons, CNA Financial Corp.'s Larwin Group, and others until they became among the most celebrated victims of housing's last down cycle.

What is new is that U. S. Home is expanding despite a recession already unfolding in its business. Odom reasons that even during periods of high interest there will still be some customers for new homes, and large builders—prudently financed—will be able to raise the money to continue building. Many small builders will not find construction financing now, he believes, and as a result, U. S. Home can grow by capturing a larger share of a smaller market. Odom also is taking steps to assist prospective buyers to obtain financing. "A company can grow in the gap" between housing start declines and less rapidly falling demand, he contends.

Because U. S. Home lined up considerable construction financing last year to carry it through a rough period this year, many analysts believe Odom's plan is surprisingly solid. Further, they seem impressed with what Odom has already done to change dramatically the company's checkered history.

U. S. Home was pieced together in the late 1960s and early 1970s by two New Jersey homebuilders, largely through acquisitions of other builders, including Odom's own Houston company, which was acquired in 1971. But the entrepreneurs who built up U. S. Home never pulled the company together into a unified organization. During 1973 and 1976, for example, three presidents came and went. The 1974 downswing caught the company with huge inventories of unfinished land and unsold houses and condominium projects. In 1975, U. S. Home lost $2.9 million.

Meanwhile, Odom was prospering. He had left U. S. Home in 1973 after a dispute with management and formed another homebuilding company that made money every year, including 1974 and 1975. In late 1976, U. S. Home directors asked Odom to come back. In February, 1977, he became president, and a few months later, chairman.

For the three years since Odom has been chief executive officer, U. S. Home's sales have grown 116% to $935 million in 1979, and earnings have increased 277% to $41 million. U. S. Home stock has doubled in price since early 1977, and just recently, Société des Maisons Phénix, France's largest homebuilder, successfully tendered for 16% of U. S. Home shares. The tender was both an investment and a way of getting into the U. S. market, explains Maisons Phénix Vice-President Jacques Deschamps.

But Odom's drive for growth is far from satisfied. Even as the country's biggest homebuilder, U. S. Home's 1979 sales of 14,000 units represent only 0.8% of the market, a figure the chairman terms "downright embarrassing."

Deeper thinking. Odom contends that individual builders have failed to grab substantial chunks of this market because they have been unable to put together a single, big organization that can manage the nation's highly diverse housing markets. His confidence that U. S. Home will be the first to do so thus rests largely on an extraordinary attempt to find, train, and motivate new managers.

Odom uses a variety of techniques. Prospective employees must take a battery of personality tests, whose results Odom immodestly insists must match a profile established when he and some of his top managers took similar tests. Recruits who "pass" these tests not only receive professional training but also are assigned to read 45 books—ranging from Saul Gellerman's *Management by Motivation* to Plato's *Republic*—designed to make them deeper thinkers.

Managers of the company's 42 divisions are all expected to know how to build a house, so Odom has focused on training construction superintendents to take these positions. Finally, to prevent undermanaged expansion, Odom has decreed that no division manager can enter a new geographical market before having at least one subordinate well-trained enough to replace him.

Critics have charged that Odom's approach is bound to create cookie-cutter managers. But even those critics concede the system seems to work. "If you look at the bottom line," observes one outsider, "the company is doing better than it has ever done in its history."

Odom has achieved that record, of course, during three years of a generally strong housing upswing. Says industry analyst Stanley D. Salvigsen of Cyrus J. Lawrence Inc.: "Odom tells a good story, but it will take the recession to prove him right or wrong."

Fast turnover. Yet Odom claims the recession is an opportunity. Higher profits in homebuilding require faster turnover, he says, and a downturn makes quick construction easier because labor and materials become readily available.

This theory works, of course, only when a company has sales. U. S. Home's basic strategy for keeping sales up is not much different from that of other large builders: It appeals mainly to the first-time home buyer with single-family suburban tract homes, priced less than $75,000. But in another area, U. S. Home has shown its special agility. It makes sure that mortgage money is available to finance every home it builds.

In the last three years, the company has revamped its building practices so that 80%, rather than 30%, of its homes now contain safety and other features required to qualify for government-backed mortgages. Actual financing is provided to about 20% of U. S. Home's customers through the company's own in-house mortgage operation. For the rest, it arranges financing from conventional lenders. In October, 1978, U. S. Home raised $15 million in mortgage money, selling the first package of mortgage-backed securities for 95% loans ever to receive a AAA rating.

Taking a loss. The company is not afraid of swallowing some financing costs, if necessary, to make money available for its customers. Although the company does not reduce interest rates on the mortgages it makes, it is willing to make other concessions. Last summer, for example, Odom and his five division presidents in the Houston market grew concerned about going into winter with too much inventory. So in July and August, before sales had slipped too badly, they offered $18 million worth of mortgages at 3% down, with a maximum $450 in closing costs. At the time the usual downpayment for conventional mortgages was 10%, with closing costs run-

U. S. Home still builds on speculation and retains a large inventory of lots

ning as high as $1,100 per sale. In two months the company sold 350 houses under this program. The expense, Odom says, "came out of the division's profits, but it increased penetration remarkably."

Odom also has taken timely steps to obtain construction financing to get through the present high-interest cycle that is restricting the operations of many smaller builders. Where most builders finance each project with short-term money, borrowed against the individual project, U. S. Home has adopted long-term financing methods similar to those used in manufacturing. The company has secured $140 million in fixed-interest debt, half of it last August at 10¾% in the biggest private placement ever by a domestic homebuilder. An additional $50 million was raised in a public placement of 10-year notes at 10% in 1977. There is also $150 million in debt through lines of credit with commercial banks and stockholders' equity of about $166 million.

The bottom line is that U. S. Home's cost of money averages only about 8%, while other builders are paying 15% to 20% in some markets today for short-term construction loans.

For a company that claims to be lean and ready for a recession, U. S. Home holds an extraordinarily large inventory of land and is highly leveraged. Its debt to equity ratio was 2-to-1 at the end of 1979. But chief financial officer Frederick E. Fisher says that 9% of the debt is nonrecourse loans backed by developed and undeveloped land. Fisher and Odom are working to set that land aside in "land banks," puppet corporations whose sole function is to hold the property. U. S. Home thus controls the land while getting the debt off its balance sheet.

U. S. Home has already set aside $67 million worth of land in a company called Homecraft Land Development Inc., which is 20% owned by U. S. Home. Senior Vice-President Harlan Smith owns the other 80%. Debt on this land is set up so that U. S. Home does not make a single interest payment for the first five years, and by then most of the land should be carved into lots and sold to individual homeowners.

Other builders achieve similar results by taking options on land held by local developers. But Odom says his company intends to grow too fast to rely on other developers to provide it with lots. "We're the largest end-user of finished lots in the world today," he claims. "There are no developers who can supply us with the number of lots we need, and we will not put U. S. Home at risk in dealing with third-party developers." The company likes to keep a nine-month supply of finished lots and three to four years' worth of undeveloped land available at all times. It currently owns or controls more than 50,000 lots of varying sizes in the 15 states in which it does business. Odom notes that owning all this land has one other benefit: "It limits competition."

Condominiums. Odom also is convinced that condominiums will grow in popularity as energy costs rise and family units get smaller. The company therefore has been buying land at close-in sites in most major cities and has outlined a two-year plan to sell 2,500 condominium units for $100 million. In 1981 and 1982, the company hopes to build and sell an additional $200 million worth.

Another aim is to capitalize on what Odom predicts will be one of the fastest growing segments of the housing market by the mid-1980s—retirement homes. U. S. Home is currently developing three major retirement communities and will open a fourth near Washington, D. C., this year and a fifth in Houston in 1981. Odom says the demographics are so favorable for these projects that "we don't even look at them as risks."

For the long term, Odom is more concerned about shortages of labor and materials as the industry climbs into the next boom. If housing starts fall to 1.3 million units this year from 1.7 million in 1979, as predicted, that will leave several hundred thousand potential buyers whose pent-up demands will have to be met when money loosens up and construction takes off again. But Odom admits he does not have many solutions for this problem. Ironically, he says, "We're better positioned for the downturn than for the next peak." ∎

QUESTIONS

Magazines Targeted at the Working Woman:

1. Conditions now appear to be favorable for the publication of magazines targeted specifically at the working woman. Discuss.

2. Specifically, how do the new magazines *Savvy* and *Enterprising Woman* intend to take advantage of the opportunity afforded by the growth in the number of working women?

The Investor Excitement over New City Hotels:

1. From an investor's point of view, what are the pros and cons of investing in the hotel industry at the present time?

2. What impact has the general interest by investors had on the strategies of firms such as Marriot or life insurance companies?

The Microchip Revolution: Piecing Together a New Society:

1. In what areas and for whom does the "microchip revolution" offer opportunities?

2. What are the major contingencies that will determine whether entering the microelectronics industry is a viable strategic alternative for a firm?

The Shrinking Standard of Living:

1. What are the long-range strategy implications for U.S. businesses in response to the shrinking standard of living?
2. Rising oil prices are behind many of the major problems facing the U.S. economy today. Explain.

Southeast Banks: Set for a Slump:

1. Describe the profile of the major regional banks of the Southeast prior to the 1974 recession and at the present time.
2. What were the most influential factors in their adoption of a more conservative operating strategy?

Antibusiness Forces Aim at Corporations:

1. Discuss the impact that the Americans concerned about corporate power coalition could have on the typical U.S. firm.
2. What sectors of the environment are involved in this movement? Does this have any bearing on the potential impact this coalition could have on American business? Explain.

A UN Space Treaty That Could Zap Industry:

1. Why is the potential passage of the "moon treaty" causing so many U.S. firms to worry?
2. Discuss the impact the "moon treaty" itself would have on business organizations in general.

U.S. Autos: Losing a Big Segment of the Market—Forever?:

1. Failure to recognize and understand the wants and needs of its consumer market and to foresee crucial changes in the supply sector are the prime reasons Detroit auto makers are in a noticeably less competitive position than before. Discuss.

2. How can they overcome the threats posed by long lead times, intensive capital requirements in a tight credit market, and foreign competition? Mention the proposed strategy of the U.S. auto makers.

Luxury Car Sales Skid to New Lows:

1. How have the general status of the economy, competition, and consumer attitudes contributed to the problems now facing luxury car manufacturers?
2. What strategies are available to these "big car makers"?

Detroit's High-Price Strategy Could Backfire:

1. In what sectors of the environment are U.S. auto makers most vulnerable?
2. Describe a strategy that would help U.S. auto makers to meet these threats and that would capitalize on their strengths and minimize their weaknesses.

Tight Credit Slams Car Dealers Two Ways:

1. Tight credit conditions have had a devastating effect on the U.S. auto industry. Explain.
2. What type of auto manufacturing company is best prepared to survive in this sort of economic environment? Discuss.

What Caused the Decline: Inflation Skews the Profit Incentive:

1. Many strategy makers of today may be basing their strategic decisions on misleading information. Discuss in reference to this article.
2. What needs to be done to alleviate this problem of illusory performance results?

What Caused the Decline: Expectations That Can No Longer Be Met:

1. Discuss how the attitudes of the American public have changed since World War II.
2. How do these attitudes affect U.S. firms and the American economy as a whole?

Maine's Nuclear Vote Has Industry Jumpy:

1. Discuss present consumer attitudes and values in relation to nuclear power. Are they likely to change in the near future?
2. What do these attitudes suggest to firms who are considering strategic moves into nuclear power?

A Skewed Recession Has Hidden Strengths:

1. What factors have contributed to the differential impact that the recession has had on various industries and regions?
2. What are the implications of such a "skewed recession" for government policymakers and industry strategy makers?

Cable TV: The Race to Plug In:

1. Has the government (federal and local) proved to be a helping or hindering force in the expansion and growth of the cable TV industry? Discuss.
2. What impact do all the other sectors of the environment have on a firm's decision about whether or not to enter the cable TV industry?

The Implications of Oil Company Profits:

1. The sheer magnitude of oil company profits poses a threat to U.S. business in general. Discuss in reference to this article.
2. How could this threat be turned around into an opportunity for U.S. industry? Discuss.

Videodiscs: A Three-Way Race for a Billion Dollar Jackpot:

1. In what areas do opportunities exist for the videodisc industry?
2. How will the various sectors of the environment affect the future of this new industry?

U.S. Home: Defying a Slowdown by Continuing to Expand:

1. Make an appraisal of the internal strategic advantages and disadvantages of U.S. Home as well as of the external environment in which it must operate. Be sure to include a discussion of all major environmental sectors.
2. In light of all these factors, is U.S. Home in a position to weather the recession and to successfully implement its desired expansion strategy? Discuss.

Four.

Now that environmental opportunities and threats to enterprise strategy have been examined, Chapter 4 will focus the reader's attention on two environmental sectors which are important to strategy makers: government and unions. Because of the power of these two institutions, strategists must respond to new constraints in creative ways to ensure that their firms assume an effective strategic posture.

GOVERNMENT

The twentieth century has experienced a dramatic increase in both the size and the scope of government—federal, state, and local. Federal government employment of civilian workers grew from 239,476 to 655,265 between 1901 and 1920 (an increase of 174 percent).[1] Furthermore, the years 1920 to 1941 and 1941 to 1970 witnessed a doubling and then a redoubling of federal government employment. The number of civilians employed by the federal government grew from 655,265 to 1,437,682 between 1920 and 1941 (an increase of 119 percent), and then between 1941 and 1970 employment increased from 1,437,682 to 2,981,574 (an increase of 107 percent).[2] The importance of these statistics can be seen clearly when they are compared with the growth in total United States employment during this time period. From 1901 to 1920, total employment in the United States increased from 27,948,000 to 39,208,000 (a 40 percent increase); between 1920 and 1941, total employment increased from 39,208,000 to 50,350,000 (a 28 percent increase); and from 1941 to 1970, total United States employment increased from 50,350,000 to 78,627,000 (a 56 percent increase).[3]

Growth in government employment, however, has not been restricted to the federal government. State and local government employment of the civilian labor force has grown at an even more rapid pace. In 1977, states and localities employed more than 12.5 million people, up from 2.5 million in 1929 (a 400 percent increase).[4]

To a large extent, the growth in the size of government has been stimulated by the increased scope of government operations. Through its taxing, law making, and regulatory powers, the government has assumed direct or indirect control of many private resources. The last thirty years have witnessed a proliferation in government regulatory activity unparalleled in our nation's history. During this time the Federal Register, which publishes government regulations, has grown in size from 2400 to more than 77,500 pages. This increase reflects the voluminous regulations promulgated in agencies such as the Environmental Protection Agency and the Occupational Health and Safety Administration.

The magnitude of the shift from private to government control of our nation's resources can be illustrated by looking at selected economic data. Between 1941 and 1977, gross national product (GNP) in the United States increased from $124.9 billion to $1890.4 billion (a 1424 percent increase). However, during this period of time, federal government expenditures increased from $20.5 billion to $423.5 billion (a 1966

Two Environmental Sectors of Special Importance in Formulating Strategy: Government and Unions

128 / Readings from *Business Week*

percent increase). Additionally, state and local government expenditures increased from $9.1 billion to $265.3 billion (a 2815 percent increase)[5]—a growth rate almost twice that of GNP.

These numbers indicate very clearly that government has assumed a more dominant role in our society, and they serve as signals to strategists that the business environment is changing. In the future, successful firms must learn to anticipate and adapt to changes in government, and they must become more skillful in their dealings with government.

The *Business Week* articles in this chapter pertaining to the relationship between business and government cover a broad range of issues of importance to strategy makers. Several of these articles discuss opportunities resulting from government initiatives:

- "Truckers Quietly Get Set for Deregulation"
- "Tax Credits That Could Save Industry Billions"
- "Senate Energy Gets a Friend of Industry"
- "Using the Market in Regulation"
- "The New Case for Monopolists"
- "How Washington Spurs High Technology Companies"
- "The Court Leaves OSHA Hanging"

Additionally, many of these articles describe threats or potential threats to business which strategists must recognize and plan for:

- "What Trade Sanctions Will Cost"
- "Here Comes the Credit Crunch"
- "Credit Curbs Push Sales toward a Tailspin"
- "A Product Liability Bill Has Insurers Uptight"
- "Canada's Oil Policy Is Starting to Hurt"
- "States Seek a Slice of Oil Profits"
- "Justice Takes Aim at Dual Distribution"
- "A Bill That Will Give The Fed More Power"

All these *Business Week* articles should bring home to you how important government initiatives can be in affecting the strategic choices of planners.

UNIONS

About 21 million workers in the United States belong to one of approximately 70,000 local unions. This figure represents almost 33 percent of the eligible nonagricultural civilian labor force.[6] While union membership in the private sector is stable, union membership in the public sector is growing rapidly—from 1.5 million members in 1964 to 5.5 million members in 1974. Currently, union leaders are attempting to increase private sector membership.[7]

The relationship between business and unions is changing. Consider the effect of Douglas Fraser's appointment to the board of directors of Chrysler Corporation on that firm's strategy. One might argue that the Chrysler situation is an isolated incident—one that will not be repeated. But Fraser has announced that he intends to seek similar concessions from other automobile manufacturers.

Many of the *Business Week* articles in this chapter emphasize union involvement in two of our nation's most important industries: automobiles and steel. As union involvement in these industries increases, their potential to affect strategic decisions increases. The first article, "A New Social Contract: A Partnership to Build the New Workplace," lays the foundation for the rest of the articles in this section.

The articles concerning the automobile industry are

- "The UAW's About-Face on Import Controls"
- "How the Changing Auto Market Threatens the UAW, Too"
- "The Risk in Putting a Union Chief on the Board"
- "Can Chrysler Squeeze More from the UAW?"
- "The Price of Peace at Chrysler"
- "Ailing AMC Seeks Relief from the UAW"

The *Business Week* articles pertaining to the steel industry are

- "Steel Talks: A Costly Pact, Even with Restraint"
- "Steel Labor Is Adding Insurance"
- "Labor Cools It with Big Steel"
- "When Steel Wages Rise Faster than Productivity"
- "Edgy Steelworkers Set Their Goals High"

These *Business Week* articles demonstrate the importance of union activity and involvement in the strategic management process in firms. Furthermore, they suggest that we might be entering a new era in business-union relations.

---

[1]U.S. Bureau of the Census, *Historical Statistics of the United States, Colonial Times to 1970* (Washington, D.C., 1975), p. 1102.
[2]Ibid., p. 1102.
[3]Ibid., pp. 126–127.
[4]United States Government, *Economic Report of the President, 1978* (Washington, D.C., 1978), p. 296.
[5]*Ibid., pp. 257, 342.*
[6]Glueck, William F., *Personnel: A Diagnostic Approach, Revised Edition*, (Dallas, Texas: Business Publications, Inc., 1978) p. 647.
[7]Ibid., p. 647.

Part A

TRUCKERS QUIETLY GET SET FOR DEREGULATION

As Congress moves closer to enacting legislation to lessen the government's economic regulation of the trucking industry, the organized opposition of that industry grows more intense; at least, it does on Capitol Hill. But meanwhile, many trucking companies are quietly positioning themselves so that they can leap from the starting gate if Congress throws the industry open to competition.

"There are a number of closet deregu-

While the industry opposes easing the rules, many lines prepare for the inevitable

lationists out there," says Thomas F. Herman, president of Delta California Industries Inc., which owns two truck lines, both of which are preparing for a new environment. "We've begun doing a lot of work in management information, costing, and market research."

Commonplace although those terms may be in other industries, they are relatively new in trucking. Freight rates today are jointly set by company representatives meeting under the auspices of regional "rate bureaus," with immunity from antitrust prosecution. And the regulated trucking industry has always predicted that chaos would ensue if Congress were to do away with that system of rate-making and with the Interstate Commerce Commission's route-and-rate authority. The American Trucking Assns. has warned insistently that under deregulation, service would deteriorate while prices would rise. More to the point, some companies might go out of business, and thus the ATA has fought deregulation long and hard on Capitol Hill and at the ICC.

Quiet preparation. But the ATA is losing. The Senate Commerce Committee on Mar. 11 sent to the full Senate a bill that would remove much of the ICC's authority, and hearings are almost completed on a weaker House version. Although no major trucking company has formally broken ranks with the ATA as yet—as did several airlines with their trade association in similar conditions three years ago—what one analyst calls "a vast minority" of firms have begun strategic planning for deregulation.

"If we're forced to publish an individual tariff, we don't plan to be sitting around on our hands," says one trucking executive. Consolidated Freightways Inc. has been working on pricing strategy options for more than a year, and other industry giants, including Yellow Freight System Inc. and Roadway Express Inc., are doing the same.

The Senate bill, sponsored by Senator Howard Cannon (D-Nev.), would make it easier to enter new markets, a provision the ATA also opposes strongly. Yet many carriers are looking at new expansion. "A lot of companies are seriously determining what markets they should be in," says Michael P. McGee, director of economic and market research for IU International Corp.

Eager to grow. ICC restrictions clearly have held down expansion in the past. The commission began granting new routes more freely two years ago, and the number of formal applications since then has jumped sharply. Moreover, since the ICC offered to give any trucker authority to carry government freight in January—a step the ATA opposed—it has been flooded with queries about how to apply for the business.

A recent trend in trucking may be partly responsible for the shift in some companies' attitude toward deregulation. More and more, nontransportation companies are buying general-freight and other carriers. In the last few years, such companies as American Natural Resources Co., PepsiCo, Sun Oil, and ARA Services have bought trucking companies despite the considerable uncertainty in the industry over deregulation. "Although there could be some dislocations [due to deregulation], we feel in the long-term this was a good investment," says David D. Dayton, vice-president-financial of ARA, which last year bought Smith's Transfer Corp.

There is another, paradoxical reason why companies are beginning to think they can live with more competition. It, too, is reminiscent of the reason airlines finally switched positions. Some ICC members now use 12% as an interim desirable rate of return in deciding truck rate cases, while the ICC debates what a permanent standard ought to be—should rate regulation continue. That figure scares truckers, many of whose returns are as high as 20%. "That 12% return standard makes regulation look so awful, people are screaming about it," says Herman of DCI. "Anything is better than going back to the ICC."
∎

TAX CREDITS THAT COULD SAVE THE INDUSTRY BILLIONS

Nearly buried in the $227 billion windfall profits tax legislation is an array of tax credits that may prove nearly as controversial as the tax itself. The credits could save business $6 billion and consumers $600 million in taxes over the next decade, and they could be the making of such fledgling industries as solar power. There is, for example, a maximum $4,000 credit for consumers who install solar equipment.

What makes the new credits so controversial is that they apply almost entirely to the installation of alternative energy sources: not only solar, but geothermal, hydropower, and the like. Congress has left untouched the credits for spending on conventional energy-saving techniques—adding more insulation, for instance—and there are no credits at all for reducing consumption of conventional sources of energy.

No less controversial than the energy credits themselves is the growing tendency of Congress to write credits into tax legislation as a means of channeling spending into areas that are regarded as desirable. There is general support for the child-care credit and for the 10% investment tax credit, although some economists regard the 10% credit as too small to stimulate investment when the economy is weak and too much of a good thing when the economy is overheating and the need is to damp down investment. But the energy credits that Congress wrote two years ago are regarded as a mixed blessing at best. They have done relatively little to promote vast public spending on energy conservation while helping to draw a lot of fast-buck operators into the field.

Revisions. By shaping the new energy credits as it did, Congress has invited the wrath of a large slice of U. S. industry and prompted some new questions about the use of tax credits generally. Even before Congress finished work on the windfall profits measure, tax and energy specialists from 22 major corporations had formed an ad hoc group to press for an early revision of the credits. Owens-Corning Fiberglas Corp., a maker of insulation, is in the group, as are such vast consumers of conventional forms of energy as Alcoa, American Can, Union Carbide, and U. S. Steel.

"Basically, the credits stress new equipment but ignore the energy efficiency that comes from readjusting present equipment and processes," says Ronald S. Wishart, energy director of Union Carbide Corp. and chairman of the group. He, for one, favors a $15 credit or grant for each barrel of oil saved by a company, rather than a variety of credits that require a cash investment.

There is the further complaint by industry that in a time of tight money and record-high interest rates, and with the Federal Reserve trying to stem borrowing by big business, no program that requires additional investment by corporations is going to do much good. Indeed, by diverting some capital away from investment in new and more efficient productive facilities, it could actually do the economy some harm. The same 10% investment credit that applies to investments in new plant and equipment will also apply to investments in alternative sources of energy.

The credits cover a broad range of alternative energy sources, some of them still pretty much in the experimental stage. The real test of how well the new credits will work will almost certainly be in the solar field. The old law allowed consumers a $2,200 credit on solar installations, against the $4,000 credit in the new law. Industry sources expect sales of solar equipment to hit $200 million this year against $125 million in 1979, and they reckon that half the gain will come because of the new credit. The new law is further liberalized to permit

The new array of energy tax credits

Investment	What the new law provides	Cutoff date	Estimated revenue loss 1980-90 (Millions of dollars)
For business			
Biomass equipment to convert waste into fuel	More liberal provisions and the cutoff date extended three years. Credit remains 10%	1985	$ 648
Cogeneration equipment	A new 10% credit	1982	356
Coal gasification equipment	A new 10% credit	1982	277
Geothermal and ocean thermal equipment	Credit raised to 15% from 10% and extended to ocean thermal	1985	34
Intercity buses	A new 10% credit	1985	36
Small-scale hydroelectric facilities	A new 11% credit for power plants of less than 125 megawatts of capacity	1985	1,797
Solar or wind equipment	Credit raised to 15% from 10%	1985	1,058
Production of shale oil and similar products	A new $3-per-bbl. credit applying when domestic crude oil is priced below $23.50	1989	160
Production of engine-fuel alcohol	A new 30¢ to 40¢-per-gallon credit to apply in some cases in lieu of a tax exemption	1992	99
For consumers			
Home insulation, storm windows, thermostats	New provisions for joint owners of apartments. Credit remains at $300 (maximum)	1985	67
Solar, wind, and geothermal energy equipment	Credit raised from $2,200 to $4,000 (maximum)	1985	533

Data: BW

Government and Unions / 131

more types of installation to qualify for the credit. A solar roof panel that becomes part of the home now qualifies for the credit. Under the old law, anything that became part of the structure did not. Moreover, residential credits can now be used by two or more owners who occupy different dwellings on the same property—in apartments, for instance. The cost of the jointly purchased equipment must be divided up, but each property owner gets a separate credit.

Credit caps. Though homeowners may benefit, industry stands to gain little from the business solar credits, which were raised to 15% from 10%. Charles Feledy, energy director of United Tech-

Sales of solar equipment could reach $200 million, thanks to the new credits

nologies Corp., says, for example, that the payback of money invested in solar hot water in a factory in the north is 10 to 15 years. "The new total tax credit of 25% (investment credit plus the energy credit) might need to be 50% to be practical," Feledy says. Others note that solar energy in industry still cannot compete with oil, which is written off as a business expense and thus, in effect, gets a 46% tax credit.

The most controversial energy credits of all are those that use credit caps and phaseout formulas to stimulate a specific type of investment or to limit revenue loss. The cap will often be in terms of the size of the equipment, or the amount of investment.

Thus, hydropower units of up to 25 Mw of electric power qualify for an 11% credit. The credit gets progressively smaller as the installation gets bigger, because Congress wanted to stimulate development of small hydro systems. With a 60-Mw unit, for example, only 58¢ of each dollar invested counts toward the credit. But many regard phaseouts as too complex, while adding to the likelihood of tax disputes and even distorting what Congress had in mind.

In the case of hydropower, Congress plainly meant for business to look again at potential dam sites that had previously been regarded as too small for commercial development—hence the maximum credit for the smallest hydro units. Conceivably, however, companies, to gain the credit, might build facilities smaller than a site might sustain, which plainly is not what Congress wanted. "The tax writers had a hard time with this but found no solution," says Linda Goold, a legislative specialist with Arthur Andersen & Co., the accounting firm.

Another phaseout applies to the $3-per-bbl. credit for production of oil from shale rock or tar sands. To provide price supports for those willing to wring oil from shale and tar sands, the credit applies when the price of competing domestic crude oil falls below $23.50 per bbl. and phases out as crude rises to $29.50. The formula, Goold notes, shows the positive side of tax credits—the ability to tailor them neatly.

The formula. A basic argument against tax credits generally is that since they relate to profits, companies that are marginally profitable may lose benefits. A large credit can be offset against profits over 10 years. But a fast-growing company with modest earnings, for instance, may build up excess credits but have low tax liability. "Many companies use up the 10 years," notes Gene Knorr, a consultant with Charls E. Walker Associates, in Washington. "Also the value of a postponed credit is much less because of inflation," he adds.

The new energy credits ignore the problem. One solution favored by business is "refundable" credits—credits available in the form of cash, instead of as an offset against profits.

Despite all the furor over the credits, business and consumers will have to live with them for a while, since Congress is not likely to tackle the issue soon. And for those who can use the credits, the tax saving can be considerable. If a company buys energy-related equipment, the 10% investment credit is computed first. For 1980 the rule is that a company can take—not the full 10%—but $25,000 plus 70% of the remaining tax liability for the year. A company that owes $50,000 in taxes and earns a $100,000 credit can take $42,500, with $57,500 carried back three years and then forward up to seven years, as needed, to use up the full credit, if possible.

The energy tax credit can then be used to offset the remaining tax liability—in this case, just $7,500. The unused energy credit, like the investment credit, can be carried back three years and forward seven years. There is no 70% limit, as in computing the investment credit. And although the government, through total credits, pays 20% to 25% of an investment in energy equipment, the usual depreciation write-off is based on 100% of the investment.

"The overall complexity of the credits is unfortunate," notes Peter J. Hart of Price Waterhouse & Co. Indeed, administrative problems might be expected, especially since the law is laced with instructions to the Treasury to fill in missing details and create interpretations. This means there may be a flood of new Internal Revenue Service regulations coming some day. Still, considering that final regulations have never been written for the 1978 energy credits, it will take time for the IRS to get around to it. ∎

SENATE ENERGY GETS A FRIEND OF INDUSTRY

During Ronald Reagan's campaign for President, Senator James A. McClure was one of the Republican candidate's top energy advisers. But when McClure, a conservative Republican from Idaho, becomes chairman of the Senate Energy Committee in the new Congress, he is likely to move more slowly than some Reaganites might expect to dismantle the Energy Dept. and reshape energy regulation. "It's important not to get carried away by the euphoria of this election," he says. "There are 53 Republicans in the Senate, and they're not all going to vote the same way."

McClure, who was elected to the Senate in 1972 and who describes himself as a "pragmatist," will be faced with forging a consensus in an energy area that in recent years has become one of Congress' most factious. In the House, control by the Democrats and the return of most top energy leaders could slow the sweeping reforms the Reagan Administration will probably suggest. "We'll need to hold many an oversight hearing before we'll know just what we can and should do," says McClure.

'Our type of guy.' Even so, just the prospect of the beginning of a McClure era in the Senate has boosted the spirits of the nuclear industry he has championed since he came to the House in 1966. In addition, McClure's vote against the windfall profits tax has labeled him, according to a staffer as "pro-oil," and his outspoken support of increased leasing of federal lands for coal development has won over that industry. "He is," says a top Washington lobbyist for a major oil company, "our type of guy."

McClure stresses he will not be "a rubber stamp for Governor Reagan" and will seek "to have my imprint on any piece of legislation the Administration sends up, either before it gets here or after." Whereas Reagan once called for abolishing the Energy Dept., and more recently has talked of dismantling sections of it, McClure prefers "to wait and see." He says that the 1982 mandated review for the agency might be the time to think of the future. "He is anything but a yes-man," says Richard M. Fairbanks, the Washington lawyer and former Nixon Administration energy official who heads Reagan's energy transition team.

One of few conservatives to vote for the 1977 Clean Air Act Amendments, McClure is not likely to seek sweeping changes in those laws, although he acknowledges that "overexuberant administration" by federal agencies "has energy development stopped in its tracks." He will seek to return to states primary responsibility for administering air pollution and strip-mining laws.

Trimming power. McClure's vision of energy policy consists largely of "getting the government out of business." He hopes to accelerate the timetable for decontrolling both crude-oil and natural gas prices—oil controls now expire on Sept. 30, 1981, and gas price controls are scheduled to be phased out in 1985. He also wants to trim the federal government's power to force utilities and industry to convert to coal, perhaps by using tax credits to prompt the conversion. Although he says he does not want to "gut the nation's environmental laws," he will push for changes to encourage coal to be burned in some areas and for coal ports to be built.

But the 56-year-old legislator may push for increased government involvement in other areas. Reorganizing his committee to place more emphasis on public land issues, McClure hopes to make more land available for development and to attack a water problem that he calls "our most forgotten crisis." When price controls end for crude oil, he plans to push legislation that would protect small and independent oil refiners from what he calls "the ability of major oil companies to dominate the market and swallow them up."

McClure, who is the only member of Congress to drive an electric car to work each day, also hopes to push the new Administration more deeply into energy research, despite a lukewarm attitude in the Reagan camp. In 1978 he was one of the few conservatives to support the Carter Administration's phased decontrol of natural gas, because Carter promised in return to increase funding for the nuclear breeder research program. He is a strong supporter of geothermal energy, and he says he has "made some headway" in persuading Reagan to accept at least the first $20 billion phase of President Carter's program of seed money for synthetic fuel development. "I believe in being my own man on issues like that," says McClure, "and I can be my own man as well as anyone I know." ∎

Government and Unions / 133

USING THE MARKET IN REGULATION

Government regulation is under fierce attack these days along its entire front. One has only to hear the claim, for example, that it is responsible for all the problems of our automobile industry, or other such fatuous observations that I refrain from further identifying, to understand how great the threat really is. Where would the auto companies be now, one wonders, were it not for the mandated fuel economy standards, about which they complained so bitterly?

But that doesn't mean the criticisms are baseless. Underlying the attacks are two basic complaints: Regulation is excessively costly and excessively coercive.

We in government have no choice but to believe that if we meet the criticisms of regulation that are valid, we will be in the best possible position to repel the ones that are invalid.

Of course, the most striking way in which we can meet the legitimate complaints is simply to deregulate in the many cases in which the government has intervened to protect private parties from the discipline of the competitive market. Where competition alone can effectively protect the public, this is clearly the proper remedy. I am proud of our deregulations or substantial deregulations during just the last three years of airlines, motor carriers, railroads, financial institutions, and communications, not to mention the related, but different, cases of crude oil and natural gas.

Experiments. In the many cases in which competition cannot be trusted to do the job, much can still be done to reduce the cost and intrusiveness of regulation. One of the most heartening recent developments is the increased willingness of regulators to experiment with innovative techniques to do just that. The recent report of the Regulatory Council to the President provides an encouraging summary of 376 such experiments.

Significantly, many of these techniques use or stimulate the market. Since markets leave the requisite cost/benefit comparisons to the people directly involved, who have every incentive to make the proper economic choices, they simultaneously achieve the twin goals of regulatory reform that I have already identified—imposing only costs that are justified by benefits, and minimizing coercion.

I recall a discussion at the Civil Aeronautics Board before I became chairman of how to handle the vexing problem of airline bumping. The good lawyers assembled debated at length what would be the fairest basis for setting priorities among potential bumpees: first to reserve, first to buy tickets, first to check in. For every proposed criterion of equity, it soon became clear, there was an equally valid counter-consideration.

At my first meeting on the subject, I suggested (following Professor Julian Simon, among others) that the real problem was the involuntary selection of the passengers to be bumped, and that there could not be any objection if the bumpees were permitted to select themselves in response to economic incentives. Airlines engage in overbooking because it pays. It makes perfect sense, then, to require them, when bumping becomes a necessity, to offer whatever monetary compensation is necessary to induce the requisite number of people to give up their seats voluntarily. The result will be economically efficient and uncoercive.

A market mechanism. As the Regulatory Council's report shows, there are many other situations in which regulators are experimenting with ways of achieving the requisite protection of the public merely by setting up the framework within which the market can do the actual choosing. Where, for example, it is necessary to ration portions of the limited radio spectrum, or the right to land at crowded airports at peak hours, or the amount of pollutants that may be emitted, innovative regulators are evaluating proposals to auction off the rights or distribute them more randomly while allowing people to buy and sell them freely.

Similarly, it is now almost unanimously accepted that if we ever do have gasoline rationing, we should permit free purchase and sale of the ration coupons. Such a system has the critical virtue that under it every single gallon of gasoline that anyone uses has to be worth at least as much to him as it would be to someone else, to whom he could instead choose—voluntarily—to sell the coupons.

These cases illustrate yet another closely related principle that innovative regulators are adopting: Make the rules as general and nonprescriptive as possible while still achieving the ultimate purpose. A corollary of this principle is a preference for specifying ends rather than prescribing means: Leave it to the regulatees to figure out the lowest-cost method of achieving the prescribed performance standards. The classic example is the Environmental Protection Agency's "bubble" policy, which sets overall air pollution limits for plants, rather than specifying exactly what emissions are allowed from each source, or how control is to be achieved. Du Pont Co. estimates that the bubble will cut its costs of complying with the Clean Air Act by $81 million annually.

But they do require—and their progressive adoption reflects—a changing attitude. Traditional regulators tend to be compulsively neat. They want things to be done the right way, and they have a compulsion to prescribe that way. It is only by disciplining themselves, like the House of Lords, to "withhold their legislative hands," wherever this would be consistent with the ultimate objectives, that regulators are going to preserve the defenses we have been erecting in the last decade or two of the public health and safety, of workers on the job, and of consumers in the marketplace. ∎

Monopoly is losing its bad name in court.

For 90 years the antitrust movement has ridden a wave of outrage at the dominance of industries by single companies, a wave that led Congress, in the Sherman Antitrust Act, to make it a federal crime to garner too big a portion of any market. So deep has the law's hostility to monopolies been that even companies innocent of intentionally predatory conduct have been forced to alter their business practices—for example, to license technology or to sell machinery previously available only by lease—if their

THE NEW CASE FOR MONOPOLISTS

marketplace success had let them dominate a field. As enunciated by the Supreme Court in 1948, the law was that "monopoly power, whether lawfully or unlawfully acquired, may itself constitute an evil and stand condemned."

But a string of recent court decisions shows that the old outrage at the mere fact of monopoly has cooled, especially if the monopolist champions innovation. For companies that have stitched together production and marketing strategies to become first in their field, the change provides elbowroom to try new ideas, even if they squeeze smaller competitors in the process. And for those smaller companies, winning a private antitrust suit will be harder.

In September, for instance, U. S. District Judge Malcolm M. Lucas in Los Angeles threw out a monopolization charge that a small auto-parts maker brought against W. R. Grace & Co. Even though Grace once had 100% of the market involved—a decorative wheel for sports cars—Lucas ruled that the later entrance of others into the field proved that Grace had no monopoly power.

Private suits. The cases earlier this century establishing the original tough rules against monopolists were filed by the government. Most of the new monopoly law is being written in cases waged by small competitors of industry leaders. The competitors' interest is not to benefit the public but to ensure their own prosperity—or survival. Nevertheless, the precedents that monopolists are establishing in fighting these corporate suits influence the government, too.

The most significant indicator of the new attitude toward monopoly came in October, when the Federal Trade Commission dismissed an attempt by its staff to undo Du Pont Co.'s rapid extension of its capacity to produce titanium dioxide, a chemical brightener used in paint and paper. Du Pont's expansion was tied to a cheaper process that the giant chemical manufacturer developed. Explaining the unanimous decision, Commissioner David A. Clanton wrote that "the essence of the competitive process is to induce firms to become more efficient and to pass the benefits of the efficiency along to consumers. That process would be ill-served by using antitrust to block hard, aggressive competition that is solidly based on efficiencies and growth opportunities, even if monopoly is a possible result." Clanton pointed to several preliminary victories by International Business Machines Corp. in private suits as evidence that his reading of the Sherman Act tracks the latest judicial thinking.

In the past judges have often decided that whatever policies a monopolist has been following to stay successful must be the kind of overt actions banned by the Sherman Act. What is new is that some courts are beginning to focus on the benefits to society of the very practices that keep a monopolist entrenched. If there is enough of a plus for customers, the courts are deciding that the practices cannot in good sense be called unlawful.

Most experts think that trend will broaden. The line of decisions that brands almost any business policies of a monopolist unlawful "will become increasingly obsolete," predicts Betty Bock, a consultant on antitrust matters for the Conference Board.

The changed judicial attitude toward monopolies stems from growing concern that innovation is lagging in the U. S. and that clamping down on risk-taking companies will stifle technological experimentation. Du Pont Chairman Ir-

If they benefit the public, monopolies may not automatically be illegal

ving S. Shapiro made the point repeatedly in lashing out at the FTC titanium dioxide case. In one private suit against IBM, the U. S. Court of Appeals in Denver said that "technical attainments were not intended to be inhibited or penalized" by the Sherman Act. And last year, in overturning much of a monopolization ruling against Eastman Kodak Co., the U. S. Court of Appeals in New York insisted that "innovativeness" is a marketing route open to a monopolist.

Burden of proof. In fact, Boston attorney Thayer Fremont-Smith noted at last month's annual New England Antitrust Conference that so much concern is developing for spurring new products and processes that, he predicts, courts will begin to presume legal any conduct that monopolists could argue would encourage innovation. The burden would then be on plaintiffs to prove that the conduct in question does not benefit the public.

Such a standard would most aid companies in new markets or those in which the technology is changing rapidly. These are the markets where one company is likely to dominate. "The Xerox machine created a short-term monopolist," says Donald I. Baker, former Justice Dept. antitrust chief, "but it has now been caught up with."

The problem is that the emerging standard requires judges or juries to make technical decisions. Monopolists that dominate their markets by developing better products will be within the law. But when success stems from something other than engineering superiority, it may still violate the Sherman Act. Just two years ago, the FTC branded Borden Inc. a monopolist in the lemon juice market because the commissioners decided that Borden's Realemon brand was neither a superior enough product nor the result of sufficient production efficiencies to account for its capture of 80% of the total market. Thus the lesson for corporate legal departments is that they must find ways to make complex technological distinctions understandable to those in a courtroom who must distinguish between monopolization and the fruits of superior knowhow. ∎

Government and Unions / 135

How Washington spurs the high-tech companies

Small business in general and the high-technology companies in particular have suddenly become the darlings of Washington. In October, Congress passed several bills that will make it easier for small companies to raise capital and ease the regulatory burdens of venture-capital firms that invest in fledgling enterprises, especially the high-tech companies. And another 75 to 80 bills to spur industrial innovation have been proposed, a measure of both the concern over the slowdown in productivity and the determination to maintain the nation's technological lead over its international rivals.

Tax favors. Most important is the Senate Finance Committee's proposed Tax Reduction Act of 1980. The bill, or one very much like it, stands a strong chance of being passed next year. It contains a variety of measures to encourage R&D, provide new incentives to investors, and aid small growth companies. They include:

- A 25% tax credit on the increase in R&D outlays above the average for a prior three-year base period. This includes generally "all such costs incident to the development of an experimental or pilot model, a plant process, a product, a formula, an invention or similar property, and the improvement of already existing property of the type mentioned." It also includes the cost of obtaining a patent.
- An increase in the capital gains exclusion from 60% to 70%, which would cut capital gains taxes to a top rate of about 21% from the present 28%. Capital gains are especially important to investors in new high-technology companies that normally plow back all earnings into the company and so pay no dividends.
- Creation of an "incentive stock option" to treat gains on stock options as capital gains rather than ordinary income. This should make it easier for high technology companies to grant stock options to employees.

Other parts of the Senate Finance Committee bill will also aid small business, although more indirectly. The bill calls for a two-phase reduction in the corporate income tax's top rate to 44% from 46%; an increase from five to seven in the number of brackets within the corporate rate structure; a 40% speedup in tax write-offs for plant and equipment through a combination of changes in the depreciation allowance and the investment tax credit; immediate expensing of up to $25,000 of the cost of most depreciable property; and an increase from $150,000 to $250,000 of the earnings a company can retain to meet reasonable business costs without having to pay the accumulated earnings tax.

Help from the SEC. Washington sees the need for sharpening the U. S. technological edge by eliminating a variety of other disincentives inherent in federal trade, patent, antitrust, and regulatory policies. The Securities & Exchange Commission put into effect a program in April, 1979, that greatly reduces the paperwork for small companies selling stock to the public. More than 100 small companies, many of them high-tech, have availed themselves of the SEC's short-form registration to raise capital.

The SEC has relaxed Rule 144, relating to insiders' sales of stock, which essentially permits the financiers of these companies and their managers to sell restricted securities more frequently and in larger quantities. This increases the liquidity for those investing in young companies and frees up significant amounts of capital for new investment.

With strong SEC support, Congress recently passed the Small Business Investment Incentive Act. Among other things, it increases the incentives for venture-capital firms to provide seed money. Venture-capital firms, for example, can now base their fees on how well the startup companies perform, even after they have provided the initial financing.

Already on the books is the Regulatory Flexibility Act, which requires federal agencies to consider the impact new regulations would have on small business, and to cut paperwork and similar burdens where possible.

Antitrust protection. The Justice Dept. is on the verge of issuing guidelines that will tell companies just when and how they can conduct joint research or share research results without fear of antitrust action. This should spur cooperation between companies.

A greater sense of realism is emerging in another area of vital interest to high-tech companies: patent policy. Each government agency has its own procedures, but in general the federal government retains title to any patent developed even partly with public funds. Congress has before it a spate of bills that would do everything from making the Patent Office separate from the Commerce Dept. to giving universities and small businesses patent rights to work even when it is sponsored by the government. The government has tens of thousands of patents gathering cobwebs on its shelves.

Yet, in the long run, the biggest indirect boost to high-technology companies may come from the federal R&D budget, which the White House science adviser, Frank Press, calls "the ultimate statement of science and technology policy." From 1968 to 1978, government R&D spending in real dollars declined sharply. President Ford started a small upturn in his final budget, and Jimmy Carter endorsed somewhat more R&D funding in every budget since. And the trend, most experts agree, is likely to continue.

THE COURT LEAVES OSHA HANGING

The U.S. Supreme Court's decision on the Occupational Safety & Health Administration's disputed benzene standard was an apparent victory for industry: The court threw out OSHA's standard limiting levels of benzene in the workplace to 1 part per million. But both OSHA and the industries it regulates had hoped that the court's ruling would clarify just how much OSHA can ask industry to spend to protect workers. Instead, the sharply divided decision provided more confusion than guidance on the way the agency can fulfill its mandate to ensure workers' safety and health.

"We thought we hit a home run," explains Basil J. Whiting Jr., the Labor Dept.'s deputy assistant secretary for OSHA, "but they're telling us to go back to first base. We've been cast adrift without any clear guideposts." Indeed, the court's 5-4 vote leaves wide open many long-simmering issues that are at the heart of industry's complaints against OSHA. The justices embraced industry's argument that there is no such thing as an "absolutely safe" workplace, but they did not suggest how OSHA should decide how much hazard is too much. Nor did they offer advice on weighing costs against benefits or deciding how much evidence of harm is cause for regulatory action. Thus the decision "opens the way to a whole mass of questions" on how costs and acceptable risks will be determined, notes Robert C. Barnard, an attorney who represented the industry-funded American Industrial Health Council in opposing the rule.

Nonetheless, the July 2 decision does free industry from the burden of reducing levels of benzene, a suspected carcinogen, from the present standard of 10 parts per million to 1 part per million—at a cost estimated by OSHA to be $500 million in the first year alone. And it provides industry with important legal ammunition in its fight over OSHA's controversial cancer policy, which is already being challenged in the lower courts.

'Sketchy at best.' Like the benzene standard, the agency's cancer policy is based on the idea that there is no safe level of exposure to a cancer-causing agent and that exposure must be reduced to as low a level as technically and economically possible. But the high court, upholding an October, 1978, judgment of the U.S. Court of Appeals in New Orleans, did

'A new bubonic plague' has to hit before OSHA can act, says one union leader

not accept that argument. Instead, it agreed with petroleum, petrochemical, steel, and rubber industries trade associations, which claimed the benefits of the more stringent standard were unproven. Justice John Paul Stevens' plurality opinion said that data were "sketchy at best" supporting OSHA's contentions that the 1-part-per-million benzene standard would cut the incidence of leukemia and other blood disorders among workers. Cutting exposures to the lowest feasible level "would give OSHA power to impose enormous costs that might produce little, if any, discernible benefits," wrote Stevens.

Moreover, the court underscored the possible use of its ruling as a precedent in cancer policy litigation. In a footnote, the justices pointed out that OSHA's "cancer policy indicates that the possibility" of costly controls producing little benefit "is not merely hypothetical."

The court's endorsement of some form of risk analysis was long-awaited by industry. "OSHA's going to have to be more responsible by making sure it is protecting people from real hazards," says Malcolm R. Lovell Jr., president of the Rubber Manufacturers Assn. But labor sees the decision as "crippling." Unions fear that the court was paying lip service to scientific uncertainty and that OSHA will be forced to set standards based on data, not on existing hazards. "They're institutionalizing the body count, telling us we've got to come up with a new bubonic plague before OSHA can do anything," says Anthony Mazzocchi, safety and health director of the Oil, Chemical & Atomic Workers Union.

Next case. Clearly, OSHA will have to make some hard choices about acceptable risk in the future. But both labor representatives and OSHA insiders are cautiously optimistic that other standards now being challenged in the courts will hold up under future tests of evidence demonstrating significant harm. Futhermore, the Supreme Court may be willing to tackle the issues it avoided in its benzene decision.

On the same day it issued that ruling, it agreed to review OSHA's $250 million coke oven emissions standard in its next term. There is general agreement that OSHA has better data justifying the need for the coke oven rule, and in its decision the court may pin down what it means by "significant risk" and what it expects in the way of cost-benefit analysis. "I don't buy industry's first knee-jerk reaction that they've got us on the ropes now," says Bailus Walker, director of health standards for OSHA. ∎

What trade sanctions will cost

President Carter's crackdown on U.S. trade with the Soviet Union, and his call for allied support for such economic retaliation, have fired a hot debate within the Administration and with U.S. allies over how, or even whether, the economic pressures should be applied. At stake are U.S. exports that totaled $3.4 billion last year, and another $15 billion worth of sales to the Russians by other Western countries.

Besides embargoing shipment of 17 million tons of grain, Carter struck at U.S. exports of nonfarm products to the Soviets that totaled $800 million last year, including $160 million worth of high-technology items. In rapid fire, he:

■ Halted processing of applications for licenses to export high-technology products, pending an interagency review.
■ Suspended temporarily existing licenses, so that U.S. companies at present cannot ship any industrial goods that require such permits.
■ Denied eight license applications, including one requested by Western Electric Co. to provide $1 billion worth of telecommunications equipment and technology to the Soviets.

At issue in the debate over such measures are both their effectiveness as a means of pressuring Moscow to halt its aggression and their impact on the sagging U.S. balance of payments and the international competitiveness of U.S. manufacturers. Carter's cutback in grain shipments will cost the U.S. $3 billion in current farm exports, but the restrictions on manufactured goods may have longer-term negative effects on U.S. industrial exports.

Apart from defense-related items, businessmen insist, most goods that the U.S. embargoes will be obtained by the Russians from other sources. William H. O'Connor, director of government affairs for Houston's Geosource Inc., for example, says the Soviets can go to alternative suppliers for the $12 million worth of seismic data-gathering and -processing equipment they have contracted to buy from his company. Geosource "wrestled its business away from the French," O'Connor explains.

But other U.S. manufacturers doubt that they will be seriously hurt by the sanctions, because the Soviet market is

Carter's curb on trade with Russia involves U.S. exports that totaled $3.4 billion last year.

marginal for most U.S. companies. Western Electric says that the telecommunications project—which reportedly called for the addition of 1 million telephones to the meager 25 million now installed in the Soviet Union—was dormant and had never reached the stage of detailed discussions. And Baker International, of Orange, Calif., is not greatly upset by the possible loss of its $15 million in annual sales of oil-field equipment to the Soviets, out of $1.5 billion in anticipated revenues this year. "If we become *persona non grata* in Russia, we'll just move on," says Vice-President Frank L. Scott.

Such unconcern provides ammunition for hard-liners in the Administration,

Business fears long-term export losses. Problems for the payments balance

led by Carter's national security adviser, Zbigniew Brzezinski, who have now gained the upper hand in the long-running debate on economic policy toward the Soviet Union. Brzezinski argues that the U.S. should try to deny to the Russians not only items of potential military value but also anything that could significantly improve the Soviet Union's economic efficiency and growth.

Keeping options. Ranged against Brzezinski and his supporters in the White House and Defense Dept. are officials in the Commerce Dept., State Dept., and Office of the Special Trade Representative, who argue for tightening up on sales to the Russians but preserving a framework for long-term trade if the Kremlin backs off from its aggression.

Carter has asked for policy recommendations to be submitted to him by the first week in February. The temporary halt to all exports of goods and services to Russia that require validated export licenses is expected to last at least a month. After that, the list of high-technology exports that will continue to be restricted will depend partly on the Administration's success in getting an agreement on concerted action with Europe and Japan under the Paris-based Coordinating Committee (COCOM), which has been reviewing its control lists for trade with Communist countries for the past year. Officials who oppose Brzezinski's hard line attach overriding importance to acting in parallel with the allies. "Any export we cut off together we can restore together," says one. "If we act alone and our COCOM partners pick up the business, the Soviets aren't hurt but we are."

If the Administration adopts such a criterion, it can count on some support from its allies, mainly in tightening controls on products that have military-related applications. A Bonn government source hints, for example, that Germany may announce a temporary ban on exports to Russia of various types of equipment including machine tools and complete plants involving microelectronic technology.

"We are going through these goods category by category to determine which should be on a taboo list," says this source. "We are consulting with our NATO allies, and we will consult with German industry." But French officials insist that they will resist any attempt to expand the COCOM list beyond strictly defense-related items to make it an instrument of broader economic pressure, as Brzezinski advocates.

Maintaining ties. Moreover, French and German officials and businessmen continue to stress the need to maintain business ties with the Soviets as a means of pursuing detente. Thus, Germany's Krupp expects to deliver $175 million worth of electric furnaces for a steel plant at Kursk under an order it received last March, and France's Thomson-CSF, a competitor of Western Electric, will proceed with two plants that it is building in the Soviet Union.

For Western high-technology controls to have any significant effect, however, European and Japanese competitors must refrain from moving in to take over projects that U.S. companies abandon because of the economic sanctions. The French say they will respect the U.S. embargo in such cases—but only if the American company has signed a contract with the Russians. Such a rule would not prevent France's Pechiney Ugine Kuhlmann, for one, from pushing its bid to build a $600 million aluminum smelter in Siberia following this month's decision by rival Aluminum Co. of America to drop out of the competition.

Technical lead. Such an outcome would strengthen the argument of trade hard-liners in Washington, who reject the contention of U.S. businessmen that Europeans and Japanese are able to supply the Soviets with almost anything the U.S. refuses to sell. The economic cold warriors argue, on the contrary, that U.S. policy has underestimated the technical lead that this country still has in many areas. Officials at Nippon Steel in Tokyo question, for example, whether computer systems and software could be supplied from non-U.S. sources for a $363 million dynamo steel plant that it has contracted to build in the Soviet Union with Armco Inc., which proposes to obtain automation equipment from General Electric Co.

Such questions will be critical in the skirmishing over export controls, because availability of products from other sources is one of the criteria imposed by Congress in the 1979 Export Administration Act to limit the President's authority to curb exports for foreign policy rather than military security reasons. In the current political climate, congressmen will probably not look too closely at Carter's reasons when he reports to Congress, as the law requires, on the grain embargo and other export restrictions. But U.S. machine-tool builders, whose share of the big Soviet-bloc market has dwindled to less than 1%, are worried that the restrictions on doing business with the Russians will also inhibit sales to other markets—particularly if the curbs are given a defense label. "The industry has no quarrel with the bottom line, but we are concerned about the implication that the Administration is calling them national-security controls and not foreign-policy controls," says James A. Gray, president of the National Machine Tool Builders' Assn. "Certainly we're out of business in the Soviet Union for some time, but I'm worried about the U.S. licensing becoming even more complex and U.S. producers getting cut out of other markets." ■

HERE COMES THE CREDIT CRUNCH

Invoking the martial law powers of the 1969 Credit Control Act as a final blow to an economy that has been stubbornly resisting recession, President Carter has dramatically upped the odds for a full-blown credit crunch. The selective credit squeeze that is already hitting housing, small businesses, and some consumer sectors can be expected to sweep the economy in coming weeks.

Unless the Fed flinches, all but the most creditworthy corporations will soon find credit scarce at any price. Increased bankruptcies seem inevitable. And there is a growing sense that strains on the banking system are reaching the point where a large financial institution or corporation could collapse.

With the prime rate now hitting 19%, with banks paying effective rates of 23% to sell three-month certificates of deposit, and with big corporations under the gun for the first time since World War II to report on their credit use to the Fed, the deep strains in the financial system will only intensify. The further plunge in February housing starts to 1.3 million annually from 1.4 million in January—provoked by the Fed's earlier tight money policy—is the forerunner of what is to come.

Savings flows, which the Fed hopes to redirect to banks and savings and loans by putting a stiff 15% reserve requirement on popular money market mutual funds, are more likely to spill out now in the money market. Because money fund yields will be lower, savers will probably increase their Treasury bill purchases. On Mar. 17, close to one-third of the $3.3 billion sold went to small investors. And with the depressed bond market closed to all but a handful of top-rated utilities, credit demands at commercial banks will build to a fever pitch.

'Not cosmetic.' The flash point for these converging borrowers—as it has been in all previous credit crunches—will be the banking system. But the trigger will be in the hands of the Fed. With the powers it now has, there is little question that the Fed can control loan growth to the 6%-to-9% range it has set for the banking system. It can restrict corporations, consumers, and investors at the source—but the risks to the economy and costs to growing companies will be high.

As bankers and corporate executives combed through some 40 pages of credit control regulations, the dominant question was: How serious is the central bank? "I believe they are [serious]," says Beryl W. Sprinkel, economist for Harris Trust & Savings Bank in Chicago. But, he warns, "We have loan commitments to honor. If there is a conflict between their goals and our word to long-standing customers, then something will have to break."

Fed officials are aware of the conflict. After briefing executives of 50 large domestic banks and top U.S. officers of 15 foreign banks on the new program in Washington on Mar. 17, Fed Vice-Chairman Frederick Schultz said: "This is not cosmetic, and there very well may be conflicts. It is up to the banks to do the rationing. We will be watching them."

Low reserves. Companies and banks have heard that kind of tough talk from the Fed before, of course, only to see the resolve fade. Now, say many economists, things are different. "Financial institutions cannot operate for any long period in this environment," says Jerry L. Jordan, an economist at Pittsburgh National Bank. "Ninety-five percent of the financial institutions may be sound. But

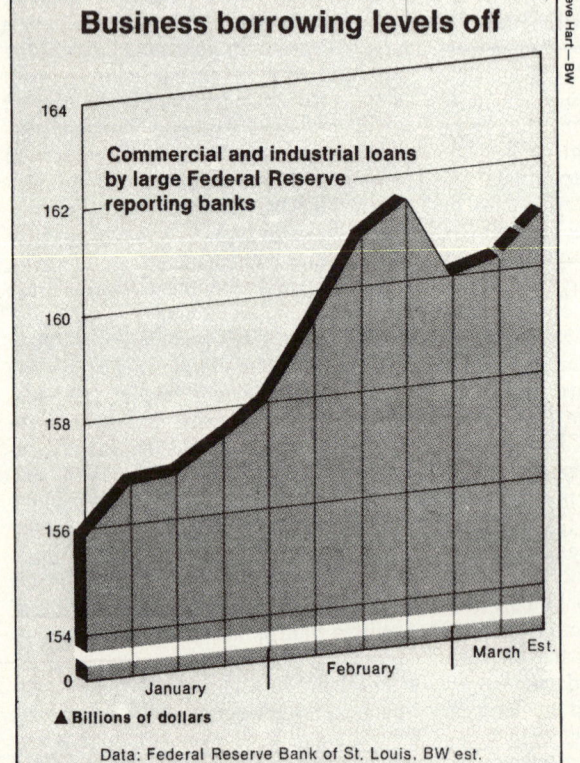

Business borrowing levels off
Commercial and industrial loans by large Federal Reserve reporting banks
Billions of dollars
Data: Federal Reserve Bank of St. Louis, BW est.

'NOW COMES THE TRICKY PART...'

it is that other 5% that will make the difference," he warns.

Fed officials share the worry that the strain may be too much for some institutions. They publicly signaled their concern by holding the emergency borrowing discount rate at 13% when they boosted the rate for larger banks to 16% on Mar. 14. Says Fed Chairman Paul A. Volcker: "The quicker we get through this period the better."

The paradox is that large banks themselves still feel flush with cash. That was a major reason that few refused the major corporations' requests for massive lines of new credit in the days preceding the Carter program. "In terms of our ability to sell large CDs, we're well below the peaks that we were at in 1974," says Bankers Trust Co. economist Jay N. Woodworth. But broad statistical measures of banking system tightness are at peaks. "The ratio of purchased funds to loans is up more than 40% from 1974 levels, and reserves are as low as they were in 1974," says Allen Sinai, of Data Resources Inc. "There will be financial failures and bankruptcies, and some banks may be required to do a very large amount of inventory financing in the next few months," he says.

Offshore loans. Credit markets are also throwing off symptoms of tightness. Multinationals are scrambling to nail down offshore loans from foreign banks in the hope of beating the Fed's domestic restrictions, and some companies are beginning to work out swaps of dollars for foreign currencies in an effort to get around the Fed (page 38). Low-rated companies, meanwhile, are sprucing up their credit ratings by buying letters of credit from their banks (page 84). And, predicts George A. Needham, managing director of First Boston Corp., there will be a dramatic increase in filings of convertible debentures and other forms of equity financing, which seems not to be covered by the Fed regulation.

The Fed will get to show its resolve soon. Its 6%-to-9% limit on bank loan expansion will bite as companies enter a peak seasonal borrowing period. Heavy Treasury borrowing, such as the $6 billion in bills sold Mar. 19, will make market pressures even greater.

But five days after the Fed announced its program, many companies contacted in a BUSINESS WEEK survey were still unaware that they will be required to report to Fed district banks on commercial paper and offshore borrowing. Some 300 selected companies will get a special review if they are using the commercial paper market heavily, warns Vice-Chairman Schultz. But to the extent the Fed closes that route, and some borrowers already cannot sell commercial paper, they will turn to their banks for funds.

Mounting complaints. Hypersensitive financial markets began questioning the Fed's monetary resolve only hours after

Many companies do not know they must report to the Fed on credit use

they opened on Mar. 17 and 18, when market rates failed to take off. While the Fed's program sopped up $1.4 billion in new bank reserves overnight, some analysts now fear the central bank will offset the policy by pumping new funds into the system.

In the political world in which the Fed operates, the concern will be about a crunch. Already, complaints over credit card restrictions are mounting, and they will snowball if only top-rated corporations are getting loans.

With business borrowing continuing to rip, the immediate test for the Fed will be how tough it will be on business credit. Or as Pittsburgh National's Jordan puts it, the test is "how long it will be before something snaps." ■

Government and Unions / 141

CREDIT CURBS PUSH SALES TOWARD A TAILSPIN

The Fed's new controls take a bite out of credit cards.

As inflation has eroded buying power over recent months, retailers have known that the free-spending habits of consumers would change. Sagging sales reported for February and March suggest that is what is happening, and the expectation is that the Federal Reserve's consumer credit restrictions, announced on Mar. 14, will send sales into a tailspin.

"We had already begun to see consumer credit, as a percentage of income, start declining six months ago," claims Jay A. Levine, chief corporate economist for Sears, Roebuck & Co. "The credit controls wiped out what little strength was left." Levine thinks industry-wide sales, in real terms, will be down 4% to 5% in each of at least the next two quarters. Retail sales in March totaled $77.2 billion, seasonally adjusted, up 6.9% from March, 1979, but off from the February total of $78.2 billion, which in turn represented a drop from January's $79.5 billion.

Ever since Christmas, retailers have been clearing the decks for a sales debacle that has not arrived. Sales have not made spectacular increases, but they have not fallen off much either, and some retailers in some regions have done quite well. On Apr. 15, for example, K mart Corp. announced a 2¢-per-share first-quarter dividend increase to 23¢.

But in constant dollars, they have been virtually flat for a year. That is why many retailers are viewing credit restrictions as the end of the recession's beginning, and are adjusting their operations accordingly.

Credit pinch. Citing the high cost of floating funds, San Diego-based Walker Scott Co., a chain of 12 Southern California department stores, has suspended its financing on major appliances. And although it will still open new credit accounts, it has taken all its new-account signs down in its stores. "We're running about even with last year and struggling like hell to stay that way," groans Robert J. Dicker, president of the chain.

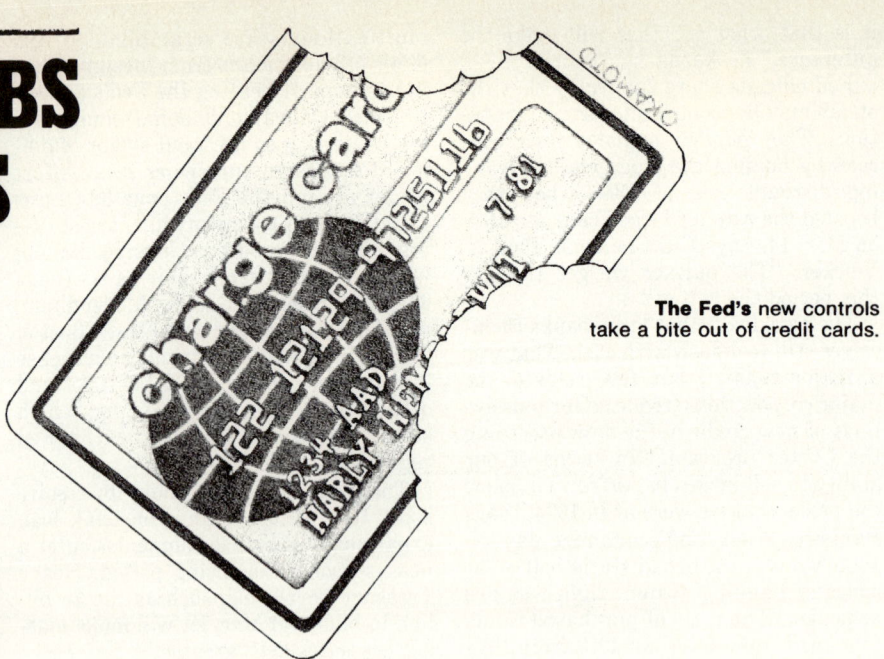

Hess's Department Store, Inc. has "tightened" the criteria for new accounts in its 18 stores, says Irwin Greenberg, president. In May, Hess's will make credit card customers increase their minimum payments from one-tenth of outstanding balances to one-sixth.

Even stores that are doing well are not escaping the credit pinch. K mart, the nation's second largest retailer, has averaged an 18% annual increase in sales in recent years and plans to boost its sales a minimum of 14% in 1980. But Chairman Robert E. Dewar concedes that major appliance sales have recently been "weak, due to high finance charges and more restrictive credit."

Some retailers, however, see an opportunity in the new pressure on bank cards. Carson Pirie Scott & Co., the Chicago-based retailing giant, is still pushing use of its own credit cards to encourage sales. "Overall, the department stores might be the beneficiaries, with bank cards beginning to charge fees," maintains John E. Cotter, executive vice-president for marketing. Nevertheless, Carson Pirie is in the process of "updating" its credit policy by increasing minimum payments and shortening the repayment schedule for some items.

Most retailers are also running leaner inventories and revising fall buying plans downward. Specialty stores have

'People are buying less but better,' observes an Altman's executive

been especially hard hit. For example, at Judy's Inc., a 53-store women's apparel chain in the Southwest, management has cut an average of one full-time employee per store, and it is considering trimming some of the goods it sells. "We've got to keep a fashion image, but a tight inventory policy dictates being a little shy of the far-out items," explains Ben G. Sumner, vice-president.

Aggressive answers. Many stores are mounting intensive sales promotions to maintain or increase floor traffic. Hess's, which expects spring and summer sales to keep 3% to 5% ahead of sales for the same period last year, is gearing up for sales and earnings gains of up to 12% in the fall by taking "a very, very aggressive stand," according to Greenberg. The company is planning to open three new stores in the fall.

As sales slip and buying power shrinks, consumers are concentrating more and more on quality goods, regardless of price. "The upper price points are holding up well," says George M. Hanley, vice-president of B. Altman & Co. in New York. "People are buying less but better because they are interested in putting their money in something that has more value." Cotter of Carson Pirie adds that "the consumer is more aware than ever before" because of tight money, and is "looking for quality and value, which can be synonymous."

In the troubled months ahead, most companies plan to stress caution. Modern Merchandising Inc., a Minneapolis-based retailer, has cut back on initial ordering, relying instead on reorders as the need arises. "Rather than actively chase sales, we're going to try to control expenses, watch inventory, and keep interest costs down," explains James Roitenberg, vice-president. ∎

A PRODUCT LIABILITY BILL HAS INSURERS UPTIGHT

"We haven't folded our tent," said Donald L. Jordan, assistant vice-president for the 130-member Alliance of American Insurers, after the first product liability bill ever to reach the floor of the House passed by an overwhelming 332-to-17 vote. The alliance and most of the rest of the insurance industry are determined to fight to kill the legislation in the Senate because they fear it is the prelude to federal regulation. But the insurers face a lonely battle, for arrayed against them are not just the Carter Administration, consumer groups, and small business but also the unlikely coalition of Ralph Nader and the National Association of Manufacturers.

Known as the Risk Retention Act, the bill offers business two possible solutions to the threat of potentially ruinous damage suits, burgeoning premiums, and the inability of some companies to buy product liability insurance at any price. One way is to form self-insurance cooperatives, called risk-retention groups, whose members would share all or part of their product liability exposure. The cooperatives would be administered by the Commerce Dept., but they would be self-policing and self-sustaining. Alternatively, companies could buy insurance as a group, a practice prohibited in 45 states, presumably at lower rates than they could get on their own.

"It is a classic market solution—voluntary and self-supporting," says Victor E. Schwartz, a former law professor at the University of Cincinnati who helped draft the legislation as a consultant to Commerce. Schwartz was chairman of the government's interagency task force that issued a study on the product liability problem two years ago. He also wrote a textbook on tort law and is considered by lawyers to be an authority on product liability.

Regulation issue. Like the bill's House sponsor, Representative Richardson Preyer (D-N. C.), Schwartz is confident that risk-retention group purchase of coverage would promote competition among insurers and reduce liability premiums. And, says Schwartz, it could be achieved "without more regulation of the insurance industry."

Insurers vehemently disagree. They argue that rates have stabilized, and that while the groups build up reserves, their members' assessments will exceed the premiums of commercially available insurance. They further contend that risk-retention groups can be formed—and indeed that they operate—under existing state law.

But their greatest concern by far is that even a modest involvement now would give the government a foot in the door for eventual regulation of the industry. "I appreciate their concern,"

The Risk Retention Act, insurers say, would open the door to regulation

Schwartz says, adding that he does not advocate federal regulation.

Time factor. The insurers' main chance of heading off the legislation in the Senate lies in the dwindling time left in this Congress. The Senate Commerce Committee has not yet begun hearings on the product liability issue; it will hold off at least until the Federal Trade Commission legislation is completed. If opponents of the Risk Retention Act can keep the bill from reaching the Senate floor before early summer, it could get dropped as Congress rushes to adjourn for the election campaigns.

Schwartz considers risk retention only part of the answer to the product liability problem. Also needed, he says, is tort reform along the lines of the Uniform Product Liability Law that Commerce proposed last year.

Designed as a model law for the states, such a law would supplant the present hodgepodge of negligence and liability theories. Schwartz thinks it would "help bring about better predictability in rate-making and remove excess costs from the system." The model law has been introduced in Kansas and Massachusetts, and other states, including California, are studying it. ∎

Government and Unions / 143

CANADA'S OIL POLICY IS STARTING TO HURT

A proposal to give Canada's federal government new power over the nation's energy resources—including wresting control away from non-Canadian companies—is already having a negative effect. The Alsands consortium headed by Shell Canada Ltd. on Nov. 21 announced that it was canceling plans to spend $200 million in 1981—part of an $8 billion project—to open Alberta's oil sands for commercial development. Three days earlier, Imperial Oil Ltd., Exxon Corp.'s Canadian subsidiary, said it would mothball its Cold Lake tar sands project in northern Alberta.

A BUSINESS WEEK survey, moreover, suggests that all of the major energy companies operating in Canada are ready to make significant cuts in their spending plans. "Most companies are going through a process of total reevaluation of their Canadian strategy," says Donald J. Taylor, a Shell Canada senior vice-president. There is concern in the industry that, unless the government of Prime Minister Pierre Elliott Trudeau revises its proposal, oil and gas exploration could be slashed by as much as half by next spring.

Trudeau's proposal calls for turning over to Canadian ownership 50% of the oil and gas assets of foreign multinationals, which now hold 70% of the country's energy assets. The proposal would also set a broad new role for the state-owned oil company, Petro-Canada; impose higher federal taxes; and fix production incentives that sharply penalize non-Canadian companies.

Profits crunch. The Alsands consortium is delaying its $8 billion project pending resolution of a bitter dispute between Alberta and Ottawa over the Trudeau plan's impact on provincial revenues. Alberta Premier Peter Lougheed is refusing to grant permits for further work on oil-sand crude oil refining until the federal government meets his demands, which include raising oil prices to 85% of U.S. levels. Indeed, the combination of a $15.50-a-bbl. price ceiling on oil and an 8% production tax will slash first-quarter earnings by 30%, according to oil industry estimates.

As a result, development activity, particularly in Alberta, is already being slowed. Oil experts are predicting that as many as 40% of Canada's 500 rigs will be shut down, with the crunch coming after the spring thaw, when companies traditionally move to new sites.

Ironically, the most certain result of the national energy proposal will be to force rigs to head south of the border. With returns in the U.S. three times higher than in Canada, small, aggressive exploration companies are leading the charge. One of the most active, Canadian Hunter Exploration Ltd., has announced that it plans to spend its entire $100 million exploration budget for 1981 in the U.S.

Nervous bankers. In Newfoundland, Premier A. Brian Peckford is pressing ahead with demands for provincial ownership and control of the potential 1 billion bbl. of oil in the Hibernia field off Labrador, now classified as federal lands. Ottawa is prepared to fight Newfoundland in court, and if the ruling goes against his

Ironically, Trudeau's energy plan will force rigs to head south of the border

province, Peckford vows to use "other means" to gain control and to hold up development in the meantime.

With the prospect of the bottom falling out of the oil economy, Canadian bankers are growing nervous. "I think the government went beyond what they hoped to achieve. I think there will be some compromises," says Ralph G. Sultanis, vice-president of Royal Bank of Canada, the nation's leading lender. Parliament is now working on the details of legislation for the energy policy and Energy Minister Marc Lalonde is meeting with oil executives to discuss their grievances. But only optimists expect the government to back down on the major issues of Canadian ownership and the enhanced federal share of production revenues. Declares Lalonde: "We know what we are doing."

The chaos can only spell long-term difficulties for Canada's attempts to raise some $200 billion in foreign capital markets to ensure energy self-sufficiency by 1990. "Canada now rates among the bottom quarter of countries as a favorable place to look for oil," says Alex H. Massad, an executive vice-president of Mobil Oil Corp. In recent days the only winners on the battered Toronto Stock Exchange—socked with paper losses of $5 billion in recent weeks—have been the small Canadian oil companies with a majority of their drilling in U.S. fields.

Lalonde, however, is mindful of the risks, and he states flatly that Canada can do the job with or without the multinationals. "We are prepared to face the short-term consequences of a long-term policy for which there is no alternative," he says. Oil executives believe that view is naive and predict that the dollar outflow will increase. Says Robert W. Sparks, president of Texaco Canada Inc.: "I'm very skeptical they will achieve what they want. I doubt the plan will work." ■

States seek a slice of oil profits

A New York federal appeals court is now weighing an opinion that will go far toward deciding how much freedom a state has in taxing the windfall profits of the big interstate oil companies. The Second U. S. Circuit Court of Appeals heard arguments on Oct. 30 and will rule soon on a bitter contest pitting the oil industry against the state of New York, which appealed a lower court decision. Hundreds of millions of dollars, maybe billions, ride on whether New York can tax the gross receipts of oil companies with retail outlets in the state and at the same time block the companies from passing the tax on to consumers.

New York vs. the oil companies could even end up in the Supreme Court because of the various constitutional questions posed. Meantime, the parties

The Energy Dept. says oil profits tax laws tread on federal territory

in the case—a list of international oil companies including Amerada Hess, Atlantic Richfield, Gulf, Mobil, and several regional companies—are hoping that the appellate court will uphold a Sept. 5 district-court decision that clipped the wings of New York State. The state can levy its 2% tax on gross earnings, said the lower court, but it cannot deny the companies' right to pass the tax along to consumers. This restriction, said the court, is unconstitutional, because it conflicts with federal laws that govern the pricing of petroleum products.

Federal territory. Adding fuel to the oil companies' argument is a declaration two months ago by the Energy Dept. that a similar tax in Connecticut could be passed on to consumers, if the oil companies so desired. Energy, too, said New York was trodding on federal territory with its tax law.

"Naturally, we want freedom to pass the tax along," says William M. Fischbach, tax director of Atlantic Richfield Co. in Los Angeles. He and others in the oil business fear that if New York is able to levy the tax with the restriction against its being passed through to the consumer, other states will follow. "If this happens," Fischbach adds, "we would hope that Congress would intervene with a law limiting a state's right to prohibit pass-through."

The conflict was sparked last winter when the $227 billion federal windfall profits tax was signed into law. It goaded the states into exploring oil windfall taxes of their own. "Now it's a battle that puts the oil producing states and the consuming states of the Northeast and Midwest into separate camps," says Richard J. Krol, a state tax specialist with Coopers & Lybrand, the accounting firm. Producing states such as Oklahoma and Texas can freely levy "severance" taxes based on the removal of oil from the ground, but the consuming states, explains Krol, have had no parallel or offsetting method of taxation. "The new 2% gross earnings taxes, like New York's—are one answer."

Of course, the consuming states want oil windfall money. But,

A court will soon decide if states can stop the pass-along of new taxes.

Krol adds, "they also want the companies and not consumers to pay, partly because of what they consider to be 'fair'—and partly because of politics."

Industry's argument. The oil companies, however, claim that the consuming states already have a way to latch on to windfall profits. "The existing state income tax laws in New York and other states have cost us more, as we've earned added profits," says John J. Ross, chief tax officer of Gulf Oil Corp. in Pittsburgh. He points out that from 1978 to 1979, Gulf's profits went from $785 million to about $1.3 billion. "Our profits went up 68%, while our New York income taxes rose by 131%," says Ross.

For their part, New York tax officials note that the New York State income taxes of all the major interstate oil companies rose from $20 million in 1978 to about $42 million in 1979. For 1980 this figure will reach some $60 million, they say. By contrast, the new 2% gross receipts tax in New York aims at revenues of about $230 million a year. "This money," says New York Tax Commissioner James H. Tully Jr., "will be used for mass transit needs, particularly in New York City."

Legal impediments. Constitutional issues posed by the 2% tax are complex and confusing. "The idea of preventing pass-through to the consumer brings up the question of taking property 'without due process of law' under the 14th Amendment," says Robert H. Bork, professor of constitutional law at Yale Law School. "This may also be arguable under the Fifth Amendment, which prohibits taking property 'without just compensation,'" he adds.

The prime constitutional question, however, arises under the "supremacy clause" of Article VI of the Constitution, explains Bork. "Since the Energy Dept., operating under the Federal Energy Act, has authority to control the pricing of petroleum products, it can be argued that the New York 2% gross-receipts tax is out of bounds. It steps into a field that has been preempted by Congress."

"Preemption by the federal government is our basic position," says Fischbach of Atlantic Richfield, adding that "this is the kind of question that may go to the Supreme Court." Tully agrees that the high court may eventually hear the case. "But even if our tax is held to be preempted," says Tully, "there are other possibilities."

He notes that the federal Energy Act expires on Sept. 30, 1981. "If Congress takes no action to extend the law, we'd be relieved of our problem," Tully says. "We could simply pass our 2% tax into law again."

Tully also hopes that if New York loses its case in the courts, Congress will provide it with legislative relief. One idea, he explains, "is that a new law might permit the oil companies to deduct taxes such as our 2% tax from their federal windfall profits taxes. We'd then be allowed to prohibit pass-through to the consumer."

"Mobil and Shell have now said that they will not pay the tax, pending the outcome of the case," adds Tully. "We consider this an evasion, and criminal proceedings may be brought." Gulf Oil has taken a more conservative step. "We paid the tax under protest, and this is no mere gesture," says Ross. "It protects our right to file a claim for refund and litigate the validity of the tax later on." ∎

Government and Unions / 145

JUSTICE TAKES AIM AT DUAL DISTRIBUTION

The risk to businessmen of competing with their customers is getting a lot greater. "Dual distribution" arrangements, in which companies sell some of their output directly to consumers and some through independent wholesalers or retailers, have always raised antitrust questions. But for the first time the U.S. Justice Dept. is prepared to bring criminal charges against such schemes. Several grand juries are probing dual distribution setups; corporate executives could face criminal prosecution for devising marketing programs that use the muscle of a supplier to keep a competitor in line.

"I don't plan at this moment to contend that dual distribution as such is illegal, but rather that dual distribution does in fact—I don't think there's any question about it—pose antitrust problems," says Sanford M. Litvack, antitrust chief at Justice. What is he looking for in the current investigations? "Price fixing, geographic allocations, customer allocations, those are the kinds of things," he explains.

Crying foul. Private antitrust lawyers are already arguing that it is not fair to switch signals on company officials and bring criminal cases for actions that in the past have always been treated merely as civil violations. But there is no doubt that dual distribution always had the potential for trouble. One example: B. F. Goodrich Co. is currently facing suits from California, Colorado, and other Western states for selling tires through both franchised dealers and its own stores. The plaintiffs seek damages for all motorists who brought Goodrich tires in the region, and they claim that the rubber company used its double role as manufacturer and retailer to fix prices of its products and divide up markets between company-owned and independent stores.

Antitrust experts say they have always warned their clients against letting dual distribution arrangements become a cover for disciplining discounters, but they expect to be listened to more carefully now that criminal prosecution is a possibility. The new Justice position, "I think, makes the advice more effective, though it won't change the advice," predicts Cleveland lawyer Carl L. Steinhouse, chairman of the criminal practice committee of the American Bar Assn.'s antitrust section.

The new interest at Justice—which has generally left litigation over such issues to the Federal Trade Commission—flows directly from Litvack, who took over as head of the Antitrust Div. in January. "Five years ago you would have to do cartwheels off the Empire State Building to get anyone at Justice interested in dual distribution," insists Chicago lawyer Paul E. Slater, an expert on distribution problems. But Litvack is looking for consumer cases, and he has goaded staffers into paying more attention to schemes that turn suggested list prices into more than mere suggestions.

Protection. Ironically, the new attention on dual distribution comes just when the economic downturn may stimulate more manufacturers to enter wholesaling or even retailing. If slow sales force some distributors out of business, marketers expect companies to protect themselves in the territories affected by taking on the selling jobs themselves.

The need to cover such sudden distribution vacuums has always been a major reason companies have started peddling their own wares. For instance, between 1973 and 1978, IC Industries Inc. took over 19 local Midas Muffler shops in what were deemed "distress situations;" most of them remained in IC hands for less than a year. ∎

Working both sides of the street: Dual traders now risk antitrust action.

A BILL THAT WILL GIVE THE FED MORE POWER

Buried in the banking reform bill that Congress is expected to pass soon (table) is a significant strengthening of the Federal Reserve System, giving the central bank broad new powers to control monetary growth.

So sweeping is the provision that some legislative drafters are themselves astonished. Says the Senate Banking Committee's chief economist, Steven Roberts: "With this bill, you won't have any need for a credit control act. The Fed can do it all." The Fed's authority to control the growth of checking accounts by raising reserve requirements will be extended to 40,000 financial institutions from 5,600 now. The bill provides the Fed with emergency authority to boost reserve requirements to any level it likes, breaking through whatever nominal limits Congress sets. And it gives the central bank room to put a new kind of marginal reserve requirement on checking accounts whenever it feels high turnover money is expanding too rapidly and is exacerbating price increases.

Political will. The bill, approved Mar. 6 by a congressional conference committee, is likely to focus credit market attention on the Fed's political will, not just its institutional ability, to control money. Until now, Fed officials have successfully made that issue secondary to their membership problem. In statement after statement in recent months, they have suggested that moving too aggressively to control the quantity of money in the economy by raising reserves might backfire, driving more and more banks out of the Fed system because of the high cost to banks of leaving interest-free reserves with the Fed.

Now, with the membership issue settled, the credit markets are likely to be increasingly skeptical if money growth continues on the order of the 8.4% pace of January and February. Therefore, two important policy changes that affect banks and their borrowers could be in store. One is a floating discount rate. Congress is pressuring the Fed to close the gap between the 13% discount rate and the 17% rate that banks must pay to borrow overnight money. It would like to see the discount rate float because that would allow a sharp drop if the economy slows. "If the Fed controls the rate, it might take forever to bring it down," says one lawmaker.

Psychological impact. More important, the Fed's ability to nip money growth before it sets off on an expansionary trend is critically important to calm inflation-scarred markets right now, and the simplest way to do that would be for the Fed to get banks to post reserves in the same week they take deposits, not two weeks later as is now the case. Again, the Fed excuse for not acting has been that the imposition of synchronous reserve reporting might drive more banks away. But that excuse will look a lot less credible now, and with the banks locked in, the Fed may soon act.

But the biggest impact will be psychological. Thousands of financial institutions will be reporting to the Fed each week. If forced to increase their interest-free—and non-profit making—reserves with the Fed, the impact on their earnings will be direct. "Suddenly, Fed pronouncements will take on a new coloration," says one S&L executive. Fed Chairman Paul A. Volcker has never debated the Fed's ability to control the money supply in a technical sense. It has always been the costs he stresses. Now, with tentacles that can be extended across the U.S. depository system, the loss of member banks to control is a moot issue. ∎

What the financial reform bill will do

New services

Authorize nationwide negotiated order of withdrawal accounts effective Dec. 31

Permit federally insured credit unions to continue to offer share drafts

Permit commercial banks to continue to offer automatic transfer accounts

Lending authority

Provide expanded lending powers for federal savings and loan associations

Provide limited business loan and deposit powers for federal mutual savings banks

Interest ceilings

Phase out Regulation Q ceilings within six years by gradually increasing ceilings to market rates

Preempt state usury laws for mortgage loans, allowing states the right to reestablish ceilings during first three years

Preempt state usury laws for business and agricultural loans in excess of $25,000 for three years, allowing any state to reestablish the ceilings at any time

Permit state-chartered depository institutions to make any loan at 1% above the Federal Reserve discount rate irrespective of state usury laws

Permit the National Credit Union Administration to lift the 12% usury ceiling for federal credit unions for up to 18 months

Customer protection

Increase the amount of federal deposit insurance to $100,000 from $40,000

Simplify truth-in-lending disclosures

Branching

Prohibit the establishment of bank trust offices across state lines for 18 months

Prohibit foreign bank acquisitions until July 1

Fed membership

Require all depository institutions to keep reserves with the Federal Reserve System. The reserves would apply against transaction accounts and nonpersonal time deposits

Part B

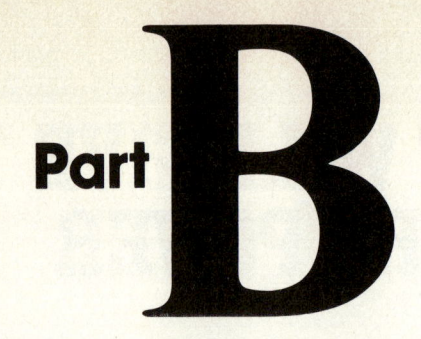

A NEW SOCIAL CONTRACT

A partnership to build the new workplace

Our will is always for our own good, but we do not always see what that is; the people is never corrupted, but it is often deceived . . .
—Jean Jacques Rousseau

Rousseau's point in this passage from *The Social Contract* is that people often fail to perceive what is in their own best interest. In the case of labor and management, where the goal of both is to remain in business, the two sides have too often behaved as if there were an unbridgeable gulf between worker and boss. It is almost as if they were trying to perpetuate a class-struggle notion in one of the least class-conscious of nations. But a social contract in the U.S. can work only if labor and management see where their interests coincide and put the energy they employ as adversaries to work solving mutual problems.

These problems arise at three levels: in national policy-setting forums, at the bargaining table, and in the workplace. An inertia that defies easy change exists at each of these levels, but increasing numbers of labor and business leaders and workers—especially in declining industries, such as steel, autos, and electrical equipment—are beginning to recognize that the survival of their institutions and jobs is threatened. "The work force today is better educated, and there is a deep understanding that we are in economic difficulty," says Frank P. Doyle, vice-president for employee relations at General Electric Co. Adds Douglas A. Fraser, president of the United Auto Workers: "Things have to get sufficiently bad before we address the problem, and maybe we're reaching that point."

The best signs of progress toward establishing a "collaborative relationship," as labor economist Jack Barbash defines what is needed, are occurring in the shops and factories. Increasingly, unions are cooperating with managements in installing new work relationships—some fairly radical in nature—that seek to give workers a voice in workplace decisions, eliminate the old authoritarianism of supervisors, and improve product quality and output. Perhaps more than anything else, these programs try to reduce the conflict between workers and bosses and substitute "problem-solving skills for adversarial skills," says Delmar L. Landen Jr., director of organizational research and development at General Motors Corp. "There's no question that the organizations capable of doing this more effectively will be the ones best able to cope with a rapidly changing social, political, and economic environment," he says.

These programs are under way in enough places to constitute an important new trend in industrial relations, although only a minority of companies and few unions are involved in them. But there can be no social contract in the U.S. unless top business and labor leaders cooperate in determining—along with government and other interest groups—broad economic goals for the country (page 88).

But top AFL-CIO leaders and corporate executives have been keeping one another at arm's length ever since the bitter battle two years ago over legislation to reform federal labor law. Even the major unionized corporations backed the successful attempt by business to defeat the proposed bill in what Labor Secretary Ray Marshall calls an "emotional and irrational crusade." Moreover, the unions perceive that management is sparing little effort to do without them. Many companies are "ambivalent about whether they should work with unions to improve collective bargaining or keep unions on the defensive and move into the nonunion area," says Thomas A. Kochan, associate professor of labor relations at Cornell University.

AFL-CIO President Lane Kirkland is now in Europe, but his executive assistant, Kenneth Young, says that top-level cooperation is possible only if management recognizes that "organized labor has a role to play in American society. We still feel it as a gut issue that management is trying to knock us out of the box at every opportunity." Some businessmen say that until the unions get over their "hang-up" about labor-law reform, it will be difficult to obtain "across-the-board co-

148 / Readings from *Business Week*

operation," as a business trade association official puts it.

Cornell's Kochan points out in a new book on industrial relations that efforts to "develop a dialogue and consensus at the national level" have occurred periodically through most of this century. The most successful attempts came during the two world wars, when important industrial relations reforms were made. In each case, after the war ended, "the absence of an external threat to society led the parties to return to their previous power struggles and conflicts," Kochan writes. But he believes now that the economic stimuli "to start the change process" are once again present, particularly in heavy manufacturing industries. "The link we're missing," he adds, "is an organizational mechanism at the national level that can turn stimulus into real action. It requires direct leadership by the federal government."

Lloyd Ulman, an economist at the University of California at Berkeley and a public member of the President's Pay Advisory Committee, says he sees "something like a social contract principle" now emerging. In tripartite discussions, the government might agree to take steps that would shore up weakened industries. "Then the government could say to unions and companies, 'In exchange for job protection, you give us wage restraint,'" Ulman says. But he warns that greater cooperation between labor and management raises the danger of "collusion" by the two sides in pressuring government for subsidies or quotas on imports.

An amelioration of the adversary relationship is also necessary in collective bargaining, and leadership at the top could create a climate to make that change easier. This does not mean that a top committee could impose change on collective bargaining practices in specific industries. The U.S. bargaining structure is much too decentralized for that. Moreover, GE's Doyle has reservations about a top-down approach that "doesn't allow you to confront day-to-day conflict. The high level of discussion is not terribly useful down where the real accommodation takes place," he says.

But negotiators must be encouraged to change past practices that no longer conform to economic reality. For example, Arnold R. Weber, president of the University of Colorado and a noted labor economist, urges a "new configuration of bargaining structures" in the steel, auto, and rubber industries (page 82). Weber also believes these unions must reassess their high wage and benefit levels. "Those were fine when they were operating in a protected market environment and a low rate of inflation, but now the unions have got to choose between unemployment and wage increases," he says.

Nobody is seriously suggesting that collective bargaining be shorn of its adversary nature; it would then no longer be bargaining. A certain amount of tension and brandishing of power is necessary if labor and management are to divide up the gains that they jointly produce. However Barbash, a former union official and now a professor of economics at the University of Wisconsin, says the U.S. no longer has the resources to permit the two sides to indulge in constant warfare. "There is a good deal of macho which has nothing to do with bargaining," Barbash says. "What we need is for two guys who don't call each other names to sit down and bargain a contract. Union democracy makes it difficult to get away from the pageantry, but there's nothing left these days for game-playing." Unions, however, are political organizations, and the necessity of getting elected gives union leaders a vested interest in playing the adversary role to the hilt. But economic adversity tends to undermine the demagogue's standing with the rank and file.

There is more reason for hope, however, in the work-practice reforms that are being introduced on the factory floor. The movement has been under way for about 10 years, mostly in non-union plants but now increasingly in unionized ones, with union cooperation. One purpose is to "unfreeze" the antagonistic worker-boss climate that exists in many plants and inhibits productivity growth. Above all, most of the programs try to involve the worker more deeply in the production process by seeking his ideas. "Management is getting away from the old, 'I'm the boss, you're the hoss' attitude," says Raymond Calore, president of UAW Local 664 at Tarrytown, N.Y., where the union and General Motors Corp. have a successful "quality of work life" program.

In addition to quality of work life—or QWL as it is known—the programs go by a variety of names, including worker participation, labor-management teams, and industrial democracy. Nobody knows how many companies have these programs, although the number must be in the hundreds. GM alone has QWL programs at 66 plants, and even the conservative steel industry is experimenting with new shop-floor relations.

In April the nine major steel companies and the United Steelworkers agreed to set up "labor-management participation teams" in certain plants to deal both with quality and production problems and workers' complaints about the job. This concept was proposed and pushed by two companies that already have work improvement projects under way, Jones & Laughlin Steel Corp. and Bethlehem Steel Corp. Bethlehem has gone so far as to bring an outside consultant into its Los Angeles Works to hold consciousness-raising seminars for steelworkers and particularly to induce foremen to get more teamwork from their crews by reducing antagonisms. The result: a 30% increase in daily output on two rolling mills in the first weeks after the training ceased last month.

Some 15 years ago, two American personnel consultants introduced "quality control circles" in Japanese industries. The circles, consisting of committees of workers and supervisors who meet to discuss product-quality improvement, have proliferated in Japan. Says Thomas J. Murrin, president of Westinghouse Electric Corp.'s Public Systems Co., the use of the circles is the "single most significant explanation for the truly outstanding quality of goods and services" produced in Japan.

'The communication is better'

U.S. companies are now rediscovering the circle concept. Westinghouse, for example, has established 150 "quality circles," as it calls them, at 50 locations. At its Baltimore defense complex there are 63 circles, which range from 6 to 10 members and cover 4,500 blue-collar workers. Supervisors who run the weekly circle meetings make no secret of the fact that their purpose is to find better ways of producing quality goods, not to serve as a sounding board for all worker complaints.

"You have a better relationship with your supervisor, the communication is better, and you really feel part of it," says Cardell Jones, a circle member who assembles microcircuitry for components of weapons and radar systems. Ronald Shenton, an inspector, says he often tells management "things that make them mad," but he is a zealot about quality and believes that "if you don't come up with better quality, you lose."

So far, three unions that represent workers at Baltimore have not objected to the circles, but Thomas Rostkowski, president of Local 1805 of the International Brotherhood of Electrical Workers, says he is demanding a union co-chairman in each group. Still, several of the workers told a reporter that their concern for their own job was more important than whether the union approved of the circles. And Westinghouse says the circles have made changes resulting in more than $1 million in savings in the two years of their existence. The company's defense business is booming, and Murrin says that "we can virtually assure our current employees in Baltimore that they will not be put out of work by robots or quality circles."

The ability to guarantee job security appears to be one of the most important trade-offs that management can offer to induce worker cooperation in work-improvement projects. "When you're making a radical shift that is very threatening to the whole organization, you need good job protection," says Jerome M. Rosow, president of Work in America Institute Inc. Workers understand, he says, that by improving quality and productivity "they'll be more competitive, they'll increase their company's share of the market, and, in the final analysis, they'll keep their jobs."

This is one of the factors that helped make the program at GM's Tarrytown assembly plant one of the most successful of QWL programs. By 1971, after a decade of changes in the work force, Tarrytown was in trouble. Absenteeism was high, product quality was poor, and union-management relations were so bad that as many as 1,000 grievances clogged the grievance procedure at a time. "Everybody was mad at one another," says the UAW's Ray Calore. "The foremen felt you had to have severe discipline, push and shove. The generations had changed, but they hadn't changed." It became apparent to him, Calore says, that GM management might not invest more money in Tarrytown.

Calore and local management began to meet informally to solve the labor problem, and the program became a formal one when the UAW and GM agreed in 1973 to embark on a QWL program throughout the corporation. The core of the program at Tarrytown involved three-day orientation sessions for all workers in the plant and those who have been hired since. In these meetings, company and union goals were explained, workers were shown the interrelation of one assembly-line job to another, and they were given a chance to meet workers from other departments. "They ended up knowing more about the plant than the supervisors," Calore says.

At the same time, the UAW local and plant management met frequently to solve problems as they arose rather than waiting for the next round of local negotiations or the filing of grievances. Supervisors stopped applying discipline in a heavy-handed way, absenteeism dropped, and product quality improved. The grievance backlog seldom exceeds 20 or 30 complaints at a time. "We're no longer involved in the adversary rat race," Calore says. "What we're trying to do is create an atmosphere in the workplace so a person has the same freedom of expression and dress that he has at home."

A job on the Tarrytown assembly line is still not a creative joy, and the line still turns out a car a minute. But bosses no longer intimidate workers, and an easy-going atmosphere permits socializing on the job. Moreover, Tarrytown is now one of only three GM plants that produces the popular Chevrolet Citation, Pontiac Phoenix, and Buick Skylark. While 135,000 other GM workers are on indefinite layoff, Tarrytown's full force of 4,600 hourly employees works nine hours every day as well as three Saturdays every month.

The UAW says it cooperates in QWL programs to make jobs more satisfying for workers; if the programs also increase productivity, that is a side benefit, the union says. GM, meanwhile, does not crow about boosting productivity so as not to turn workers against the program.

But as Rosow says, "GM is smart enough to know if you improve the quality of work life, you improve efficiency. It isn't that you make the people happier. You make them more effective, and that produces satisfaction." ∎

THE UAW'S ABOUT-FACE ON IMPORT CONTROLS

Walter P. Reuther and other founders of the United Auto Workers cherished the concept of free trade as a bulwark against the international trade wars that helped spawn the Depression. But now, 45 years after its formation, the UAW has reluctantly joined the protectionist ranks of many other trade unions that feel threatened by foreign competition. On Jan. 14, the auto union announced that it had decided to seek import controls on Japanese cars. "You can't have fair trade," UAW President Douglas A. Fraser says, "when we do all the giving and they [the Japanese] do all the taking."

This shift in policy occurred just as the UAW was preparing for a major change in leadership that will bring younger members to the fore by 1983 to replace Fraser and the retiring Reuther generation. The new leaders are likely to be faced with a set of economic issues not encountered by Reuther, the ideological father of the UAW, and more than ever the union will be focusing on legislative and political solutions for its problems.

On Jan. 12, the union's executive board, acting as a political caucus, nominated four men to be elected to top posts at a June convention. They will replace Reuther-era veterans Irving Bluestone, Ken Bannon, and Duane (Pat) Greathouse, now vice-presidents, and Secretary-Treasurer Emil Mazey, all of whom are retiring. The nominees, currently regional directors, are Stephen P. Yokich, age 44; Owen Bieber, 50; Ray Majerus, 55; and Donald F. Ephlin, 54, who is likely to replace Bluestone as the UAW's chief negotiator at General Motors Corp. When Fraser retires in 1983, his successor will probably come from this new group. Ephlin, once a local union president and for 17 years an assistant to former UAW President Leonard Woodcock, may have the best credentials for the top post. He calls himself a "pragmatic liberal" who believes in Reuther's social activist philosophy.

Until now, the union was able to negotiate militantly for big wages and benefits in an industry that expanded virtually nonstop and enjoyed large productivity gains. But the new leaders face the prospect of a trimmed-down work force and a car-buying public increasingly addicted to small foreign cars. In 1979, Japanese car producers claimed 16.7% of the U. S. market, even as one in four of the UAW's 750,000 U. S. auto workers was laid off. With prices rising much faster on small Detroit-built cars, the number of Japanese imports is likely to rise.

Foreign plants. Fraser is demanding that the federal government hold Japanese imports for the next four years to 1977 levels of 1.4 million units through an "orderly marketing agreement." Fraser also wants the U. S. to adopt "local content" rules, common in other countries, that would require part of each Japanese car sold here to be made in the U. S. "If the Japanese won't agree to a timetable" for setting up plants here, the union leader declares, "then it's time to start fighting on this issue."

The impact of the UAW's policy shift was blunted somewhat by Honda Motor Co.'s Jan. 12 announcement that it plans to build an auto assembly plant next to its motorcycle plant in Marysville, Ohio (page 112). Fraser wants Toyota Motor Co. and Nissan Motor Co. to follow Honda's lead. But they are unlikely to shift their production willingly because of the unfavorable dollar-yen relationship and because UAW wage rates are roughly double those in Japan.

Salary demands. Indeed, union concessions on wage rates, given to Volkswagen when it became the first foreign company to make cars in the U. S., may end. UAW workers at VW's South Charleston (W. Va.) stamping plant have been on strike since Jan. 2, demanding a heftier General Motors-style contract. That strike has also closed VW's Westmoreland (Pa.) assembly plant, halting production of 1,000 VW Rabbits per day.

U.S. auto makers share Fraser's view toward Japan but want to avoid disrupting trade relations elsewhere, since they have extensive foreign operations themselves. "Those who benefit from the market should contribute to the market," says Ford Motor Co. President Philip Caldwell. However, the Carter Administration has been trying to break down "local content" barriers to U.S. car exports, and it fears that moves to force foreign manufacturing here would endanger this effort.

Fraser's abrupt turn away from the traditional UAW free-trade stance highlights an identity crisis within the union. Increasingly, the UAW has been haunted by doubts about its waning militancy and eroding membership base. No longer is it Reuther's brash, young vanguard of the working classes, but rather, a middle-class institution in a maturing industry trying to defend its turf. "It could be," theorizes one auto company negotiator, "that the UAW's ideological leadership of the labor movement could be up for grabs."

How the changing auto market threatens the UAW, too

If the influx of auto imports is forcing the U.S. auto industry to change gears rapidly, it is also prompting the United Auto Workers to make drastic changes in strategy that will affect the companies as much as their workers. To avoid an enormous loss of jobs, the union has reversed its traditional free-trade philosophy and is seeking restrictive legislation on imports. It will also try harder to win a four-day work week at the Big Three auto makers to spread the work. But the first strategy may not succeed, and the second may create serious bargaining and political conflicts within the union.

"The long-range goal has to be to get the Japanese to locate here and produce here," says UAW President Douglas A. Fraser, who outlined UAW proposals for import restrictions on Mar. 7 before the House Ways & Means subcommittee on trade. Fraser failed, in a trip to Japan in mid-February, to persuade the Japanese to voluntarily build U.S. plants soon. So he urged the subcommittee to recommend enactment of "local content" rules that by the mid-1980s would require Toyota, Nissan, Honda, and other importers of more than 200,000 units a year to make in the U.S. at least 75% of each car they sell here. He also proposed that Congress ask the Japanese to restrain exports to the U.S.

Layoffs. Fraser is facing two related but separate problems. Slumping sales of full-size and mid-size cars have indefinitely idled 25% of the UAW's 750,000 members at the Big Three, and UAW insiders fear that many of these layoffs could become permanent if imports keep their current 27% of the market. Moreover, even if imports drop to a more normal 15% to 20%, UAW staffers think that the Big Three's changeover to smaller cars could cut the industry's work force nearly in half by the early 1990s, because the labor content of a subcompact is only two-thirds that of a standard-size car. This "worst case" UAW estimate assumes slow market growth to 15 million cars and trucks a year in North America, plus a strong effort by Ford, GM, and Chrysler to increase the share of foreign-made parts in their cars from the current 3% to the maximum 25% allowed by the federal law that sets standards for gasoline mileage.

The UAW's new strategy replaces its partially successful effort over the past 30 years to fight imports by helping foreign unions "harmonize" their wages with those of U.S. auto workers. Now, the union probably will have to put a much higher bargaining priority

UAW President Fraser: Pushing to restrict imports and spread the work.

on job-preserving provisions, such as more paid time off and restrictions on plant closings. To win these immediately, the UAW would have to accept more moderate wage and benefit improvements. This could cause internal upheavals in one of the country's most politically stable unions.

Uphill battle. Fraser does not blame the Japanese for this year's layoffs. Instead, he blames the Big Three for moving too slowly to make small cars, a step the late Walter P. Reuther urged as early as 1949. But Fraser argues that the Japanese alone have expanded their U.S. market share to 22% largely because U.S. import laws are generous. Most other countries already have local-content rules, and Fraser notes that Japan even requires part of each Boeing commercial jet it buys to be made by Japanese workers. "If it's good enough for us, it's good enough for them," he declares.

Still, his campaign for U.S.-based Japanese plants faces an uphill battle. Fraser will get little help from the Carter Administration. "While we have a serious problem, the industry cannot make a legitimate case for trade restrictions," says one top Administration trade official. He adds: "Any such bill would become a Christmas tree [for other industries], and the President would veto it." Similarly, the Big Three oppose quotas because they want to sell more cars abroad. They fear that new U.S. import restrictions might jeopardize this effort.

Labor costs. Without trade law pressure, it is unlikely that the Japanese will bow to Fraser's demands except in token fashion. The main deterrent to locating in the U.S. is the cost of U.S. labor. According to the Bureau of Labor Statistics, the average Japanese auto worker's wages and benefits in the first half of 1979 were only half the $13.72 an hour earned by the average U.S. auto worker. And that figure will exceed $20 an hour by 1982 if inflation stays in double digits.

If the Big Three regain their market share, as they predict, the biggest dispute may yet come over small-car changeover in the U.S. The union almost certainly will try to win restrictions on the use of foreign-made parts in domestic cars. Indeed, regional UAW leaders are already taking a suspicious view of Ford's plans to build a new small-engine plant in Mexico. And Fraser says he will try to spread the work even further by winning more of the "paid personal holidays" the union has won in its last two contracts. "The four-day week is going to come as sure as I'm standing here," he declares. "The only question is how soon we're going to get there."

THE RISK IN PUTTING A UNION CHIEF ON THE BOARD

United Auto Workers President Douglas A. Fraser believes that most U.S. labor leaders "look into the future through a rearview mirror." Not so Fraser. Like his mentor, Walter P. Reuther, he welcomes new ideas and, indeed, eagerly pursues ways of establishing industrial relations precedents. Fraser's latest innovation, gaining a union seat on the Chrysler Corp. board of directors, could turn out to be a breakthrough that leads organized labor in a totally new direction. But it also carries some legal and bargaining risks for Fraser, and the concept—alien to the social and economic structure of the U.S.—is not likely to spread rapidly, although it will spread.

Barring unforeseen circumstances, Fraser will be elected to the Chrysler

Board membership is one element of a trend toward more say for workers

board at the annual meeting in Rockford, Ill., on May 13. It will be the first time that a union leader has sat on the board of a major U.S. corporation, although there are a few examples of worker representation on the boards of small companies. Chrysler Chairman Lee A. Iacocca offered to nominate Fraser to the board as a quid pro quo for wage and benefit concessions made last fall by the UAW and for the union's cooperation in lobbying for the company's government loan guarantee plan. With management supporting the nomination, Fraser's election to the 20-member board is certain.

Joint committees. Not surprisingly, the board role for Fraser has been attacked by many corporate executives, who contend that it poses a conflict of interest for the labor leader. U.S. unions for the most part also remain hostile, although the concept's acceptance by the powerful and innovative UAW encourages other union leaders at least to think about the previously unthinkable.

Fraser, who has the security of knowing that he has almost complete political control in his union, argues that the idea will spread. "Almost inevitably, workers are going to realize it's not enough for the labor movement to react to decisions made by management," he says. "We've got to be where the decisions are made." Adds a company labor negotiator: "I think the idea is hokum, if well-intentioned hokum, but by the mid-1980s it will have slipped in elsewhere."

Board representation for workers is only one element of the most important new trend in industrial relations since collective bargaining was institutionalized in the 1930s. Workers in increasing numbers, and in many industries, are seeking and getting a voice in management of the workplace. This is happening mainly on the shop floor, where workers and lower-level supervisors are participating in labor-management committees set up under "quality of work life" programs to make jobs more challenging, rewarding, and productive. Growing numbers of corporations are also borrowing from Japan the concept of quality-control circles, in which labor and management jointly decide how to improve production processes. And the increasing use of employee stock ownership plans (ESOPs) is creating a worker demand for a voice in company operations—and in some companies for membership on the board.

So far, the trend has been to democratize the workplace from the bottom up, rather than to follow the model of board representation for workers, or "co-determination," that is common in Europe, especially West Germany. Co-determination laws have been on the books in Germany since 1951, and in many ways that country, with its homogeneous population and hierarchical social structure, is well-suited to the top-down democratization of corporations embodied in the worker-director concept. Bargaining in Germany parallels this top-down structure, while in the U.S. it is much more diffused and localized. Moreover, state corporation laws in the U.S. do not provide for "special-interest directors" to represent the interests of only one group of shareholders or employees on a corporate board.

Indeed, the legal problems that Fraser will face as a Chrysler director may be the first and surest test of whether co-determination has a future in the U.S. Courts have consistently held that a director has a fiduciary responsibility to represent all shareholders equally. But in describing his anticipated role, Fraser has repeatedly said that he would "represent the workers and the consumers." This has led critics to declare that a conflict of interest is unavoidable.

Two law professors and legal authorities on corporate governance, Donald E. Schwartz of Georgetown University and Alfred F. Conard of the University of Michigan, agree that Fraser's dual role as union chief and director represents, on the surface, a conflict. "There are times when the interests of the union and the interests of all the shareholders will conflict," Schwartz says. "But the conflict can be resolved, just as conflicts have been resolved when bankers sit on the board." Conard points out that Fraser will most likely be outvoted by other directors on issues where workers' interests are opposed to those of other shareholders. "There is no significant chance that a court will find that a board, made up as this one is, voted for something that the directors did not reasonably believe would be in the best, long-term interests of the corporation," Conard says.

Threefold duty. In a proxy statement recently mailed to all Chrysler shareholders, Fraser defines his role in a way obviously meant to allay criticism: "I believe my activities as a director will advance the interests of the broad Chrysler community—shareholders, workers, suppliers, dealers, consumers, and the public." The statement was drafted after UAW lawyers analyzed court decisions on fiduciary responsibility. John A. Fillion, the union's general counsel, cites court rulings that say a corporation has a threefold duty: to its shareholders, its employees, and the public. A director, therefore, Fillion says, is similarly obligated. "Under the evolving law of the responsibility of directors, Doug stands no greater danger of a conflict of interest than any other board member with a traditional background," the lawyer adds. "If there is a conflict, we'll back off."

Chrysler employees and retirees currently own about 30% of the company's common stock. Under an ESOP plan linked to the government loan guarantee program, Chrysler must contribute $162.5 million worth of new stock to active UAW members over four years. By the end of that time, Fraser estimates, members of his union will own 15% of the common stock outstanding, assuming an average market price at the time of issue of $10 per share. The result will be "a remarkable overlap in the identity of interests between shareholders and Chrysler workers," Fillion says. Still, under U.S. law a director may not represent both a single constituency, such as employees, and all shareholders.

Antitrust constraints. Other potential conflicts could have an adverse impact on the UAW's relationships with General Motors Corp. and Ford Motor Co. Both companies have spoken out emphatically against the principle of auto union representation on the board of a major competitor. In the past the companies have routinely shared information with UAW

Government and Unions / 153

leaders, but they worry now that such disclosures, while Fraser sits on the Chrysler board, may violate the Securities & Exchange Commission's antitrust rules.

At Ford, top management has met periodically with Fraser and other UAW leaders to discuss such matters of mutual interest as Ford's market share and design prospects for new cars. "We want to keep up communications with the UAW, and we trust Doug," says Peter J. Pestillo, Ford's labor-relations vice-president. "But could we offer the kinds of disclosures we have in the past under the SEC rules?" Adds B. Patrick Crane Jr., GM's director of labor relations: "We have all kinds of constraints on what we're allowed to talk to our competitors about, and I think we'd have to give some serious consideration to what we'd be willing to discuss with the UAW."

Another major problem arises in deciding which issues Fraser can discuss and vote on as a Chrysler board member without raising conflict of interest. In his Chrysler proxy statement, Fraser declares that he will not discuss or vote on "issues of collective bargaining strategy by the corporation vis-à-vis the UAW." But he will vote on "collective bargaining policies," among other topics that affect workers. "I've been in this business for many years," says one labor relations executive, "and I have trouble seeing how you differentiate between strategy and policy."

Drawing lines. The UAW's Fillion differentiates this way: A policy matter might involve a new principle in bargaining—for instance, whether Chrysler should be willing to negotiate more extensive workplace democratization provisions with the union. A "strategy" issue, by contrast, might involve specifically how the corporation will oppose a set of labor demands, possibly by locking out workers or taking a strike. "I'm fairly optimistic about being able to draw the line between the two," the attorney says.

As far as is known, there are no legal precedents involving conflict of interest cases against "special-interest directors" in the U.S. Critics have attacked the idea of directors being elected on the basis of representing blacks, other minorities, women, or environmentalists. But union representation on a board has occurred so rarely that examples are practically unknown. One is South Bend Lathe Inc., where the workers took over the company in 1975 under an ESOP. An official of a United Steelworkers local now sits on the board.

Another example is the small Providence & Worcester Co. in New England. For many years, this company merely leased its track and right-of-way to other railroads. When it converted to an independent operating railroad in 1973, it asked Charles Luna, who had just

Can a labor leader who is also a board member vote on bargaining strategy?

retired as president of the United Transportation Union, to join the board. He served for four years before resigning to pursue his duties as a director of Amtrak full-time. Joseph R. DiStefano, secretary and general counsel of the railroad, says that Luna's presence on the board fostered "good relations with our unionized employees," and a conflict of interest never arose.

At Chrysler, Fraser wants to use his board position to help the company survive and to bring more democracy to the workplace. He especially believes that he can stimulate worker cooperation in making Chrysler's plants more productive. "I think we know the industry better than management," he says. "I'll be the eyes and ears and transmit the ideas of hundreds of thousands of workers to the board." Eventually, Fraser wants to get "worker input" into management decision-making at all levels of the company, involving such matters as work and production scheduling, production standards, safety and health, product planning, and quality control.

Fraser realizes that he will be voted down by other directors on major issues, such as plant shutdowns, but he believes that at least he will "moderate positions, if not change them." However, some observers question whether Fraser's position will give him "responsibility without power," as one puts it, and thus hurt him politically. But for all these potential problems, if the worker-director idea is to succeed anyplace in the U.S., it will most likely be at a company, such as Chrysler, where survival is at stake. ∎

CAN CHRYSLER SQUEEZE MORE FROM THE UAW?

By linking federal loan guarantees for Chrysler Corp. to a three-year wage freeze for the company's employees, congressional opponents of a bailout may have designed an aid package that is destined to self-destruct. The United Auto Workers rejected such a freeze out of hand at a Dec. 3 meeting. The UAW has indicated that it will grant some further concessions to help Chrysler survive, but one of the few remaining options—reopening its recently signed contract with Chrysler—poses major logistical problems and political risks for the union's leaders.

The UAW's move will be the key to passage of an aid bill agreeable to all sides. UAW President Douglas A. Fraser is lobbying intensively on Capitol Hill, hoping to reach an understanding before Congress adjourns on Dec. 21. To dramatize the UAW's opposition to the three-year wage freeze proposed by the Senate Banking Committee, Fraser summoned the UAW's 233-member Chrysler Bargaining Council to Washington on Dec. 3. "Almost to a man, they said that they would rather shut down the shop than take a three-year freeze," says a top UAW official.

But this leaves the auto union in the vulnerable position of seeming to pull the plug on Chrysler's survival hopes, unless it can soften the sacrifices demanded of workers in the bill approved by the Senate committee. It is becoming clear that the UAW can compromise only by taking the painful course of reopening the contract and making concessions short of a three-year freeze. The pact signed by the UAW and Chrysler on Nov. 27 provides wage and benefit increases estimated to cost $1.1 billion over three years. UAW concessions in that contract will cost Chrysler $203 million less than the pattern settlement at General Motors Corp. At best, union leaders expect they can squeeze only another $200 million out of the pact without risking rejection by the rank and file.

Political problem. To reopen the contract, the UAW must first get the approval of its Chrysler Bargaining Council. Union officials say they also would seek rank-and-file approval, probably through simple majority votes of members attending meetings at the 69 Chrysler local unions. This immediately poses a political problem for Fraser: Only a few weeks ago he recommended acceptance of a Chrysler pact, and now he will have to concede that he was wrong in estimating what it would take to persuade Congress that the workers were sacrificing enough.

Nevertheless, the workers probably would approve a contract reopening to save their jobs. Fraser's problem is reaching an understanding with key congressional members before Dec. 21 on the total concessions the union might make. The UAW is aiming for an "equity of sacrifice" between workers, bankers, and the company. But it wants to work out the specifics of its concessions in talks with Chrysler.

This means that the UAW may wait for a bill to emerge from Congress before it reopens the Chrysler contract. The bill probably would specify that Chrysler would only get the loan guarantees if and when the UAW ratifies the new

The union failed to convince Congress that workers were sacrificing enough

pact—and that might take a month or more. The first contract was approved by only a 69% majority, and many workers oppose any further wage cuts. The ratification problem is compounded by the steady rise in the number of laid-off Chrysler workers. Eligible to vote on the pact, they would have little to lose if it is rejected.

Court action? Even if a new settlement is ratified, wildcat strikes could ensue, and skilled workers might defect to other auto companies to avoid the wage cuts. UAW officials also worry that renegotiating the contract at lower terms might leave the union open to lawsuits by members, who could argue that the union had violated its duty of "fair representation" under federal labor law. Such suits might have little chance of success, but they would be troublesome to the union.

The UAW has already rejected other possibilities for helping Chrysler, such as using its strike fund to buy stock or to loan money to the company. This idea conflicts with the union's constitution. Fraser has said he would support a congressional proposal that the union can "make an additional contribution by having workers buy stock" in Chrysler. But the aid bill opponents probably will demand more than that. ∎

THE PRICE OF PEACE AT CHRYSLER

Leaders of the United Auto Workers faced an unenviable task in negotiations this year at Chrysler Corp. The ailing No. 3 auto producer was demanding a two-year wage freeze in place of the pattern-setting agreement the UAW won at General Motors Corp. in September, and adamant UAW opposition to concessions would have jeopardized the jobs of nearly 100,000 Chrysler workers—as would have a strike. The union did make costly concessions in a new agreement reached on Oct. 25, but in the least painful way possible. In return, it won noneconomic demands that could have important ramifications for labor-management relations in the U. S. These include a seat on Chrysler's board for UAW President Douglas A. Fraser and more say in pension investment decisions.

Social projects. Chrysler workers are expected to ratify the new package by Nov. 15, even though their total wages and benefits over the next three years will average some $2,000 less per worker than their peers at GM and Ford Motor Co. will get. The workers know they must make sacrifices if the company is to survive. Moreover, the new contract does not restrict the union's cost-of-living adjustment (COLA), an important consideration with inflation running at 13% annually. As a Chrysler director, Fraser is likely to push for more worker say in decisions on plant closings. And, the union won a limited ability to make the pension funds of Chrysler employees work to their advantage well before these people retire.

The union and Chrysler agreed that, in the future, part of the company's pension contributions will be used to fund "socially desirable projects," rather than to buy common stocks or government securities, as in the past. A joint committee of union and management representatives will suggest specific investments to the Chrysler pension fund trustees, such as home mortgages, health maintenance centers, and nursing homes in communities with Chrysler plants. This is aimed at saving decaying urban centers and preserving union jobs in the North. The money available for such uses will be 10% of what is left each year after annual expenses of the fund are subtracted from investment earnings and new contributions. In 1978 this would have been about $7 million.

This provision, which the UAW had demanded in every set of auto talks since 1964, is what Richard Prosten, research director of the AFL-CIO's Industrial Union Dept., calls a "very important first step" in a new strategy unions are developing to win their organizing and social goals. Union pension funds have about $250 billion in assets. About $60 billion is jointly managed by union and company trustees, but the rest is controlled by trustees appointed by management. At Chrysler, the UAW has managed to get a say in investments in a way that union bargainers say lets them avoid the fiduciary responsibility that joint trusteeship would bring.

In a related provision, the union won the right to name up to five companies each year whose stock it wants the pension fund to shun because of their involvement in South Africa and their failure to endorse the "Sullivan principles" of racial equality. As of Dec. 31, 1978, the Chrysler-UAW pension plan had $30 million, or 6% of its total stock holdings, invested in 26 companies that the American Consulate General in Johannesburg says have yet to sign the statement of principles authored by the Reverend Leon Sullivan of Philadelphia. Among the nonsigners is Chrysler itself.

Most managements bitterly oppose such provisions, but for Chrysler they seemed a small price to pay. Even if it gets the $750 million in government-guaranteed loans it wants, the company must raise about $1.4 billion in working capital by 1982 to stay afloat while it revamps its lineup of cars. In early October the union in effect lent Chrysler $200 million by agreeing to let it skip contributions to its UAW pension fund in 1979 and 1980. The new pact will save an additional $203 million, bringing Chrysler's total saving from the UAW to $403 million over the next two years. "If the government and the bankers come through the way we did," declared UAW

For the UAW, a greater say in decision-making, but lower wages than at GM

Vice-President Marc Stepp, "it will give Chrysler a clear opportunity to survive."

The UAW's concessions come in four areas of the contract. First, the company will save about $59 million in wages. This will be achieved by delaying the effective date of the union's traditional 3% annual wage increase by six months in the first year, four months in the second, and two months in the third. Chrysler will continue to pay $1.37 per hour in accumulated cost-of-living adjustments from the expiring contract, but this will be paid in a lump sum at the end of each quarter, rather than immediately rolled into each worker's weekly pay. The effect will be an interest-free loan to the company of about $30 million.

Time off. The union's COLA formula was preserved, including an improvement in the third year from a penny per hour for each 0.3-point increase in the consumer price index to a penny for each 0.26-point rise. This by far is the most lucrative part of the UAW wage settlement, and it could make savings from other concessions in the Chrysler contract far less meaningful if inflation continues at its 13% pace.

The biggest savings will be in paid time off. Instead of eight "paid personal holidays" won in the first calendar year of the new GM pact, Chrysler workers will get no paid personal holidays until 1981. They will match GM workers at nine days in 1981 and then go beyond the pattern with 11 days in 1982 vs. nine at GM and Ford. The savings to Chrysler will be $73 million by 1982, although the days the union will get back in the third year will cost $18 million.

The third area of savings is in sickness and accident pay. This has been a vexing problem at Chrysler, whose aging, inner-city Detroit parts and assembly plants have had higher sickness and accident costs than Ford's and GM's. To cope with this, the new agreement will require an employee to miss four work days before he can start getting sickness and accident pay. Weekends no longer count, and "S&A" pay is virtually frozen for two years. The total savings: $24 million.

Pension savings. Roughly one-quarter of the $203 million in savings will come from below-pattern increases in pension benefits, although payouts to both present and future retirees will rise sharply. All improvements are delayed until Jan. 1 and will start at only 70% of the increase at GM. They will rise gradually, matching the GM pattern by May, 1982.

156 / Readings from *Business Week*

Ultimately, pension benefits for new Chrysler retirees will jump 27%, from $14.33 to $18.25 per month per year of service. Early-retirement benefits for those too young for Social Security will rise from the present maximum of $700 to $915 a month.

Chrysler will thus save about $49 million in pension costs by 1982. By the end of the contract, however, Chrysler's pension costs would again be the highest of the Big Three, rising by one-half to about $1.70 per hour per active worker. "We're on the horns of a severe dilemma here," admits Melvin A. Glasser, head of the UAW's Social Security Dept. and an

The UAW's concessions represent a $203 million savings for Chrysler

architect of the Chrysler settlement. "We wanted to give the company maximum relief, but we also wanted to keep the incentives for early retirement because we expect lower overall employment levels in the company."

With some 29,000 hourly workers laid off indefinitely, Chrysler has only 82,000 active hourly workers in the U.S. and Canada. In addition, the UAW represents 10,000 unionized salaried workers. The impending shutdown of Chrysler's largest assembly plant, in Hamtramck, Mich., will cost about 6,000 more jobs, and other cuts are expected. "We expect to see a pattern more like that at Ford Motor Co.," says Glasser, noting the traditionally lower manpower and higher overtime at the No. 2 auto maker, where Lee A. Iacocca and much of Chrysler's new management team earned their reputations for cost control. ∎

AILING AMC SEEKS RELIEF FROM THE UAW

Coming on top of sagging car sales, substantial labor cost increases have exacerbated the financial plight of U.S. auto makers this year. And fifth-ranked American Motors Corp. may be the next example. The two-year contract covering 11,000 AMC workers expires on Sept. 16, and the company wants concessions similar to those the United Auto Workers granted Chrysler Corp. last year. But unlike Chrysler, which needed a government bailout to avoid bankruptcy, AMC is being bankrolled by France's government-controlled Renault. Thus the UAW is taking a skeptical view of AMC's pleas for aid, and the result could be a settlement that will leave the company in deeper trouble—and more dependent on Renault.

"With Renault in the picture, the company will have a tough time pleading poverty," says Terry K. Gorman, president of UAW Local 1285 at AMC's Brampton (Ont.) assembly plant. Last year, Renault agreed to pump $200 million into new-product development at AMC in return for an eventual 22.4% slice of AMC's common. This year, Renault has provided $90 million in credit to help cover what analysts say will be a $150 million loss on sales of about $2.8 billion for AMC's fiscal year ending Sept. 30.

The problem is that other U.S. producers have new compact cars coming out this fall, while AMC will have no new U.S.-built products until late 1982. Then the company plans to market a Renault-designed front-wheel-drive car to be built at its Kenosha (Wis.) plant. But continued losses in the meantime could add up to a cumulative cash shortfall of $200 million, unless AMC's sagging sales of Jeeps make an unexpected rebound. Lenders are reluctant to finance such a large deficit. And even well-heeled Renault may think twice before doubling its initial investment—unless AMC workers bear part of the burden. As one AMC executive puts it: "We need money—and lots of it."

Relief possible. Prodded by Congress, the UAW agreed to delay phasing in at Chrysler the wage and benefit increases it won last September from General Motors Corp. This will save Chrysler $2,000 per worker in the first two years of a three-year package that eventually will match GM pay levels. But AMC is unlikely to do as well. "This is not another Chrysler," says Raymond E. Majerus, the UAW's newly elected secretary-treasurer and the union's chief bargainer at AMC. "There's nothing wrong with AMC that a better market won't cure."

"Off-pattern" labor contracts are nothing new at AMC. Heading for its fourth loss in 11 years, the company has perpetually won exemptions from the hefty increases at GM, Ford, and Chrysler. In recent years, however, AMC workers have regained "parity." As of last September, when GM's prior contract expired, AMC estimated its costs at about 50¢ more per hour worked than GM's $15.10, because of higher pension expense and a higher ratio of company-paid union representatives at Kenosha. Since then, GM's average hourly labor costs have soared to $18 in the second quarter. AMC's costs, on the eve of a new contract, are about $17 an hour.

AMC has traditionally offset its higher labor costs through production efficiencies, including faster line speeds at Kenosha. But as the rest of the auto industry overhauls its plants to make smaller cars, this advantage will be harder to maintain. That could mean renewed pressure by management to modify the long-standing right of UAW workers to turn down overtime at Kenosha.

Overtime ills. Union officials claim AMC workers readily volunteer for overtime. But company managers say the refusal of even a few workers effectively prevents AMC from running its two lines at Kenosha more than eight hours per shift or five days a week. "When you need the overtime is exactly when you can't get it," laments one former AMC executive. The company's last try at imposing overtime requirements led to a three-week strike in 1974, which the company lost.

Another key issue this year will be the union's demand for management neutrality in UAW organizing drives at AMC's three nonunion plants. And Majerus puts high priority on winning a UAW seat on AMC's board of directors, as UAW President Douglas A. Fraser did at Chrysler. This may prove to be less of a sticking point than it would be at other companies because half of Renault's 16 directors are already employees from all levels of the company. ∎

STEEL TALKS: A Costly Pact, Even With Restraint

Both sides acknowledge that the contract could well exceed 30%

The United Steelworkers and the basic steel industry faced a crucial problem as they began contract negotiations on Feb. 5: Historically, high wage and benefit rates tend to develop a runaway momentum during a time of double-digit inflation, making inflation catch-up and bargaining restraint incompatible goals. The USW, worried about plant shutdowns and a continuing flood of steel imports, has indicated some willingness to hold itself in check at the bargaining table. But the steel compensation package is already so rich that even the barest of USW gains will increase labor costs in new three-year pacts by more than 30%.

The eventual agreement, covering 286,000 workers at nine major companies that bargain as a group, will become the pattern for other steel producers and fabricators (with 169,000 employees) and for the aluminum and nonferrous metal industries. It will thus be the most critical settlement of 1980 and may provide the biggest test of the Carter Administration's response to wage packages that seem unresponsive to the fight against inflation. The new voluntary wage guideline, a range of 7.5% to 9.5%, is so loose that it is unlikely to influence steel bargaining. "I don't expect to have any guideline problem from what I've observed of other settlements under the guidelines of the past year," declares J. Bruce Johnston, the steel industry's chief negotiator and vice-president of employee relations at U. S. Steel Corp.

Company and union negotiators were not talking publicly about the potential 30% plus bargaining outcome as talks opened in Pittsburgh. Their deadline is still two months away. But the gap between the two goals—catch-up and restraint—was apparent in the general positions outlined by both sides' top negotiators for hundreds of local and union management people in the opening "sound-off" meetings.

The USW's highest priority, President Lloyd McBride declared, is raising the pensions of some 140,000 current retirees to ease the impact of inflation. This costly item is only one of many wage and benefit improvements sought by the USW. Company officials took an opposing tack. Citing steel's troubles in raising capital for new plants and expanded capacity, the company men urged steelworkers—whose average hourly wage of $11.35 ranks second only to that of coal miners—to rein in their expectations. "The time has come," one company negotiator told the unionists on Feb. 6, "to slow down the rate of your advantage compared to other workers."

Divisive issues. There is some sentiment for moderation in the USW ranks, particularly in plants that have yet to be modernized and are considered marginal. Since 1977, full and partial plant closings have cost 35,000 jobs and reduced U. S. production capability by 5 million tons. Still, the recent plant closings have stirred great anger in hard-hit communities such as Youngstown, Ohio, where a group of workers recently took over a U. S. Steel office building for a day. This sort of reaction is hardening the USW's demand for restrictions on the companies' ability to shut down plants and for improved early pension and layoff benefits for workers idled by closings. The union is also demanding a higher-yielding cost-of-living adjustment (COLA) formula and improvements in safety and health provisions, benefit plans, and the quality of work-life in steel plants.

Indeed, the issues facing the USW and the industry are more divisive this year than in any bargaining round since 1971. The two sides avoided a national strike that year only by postponing the walkout deadline. In 1974 and 1977 bargaining was conducted under the Experimental Negotiating Agreement (ENA), which prohibits the union from mounting a national strike but commits the companies to extensive wage improvements even before negotiations begin. The ENA produced big settlements in 1974 and 1977, enabling steelworkers to pass even auto workers in wages. The 1980 talks are also being held under the ENA, but the companies—increasingly sensitive to outside criticism of steel's high wage structure—threaten to cancel the ENA for future bargaining if they dislike the outcome this year.

A 30% package. "The Steelworkers have to be concerned whether they have an industry left to bargain with," says one top steel executive. "It's absurd to think we can go on with slot-machine unionism, in which you pay your dues and once every three years you pull the chain and a big pot of gold falls out of the industry." But while they use this rhetoric, many steel management people concede that the USW's McBride—a tough negotiator who has political control of his union—understands the industry's problems. But he does not fully accept all of the industry's arguments, declaring: "The American steel industry is in better shape than any other group of steel producers in the world." But one highly placed union source says, "There is a recognition that the industry is not a bottomless cash pit and that the massive settlements are a thing of the past."

But union and management sources say the settlement is unlikely to fall below 30% for three years, even if the USW curbs its demands. Steel's total hourly employment cost of $16.80, which includes wages, benefits, and government-mandated costs such as the Social Security tax on employers, is already one of the highest in the U. S. And labor costs escalate rapidly with the ENA's guarantees—a 3%-per-year wage increase, a $150 one-time bonus for each steelworker, and a COLA formula that calls for a quarterly payment of a 1¢-per-hour increase for each 0.3 point rise in the consumer price index.

In fact, say company officials, if current steel contracts were merely extended for three years without any im-

Government and Unions / 159

provements beyond those already guaranteed, labor costs would rise 32% at a 10% annual inflation rate. This includes increases of about $3.72 per hour in wages and COLA payments and $1.70 for other items, including the cost of maintaining current health benefits as inflation pushes up health care prices at an assumed 12% per year. Even a 9% inflation rate will produce a 30% package.

Pension demands. Last year's United Auto Workers settlement at General Motors Corp. amounted to a 33% increase in total hourly employment costs, assuming 9% inflation, and it included hefty pension increases. The steel producers say they are determined to shave a few percentage points from the General Motors settlement in their final package. "There's no way we're going to track GM this year," a top steel man said a few months ago.

But it will be difficult to bring steel in under GM and still grant major USW demands, particularly pension increases for current retirees. Although Social Security boosts have softened the impact, in most cases, their monthly stipends have been badly eroded by inflation. A worker who retired with 30 years' service in 1975 received $352.50 per month then under steel's minimum pension formula. He has had only one pension increase, of 5% in 1976, while consumer prices have risen by 37%. The USW hopes to persuade the steel companies to raise pensions of those retirees by $90 to $100 a month, about the same increase the UAW won at GM.

In the past, steel companies typically raised current pensions by no more than $15 per month during a three-year contract. But most likely, the majority of active workers in tightly knit steel communities would willingly give up some of their wage package to help their pensioned fathers. McBride emphasized at a news conference that the union would "take a portion of whatever might otherwise come out of bargaining and apply it to the pensions of retirees."

An April target date. How much the actives would be willing to give up while inflation erodes their paychecks is by no means clear. The UAW agreed to divert 14¢ of future COLA payments to help finance pension increases. The steel union has always opposed COLA diversion, but McBride may change this policy—or he may agree to divert a portion of the 3% wage guarantee to pensions. Local USW officers say that rank-and-filers will be willing to sacrifice big wage increases but not COLA. Still, diversions could not completely offset the increased costs of pension improvements. Every boost in existing pensions will require an equivalent increase in the pension rates of future retirees to maintain the historic relationships.

The GM settlement raised all pensions by 27% to 40%, at a cost estimated at 55¢ per hour over three years. This can be only a very crude measure for steel because of differences in pension plans and actuarial assumptions. But steel's cost will be greater because three active workers support each pensioner at GM, while the steel ratio is less than two to one. "The GM pension is out of the question," a company negotiator declares.

USW and industry negotiators have set Apr. 14 as a target date on national issues; under the ENA, unresolved items will then go to binding arbitration. The contentiousness of the issues this year makes it likely that arbitration will be invoked for the first time, and an unhappy outcome for one or both sides could spell the end of the ENA for future bargaining.

'Contracting out.' There are several tough issues in addition to pensions. The USW is demanding restrictions on the companies' ability to bring contractors into steel plants to perform construction, rehabilitation, and maintenance work. A joint study by the union and the industry revealed that more than 11,000 contractor employees worked on maintenance and repair jobs inside some 25 plants over a seven-year period ending in 1977. For the entire industry, the study found, this translates into about 5% of all employment of craftsmen members of the USW. These craftsmen become incensed when contractors are at work in the plants while they are laid off.

The companies contend that they must resort to "contracting out" to keep costs down. One possible solution may be to negotiate the size of a minimum base force of craftsmen on a plant-by-plant basis. The companies could guarantee these jobs and be free to hire contractors when the need for workers exceeds this number. But companies would also like to increase the productivity of steelworker craftsmen by merging some of the 26 separate crafts to create more versatile groups of workers.

Another major issue is discipline. Many USW local union officers contend that employers have stepped up discharges of workers for cause. At one large mill in Gary, Ind., firings recently averaged 20 per month. The companies

The steel pact, in setting a pattern, will be 1980's critical settlement

cite tardiness, absenteeism, and insubordination, and local union officials admit that absenteeism runs extremely high, especially among young workers. But locals charge that many firings are arbitrary, and although the union can win reinstatement and back pay in arbitration, the companies' right to fire a worker is unlimited.

McBride wants to prohibit an employer from terminating a worker before his guilt is proved, except in the most egregious cases. The companies balk at this demand on grounds that it would erode their authority in the work place. But the USW is also pressing other demands to enhance the "dignity" of workers, including restrictions on industrial spying, search and seizure, and the unauthorized use of employees' medical records. The union is demanding a greater voice "in all matters involving hours of work, lunch period practices, and the scheduling of work." ∎

STEEL LABOR IS ADDING INSURANCE

As their old strongholds in manufacturing continue to dwindle, industrial unions increasingly are stepping out of their original jurisdictions to organize the fast-growing service industries. This effort to sign up service workers has caused some unlikely crossing of traditional union boundaries. But many union officials now feel that "whoever grabs them, gets them," as one leader says. The newest example of this trend is a likely merger between two unions with once-diverse interests: the United Steelworkers and the Insurance Workers International Union.

Officers of the USW, with 1.2 million members, and the IWIU, with 20,000 members, are considering a proposed merger agreement recently completed by negotiators for both unions. The only big unresolved issue is how to integrate the two unions' dues structures, says Joseph Pollack, president of the Insurance Workers. Pollack hopes to present a final proposal to his executive board within two weeks and to recommend membership ratification either in a special convention or a rank-and-file referendum. "We're close to agreement, and I think we can work it out," he says.

The open field. Such a merger would give the USW an opening to jump into the largely unorganized financial services field. Powerful and well-financed, the USW is active in organizing nonunion workers and has a $90 million strike fund to support bargaining. In the proposed merger agreement, the USW pledges "to make every effort to organize the vast numbers of unorganized" insurance workers.

The Insurance Workers mainly represents insurance agents at Prudential, Metropolitan, and John Hancock. Although organized in 1937, the union has been frustrated by the companies' resistance to unions and by an improvement in agents' working conditions. Its membership has not increased in years. About 1 million agents and workers in insurance company offices remain nonunion, Pollack estimates. "With the money and personnel available at the Steelworkers, we can break out of this beachhead the companies have held us in for 40 years," he adds.

The USW has become a conglomerate union as employment in steel has shrunk. Less than half of its membership is now in basic metals. It represents workers in many other manufacturing industries and has an Office, Technical & Professional Dept. devoted to some 40,000 white-collar members. Many of these are employed in steel-company offices, but several thousand work in service jobs that have some affinity with financial occupations. "We see 2 million financial workers unorganized, and we're going after them," says one USW man.

Springboards. The USW is not the only major union seeking workers in new jurisdictions. The International Brotherhood of Teamsters, with 2 million members, is organizing workers in every conceivable kind of store and office. The once-independent District 65, Distributive Workers of America, representing 35,000 workers—mainly in office and technical jobs—at universities, publishers, and retail stores, affiliated last year with the United Auto Workers. This was to be the "springboard for a major organizing drive." Says District 65 President David Livingston: "The fact we are able to say we are District 65, UAW, is a tremendous aid in organizing."

The Service Employees International Union and the Retail, Wholesale & Department Store Union, both of which have large health-care units, are well along in merger talks that would create "one big hospital union," among other things. The American Federation of Teachers, once exclusively in education, has jumped into the health care area and has already organized some 20,000 nurses. The United Food & Commercial Workers, established only last year by a merger, is about to gobble up the 35,000-member Barbers & Beauticians International Assn. The Barbers Union is now in the process of ratifying an agreement with the UFCW, and the merger is expected to become effective in September. "UFCW has their eye on 1.5 million unorganized barbers and beauticians in the country and thousands more in Canada," says Richard A. Plumb, president of the Barbers.

The Insurance Workers began looking around last summer for a stronger partner to beef up its organizing activities. It

Financial services present a fertile field for labor organizers

began negotiations with the small Office & Professional Employees International Union, but a USW staff man heard of the talks and lured the insurance union away from the OPEIU, which is growing but has less than 100,000 members. The IWIU and the Steelworkers are now negotiating the final dues issue. Steelworkers pay dues equivalent to two hours' wages per month, averaging $13. But insurance agents, who are not paid on an hourly basis, pay only $9.50 per month.

The USW is not commenting publicly about the proposed merger. If it comes about, the IWIU's five officers and eight staffers would join the USW staff, and Pollack would direct an insurance workers' division as an aide to USW President Lloyd McBride. ∎

Government and Unions / 161

Labor cools it with Big Steel

A joint effort to dampen worker alienation and to increase productivity

The steel industry's labor settlements have often set national bargaining trends, but this year's pact is more significant than most. While inflation's impact on wages and benefits makes it costly, the agreement shows a move toward moderation to fit the reality of the U. S. steel industry's competitive decline. Perhaps more important, the settlement may signal a fundamental shift in steel's labor relations—away from the traditional adversary confrontation between workers and bosses and toward a more cooperative approach to common problems in the workplace.

This step toward cooperation is only one of many provisions in a three-year pact that won overwhelming ratification by a United Steelworkers delegate body on Apr. 15 in Pittsburgh. The USW and nine major companies that negotiate as a group reached agreement only hours before an Apr. 14 deadline for submitting the issues to binding arbitration; industrywide strikes are prohibited under steel's bargaining procedure. The companies granted hefty wage and pension improvements—including significant increases for 140,000 current retirees—in a package that raises labor costs by about 34.5%, assuming a 10% annual inflation rate. But it was the experimental program to improve relationships in the mills that might prove most significant in the long run.

Participation teams. The USW and the companies agreed to set up "labor-management participation teams" in each operating unit of selected plants as a step toward a broad-based effort to make jobs more meaningful for workers and more productive for the companies. The teams would discuss such problems as production efficiency, product quality, safety and health, employee morale, absenteeism, and how foremen deal with workers. They could make decisions that do not change the union contract or interfere in the grievance procedure.

The idea is not new; many U. S. companies are experimenting with such concepts. Some experts believe that labor and management inevitably will have to adopt work-improvement ideas to relieve worker alienation and to speed lagging productivity growth rates. But the steel settlement, which covers 286,000 workers at U. S. Steel, Bethlehem, Jones & Laughlin, Republic, and five other producers, is the first union-management agreement to experiment with such ideas on an industrywide basis.

Basic steel's economic terms, meanwhile, will be extended to 169,000 workers at smaller steel producers and fabricators. The USW likely will try to improve on the steel package in talks with the more healthy aluminum industry, where contracts covering 51,000 workers expire on June 1. The steel terms also will influence USW bargaining this summer in the copper, lead, and zinc industries, as well as current talks covering 600,000 workers in the Bell System. The Communications Workers union has also made pension increases for present retirees a top priority.

With the steel companies anticipating possible increases in steel imports and further domestic plant shutdowns, management made a major effort to hold the

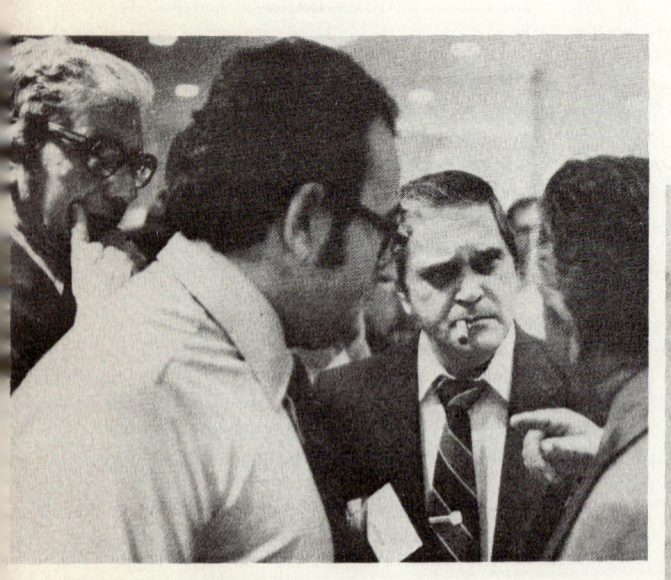

Photographs by Bud Harris

Conferring: Unionists (above) and their leaders (right) won raises, but the program to improve relationships in the mills was more significant.

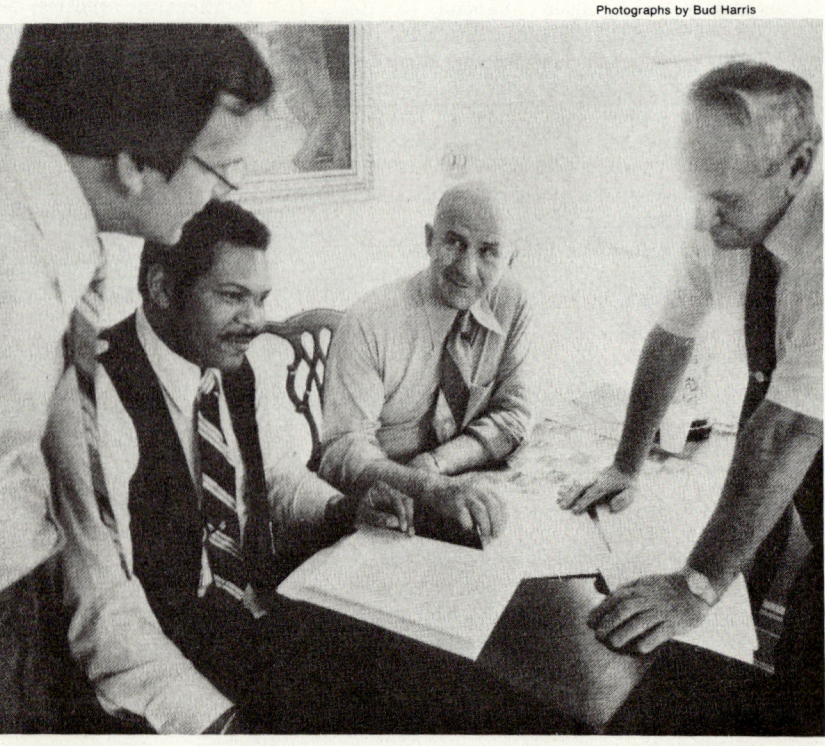

line. Finally, at about 6 p. m. on Apr. 14, USW Vice-President Joseph Odorcich, filling in for President Lloyd McBride, who was hospitalized, reached a tentative agreement with J. Bruce Johnston, a U. S. Steel Corp. vice-president and the industry's chief negotiator. With 400 local union presidents waiting impatiently to ratify a pact, Odorcich came close to walking out without a settlement. Had the issues been forced into arbitration, the outcome might have made one or both sides unhappy with the ENA. Indeed, the industry is reluctant to renew the ENA until local bargaining is finished.

The package that Odorcich brought to his members includes straight wage increases of 84¢ an hour over three years for the industry's average job class, and this figure rises to $1.03 including an increase in the incentive pay base (about 90% of steelworkers are covered by incentive plans). Increases in pension and other benefits amount to about $2.23 an hour, and steel's cost-of-living adjustment (COLA) will produce $2.32 an hour at 10% annual inflation. At steel's total hourly compensation base of slightly more than $16, these increases amount to a 34.5% package. This would have been high in the days before double-digit inflation, but it actually represents some moderation.

Negotiating: U. S. Steel's Johnston got the unions to drop several demands.

Labor's concessions. The USW agreed to divert a COLA payment that is due May 1, and that will amount to 30¢ to 32¢ an hour, to help finance the pension increases. Furthermore, the union dropped several major demands, including one for an improved COLA that would have kept steelworkers abreast of workers in the rubber and auto industries. The USW also retreated on demands for more paid time off the job and a voice in pension fund investments. It made only slight gains in improving benefits for workers idled by plant shutdowns. "The industry was very reluctant to open itself up to possibly uncontrollable costs if more shutdowns are necessary," says one USW negotiator. Adds another: "We were determined not to do violence to the industry as an institution."

Rank-and-file union officials were satisfied with the pact because it solved some vexing noneconomic problems and raised pensions for current retirees. The pension rates for all of these retirees were brought up to a minimum of $12 per month per year of service, which more than doubles the stipend of workers who retired before July 31, 1966. "You've got to feel you're paying back the people who built the union for you," says one union staff man.

Some analysts were critical of the steel pact. "It's a generous settlement for an industry that's hurting," says Peter L. Anker, vice-president of First Boston Corp. He estimates that a 4% steel price rise would be needed to cover the increase in steel labor costs in just the first year of the new contract.

While the steel companies lost a bid to win several givebacks, they did gain some contract changes that will cut costs. And the labor-management participation teams grew partly out of proposals made by Thomas C. Graham, president of Jones & Laughlin Steel Corp. Some USW leaders have long urged that management give workers more participation in workplace decisions to enhance their "dignity" as workers and to improve working conditions. With the USW, and J&L and Bethlehem in particular, pushing these twin concerns—improvements in productivity and job conditions—the negotiators developed the team concept.

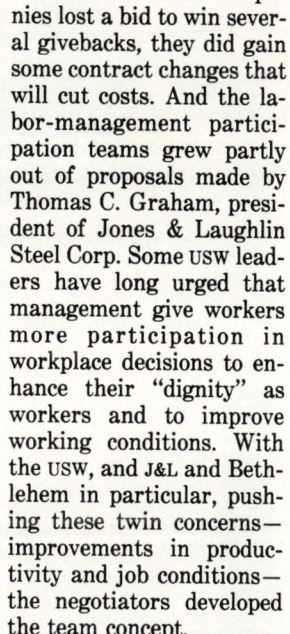

At first, teams will be set up in at least one plant at each of the nine companies if the workers and local management agree. Members will meet on company time to discuss work-related problems. Says one union negotiator: "We're really trying to change the adversary relationship, and it can work only if management realizes that workers won't accept the master-servant relationship on the job any longer." ∎

Government and Unions / 163

WHEN STEEL WAGES RISE FASTER THAN PRODUCTIVITY

Collective bargaining in the basic steel industry has produced an unparalleled record of peaceful negotiations—20 years without a nationwide strike—and has pushed steelworkers to the top of the wage heap. Yet the industry has long been in trouble because of import penetration, low profits, and a lack of capital to build modern mills. Now it is crying out for government help to halt its competitive decline, even as it is on the brink of negotiating another costly labor settlement. The question is whether the bargaining process in steel—generally regarded as among the most sophisticated in U.S. industry—can reflect the economic reality of the industry in 1980. Ironically, given historic wage trends, it may not be able to do that.

The outcome of this year's contract negotiations covering some 350,000 steelworkers is likely to indicate a shift toward wage moderation. As top negotiators for the United Steelworkers of America and the industry met in Pittsburgh's William Penn Hotel for the final days of hard bargaining, a USW willingness to trade off part of its guaranteed 3%-per-year wage gain was already apparent. Although USW President Lloyd McBride had to undergo emergency abdominal surgery as negotiations reached the critical stage, Vice-President Joseph Odorcich took over as chief negotiator to deal with an industry team headed by J. Bruce Johnston, a U.S. Steel Corp. vice-president. The two sides expected to reach tentative agreement within a few days on a new, three-year economic package so that it can be presented to a union conference for ratification on Apr. 14 or 15.

High wages, low marks. But any wage moderation short of a pay cut—and the USW has no intention of going that far—will not reverse steel's historic trend of paying ever higher labor costs as the industry sinks deeper into trouble. For perhaps the first time in U.S. bargaining history, it appears that some costs of employing union labor—particularly wage escalation plans and health care benefits that float upward with medical price inflation—have become uncontrollable. The steel industry pays the highest compensation bill in the nation for the labor of industrial workers—about $16 an hour, including wages and benefits—and there is almost no way it can escape at least a 30%, three-year settlement in 1980, assuming a 10% annual inflation rate, no matter how willing negotiators are to compromise.

Indeed, the steel labor situation perplexes bargaining experts. In January, average hourly earnings in steel were $11.30, compared with only $6.95 in all manufacturing. Ten years ago steelworkers had only an 87¢ advantage over all-manufacturing employees, but they rapidly widened the gap during the 1970s—even while negotiating under a no-strike agreement—with big wage increases and a high-yielding cost-of-living adjustment (COLA) plan. "If you look at the factors that normally affect wage bargaining, such as productivity and profits, you can't help wondering what in the world steel is doing way up there," says one labor economist.

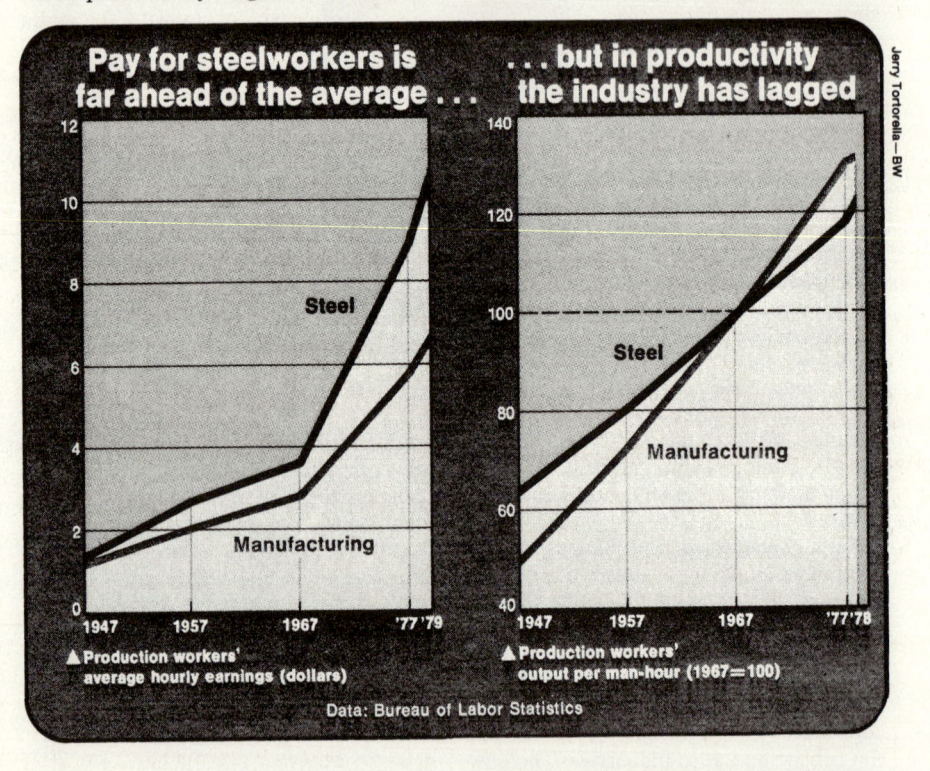

The productivity-wage relationship in steel is especially striking. The last year in which steelworkers received contract improvements that were negotiated to end a strike was 1962. In the peaceful 16-year period between 1962 and 1978, production workers' output per man-hour in steel showed a compound annual average increase of 2%. In the same period earnings shot up at a 7.3% annual rate.

Even adjusted for inflation, the yearly increase in hourly earnings was 2.3%, and steel's total hourly employment bill—including wages, benefits, and government-mandated costs such as Social Security taxes—rose even faster, at a 3% annual rate.

Productivity in the total private economy rose at a 2.3% rate from 1962 to 1978. One widely held concept among economists of a proper wage-productivity relationship is that compensation may rise at the same rate as national productivity unless an industry's output growth is less than the national average. In that case, the industry's wages ought to be less than average. Steel clearly does not fit the concept. While its yearly rises in compensation exceeded productivity growth, the industry's average annual return on stockholders' equity averaged only 6.5%, considerably lower than the 12.1% in manufacturing. Steel's poor profits picture can be attributed to other factors, including management mistakes, but labor bargains over the years share some blame for a drying up of internally generated capital for investment in new plant and equipment.

Some reasons why. Still, employment costs as a percentage of total operating costs in the steel industry declined from an average of 40.3% in 1960 to 33.9% in 1978, while the costs of energy and materials rose. Certainly, labor has played only one tune in what is becoming a crashingly discordant symphony. The USW takes the position—with some justification—that steelworkers ought to be highly paid. Steel mills are dirty, hot, uncomfortable, and in some areas quite hazardous, and steel production jobs require more skill than most industrial

164 / Readings from *Business Week*

occupations. "We place high values on production skills," agrees a steel-industry labor relations executive. "I don't think steel deserves to be too far down the economic ladder."

But this does not fully explain why the USW, bargaining in an essentially declining industry, has been able to outstrip even the powerful United Auto Workers in the auto industry, until recently a high-productivity, high-growth industry. In 1946 average hourly earnings stood at $1.35 in autos and $1.32 in steel. By last December, steel's $11.30 per hour was well above the auto industry's $10 per hour. USW leaders have long felt highly competitive with the UAW, partly because of unfavorable—and largely unfair—comparisons that are made about the two unions. Whereas the UAW is pictured in the vocal liberal community as militant and progressive, the USW is regarded as stodgy, conservative, and undemocratic, although on the whole it is every bit as democratic as the UAW. "We were harassed, criticized, and demeaned," says a former USW negotiator, "and all these influences added up to an attitude that we had to show these guys in negotiations."

But the high labor costs have given steel management an incentive to introduce laborsaving technology. Between 1960 and 1979, steel's production force shrank from 449,900 workers to 339,200, a 25% drop. The USW, which does not oppose new technology, has knowingly accepted that price. Arnold R. Weber, a noted labor economist and currently president of the University of Colorado at Boulder, cites steel's workforce reduction and sluggish productivity growth in assessing what has happened. "If the purpose of collective bargaining is to be closely attuned to economic realities and to adjust to them, it clearly hasn't accomplished that in steel," he says. "If the purpose is to establish a framework for decision-making through which workers make choices between high wage levels and [low] employment, it has. Maybe the workers and the union made the wrong guess."

The USW has accepted lower employment along with higher wages

Bargaining power. A number of other factors have played important roles in the bargaining decisions that have been made in steel. The USW has all but a few basic steel mills under contract in the U. S., giving it extraordinary power in industrywide negotiations. The steel industry's concentration and pricing policy have enabled it to pass on a large proportion of increased labor costs in price rises. And the political milieu in which bargaining has occurred has been enormously important. Nationwide steel strikes were highly visible, and U. S. political leaders came under intense pressure to bring them to a halt, at whatever price.

Indeed, the federal government began to intervene in steel wage and price decisions quite early in the bargaining relationship, and this had—it appears in retrospect—an adverse and still lingering impact on the quality of the steel bargains. The USW conducted five major steel strikes between 1946 and 1959, culminating in the 116-day strike of 1959. In most of these strikes, steel prices were as much an issue as wages, and typically labor, management, and the government engaged in a three-way negotiation—like a ritualistic dance around the Maypole—that in the end skewed the wage-price relationship.

"We took five strikes in 14 years to hold down wages," complains a top company negotiator. "But in a basic industry like ours, the union won't let you win a short strike, and the government won't let you win a long one. Anytime you take a strike, the government cuts your legs out from under you."

Further, the industry complains, the government clamped down on steel price rises in nonbargaining years, particularly when steel was at the peak of its cycle and should have been able to reap good profits. Ben Fischer, who retired in 1978 after 34 years on the USW staff and is now a lecturer and a consultant, says this deep government involvement in steel's affairs has had a deleterious effect on bargaining. "Anytime the government gets involved in bargaining, it's advantageous to the union," he says. "And an industry under attack tends to seek the cooperation of its union. To some degree, this has actually had the effect of facilitating liberal wage settlements."

Allies. Management, in other words, tends to respond to union support for its pricing policy and for legislative campaigns to stem the flow of imports by—in effect—being accommodating in bargaining. The USW carried out its part of the bargain. Under I. W. Abel, McBride's predecessor as president, the union campaigned for import restrictions. Instead of attacking steel price rises, it announced support for them. Abel was one of the few labor leaders who backed accelerated depreciation and amortization for industry, and in the early 1970s he even appeared in magazine ads to promote productivity-improvement campaigns in the steel mills—an act that drew severe criticism from militant USW members.

It was also under Abel that the USW negotiated the "experimental negotiating agreement" (ENA) with the steel industry in 1973. The ENA proscribes industrywide strikes and substitutes arbitration of unresolved issues. The ENA provides the USW with substantial guarantees, including wage increases of 3% per year, a $150-per-worker bonus once every three years, and continuation of a lucrative COLA provision and fringe benefits. In 1974 and 1977 the union won fat contracts under the ENA procedure without having to strike or submit issues to arbitration.

Between 1973 and 1979, steel's total hourly labor costs shot up from $7.68 to $16.80, a 119% boost while the consumer price index rose 63%. The union and the industry, perhaps out of a feeling of being mutually embattled by critics, seemed to draw closer together in bargaining. Jack Stieber, director of the School of Labor & Industrial Relations at Michigan State University and a longtime student of steel labor, pointed out this high degree of accommodation in a recently published analysis. The ENA, he wrote, "represents an important step" away from adversarial relations and toward a "more cooperative relationship." He added: "The question is whether it comes at too high a price."

Some industry executives, particularly at U. S. Steel, have raised the same question in suggesting that they might cancel ENA for use in 1983 negotiations. That would mean a return to the national strike threat and widespread hedge-buying by steel customers. This would probably increase the influx of steel imports, which accounted for 18.4% of the domestic market in February.

An aid to compromise. But both sides really want to retain the ENA, whatever its shortcomings, and this is why the 1980 negotiations have so far been characterized by a spirit of compromise. The USW and nine major steel companies that bargain as a group got through a critical early stage in local-issues bargaining without having to invoke an arbitration provision that probably would have created a conflict atmosphere in bargaining. In this case, the USW conceded that the issue of incentive-pay coverage—that is, union demands for the extension of incentive pay plans to workers not now covered—was an economic issue and not negotiable at the local level, as many local unions contended.

In the economic talks, it appears likely that the union will agree to divert a portion of the 3% annual wage boosts that are guaranteed by the ENA to help pay for benefit improvements such as costly pension increases for some 140,000 current retirees. "Our people are not too concerned with a great big wage increase, but they are concerned about the older people," says one USW official privately. "If we can make retirement secure and attractive enough, there will be a lot of lucrative jobs opened up for younger workers."

USW and company negotiators are also

discussing ways of improving productivity in the steel mills, a subject that seldom gets a hearing at the bargaining table because of workers' suspicion that productivity means speedup. The USW has also broached the idea of a stock

Critics are asking if the 'no-strike agreement' is worth the price

option plan for workers as one means of increasing their income security as well as their interest in the company. But even if the USW agrees to slice a percentage point or so off the straight wage increase, the new terms will be costly. Steel's compensation base is already so high that the cost of merely continuing the current COLA and benefit plans, along with some wage increase, will raise labor costs by at least 30% over three years, with 10% inflation.

This is one reason why government officials generally are not sympathetic to steel's pleas for help in raising capital and cutting back imports. "The above-average wage gains in the past have helped give them the problem they now have," says a government economist. "Today, we are locked into the ENA, and I just don't think it is needed any more." ∎

EDGY STEELWORKERS SET THEIR GOALS HIGH

Next year's contract negotiations in the basic steel industry—the most critical labor talks of 1980—will present a major paradox to union and company bargainers. The United Steelworkers, worried about the severe contraction of the industry, wants to preserve jobs by cooperating with management in areas such as combatting steel imports. But the failing health of the industry, along with inflation, have created sharp conflicts for bargaining that endanger a major cooperative effort between steel labor and management: steel's no-strike agreement.

This became apparent as the USW's 560-member Steel Industry Conference (SIC) on Dec. 7 voted approval of bargaining goals for the industrywide talks, which begin in Pittsburgh next February. The union's priorities include major pension improvements for future retirees and workers idled by plant shutdowns, sizable inflation protection for the pensions of current retirees, major improvements in the USW's "lifetime security" program, and one-year prenotification provisions for plant closings. In addition, the USW will seek a "substantial" wage increase for active workers, a higher-yielding cost-of-living adjustment (COLA) provision, and restrictions on the companies' ability to bring building trades workers into the mills to perform maintenance work.

The income and job security demands have strong emotional backing because of the shrinkage of the domestic steel industry. Since the last steel contract was negotiated in 1977, some 20,000 steelworkers have been affected by plant closings. Additional shutdowns announced recently by U.S. Steel Corp. and Jones & Laughlin Steel Corp. will eliminate another 14,500 jobs.

Arbitration. There can be no nationwide strike in 1980 because the USW and the nine companies that bargain as a group have already agreed to conduct talks under the experimental negotiating agreement (ENA). Issues that remain unresolved as of Apr. 20 must be settled by an arbitration panel. The plant shutdown issues, along with the USW's demands to ease the impact of inflation on wages and pensions, will be tough to resolve. But resorting to arbitration could kill the ENA for the future because one or both sides might be unhappy with the result. SIC, by a vote of 313 to 73, reaffirmed support for using the ENA procedure in 1980 bargaining, despite the protests of dissidents. USW President Lloyd McBride said this decision will enable both sides to conduct "cohesive" bargaining and that it "leaves us free to join hands [with management] on problems, such as trade, that affect both the industry and the workers."

The USW acknowledges the industry's predicament. Its chief economist, Edmund Ayoub, told the SIC delegates that steel wages will rise 41.7% during the current three-year contract; average hourly earnings are $10.96. But Ayoub also told the meeting that "in spite of billions of dollars in capital expenditures, we've had a decline in steelmaking capacity, and this is serious. We ought to be at least cognizant of these underpinnings."

Bird-dogging. McBride has also conceded that the industry has major problems, and industry leaders feel that he will recognize them in bargaining. For now, however, he is maintaining a tough bargaining position, just as the industry—from the union's point of view—appears to be using the plant shutdowns to create job-loss fears that will moderate the union's ultimate demands. But McBride has taken steps to establish worker-management "alert committees" at individual plants to head off closings "well in advance of a crisis." McBride adds: "Where we see poor maintenance or failure to innovate and stay modern, we will make such matters a subject of discussion with management."

The steelworkers plan to speak up when they spot a failure to innovate

The USW is also resisting company efforts to split some 12,000 steelworkers employed in subsidiary operations, such as fabricating plants and steel service centers, away from the basic steel pattern. Some of U.S. Steel's shutdowns are in these operations. At a Dec. 5 meeting, 78 local union presidents who represent workers in the subsidiaries voted unanimously to remain under the basic terms.

Even if the union agreed to a below-pattern settlement in the subsidiaries, "the companies wouldn't give us any insurance that the plants wouldn't still be shut down," says Walter Stewart Jr., president of a local at a U.S. Steel supply plant in St. Louis. However, the subsidiary locals said they would be willing to give the companies more flexibility in making job assignments and scheduling vacations, to make them more competitive. ■

QUESTIONS

A. Government

Truckers Quietly Get Set for Deregulation:

1. How will the deregulation of the trucking industry affect the operating strategies of firms in the business?
2. Is deregulation a positive factor for the trucking industry?

Tax Credits That Could Save Industry Billions:

1. What sort of opportunities are afforded to business as a result of these energy tax credits?
2. How effective are the government tax credits in encouraging energy conservation by business?

Senate Energy Gets a Friend of Industry:

1. Which parts of the business sector will probably benefit most from the appointment of James McClure as Chairman of the Senate Energy Committee?
2. Is Mr. McClure probusiness, antibusiness, or neither? Explain.

Using the Market in Regulation:

1. How can government regulation of business become more consistent with the "free market" philosophy of the U.S. economy?
2. Does the trend appear to be toward a more or less regulated business environment? Discuss.

The New Case for Monopolists:

1. Contrast the past and present attitudes of the courts toward monopoly.
2. For whom is the reversal in attitudes beneficial? How?

How Washington Spurs High-Tech Companies:

1. Recently government action appears to be having a facilitating effect on the operations of small businesses. Discuss. Mention the areas of the government involved and what each is doing.
2. Discuss how such actions will help not only high-technology companies but U.S. business as a whole.

The Court Leaves OSHA Hanging:

1. Discuss the Supreme Court's decision in the benzene case and the implications this presents for the future.
2. What roles do the courts and regulatory agencies play in regard to the business sector and the market as a whole?

What Trade Sanctions Will Cost:

1. The increasingly dominant role the government plays in our society is illustrated in this article. Discuss.
2. What does this suggest in terms of the ability of a firm to freely market its products?

Here Comes the Credit Crunch:

1. How are U.S. companies obtaining the funds they need in the tight credit environment?
2. During the "credit crunch," will the Fed's actions be a positive or negative factor for the business community?

Credit Curbs Push Sales toward a Tailspin:

1. What impact have the Fed's credit curbs had on the consumer and retailer segments?
2. How have retailers adjusted their credit and operating strategies in response to these curbs?

A Product Liability Bill Has Insurers Uptight:

1. To whom does the proposed product liability bill pose a threat and in what respect?
2. Discuss some of the factors that might justify the need for such a bill.

Canada's Oil Policy Is Starting to Hurt:

1. Canada's oil policy may well backfire and have a strong negative impact on the Canadian economy. Explain.
2. How does this policy affect U.S. business?

States Seek a Slice of Oil Profits:

1. Why is the outcome of the New York Federal Appeals Court decision of such great importance to the entire oil industry?
2. Discuss how this article illustrates the extensiveness of government involvement in the operations of the oil industry.

Justice Takes Aim at Dual Distribution:

1. How and why does the new stance on dual distribution by the Justice Department pose a threat to U.S. firms?
2. What type of strategic decisions will be most affected by the new stance?

A Bill That Will Give the Fed More Power:

1. What will be the scope of the Fed's power as a result of the banking reform bill?
2. Will the new authority thus bestowed upon the Fed enhance its ability and/or inclination to work actively toward controlling the money supply? Discuss.

B. Unions

A New Social Contract: A Partnership to Build the New Workplace:

1. What is required for widespread adoption of a cooperative management-employee relationship?
2. How have companies helped to further this cooperative atmosphere?

The UAW's About-Face on Import Controls:

1. What has caused the UAW to shift its position in regard to the issue of import controls?
2. Discuss the extent to which U.S. auto makers and the UAW are in agreement on this issue.

How the Changing Auto Market Threatens the UAW, Too:

1. What effect will the UAW's strategies have on the U.S. auto industry if they are successfully implemented?

2. What is the nature of the relationship between the problems facing the U.S. auto market and those facing the UAW?

The Risk in Putting a Union Chief on the Board:

1. Discuss potential conflicts created by having UAW's Fraser on the board of Chrysler.

2. What role does Fraser hope to play in influencing Chrysler operations?

Can Chrysler Squeeze More from the UAW?:

1. How crucial is the UAW's support to the survival of Chrysler Corp.? Discuss.

2. What factors may make the achievement of a mutually acceptable agreement between UAW and Chrysler difficult if not impossible?

The Price of Peace at Chrysler:

1. Specifically what did the UAW and Chrysler agree to on their recent negotiations?

2. What tradeoffs were involved on both sides in this agreement?

Ailing AMC Seeks Relief from the UAW:

1. The future financial position of AMC will depend to a large extent on the actions of the UAW during upcoming contract negotiations. Explain.

2. How is the UAW attempting to become more of a controlling factor in the operations of AMC?

Steel Talks: A Costly Pact Even with Restraint:

1. What are the critical issues to be addressed in the contract negotiations in the steel industry?

2. What external factors have an impact on the eventual outcome of the steel talks?

Steel Labor Is Adding Insurance:

1. How are union leaders attempting to reverse the trend of stable union membership in the private sector?

2. What does this suggest about the future scope of union influence in the business sector?

Labor Cools It with Big Steel:

1. Discuss the new role (relationship) the union hopes to have in the future in relation to business.

2. Specifically what is the USW doing to further this end?

When Steel Wages Rise Faster than Productivity:

1. What impact does the USW have on the current economic position of the steel industry?

2. Discuss the nature of the bargaining position of the USW and the impact it has on the steel industry.

Edgy Steelworkers Set Their Goals High:

1. Is the relationship between the USW and U.S. steel companies best described as adversarial or cooperative? Discuss.

2. Has the health of the industry proved to be a helping or hindering factor in the negotiations? Explain.

Government and Unions / 169

Five.

process in the firms. Remember also that the key to selecting an appropriate strategy is finding the proper match between the opportunities and threats in the firm's environment and the firm's strengths and weaknesses.

In the internal appraisal part of the strategic management decision process, the manager takes a hard look at where the firm is leading from strength and where it must fight from a weak position.

ronment. The four most frequent factors examined for advantages or disadvantages are marketing, operations, finance/accounting, and personnel/management. A sample list for each factor that managers can appraise is

I. Strategic advantage factors: marketing.

   A. Competitive structure and market share: To what extent has the firm established a strong market share in the total market or in its key submarkets?

   B. Efficient and effective marketing research systems.

   C. Product mix: What is the quality of products and services?

   D. Product-services line: How complete is it? What is the new product leadership and product mix? What phase of the life cycle are the main products in?

   E. Efficient and effective channels of distribution and geographic coverage, including international efforts.

   F. Pricing strategy for products and services.

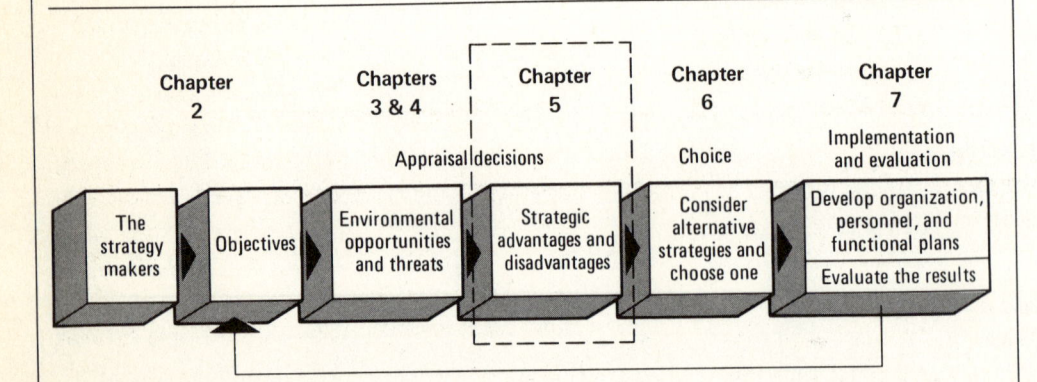

Exhibit 5-1: A MODEL OF THE BUSINESS POLICY AND STRATEGIC MANAGEMENT PROCESS.

Exhibit 5-1 shows that the second part of the appraisal decision process is the assessment of internal strategic advantages and disadvantages. While the *Business Week* articles in this chapter focus on the internal appraisal, the reader should remember that this part of the business policy and strategic management process cannot be separated easily in reality. Thus, as you read the articles in this chapter, pay close attention to the interrelationships between the environmental appraisal process, the internal assessment process, and the choice in effect, the manager is developing a strategic advantages profile: a systematic evaluation of the firm's strategic advantage factors weighted by the significance of each factor for the firm in its envi-

Assessing Strategic Advantages and Disadvantages

170 / Readings from *Business Week*

G. Efficient and effective sales force: Are there close ties with key customers? How vulnerable are we in terms of concentration of sales to a few customers?

H. Effective advertising: Has it established the company's product-brand image to develop loyal customers?

I. Efficient and effective marketing promotion and packaging.

J. Efficient and effective service after the purchase.

K. Efficient and effective evaluation of marketing policies.

II. Strategic advantage factors: operations.

A. Raw materials cost.

B. Raw materials availability.

C. Efficient and effective inventory control systems.

D. Efficient and effective facilities: Are they productive? Are the facilities' capacities overutilized or underutilized given the current demand.

E. Degree of vertical integration of operations.

F. Efficient and effective management information systems.

G. Efficient and effective equipment for production and/or office.

H. Strategic location of facilities and offices.

I. Efficient and effective operations procedures: production design, scheduling, output, and quality control.

J. Lower total costs of operations compared with competitors.

K. Efficient and effective research and development unit: basic and applied research.

L. Patents and similar legal protection for products, processes, and similar trade secrets.

III. Strategic advantage factors: finance/accounting.

A. Low cost of capital relative to industry and competitors because of stock price and dividend policy.

B. Effective capital structure, allowing flexibility in raising additional capital as needed; financial leverage.

C. Amicable relations with owners and stockholders.

D. Advantageous tax conditions.

E. Barriers to new entry because of high entry costs.

F. Efficient and effective financial planning, working capital, and capital budgeting procedures.

G. Efficient and effective accounting systems for cost, budget and profit planning, and auditing procedures.

IV. Strategic advantage factors: personnel/management.

A. High-quality employees and managers.

B. Low labor costs.

C. Effective relations with trade unions.

D. Efficient and effective personnel relations policies: staffing, appraisal and promotion, training and development, and compensation and benefits.

E. Corporate image and prestige.

F. Effective organizational structure and climate.

G. Company size relative to industry.

H. Strategic planning system.

I. Enterprise's record for reaching objectives: How consistent has it been? How well does it do compared with similar enterprises?

J. Influence with regulatory and governmental bodies.

K. Balanced functional experience and track record of top management: Are replacements trained and ready to take over? Do the top managers work well together as a team?

This chapter includes *Business Week* articles describing firms in a variety of industries attempting to use their strengths in the pursuit of their objectives. As you read these articles identify the strength(s) upon which each firm is developing its strategy. Additionally, three articles in this chapter discuss competitive strengths from a macroperspective. They examine the firms in the United States as a whole and compare their strengths with the strengths of foreign firms. These three articles are

- "The Decline of U.S. Industry: A Drastic New Loss of Competitive Strength"
- "A Policy for Industry: Technology Gives the U.S. a Big Edge"
- "Will It Work: What the U.S. Can Learn from Its Rivals"

All the *Business Week* articles in this chapter will help you understand the internal assessment as an input to the firm's decision about choice of a future strategy.

THE PROBLEM
THE DECLINE OF U.S. INDUSTRY

A drastic new loss of competitive strength

U. S. industry's loss of competitiveness over the past two decades has been nothing short of an economic disaster. Even in 1960, well after the economies of Europe and Japan had been reconstructed, the U. S. accounted for more than one-fourth of the manufacturing exports of the industrial nations, while supplying 98% of its domestic market. Since then, the U. S. not only has been losing market shares both at home and abroad, but the decline actually has been accelerating.

In the 1970s the U. S. lost 23% of its share of the world market, compared with a 16% decline during the 1960s. U. S. manufacturers' share of the domestic market also fell more in the most recent decade than earlier. The losses in the 1970s are particularly telling, because they came in the wake of a 40% depreciation in the value of the dollar, which made U. S. exports cheaper and foreign imports more expensive. The decline in the U. S. position in the 1970s alone amounted to some $125 billion in lost production and a loss of at least 2 million industrial jobs.

Few industries have been exempt from the erosion of U. S. industrial power. Even sectors where the U. S. still racks up tremendous trade surpluses have been losing their share of the world market steadily. The aircraft industry, for example, exported nearly $10 billion worth of products last year, while only $1 billion worth of planes and parts were imported. Yet U. S. domination is by no means as complete as it once was. America's 58% share of world airplane exports last year represented a significant decline from the 66% share of a decade ago. Further erosion is almost inevitable as the European airbus attacks the U. S. monopoly of widebodied jets.

Other research-intensive industries also are having trouble holding their own, although the depreciation of the dollar has improved their price-competitiveness. The U. S. share of plastics exports, for example, has dropped from 27.8% in 1962 to 13%. In organic chemicals, where the U. S. position actually improved in the 1960s, U. S. exports now account for only 15% of world trade.

Another example is the U. S. drug industry. Once a technological trailblazer, that industry is now well on the way to becoming a producer of standard products, since the task of bringing a new drug to market, made arduous by regulation, has reduced considerably the payoff from innovation. Its 27.6% of world exports in 1962 has dropped to just 15%. And while the U. S. still exports more drugs than it imports, the difference is shrinking rapidly.

The trade balance in machinery is still impressive, reaching a record $16.7 billion in 1979. Yet only the computer industry has maintained its position over the last two decades—and even

How U.S. manufacturing's market share has been shrinking at home...

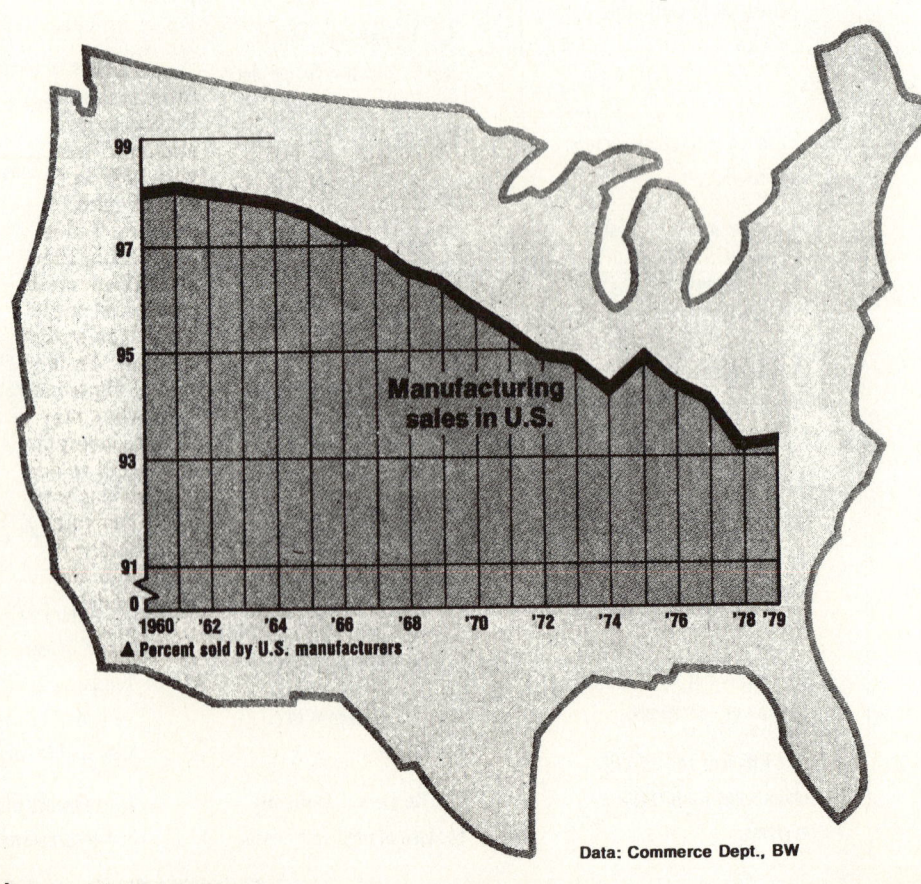

▲ Percent sold by U.S. manufacturers

Data: Commerce Dept., BW

The decline in the U. S. position in the 1970s alone amounted to some $125 billion in lost production and a loss of at least 2 million industrial jobs

there, America may soon have to make room for the Japanese. Agricultural machinery already is under siege, not only in the world market but in the domestic market as well. The U. S. share of world exports has slipped from more than 40% in 1962 to less than 25% last year. One problem is that the industry increasingly has concentrated on making big and expensive equipment that is appropriate only for the U. S. market. The U. S. no longer makes any farm tractor under 35 hp., which means, among other things, that it has now largely excluded itself from developing countries.

The textile machinery industry, which used to be a strong trade performer for the U. S., now has moved into the deficit category. The U. S. share of world exports of textile machinery is less than 7%. It was more than 15% in 1962. Meanwhile, U. S. manufacturers supplied only 54% of the domestic market for textile machinery last year, in sharp contrast to the 93% share they held in 1962. So, ironically, the technological upgrading of the U. S. textile industry, one of the few successful responses to competitive pressures, has been accomplished largely by using foreign equipment.

In metal-working machinery, the U. S. has been overwhelmed by West Germany. The two countries were neck and neck in the early 1960s, with each having about a third of world exports. Now the U. S. share is down to 21%, while Germany's is close to 40%. Much of the problem seems to be the reluctance on the part of the fragmented U. S. industry to build enough capacity to serve the market in periods of peak demand.

Meanwhile, the failure of the U. S. machine tool industry in its own market has been dramatic. Over the last decade, the domestic manufacturers' share of the U. S. market for metal-forming machine tools has dropped from 93% to 75%, while their share of metal-cutting machine tools has gone from 89% to 74%. The equivalent figure for both categories was 97% in 1960.

Outdated steel plants

The U. S. steel industry was still putting up open-hearth furnaces in the late 1950s, while the Japanese were building modern steel plants that used the basic oxygen process. Ironically, the basic oxygen process was a U. S. invention. "The U. S. steel industry is still living with the consequences of its own conservatism," says economist Walter Adams, of Michigan State University. And only the protection of "voluntary" quotas and trigger-price mechanisms has allowed it to retain its 85% share of the domestic market.

Detroit's failure to build sufficient small-car capacity was largely responsible for last year's surge in imports that gave foreign auto producers nearly 30% of the U. S. market on the basis of units sold. But the competitive problem of the auto industry is a long-standing one. Imports, which were negligible in 1960, had captured nearly 15% of auto sales only a decade later, mainly because American companies chose to ignore that many customers were returning to the idea of simple and efficient transportation that Henry Ford had pioneered. This gave foreign companies an opening that they were able to exploit when oil price increases made the big American car obsolete. The result has been not just to reduce Detroit's profits and bring Chrysler Corp. to the brink of oblivion but to shrink the market for the supplier industries.

The most obvious area where U. S. manufacturers have ceded their own market is consumer electronics. In 1960 about 95% of radios, television sets, and the like were supplied domestically. By 1979, imports had captured more than half the market. The U. S. no longer even makes radios, and black and white TV sets are now almost all of foreign manufacture. Not only are U. S.-made color television sets now assembled largely from foreign-made components, but an increasing number come from Japanese companies that have set up U. S. plants to escape the impact of the so-called "orderly marketing agreements." The Japanese captured the TV

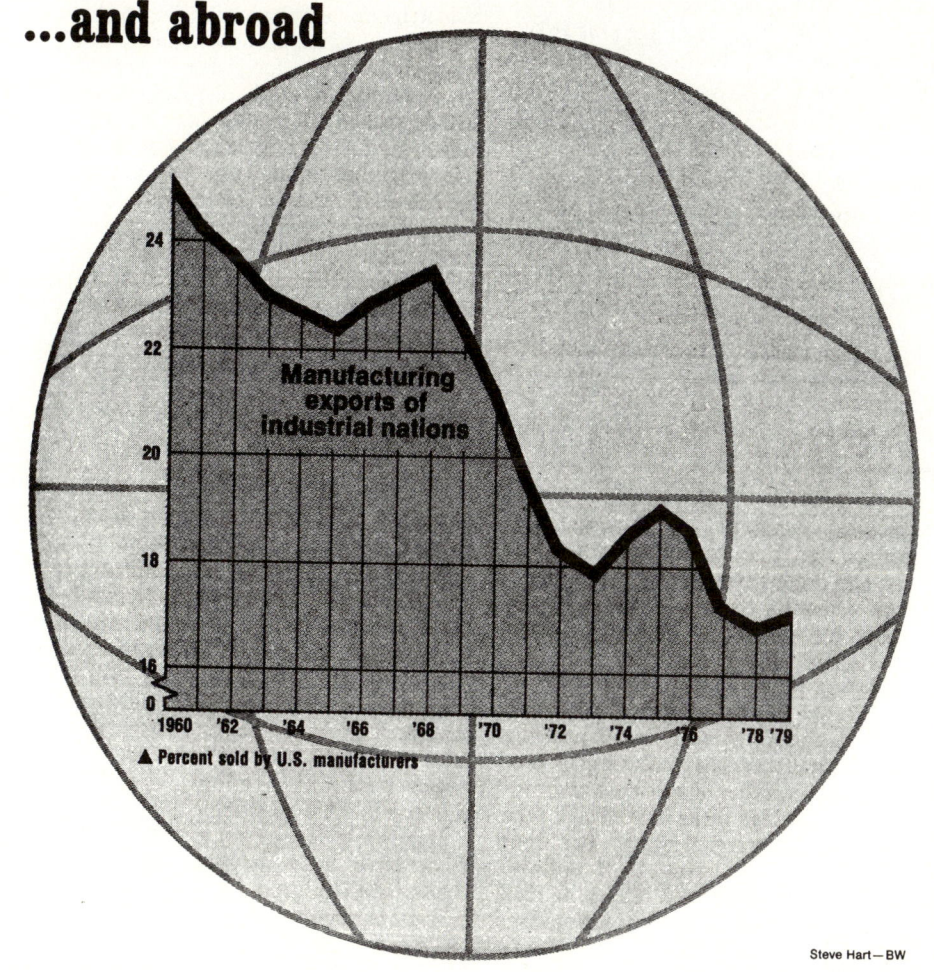

...and abroad

Manufacturing exports of industrial nations
▲ Percent sold by U.S. manufacturers

Steve Hart—BW

Assessing Strategic Advantages and Disadvantages / 173

Key industries hardest hit in the U.S. market...

Ranked by total sales of industry
Percent of market

	1960	1970	1979
Autos	95.9%	82.8%	79.0%
Steel	95.8	85.7	86.0
Apparel	98.2	94.8	90.0
Electrical components	99.5	94.4	79.9
Farm machinery	92.8	92.2	84.7
Industrial inorganic chemicals	98.0*	91.5	81.0
Consumer electronics	94.4	68.4	49.4
Footwear	97.7	85.4	62.7
Metal-cutting machine tools	96.7	89.4	73.6
Food processing machinery	97.0*	91.9	81.3
Metal-forming machine tools	96.8	93.2	75.4
Textile machinery	93.4	67.1	54.5
Calculating and adding machines	95.0*	63.8	56.9

Data: Commerce Dept., BW

...and in world markets

Ranked by size of U.S. exports
Percent of world exports

	1962	1970	1979
Motor vehicles	22.6%	17.5%	13.9%
Aircraft	70.9	66.5	58.0
Organic chemicals	20.5	25.7	15.0
Telecommunications apparatus	28.5	15.2	14.5
Plastic materials	27.8	17.3	13.0
Machinery and appliances (nonelectric)	27.9	24.1	19.6
Medical & pharmaceutical products	27.6	17.5	16.9
Metal-working machinery	32.5	16.8	21.7
Agricultural machinery	40.2	29.6	23.2
Hand or machine tools	20.5	19.1	14.0
Textile & leather machinery	15.5	9.9	6.6
Railway vehicles	34.8	18.4	11.6
Housing fixtures	22.8	12.0	8.1

Data: Data Resources Inc., BW estimates   *Estimated

---

market not because of lower labor costs but because of superior management and technology. The videotape recorder has become something of a symbol for the waning entrepreneurial spirit of American industry. Invented in the U.S., it was left to the Japanese to devise the techniques of mass production.

For some industries, of course, the decline in American competitiveness was inevitable. In labor-intensive industries such as apparel or shoes there is simply no way that U.S. manufacturers can hold back the import tide. It has only been the existence of quotas and orderly marketing agreements that has allowed domestic companies to retain 90% of the U.S. apparel market, and there is no way to arrest the decline permanently. The depreciation of the dollar and the general increase in the level of Japanese wages pretty well has eliminated Japan as a competitive factor in the U.S. apparel market. But production has shifted to the newly industrializing countries of Asia and Latin America, where labor is even cheaper. Other labor-intensive industries inevitably will move in the same direction.

This shift in world trade will have relatively little effect on other industrialized countries, where unskilled labor is now in short supply. But the U.S. has large numbers of unskilled workers who still depend on relatively unsophisticated industries for employment. This makes reindustrialization a more difficult task for the U.S. than for either Europe or Japan. Unlike the U.S., they can concentrate single-mindedly on the high-technology areas that, in the long run, will pay the biggest dividends in terms of living standards and economic power. ∎

A SOLUTION

A POLICY FOR INDUSTRY

Technology gives the U.S. a big edge

If the U. S. can forge a new social contract centered on growth, increased competitiveness in world markets is an achievable goal. The U. S. possesses many rich resources—in technology, energy reserves, and manpower—that can be better exploited to bolster trade. Its multinational corporations are still the most dynamic element in the world economy. With the proper government policies, many industries and products have enormous potential for growth.

To the extent that America's vaunted industrial machine may be squeaking, it is not for want of technological oil. In fact, to most technologists the 1980s look rosy. While none disputes that a few nations are closing the gap and in certain narrow areas even surpassing the U. S. in innovation, this does not mean American ingenuity and inventiveness are being crippled in the process. Those who suggest otherwise overlook the vexing fact that many foreign innovations continue to be built on U. S. developments, on concepts that American companies have, for various reasons, failed to exploit as fully as the Japanese or Germans. "I am absolutely convinced," says Friedrich Schroeder, a native German who heads corporate development at Hewlett-Packard Co. (HP), "that the U. S. will be the leading technological country to the end of this century."

A renewed climate

Remove some economic and political impediments to make the U. S. business environment more comparable to that in Japan or Germany, technologists contend, and existing American technology will contribute to a rapid revitalization of manufacturing. Such a change would also help the U. S. maintain its lead in today's high-technology areas, as well as give America a leg up in such emerging technologies as biological engineering.

However, executives at high-technology companies insist that any government policy aimed at reindustrialization must be grounded on a clear appreciation of what modern technology is about, its implications, and especially its accelerating pace. Lacking such understanding, they fear that any cure devised in Washington could be worse than the disease.

Some executives in California's citadel of high technology, Silicon Valley, are pushing hard on Washington. HP Chairman David Packard, for one, feels that the U. S. lead in computers will face a strong challenge by the 1990s. In other fields, the U. S. edge in implementing technology is already slipping. A study of innovation between 1953 and 1973 for the National Science Foundation (NSF) produced these statistics: In the 1950s the U. S. was the first to market 82% of all major innovations; by the late 1960s, though, the share had dropped to 55%.

One explanation of the apparent downturn, says Robert M. Coquillette, executive vice-president at W. R. Grace & Co., is that U. S. industry has been living off technology conceived during the Depression, when there was scant incentive to exploit new knowledge, and World War II, when the emphasis was on military applications. Jacob E. Goldman, senior vice-president and chief scientist at Xerox Corp., sees a similar pattern. Most of the major technological forces that are shaping today's world, he observes, stem from discoveries made before 1970—the whole microelectronics revolution, color television, a host of new drugs, the Polaroid camera, and of course xerography. To drive home his point, Goldman notes: "One is hard put to compile a list of innovations in the last few years that matches any equivalent span of time in the 1950s or '60s."

What troubles many executives is that U. S. industry is liquidating its technological capital at the same time that economic factors are forcing companies to stress short-term, applied research instead of the longer-range programs that are more likely to give birth to new scientific breakthroughs. HP's Packard and others favor giving industry a federal shot in the arm to encourage basic research and development, but they stress that the objective must clearly be to foster still faster progress and create new business opportunities, not to try to prop up ailing businesses to satisfy outmoded economic principles. "What I find most distressing," says John L. Nesheim, treasurer of National Semiconductor Corp., "is that taxpayer dollars are directed toward dying things rather than growing things."

Information replaces goods

Numerous studies have documented that the U. S. has been in the throes of an historic transition for the past two decades. The old industrial society that generated wealth in the form of capital goods and manufactured products is giving way to a new society valued in terms of intangible assets, such as knowledge and information processing. In fact, for 15 years more people have been working at processing information than any other type of job (chart, page 104)—and today in more than all other jobs combined. The two worlds are fundamentally different, so the new information-based society cannot be gauged with the economic yardsticks formulated for the old world.

For example, Vincent E. Giuliano, senior consultant on information processing at Arthur D. Little Inc. (ADL), points to the data-processing and aerospace industries. "What those industries are really selling," he notes, "is a package of knowledge in hardware form." In such industries, he adds, "human capital—the investment in skills and knowledge of people—becomes ever more important, but the [economic] measures we use simply ignore the vast current rate of investment in human resources."

A workable strategy for reindustriali-

Assessing Strategic Advantages and Disadvantages / 175

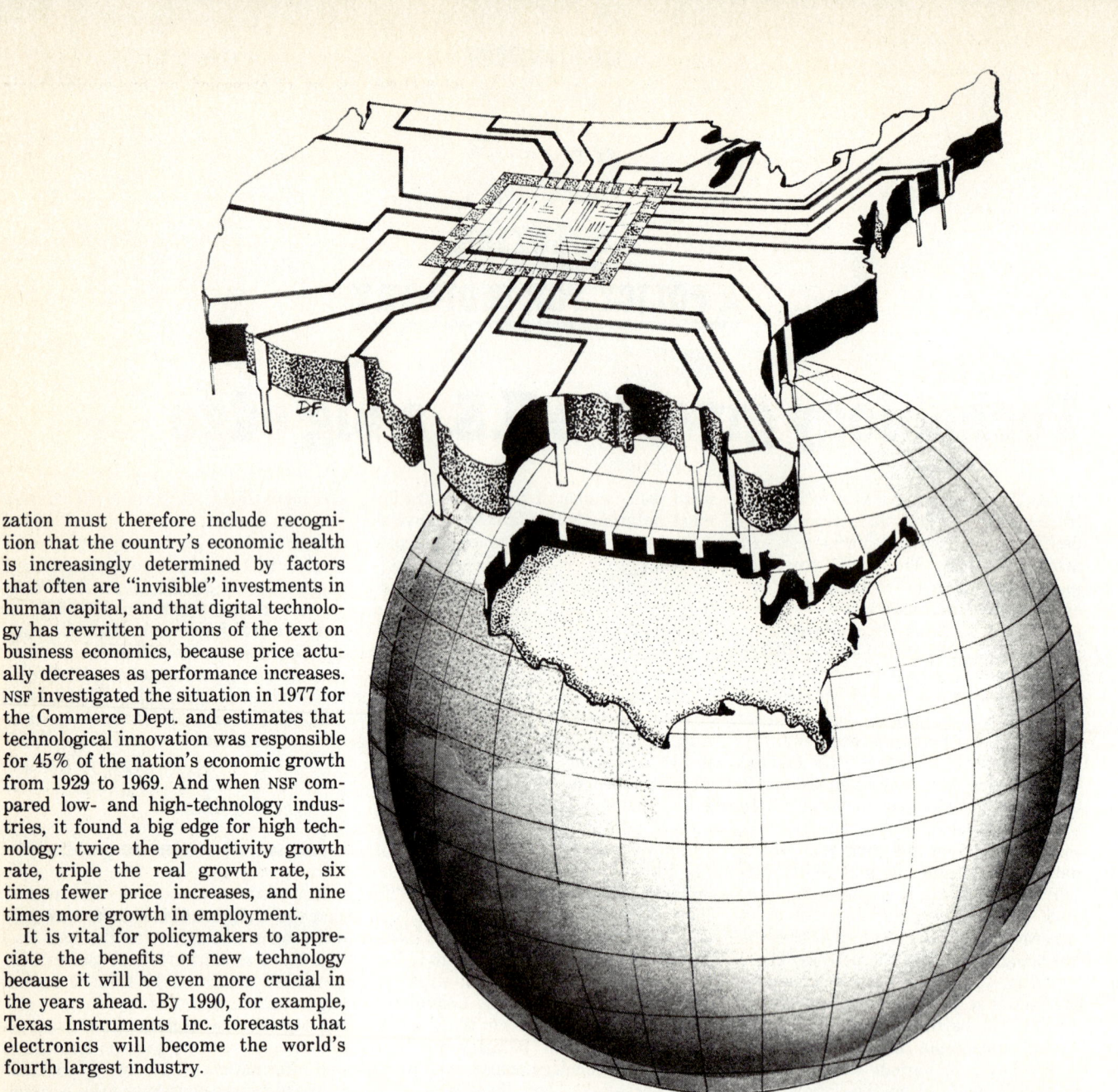

zation must therefore include recognition that the country's economic health is increasingly determined by factors that often are "invisible" investments in human capital, and that digital technology has rewritten portions of the text on business economics, because price actually decreases as performance increases. NSF investigated the situation in 1977 for the Commerce Dept. and estimates that technological innovation was responsible for 45% of the nation's economic growth from 1929 to 1969. And when NSF compared low- and high-technology industries, it found a big edge for high technology: twice the productivity growth rate, triple the real growth rate, six times fewer price increases, and nine times more growth in employment.

It is vital for policymakers to appreciate the benefits of new technology because it will be even more crucial in the years ahead. By 1990, for example, Texas Instruments Inc. forecasts that electronics will become the world's fourth largest industry.

Microelectronics revolution

Barring some spectacular breakthrough, the most significant driving forces in high technology for the balance of this decade will be continuations of two current trends in electronics. First is the steep decline in the price of computing power. Second, and linked to the first, is the spread of the microprocessor into an ever-widening array of products. Together, these two trends will profoundly affect every aspect of daily life—and virtually every commercial and consumer product that runs on electricity. Indeed, computers and microprocessor chips soon will be so ubiquitous that any electrical product without one or the other will have about as much sales appeal as an antiquated "cat's whisker" crystal radio.

Microelectronics will be the keystone technology not only because it is the world's fastest-growing industry. Even more potent than its sheer dollar volume is its pervasiveness. There will be few markets where "dumb" products can long compete against more sophisticated, computerized units. And once a market embarks on a computerization race, the rules of the game change forever.

Just making "smart" products and replacing mechanical functions with less expensive and more reliable semiconductor devices will suffice only temporarily. Given the rapid progress in packing more and more intelligence onto smaller and cheaper chips, remaining competitive will require that the electronics content of products be updated continually. In addition, the increasing capabilities of microprocessors will mean that more and more knowhow and functionalism will reside in the chip, and this will make it easier for a company to jump into a market by simply buying the proper semiconductors or copying a competitor's electronics hardware.

Thanks to computerization in two other disciplines, computer-aided design (CAD) and computer-aided manufacturing (CAM), it will be progressively less expensive for companies to practice ongoing innovation. "CAD-CAM will begin an industrial revolution of its own," says Guy L. Fougere, a vice-president at ADL. A company that uses an integrated CAD-CAM system not only can turn out new product designs much faster, but also can program the computer to make sure that the designs provide quality and reliability as well as the lowest possible manufacturing costs. And the digital output from the CAD computer can be simply plugged into the CAM system to reprogram the plant's manufacturing computers. "If you are not pretty well steeped in CAD-CAM, in 10 years you have a pretty good chance of being nonexistent," asserts Walter L. Abel, vice-president of research and development at Emhart Corp.

All signs thus point to a churning acceleration in product life cycles, paced by developments in microelectronics. The implications are staggering. Except for commodity-type items, many mature industries will be forced to march to a faster drummer. "We are talking about a product cycle that is 3-to-4 years, not the 10-to-12 we were getting a decade ago," notes J. Roy Henry, executive vice-president of Burroughs Corp. "And it could narrow further."

pacesetter. "For years, we set our targets by following the U. S.," says Hiroshi Watanabe, executive managing director for research and development at Hitachi Ltd. "But lately we've come close to America, if not up to her level. That means we must now become a creative leader by ourselves." But that is proving unexpectedly difficult, he concedes, and many Japanese frankly worry whether their culture's groupthink mentality is conducive to invention.

That may explain why U. S. semiconductor companies are almost universally confident of maintaining their lead. J. Fred Bucy, president of Texas Instruments, declares stoutly that semiconductors are not going to go the way of cars, steel, and consumer electronics. "There

Germans have thus concentrated to the point of obsession on fine-tuning their technology. But in recent years they have begun to approach the point of diminishing returns in their penchant for reengineering—at the same time that mechanical processes everywhere are giving way to electronics. The German government has poured millions into the development of microprocessors, but the companies it supports have been unable to close the gap.

"Basic innovation is lacking," admits Klaus Luft, vice-chairman of Nixdorf Computer. The Ministry for Research & Technology is now considering proposals to rectify the lag, because some officials there believe that Germany's machine-tool export "pillar" will face a crisis by 1985 if it does not keep pace with developments in microelectronics.

American machine-tool builders are also looking over their shoulders. Imports now account for more than twice as big a slice of the domestic market as in 1973, when it was 10%. "The gap has been closing in technology," says James A. D. Geier, president of Cincinnati Milacron Inc., in part because "it's always easier for the No. 2 person to catch up." Geier is hardly ready to throw in the towel, though. He points out that "my company is now producing very few machines that don't have full or partial computer control."

Information handling is already America's biggest employer

▲ Percent of total U.S. labor force
Data: Stanford University Institute for Communications Research

International cash flows

The industry also is concerned about trends in international trade, because Japanese, German, and other competitors are developing cash flows in markets that are verboten to the U. S. "Over 50% of all machine tools consumed outside the U. S. go to East bloc countries," notes James A. Gray, president of the National Machine Tool Builders Assn. But because of export policies, he complains, these markets are closed to U. S. suppliers. Eventually, he fears, this means that foreign producers will "generate more profits in world markets and reinvest a part of those gains in R&D."

The same message echoes from industry after industry—aircraft, appliances, steel, even textiles and shoes: Technology is not lacking; the knowhow that is needed exists; however, U. S. companies cannot raise the capital necessary to put the technology to work. Says Robert M. Dunn Jr., an economics professor at George Washington University: "Investment in plant and equipment that increases capital stock is critically tied to technological advance. Very few new inventions or productive improvements can be used with old machinery."

Harold T. Barraclough, program man-

Under such conditions, an incremental improvement in a product will give a manufacturer an edge for no more than a couple of years before another company makes a one-up change, and any country that does not have thriving semiconductor and computer industries will be at a severe disadvantage. The Japanese in particular are determined not to allow that to happen. They have launched a concerted, national campaign to close the technology gap.

Can Japan invent?

But there are grave questions even in Japan as to whether the Japanese can ever displace the U. S. as the world's

is a big difference in awareness today of the capabilities of the Japanese," he points out, "unlike the attitude that existed here 15 to 20 years ago, [when] U. S. industry was caught napping."

England, France, Germany, and other Western European nations are anxious to build their own semiconductor industries, too, if only for reasons of national pride. So far, though, none shows signs of overtaking Silicon Valley. For example, Germany has problems much deeper than Japan's when it comes to electronics, although in other areas it is a world-class leader. "German exports consist of three pillars—autos, chemicals, and machine tools," notes Hermann Schunck, a director at the federal Ministry for Research & Technology. "We can't afford to let one of those pillars crumble." The

ager for advanced development at SRI International, agrees that "high technology by itself can't save low-technology industries. If U. S. Steel Corp. has no profits," he explains, "it cannot afford a new process to improve productivity." The only solution that he sees is "to let the capitalists go by taking off the restraints on capital."

If capital is essential to applying technologies that already exist, it is even more crucial to nurture the emerging technologies that will form the industrial foundation of the 1990s and beyond. Of particular importance to the future are new sources of energy, biological engineering, and so-called supermaterials. Most work in these fields is still concentrated in research laboratories and funding has not been a major problem, although federal funds are being pruned somewhat.

For instance, while Atlantic Richfield Co. is strapped for cash in most of its businesses, when it comes to photovoltaics—electricity from the sun—the company maintains an open checkbook. Photovoltaics, explains Chairman Robert O. Anderson, "comes as close to being a Daddy Warbucks solution [to the energy crisis] as anything you can find." ARCO will not divulge its budget or investment to date in solar energy—insiders say privately that total spending over the next five years will be more than $200 million—but one recent example of its largesse occurred earlier this year, when ARCO signed a $25 million licensing agreement with Energy Conversion Devices Inc.

Solar energy's future

ECD is the company founded by controversial inventor Stanford R. Ovshinsky, who believes that more efficient photovoltaic cells can be made from amorphous silicon, a material that is much cheaper to produce than the silicon crystals now used for semiconductors. ARCO hopes that such a development will reduce the price of solar cells, now running about $7 per watt, to the 70¢ a watt figure set by the Energy Dept. as a target for the mid-1980s.

And if the cost is cut further with volume production, the sun could furnish a good portion of energy needs by 2000. Researchers at Argonne National Laboratory, Brookhaven National Laboratory, and a couple of university labs even foresee the development of artificial silicon leaves that could be more efficient at utilizing the energy of sunlight than natural plants.

A study last year by the Harvard Business School's energy project states that solar energy—defined as including all sun-dependent sources, from wind to wood burned in stoves—could account for 20% of turn-of-the-century supply. And with innovation in such areas as orbiting solar-power satellites and ocean-temperature energy conversion (OTEC), Peter E. Glaser, an ADL vice-president and solar-energy expert, pre-

Harnessing the sun is the promise for semiconductors. Solar cells of silicon leaves

dicts that solar energy's contributions 50 years hence could amount to 80% of U. S. electricity and 50% of nonelectrical energy.

Proponents of other emerging sources of energy are equally enthusiastic. Melvin B. Gottlieb, director of Princeton University's Plasma Physics Laboratory, believes that in the 21st century "the majority of our power could be generated through fusion." The process liberates more energy than present nuclear fission techniques and does not create long-term radioactive pollution.

Magnetohydrodynamics (MHD) is another source of future energy that should reach the demonstration-plant stage in the 1990s. Meanwhile, MHD research may pay off later this decade in improved methods of burning coal. Bert Zauderer, a manager of General Electric Co.'s MHD program, says that he expects "a tremendous spinoff in coal-combustion technology that will benefit the country a lot sooner than MHD will."

In materials, there is mounting concern regarding the focus of research. A recent NSF study, *Science & Technology: A Five-Year Outlook*, states that "the forces that mold the materials enterprise are shifting to an uncommon degree from the purely technological to social and economic factors." Nevertheless, in comparatively high-technology disciplines—polymers, composites, ceramics, and superalloys—considerable progress is being registered. For example, the NSF believes plastics in Detroit's cars will grow 50% by 1985.

Biotechnology diffusion

Perhaps the most exciting new technology on the horizon is biological, or genetic, engineering. Some biotechnology enthusiasts hail it as the semiconductor industry of the 1980s and '90s. However, it is unlikely that biotechnology will create a concentrated industry of its own, like semiconductors. Instead, it will diffuse into such industries as chemicals, drugs, food, and energy. The first commercial applications should begin appearing later this year, and by the late 1980s, according to a study by International Resource Development Inc. (IRD), biotechnology will be producing several drugs, including insulin and interferon and perhaps morphine, in sufficient bulk to avert worldwide shortages that would otherwise occur. Biotechnology is "the ace card for the 1980s," says IRD's Ruth Lipsitz.

Fundamentally, then, America's technology base is still the envy of the world—diverse, progressive, and vital. Warning signals have cropped up in the last decade, but they are not symptomatic of inherent weaknesses in the science and technology communities; rather, the causes are economic and are thus susceptible to economic cures. ∎

WILL IT WORK?

What the U.S. can learn from its rivals

Japan, the world's most successful industrial society, energizes its economy and steers business along fast-growth tracks by means of a pervasive national industrial plan. Its strategy is to identify and promote industries with the best prospects for developing new technologies and exploiting world market opportunities (chart, page 139) while shifting workers out of declining industries.

By contrast, West Germany—although it is Europe's industrial powerhouse and the world's most formidable exporter—has made only pro-forma attempts at setting national industrial priorities. Instead, it relies primarily, as it has since 1948, on market forces and on decisions by individual companies to channel resources into industries with the highest growth potential. Britain, in another contrast, failed to halt a long slide from being one of Europe's richest countries to being one of its poorest, despite nearly two decades of government-directed efforts to reshape the economy through a network of government-business-labor councils—and despite $130 billion of government grants, subsidies, and equity investments aimed at propping up a variety of industries.

What Japan's experience demonstrates is that coherent national planning can be a potent instrument for improving a nation's economic performance—to the point, in Japan's case, where it may soon challenge the U. S. for global industrial supremacy. But Germany's impressive achievements without a national industrial strategy, and Britain's decline despite efforts at industrial planning and promotion, point to a more fundamental factor in economic performance. What Japan and Germany both have, and Britain lacks, is a broad national consensus among social groups on basic economic priorities. A primary focus of this consensus in Japan, Germany, and other economically successful countries is productivity, perceived as the key to jobs, prosperity, and even national security. In Britain, by contrast, "we have never had the sense of urgency about productivity of the Germans or even the French," says Rupert N. Hambro, executive director of Hambros Bank Ltd.

The U. S., if it is to succeed in reindustrializing, will have to create an understanding throughout society that productivity is crucial to the achievement of other national goals. Whereas formerly Japanese flocked to the U. S. to learn technology, Americans are now going to Japan to study productivity, notes Hiroshi Watanabe, managing director for research and development at Hitachi Corp. "The problem in the U. S. is not one of technology but of economics and politics," he says.

Joining the scramble

In the 1980s the U. S. also will have to adopt international competitiveness as the touchstone of its industrial strategy if it hopes to match the performance of the economically successful nations. What that will require is a wide agreement by workers, managers, and political leaders that the nation as a whole, and each individual company—if it is dependent on overseas markets or vulnerable to inroads by foreign products—must be internationally competitive. "You have to look at the exposed sectors of the economy," says Bruce R. Scott, a professor at Harvard's graduate school of business administration who has analyzed the performance of European economies. "The tests are: 'Can you maintain market share?' and 'Can you do it profitably?'"

That is why the U. S. will have to join in the scramble for world market shares, a crucial element in the "export-led" growth strategies of Germany and Japan, as well as "new Japans" such as Korea, Taiwan, and Singapore. "Exports have played a key role in each of these success stories—each has been able to achieve a high or rapidly rising market share in the world trade of manufactured goods," Scott says. "This export performance has put pressure not only on American companies and American workers but on other industrialized countries as well."

The effort to develop a national industrial strategy, and the debate that it stirs, should itself help to create a greater sense of urgency in the U. S. about these issues. Other countries' experience although not entirely applicable to the U. S., suggests policies that have proven effective in dealing with the critical problems that the U. S. now faces—and warns of policy pitfalls to avoid.

JAPAN. A 357-page compilation of data, charts, and analysis, issued in April by the Ministry of International Trade & Industry under the title "Industrial policy vision of the 1980s," is being studied by Japanese businessmen as an authoritative investment guide. By pinpointing industries that MITI considers to have the best growth potential, the report indicates the types of investments that are likely to be eligible for official financial assistance and incentives.

Although it carries MITI's imprimatur, the report is actually a product of Japan's broad policymaking consensus. Thus the shaping of Japan's industrial strategy for the 1980s also shows how consensus works to enlist virtually all sectors of Japanese society in a coordinated productive effort. The choice of favored industries was approved by an advisory board called the Industrial Structure Council, composed of more than 50 representatives from government, business, and academia. The document is the outcome of 10 to 15 industrial policy meetings at which consumers, labor unions, and other groups were represented, and of countless smaller sessions between MITI officials and these groups over endless cups of tea. Sessions of the council, according to Kiyohiko Fukushima, economist at Tokyo's Nomu-

Assessing Strategic Advantages and Disadvantages / 179

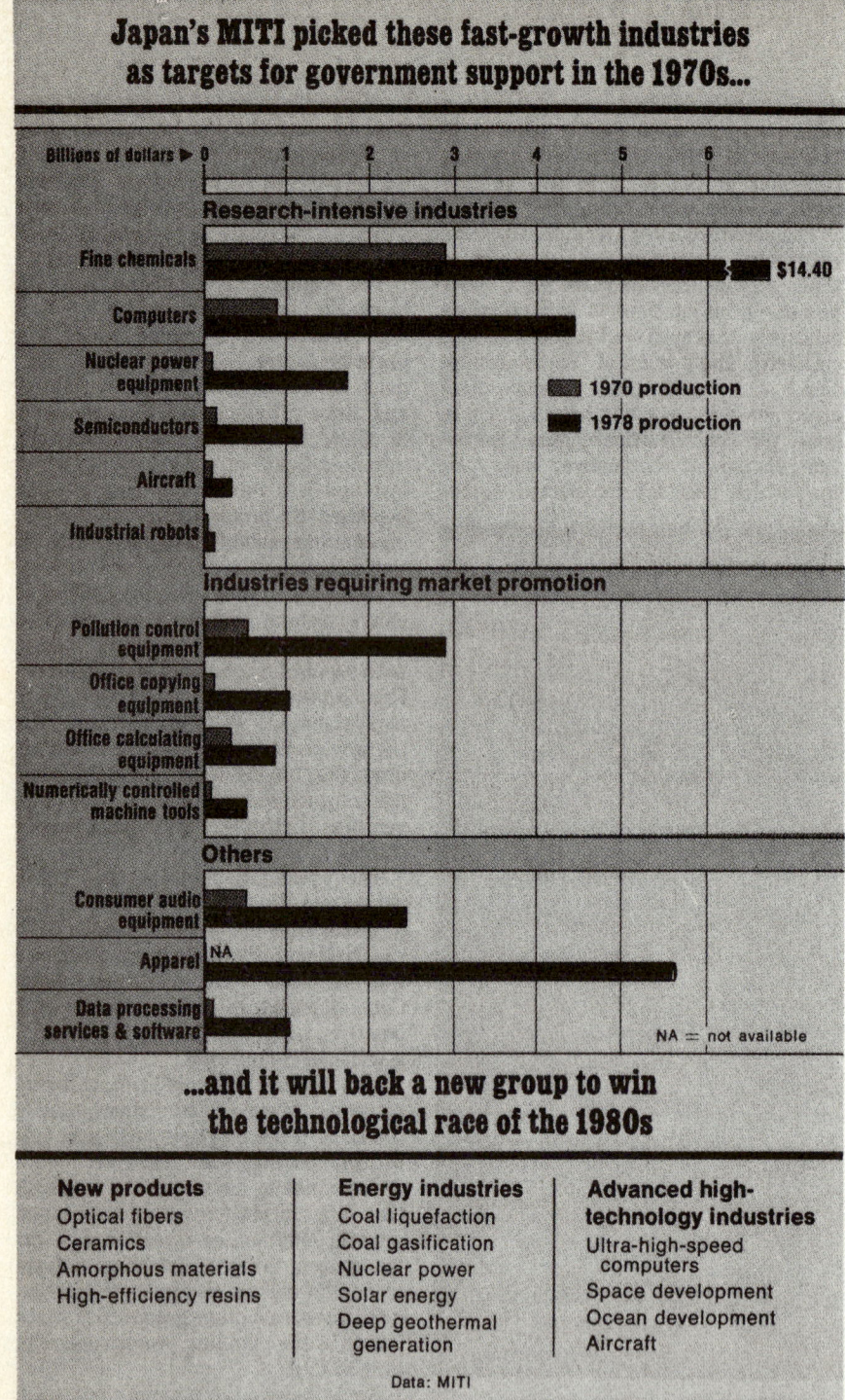

Japan's MITI picked these fast-growth industries as targets for government support in the 1970s...

Billions of dollars ▶ 0 1 2 3 4 5 6

Research-intensive industries
- Fine chemicals — $14.40
- Computers
- Nuclear power equipment
- Semiconductors
- Aircraft
- Industrial robots

■ 1970 production
■ 1978 production

Industries requiring market promotion
- Pollution control equipment
- Office copying equipment
- Office calculating equipment
- Numerically controlled machine tools

Others
- Consumer audio equipment
- Apparel — NA
- Data processing services & software

NA = not available

...and it will back a new group to win the technological race of the 1980s

New products	Energy industries	Advanced high-technology industries
Optical fibers	Coal liquefaction	Ultra-high-speed computers
Ceramics	Coal gasification	Space development
Amorphous materials	Nuclear power	Ocean development
High-efficiency resins	Solar energy	Aircraft
	Deep geothermal generation	

Data: MITI

---

commercial banks that take the JDB's actions as a signal of official support for the borrowers.

In research and development, the collective judgment of industrial managers largely determines how big government subsidies should be spent. "When MITI makes policy, it is not really their policy but is based on the consensus of Japanese industry," says Hitachi's Watanabe.

Right now, MITI is wholly or partly funding nine "large projects" by Japanese companies working in teams to develop technologies ranging from steel production and jet engines to automated factories and "alternative" energy sources. A computerized pattern-recognition project, for example, will end this year after spending $100 million of MITI money since 1971.

IBM and Texas Instruments

Although many such Japanese arrangements would be difficult to graft onto U.S. society, some Japanese observers think that the cultural barriers to such adaptations have been exaggerated. "Japanese-style management can be done in the U.S.," says Nomura's Fukushima. "Successful firms like IBM and Texas Instruments don't have trade unions. The key to their success is how their system is suited to obtain their objectives, how they give their workers dignity and pride."

GERMANY. In sharp contrast with Japan's system of detailed "administrative guidance" to industry, the Federal Republic pursues a steady, anti-inflationary "macroeconomic" policy that creates a climate of investor confidence but leaves it to corporate managers to decide where to invest. The result has been a 9% average real increase in investment in the past two years, and an expected 10% rise this year.

Bonn's hands-off industrial strategy is a corollary of the market-oriented philosophy that Germany has pursued since 1948 when Economics Minister (later Chancellor) Ludwig Erhard launched the country's "economic miracle" by sweeping away postwar controls. One major difference between Germany and the U.S., which also relies primarily on the market to shape the pattern of industry, is that Washington has discouraged investment by failing to control the price spiral.

Moreover, German management and labor, unlike their U.S. counterparts, have achieved a tacit consensus to avoid inflationary wage outbursts. Since 1975 unions have settled for nominal pay increases that are only slightly above the inflation rate. The resulting gradual increase in real wages gives German companies an incentive to keep investing in

ra Research Institute, are like "a big meeting of relatives . . . they all know each other and can readily compromise their interests."

In the broad context of Japanese consensus, one such compromise was the settlement of this year's spring labor "offensive" with wage increases well below the rise in the consumer price index. Because workers recognized that they would ultimately suffer if their companies were hurt, Fukushima says that "it was easy to persuade the unions to take only small salary increases."

The development of advanced products and new techniques that MITI will promote in the 1980s is a continuation of the emphasis on "knowledge-intensive" industries that began in 1970. Financing for investments in such industries will be provided by MITI in collaboration with the Ministry of Finance and the government's Japan Development Bank. In fiscal 1980, JDB will lend around $4.5 billion. But the government's lending will also trigger a large volume of loans by

180 / Readings from *Business Week*

WILL IT WORK?

order to raise productivity and maintain their competitiveness in vital export markets. Even Fried. Krupp, in the troubled steel industry, has spent heavily on a complete revamping of production facilities. By contrast, in the U.S., where real wages have decreased, the capital-intensity of industry has also declined.

A key to Germany's high investment rate is the country's financial structure—a network of close, stable links between industrial companies and banks that encourages companies to invest with an eye to long-term growth. In the U.S., where corporate financing is heavily dependent on public capital markets, managers are forced to emphasize short-term performance instead. As a result, although American corporate planning techniques are better than those of German companies, according to Herbert H. Jacobi, a partner at Frankfurt's BHF-Bank, "German planning decisions are better."

German bankers typically sit on the boards of companies that they regularly lend to and discuss future activities of companies at a much earlier stage than their American counterparts. One benefit, for Volkswagenwerk, of such long-term relationships was the debt moratorium, never publicly admitted, that the auto maker's banks quietly allowed in 1975 at the depth of the auto industry recession to enable it to finance new models to replace its aging Beetle.

The counterpart of German corporate managers' close ties with bankers is their regular consultation with labor unions—a major element in Germany's relatively tranquil worker-management relations. The system of "co-determination," which puts union representatives on corporate supervisory boards, helps to head off confrontations. More important, though, is the postwar shop rules law, which provides for elected worker representatives to serve on behalf of all employees and makes it illegal for them to work against the company's best interests. Managers, for their part, are required to keep workers' councils, roughly equivalent to union locals, constantly informed about company plans. "The essence of the German system," says an observer, "is that there are few surprises."

FRANCE. The nearest thing to central planning in the West since World War II is the system of "indicative" plans that the French launched in 1947. They are a far cry, of course, from the economic "command" system of Communist countries because the French system relies on incentives and administrative nudging to achieve its objectives. But measured by France's real growth rate, which averaged 4% in the past 10 years, indicative planning has been successful.

The original purpose of the plans was to provide businessmen and other decision-makers with a "macro model" that projects future economic activity as a guide for investments, wage bargaining, and other activities. But the attempt to fit all sectors of the national economy into neat input-output grids has become less and less relevant as France—once insulated by protectionist policies—has become increasingly integrated with the world economy.

Instead of trying to devise policies for entire sectors, such as steel, autos, or electronics—which may each contain both successful companies and failures—French thinking is now shifting to "strategic planning." What this means is that the government will indicate industrial areas that it considers promising and listen to concrete investment proposals for ventures that may merit official support (table).

The upcoming plan for the 1981-85 period was developed from an initial set of broad aims or "options" drawn up by the National Planning Commission. It was discussed by the Economic & Social Council, made up of representatives of business, labor, and other groups, and by a series of committees.

The political difficulties in indicative planning, however—in France, and in the U.S., if such an approach were tried in this country—are reflected in the decision not to include in the upcoming plan any formal targets for economic growth, inflation, or investment. A major reason is that the targets imply trade-offs among the interests of business, labor, and other groups that participants in the planning process are reluctant to face.

Nevertheless, the planning process itself is important in France because the French social consensus is fragile, with labor-management relations that are embittered by antagonisms between politically motivated union leaders and backward-looking managers. Discussions of the plan are one context in which businessmen and labor leaders work closely together.

BRITAIN. The industrial planning and promotion mechanisms created in Britain over the past two decades by both Conservative and Labor governments are being drastically cut back by Prime Minister Margaret Thatcher, a firm be-

The French will channel official support to strategic growth sectors

Strategic industry	Objectives	Actions planned
Electronic office equipment	To achieve a 20% to 25% world market share and avert an anticipated $2 billion trade deficit in such products by 1985, on present trends	In strategic sectors, the government will negotiate "development contracts" with individual companies, setting specific goals for sales, exports, and jobs. Companies that make such commitments will receive tax incentives, subsidized loans, and other official aid
Consumer electronics	To create a world-scale group including TV-set and tube makers that will each rank among the top three globally; to eliminate the $750 million annual trade deficit in such products	
Energy-saving equipment	To ensure that government grants to companies and households to install such equipment are spent primarily on French products	
Undersea activities	To recapture second place in the world (after the U.S.)	
Bio-industry	Objectives not yet defined	
Industrial robots	Objectives not yet defined	
	The six strategic industries together are expected to add $10 billion in sales and double their work force to 135,000 by 1985	

Data: CODIS

Assessing Strategic Advantages and Disadvantages / 181

WILL IT WORK?

liever in the free market. Instead, she intends to rely basically on macroeconomic policies—including government spending restraints, monetary measures to reduce inflation, and a shift in taxes from income to consumption in order to stimulate investment.

Thus she is curbing the National Economic Development Council (NEDC) and the National Enterprise Board (NEB), both designed to operate on the strategic planning principle of picking industrial "winners" and channeling government support to them. Both had some success in this role, although not nearly enough to offset the debilitating effects on industry of fundamental British ills, ranging from the disastrous "stop-go" economic policies of previous governments to the near-warfare between trade unions and employers.

The NEDC, set up in 1961, served at its peak as the umbrella for working parties, made up of representatives of the government, the Trades Union Congress, and the Confederation of British Industry, for each of 38 industrial sectors. Their purpose was to identify viable investment prospects and recommend government support for them.

The NEB, set up in 1975, is specifically aimed at guaranteeing and financing investments, including share purchases, in internationally competitive, export-oriented industries. In fiscal 1980-81, NEB will get only $150 million for new investment and will concentrate mostly on high-technology ventures in microelectronics, computer software, office equipment, and possibly biotechnology.

Thatcher also is expected to halt the huge bailouts, by previous Conservative and Labor governments, of industrial "losers," ranging from Clydebank shipyards to British Steel Corp. And she is slashing heavy "regional development" grants for financing of industries and infrastructure in depressed areas.

ITALY. Based on a trio of state-controlled holding companies that funnel investment into industry (table, below), Italy's industrial strategy worked fairly well until 1973 in building up steel, shipbuilding, chemicals, and other heavy industries. Guido Carli, former governor of the Bank of Italy and now president of L'Union des Industries de la Communauté Européene, a Western European manufacturers' association, argues that such an approach was an effective means of developing key sectors of the economy that private companies alone could not finance. But since the oil crisis plunged many Italian companies into heavy deficit, the holding companies have become channels for massive government bailouts of money-losing ventures and for political logrolling.

Spreading unemployment also shifted the main emphasis of Italy's state capitalism from strengthening key industrial sectors to creating jobs, especially in poor southern regions, and maintaining employment in other areas. But lush government financing and tax breaks for investors, together with a ruling that 80% of new outlays by state-run companies must go into the *mezzogiorno*, backfired. "With all that money being offered, companies built capital-intensive, not labor-intensive, industries," says economist Luigi Spaventa, an independent leftist member of Parliament.

The expanding government role in industry also created other problems, including a pattern of careless lending by financial institutions to dubious ventures. "Any financing for an investment in the south had pretty much a government guarantee, so the lending institutions did not do their homework," says Bruno Brovedani, chief economist of the Banca Nazionale del Lavoro. Moreover, businessmen, as well as labor unions, lobby the government to take over failing companies.

Economist Romano Prodi, a former Minister of Industry, says American colleagues assure him that the U.S. could avoid the kind of political interference that has undermined Italy's industrial strategy. But his answer, he says, is always, "I have my doubts."

The U.S. can achieve an industrial renaissance, the experiences of other countries suggest, by channeling resources into industries with the potential for adaptation and growth instead of attempting to shield declining sectors against inevitable change. To mobilize support for such a program, a coordinated effort to establish national priorities—with the participation of all social groups, as in Japan—can serve as a framework to rally competing interests around a common goal (page 146).

By encouraging research and development, the U.S. can keep in the forefront of technology, but developments in other nations show that technological advances alone are not enough. If the U.S., like Germany, adopts a firm, noninflationary approach to managing its economy instead of persisting in futile attempts at fine-tuning, it should be able to give businessmen the confidence to invest more while assuring workers that their wage gains will be real, not illusory.

Above all, the lesson of the industrially successful nations is that a national consensus can be built on the fundamental importance of productivity as the bedrock of prosperity and, ultimately, of national strength. The U.S., if it recognizes this need, can certainly do no less. ∎

In Italy, aid to state-run companies has become a prop to inefficient money losers

Government holding company	Activities	Number of employees	1978 sales	1978 losses	Debt at yearend 1978
			—Billions of dollars—		
Istituto per la Ricostruzione Industriale (IRI)	Controls 559 banks, steel mills, airlines, electronics manufacturers, auto maker Alfa Romeo, and other companies	545,000	$18.8	$1.4	$24.8
Ente Nazionale Idrocarburi (ENI)	Controls 229 companies engaged in oil production, refining, engineering, fiber manufacturing, and other activities	120,000	15.9	0.2	9.0
Ente Partecipazioni e Finanziamento Industria Manifatturiera (EFIM)	Controls 41 companies engaged in mining, metallurgy, food processing, and other activities	31,000	2.7	0.1	1.7

Data: Ministry of State Participations

182 / Readings from *Business Week*

CAN CANON COPY ITS CAMERA COUP?

One company's technology clearly dominates the market for copying machines that churn out duplicates on ordinary paper—and it is not the "Big X." More than half of the 2 billion plain-paper copiers sold worldwide last year, including such brands as Savin, Sharp, and Saxon, are based at least in part on technology licensed from Canon Inc. That may come as a surprise in the U.S., where Canon is known primarily for its cameras and has been a negligible factor in the copier market.

On Jan. 15, Canon unveiled what Executive Director Keizo Yamaji calls "our most major innovation so far"—a simplified machine that combines such developments as a fiber optics system not much bigger than a ruler, which replaces the conventional, bulky ground-lens optical system, with a new toner, or "ink," that eliminates much of the mess and bother associated with plain-paper copiers. The upshot is machines that are smaller, more reliable, and cheaper—and what Yamaji feels is a shot at the No. 1 spot in plain-paper copier sales.

Yamaji's optimism may not be quite as far-fetched as it first appears. Canon machines already account for nearly 20% of current sales worldwide, he claims, although they now have less than 10% of the U.S. market. And Fujio Mitarai, president of Canon USA Inc., whose sales last year were up 55% over 1978, "confidently" expects a gain of at least 75% this year.

'Market-buster.' Canon has demonstrated that it can capture U.S. market share rapidly. In the camera business, it was an also-ran as recently as 1974. Today, thanks to product innovations and major advertising campaigns, it is the leading brand in the U.S. 35-mm camera market. Mitarai figures that what Canon has done in cameras, it can do in copiers. "We established Canon in the camera business in the 1970s," he says. "In the 1980s, I want to establish Canon in the business machines field," and he has budgeted $10 million for advertising to help do it.

The first copier to feature the new technology is a desk-top unit, only a bit bigger than an electric typewriter, that can crank out as many as 20 copies a minute and can handle paper as big as 11 x 17 in. It costs $4,000.

At that price, with those features, says Melody Johnson, a consultant at Quantum Science Corp., which tracks high-technology markets, "they've got a market-busting product—if the thing is reliable." Another market researcher figures that the machine is so mechanically simple that "it could be sold at retail down to $3,000." David G. Jorgensen, office equipment analyst for Dataquest Inc., a Cupertino (Calif.) research company, terms the new copier "impressive—there's just nothing that touches it." He adds that Canon has developed a good dealer network, and, if everything stood still, he thinks that Canon might have a chance at grabbing a big share of the U.S. market. But Canon is aiming at a moving target, he notes. "We haven't seen the final salvo from Xerox by any means."

The first competitors to feel Canon's new muscle are likely to be the companies that now license its older technology; they will not be offered the new technology. However, Gabriel S. Calin, executive vice-president of Savin Corp., says he is not worried. "I'm not familiar with the new machine," he says, "but nothing in our future plans depends on Canon technology." But Ken Fukae, vice-president of the U.S. subsidiary of Minolta Camera Co., a rival that also builds copiers, admits: "It's going to give us a little competition." ■

FORD RESTS ITS FUTURE ON TOUGH COST CONTROLS

The problems at Ford Motor Co. could hardly be more obvious. The company's domestic car business is headed for perhaps $1.5 billion in red ink this year, on top of a $1 billion loss in 1979. Booming overseas sales have kept the No. 2 auto maker healthy overall, but its executive shuffle on Mar. 13 leaves no doubt that Ford intends to pave its road to domestic recovery with tougher cost controls and a rethinking of its product plans.

"We've got to zig instead of zag, as we had planned originally," concedes Philip Caldwell, Ford's new chairman. Caldwell, who became president in 1978 and chief executive officer last October, hopes to resuscitate his company's U.S. auto operations with the help of a cadre of financially oriented executives who have been seasoned in Ford's highly profitable overseas operations. The new lineup also signals the end of any remnant of the flamboyant, product-and-marketing tilt the company acquired in the late 1970s under the presidency of Lee A. Iacocca, now chairman of Chrysler Corp. Ford's top management now includes:

DONALD E. PETERSEN, 53, president and chief operating officer. Petersen, described by colleagues as a "meticulous manager," is former executive vice-president of Ford International Automotive Operations, credited with keeping Ford in the black last year.

HAROLD A. POLING, 54, executive vice-president of Ford North American Automotive Operations. Poling was controller for several Ford divisions, served as president and then chairman of Ford of Europe, and became executive vice-president of corporate staffs last April.

Henry's rap. Ford has already indicated that it will slash about $500 million from the $4 billion that it planned to spend on product programs this year. Insiders say that the company is now reviewing those programs in an effort to cancel or combine some car lines—even at the risk of giving up some auto market segments. "The market is pressing us," frets Caldwell. Short term, he admits, "we're absolutely exposed."

Ford's bind prompted Moody's Investors Service Inc. on Mar. 19 to downgrade its rating of Ford senior debt and tax-exempt issues from AAA to AA. Moody's also downgraded the debt of Ford's financial subsidiary. "They don't have the cars that are selling," says a Moody's spokesman. Ford and its competitors are locked into the new cars they can offer over the next three years (BW—Mar. 24).

The problem is particularly acute at Ford, which, at the insistence of Henry Ford II, was philosophically opposed to "downsizing" its larger cars until last summer—almost six years after General Motors Corp. realized smaller cars were inevitable. "Two years ago [Ford] did big cars instead of small, front-wheel-drive vehicles, and it's killing them now," says a source close to its product planning. "That rap lies with Henry."

Insiders say Henry Ford was convinced that most American car buyers would never accept vehicles much smaller than the compact Fairmont—roughly equivalent to the largest car Ford sells in Europe. "There was almost a preoccupation about keeping our larger cars around, because we thought that's what the public wanted," adds Bennett E. Bidwell, vice-president of Ford's Car & Truck Group.

With its product plans largely committed through 1983, Ford has little choice in the short run but to try to trim its losses in the U.S. auto market with spending cuts. Yet any reductions in its future product programs could end up only prolonging its domestic problems by handing GM and imports still more time to grab additional market share. Ford's slice of the U.S. car business has already dropped from 23% to 17% over the past year, a loss of roughly $3.5 billion in sales revenues.

Short on savvy? Ford has allowed implicit blame for its U.S. sales problems to rest with William O. Bourke, 52, former head of the company's North American auto business, who will take early retirement in May. Ironically, Bourke was brought to his U.S. post from Ford of Europe by Henry Ford as the eventual heir to the presidency. But Ford's decision to replace Iacocca with Caldwell changed the tenor of top management. Friends of both men say Bourke's blunt, outspoken manner grated on Caldwell and helped swing the presidency to the more soft-spoken Petersen.

Company observers have little doubt that Ford's new management team can rein in its domestic cost problems. But some worry that the heavy financial bias of the executives will leave Ford dangerously short on savvy marketing and product leaders just when it needs them most. "There ought to be a heck of a good product guy somewhere in the top half-dozen people," says one ex-Ford executive, "but now, I don't see one."

WHY CONSUMER PRODUCTS LAG AT TEXAS INSTRUMENTS

The news was surprisingly good at the Apr. 17 shareholders' meeting of Texas Instruments Inc. President J. Fred Bucy kept the affair—jam-packed as usual—definitely upbeat by reporting a 32% jump in both net income and sales for the first quarter. On top of that, he said that the company had decided to raise its 1980 spending plans for new plant and equipment by 31% over last year, to $570 million, and for research and development by 27%, to $135 million.

With sales now running near a $4 billion annual rate, the TI president told stockholders that the company had raised its $10 billion sales goal for the late 1980s to a breathtaking $15 billion. Last year, TI hit a goal set in 1966 by reporting sales of $3.2 billion.

What did not come out at the meeting was that one of the three legs that TI needs to support its 20% growth rate in the 1980s is tottering. To meet its ambitious goals, TI has counted on three primary market thrusts—semiconductor devices, distributed computing, and consumer electronics. And TI is losing ground in its pursuit of a consumer electronics franchise. Eight years ago, TI figured that it alone among the semiconductor companies had the technological savvy to come up with innovative consumer products, the financial muscle to launch them, and the manufacturing skills to drive prices low enough to grab a dominant market share.

Volatile market. But TI's consumer revenues last year hardly grew at all. Industry analysts figure that this business accounted for little more than $400 million, lagging considerably behind its plan. Worse, the Consumer Products Group's contribution to pretax profits dipped from an estimated $28 million in 1978 to a minuscule $2 million.

The company blames its profit problems squarely on the digital-watch business, citing "cost problems and competitive pricing pressure." But as TI's major consumer electronics markets mature, there are increasing signals that the company's vaunted management systems are too burdensome a process for the volatile consumer marketplace. The watch business, in fact, is the poorest performer in a product portfolio whose 1979 performance was stalled by TI's inability to produce. Here is how 1979 looked:

WATCHES. Estimates of TI's loss in digital watches alone topped $10 million as the company's image withered from that of the unquestioned leader to that of merely another importer. Half of its models were purchased offshore for sale under the TI label.

CALCULATORS. TI watched all year as Japan's Sharp Corp. and Casio Computer Co. chipped away at its share of the low-priced consumer calculator market. Sales of TI's highly profitable professional calculators remained strong, but a revitalized Hewlett-Packard Co. leapfrogged past TI's technical dominance with a powerful new model.

The changing revenue mix...

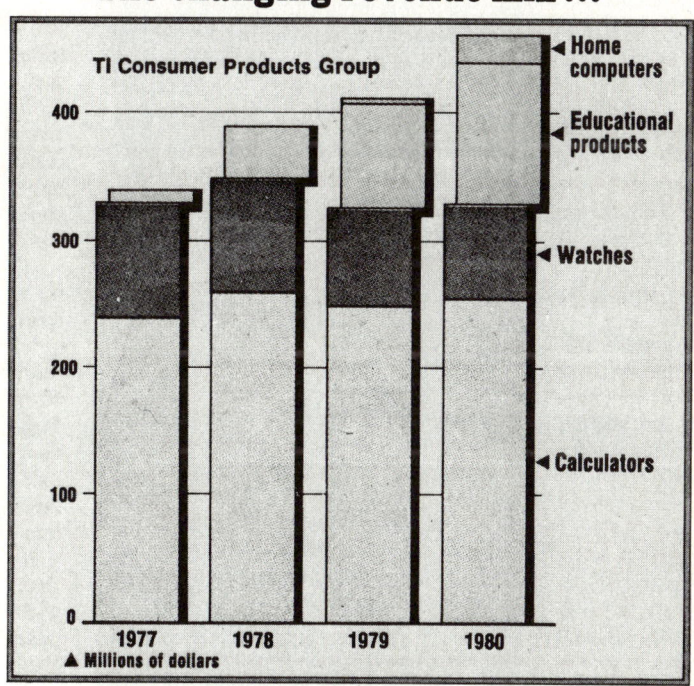

TI Consumer Products Group

(Bar chart showing 1977, 1978, 1979, 1980 with segments for Home computers, Educational products, Watches, Calculators. Millions of dollars, axis 0–400.)

...and a profit problem

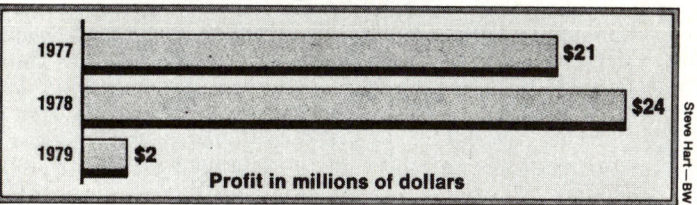

Year	Profit in millions of dollars
1977	$21
1978	$24
1979	$2

Data: Dataquest Inc., BW estimates

HOME COMPUTERS. TI took the wraps off its long-delayed and much-awaited home computer, but production snafus kept it off the market until late December. Now, as production volume heads up, TI has yet to back the product with the massive promotion needed to introduce a new product category to the public. Such support might persuade consumers that the benefits of the $1,400 machine outweigh its unexpectedly hefty price.

EDUCATIONAL PRODUCTS. TI's big headstart in electronic learning aids, such as the talking Speak & Spell, remains unchallenged, but semiconductor chip shortages—exacerbated by TI's conservative forecasting a year ago—reined in the growth of this business.

TI is betting its consumer business almost wholly on its semiconductor knowhow and on its ability to design and produce large-scale integrated (LSI) circuits—microprocessors and complex chips that synthesize speech. Such circuits made digital watches and calculators feasible, and they serve as the guts of such novel TI products as Speak & Spell and talking language translators. "Our consumer strategy is based on innovative applications of LSI—the source of our strength," says C. Morris Chang, TI's consumer group vice-president. "And the market is exploding as the cost of LSI passes the consumer threshold."

Yet those complex chips are at the root of TI's 1979 consumer problems. The company—indeed, the whole semiconductor industry—was caught without enough production capacity to satisfy last year's booming demand. While TI's semiconductor group had a sellout year, as reflected in its 14% pretax profits on $1.5 billion in sales, TI's consumer group had to make do with fewer chips than it needed. So it used the precious commodity for its sophisticated and higher-priced products, choosing to give up market share in watches and inexpensive calculators. Still, demand overwhelmed capacity for popular products. TI closed its order books for Speak & Spell in September, and put off producing such new products as the translator and computer until yearend. The

Assessing Strategic Advantages and Disadvantages / 185

company is now taking major steps to correct its production-capacity problems. Five chip-fabrication lines, each costing $40 million to $60 million, are under construction.

Annual pessimism. But TI's consumer ills go deeper than chip shortages. The company is run by well-oiled, sophisticated financial models, and its conservative operating ratios impose constraints that force managers to play down estimated growth. "Every October," says one, "TI forces itself to prepare for a recession the following spring. Managers give numbers they know are too low, and when the recession doesn't come, they scramble to get the parts they knew they needed in the first place." If TI consumer managers had been allowed to plan for bigger growth, he adds, they would have been allotted a larger share of the semiconductor group's production.

TI management's insistence on formalized planning does not mesh well with the fast-paced consumer marketplace either. "TI's equations are fine for the high-flying semiconductor business, but they leave no room for the entrepreneurial decisions a consumer business needs," says a former TI marketing manager. If a manager quickly decided to build more calculators, for example, it would take too long to get the product to market. "TI's approach is pretty much to plan it one year and do it the next," says a former technical manager. That works when TI is pioneering new markets, he says, but not when the company is trying to sustain its share of the maturing watch and calculator markets.

Turning to Japan. TI managers were late, for example, in spotting the big trend toward "fashion" calculators. These models, which play tunes and include built-in clocks, alarms, or notebooks, were initially labeled as fads by TI. Consequently, the company was forced to go to Japanese suppliers to fill out its line.

Calculator margins dropped as a result. TI's share of the consumer calculator market, which had risen until 1978, was eroded last year by both Sharp's basic line and Casio's specialty products. That loss was offset by gains in desk-top calculators, where TI competes with Sharp and Canon Inc.

Except for professional calculators, where TI's engineers-turned-managers understand their ultimate consumer, the company simply does not listen to the market as well as its competitors do. "Most people in the consumer business let the market decide what the appropriate product is," says analyst Benjamin M. Rosen of Rosen Research Inc. Adds a former TI watch manager: "TI gives lip service to being customer-oriented. But when it comes right down to it, they consider it their first duty to take TI technology to the outside world."

It seems clear that the company's home computer and educational products are the key to its future growth in consumer products. "In calculators, we saw rapid growth and then a leveling off. And then in watches, growth followed by consolidation," explains TI Vice-President Ronald J. Ritchie. "We've added new categories, and because of the potential product spectrum, I think we're getting ready for explosive growth again."

That growth will also be fueled by TI's patented version of the razor-blade ploy: Solid State Software. "Solid State Software is a growth opportunity we haven't had up to now," says Ritchie. Developed for TI's programmable calculators, these tiny plug-in semiconductor memory modules enable the calculator to perform new tasks. For the home computer, a customer can purchase modules storing programs to play a variety of games and set up personal-finance plans. By summer, two new products—Speak & Read and Speak & Math—will spawn their own families of plug-in modules, as will most future TI educational products.

'Forward pricing.' While there are few signs that TI is loosening its tight management style to accommodate its consumer business, one long-standing practice is changing. TI has tempered its strict adherence to "learning curve" pricing, a formula that requires the introductory price of a product to be tied to an estimate of future volume. Such "forward pricing" won TI dominance in semiconductors, calculators, and—in the initial stages—watches.

TI is now pricing products in relation to supply and value. The company often asks for a premium for its technology edge and, when it no longer enjoys that edge, for its brand name and reputation. The company, for example, has boosted the price of Speak & Spell by 36%, to $75. "That reflects our ability to supply a certain volume," explains Ritchie. "Demand is vastly exceeding supply, so there is a different price point we want to—we need to—sell it at."

While better profit margins may pull TI's consumer operations out of their short-term woes, they will not be of much help to the group in meeting its part of the company's $15 billion goal. "I love two-thirds of their strategy," says Daniel L. Klesken, a Dataquest Inc. analyst. "But I wouldn't want to manage a strategy that has to compete with the Far East, and that's what they're doing with their consumer business."

TANDY'S NEXT BIG DRIVE INTO HOME ELECTRONICS

No one was more surprised than Tandy Corp. when its personal computer became an overnight sensation. Its 7,600 Radio Shack outlets have already sold more than 200,000 TRS-80s, giving the Fort Worth company at least half of this fast-growing market. Now Tandy will open a second consumer electronics market that it hopes will be as successful as the personal computer. On May 27, it will launch a massive campaign to sell a new product that will turn any home telephone and television set into an information retrieval system that will enable customers to tap banks of information in such areas as weather, sports, airline schedules, and stocks and bonds. The new device, called the TRS-80 Videotex, which the company points out is not a computer, will retail for slightly less than $400.

The idea of turning the TV set into a display for calling up computerized information relayed via telephone is not new. Several companies are experimenting with such systems, and any home computer with the right attachment can be used to plug into the growing number of data banks. But Tandy is counting on its manufacturing and massive marketing capabilities to overwhelm competitors—such as Knight-Ridder Newspapers Inc.'s Viewdata Corp. of America, which will soon start test-marketing a system in Coral Gables, Fla. (BW—Feb. 18).

Delivering information. Tandy will begin taking orders for Videotex immediately, according to Lewis F. Kornfeld, president of Tandy's Radio Shack Div. Within a year or so, he claims, the product will be at nearly all Radio Shack outlets. "We feel we are close to providing this kind of product at the ideal price in the ideal time frame and with the ideal distribution system," he says.

CompuServe Inc., the H&R Block Inc. subsidiary that will manage the network delivering information to Videotex users, is equally confident. "This is the first time anyone has put together a distributed system that can really reach the consumer at the retail level and still manage the information-delivery side of

With Videotex, a telephone can tap data banks for display on a TV screen

the business," says Jeffrey M. Wilkins, president of CompuServe.

Initially, CompuServe will provide Videotex subscribers with access to newspapers, wire services, and stock and bond prices for $5 an hour. "We will be adding a number of other information suppliers to the system in the near future," says Wilkins.

The only link. Videotex consists of a "black box" that connects television and telephone, a small memory bank, and a keyboard. The keyboard enables the user to call up the information required, while the memory allows information to be printed out on the screen after the telephone connection is severed. The keyboard also gives a user the ability to communicate with other Videotex users over the CompuServe network.

Tandy claims that its machine is the only one that will link any kind of television set with any kind of telephone. It plans to sell $200 decoders to users of its TRS-80 personal computers, as well as other personal computers, and to give them access to the information service. At least one industry expert is already giving the new Tandy product mixed reviews, however.

"I think that there are enough computer-communications buffs out there to buy [the Videotex] by the scores and even thousands," says N. Richard Miller, a vice-president with Diebold Inc. in New York. But he adds: "The longer-term market still has to be proven. How easy will it be for people to seek out the information they want, and how costly? The $400 still sounds like a high price for the basic equipment." ∎

WHERE K MART GOES NOW THAT IT'S NO. 2

S.S. Kresge Co. in 1962 began a blitzkrieg expansion, transforming itself from a sleepy variety store chain into one of the new breed of national discounters offering low prices, value, and service for a quick turnover of merchandise. The formula proved so successful that the Detroit-based company, now known as K mart Corp., today has 1,900 units blanketing the country and has vaulted past J. C. Penney Co. to become the nation's second-largest retailer. Last year, K mart's $358 million earnings exceeded Sears, Roebuck & Co.'s $349 million in merchandising net income, and many analysts predict that by 1985, K mart will have surpassed the Chicago-based giant in dollar sales volume. K mart's 1979 sales amounted to $12.7 billion, while Sears' merchandising revenues were $17.5 billion.

But although K mart is within fingertip reach of retailing's pinnacle, it is also nearing a dangerous crossroads. The recession, increasingly fierce competition, saturation of major markets, and soaring operating costs are making it nearly impossible for K mart to maintain its 20% annual growth rate. Moreover, the growing strength of such regional discounters as Wal-Mart Stores Inc. and Caldor Inc. have underscored K mart's merchandising weaknesses, particularly in apparel. As a result, the company is now projecting a modest 12% annual growth rate for the next three years—much of that dependent on a continuing addition of new stores. K mart management must decide whether to accept slower growth and concentrate on internal productivity gains, or to diversify and acquire other businesses that offer higher growth potential.

K mart seems unsure of which direction to pursue. Earlier this year, the company made its first tentative step toward diversification when it acquired Furr's Cafeterias Inc., a small chain in the Southwest. Still, executives insist that the retailer's future lies in fine-tuning its merchandising skills to reap larger profits from existing operations. "There will be no change in direction, but a change in emphasis," declares Robert E. Dewar, K mart's chairman since 1972. One change will come at the company's annual meeting on May 27, when Dewar, 57, will turn over the chairmanship to Vice-Chairman Bernard M. Fauber, also 57, who became chief executive officer in January. Explains Dewar, who remains a director: "We have to do something different."

Boosting turnover. There is a sense of urgency because K mart is losing momentum. Preoccupied over the past five years with building more than 175 new stores annually, the company, according to many competitors and industry analysts, lost sight of the need to maximize profit from every square inch of store space. Fauber concedes the problems. One immediate goal, for example, is to boost inventory turnover in the stores by 50% within five years. "We looked good at one time, but we've slipped throughout the years," the incoming chairman says.

Inventory turnover, a key measure of a retailer's success, has dropped from 8 times a year at K mart in the 1960s to 3.8 last year. By comparison, general merchandise retailers on the average turned over their stocks 4.7 times last year, and discounters managed 4 turns.

Moreover, K mart's earnings growth is lagging behind sales—the latter rose 12.8% last year while net income was up only 4.2%—and profit margins fell from 2.9% in 1978 to 2.8% last year. The company's goal is a 3% margin. Meanwhile, selling, general, and administrative expenses rose from 21.5% of sales to 22.5%, a trend the company fears will continue. Part of the drag was a disappointing fourth-quarter performance, when profits dropped for the first time in six years largely because of excessive markdowns.

Of course, many of K mart's difficulties are shared by other retailers facing a gloomy period as consumer spending and borrowing falter. Profits for the first quarter dropped 58.9% at Penney and 60% at Sears as rising unemployment and credit curbs took their toll. In contrast, K mart's profits dipped 13.2% in the quarter, partly because it is less affected than are other retailers by government efforts to restrain credit. The company's Thrifty credit card was dropped in 1974, and, while the chain has accepted bank cards since 1970, their use represents only 10% of sales.

The recession has already altered K mart's expansion plans. Last year its performance was bolstered by the opening of 193 new stores. Plans called for 2,400 K mart stores by 1984 and 3,000 by 1989, but the goal is now under review. Snaps an executive of a Midwest discount chain: "If they were to stop opening stores, would they be doing 12% to 15% increases? I hardly think so."

Wetting their feet. Indeed, on a store-for-store basis, the company is posting sales gains of only 5% to 6% a year, about even with the rate of general merchandise inflation. "I'm not optimistic about K mart's prospects this year, and [I] expect results to be flat," says Stanley Iverson, an analyst with Chicago-based Duff & Phelps.

That prospect may be one reason K mart is now considering acquisitions. Executives describe the recent purchase of Furr's as a logical outgrowth of the cafeterias that K mart operates in its stores, and they say it met their profitability, management, and growth criteria. But Furr's, with 76 units, adds less than 1% to K mart's sales and is in a field vulnerable to cutbacks in customer spending. The acquisition's primary function is to serve as a learning and testing experience. "They're getting

188 / Readings from *Business Week*

their feet wet," says Stuart Robbins, an analyst with Paine Webber Mitchell Hutchins Inc. "If it works out well, they will probably do several small deals like this until they make up their mind what direction to take." Robbins suggests that to bolster its return on investment, K mart might want to look outside the retailing sphere to such rapidly growing areas as electronics.

The diversification issue was controversial enough to drive out Vice-Chairman Walter H. Teninga last May, after 23 years with K mart—a remarkable event for a company that claims an "infinitesimal" management turnover. Teninga was the chief development officer, and he oversaw the diversification planning that began in 1977. Yet no moves were made until after his departure, when K mart in 1979 offered $200 million for Morrison Inc., an Alabama-based cafeteria chain. K mart backed off once the 384-unit Morrison rejected the offer. It then acquired Furr's for $70.4 million. While some say Teninga was eased out to make way for Fauber, the company line is that management was unwilling to diversify as aggressively as the former vice-chairman wanted.

Indeed, K mart's inertia is born of its success. The basic strategy established by company founder Sebastian S. Kresge in 1899 still stands. "Sebastian had a better idea—sell a lot at a low margin," says Chairman Dewar. "And that concept is still here today." S. S. Kresge Co. branched out from variety stores in 1960, when profits began declining. Experimental conversion of Kresge stores into Jupiter discount units led to the introduction of the first K mart in 1962. By 1977, K mart units were contributing 96% of Kresge's sales and earnings, and the corporate name was changed.

Saturation. Much of K mart's growth came at Sears' expense during the 1970s, as the Chicago giant first upgraded its merchandise and then slashed prices when its customers became confused and turned to alternative retailers. From 1974 to 1978, K mart revenues grew 21%, and the company accounted for 6.1% of total general merchandise, apparel, and furniture sales. During that period, Penney's sales grew only 12.6%, and Sears' 11%. When Sears engaged in heavy promotional activity in 1977 to win back lost market share, it triggered a price war among the nation's 28 leading retailers. These leaders now account for 41% of general merchandise, apparel, and furniture sales, up from 36% in 1974—wiping out weaker competitors and making further gains more difficult and expensive, especially since major markets have become saturated. By now some 276 of the country's major metropolitan areas have outlets of at least five of the leading 28 retailers.

The development is prompting many retailers to explore prospects in smaller towns and the suburban fringes. But a new crew of general merchandisers and discounters—including Wal-Mart, Caldor, and Fed-Mart—has already entrenched itself in these markets while the major retailers have been off building in urban areas. The sales productivity of these newcomers, with inflation and store expansion factored out, is impressive. From 1974 to 1978, Caldor's real gain was 30%; Fed-Mart's, 37%; and Wal-Mart's, 47.5%. K mart's real gain of 12.6% during that period looks impressive only against Penney's 6.9% gain or Sears' 0.5% decline.

K mart believes it is well-positioned to plumb both the urban and small-town markets. It claims that only 60% of its urban market potential has been reached, based on a new strategy of locating stores as close as 3 mi. from each other; previously, 10 mi. had been considered the optimum distance. Moreover, with 400 units in operation, K mart is one of the few major retailers that already has a strong presence in smaller market areas. These scaled-down units—40,000 sq. ft. to 73,000 sq. ft., compared with the typical K mart of 84,000 sq. ft.—will account for nearly half of the company's new stores in the future. K mart's primary shopper is between 25 and 44 years old, with a household income ranging from $15,000 to $35,000, a demographic group that is growing rapidly. The company is also optimistic because shoppers are becoming polarized between low-margin and high-priced stores, a trend that is expected to accelerate as the economy worsens and middle-class households "trade down" for goods. "A lot of volume just flows on," says Dewar. "The buyer will be there."

Today's consumer, however, is demanding more value for the dollar, and K mart is striving to upgrade its merchandise quality to draw former department-store customers. The company's aim is to attract shoppers by offering the lowest possible prices on a wide array of commodity merchandise, then lure those customers to other areas of the store that offer more discretionary, higher-margined goods.

Poor image. But, says Michael G. Wellman, director of planning and research, "we still suffer from the image that our shoppers are blue-collar, low-income people. So we are in a series of constraints in adding better quality and yet not improving our gross margins."

To upgrade its appeal, K mart has added 14-karat gold jewelry, higher-quality house paints, and Book Korners, which features best-sellers at 25% off list price. The biggest push, however, is in softgoods that offer the best opportunity for increasing margins. For example, Russell A. Hansen, executive vice-president of merchandising, is putting half of his men's sweater merchandising dollars this fall into more than 70,000 acrylic loop sweaters that will sell for $18 to $20, compared with the usual K mart price of $11. The company will pay $12 per sweater and achieve a margin three to five points higher than usual on a lower-priced item.

Whether K mart will be able to sell the sweaters, though, is questionable. The chain does not have a reputation as a good merchandiser, particularly for higher-priced, discretionary items. "They're not as good as they should be, and they're not cutting it in apparel," says analyst Robbins. "What's needed is better presentation, better store housekeeping, and more new products." The chain only recently converted its apparel departments from "bargain" table displays to racks, and although that is an improvement, it is still stark and not conducive to impulse shopping. Apparel sales declined from 12.7% of total revenues in 1978 to 11.8% in 1979.

New layout. Even in the company's strongest departments, sales are lagging. "We're a major factor in the home-center business, but we haven't succeeded as we wanted to," says planning director Wellman. The chain is now consolidating its paint, hardware, and lumber departments into unified home centers of 20,000 sq. ft. and adding new hardware products. "We do a great job of bringing people into the stores, but we don't fully satisfy their needs," says Fauber, who is expected to make important changes to upgrade the type of goods K mart carries and the way these goods are presented. This summer, the incoming chairman says, K mart will begin testing a new store layout and colors featuring a more sophisticated earth-tone motif to replace the present white-and-pastel theme.

Fauber aims to increase store productivity and decrease operating costs. That is one reason why pharmacy and optical departments have been added to some stores, and why more in-store services such as dental clinics are under consideration. At the same time, all new and

K mart faces a crossroads: Should it accept slower growth or try to diversify?

remodeled stores have had their ceilings lowered by two feet and lights placed farther apart to reduce energy costs. K mart is installing a new data processing system, nicknamed KIN for K mart Information Network, to cut costs and facilitate the flow of information.

Slow to computerize. The snail's pace at which the chain has computerized its record-keeping until now astounds many observers. As late as last year, corporate headquarters was still grappling with an annual avalanche of 24 million invoices mailed in from the field, which had to be fed into a central computer to produce analyses that were then mailed back to store managers. KIN will eliminate the paperwork, but all stores will not be plugged into the system until 1984—14 years after the company began studying the idea. Even then, the system falls short of the direct point-of-sale (POS) monitoring that major competitors began using several years ago.

The company's extreme caution makes its recent plunge into box stores all the more remarkable. Popular in the Sunbelt and growing elsewhere, box stores sell groceries from cartons at cut-rate prices. When K mart suddenly opened one last October in a vacant building adjoining one of its branches in Detroit, sales were 30% below plan, and the store closed less than a month later. Says Dewar: "It wasn't a full commitment. We really do believe in experimentation." But observers think the box store was dropped to avoid a confrontation with the United Food & Commercial Workers Union, which has been trying to organize K mart for years.

In short, the conservative policies that have fueled K mart's success in the past now threaten the innovation needed to maintain momentum. Company officials shrug off such criticism, preferring to describe themselves as "frugal." But the question is whether K mart can pace its competitors in the 1980s with only minor adjustments to its basic strategy. ■

WORD PROCESSING

WANG'S GAME PLAN FOR THE OFFICE

With such giants as International Business Machines Corp. and Xerox Corp. moving full tilt into the automated office market with products that are setting new price and performance standards, competitors and customers alike have been eager to see how Wang Laboratories Inc. would respond. The Lowell (Mass.) company is in the spotlight because it managed to parlay an early lead in word processing systems into spectacular growth and dominance of the market for large, shared word processing systems. But Wang lacks many of the system components that would make it a full-line office supplier.

Now Wang is making it clear that it intends to match everything that its larger competitors offer—and more. "Our whole thrust in office automation is to create our own direction and play in our own ball park," says Frederick A. Wang, vice-president for market planning and development. The first major move in this strategy will come on Dec. 9, when the company is expected to announce the Wangwriter, its smallest and lowest-priced word processor.

That announcement has been looked for since June, when IBM brought out its low-cost model, the Displaywriter (BW—June 30). But Wang will surprise the industry, according to experts who have been briefed on company plans. For one thing, Wang plans to make it possible for all its word processing equipment to communicate easily with the enormous base of IBM mainframe computer systems installed at many companies. And it will also unveil its concept for a local network to link machines together in the office.

"Wang is already No. 1 in word processing," notes Patricia B. Seybold, editor of *The Seybold Report on Word Processing*. "It is clearly trying to claim the No. 1 position in office automation."

A basic system. The linchpin of this effort will be the company's new Wangwriter. A very basic word processing system with a 24-line TV-like display, the desktop unit will cost $7,500, dropping to $7,125 in quantity orders. This pricing undercuts the Displaywriter, which starts at $7,895, but the Wang product is somewhat more limited than its IBM competitor. The Wangwriter, for example, comes equipped with a less powerful processor and will be sold only with a 20-character-per-second (cps) printer, while IBM offers three printers with speeds of 15 cps, 40 cps, and 60 cps.

Nonetheless, observers believe that the Wangwriter has one advantage that will make it a winner from the start: availability. Wang claims that it has 500 machines ready to ship now, and promises delivery within three months for all subsequent orders. IBM customers, on the other hand, report that they are faced with up to a year's wait for their Displaywriters. IBM itself is quoting 38 weeks delivery. "If Wang can keep delivery dates down, it will drive IBM mad," comments Amy D. Wohl, president of Advanced Office Concepts Corp. in Bala Cynwyd (Pa.).

At the same time, the Wangwriter could prove to be just the tonic that Wang needs for its ailing service reputation. Its sales, which grew an average 70% annually over the last three years and reached $543 million in the year ended June 30, had outdistanced Wang's ability to service its products. But the Wangwriter, like IBM's Displaywriter, is equipped with built-in diagnostic circuitry to help repairmen correct problems more quickly. "The Wangwriter is a highly reliable product with low-level support and service," says one veteran industry observer. "It will help Wang get on its feet in support and service."

First-time users. Wang is counting on its new word processor as the entrée to lucrative new markets. Already the company has hired 100 new sales people to push the Wangwriter as a stand-alone (self-contained) unit solely to first-time users of word processing equipment. Until now it has lacked the products to make it a force in this market. Even though Wang holds 46% of the market for shared-logic systems—clusters of word processing workstations that rely on a central processor for logic and memory—it accounted for only $40 million of the $750 million worth of stand-alone models sold last year.

Now the company hopes to change that. "With the Wangwriter, we have made text-editing functions cost effective for the secretary who doesn't spend all day typing," Wang claims. "We expect the Wangwriter to substantially increase our market share in the electronic typewriter and stand-alone word processor marketplaces."

Wang also expects the Wangwriter to help boost its sales to big business. Now, only 25% of Wang's sales come from large corporate customers. But the company aims to increase that figure to 60% by 1990, and the Wangwriter is crucial to that kind of growth. The machine is priced for national accounts at $6,900 for small volumes, dropping to $6,525 for larger quantities. And, within a year, the machine will have communications capabilities that will tie it into Wang's own electronic mail system, outside computer

Assessing Strategic Advantages and Disadvantages / 191

time-sharing networks, as well as IBM mainframes. As a result, the Wangwriter will become a low-cost terminal alternative for companies with IBM systems, according to Wang.

Data exchange. Wang is betting that by also making its VS minicomputers compatible with IBM mainframes, they can act as a similar draw for large corporate users who need distributed processing. Indeed, the company expects that just the promise of this capability—still 18 months off—will boost 1981 sales of VS systems to $300 million, up 71% from $175 million this year.

Some observers acknowledge that the company's highly optimistic forecast could be in the ball park. "Wang has significantly enhanced its word processing position in national accounts that have IBM mainframes," says one industry expert. "They are already the incumbent in the office. Now it will be harder than ever to displace them."

Outsiders are not quite so sanguine, however, about Wang's blueprint for a local network. The company claims that its offering will go further than that of such competitors as Xerox's Ethernet, because it will handle all types of information—words, data, images, voice, facsimile, and graphics—on a wide-band coaxial cable that will connect users within a building to one another and to outside communication networks. But the Wang network will not be available for two years, and Wang watchers suggest that the company may be offering more than it can deliver. "Wang has traditionally had trouble with communications technology," says editor Seybold. "The question is whether Wang can implement a broad-band network in time to satisfy its customers."

Cool. Not surprisingly, Wang's competitors evince little concern over the company's latest moves. "The Wangwriter opens up the market for everyone that's in it," says Wesley E. Cantrell, president of Lanier Business Products Inc., the Atlanta-based company that dominates the stand-alone market with its "No Problem" line of word processors.

But Wang clearly does not intend to be left behind in the race to supply the office of the future. And if the company can deliver on its promises, the chances are it will not be. "Wang is going to come out looking like the company that is ahead of everyone else," says consultant Wohl. "And that's crucial to maintaining their marketing momentum." ■

192 / Readings from *Business Week*

KEY PHARMACEUTICALS: Bidding for Growth through Unique Products

For most of its 33 years, Key Pharmaceuticals Inc., of Miami, hovered near the bottom of the drug industry. It was among the tiniest U.S. drug manufacturers, with annual sales of only $2.1 million as recently as five years ago and losses in the early 1970s that appeared to make its case terminal. Now, the company has more than recovered. Major breakthroughs in new products for asthma and heart disease are expected to push sales this year to $25 million—up nearly four times over the past two years—and net earnings as high as $4 million. More important, new agreements with giant foreign companies, including Japan's Mitsubishi Chemical Industries Ltd., hold the potential for making Key a more significant force in the pharmaceutical business in the 1980s, with sales well over $100 million per year.

Most unusual is the way in which Key has achieved its success. It has followed a single plan: never to take on the expense of developing new drugs, but to focus on improving ways to deliver existing drugs to the body. Key's newest product—and the one with the most potential—is a radically new way to administer nitroglycerin to victims of angina pectoris. The product, Nitro-Dur, is a round plastic strip, like an adhesive bandage, which the patient affixes to his arm. Nitroglycerin from the strip gradually seeps through the skin for 24 hours. This would replace the method that millions of patients now use—placing a tablet under the tongue when an attack begins. The alternative has been to smear a messy nitroglycerin ointment on the chest, where it permeates the skin but can stain clothing.

Recognizing limits. The average large pharmaceutical house spends an estimated eight years and $50 million bringing a new drug to market. Nitro-Dur, just coming on stream for Key, took three years and less than $1 million. Key's small size, concedes Michael Jaharis Jr., president and chief executive officer, means that Key "can never hope to break into the ball game" of developing new drugs. Jaharis' strategy is built on a recognition of his limitations.

Those limitations were extreme when Jaharis took office in 1971. Founded in 1947, Key had languished for decades trying to sell over-the-counter skin creams and a small number of drugs, including a nitroglycerin tablet called Nitroglyn, introduced in 1954 and now passé. In 1969, the company, with sales of just $1.2 million, sustained a catastrophe within its small management team. Sales manager Carl Brasfield died, and President Jack Kantor became seriously ill, just a year after the death of Chairman Nathaniel Klein.

Jaharis, a former director of ethical drugs at Miles Laboratories Inc., and Phillip Frost, Key's current chairman and a physician, acquired a controlling interest in the company and moved into the top jobs. They found, according to Jaharis, "a ship going down." Key had a loss of $521,085 in 1969—an amount equal to nearly half its revenues. Jaharis quickly closed two foreign plants and instituted rigorous financial controls while he beefed up funds for product development and marketing.

Right now, Jaharis is riding the coattails of the company's first big product, an asthma treatment called Theo-Dur. This drug is merely theophyllin, a medication known and used for 50 years, but it is contained in a "sustained release" capsule, swallowed by the patient, that releases the medicine in even amounts over 8 to 12 hours. Other drug companies have also made time-release asthma medicines, but Key's has won a rare clearance from the Food & Drug Administration for promotion as a "zero-order release" drug—meaning that the timing mechanism is so efficient as to be nearly perfect. "That doesn't exist with any other product," boasts Frost. Theo-Dur alone is expected to account for 70% of Key's total sales this year and has become the most prescribed theophyllin medicine for asthma, according to Pharmaceutical Data Service Inc., a Phoenix market research company.

Nitro-Dur is just beginning to be reviewed by physicians. It has been undergoing tests for six months at the Uni-

The costly development of new drugs was not the path for a small company

versity of Michigan's medical school, where Bertram Pitt, chairman of the cardiovascular department, says it has "worked the very way it should have." Key has entered into preliminary agreements with four foreign drug companies to sell Nitro-Dur outside the U.S. market, which Key is holding for itself. These companies would pay Key $6.2 million for licenses, and royalties from foreign sales would supply future income.

Jaharis is hoping that Nitro-Dur will be just one of a family of drugs delivered by plastic strip. Key contends that up to one-third of all current prescription drugs could be administered this way, including hormones, contraceptives, and burn medicines.

The Japanese connection. Key got the money to finance production of Nitro-Dur last year, when Mitsubishi Chemical, a subsidiary of Mitsubishi Corp., bought 10% of the company's common stock through a new issue for $4 million. In August, Mitsubishi bought an additional 100,000 shares, or 1.7%, this time from Jaharis and Frost, each of whom was paid a cool $1 million. The two men still control 28% of Key's total shares. Perhaps the most significant part of the Japanese connection is a new agreement by which the two companies will set up joint research efforts. The products that come from the joint venture are to be sold by Key in Western countries and by Mitsubishi in Asia.

Although Jaharis started with a plan tailored to Key's small size, the company may now outgrow that strategy. "In the next 10 to 20 years," Jaharis declares, "we're looking to build a major company." ∎

MOBIL'S SUCCESSFUL EXPLORATION

Making people remember it is an oil company

When Mobil Corp. purchased Marcor Inc. six years ago, it set off a storm of protest. Many congressmen quickly concluded that Mobil was simply using the rich profits it earned from the fourfold price increase that accompanied the Arab oil embargo to finance a plunge into nonenergy businesses, and they held up Mobil as a reason why restrictive legislation against the oil companies was needed.

Oil executives were equally upset by Mobil's move. It undermined their argument that their embarrassingly high profits were needed to finance expanded exploration programs to reduce the nation's dependence on Mideast oil. Within Mobil itself, many executives concluded that the $1.7 billion acquisition of Marcor, the parent of Container Corp. of America and Montgomery Ward & Co., was Mobil's first step out of the oil business. Even before it became a fact, critics began labeling Mobil as a conglomerate, and that image persists. "People forget we're an oil company," complains William P. Tavoulareas, the company's president.

Indeed, it has been so well-forgotten that hardly anyone has noticed that Mobil is racking up one of the hottest exploration records in the oil business today. Ironically, the Marcor acquisition—for all the attention paid to it—turned out to be a diversion from the course Mobil had charted more than a decade before: reducing its heavy dependence on Mideast crude by building a strong exploration program where previously it had one of the industry's weakest.

The Marcor deal was made just as Mobil was beginning to flex its new exploration muscle. It now seems that Mobil's top management—a collection of conservative financial men—suddenly

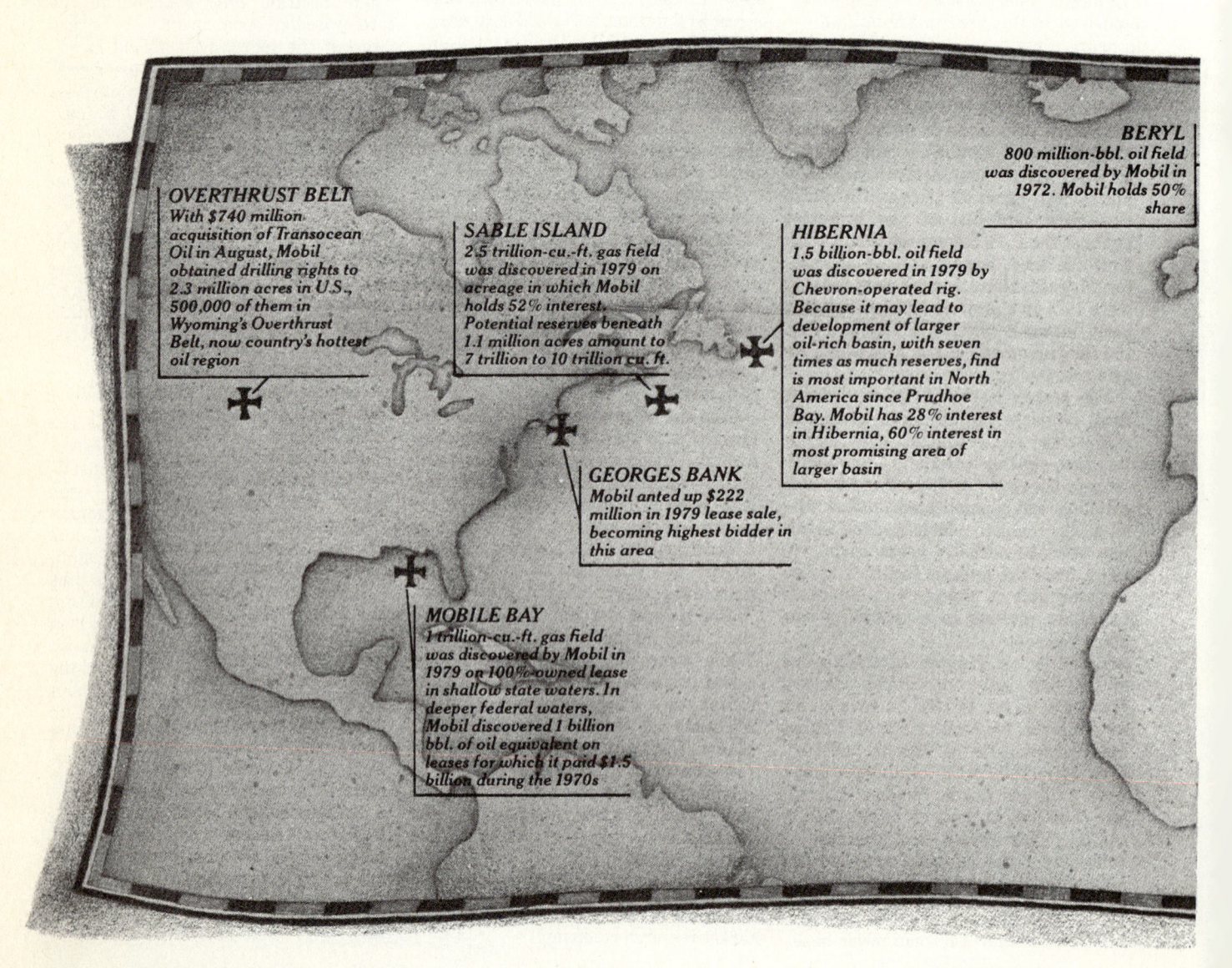

OVERTHRUST BELT
With $740 million acquisition of Transocean Oil in August, Mobil obtained drilling rights to 2.3 million acres in U.S., 500,000 of them in Wyoming's Overthrust Belt, now country's hottest oil region

SABLE ISLAND
2.5 trillion-cu.-ft. gas field was discovered in 1979 on acreage in which Mobil holds 52% interest. Potential reserves beneath 1.1 million acres amount to 7 trillion to 10 trillion cu. ft.

GEORGES BANK
Mobil anted up $222 million in 1979 lease sale, becoming highest bidder in this area

MOBILE BAY
1 trillion-cu.-ft. gas field was discovered by Mobil in 1979 on 100%-owned lease in shallow state waters. In deeper federal waters, Mobil discovered 1 billion bbl. of oil equivalent on leases for which it paid $1.5 billion during the 1970s

HIBERNIA
1.5 billion-bbl. oil field was discovered in 1979 by Chevron-operated rig. Because it may lead to development of larger oil-rich basin, with seven times as much reserves, find is most important in North America since Prudhoe Bay. Mobil has 28% interest in Hibernia, 60% interest in most promising area of larger basin

BERYL
800 million-bbl. oil field was discovered by Mobil in 1972. Mobil holds 50% share

lost their nerve and began to doubt the wisdom of putting all their chips behind a segment of the oil business that had been largely foreign to them.

Marcor was an aberration, however, not part of any far-reaching diversification plan, and Mobil has gone on to make a string of oil and gas strikes that would be unique even for such traditionally successful explorers as Standard Oil Co. of California (Chevron) and Standard Oil Co. (Indiana) (Amoco). The discoveries seem to have given Mobil's top management an unaccustomed confidence in exploration ventures, the very element that was missing, even though the company first made a commitment to a strong exploration program in the 1960s. Now, Mobil's top managers insist that they are not interested in making another diversification hedge and concede that Marcor would not be bought if the decision were to be made today (page 116). "We've hit on some kind of formula in exploration," says Tavoulareas. "We hope we are in a cycle where each year we can find a big field, and if we do, I'm not worried about our future."

In just the last 18 months that formula has given Mobil a major piece of the action in nine giant oil and gas discoveries, each of which will net Mobil the equivalent of at least 100 million bbl. of new reserves. The largest and most publicized is Hibernia, the major oil field discovered a year ago by a Chevron-operated rig drilling 200 mi. off the east coast of Newfoundland. With a 28% interest—the largest—in the field, Mobil stands to gain 400 million of the estimated 1.5 billion bbl. of oil found in the Hibernia structure.

Seeking safer ground

Were it not for a batch of smaller but still impressive discoveries around the globe, Hibernia might easily be considered a fluke for Mobil, because nearly all the drilling leading to the discovery was financed by Chevron and Gulf Oil Corp. This work earned them an interest in the Hibernia block, which once belonged entirely to Mobil (page 115). In addition to Hibernia, however, Mobil has the largest stake in major gas discoveries made since the beginning of last year off Nova Scotia, off the coast of Cameroon, in Mobile Bay on the Gulf Coast, and onshore in Germany. According to outside estimates—and privately confirmed by Mobil exploration executives—Mobil's share in these finds, along with four other oil and gas discoveries in the 18 months, amounts to the equivalent of 2 billion bbl. of oil. That figure—yet to be added to the company's books—is equal to 40% of Mobil's current reserves. Beyond that, the undiscovered but potential reserves now estimated to exist on Mobil's acreage surrounding these discoveries could add 5 billion bbl. more.

"Mobil was an also-ran in exploration," says Owen D. Thomas, vice-president of exploration at Phillips Petroleum Co. "This puts it in the forefront of the exploration business, in the same league with Chevron and Amoco." Adds Bruce E. Lazier, vice-president and energy analyst for Paine Webber Mitchell Hutchins Inc.: "In the 1970s, Mobil has been transformed from the worst of the internationals in oil exploration into the best."

If Mobil's recent finds come close to reaching their potential, they will have an enormous impact not only on the

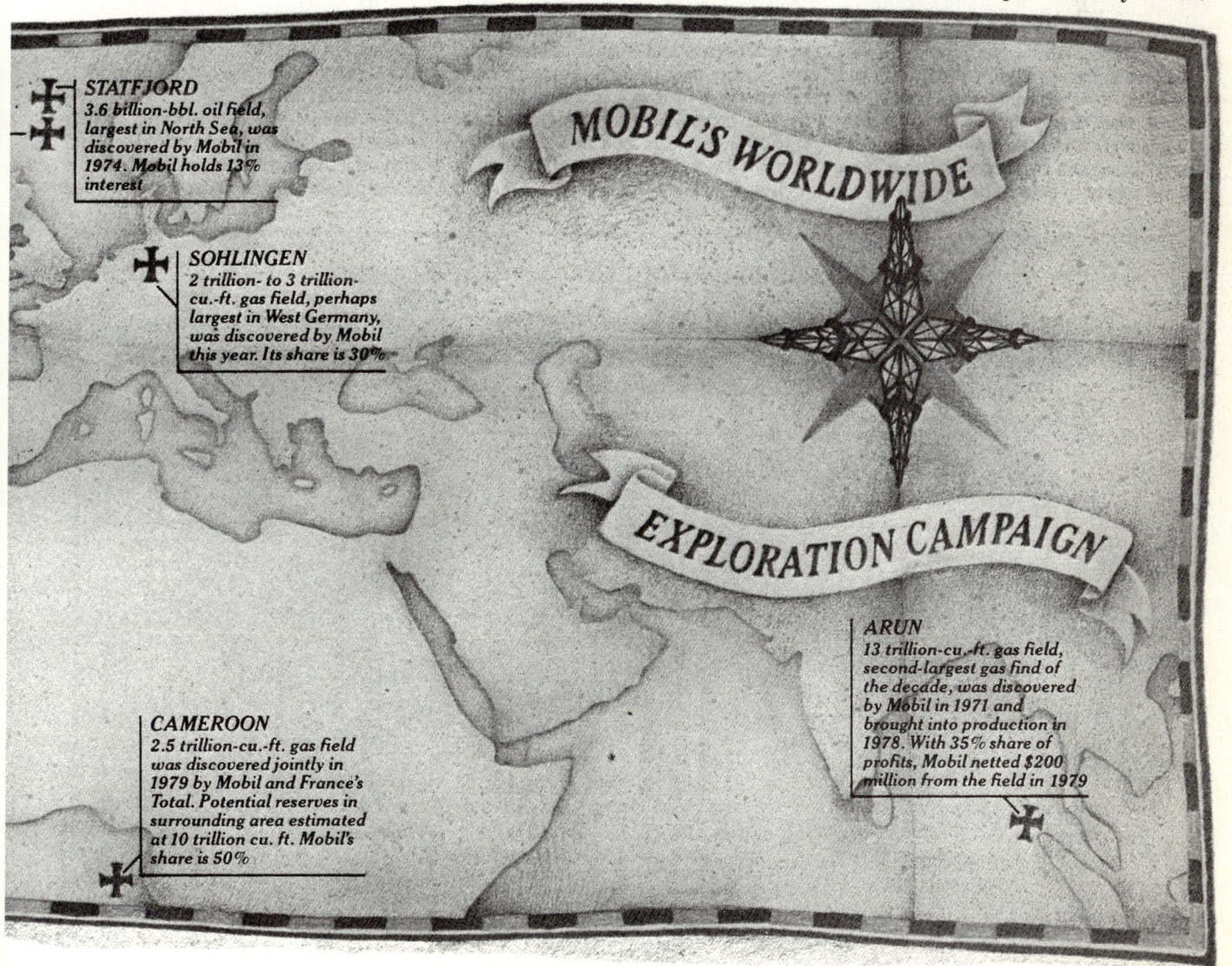

MOBIL'S WORLDWIDE EXPLORATION CAMPAIGN

STATFJORD
3.6 billion-bbl. oil field, largest in North Sea, was discovered by Mobil in 1974. Mobil holds 13% interest

SOHLINGEN
2 trillion- to 3 trillion-cu.-ft. gas field, perhaps largest in West Germany, was discovered by Mobil this year. Its share is 30%

CAMEROON
2.5 trillion-cu.-ft. gas field was discovered jointly in 1979 by Mobil and France's Total. Potential reserves in surrounding area estimated at 10 trillion cu. ft. Mobil's share is 50%

ARUN
13 trillion-cu.-ft. gas field, second-largest gas find of the decade, was discovered by Mobil in 1971 and brought into production in 1978. With 35% share of profits, Mobil netted $200 million from the field in 1979

Illustration by Kirsten Soderlind

Assessing Strategic Advantages and Disadvantages / 195

company's profits but also on its competitive position. These discoveries will give it a more secure crude supply than it has ever had. As Mobil develops its new oil and gas fields, it seems certain that it will increase its total reserves during the first half of the 1980s, quite possibly becoming the only major to accomplish that through exploration. Although it is impossible to predict exactly how much help the new reserves will provide, there is little question that they will greatly alleviate Mobil's most serious competitive handicap: It is among the most crude-short of the majors. Last year its net oil production accounted for only 30% of its refineries' needs. And the new reserves will finally begin to reduce the company's dependence on oil from the Middle East, which has accounted for more than half of Mobil's supply since the mid-1960s.

That reduced dependence could not be more timely. The war between Iraq and Iran provides further evidence that supplies from the Middle East are insecure. And because of the desire of Saudi Arabia to market much of its own oil, rather than sell through Mobil and the other Aramco partners, Mobil's biggest single source of crude is extremely vulnerable. Mobil's discoveries around the world will not give it the security of supply enjoyed by some domestic majors, such as Amoco, but they clearly improve Mobil's position among the internationals, particularly those such as Texaco Inc. that have fared poorly in exploration.

It is ironic that Mobil should suddenly emerge as a leader in international oil exploration. In the 1950s and 1960s, Mobil concentrated on improving its downstream refining and marketing operations, not on exploration. Indeed, it sometimes acted as if refining and marketing were the only segments of the business it cared about. In the late 1940s, when Chevron and Texaco offered Mobil and Exxon each a 20% share in their lucrative production concession in Saudi Arabia, Exxon persuaded Mobil to take only 10%, while it took 30%. This decision cost Mobil more than $3 billion in profits. Similarly, in 1949 the company sold at cost to Conoco Inc. and Newmont Mining Corp. a half interest in all its oil and gas leases in unexplored areas of the Gulf of Mexico. Later, the areas turned out to be highly productive. As late as 1965, Mobil relinquished acreage in Libya that was promptly picked up by Occidental Petroleum Corp. Oxy found more than 2 billion bbl. of oil on the property.

Throughout this period, Mobil's board—dominated by refining, marketing, and finance specialists—consistently rejected or only weakly supported drilling prospects proposed by the company's exploration staff. That staff was one of the first to perform seismic work on Alaska's North Slope, and it vigorously pressed the company to get into the action there. But the board, clearly uncomfortable with taking exploration gambles, did not show similar aggressiveness in bidding when the acreage was auctioned by the state beginning in 1965. Mobil did not even bid on what later became the Prudhoe Bay field. "The financial people in this company did a disservice to the exploration people," concedes Rawleigh Warner Jr., Mobil's chairman, who himself rose through the financial ranks. "The poor people in exploration were adversely impacted by people [in the company] who knew nothing about oil and gas."

The Marcor purchase seemed merely to continue this management discomfort with oil and gas exploration. At the time of the purchase, some observers believed diversification made business sense for Mobil. To all appearances, the company was hopelessly unprepared to replace the Mideast oil it had easily purchased—and was just as easily losing as the Saudis nationalized their oil.

Such perceptions were off the mark. Long before the Marcor deal, Mobil had carefully planned a sweeping reorganization to make the company an exploration powerhouse and diversify its oil sources. It had quietly acquired drilling leases in dozens of unexplored areas around the world. It had centralized a once-fragmented exploration group, elevated its status within the corporation, and given it better access to the board.

A full plate

Now, Mobil's commitment to oil and gas exploration is so strong that the

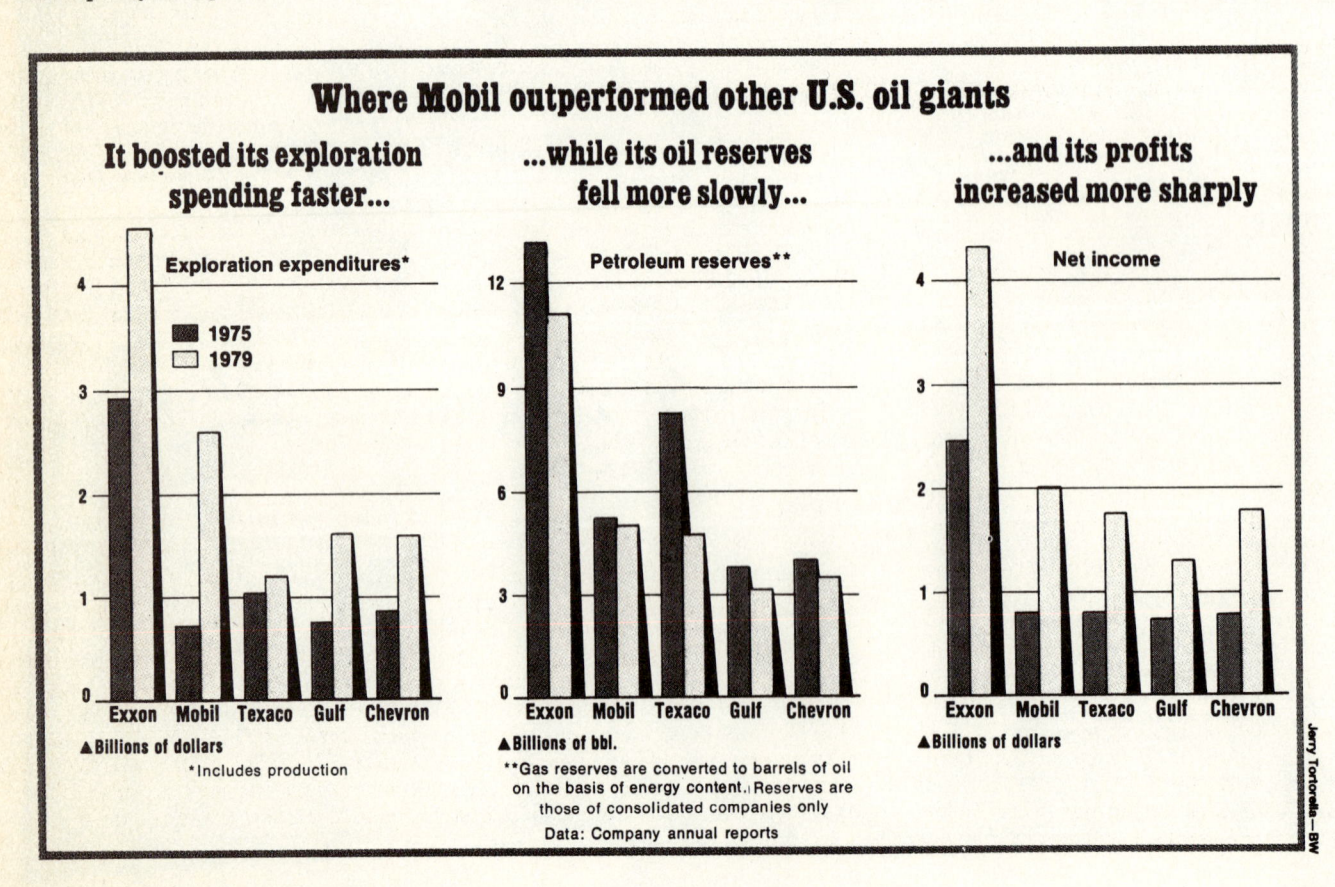

Where Mobil outperformed other U.S. oil giants

It boosted its exploration spending faster...

Exploration expenditures*
■ 1975
□ 1979
▲ Billions of dollars
*Includes production

...while its oil reserves fell more slowly...

Petroleum reserves**
▲ Billions of bbl.
**Gas reserves are converted to barrels of oil on the basis of energy content. Reserves are those of consolidated companies only
Data: Company annual reports

...and its profits increased more sharply

Net income
▲ Billions of dollars

company has shown much less interest than other oil majors in diversifying beyond oil into other energy forms. Some companies are planning huge investments in oil shale or coal liquefaction, for example. But Mobil has been content just to line up reserves.

One big reason is that Mobil's plate is suddenly full of oil and gas projects. Several of its recent discoveries have apparently opened up new petroleum provinces, the development of which could keep the company busy for at least the next five years. More important than Mobil's interest in Hibernia, for example, is the commanding control it has over the drilling rights for the geologic area around the discovery. Called the Jeanne d'Arc Basin, a 50 x 200 mi. geologic depression, the province contains about a dozen structures. Despite some recent disappointments at Ben Nevis, a structure adjacent to Hibernia, where oil was found, but not in commercial quantities, executives at Gulf Oil (which has 25% of Hibernia) and Chevron (which has 22%) estimate that the drilling done so far suggests that the area has a reserve potential of as much as 10 billion bbl. That would make it the largest oil find since Prudhoe Bay was discovered in 1968.

Potential is not the same as proven reserves, of course, and the governments of Canada and Newfoundland must settle their conflicting claims to jurisdiction over the territory before the area can be developed (BW—Sept. 15). Still, Mobil has a 60% interest in the 6 million acres considered the most promising in the basin, and even after adjusting for equity changes now being demanded by the government of Newfoundland, Mobil's share of potential reserves could reach 4 billion bbl. "It will do for Mobil what Prudhoe Bay did for ARCO and Sohio," predicts Paine Webber's Lazier.

Mobil's exploration successes began popping up in the early 1970s. In 1971 the company discovered Arun, a 13 trillion-cu.-ft. gas field in Indonesia that ranks as the second-largest gas find of the decade. To exploit the field, a liquefied natural gas plant was built by Pertamina, the Indonesian state oil company. It began making deliveries to Japanese utilities in 1978 and reached full production last year, when Mobil netted more than $200 million from Arun. Mobil's production and profits from the field could more than double by the mid-1980s under LNG agreements that Pertamina has made with other Japanese and U. S. utilities.

Although a late entrant in the North Sea, Mobil found Statfjord in 1974, the largest oil field in the region. And in the frantic rush for federal leases in the Gulf of Mexico during the 1970s, Mobil was one of the most aggressive bidders.

The Hibernia strike: Luck and lost chances

Mobil Corp. may have carefully constructed an elaborate exploration effort, but last year's discovery of Hibernia—possibly the largest oil find in North America since Prudhoe Bay—came only after years of errors, false steps, and missed opportunities. In the end, luck played a big part. In that, Hibernia is no different from the major oil finds of the past, computers and modern seismic techniques notwithstanding.

Although Mobil picked up the rights to drill for oil off Newfoundland in 1965, it was 14 years before a rig operated by Standard Oil Co. of California (Chevron) finally made the Hibernia discovery on Mobil's acreage. During the first half of that period, no holes were drilled.

Mobil was content merely to perform seismic activity in the Newfoundland area, which was enough to satisfy the minimal work requirements of the 12-year leases, and it concluded that there were better prospects to drill first. The decision was influenced by results in the vicinity of Mobil's Newfoundland block, where other companies had previously drilled nearly 50 unsuccessful wildcats.

Farming out. If Mobil had drilled its area aggressively, it probably would still hold title to all 1.5 billion bbl. of oil discovered at Hibernia and all of the almost 10 billion bbl. of potential reserves estimated to exist in the surrounding region known as the Jeanne d'Arc Basin. Instead, Mobil got others to do the drilling by offering them farm-outs—shares in its acreage position in exchange. Mobil now has only 28% of Hibernia and 60% of the most promising area of the Jeanne d'Arc Basin.

The first company cut into the play was Gulf Oil Corp., which in the early 1970s spent $20 million to drill six wildcats in return for a 25% interest in Mobil's 13 million acres. Mobil put up $3 million—all it was to invest in Newfoundland until after oil was found.

The drilling yielded only a small show of oil. Gulf and some executives at Mobil Oil Canada Ltd. argued for drilling another wildcat—this one at Hibernia—but Mobil refused to go along. In 1977, Mobil and Gulf decided to renew the permits on about 6 million acres. By then, Petro-Canada, the state-owned oil company, claimed 25% of almost half those acres, reducing Mobil's share of Hibernia to 54.5% and Gulf's to 18.5%.

Missed opportunities. To meet the tougher work rules required under the renewed permits, Mobil again decided to farm out, selling 22% of the Hibernia section to Chevron and an additional 7% to Gulf, which raised the latter's interest back to 25%. These two partners, along with Petro-Canada, then agreed to drill a $40 million wildcat on the Hibernia structure. Chevron picked the location and drilled the P-15 well that last September resulted in a 20,000-bbl.-a-day discovery. Chevron claims that its interpretation of the Mobil data showed a much better drilling prospect than Mobil realized. "We instigated the whole Hibernia play. We saw a lot more on this block than Mobil," says Gerald G. L. Henderson, senior vice-president of exploration for Chevron Standard Ltd. "They farmed out because they didn't think it was worth drilling."

Mobil insists that it saw the same structure that Chevron did and only wanted to spread the risk of another dry hole. Beyond that, it reminds other oil companies, including Chevron, that they blew a golden opportunity to get an even bigger piece of the action in 1977, when Mobil offered to farm out all 6 million acres in the Newfoundland basin, not just the 8% containing the Hibernia structure.

Chevron did not take the bait until 1978, when it agreed with Mobil Canada executives to drill in order to earn what it thought was a share in all 6 million acres. But Mobil's corporate executives by then had decided to farm out only the much smaller Hibernia block. "I didn't get mad," recalls Chevron's Henderson. "I got furious."

Yet, Mobil's Graves believes that Chevron accepted the lesser offer because it had leased an offshore drilling rig that was not being used. By drilling a wildcat at Hibernia, Chevron could write off 90% of the cost of the rig against Canadian income taxes. Under that interpretation, the explanation for Hibernia becomes a tax break. "It probably influenced their taking the farm-out more than anything else," speculates Graves. "But when someone farms into a property and discovers oil, they become the smartest people in the world."

But unlike some other majors who spent heavily in the Gulf, Mobil's big bids led to some big reserves: Its finds in the Gulf during that period were equivalent to roughly 1 billion bbl. of oil—more than any other oil company.

Production of such discoveries partly explains why Mobil's income increased nearly 145% in five years to $2 billion last year, resulting in a pretax return on investment of 50%—the highest of the five U.S.-based international oil companies. Mobil's income growth also was greater than that of the other internationals, even though declining profits at its Montgomery Ward subsidiary last year produced a drag on corporate earnings. The older discoveries also explain why Mobil's 8% decline in oil and gas reserves during the last five years was the slowest reserve drop experienced by a U.S.-based international.

The roots of this transformation go back to the Suez crisis in 1956, when Mobil's Mideast oil supplies were badly disrupted. To keep the company's refineries running, Mobil paid dearly to acquire and transport replacement crudes. The episode severely penalized its earnings during the late 1950s.

Reacting to that, Mobil reorganized in 1959 to grant exploration a higher priority in the corporation. Exploration operations—previously split between the parent company and two acquired subsidiaries—were pooled. Since then, Mobil has steadily centralized drilling decisions to make sure that prospective sites are drilled because they look better than others proposed and not, as sometimes was the case, because they are promoted more strongly by certain local affiliates. A planning department also was created in the 1959 reorganization, and the senior planning officer was given a seat on the board in order to counter the board's bias for refining and marketing investment. Eventually, all proposed projects were scrutinized by planners and justified by economics, not corporate politics. "You had a lot of logrolling in this company," admits Tavoulareas, referring to the way refining and marketing executives supported each others' proposals at the expense of exploration.

Mobil also laid the groundwork for its recent discoveries by embarking on a massive but little-noticed drive to acquire drilling rights in unexplored regions that were found to be promising by the company's studies. During the 1960s, Mobil quietly doubled its land position to nearly 100 million acres. Because these drilling rights were acquired as long as 15 years ago, they have become incredible bargains. For example, Mobil paid $37,000 for the rights to 13 million acres off Newfoundland in 1965. By contrast, it paid as much as $36,000 an acre in the Gulf of Mexico 10 years later.

During this stage-setting period, Mobil dramatically upgraded its exploration technology. In the early 1970s, Mobil, along with Gulf and Shell Oil Co., pioneered the development of Bright Spot, a method of analyzing seismic data that pinpoints the presence of natural gas in geologic formations.

Aggressive bidding

More recent improvements may well have made Mobil the leader in offshore geophysics work. The company's $14 million geophysical vessel, the T. W. Nelsen—considered by many the industry's most sophisticated—was launched two years ago. Because of its unique ability to reposition seismic equipment immediately in order to obtain better readings, Mobil says that the ship can map geologic structures more completely and insists that this explains why it bid so aggressively at last December's sale of federal drilling leases for the Georges Bank area off Massachusetts. Mobil spent $222 million at the sale—more than one-quarter of the money the government took in. While it is common in the industry to conclude that Mobil simply overestimated the value of the tracts being auctioned, some major oil company executives suspect that Mobil saw more valuable structures in the area because it had better data. Says one: "Mobil has been a little better in gathering and interpreting seismic data offshore, and the industry was shaken by those bids because there is the belief Mobil was able to do something the others were not."

Having strengthened its exploration arm, by 1970 the company was finally ready to implement its drilling strategy: It would search for a relatively small number of large fields, particularly in frontier areas. While better returns can often be made by doing just the reverse, Mobil reasoned that it needed to find enormous reserves to improve appreciably the security of oil supplies for its refineries. "Mobil's exploration accomplishments in recent years have been intensive rather than extensive," says Richard Nehring, a resource analyst with Rand Corp.

As such, Mobil's exploration program

The Marcor deal: Bad timing, bad business

Politically, the timing of Mobil's purchase of Marcor Inc. could hardly have been worse. But it also was bad from a business standpoint: Many of the reasons that led Mobil's managers to acquire Marcor no longer apply or are not as important as they once seemed to be. Furthermore, Mobil's management should have been able to see at the time that the company's prolonged effort to build an efficient exploration department was at last about to start paying off. "We probably wouldn't buy Marcor this year, right now," concedes William P. Tavoulareas, Mobil's president.

The purchase was six years in the making. Mobil was seeking a source of domestic earnings to offset the possibility that it would lose most of its foreign profits through expropriation of its overseas oil. At the same time, the company was seeking a haven in case federal regulation of the oil industry became too nettlesome. Mobil also was looking for a business that it thought could someday become as profitable as oil without draining the corporate treasury. Four Mobil planning analysts for several years screened scores of possible candidates before settling on Marcor.

By all counts, the deal looks far less attractive today. Mobil still has heavy overseas earnings, but they are now better diversified out of the Middle East. The government is far less threatening to the oil industry than it was in 1974. And with the oil price increases of the last six years, there is no way even a healthy Marcor could match oil industry returns. Last year, Marcor earned $98 million after taxes, yielding a paltry 5% return on Mobil's $1.7 billion investment. This year, Marcor has ceased to be self-supporting because of problems at Montgomery Ward & Co.

Financing. Ward's management improved merchandising in the retail chain but relied heavily on credit to do this. As interest rates have soared, Ward's earnings have plummeted, and the company lost $82 million during the first half of 1980. To maintain the unit's bond rating, Mobil was forced to pump $200 million into Montgomery Ward.

Mobil still defends the purchase, although the rationalizations sound increasingly contrived. If everything "went to hell in the oil business," says Tavoulareas, the deal has permitted Mobil to develop an expertise in two areas that could provide a base for intelligent diversification deeper into retailing or paperboard packaging. Without such knowhow, he says, "don't think you can diversify outside your business and do very well." There is no better proof of that than Mobil itself.

often appears to be expanding more slowly than those of competitors; its approach does not require massive increases in staff or in the number of wells drilled each year. In fact, Mobil virtually shut down its domestic onshore exploration effort because it figured the remaining oil and gas deposits were too small to bother with.

The new program did require opening the corporate treasury to the exploration department, and when Mobil at last put its new strategy into operation, it began spending on exploration risks with unaccustomed ease. The first evidence of this change appeared at the federal offshore lease sales for the Gulf of Mexico. Mobil had been a rather feckless bidder until 1970, but during the last decade the company tied Exxon for the acreage in the Gulf, with each company ponying up $1.5 billion. More surprising, Mobil continued to bid aggressively even after suffering major setbacks at the Baltimore Canyon, off New Jersey, and the Destin Anticline, off the west coast of Florida. Mobil had spent a total of $363 million for leases that yielded only dry holes. Says Tavoulareas: "You've got to be willing to put up the dough and not flinch."

Mobil's spending on exploration picked up still more momentum during the latter half of the 1970s. Excluding money spent on acquiring other oil companies, Mobil's outlays on exploration and production (capitalized and expensed) has grown 150% since 1975—faster than any of the top 10 U.S. majors. Now, Mobil also is spending on the one area it had ignored—domestic onshore—where Chevron, Amoco, and others have made impressive gas discoveries. In playing an obvious catch-up game, Mobil is acquiring domestic oil companies primarily to obtain acreage near the hot domestic plays. Last year it spent $782 million to acquire General Crude Oil Co. from International Paper Co., and in August, it agreed to purchase Esmark Inc.'s Transocean Oil Inc. for $740 million. In that deal, Mobil will pick up mineral rights on 2.3 million acres in the U.S., including 500,000 along the Overthrust Belt in Wyoming, currently the country's busiest exploration region. "We probably made a mistake by deemphasizing onshore, because those fellows who stayed had success," says Tavoulareas.

Curiously, the one ingredient Mobil did not need in making its bolder move into exploration was the explorers themselves. The fact that Mobil already had skilled exploration executives may have come as a surprise even to the company's top management, which is a measure of just how suppressed the oil explorers were in the Mobil organization. When Mobil's top executives decided to push exploration harder, they felt compelled to ask outside experts whether the company had actually hired top-notch exploration talent. They were assured it had.

Much of that talent existed in Mobil Canada Ltd., which in the 1950s and 1960s established an impressive drilling record. Shortly after its belated entry onto the Canadian scene, Mobil discovered the Pembina field in 1953, the largest oil field found in Canada until last year's Newfoundland strikes. Suddenly, Mobil Canada was swamped with prospects, and it rapidly recruited young geologists to get them drilled. "They really socked you with responsibility early," recalls Robert R. Graves, Mobil's vice-president of exploration, who was hired by Mobil Canada right from college in 1953. "On my first day, I was told to supervise six drilling rigs, pick all the locations, and report back on what I'd found."

Canada proved to be an invaluable training ground, and it is not surprising that Mobil's exploration department is now heavily sprinkled with Canadians, including the No. 1 and No. 2 executives in the department and the head of the Exploration Service Center in Dallas. There are so many Canadians in the exploration department that they are internally referred to as the "Canadian Mafia."

Some critics charge that, despite its recent success, Mobil is still too timid and has not completely transformed itself from the days when finance men made the decisions on what leases to buy and where to drill. They point to Hibernia as an example. If Mobil had drilled the wells instead of farming them out, it could today have had all of it, instead of just 28%—and all the surrounding area as well. "Mobil always wants to share the risks," says H. R. Hirsch, senior vice-president of Superior Oil Co. and a former Mobil exploration executive. "Most of its recent discoveries are based on a damn fine land acquisition program of the 1960s, but they are made with wildcats that should have been drilled years ago."

Still, Mobil's strategy of acquiring acreage and farming much of it out for drilling—a common practice—spreads the company's exploration funds. That many oilmen only begrudgingly acknowledge Mobil's exploration accomplishments may be explained by their view of the company as an industry maverick that is hardly deserving of such success. Mobil has frequently adopted political positions that do not square with those of the industry. The Marcor acquisition, because of its timing, demonstrates Mobil's lack of sensitivity to oil industry politics.

But today, Mobil's focus is on oil, as opposed to other forms of energy. With its vastly expanded exploration budget and its purchase of domestic oil companies, Mobil lately has begun acting more like an oil company than even some traditionally exploration-oriented majors. ∎

IOWA BEEF:
Moving In for a Kill by Automating Pork Processing

Just over a decade ago, Iowa Beef Processors Inc. revolutionized the beef slaughter industry by establishing low-cost, highly efficient packing plants in the heart of rural cattle-producing areas. By using new, automated meat-cutting and packaging techniques—with unskilled, often nonunion labor—and by slashing transportation costs, Iowa Beef Processors (IBP) stampeded over its competitors to become the largest U.S. beef packer, with 19% of the market. Not content with that share, the company intends to capture as much as a quarter of the market by 1984. But even those plans are not aggressive enough for the Nebraska-based management. Having proven that its strategy works, Iowa Beef is now planning to attack the pork industry with equal vigor.

A lender's dream. Iowa Beef's moves come at a time when many of its competitors, which are operating with antiquated plants and staggering labor costs, have watched earnings steadily erode in recent years. The Fresh Meats Div. of Swift & Co. has performed so poorly that on June 26 its parent company, Esmark Inc., announced its intentions to close down certain units and to attempt to sell off what remains as a separate company. And although Armour & Co. made a profit last year, Gerald H. Trautman, chairman and chief executive officer of parent company Greyhound Corp., told shareholders in the annual report that the subsidiary has "a long way to go to generate earnings proportionate to their asset base."

This is hardly a problem for Iowa Beef. Last year the company registered earnings of $42.7 million on sales of $4.2 billion, its ninth consecutive year of earnings gains and an outstanding performance in an industry where margins are traditionally slim. And Iowa Beef boasts a 22% five-year average aftertax return on equity and a 17% five-year average increase in earnings per share. A new $96 million beef facility, which starts up next December in Kansas, will be paid for out of cash flow. And its $300 million capital spending plans for the next five years could well be financed in the private debt market. With a 3-to-1 ratio of current assets to current liabilities and a 0.2-to-1 ratio of debt to equity, Iowa Beef is a lender's dream.

Iowa Beef is taking that strength into the $20 billion pork-processing industry. The company, which currently has a small "custom-kill" operation that supplies pork to Armour, now plans to expand these operations with a new plant costing some $100 million—a move that is sending chills through the pork industry. Although some larger producers have modernized, much of pork processing today is in the same state as beef processing in the 1960s, when Iowa Beef entered the market: It is rife with high-cost, labor-intensive plants, some dating back 60 years and located in areas where agriculture is no longer dominant. "Pork has been there for 25 years waiting for someone to automate and upgrade," declares Robert L. Peterson, Iowa Beef's president and chief executive officer, who makes it clear that this is exactly what his company intends to do.

Iowa Beef's moves into pork are fueled by more than a simple recognition of an opportunity to modernize another antiquated industry. With its new beef plant, it will have a facility in every major producing area not already dominated by another company. For years, Iowa Beef has been under scrutiny for antitrust violations, and it is even now facing a series of lawsuits brought in Dallas by a group of small cattle feeders. In Washington, meanwhile, legislation has been introduced to restrict any producer from controlling more than 25% of the beef market—the share Iowa Beef will approach when it completes its new plant. So while the company plans some growth through such means as offering portion-controlled beef to supermarkets, there is a strong awareness in the company that it cannot continue to grow in beef at the rate it has in the past.

Lean on bacon. Pork processing thus appears to be a natural diversification. But Iowa Beef is likely to wait until its new beef plant is operating at full capacity in 1984 before it goes heavily into the new business. By then the company expects the pork industry to be even more consolidated than it has become during the last five years. With smaller processors dropping out or being swallowed by larger companies and with old plants closing up, the number of pork-processing plants in the U.S. dropped 15% from 1974 to 1978, while the number of hogs slaughtered remained constant.

When Iowa Beef enters the pork market, it will find itself up against the old-line meatpackers it locked horns with a decade ago in the beef industry—Oscar

---

Swift gets an order: No more fresh meat

On June 26, Esmark Inc.'s president and chief executive officer, Donald P. Kelly, made good an earlier threat: He announced his intention to close three meatpacking plants and sell off the nine remaining plants of subsidiary Swift & Co.'s Fresh Meats Div. Less than two years before, Kelly had put Swift on notice that he expected sharp improvements or the ax would fall. By the end of 1979, however, those improvements had not materialized. Although sales, at $4.5 billion, were up 11.2% over 1978, operating earnings had plunged 34.6% to $23.6 million. Kelly hotly criticized this performance, and shortly thereafter, Swift's then-president, William S. Watchman Jr., resigned.

The decline at Swift came despite furious efforts to speed up a decade-old plan to close high-cost, noncompetitive plants. But the company's labor costs continued to soar, and the president of the Fresh Meats Div., John A. Copeland, now says that the company often gave in to union contract demands rather than take a strike that would spill over onto Esmark's bottom line. Indeed, in announcing his plan for Swift, Kelly pinpointed exorbitant labor costs as the obstacle Swift had been unable to overcome. "Time and again we went to the union and asked for concessions to make us competitive," Kelly explained. "It's abominable that Swift had to close as many plants as it had to."

Fourth place. Esmark will retain Swift's extensive line of processed foods—such as Butterball turkeys and Sizzlean pork breakfast strips—because they fit into Esmark's plan to concentrate on strong, brand-name consumer products. But the demise of the fresh meat operation marks the end of an era for the 125-year-old meatpacker, the industry leader in beef until the mid-1970s. Since then,

Mayer, Geo. A. Hormel, Wilson Foods, and Armour. But its competitors in pork have one significant advantage. Unlike most beef, which is slaughtered and sold as a commodity, 50% to 75% of the hog is processed into products such as bacon, hot dogs, and cured hams, and sold under well-known brand names. "IBP knows how to keep costs down, but it doesn't have a well-known brand," says Patrick J. Luby, vice-president at Oscar Mayer & Co. "They will have to spend a lot of money going up against our bacon or Hormel's hams."

Iowa Beef is not fazed by the prospect of significant spending. With the company's financial clout, Peterson says Iowa Beef could either purchase an existing pork product brand or hire a marketing team to start its own. Many observers believe that the company will take this route simply because margins on products such as ham and hot dogs are three times more than on fresh meat. But another route under consideration is a custom-kill operation that would also provide processed products as a private-label manufacturer for supermarkets and other packers.

If Iowa Beef decides to go into pork with a custom-kill operation, it stands to benefit from the same strategy that made its beef operation a success. That strategy developed out of founder Currier J. Holman's notion that there were more efficient ways to process and market beef. After slaughter in rural plants, Iowa Beef ships compact "boxed beef" cuts to be carved into retail portions at supermarket warehouses, disposing of cattle byproducts locally. By eliminating the truck space and diesel fuel required to ship carcasses, Iowa Beef figures that it cuts transportation costs by 25%.

Iowa Beef's most significant savings by far, though, have been in labor costs, which several analysts estimate to be as much as 40% below some of its competitors. The company has managed to keep unions out of 5 of its 10 plants. And although many competitors in recent years have adopted some of Iowa Beef's methods and closed down or modernized old plants, all are still tied to the master contracts with the United Food & Commercial Workers Union, which includes meat cutters.

Six-day weeks. Iowa Beef has faced eight strikes since 1965, including a 14-month strike at its major packing plant in Dakota City, Neb., which ended in November, 1978, with the union settling for less than the company's initial offer. Peterson is prepared to fight now to keep unions out of the company's pork plants. "No is a popular word at IBP," he boasts.

Iowa Beef's reputation for toughness in its labor dealings is reflected in its equally tough demands on its corporate staff. Salaried managers are required to work six-day weeks. The company's management turnover, however, is low, and bonuses and salaries are generous for upper management. "There's no frivolity at IBP," says Kevin McCullough, former Iowa Beef marketing research manager and now president of Colorado Management Consulting Partners in Boulder. "They're like the University of Texas football team—they never stop."

Peterson, who took over after founder Holman's death in 1977, is also attempting to rid the company of the tarnished image it acquired after Holman and the company were convicted in 1974 of conspiracy to commit bribery in order to get the company's boxed beef into the New York market in 1970. Peterson especially wants to dispel this image on Wall Street. Meeting with security analysts in New York recently, Peterson's first order of business was to insist that the company had no ties to organized crime and that none of the company's current executives were involved with the earlier charges.

Although the company faces no further charges, its troubles are far from over. In addition to the antitrust suits now in preliminary stages in U.S. District Court in Dallas, Representative Neal D. Smith (D-Iowa) has introduced two bills aimed at preserving competition in the meat industry by limiting a single meatpacker's share to 25% of the market. Although the new bills have little likelihood of passage this year, they demonstrate the scrutiny under which Iowa Beef must operate.

Iowa Beef's moves could also trigger a competitive thrust from other "new breed" packers that followed tactics similar to Iowa Beef's in the beef market of the 1960s, such as Spencer Foods Inc.— which has already expressed an interest in pork—and Cargill Inc.'s MBPXL Corp. unit. But few doubt that Iowa Beef will be successful if it sweeps into the pork industry as it did with beef. "Iowa Beef is absolutely driven to be the lowest-cost producer," says former marketing manager McCullough. "It's going to apply that to the pork business." ∎

Swift has dropped to fourth place. Operating profits have plummeted 70% over the past five years, and Swift's contribution to total corporate earnings is just 11%, even though it generates 66% of sales. All this has come about even though Swift has shut down 27 inefficient packinghouses since 1968. To offset the $200 million to $300 million in write-downs associated with the planned plant closings and sales, and to generate capital for new investments, Esmark also wants to sell its Vickers Energy Corp.

Esmark's plan to rid itself of Swift is the harshest action taken to date by the so-called old-line meatpackers, which include Greyhound Corp. subsidiary Armour & Co. and LTV Corp.'s Wilson Foods Corp. To remain competitive with such new-breed packers as Iowa Beef Processors Inc. and Cargill Inc.'s MBPXL Corp., old-line packers have shuttered aging plants in urban markets, shifting production closer to cattle feedlots. But the older packers still have labor contracts in which wages and benefits are typically 40% higher than those of their new competitors.

Swift did try to salvage two of the three plants it is closing. In last-minute overtures to the United Food & Commercial Workers Union, which represents meat cutters, Swift proposed an employee stock ownership plan and asked for concessions in current contracts. But Copeland concedes that the offer was vague, and the union rejected it. Lewie G. Anderson, assistant to the director of the union's packinghouse division, describes Swift's proposal as "ridiculous." He contends that, since 1968, Esmark has moved out of fresh meat so resolutely that "there was nothing the union or the workers could do about it." Anderson says the union's intent is to solve its industrywide problems by bringing compensation levels at all packinghouses up to the levels at the old-line companies. Even so, Swift's immediate dilemma is exemplified at its Moultrie (Ga.) plant, where wages of $14 per hour are almost twice the rate of its local competitors.

Selling abroad? Swift now wants to sell its remaining five pork plants, one beef plant, one chicken plant, and two lamb plants, which have combined sales of $1.9 billion and more competitive labor costs. With future pension costs covered by the cash he expects from the Vickers sale, Kelly reasons that the pared-down operation will be attractive to suitors— most likely a European company.

Still, whoever buys Swift's remaining fresh meat plants might find new problems lurking. Iowa Beef is now proposing to begin slaughtering pork, and many of its plants are nonunion. This raises the specter that all unionized pork plants such as Swift's could become noncompetitive. Such an occurrence, admits Kelly of Esmark, could certainly throw the rest of Swift's fresh meat plants into a threatening "different ball game."

Assessing Strategic Advantages and Disadvantages / 201

PPG INDUSTRIES:
Still Relying on Glass —
But Now In Growth Areas

In downtown Pittsburgh, executives at PPG Industries Inc. are abuzz with final preparations to build a $100 million headquarters. Lavishly sheathed in glass, the edifice not only will house the company but also will describe its business. PPG, also a maker of chemicals and coatings, remains dependent on glass production for more than one-third of its revenues, even though it dissolved its former name, Pittsburgh Plate Glass Co., more than a decade ago. And PPG is even more dependent on limited markets: Transportation and construction industries account for 40% of PPG sales, mainly through the purchase of glass products.

The danger of such reliance has seldom seemed more apparent. Auto and housing markets are depressed. And for the long term, the two markets are changing in a way threatening to glassmakers. Since 1973, auto downsizing already has reduced the amount of glass used in the average car by about 10%. In construction, ordinary flat glass, of which PPG is the leading U.S. producer, is synonymous with energy loss. Although an orderly retreat from these markets might seem prudent, PPG is launching an aggressive marketing and capital investment program that will maintain the company's existing dependence on them by expanding its position in a few healthy niches of otherwise sickly fields.

Management, credited by outsiders as top-notch in the fields it knows, has picked an essentially conservative path under L. Stanton Williams, chairman and chief executive since last January. "We see no need to risk diversifying into industries we know nothing about," says Williams.

A new Texas plant. Instead, Williams is trying to establish PPG as the clear leader in growth segments of autos and construction, including fiber glass-reinforced-plastic (FRP) auto parts and insulating building glasses. Thus, PPG, far from pulling back from Detroit, has increased its fiber glass sales staff in that city from 10 to 16 persons in the last two years. More significantly, Williams has budgeted a five-year capital spending program of $1.5 billion, 50% higher than during the last five years. As much as one-quarter of the money will be devoted to fiber glass, mainly to build a huge plant near Midland, Tex., designed to boost PPG's total capacity 64% to 650 million lb. per year. The plant will produce materials for the FRP sought by the auto industry to reduce car weight by replacing steel parts.

PPG's investments also are dedicated to increasing capacity to produce the construction glasses that save energy—and from which PPG can expect high profit margins through its already established market leadership over such competitors as Libbey-Owens-Ford Co. and Guardian Industries Corp. Specifically Williams intends to take advantage of the company's early entry and dominant position in multipane windows and reflective glasses.

From a standing start five years ago, PPG has raised to about 20% its volume of construction glass destined eventually for insulating purposes. And outsiders suggest that the corporate five-year plan might boost insulating glass to 40%.

Higher pretax margins. Profits in glassmaking should rise in tandem. Because of specialization and plant modernization, PPG has already boosted its pretax margins in glass from 1.1% in a recessionary 1975 to 16.8%. In stark contrast, Libbey-Owens-Ford, the dominant maker of auto glass but second to PPG in construction glass, has seen its operating margins fall from as high as 20% in the early 1970s to 8% a year ago. Nationwide, the construction industry is increasing its consumption of insulating glass at 15% per year, compared with just 2% to 3% for ordinary flat glass. Thanks to that, analysts say, producers of the insulating varieties can command profits sometimes more than double

An early lead in multipane windows. Detroit wants to use far more fiber glass

those of flat glass unit for unit. "For the next five years, or even longer, PPG will probably be a less cyclically impacted company," observes John P. Henry, an analyst for E. F. Hutton & Co.

Insulating glass has been made even more attractive by the 50% increase in home heating oil in just the last six months, but rising energy prices are also sparking PPG's drive into fiber glass. Noting Detroit's scramble to meet tough federal requirements for more fuel-efficient cars, Williams explains coyly that "government regulations do represent opportunities for some companies."

Fiber glass wheels? Auto makers, while cutting the total amount of glass purchased because cars are smaller, nonetheless plan a voracious increase in the use of fiber glass. FRP, already used to make body parts ranging from dashboards to trunk doors, is expected to nearly double to as much as 350 lb. per car by 1985. To stay ahead, PPG is now bringing out a stronger fiber glass compound it hopes can be used for auto structural parts such as wheels and door beams. Williams says he is encouraged that Ford Motor Co. has just begun testing the first product of this kind—a bumper support for the company's XD Falcon, built and sold in Australia.

For the time being, even PPG's competitors grant that there ought to be room for everyone in the growth segments the Pittsburgh company has selected. "There is a fantastic opportunity for the entire industry in Detroit," says James S. Hearons, vice-president of Owens-Corning Fiberglas Corp., the only company that tops PPG in fiber glass production. In question is how PPG's determination in sticking with autos and construction will work out when all of its competitors are drawn, as they are expected to be, toward the same growth sectors. ■

QUESTIONS

The Decline of U.S. Industry: A Drastic New Loss of Competitive Strength:

1. The fall in competitiveness of American firms is the result of events both within and beyond the control of U.S. firms. Discuss.
2. Address the scope of the declining competitive position of U.S. industry.

A Policy for Industry: Technology Gives the U.S. a Big Edge:

1. Discuss the nature of the United States's "technological edge" and the opportunities it suggests for the future.
2. What external factors and conditions will influence whether the United States will be able to maintain its edge?

Will It Work: What the U.S. Can Learn from Its Rivals:

1. How does the industrial strategy of the United Sates compare with the strategies of foreign countries? Address major strengths and weaknesses.
2. How can the United States improve the performance of its industries? Discuss practices of foreign countries that could be adopted by the United States.

Can Canon Copy Its Camera Coup?:

1. Identify the major internal aspects of Canon that will help it to become a leader in the copier business.
2. Given the firm's environment, which of these strategic advantage factors is the most important? Discuss.

Ford Rests Its Future on Tough Cost Controls:

1. What effect do the current personnel and management of the Ford Motor Co. have on the type of strategies it is likely to implement in the future?
2. Evaluate Ford's past and present strategies and suggest what sort of strategy is called for in the future.

Why Consumer Products Lag at Texas Instruments:

1. Identify the major forces behind the poor performance of TI's consumer products division.
2. How does TI propose to improve the effectiveness of its consumer strategy? Mention the strengths and weaknesses that must be considered.

Tandy's Next Big Drive into Home Electronics:

1. In what respects is Tandy Corp. in a strong competitive position in the home electronics market?
2. What factors will determine whether Tandy's new move into home electronics will prove to be as successful as its sales of home computers?

Where K Mart Goes Now That It's No. 2:

1. How has K Mart's conservative (frugal) operating philosophy been translated into strengths and weaknesses for the company?
2. K Mart is considering two possible strategies to pursue in the future: diversification and focusing on trying to achieve internal productivity gains. What are the advantages of each strategy?

Wang's Game Plan for the Office:

1. Make an internal appraisal of Wang Laboratories Inc.
2. Assess the external environment in which Wang must operate.

Key Pharmaceuticals: Bidding for Growth through New Products:

1. Agreements with foreign companies and innovative and strong product development efforts have helped to turn around Key Pharmaceuticals Company. Discuss how.
2. How does the strategy developed by CEO Jahares capitalize on the firm's strengths while taking into account its weaknesses?

Mobil's Successful Exploration: Making People Remember It Is an Oil Company:

1. In the 1950s and 1960s top management's risk aversion played a key role in placing the company in a "crude short" position. Explain.
2. Compare and contrast the internal status of Mobil Corp. now with its status prior to the 1970s.

Iowa Beef: Moving in for a Kill by Automating Pork Processing:

1. What are Iowa Beef's most notable strengths?
2. What were IBP's three proposed strategic alternatives for entering the pork industry? Given IBP's internal strengths and existing external conditions which is most viable?

PPG Industries: Still Relying on Glass—But Now in Growth Areas:

1. In what area do the majority of PPG's strengths lie? Discuss.
2. How does PPG's new strategy match up with the important internal and external factors?

Six.

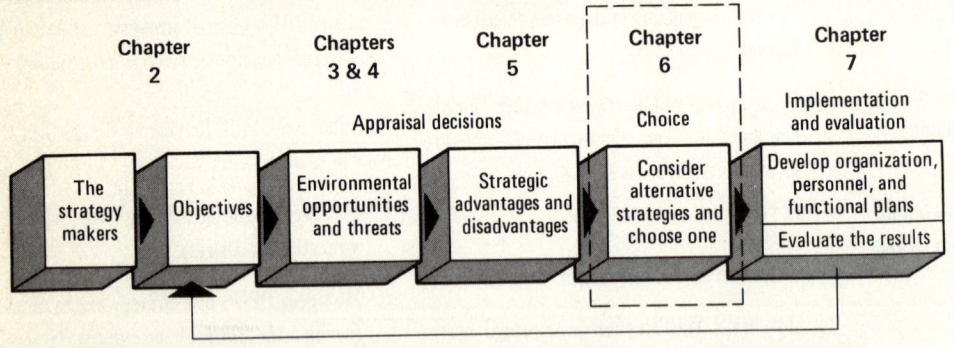

Exhibit 6-1: A MODEL OF THE BUSINESS POLICY AND STRATEGIC MANAGEMENT PROCESS.

- Chapter 2: The strategy makers
- Chapters 3 & 4: Objectives; Environmental opportunities and threats (Appraisal decisions)
- Chapter 5: Strategic advantages and disadvantages
- Chapter 6: Consider alternative strategies and choose one (Choice)
- Chapter 7: Develop organization, personnel, and functional plans; Evaluate the results (Implementation and evaluation)

As the model of the business policy and strategic management process shown in Exhibit 6-1 indicates, this chapter focuses the reader's attention on the choice process. In choosing a strategy, strategy makers compare and contrast the results of the appraisal decision process, and they identify strategic alternatives. These alternatives should reflect a match between the firm's strengths and weaknesses and opportunities and threats in its environment. Ultimately, one or more of these alternatives will be chosen for implementation.

If the environment offers major opportunities which match up with major internal strategic advantages, the conditions are right for a growth strategy.

If the environment offers threats that match up with major strategic disadvantages, the conditions are right for a retrenchment or turnaround strategy.

If the environment and strategic advantages signal growth in one part of the firm and disadvantages and threats match up in another part, the conditions are right for a combination strategy.

If no major changes are indicated from the environmental and strategic advantage appraisals, the firm will choose a stability strategy.

Let's describe each grand strategy in more detail for a moment.

A stability strategy is one that an enterprise pursues

- When it continues to serve the same or very similar customers.
- When it continues to pursue the same or very similar objectives (adjusting the expected level of achievement about the same percentage each year).
- When its main strategic decisions focus on incremental improvement of functional performance.

Strategy makers might choose a stability strategy for one or more reasons. For example,

- The strategy makers believe the enterprise is doing well. Thus, they perceive no need to change.
- The strategy makers are risk averse, and a stability strategy is less risky than other strategies.
- The enterprise has grown rapidly in the past, and the strategy makers believe the time has come to focus on creating a more efficient and manageable operation.
- The enterprise is experiencing pressure from the government with regard to antitrust actions.

A growth strategy is one that an enterprise pursues when its strategy makers formulate objectives which are significantly higher than the enterprise's past achievement level. The most frequent change in objectives in a growth strategy is to raise the market share or sales objectives.

Why might an enterprise pursue a growth strategy? Consider these reasons:

- The strategy makers equate growth with success.
- The industry or industries in which the enterprise does business is or are growing rapidly. Thus, a choice not to grow is a choice to sacrifice market share.
- The strategy makers believe society benefits from growth.
- The strategy makers are motivated toward high achievement levels.

There are a wide variety of growth strategies. For example,

- Firms can grow by acquiring other firms (external growth).
- Firms can grow horizontally—that is, in the same type of business.
- Firms can grow vertically—that is, moving forward and acquiring or developing firms in the market channel or moving backward by acquiring or developing suppliers.
- Firms can grow internally by offering existing products to new markets or by creating new products for existing markets.

Exhibit 6-2 provides examples of growth strategies available to the J. M. Smucker Company. Notice that Smucker's can vertically integrate forward by developing their own retail stores or by acquiring existing retail outlets. Likewise, Smucker's can vertically integrate backward by developing their own sources of supply or by acquiring existing suppliers.

If Smucker's desires to grow horizontally, they have several options from which to choose. For example, they can

Considering and Choosing Strategies

204 / Readings from *Business Week*

Exhibit 6-2: POTENTIAL GROWTH STRATEGIES FOR THE J. M. SMUCKER COMPANY

	INTERNAL	EXTERNAL	INTEGRATED PLAN
VERTICAL			
Forward	Build Smucker stores to sell products in	Acquire or merge with XYZ stores	Develop firm either vertically or horizontally
Backward	Develop Smucker's orchards, glassworks, box factories, etc.	Acquire or merge with ABC orchards, and so on	
HORIZONTAL			
Similar products	Develop Smucker's peanut butter, honey, and similar goods	Acquire or merge with Sioux Bee Honey, Jumbo Peanut Butter, and so on	Develop a concentrically diversified firm
Different products added	Develop products similar to the present line, such as fruit, fruit candy	Acquire or merge with firms that fit company's personality	Develop a concentrically diversified firm
No product scope defined (conglomerate)	Develop and market products which fit corporate image	Acquire or merge with firms that fit firm's image	Develop a conglomerate multi-industry firm

- Develop products similar to their existing product line internally.
- Acquire firms producing products similar to their existing product line.
- Expand their product line by developing different, but related, products internally.
- Expand by acquiring firms producing related products which will expand their product line.

Finally, Smucker's can expand by using a conglomerate diversification strategy. Under this option, Smucker's can either develop divisions internally or acquire firms producing products which are not closely related to their existing product line.

A retrenchment strategy is one that an enterprise pursues when it decides to improve its performance in reaching its objectives by

- Focusing on functional improvement, especially reduction of costs. (A reduction of costs strategy is also called a turnaround strategy.)
- Reducing the number of functions it performs by becoming a captive company.
- Reducing the number of products it produces and/or markets it serves.
- Liquidating part or all the assets of the enterprise (the ultimate retrenchment strategy).

Retrenchment strategies are used when strategy makers believe performance in a product line, division, or company in question is less than satisfactory and prospects for improvement are not good. By retrenching, the strategy makers free up some of their resources for more productive use elsewhere.

An enterprise pursues a combination strategy when its main strategic decisions focus on using more than one grand strategy (stability, growth, and retrenchment) at the same time in one or more divisions of the company. Another form of the combination strategy uses several grand strategies over a period of time. For example, a firm's strategy makers may choose a strategy which calls for rapid growth followed by stability.

Each of these strategies is effective when the environmental appraisal and internal assessment dictate their choice. Stability is the most frequently chosen strategy, followed by growth, and lastly retrenchment. The strategy makers choose the strategy that represents the best match between their firm's strengths and weaknesses and opportunities and threats in the environment. Their choice is influenced by their past strategic choices, their willingness to take risks, and their power to make a choice.

This chapter of the book provides many descriptions of *Business Week* cases on strategies considered and/or chosen by firms. The first article, "An Oil Giant's Dilemma: Investing a Mountain of Cash before the Oil Runs Out," describes the strategic choices facing the Standard Oil Company of Ohio (SOHIO). SOHIO must develop a strategy which will ensure their profitability after they deplete their oil assets in Alaska. Since SOHIO produces products in many industries and their management expertise is narrow, SOHIO can be expected to adopt a combination strategy as they seek growth in some industries and stability or retrenchment in others.

Although stability is the most frequently pursued strategy, magazines like *Business Week* do not write many articles describing stability strategies. Retrenchment and growth strategies tend to make more interesting reading for the subscribers.

A number of articles in this chapter describe growth strategies. These articles include

- "Deere: A Counter-Cyclical Expansion to Grab Market Share"
- "LTV: On the Acquisition Trail Again, but Now in Aerospace and Energy"
- "Nabisco: Diversifying Again but This Time Wholeheartedly"
- "Baker International: A Growth Wizard Divides to Conquer"
- "Western International: A $1 Billion Expansion in the Face of Recession"
- "Ramada Inns—Renovating Rooms and Rushing into Gambling"
- "Citibank: A Rising Giant in Computer Services"
- "Caterpillar: Sticking to Basics to Stay Competitive"

This chapter also contains some retrenchment articles. These include

- "Why Esmark Sold a Profitable Subsidiary"
- "Kaiser Steel: The Strategic Question Is Whether to Liquidate"

Other articles included in this chapter are

- "The Chores Facing Polaroid's New CEO"
- "Could Bankruptcy Save Chrysler?"

These articles will help you understand the grand strategies and the choice process.

Investing a mountain of cash before the oil runs out
AN OIL GIANT'S

Just 10 years ago, Standard Oil Co. (Ohio) was a regional refiner and marketer, eking out a modest living. Today it is swimming in money. Once severely short of crude, Sohio's bonanza from its huge reserves of Alaskan oil skyrocketed 1979 profits to $1.2 billion, a phenomenal 2,200% blast in just one decade. This year those profits will come in closer to $2 billion. A distant 17th in earnings in 1970, Sohio has now joined the exclusive society of oil industry giants: Its net income for the first half of 1980 ranks No. 6, and its 15.9% return on $2.8 billion sales for the second quarter is far and away the highest in oil's major leagues.

But the very speed of Sohio's rise to Croesus-like wealth has caught its managers in a maelstrom. Trained to operate a company of decidedly shorter horizons, they have only general notions about what to do with their riches and have implemented no plans to maintain their magnitude. The company has ballooned in size so suddenly that it lacks the staff, expertise, and investment vehicles to make decisive use of its money. Yet Sohio's leaders recognize that delaying new investment will draw harsh criticism from politicians, because Sohio is now reaping a windfall beyond any other oil company. Cash and marketable securities have reached $2.5 billion and are still growing. Return on investment, just 3.6% in 1976, leaped to 25.2% by June 30. And the pressure to deploy the resources is heightened all the more by the fact that Sohio's oil at Prudhoe Bay, its only big asset, is quickly draining, with nothing in the wings to replace it.

Sohio is now in a three-way dilemma: It must use its cash rapidly, it sees too few areas for U.S. oil investments, and it says it has decided that its main hope for the future is in diversification outside conventional energy, where it has had little experience and minimal success.

To be sure, not all of Sohio's unpreparedness is its own fault. Just 18 months ago, Sohio was burdened with debt and strapped with exorbitant production and transportation costs for its oil, then selling at $13.66 per bbl. A number of industry analysts suspected that the company had made a bad deal when it decided in 1969 to trade majority ownership in itself to British Petroleum Co. in exchange for the undeveloped Prudhoe reserves. Its subsequent $6.2 billion investment in those reserves left the company hard-pressed for cash.

But four events occurred that Sohio's executives never anticipated, and they rapidly changed the company's fortunes. They were:

- The near-tripling in world oil prices in the last 19 months, which has caused Sohio's average market price to jump to $25 per bbl. and its wellhead price (market price less transportation costs) to rise from $5.37 to $16.50 per bbl.
- A 25% increase, to 1.5 million bbl. per day, in the amount of Alaskan oil being pumped through the Trans-Alaska Pipeline system. Sohio owns 53% of the daily output.
- An increase from about 400,000 bbl. to 600,000 bbl. a day in the amount of its oil that Sohio has been able to land on the West Coast, partly because of shifts and drops in Iranian crude deliveries. This has cut the high cost of transporting most of the company's oil by tanker through the Panama Canal.
- Gradual federal decontrol of Alaskan

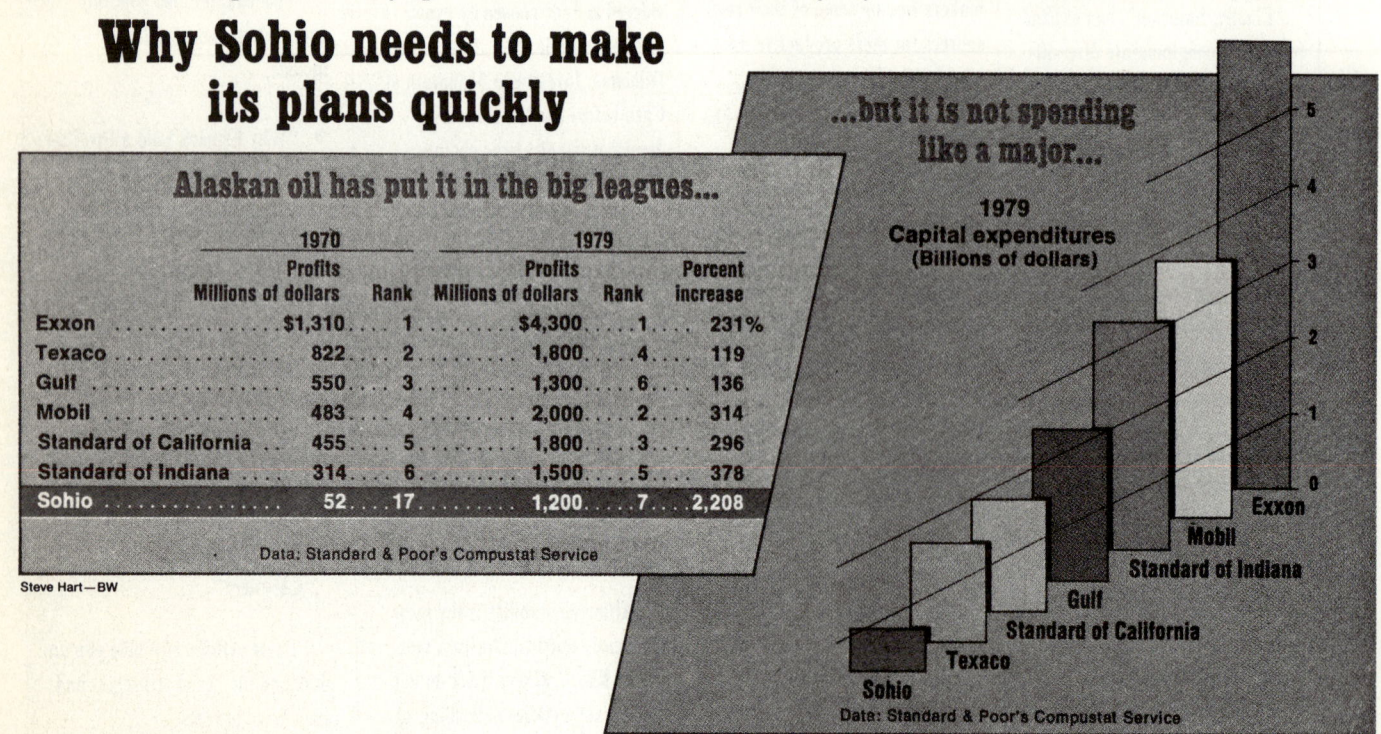

Why Sohio needs to make its plans quickly

Alaskan oil has put it in the big leagues...

	1970 Profits Millions of dollars	Rank	1979 Profits Millions of dollars	Rank	Percent increase
Exxon	$1,310	1	$4,300	1	231%
Texaco	822	2	1,800	4	119
Gulf	550	3	1,300	6	136
Mobil	483	4	2,000	2	314
Standard of California	455	5	1,800	3	296
Standard of Indiana	314	6	1,500	5	378
Sohio	52	17	1,200	7	2,208

Data: Standard & Poor's Compustat Service

Steve Hart—BW

...but it is not spending like a major...

1979 Capital expenditures (Billions of dollars)

Exxon / Mobil / Standard of Indiana / Gulf / Standard of California / Texaco / Sohio

Data: Standard & Poor's Compustat Service

206 / Readings from *Business Week*

DILEMMA

oil prices. Currently, one-third of the oil can sell at world price levels. By December, 55.2% of the oil will be sold at prices fixed by OPEC.

But even though these four elements have combined to propel Sohio into sudden wealth, they should not have taken Sohio's managers completely unaware. The disruption of Middle Eastern supplies has long been a likely possibility. It could have been expected that Alaskan oil would become more important, higher priced, and ultimately would find refineries or pipelines on the West Coast. Sohio had factored "best" and "worst" case contingency plans into its thinking, but these were not far-reaching enough and did not identify specific areas and companies in which to make investments and build staff and expertise. Such contingency planning is admittedly difficult: The scope and nature of possible disasters or bonanzas almost certainly require the most original thinking that a company is ever called upon to do.

As it is, Sohio's chairman, Alton W. Whitehouse Jr., declares that "the payoff has been higher and faster than we expected." Yet Whitehouse, an attorney who negotiated the BP deal, must scramble now to enjoy its rewards.

The company is in a position unique in its industry. It obtains nearly 90% of its cash flow from Prudhoe. Already, 13.4% of this field's original reserves of 9.4 billion bbl. are gone. In seven years (chart), more than half the oil will have been depleted. The oil that remains will then begin to flow more slowly and become more costly to extract. Even this year the new windfall profits tax on oil, plus other federal taxes, and levies imposed by Alaska—whose rates are the highest in the nation—will combine to keep Sohio's profits from increasing much further. Taxes are expected to eat up as much as 92¢ of every dollar increase in oil revenues.

This makes Sohio's bonanza strictly temporary, and it places the company at a watershed. It either must undergo what will probably amount to the biggest redeployment of assets in the annals of U. S. business, or it will end up producing what Whitehouse calls "the biggest burp in corporate earnings history." With utter irony, Whitehouse and his staff say they have concluded that

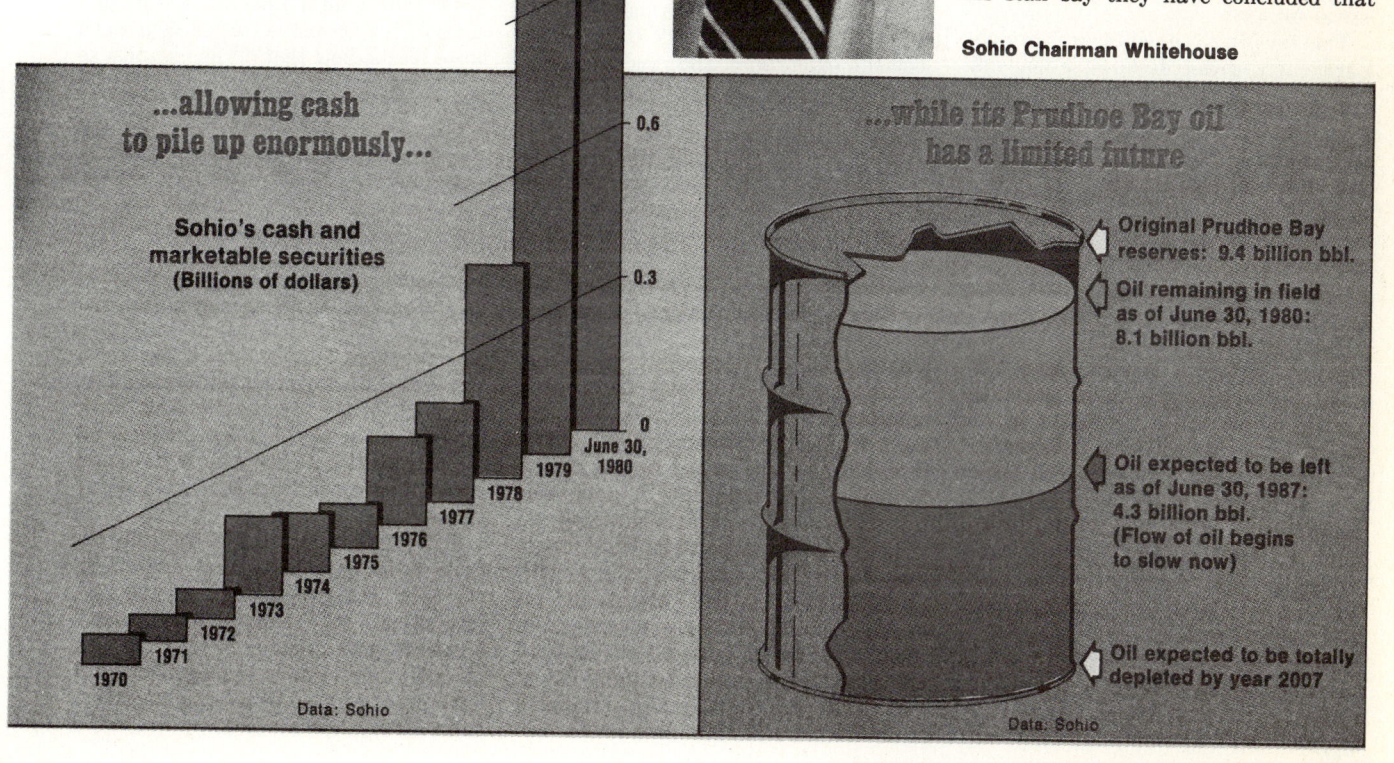

Sohio Chairman Whitehouse

...allowing cash to pile up enormously...

Sohio's cash and marketable securities (Billions of dollars)

1970, 1971, 1972, 1973, 1974, 1975, 1976, 1977, 1978, 1979, June 30, 1980

Data: Sohio

...while its Prudhoe Bay oil has a limited future

- Original Prudhoe Bay reserves: 9.4 billion bbl.
- Oil remaining in field as of June 30, 1980: 8.1 billion bbl.
- Oil expected to be left as of June 30, 1987: 4.3 billion bbl. (Flow of oil begins to slow now)
- Oil expected to be totally depleted by year 2007

Data: Sohio

Considering and Choosing Strategies / 207

the company has too much money and must spend it too quickly, when so few U.S. plays are available, to stay in the major leagues in oil. Within 20 years, they say, Sohio will be forced to obtain most of its profits from businesses other than conventional oil and gas.

Some of these new businesses will remain in the realm of energy. For example, Sohio wants to enlarge its holdings of coal. It will also try to become a power in synthetic fuels, according to Glenn R. Brown, a senior vice-president who now heads a task force of 13 planners hustling to firm up specific projects and acquisitions.

But Brown's team has picked a host of additional nonenergy businesses as targets, including nonfuel minerals, chemicals, genetic engineering, and semiconductors and other information processing equipment. Says Brown: "Even if our intent was to spend as much money as we could in energy in a timely and profitable way, we couldn't spend all the money available to us."

Sohio, which has not previously disclosed these plans, has thus become the first major oil company to make plain that it views diversification out of conventional energy not merely as a hedge against declining oil supplies but as the main path to its livelihood within the next two decades. In the next 10 years alone, according to a Sohio plan being revised because it was not aggressive enough, conventional oil and gas would be reduced to 75% of its business. Especially because it is owned mainly by a British company, Sohio may now find itself bearing the brunt of public criticism for siphoning oil dollars into nonenergy ventures at a time of dwindling world supplies.

This turn in circumstances is bizarre. For nearly seven decades, Sohio officials have patiently awaited a return to greatness in oil. Sohio was the base of John D. Rockefeller's Standard Oil empire, which began with a refinery in Cleveland, Sohio's headquarters city. Rockefeller then spent 41 years building the mightiest corporation the world had ever seen, until the federal government used antitrust law to break up the company. Out of 34 pieces, Sohio, the cornerstone, was relegated to the role of a crude-poor, regional refiner and an operator of gasoline stations in its home state.

Sohio's own timidity and ineptitude in finding new supplies of crude caused it to remain relatively insignificant until 1969, when former Chairman Charles E. Spahr bought BP's Prudhoe oil in exchange for a special issue of common stock calculated to give BP 53% ownership of Sohio when the company's Alaskan production hit a steady level of 600,000 bbl. a day—a point reached last Sept. 28. Now, the magnitude of Sohio's success has made it so large a part of BP that both companies are working to prevent an equally drastic failure when Prudhoe plays out. Sohio and BP began their marriage with a great deal of autonomy, but the companies are now growing much closer. They have set up a joint research and development committee and have exchanged directors and planning information. BP's and Sohio's future plans, says Robin W. Adam, a managing director of BP, "must be coordinated," if not necessarily the same.

But even with BP's help, there is no assurance that Sohio can develop the expertise and management infrastructure, and find the proper opportunities, to maintain its new size. In stark contrast with its peers in oil, which long ago acquired large and sophisticated staffs and widespread expertise along with plants, strategies, and vehicles for investment, Sohio has yet to emerge from the mold of the regional player. Its total employment has been essentially flat at 22,000 for the last decade, compared with industry leader Exxon Corp.'s 169,000. Sohio is just now studying how many employees to add. And Sohio still leases cramped headquarters space in buildings spread all around downtown Cleveland. More important, Sohio's past forays into nonoil ventures—coal, chemicals, and hotels—often have been marked by lack of success or commitment as the company focused on developing Prudhoe.

As if that were not enough, Sohio is the one oil major that still has a distinct dearth of knowledge within the key potential profit sector of its own business: exploration. The company has developed substantial knowhow in Alaska since it spent $27 million in 1978 to buy BP's Alaskan exploration and production operation, which provided a core of 60 exploration staffers and a fount of Arctic-area geological data. But outside of Prudhoe, Sohio has had among the worst exploration track records. The company now produces 702,200 bbl. a day from Prudhoe, not including additional barrels sold to pay royalties to Alaska. In the rest of the world, Sohio produces an inconsequential 19,600 bbl. a day, and even that is down from 30,600 bbl. a day 10 years ago.

Sohio is run by executives who cut their teeth on refining and marketing, currently the two least-promising sectors of oil. "We're a peculiar group," observes one insider. "If you look through our senior management, all have been involved in refining and marketing. Two or three were involved in the [Alaskan] series of great decisions. But none has ever been involved in the pursuit of oil and gas. We were never really there."

Now the company is trying to overcome its oil handicaps on a crash basis. Sohio's exploration operation, still led by erstwhile BP executives, has become an open hiring hall that is attempting to add 155 new employes by Dec. 31 to a staff that still numbers just 230. Since 1978, Sohio also has quadrupled its unexplored domestic leaseholdings to 2.73 million acres, mainly by trading $142 million worth of stock in December to acquire two Denver-based energy companies, Webb Resources Inc. and Newco Exploration Co. The company expects to spend more than $100 million this year to drill as many as 70 exploratory wells, up from just two in 1979, and it has budgeted $3 billion in constant 1980 dollars for further exploration during the next 10 years, not including more land acquisitions.

Such plans are impressive in comparison with Sohio's past record in oil prospecting. But Whitehouse is the first to admit they will not be enough to solve the company's basic challenge: to replace the 5 billion bbl. of oil at Prudhoe that has made Sohio the nation's largest owner of domestic reserves.

Indeed, outsiders agree, Sohio is too late an entrant to make itself a major force in exploration: It lacks geological data and it has little chance of picking up good drilling sites or trained technicians because of shortages of each. "When Sohio started getting cash in 1978, most of the good acreage had already been snapped up," notes Richard Nehring, an analyst with Rand Corp. in Santa Monica, Calif.

Sohio's total acreage, in fact, pales next to that of the domestic industry leader, Standard Oil Co. (Indiana), which holds an immense 34.9 million acres. The scramble to develop such large tracts, now that oil has become so lucrative, has caused an industrywide shortage of petroleum geologists, engineers, and other skilled oilfield workers. The shortage has caused intercompany raids on existing employees. For example, Indiana Standard's subsidiary, Amoco Production Co., saw turnover of employees in 1979 run to a serious level of 20% to 30%, says exploration manager Anthony L. Benson. "Even the major companies [in exploration] are having a very tough time getting and keeping good people," says Benson.

These limitations have left Sohio with two other options in oil: foreign exploration or the acquisition of a company that holds U.S. oil reserves. Neither is of much interest to Sohio, says Whitehouse. He has studiously avoided looking for oil outside the U.S., where he says political risks are too high. So far, the company's only involvement is in Algeria, where Sohio has agreed to join with state-owned Sonatrach to explore

900,000 acres, because Algeria requires such ventures of companies in lieu of a $3-per-bbl. premium otherwise required to buy Algerian oil.

Sohio seems content to leave foreign exploration to its parent. BP has doubled its own exploration spending during the last two years, and Adam says that push will be accelerated. BP traditionally was crude-rich, but it has been forced to become a net buyer of oil because of the disruption of oil from Iran and Kuwait and the nationalization of Nigerian fields, where BP had major interests.

Whitehouse says he has "not ruled out a major acquisition" of proven U.S. oil reserves, but he looks askance at the potential profitability of such a move. "Nobody is going to get any bargains," he asserts. "People who own oil that's already been discovered can calculate its future value as well as we can, so the return would be somewhat mundane," adds Paul D. Phillips, senior vice-president for finance and administration and a key influence in top management.

The whole spate of problems that Sohio sees in conventional oil and gas are what has led its planners to draw hasty plans to diversify. Last October, after less than a year of preparation, they presented the board with a $25 billion, 10-year spending plan, with the money split evenly between the company's existing business and a host of proposed developments in coal, synthetic fuels, minerals, information processing equipment, chemicals, and other high-technology businesses. This was the plan designed to reduce cash flow from oil and gas from 90% to 75%. Further investments in nonoil properties were to reduce the contribution of oil and gas to less than 50%.

But it is a measure of the speed of change in Sohio's cash-rich environment that this plan has already been sent back for revision. In just the last few months, Sohio officials say, they have come to realize that their prior projections of the amount of money available for expansion were far too low. The company is now working on a plan whose total expenditures would exceed the $25 billion by 1990. "In the space of just five or six months, our cash flow situation just turned around astronomically," exclaims David J. Atton, manager of corporate planning. "All of a sudden, our nice, orderly schedule of getting ready to make large discretionary investments by 1982 has had to be crunched right up to today."

Aside from the time pressure imposed by the draining of Prudhoe, Sohio executives feel they must invest quickly to avoid a hostile public reaction to the enormity of their windfall. During the years when the company pushed debt to $5.1 billion, or 74% of total capital, to finance continual cost overruns at Prudhoe and on the oil pipeline, Sohio's hard-pressed managers could scarcely wait for the arrival of what they came to call the "green mountain"—the cash that would eventually accrue from the sale of the oil. Now, however, the mountain has grown "clearly very conspicuous," worries planner Atton. "I think people [here] feel that a very important factor is what the impact of this cash buildup is going to be in public circles. If you have too much cash on hand, maybe somebody will help you get rid of it, somebody who in our view has no right to it."

Thus, while Sohio executives will not telegraph their next move, outsiders expect that a major acquisition to spend some of the money could come at any time. Already, Sohio has made some use of its windfall by using huge chunks of cash to prepay long-term debt. In 1979 the company was due to pay $241 million but actually paid off $829 million of bonds, bank debt, and other obligations. This year, financial chief Phillips says, he may retire another $150 million in debt, although payments of just $97.5 million are required.

Still, the $2.5 billion hoard is growing, and Phillips' debt reductions have enhanced profitability. The debt retirements are expected to help reduce Sohio's interest expense from $439 million in 1979 to $350 million this year, while the company's interest income from the cash has jumped from $81 million to an estimated $200 million—an amount that itself is higher than Sohio's entire profits in any year until 1978. At the same time, Phillips has managed to trim debt to $4 billion, or 47% of capital. He says he now wants to cut that figure further to between 30% and 40%.

This will give Sohio the borrowing power it lacked when debt was high, adding to what has become the company's new embarrassment of riches. If, however, the company is required to help finance the proposed natural gas pipeline that would carry Prudhoe's untapped cache of some 26 trillion cu. ft. of natural gas to market in the lower 48 states, Phillips says it may well exercise that borrowing power. Sohio owns 25% of the gas. Even at currently controlled domestic prices, the company's portion of the Prudhoe reserves would be worth more than $15 billion. Phillips estimates Sohio's share of the pipeline's construction costs at more than $2 billion, an amount that appears easy to afford.

Sohio, however, has never built a major gas pipeline. Nor, without acquisitions, will it have the technicians to back up its most ambitious plan—to spend up to $5 billion to become a major in the synfuels game. Indeed, the company is in the second decade of management trauma. As a strictly regional concern entering the 1970s, Sohio was forced to ask its limited number of managers to perform tasks far above their level of know-how. In just one instance, Whitehouse dispatched a young engineer with no financial training, Ronald A. McGimpsey, to back up Phillips in trying to arrange what became the largest private debt placement in history to finance the Alaskan oil pipeline. McGimpsey, a quick study, is now Sohio's treasurer.

But the new scramble will be far more pervasive. Sohio is discovering that management capability problems can grow in geometric proportion to a company's size. Sohio is filling out its executive ranks as quickly as possible with new officers, mostly lured from other large corporations, to provide better depth. In just the past several months, Sohio has raided three other oil company managements to hire a new controller, a senior vice-president for petroleum engineering, and a new chief executive for Sohio's faltering coal subsidiary, Old Ben Coal Co. The Company also has lured Thomas C. Norris of Consolidation Coal Co. to be a vice-president of corporate planning, and James P. Burgoon, a planner at Diamond Shamrock Corp., to be vice-president of planning and development at Sohio's chemicals and plastics company, Vistron Corp. "We will expand our management group rapidly and adroitly, by every means available, as we move to a large and inevitably more complex company," Whitehouse declares.

The posts that Whitehouse is giving to the new managers clearly indicate the company's future business interests. Most notably, Whitehouse has picked John R. Miller to replace Joseph D. Harnett as Sohio's president and second-in-command. Harnett, a refining and marketing operations specialist who lost to Whitehouse in a race to succeed Spahr in 1978, retired at age 62 on Aug. 1. Miller, although heavily involved in the Alaskan adventure, has most recently been senior vice-president for technology and chemicals rather than an oilman. Trained as a chemical engineer, Miller is perceived as more broadly qualified than Harnett to lead a diversified company.

As the day-to-day operations chief, Miller will face the awesome task of implementing Sohio's plan to become a big force in synfuels—a business in which the economics remain questionable and technology is still evolving. Even so, chief planner Brown says his target is to be producing, alone or through joint venture, as much as 100,000 bbl. a day of shale oil by 1990. This, he estimates, will cost between $2 billion and $4 billion. Sohio currently has shale oil reserves of 1 billion bbl. Brown says his plans also call for start-

Considering and Choosing Strategies / 209

ing construction of a coal gasification plant with a capacity of 250 million cu. ft. per day by the late 1980s, at an expected cost of more than $1 billion. These projects, he says, would make Sohio "one of the major players in the synfuels game."

Indeed, such plans are ambitious by any measure. Exxon, one of the more bullish companies about the future of synfuels, predicts an industrywide U. S. production level of 1 million bbl. a day of oil and 1.6 billion to 2.7 billion cu. ft. of gas. To meet its goals, Sohio would have to carve out a huge 10% of the shale oil business and probably a larger share of synthetic gas. Whether money alone will enable the company to accomplish that is an unanswered question. "There will probably be no more than 10 majors in synfuels, and Sohio should be one of them because of its capital capabilities," suggests an optimistic Thomas A. Petrie, an analyst with First Boston Corp. But even Brown's superiors are not so sure that huge market shares ought to be the ultimate goal. Within the last two months, Brown says, they have asked him to give more thought to synfuel workability and profitability than market share.

Confrontation with Congress

The company's synfuel plans are not only its most lavish but also the ones that may cause a final showdown with the government. There is already some apprehensiveness in Congress at the idea that BP, itself owned in part by the British government, is now the majority controller of the largest pool of U. S. crude. De facto control by BP of a big piece of the U. S. synfuels business, whose technical development is to be financed largely by $20 billion in federal funds, may create a direct confrontation. "I think the synfuels industry should be controlled by Americans," declares Senator Howard M. Metzenbaum (D-Ohio), a frequent oil industry critic who chairs the Senate Judiciary Committee's subcommittee on antitrust, monopoly, and business rights.

Energy Dept. officials say they have had no reason to be concerned with BP's ownership of Sohio so far, mainly because U. S. access to all Prudhoe oil is guaranteed by federal law, which prohibits exports of domestic petroleum. But political repercussions of Sohio's new plans, in synfuels and nonenergy businesses, are an unknown, because the ventures have yet to be implemented.

Energy officials and Congress have allowed diversification moves, such as Getty Oil Co.'s purchase this summer of ERC Corp., a reinsurance company, to pass without criticism. But oil industry executives continue to be nervous that any large move away from conventional oil and gas by companies larger than Getty may provoke stern governmental reprisals. "For a major to make any big nonenergy acquisition now, the political flak would be enormous," declares one. The fallout could include serious congressional consideration of the pending bill, sponsored by Metzenbaum and Senator Edward M. Kennedy (D-Mass.), that would prohibit oil companies from making any acquisitions of nonenergy companies unless those companies had annual sales volume of less than $100 million.

To avoid political conflicts, Sohio and BP officials have been extraordinarily careful to project an image of autonomy during the years that BP gradually increased its stake in Sohio. However, BP now consolidates Sohio's results with its own, making Sohio appear far too important to BP for the parent to allow its U. S. company complete freedom of action. By the end of last year, Sohio accounted for 29% of BP's $3.6 billion in profits and 36% of its $24 billion of assets. Actual cash payments to BP from Sohio dividends and special Prudhoe Bay royalties amounted to $287 million. The profit contribution and cash payment should increase dramatically this year.

For his part, Whitehouse has maintained for so long that he is an independent operator that he now shows annoyance even at the mention of the subject. "We generate our own long-range plans, period!" he snaps. "I don't foresee ever being in a posture other than that." But should management of the two companies ever disagree, BP now has legal veto power, and its officers clearly realize they hold control. "I think it would be most unlikely that any chief executive would want to push through the board a plan that he knew the major stockholders objected to," says W. Alastair L. Manson, president of BP's New York-based subsidiary, BP North America Inc., and a Sohio director.

Working with BP

So far, however, the two companies seem to be functioning smoothly together. In fact, BP already has aided Sohio in oil prospecting, production, and transportation. This summer, it will dispatch two employees to sit on Sohio's strategic planning staff. And the companies have formulated almost identical strategic plans, and appear on the verge of several joint ventures. Like Sohio, BP has been nearly 90% dependent on the oil business, but has decided to spread out. On Aug. 12 it succeeded in a $1 billion tender offer to buy Selection Trust Ltd., a minerals company with sales of $752 million in 1979. Sohio, meanwhile, has had a two-man team studying entry into the same nonfuel minerals industry, insiders say. Both companies also plan expansions of their coal holdings separately or through joint purchases.

A joint research and development coordination committee is now examining alternative energy sources, new chemicals, and coal conversion techniques. More important, BP officials confirm, Sohio's entry into some of the high-technology fields it knows nothing about may be initiated with BP's help. For example, BP has sold computer software in Britain for the last 15 years, and managing director Adam hints it would be "perfectly feasible for Sohio to serve as BP's agent should the British company decide to market its software in the U. S."

Such aid will be badly needed, judging from Sohio's track record in nonoil businesses. While it concentrated on Prudhoe, Sohio allowed its handful of enterprises in coal, chemicals, and plastics to atrophy. A hotel business, Hospitality Motor Inns, founded in 1964 by Sohio, was sold in two pieces in 1972 and 1979 for a total $41 million after the company was unable to achieve more than scant profitability.

"All our businesses other than oil were on short rations for a decade," concedes one Sohio executive. More attention will now be paid; Sohio next year will bring on stream a $100 million acrylonitrile plastic resin plant, doubling the company's capacity to more than 800 million lb. per year. This will entrench Sohio as the largest producer of this plastic, used in packaging and auto parts. Sohio's plans for coal are much larger: It will spend $1 billion by 1990 to try to at least double its reserves to more than 2 billion tons and triple annual production to 30 million tons. By 1979 standards, a level of 30 million tons would have made Sohio the nation's fourth largest coal producer.

Two troubled businesses

While it goes about making these expansions, Sohio also will have to figure out how to make chemical and coal operations more profitable. During the last 10 years, the company has more than tripled retail sales of its biggest chemical lines—fertilizer materials—to 665,000 tons per year, but the chemical company's operating income has steadily declined from a peak of $54.1 million in 1975 to $18.1 million last year on sales of $398 million. In coal, Old Ben has been a notoriously troubled operator, whose deep, high-sulfur-coal mines in Indiana and Illinois have suffered from labor and productivity problems. Coal production over the last 10 years has actually declined, from 11.7 million to 10 million tons, and pretax income last year skidded to $2.5 million, a level amazingly 22% lower than in 1978, the year of the national coal strike. As if the challenge of merely straightening out these businesses was not enough, Sohio's Brown suggests the company might now delve into a host of related ventures, mining minerals in addition to coal, and possibly moving into major petrochemicals, such as ethylene.

The company, however, does not pretend that its redeployment of assets will be easily achieved. "Prudhoe Bay," admits Whitehouse, "is a tough act to follow." Whether the BP connection will help Sohio pull it off, or hurt because it will focus even more attention on an oil company diversifying, remains to be seen. "Every step of the way, they are going to be questioned because of their unique position in Prudhoe, and because of their controlling foreign ownership," declares First Boston's Petrie. "It's not easy for an oil company to do anything today, but it's going to be more difficult for Sohio." ∎

DEERE: A Counter-Cyclical Expansion to Grab Market Share

At first glance, it would seem that William A. Hewitt, chairman of Deere & Co., has cause for concern. The Moline (Ill.) company's two principal lines—farm equipment and construction machinery—are highly cyclical, capital-intensive businesses that are slowing down. In farm equipment, the prognosis for that $19 billion worldwide market is for a period of gradually declining growth, a steady descent from this year's 12% increase. The near-term outlook for the $17.5 billion construction machine industry is far more grim: It may be in for a sickening slide, now that interest rates and tight money policies threaten to slow homebuilding activity to a crawl.

Yet Hewitt bristles at the suggestion that these trends bode ill for Deere. "We thoroughly dislike those who predict what we're going to do based on industrywide projections," declares Hewitt, who in his 24 years as chief executive has engineered the company's rise to become the world's leading farm equipment maker—and No. 2 in the U.S. construction machinery market after Caterpillar Tractor Co. In the fiscal year ended Oct. 31, 1979, Deere's earnings rose an estimated 23% to $325 million on revenues of $4.92 billion.

Plowing back. So while conventional wisdom might dictate a cautious approach to expansion or even a program of wholehearted diversification, Deere is plowing an unprecedented $2 billion back into its core businesses over the next five years. Moreover, this spending spree—much greater than the planned capital expenditures of its competitors—comes on the heels of a five-year, $1 billion program that doubled its construction-equipment facilities and added 30% to farm equipment capacity. Most of this just-ended financial barrage was aimed at launching new products—rolling out a host of new tractors and combines for North American markets, broadening Deere's construction equipment offerings, and tailoring a recently announced series of tractors for its troubled European operation.

The new plan, however, represents a determined effort to boost manufacturing capacity and efficiency, even though Deere already is the low-cost producer in farm equipment and among the leaders in construction machinery. Deere executives will not discuss precise goals, but it is clear that their strategy is to gain market share during the coming period of adversity. The approach is far more expansive than the course being followed by most of Deere's rivals. For example, the company's largest competitor in farm equipment—International Harvester Co.—has been laying off workers and slashing other operating costs in hopes of becoming as efficient as Deere (BW—June 26, 1978).

By cutting its production costs still further, Deere is trying to gain market share without a shrinkage of profitability. The company is aiming to double the anticipated industry growth rates in its two primary businesses. The farm equipment industry is expected to grow only 2% to 3% a year through 1985, while the predicted annual growth in construction machinery over the same span is nearly 5%, despite the possible drop of as much as 15% next year. Deere must also overcome recessionary pressures on its small but burgeoning and highly profitable line of consumer products, including snowmobiles, lawn mowers, and garden tractors; sales of such items have more than doubled during the past three years to $400 million.

Certainly the most striking feature of Deere's spending program is its tilt toward construction equipment. In fact, the company will be supporting that business with an estimated 30% of its capital expenditures during the next five years, almost double the portion it received over the last five. Yet Deere is set to make this commitment just when prospects for the construction equipment market seem most bleak. During the 1974-75 housing slump the company's construction machinery business suffered badly, as sales dropped 11% to $412 million in 1975, and those operations reportedly lost money that year.

'Much better.' Today, however, only 35% of the company's construction sales are tied to the housing market, compared with 50% five years before. In recent years, Deere has introduced some 20 pieces of new construction equipment, including bulldozers, loaders, and an earth-moving machine—all designed for use by contractors in road, underground sewage, and land-leveling projects. "We're in a much better position this go-round to withstand a housing falloff," says President Robert A. Hanson, who predicts that Deere's construction sales will grow twice as fast as its farm business over the coming five years. By then, construction machinery could account for 25% of Deere's sales, up from 21% now.

Deere's plan for outperforming the industry in farm equipment rests largely on catering to big farms, with increasingly sophisticated farm implements, plus huge tractors and combines, as the economies of large-scale operations become increasingly evident. Deere has targeted its marketing to the 20% of farmers who now control about 80% of total U.S. farm production. For instance, an estimated 65% of the tractors the company sells are the largest, 100-plus hp. models, compared with 52% for the industry.

Moreover, while Deere's leading share of the overall domestic farm equipment market is 31%, its stake in some niches of the market for mammoth, highly sophisticated tractors and combines, costing $60,000 to $90,000, is as high as 45%. "Deere has the biggest share of the biggest machines with the biggest profitability," observes Charles V. Bromley, an analyst with Duff & Phelps Inc.

As part of the new efficiency drive, a large chunk of cash will go toward computerizing the parts-storage and handling operations, as well as modernizing production lines with robots and other machinery. Domestically, the expansion blueprint calls for doubling to 2.5 million sq. ft. the size of its construction equipment factory in Davenport, Iowa, and building a new tractor plant in Waterloo, Iowa. Abroad, Deere is doubling its five-year capital budget to $350 million, mostly for expansions in West Germany and Spain.

Hanson foresees a "big payoff" on these investments by the early 1980s, primarily in the form of higher market shares for Deere. If he is correct, the larger gains would probably come in its faster-growing construction machine business. In that market, Deere has jumped from No. 6 to No. 2 in recent years, but its 8% share is still a distant second to Caterpillar's 33%. Some industry observers agree with Hanson. "The company's cost advantages will result in greater market share gains as it experiences a lower rate of inflation in unit costs than its less-efficient competitors," explains Mitchell I. Quain, an analyst with Wertheim & Co.

212 / Readings from *Business Week*

Deere's operating margins are already higher than most rivals. In farm equipment, for instance, its operating margins of 13.3% in 1978 compared with 12% for No. 2 International Harvester, and 11% for Allis-Chalmers Corp.

Internal funding. A key element in Deere's margin-boosting drive is the growing integration of its two businesses with the use of common components. Several of the company's heavy-duty farm and construction machines are made with essentially the same engines, transmissions, and hydraulics. This integration is particularly critical to the profitability of Deere's construction equipment because it affords this smaller business economies that otherwise would be impossible. An estimated 80% of its construction machines now contain parts that are interchangeable with the farm equipment components.

Yet Deere apparently has no intention of taking Caterpillar head-on by becoming a full-line manufacturer. For example, it has no plans to produce coal-mining and pipe-laying machines—lines dominated by Caterpillar. "It would be foolish for us to say we're out to pass up Cat," says Hewitt. Instead, it appears that Deere hopes to grab still more business away from the companies it has outdistanced recently, including Harvester and J I Case Co.

Thanks to its long tradition of financial conservatism, Deere should be able to fund its building and modernizing program primarily with internally generated capital, most analysts agree. The company sports an enviable ratio of debt to total capitalization: 0.26 to 1.

Deere's marketing prowess, as well as its money, enhance the chances of succeeding with its strategy for thriving during a several-year stretch of slowing growth. Its vaunted marketing network—3,400 farm equipment dealers and a recently beefed-up corps of several hundred construction machinery ven-

Deere is tilting its new capital outlays toward construction equipment

dors—is known for backing its products with extensive repair and parts-supply services, considered an important selling point for increasingly expensive and sophisticated equipment. One competitor observes: "The strength of Deere's dealer network is a very big influence in the success of that company."

Indeed, given Deere's marketing muscle, the one criticism of its big spending program is that it perhaps should have begun sooner. According to this view, the market-share gains Deere is hoping for are a foregone conclusion once its planned facilities begin turning out more farm and construction equipment. "Deere has the marketing power," says one analyst. "The [improved market-share] numbers just aren't there yet because of lack of capacity." ∎

LTV: On the Acquisition Trail Again, But Now In Aerospace and Energy

"A marriage made in purgatory," said one doubtful analyst. "This is not a merger," snapped another, "it's a suicide pact." Such was the derision in late 1977 that greeted LTV Corp.'s pursuit of a merger with Lykes Corp., parent of failing Youngstown Sheet & Tube Co. LTV, owner of Jones & Laughlin Steel Corp., another sickly steelmaker, jumped from eighth to third place among the nation's steel producers when the deal was completed a year later. But it also piled one great mountain of debt—Lykes' $659 million—on top of $1 billion of its own and caused observers to wonder what had happened to LTV's long-stated goal to wean the company away from its base in weak and cyclical businesses.

But the linkup with Lykes now figures as the pivotal event in a remarkable corporate comeback story. Economies resulting from that merger stand to keep LTV solidly in the black this year, one of the most traumatic the steel industry has experienced since World War II. With that, Dallas-based LTV clearly has crossed an important threshold. In terms of operating margins per ton of steel shipped, LTV has caught up with average performers such as National Steel and Republic Steel, although it still lags well behind Armco, Inland, and others that have spent heavily over the years on plant and equipment. Says David Bell, manager of research for Herzfeld & Stern, a New York brokerage firm: "They are coming up off the bottom."

So heartened is Chairman Paul Thayer by the steel operation's upbeat outlook that he is abandoning the stick-at-home attitude that prevailed at the once-acquisitive conglomerate throughout much of the 1970s. With tax-loss carry-forwards and investment tax credits that can shelter more than $1 billion in earnings over the next five to seven years, LTV managers are once again on the acquisition trail. But this time, they are searching for companies that can help LTV expand in what they see as faster-growing aerospace and oil services businesses.

Deep into debt. Texas entrepreneur Jimmy Ling, a onetime electrical contractor, built LTV (until 1972 known as Ling-Temco-Vought Inc.) into one of the highest-flying conglomerates of the 1960s. Its debt-to-equity ratio zoomed to an incredible 7 to 1 as a result of the high prices Ling was willing to pay for acquisitions. While his maneuvering made the company the 14th largest in the U. S. at the close of the decade, Ling proved more adept at buying than managing. In his largest acquisition, LTV plunged heavily into debt to buy J&L in 1968, just as the steel industry's fortunes began to wane.

When J&L began dragging down LTV in 1970, the company's directors dumped Ling, and Thayer, head of the Vought Aerospace subsidiary, was promoted to chief executive.

Thayer, a former test pilot for Vought, pulled LTV out of its precipitous dive by pruning the company back to steel, meatpacking, and aerospace operations. Still, its continuing dependence on the highly volatile steel business for as much as 50% of its revenues remained a problem. In the three downturns that hit steel in the 1970s, LTV reported deficits twice and in one year suffered an 88% drop in earnings. But in 1979, the first full year after the merger, the company turned in its best performance in a decade, reporting profits up 460% to $173.5 million on a 52% sales gain to $8 billion. This year, with industry steel shipments likely to drop about 20%, LTV's earnings are off 45% to $68.4 million on a 4% decline in sales in the first nine months.

This is an improvement over the company's performance during previous steel market slumps. Much of that lift traces directly to the Lykes merger. Continental Emsco Co., a drilling rig and oil field equipment maker that was a little-noted part of Lykes, has emerged as the fastest-growing and most profitable part of LTV. And by dint of a number of economies achieved by integrating J&L with Youngstown, the steel unit is managing—if only barely—to keep its nose above water. Thayer calculates that merger-related efficiencies already are bringing an additional $85 million to $90 million to the bottom line in steel this year. That sum alone is more than LTV's total earnings in all but two of the last 12 years. It represents an added 2¢ profit on every dollar of sales, which is about half the margin that steelmakers normally expect.

Tax havens. As a result, at least some of the cash flow that recently was used to shore up steel now is free to finance acquisitions. But the main plan is to acquire by exchanging stock, because LTV remains short of cash and borrowing power. New equity added by the Lykes purchase helped pare LTV's debt-to-equity ratio to 1.85 to 1, but long-term debt still stands at $1.4 billion, and cash on hand at just $68 million.

LTV's stock would also seem to be a poor financing vehicle at first glance, since it recently traded at only three times earnings, but analysts see the company's tax-sheltering ability as a plus. James J. Paulos, LTV's senior vice-president for finance, contends the tax havens make the stock worth six times earnings. LTV executives are now poring over a list of 146 acquisition candidates.

One goal of the new acquisition drive is to shift markedly LTV's sales mix away from its mature and cyclical food and steel businesses. Insiders acknowledge that LTV would love to sell Wilson Foods Corp., its meat and food subsidiary, which has made paper-thin profits for the past 10 years. While Thayer believes the steel operation is simply too big a part of the business to walk away from, he has no plans to expand it.

Instead, Thayer is looking to boost the contribution from Vought and Continental Emsco, whose corporate groups together produced 78% of LTV's operating income on only 16% of sales in the first nine months. By 1985 he hopes those units will represent 28% of LTV's revenues, while its steel business will drop from just over half to a third of sales.

214 / Readings from *Business Week*

"We have two major businesses—energy and aerospace—where there will be substantial room for investment and growth," Thayer declares.

So far, Thayer is finding implementation of that plan difficult. In September, LTV paid $28 million in cash to purchase Skagit Corp., a Bendix Corp. subsidiary that produces anchor winches, foundry castings, and pedestal cranes for use in offshore drilling. But there is small chance that LTV will be able to buy any sizable oil field product companies. After the 1973 oil embargo, while Lykes bled Continental Emsco of most of its cash flow to keep Youngstown afloat, such close competitors as Halliburton, Baker International, and Hughes Tool went off on acquisition binges. Now, acknowledges Paulos, "the field has been pretty well picked over and the multiples are astronomical."

Spurned offer. Thayer is encountering similar problems with potential aerospace acquisitions. LTV made its first acquisition bid since the J&L purchase last August when it offered $180 million in cash and stock for Pneumo Corp., a leading manufacturer of aircraft landing gears. But Pneumo spurned that bid as too low, although it represented a 50% premium over the market value of its stock. Explains Pneumo's Vice-President William J. Vesely, referring to LTV's steel and meat units: "LTV is in some businesses that have some pretty heavy demands on them. That probably influences what the future holds for LTV."

The success of LTV's bid to broaden its base will also ride on its ability to continue avoiding major troubles in steel. So far, opportunities for trimming transportation costs, dovetailing supplies, and shifting production from costly older plants to newer ones with idle capacity have provided LTV with a made-to-order bonanza that is staving off huge losses, if not yielding bankable profits.

Under a long-term, take-or-pay contract, for instance, Youngstown was paying dearly for iron ore not being delivered because of an unforseen plant shutdown, while J&L was paying premium prices to buy it on the open market. Now, J&L is using all of Youngstown's excess ore. Similarly, Youngstown last year closed an antiquated open hearth that used to feed processed steel called "rounds" to its seamless tube operation in Youngstown. Now J&L's basic oxygen furnaces in Aliquippa, Pa., are supplying higher-quality, lower-cost rounds.

Such improvements are the most visible results of LTV's controversial move to pick up Lykes. But perhaps the shrewdest part of the deal was the company's recognition that LTV was one of the few companies that was poor enough to buy Lykes, strange as that might seem. "It would have been almost impossible for a company with a triple-A credit rating, because Lykes would have pulled it down to a BAA in a second," recalls Paulos. "Merging with Lykes did not drag us down. We were already there." ■

NABISCO: Diversifying Again, But This Time Wholeheartedly

During the last 82 years, Nabisco Inc. has achieved great success in one basic endeavor—the making and marketing of cookies and crackers. In the U. S., its Oreo, Fig Newton, Ritz, and other brands command 40% of the market. Now, Nabisco executives say that they are gearing up for a major diversification: the introduction of additional food and nonfood items for the grocery store. Among their most ambitious targets is the salted snack business that is currently dominated by PepsiCo Inc.'s Frito-Lay Inc. subsidiary.

In the past the company has made small forays—with mixed success—into snack foods, as well as frozen foods, cereals, candy, and toiletries. But its foremost strategy was aggressive expansion into foreign markets to offset maturing U. S. markets for cookies and crackers. "We were still expanding around the world in the business we know best," says Robert M. Schaeberle, Nabisco's chairman and chief executive officer, explaining the company's success in international expansion at the expense of diversification.

Nabisco executives believe that the company can pump growth back into its domestic business by using its massive distribution system to sell other consumer goods. But the challenge will be formidable, considering the company's past attempts to diversify. Mainly because of a string of poor acquisitions and some half-hearted marketing efforts, Nabisco's toiletries and pharmaceuticals, including such products as Aqua Velva after-shave and Sominex sleeping pills, have been perennially ill. Nabisco simply failed in canned dog foods (Rival brand) and toys, and it took only a weak run at selling salted snacks. Cookies and crackers still account for some 60% of sales and a higher portion of earnings.

Says Nabisco Chairman Schaeberle: "Over the next five years, we're committed to expand in other consumer businesses using the quality image of Nabisco." To back up this plan, Nabisco may spend more than $700 million over the next two years alone to develop and promote new products and to make acquisitions in lines ranging from tape cassettes to bagged snacks. The ties between these seemingly unrelated products, says Schaeberle, are "the strengths the company has in marketing and distribution." Nabisco is one of the few national food producers that delivers directly to supermarkets, rather than using food "brokers." At Schaeberle's command is a sales staff of 3,000 plus 1,200 trucks, which will be enlarged as new products come on stream through acquisitions and joint ventures. Nabisco is considering spending up to $500 million on one major acquisition.

Executive time and capital are now free for the diversification thrust. Since 1976, Schaeberle, together with President Val B. Diehl and Chief Financial Officer C. Richard Owens, has been cutting unprofitable businesses that had accumulated in the 1960s under former Chairman Lee S. Bickmore, who retired in 1973.

The company rid itself first of XOX-Nabisco, a German biscuit subsidiary that by some estimates lost $25 million between 1969 and 1976. In 1977, Nabisco sold its Aurora toy unit, and in 1978 it closed its Rival canned dog food operation in the face of competition from dry and semimoist products. Last year the company sold another German operation, Sprengel, an ailing confectionery and snack business. Write-offs from these divestitures have totaled $23 million.

In 1979 the write-off on Sprengel alone was $17 million, causing Nabisco's profits to drop 1.8% from a year earlier to $99 million on sales that advanced 7.5% to $2.3 billion. But Nabisco's balance sheet is now in solid condition to support new investments. The company has $160 million in cash and equivalents, and its debt has been pared from 40% of total capital in 1976 to 27% this year. Return on equity did drop two points to 17.5% last year, but it is expected to approach 21% in 1980, second only to Kellogg Co. in the packaged food industry.

New markets. Aside from the opportunities that its new financial strength presents, Nabisco managers are determined to develop new businesses, because they are irked at having lost those divested. Had they been successful, grumbles financial chief Owens, their revenues "could be in the $300 million range today." These setbacks have caused Nabisco "to drop behind relative to the growth of other companies," Owens adds, "so we intend to replace [those businesses], and then some." Schaeberle has set a goal of 10% to 12% annual growth in earnings.

Part of this increase is still to be achieved with cookies, crackers, and toiletries in foreign markets. Foreign operating income now accounts for 17% of Nabisco's total, up from 11% in 1976, and while the company was stung by its losses in Germany, it views them as an aberration. In Germany, Nabisco faced strong existing national brands, plus a spate of regional bakeries and confectioners. But in France the company's annual compounded profits growth since 1973 has been a strong 32%, and in Italy it has doubled its market share in the same period.

To keep this momentum going, Nabisco is accelerating a drive into Latin America, especially Venezuela, Mexico, and Nicaragua. Unlike packaged goods

Nabisco aims to be No. 2 to Frito-Lay in snacks. Still expanding overseas

producers, such as Procter & Gamble Co., that have avoided less developed countries, Nabisco is anxious to enter them. Says President Diehl: "It's fine to talk about nutrition, but when people are really hungry what they really need is calories. Our products are good suppliers of basic calories and a certain amount of nutrition." The company will spend some $250 million in the next five years to expand foreign cookie and cracker production and improve productivity. Despite the new domestic products, says Diehl, international sales "will still be the fastest-growing part of our company."

The most ambitious move in the U. S. is into the $3 billion salted snack market, where Nabisco wants to raise its current share from about 1% to 10%, making it No. 2 after Frito-Lay, which holds 40%. As in Germany, Nabisco will have to beat not only national but also regional producers, such as Borden Inc.'s Wise and Lance Inc. of Charlotte, N. C. On a region-by-region basis, "there are already a horde of No. 2s out there," warns one competitor. Powerful national marketers, such as P&G and Standard Brands Inc., have already tried and failed to make a big dent in Frito-Lay's empire.

Nabisco's older snack brands, such as Mister Salty pretzels, have done well, but the company's first attempt to expand the business four years ago faltered because of lack of commitment, observers say. Even Nabisco executives admit that they made some bad decisions. They converted three cookie lines

216 / Readings from *Business Week*

to snacks and then "frankly started to go out with some me-too products," says Robert J. Powelson, group vice-president in charge of the Biscuit Div. Sales of these items, including corn and tortilla chips, have leveled off at about $40 million.

More ad spending. This time, Powelson says, the company is "committed 100%" to sell more. It spent $8 million this year converting a four-year-old Rival dog food plant into one that turns out snacks for people, expanding total snack-making capacity by 40%. The company is now reevaluating its seven existing snack products and is considering possible revisions of them by early 1981. Nabisco will not break out snack advertising plans, but total ad dollars for all products increased from $96 million in 1979 to $115 million this year and will probably increase 15% for 1981. "If the company accelerates their advertising commitment to snacks, it seems likely that their Nabisco label will be a valuable asset," says Peter Barry, an analyst at E. F. Hutton & Co.

With new snack capacity on line, Nabisco will increase its sales force, which it now wants to utilize as a major asset for direct distribution of a variety of products to supermarkets. In May, Nabisco entered into a joint venture with General Entertainment Corp. to help distribute its tape cassette music recordings, because Nabisco figures that a prime market, 25-to-35-year-olds, makes at least two or three shopping trips per week. If successful, says Owens, tapes will be placed in 50,000 supermarkets in four years. The company is already negotiating more distribution agreements, and in its acquisition hunt may select consumer goods that fit into its distribution scheme.

In the meantime, the company will try to use new products to prop up its toiletries and pharmaceuticals, which last year earned a scant $600,000 in operating income on sales of $149.3 million. It is bringing out a new appetite suppressant, a nasal decongestant, and a line of hair care products. In its smaller food lines, Nabisco is looking for acquisitions of small, but established, brands: It recently spent $10 million to buy Fox-Cross Candy Co., maker of Charleston Chew, a nougat and chocolate bar.

Too-fast growth. The concern about such aggressive growth plans in so many lines of business is that Nabisco may be overextending itself. "They have to be very careful the plan doesn't work backwards and wreck their efficiencies," declares David A. Goldman, an analyst at Smith Barney, Harris Upham & Co. Indeed, cookies themselves may face new competition. Frito-Lay, ironically, has moved into the market just as Nabisco has turned again to salted snacks. Last year, Frito-Lay bought Grandma's Inc. and Jack's Cookies, two regional makers, and with a national sales force fully one-third larger than Nabisco's, the PepsiCo division could be a real threat.

Nabisco, however, is aware of this, and will fight to hold its profitable base. The company is using advertising to reposition many of its cracker brands as light and healthful snacks and has been replacing artificial colors and flavors with natural ones. A new cracker, Wheatsworth, rolled out nationally this year, is selling at a $40 million annual rate, making it the most successful entry since Ritz. While Schaeberle says he can put teeth into Nabisco's diversification this time, he leaves no doubt that the rear-guard action will be just as important. Cookies and crackers, he says, "are still our No. 1 priority around the world, and we'll never back away from that." ∎

BAKER INTERNATIONAL: A Growth Wizard Divides to Conquer

Rapid corporate growth brings enormous rewards to executives who achieve it, but it also carries a built-in burden: anything less than stunning growth in the future is likely to be viewed as a poor performance. Few are more haunted by this problem than E. H. "Hubie" Clark Jr., chairman of Baker International Corp. of Orange, Calif. Clark has boosted sales and earnings of the oil field and mining equipment manufacturer by 34% a year for the last decade. He is held in near-awe on Wall Street as a result. But with Baker's sales now a hefty $1.2 billion, some of Clark's boosters are wondering if he can keep it up.

Clark thinks he can, with the help of an unusual restructuring plan. He is splitting Baker along product lines into three companies—one for Baker's oil drilling equipment, one for its oil production tools and fluids, and one for its mining machinery. Each will be run by a separate board of directors dominated by outsiders. Each company will lay its own strategy, publish its own annual report, and, ultimately, even make acquisitions without parental approval. One reason is to breathe entrepreneurial spirit into division managers, who have become the new presidents of semi-autonomous companies. Explains Clark: "They can say, 'Those tracks in the sand are mine, not Hubie Clark's.'"

Equally important, the split is designed to free Clark to become a long-range strategist searching out new growth businesses, a role he relishes. Since the split was formalized in January, Clark says he has been spending one-third of his time on planning. He has been reading, "jawing" with futurists such as Herman Kahn, "looking out the window," and brainstorming with colleagues about end-of-the-century social and economic trends. His aim is to isolate new business areas that will match Baker's past high-growth, high-profit record. Clark intends to take Baker into those fields by making acquisitions.

Maintaining Baker's growth rates through acquisition may well require some gold-plated deals. Ten years ago, Baker was a comparatively tiny company that earned $5.2 million on sales of $63 million. A combination of mergers and careful product niche-picking caused a near-20-fold increase by last year. Baker's earnings of $99 million in the year ended last Sept. 30 returned 18% on equity. For the moment, the boom in oil exploration guarantees continued fast growth for Baker's existing products, which include drill bits, drilling lubricants, and a 50% worldwide market share in "packers," mechanical plugs that maintain pressure in oil wells.

Clark maintains that the ever-increasing value of oil assures fast growth in Baker's oil equipment for at least a decade. "But," he adds, "at some point we face these markets' leveling off." The restructuring is thus designed to free Clark for planning at a time when Baker's existing businesses appear able to succeed without constant attention.

Giving subsidiaries some freedom is common enough, especially among conglomerates. But near-independence within a company like Baker, whose products and markets are closely related, may be unique. If successful, the move could become a model for other growth-bent companies. Tosco Corp., a big oil refiner whose president, Morton M. Winston, is also a Baker director, is already studying the Baker structure and other techniques for involving line managers in strategic planning for their own operations. The typical inability of such executives to do their own planning completely causes "a tension which every company must feel," says Winston.

At Baker, the corporation will still control the purse strings by allocating capital to the three subsidiaries. Still, the split is a radical change. For 15 years, all aspects of divisional operations had been tightly run by Clark, 53, a gentle-spoken engineer with a strong will and an entrepreneurial flair. Whether he really can step back remains to be seen. If he can, a fringe benefit will be to allay Wall Street's only serious criticism of Baker—that it is a one-man company. "If Clark's plane crashed, so would Baker's multiple," says John H. Hayward Jr., oil-service analyst at Merrill Lynch, Pierce, Fenner & Smith Inc.

Even in the current down market, Baker shares command 17 times earnings, or three points better than the average for oil service stocks. Part of the reason is Baker's reputation for product quality, which even competitors acknowledge. Says Jack Knowlton, vice-president for engineering and product development at Smith International Inc., a Baker rival: "Their packers are the industry standard. Baker does everything well and nothing poorly."

Possible acquisitions. Clark must now find new businesses at which he can achieve similar results. Although he has just suited up as Baker's corporate planner, Clark has some clear notions about where the company should be headed. He hopes to find another energy-connected business, but a new one with extraordinary potential. One possibility is building equipment for the emerging energy storage industry. This could include machinery to assist in overnight storage of electricity. Clark says Baker might also try to make tools to exploit natural energy storage, such as by tapping solar heat in seawater.

Clark is also delving into the future of mining. Baker entered the coal and non-ferrous-metal mining equipment fields through small acquisitions over the past eight years. Now, Clark suspects that, as has happened with aluminum, the "ore bodies of the future may be in the trash piles of today." He sees a possible role for Baker in building equipment to mine industrial scrap heaps.

One clear criterion is that the new business must involve high-technology products whose failure would cost customers dearly, as it does in oil tools. This, Clark believes, will require the kind of quality control that will limit competition and keep prices high.

Such futuristic thinking wins accolades from a key Clark colleague, Stanley Hiller Jr., a venture capitalist and Baker director. Hiller has long discussed the subsidiary split with Clark as a vehicle to free the chief executive for long-term planning—something Hiller contends most companies "wait too long" to do when existing businesses are thriving. "They stay with one product or service until they've peaked out," says Hiller. "All growth is temporary."

Separate boards. Baker's new offspring are Baker Drilling Equipment, Baker Oil Tools, and Baker Mining Equipment. A year ago, the experiment began with the creation of separate committees on Baker's full board to oversee the three companies. Now, the committees are split into separate boards, each of which is looking for additional outside directors.

Presidents of the three companies say they like the setup so far. "It's extremely helpful having the input of outside experts in making our decisions," says James D. Woods, president of Baker Oil Tools Co. When Woods' board debated a small acquisition recently, an outside director knowledgeable in the target company's industry suggested that high inventory levels at the company were abnormal and might indicate obsolete products. The suspicion proved true. Harold E. Berg, a Baker director who is chairman of Getty Oil Co., feels that time restraints alone might prevent such input at conventional corporate board meetings, where directors get only a cursory look at many issues. "Now we can concentrate more," he says.

By delivering this kind of independent attention, plus decision-making power, to bright managers, Clark's intent is to keep them from being hired away. "It's not just money that lures them," he says. "They want to do their own thing." But Clark also has devised a financial reward as unconventional as his restructuring. Managers will get fictitious shares of stock in their subsidiaries, convertible to Baker shares at a rate that grows more lucrative if the subsidiaries' performance outpaces the corporation's.

Thus motivated, Clark hopes, managers will wring more growth from Baker's existing businesses while he seeks new ones. Still, Clark seems to feel at least a twinge of nervousness about handing so much of his domain to his subordinates. He is not even a director of any of the three subsidiary companies, but Clark admits that he would quickly modify his hands-off posture if one of them developed serious operating problems. "If I see a company heading for the rocks," he says, "I would get myself put on its board's agenda and make sure the directors see the problems." ■

Western International: A $1 billion expansion in the face of recession

An obsession with quality has always outranked growth on the list of priorities at Western International Hotels Co., the UAL Inc. subsidiary that operates such glittering properties as the Plaza in New York, the Century Plaza in Los Angeles and the huge new Detroit Plaza in that city's Renaissance Center. Thus the numbers quietly under discussion these days at Western, one of the nation's largest hotel chains, come as something of a surprise. President Harry Mullikin is charting what is easily the most ambitious hotel development program in his company's 50-year history. And while other chains are heading into an imminent recession with similarly aggressive expansion efforts, Western's plan may well be the riskiest of all, because it builds nothing but high-cost luxury hotels and generally insists on taking major equity positions in each.

By 1985, Mullikin plans to add at least 22 deluxe hotels—half in the U.S.—to the company's current 53 units. The plan, which could cost more than $1 billion, is designed to boost Western's 1979 sales of $383.8 million by at least 50% in real terms in five years. Along with Cincinnati, where Western will open its newest U.S. hotel late this year, Mullikin's roster includes Boston, Dallas, St. Louis, and Miami, and there may be more. "I had three calls last week on hotel properties where the developers want an association with Western, and none of them is on our current list," Mullikin notes.

Expensive and exclusive. All the names on it, however, have one thing in common. Each will be a stylish, high-priced operation. Since its formation in 1930 by a group of hotel owners in Washington state and Oregon, Seattle-based Western has stayed with the top of the line in hotels. The cheapest double room at New York's Plaza, the company's most expensive stateside hotel, will cost its occupants $82 a night.

Each of Western's units also has its own name and identity, with no apparent link to Western. That, along with the formidable room rates, makes each of Western's hotels "a bit like a private club," says Mullikin. "You have to be on the inside to know about them." That penchant for exclusivity has paid off handsomely for Western. Its earnings have grown at a compound annual rate of 33% over the past five years to a record $22.6 million last year.

But with a recession approaching and long-term financing either extremely expensive or unavailable at any price, now would not seem to be the time to embark on a major expansion in luxury hotels that cost $100,000 a room to build. Indeed, Mullikin already has pared his list of proposed new units from 31 a year ago in light of the financial markets. Yet with Western's occupancy rates now hovering around 81%, compared with 71% industrywide, Mullikin sees no reason not to push ahead. "The easiest thing in the world for us would be to stop growing," says Mullikin, who joined Western at age 14 as an elevator operator. "But if we did, we would be out of business in 20 years. You have to continue to plant the crop."

For Mullikin, the need to build for the long term is more important than the business downturn the company is likely to suffer over the short run. "We're going to have a drop in business next year, but we'll come out of it, and the projects we're working on take two or three years to bring on line," he declares. "We don't see the logic of stopping everything during a difficult period."

While financing for the four Western hotels opening this year and next is arranged, Mullikin has yet to work out funding for the others he plans. Yet he is not worried. "I really don't know how we'll structure some of these," he admits, "but equity funds are available from associates that want to participate in Western hotels." Indeed, many industry experts believe that Western's expansion gamble will pay off. "The country is going to need a lot of class-A hotel rooms," says one competitor. "The short-term penalty you pay can be offset by the virtues of the market further down the road."

Mullikin's hotel "crop" will involve more risk than those of some other chains, because Western typically owns 25% to 30% of the hotels it manages. By assuming an equity position, Mullikin argues, Western can benefit from the cash flow from depreciation, and over the long term, receive income from the appreciation in the value of the property. But as an investor it can be left holding the bag if the property does not fare well. Other hotel companies, such as Marriott, Sheraton, and Hilton, only manage many of their properties, and they are reducing remaining ownership interests in favor of managerial contracts and franchising arrangements that offer faster growth.

Growing equity. The risks of ownership are even greater when, as now, other hotel chains are barreling into new markets. Such familiar names as Hilton Hotels and Hyatt are unfurling ambitious expansion campaigns of their own. And a raft of newcomers, including Pan Am's Intercontinental, TW Corp.'s Hilton International, and Air France's Meridien chains are rushing into the U.S. market. But Mullikin is convinced the company's ownership policy is well-founded, and he is prepared even to expand Western's equity position in its new hotels in order to support the company's expansion. "We're perfectly willing to take the additional risk, because we feel that by selecting properties properly, they won't fail," he explains.

Some observers question whether such optimism might not contribute to the creation of a glut of hotel rooms in some cities similar to the bulge of the mid-1970s that sent occupancy rates tumbling to a national average of just 62%. In Dallas alone six new hotels are under way or have been announced, Boston boasts seven properties in the works or on the drawing boards, and several ventures also are planned for each of St. Louis, Minneapolis, and Cincinnati—all cities that Western has targeted for new units (BW—Mar. 17).

Steady customers. Mullikin is counting on marketing aggressiveness, as well as Western's reliance on the business travel market, to help the company weather the impending economic downturn and any problems of oversupply. By providing such executive-oriented amenities as 24-hour room service and desks in every room, Western manages to collect fully 85% of its revenues from business travelers. These customers, Mullikin argues, often have to travel even when the economy dips. Indeed, the deep recession of 1974-75 cut only five points from Western's occupancy rates, which remained 10 points above industry average during that period.

Such relatively steady business points up the interest of Western's parent, UAL, in the company's expansion. Like such other airline holding companies as TW Corp., UAL is looking increasingly to its nonairline operations to help smooth the turbulent earnings pattern in its traditional business. Western's $22.6 million in profit last year partly compensated for the $99.5 million loss suffered by United Airlines because of a 58-day strike by machinists and the grounding of the DC-10 airplane.

But while Western is expected to finance its growth on its own, UAL is squarely behind the company's new bid. "I don't want to drain the airline to support a hotel company," explains Richard J. Ferris, UAL's president, "but I don't want to drain the hotel company to support the airline." ∎

Ever since the 1974 credit squeeze bloated the cost of a huge hotel-building program and halted refurbishing of its scruffy older hotels, Ramada Inns Inc. has been the sick man of the U. S. lodging industry. But now Ramada, the world's third-largest hotel chain—with 122 company-owned and 519 franchised hotels—is throwing away its crutches and trying to run again.

Freed from a crushing $130 million in

RAMADA INNS: Renovating Rooms and Rushing Into Gambling

short-term debt by gradual repayments, Ramada is spending $70 million to upgrade its admittedly run-down chain in order to boost room rates and occupancy levels and is betting another $200 million on an ambitious entry into gambling operations. In December, Ramada concluded a deal to buy Las Vegas' Tropicana Hotel for about $75 million. One month before, after several false starts, it finally won approval to build a $130 million hotel-casino in Atlantic City.

Ramada thinks its new growth plans can quadruple earnings by 1982, from the $16 million it is likely to report for 1979. In 1978, Ramada earned $10.2 million on revenues of $322 million, but those profits were still below the company's $15.3 million record in 1973.

Ramada's gaming and refurbishing strategy is a big switch. Growth in the past has come simply from what M. William Isbell, the company's chairman, calls "extruding" new hotels—units generally strung along highways and aimed at middle-income travelers. When the 1974 squeeze hit, Ramada had 25 hotels under construction, all financed short-term. That compared with only two projects for industry leader Holiday Inns Inc., which is triple Ramada's size.

Revolving door. Since 1974, Ramada has not started a single new hotel. Isbell believes that high credit and construction costs mean that—except for the Atlantic City project—"managing the hell out of what we've got" is the key to future success.

Outsiders agree. But they are not sure that Isbell, a shy, owlish man of 44 with a passion for ancient history, is the manager to turn that key. Isbell became president in 1970 and chairman last May, when his father, Marion W. Isbell, who founded Ramada in 1959, retired. Former colleagues describe the younger Isbell as an indecisive and suspicious autocrat who can lure talented executives but quickly alienates them. Since 1977 at least 17 top executives have left Ramada, a few through retirement, but most because of disagreements with Isbell.

Isbell blames Ramada's revolving door on "some bad picks" he has made in trying to switch the company from his father's "entrepreneurial" management style to a "professional" approach. He predicts turnover will slow because "I've finally got my team." Two current, fair-haired lieutenants are French-born Gerrard E. Hallier, executive vice-president, and Juergen Bartels, a tough, detail-oriented German who runs the North American hotel operations. Bartels is personally inspecting Ramada hotels for shabbiness. On one recent tour he plunged under a bed looking for dust, then lined up five dust balls on a dresser-top while barking reproaches at 10 assembled underlings.

Labyrinthine accounting. Former executives say the real power at Ramada is Howard E. Johnson, a group vice-president whose official job is to run a small chain of hospitals that he sold to Ramada in 1970. (He is not related to the family that recently sold its chain of motor inns and restaurants.) Insiders say that Johnson, although based in Los Angeles, spends two or three days a week "lurking" around Ramada's Phoenix headquarters and molding decisions. Isbell concedes that he uses Johnson "to bounce ideas off of."

Johnson, who is friendly with Las Vegas promoters, is largely responsible for pushing Ramada into gambling, which founder Marion Isbell avoided because of its unsavory image. Last year, Johnson and a Las Vegas crony, developer Jay Sarno of the Circus Circus hotel-casino, cooked up plans for a 3,000-room, joint-venture resort on the outskirts of the city. Ramada has also discussed joint casino ventures with Summa Corp., the gaming arm of the late Howard Hughes's empire.

But Tropicana seemed the best deal. Poorly managed and suspected of mob ties, the hotel lost its gaming license last year. Ramada, which recently got its own Nevada gaming license, is buying the hotel's operating company and half its real estate for what Las Vegas sources say is a bargain price. The company has hired Vernon Daniel, a former gaming executive at Del E. Webb Corp., to run the property.

So jumbled is Tropicana's accounting that Isbell says he cannot tell if the resort is making a profit. But the hotel is attractive, and Ramada will spend $5 million on room refurbishing. If Ramada can learn to manage a casino, outsiders predict that the venture will pay off handsomely—with 15% aftertax profit margins on revenues that analysts estimate at $60 million in 1979. Isbell sees the Tropicana as a training ground for the Atlantic City resort.

Forced neglect. When the Atlantic City hotel opens in 1981, it will contain that city's ninth casino. Outsiders fault Ramada for losing time in New Jersey by pushing a less expensive reconstruction

Considering and Choosing Strategies / 221

of an existing hotel—a scheme they say Ramada should have known authorities would reject because it did not meet their standards. But Steven Eisenberg, a gaming analyst with Philips, Appel & Walden Inc., estimates that Atlantic City's relative underdevelopment should earn Ramada a higher return than the Tropicana—possibly a 40% pretax margin, equal to $29 million in aftertax profits in the mid-1980s. Ramada's Hallier predicts that by 1982, gaming will produce 40% of the company's revenues and 55% of profits.

But to entice gamblers, Ramada must upgrade the hotel chain's shabby image. Forced neglect has severely damaged repeat business: One-third of the travelers who have slept in Ramada's beds indicate they are shunning the chain, vs. one-fifth for arch-rival Holiday Inns, according to a Ramada study.

Ramada spent $27 million in 1979 giving major face-lifts to lobbies, rooms, and restaurants of company-owned hotels, and it will spend another $33 million over the next three years on renovation. This month it will hold seven

By 1982, Ramada predicts, gaming will produce 40% of revenues, 55% of profits

regional meetings with its franchisees and their local bankers to push system-wide refurbishing. Franchisees who resist will be drummed out of the chain. "We have ways of getting rid of them," promises hotel boss Bartels.

But Bartels thinks franchisees will go along when they see how refurbishing is paying off. Spending $1 million to upgrade its Dallas airport hotel has allowed Ramada to boost room rates from $18.62 in 1977 to $26.77 by last fall, while occupancy jumped from 56.9% to 77.3%. A profitless Beverly Hills hotel is now a money-maker after a $1.5 million face-lift.

All told, Ramada has raised its average operating profit per company-owned hotel from $101,000 in 1977 to $220,000 in 1979. Isbell hopes that is just the beginning. Hotels built during Ramada's $300 million 1971-75 building boom should become increasingly profitable and will upstage competitors' older units, Isbell believes. "Extruding hotels was expensive," he says, "but it helped create a future for us."

Ramada is financing its new growth with ease. Buoyed by the gambling glamour, it sold $100 million in debentures a year ago and is completing $110 million in bank financing. Ramada has unusual collateral—utility preferred stocks, purchased for $80 million a decade ago when the company was cash-rich and Marion Isbell felt interest rates would fall. Instead, rates rose—forcing Ramada to hold the stock, now worth $54 million, or sell it and take a big earnings write-off. Recently, though, Isbell started selling chunks of the preferred to offset real estate gains. He is using the proceeds to buy utility common shares to protect Ramada's earnings.

Lack of respect. Isbell hopes his growth plans will win over Wall Street. Although its gaming plans made Ramada the most actively traded Big Board issue in 1978, analysts generally dislike Ramada as an investment vehicle because they lack respect for management. Says the research head of a major brokerage firm: "If there's a way to screw things up, they'll find it."

However, even disgruntled former executives concede that Ramada's growth strategy makes sense—with two provisos: Management must learn the gaming business, and Isbell's revolving door must finally close. ∎

CITIBANK:
A Rising Giant in Computer Services

Whenever Citicorp is mentioned, banking naturally comes to mind. But through its Citibank subsidiary, the nation's largest bank holding company is taking on the appearance of a computer company as the bank moves into an ever-broadening range of data processing markets. Its strategy, evolving slowly during the past three years, has stirred up considerable controversy, particularly among the computer companies that are the bank's new competition.

Citibank has targeted three distinct businesses. As a "systems house," the bank is combining its own programs and software with someone else's hardware and marketing the system to end-users. As a remote computing-services company, it is selling time on its own computers to outside customers. And as a software house, Citibank is selling applications software packages to customers who will run them on their own computers.

The diversification plan came about for one simple reason. New competition—from savings banks, savings and loan associations, credit unions, and brokerage houses—was putting the squeeze on Citibank's earnings by moving into such banking activities as interest-bearing checking accounts and by offering higher interest rates for deposits. "We weren't making enough money in our domestic business," acknowledges Robert B. White, the executive vice-president who heads the Financial & Information Services Group, the data processing unit Citibank set up last year. "We had to start looking at new profit and revenue sources in the domestic market, and [data processing] is one of those."

'A beautiful opportunity.' Citibank will not say how much it has invested in its move into data processing, which includes the acquisition, in the past 18 months, of the assets of five computer services companies. But the bank holding company has targeted the information services group to be a major profit center within 10 years. "In the long run," White says, "we would like to represent 10% of Citicorp's profits."

That is not small potatoes. If it happens, the Financial & Information Services Group would become a large operation in its own right, compared with most companies in the computer services industry. Last year, Citicorp reported net income of $541 million, and if the company makes its goal of 15% annual earnings growth throughout this decade, the new group—with a 10% share—could hit profits of $250 million annually by 1990.

While that forecast may sound overly

Citibank's computer services "store": The bank sells programs, other software, and time on its computers.

optimistic, industry observers are impressed by the Citibank strategy. "They have the resources in place, the people in place, the computers, the network, and the software," points out Stephen T. McClellan, a vice-president at Salomon Bros., the New York banking house. "It is a beautiful opportunity to leverage that resource and make a lot of money out of it," he adds.

Streamlining. The Financial & Information Services Group is already profitable, thanks to its being given the bank's traditional business of providing credit to its smaller, correspondent banks. The group was set up primarily to provide these banks and small financial institutions with the software and computer hardware that they would need to automate, the lines of credit to finance such moves, and data-processing and managerial consulting services. "We have identified that what these [smaller institutions] will need to compete and survive is capital funding, management expertise, and an understanding of the use of technology," White says. And he adds: "We are trying to provide that market need."

The foundation for the move into computer services was built in the early 1970s, when Citicorp decided to streamline its own back-office data processing. The giant bank became an acknowledged leader in the use of computers in banking with its "Project Paradise," a program that moved work away from central mainframe computers to smaller minicomputers that could be located at the site where the processing was needed. "We were trying to go for some combination of people, equipment, and space that would allow us to try to provide better service to our customers," White says.

This effort, which had more than its share of delays and problems, finally led to what Citibank calls its "work station approach" to banking. Traditionally, bank processing works much like an assembly line. When a letter of credit comes in, for instance, it can go through as many as six bank employees who record its arrival, check its legality, check credit and terms, and enter the letter into the bank's files. With computer terminals attached to a network of minicomputers, one person can now do the work of six. "In a simplistic sense," White says, "we were trying to take the bank back to precomputer days when one person had access to all the information about a customer."

Back-office processing. Many of the products that the new group is marketing today were born in Project Paradise. Everything—from cash and stock transfer systems to automated teller machine (ATM) systems for small independent

Considering and Choosing Strategies / 223

banks—is aimed at making more efficient the back-office processing at banks, savings and loans, and credit unions. "Most [of these] people have never paid much attention to the back office of banks," says White. By cashing in on this lack of expertise, Citibank has turned what is an operating cost at most banks into a profit center.

Citibank cannot sell computer hardware—thanks to the National Bank Act—but it has figured out ways to get around this constraint. When a customer wants to buy a letter-of-credit system, for example, the bank recommends specific hardware from several vendors and then sells its Citibank software package for a flat fee. And if a small bank wants a back-office processing system, Citibank will install Cititran, a minicomputer-based system that supports a full range of back-office operations including checking, savings, and general ledger. Citibank buys the hardware for the customer, installs the system, and takes care of maintenance and system expansions. The bank charges a monthly fee based on the size of the system and the number of transactions made.

The information services group backs all of its products with consulting and educational services, support that Citibank claims distinguishes it from its data processing competitors. "There are a lot of vendors selling hardware out there," says Alan J. Weber, president of Correspondent Resources Inc., the Citicorp subsidiary that concentrates on signing up banks with less than $300 million in assets. "But," he adds, "there really isn't anyone selling a full ATM program." Citibank, on the other hand, offers to help customers select sites for their ATMs, sends them to Diebold Inc. for the machines, trains employees to operate the system, and provides networking software to link remote machines to a host processor.

General enthusiasm. Such services take correspondent banking a step further than it has ever gone before. Traditionally, such relationships were formed as smaller banks went to the larger institutions for credit. But few of the other larger banks sell software packages or lease the systems they have developed for their own use. "We don't franchise or resell software in any way," acknowledges Douglas A. Warner III, vice-president for operations services at Morgan Guaranty Trust Co. The New York commercial bank is concentrating now on providing such services as balance and transaction information through its Morgan Account Reporting Service. It believes that the Citicorp approach may be a good idea but does not have immediate plans to follow Citicorp's move. "It is a question of time [for Morgan Guaranty]," explains Warner. "We have a full plate of [other] projects."

By moving now, Citibank figures that it will get the jump on big banks that could become competition later. The goal of its information services group is to sell its services to 20% of the 50,000 financial institutions in the U. S. "We aim to be the preeminent source of financial services," says Richard J. Matteis, president of BHC Resources Inc., the Citicorp subsidiary that concentrates on banks with more than $300 million in assets. "No bank right now has a similar strategy for the bank market."

So far, customers have generally been enthusiastic about the Citicorp offerings. Central National Bank, of Chicago, gave all of its back-office processing to Citicorp in March at the same time that the giant bank holding company bought $12 million in the Chicago bank holding company's preferred stock. "Nobody we saw would provide as complete a service," says Jackson W. Smart Jr., chairman of Central National. "We are a mid-sized bank [and] not in a position to develop sophisticated products necessary to compete with larger banks," he adds.

A legal battle. The two-part deal at Central National indicates that the Citibank group could turn out to be more than a profit center for Citicorp. It could be a wedge into nationwide banking, since the rules that prohibit banks from branching across state lines could ease in the future. "If [Citibank] gets close enough to these people in terms of doing their processing, it makes it easier to acquire them," notes Mark Biderman, a vice-president at Oppenheimer & Co., a New York brokerage firm. Citibank's White brushes aside such comments, saying, "It is not a necessary part of the scenario." But he does admit that his information services group cannot help but be a plus for Citibank as the era of national banking approaches. "Clearly," he says, "any relationship you have with anyone is going to help."

But the computer services industry is throwing up roadblocks against Citicorp's move into their markets, and these could slow down, or even cripple, some parts of the company's grand strategy. The Association of Data Processing Service Organizations Inc. (ADAPSO), whose member companies account for the bulk of the $12 billion computer services industry, has filed two actions—a court case against Citibank and an administrative proceeding against Citicorp—to prevent them from providing services that ADAPSO claims are in violation of the National Bank Act and the Bank Holding Company Act. These acts limit banks and their holding companies in offering services unrelated to their basic banking business.

"We have no problem with Citibank selling data processing services that are related to banking," says Jerry L. Dreyer, executive vice-president of ADAPSO. But he worries that Citicorp has an unfair advantage over computer-services vendors because it can cross-subsidize its data processing operations with revenues from its banking activities. "It is not right to let the bank mix an unregulated with a regulated enterprise in this way," Dreyer charges.

Confusing roles? The computer services trade group also believes that Citicorp will benefit from what Dreyer calls a "tying effect"—companies buying computer services from Citibank on the theory that they will have an easier time obtaining loans. "Banks have an opportunity to combine roles and to confuse roles with customers," charges C. Harley Booth, vice-president of Tymshare Inc., a computer services company joining the ADAPSO suit. "They are in a position to suggest more than gently that customers ought to subscribe to their computer services," he says.

ADAPSO has waged its legal battle against Citibank since May, 1977, when it first filed suit against both Citibank and the Comptroller of the Currency, who regulates national banks. Soon after the suit was filed, Citibank agreed out of court that it would not subsidize computer services with profits from other activities and, says Dreyer, it promised not to use the Citibank name for these businesses. But last year, Citicorp applied to the Federal Reserve Board, which regulates all bank holding company activities, for permission to establish Citishare Corp. as a separate subsidiary. "It was pretty transparent," claims Dreyer. ADAPSO then reactivated its 1977 suit and began an action against Citicorp requesting that the bank holding company's petition to set up Citishare—under consideration by the Federal Reserve System—be denied.

ADAPSO hopes that these two actions will clarify just how far banks can go in the data processing marketplace. "The banks are confident that the Comptroller will give them whatever they want," says Dreyer. As a byproduct of the ADAPSO suit, however, the Comptroller is planning to hold hearings on the ruling that outlines the extent to which banks can get into data processing. And the Federal Reserve has agreed to hold a hearing sometime this fall on the Citicorp request.

The ADAPSO suit cites such Citibank services as MODFUN (a credit analysis system that generates reports and balance sheet analyses) as a clear violation of the Bank Act. It is offered by Citishare, the holding company's computer time-sharing service. Another service that ADAPSO is fighting is Database, a library of financial information on 3,000 U. S. and Canadian companies. Both of these Citibank services are offered to the general public as well as to financial institutions. Even further afield from the banking business, according to the ADAPSO suit, is the system that New York City runs on Citibank computers to manage its collections of parking violations.

Here to stay. Citibank categorically denies that the services that it offers are in violation of the banking regulations. In fact, on June 23 the bank filed a counterclaim in the U. S. District Court for the Southern District of New York, claiming that ADAPSO's suit "is a sham designed solely to delay and impede the development and marketing of Citibank's financial information processing services." A Citibank statement accompanying the suit continues: "All of the Citibank services challenged by ADAPSO have traditionally been part of the business of banking." Adds White: "We are not doing anything that is illegal."

Citibank is taking care to spin off any information services group activities that stray from the banking business. Last year, for example, it acquired Lexar Corp., a Los Angeles maker of automated office equipment. When Lexar decided to market the word processing terminal that it had developed for Citibank, Citicorp sold off that part of the business to Lexar employees, who set up Axxa Corp. Still, Citicorp has a minority share in the new company, collects licensing fees on its products, and is its chief lender. Now Citicorp is spinning off Lexar altogether so that the tiny company can market its digital telephone exchange to corporate customers.

Whatever the outcome of the challenges from the computer services industry, it is clear that Citicorp is in financial data processing to stay. In fact, these operations have become such an integral part of its basic banking business that complete divestiture would require a major overhaul of Citibank's long-term corporate strategy. Predicts a confident White: "In five years, we expect to be established in each of our targeted market segments as an accepted full-service supplier." ∎

CATERPILLAR
Sticking to basics to stay competitive

The fashionable management concepts that have been shaping U. S. corporations for the past decade have made no inroads at Caterpillar Tractor Co. As other companies vied with each other to lure top MBAs from prestigious schools, Caterpillar looked to undergraduates at second-string Midwestern colleges to fill its trainee jobs. While others hired a progression of specialists and consultants to craft strategic plans, restructure organizations, and install management techniques, Caterpillar steadfastly stuck with informal planning, minimal protocol, and slow, on-the-job training.

Even when most companies of its size diversified far afield from their businesses, Caterpillar made no acquisitions at all. Instead, it plowed ahead in its three basic lines: earth-moving equipment, diesel engines, and materials-handling devices. Although most traditional competitors categorized those businesses as mature, Caterpillar consistently viewed them as great growth markets.

A single-minded focus

Indeed, Caterpillar justifiably could be labeled hopelessly old-fashioned but for its track record, which more modern companies would envy. In more than half a century, Caterpillar has suffered just one year of loss—and that was 1932, the height of the Depression. Last year the company earned a near-record $565 million on sales of $8.6 billion. "People don't look at us as an interesting, high-flying company, but our management strengths are a hell of a hurdle for competitors to overcome," says E. C. Chapman, executive vice-president for marketing. "There's no magic at all to Caterpillar's success; we just know our business better than anyone else, and we work harder at it."

To Caterpillar managers, working hard at the business means focusing almost single-mindedly on customer needs and on methods to meet them quickly. The company concentrates on building high-quality, reliable products and on ensuring complete servicing, assuming that market share will take care of itself. It has developed a series of complex yet workable arrangements with its extensive dealer network that serve the dual goal of enhancing the dealers' positions as entrepreneurs (box, page 77) and enabling them to provide exemplary service to the customer.

Those arrangements include:
- Encouraging dealers to establish side businesses in rebuilding parts. This not only boosts dealer profitability but also makes Caterpillar products more economical for customers because machines can be repaired at lower cost.
- Introducing new products only after building up a two-month supply of spare parts. This lets dealers service new offerings immediately.
- Keeping tight control of parts inventories to provide 48-hour delivery of any item to any customer in the world.
- Repurchasing parts or equipment that dealers cannot sell. This makes it relatively painless for dealers to keep a full stock of all items.

To be sure, such techniques are neither exotic nor new. But Caterpillar's ability to get—and retain—customer loyalty proves that they work. And it is just such practices, aimed at establishing long-term relationships, that will probably form the prototype for the successful "modern" company of the 1980s.

No specialists or gimmicks, just reliable, quality products

Through the 1970s, behavioral-science gimmickry, complex formulas to spot quick-payout projects, and fancy matrices to describe the perfect product portfolio—all techniques that Caterpillar consistently ignored—were considered the *sine qua non* of management sophistication. But they focused almost single-mindedly on short-term performance.

Today management experts are recognizing that the 1970s' techniques did little to bolster the U. S. economy or to keep foreign competitors from making devastating inroads in American markets. The pendulum is swinging back now to the management approaches exemplified by Caterpillar's "heartland of America" values and practices. Leading universities are again emphasizing operations courses, and companies are again promoting executives with broad-based rather than specialized skills. A back-to-basics movement is taking hold, with practices that Caterpillar has always used.

Caterpillar's stellar performance in a mature, cyclical, and intensely competitive industry is the best advertisement for its approach. Like other domestic manufacturers of construction machinery, Caterpillar contends with a highly paid work force represented by the extraordinarily powerful and strike-prone United Auto Workers. Moreover, the Peoria-based giant is the target of intense efforts by Japanese and European companies. Indeed, the combination of the competitive pressures and a sluggish overall economy caused most of Caterpillar's domestic rivals to hit the skids last year. Deere, JI Case, and Clark Equipment all suffered earnings declines, and International Harvester Co. is now pleading with 275 banks to prop up its tattered balance sheet following a $119 million operating loss in its construction line.

Yet, against the backdrop of an industrywide depression, Caterpillar increased its sales volume by almost $1 billion over 1979—a figure that topped most of its competitors' total sales. Japan's Komatsu Ltd., the closest rival in the $17 billion worldwide construction-equipment market, remains one-fourth Caterpillar's size.

Investing for the long term

Hirosuke Hiraoka, Komatsu's executive vice-president, puts his finger precisely on those elements of Caterpillar's management style that have made the U. S. company virtually invulnerable to attack. "They are very concentrated," he says. "It's the firms that veer off into other industrial areas that are vulnerable. Caterpillar stays in its specialty and strengthens itself by improving its products and services. They are not just buying up other companies the way so many Americans do."

Indeed, many Caterpillar competitors that did stray far afield of narrowly focused businesses and markets are now trying to divest themselves of the excess baggage. International Harvester's financial dilemma stems in large part from having to maintain separate plants and dealer networks in trucks, farm implements, and industrial turbines as

226 / Readings from *Business Week*

well as in construction equipment. Harvester's bankers now insist that the troubled company redirect itself into a narrower assortment of businesses.

By contrast, Caterpillar's three businesses—construction, engines, and materials handling—move in similar markets and sell their products through the same dealer network. Thus, the company need not concentrate its expenditures on serving the short-term requirements of numerous businesses. Rather, it has been consistently willing to spend today for tomorrow's growth. Construction is proceeding apace on a new diesel-engine plant in Lafayette, Ind., and this month Caterpillar announced that it will double the size of its Morton (Ill.) parts-distribution center. In 1980 alone the company spent a staggering $750 million on capital projects and an additional $326 million on research and engineering, with the bulk of those outlays going for robots, computerized machine tools, and other automated equipment geared toward making Caterpillar an even more formidable competitor in the future.

To those of Caterpillar's colleagues that have been struggling to pare expenses to the bone, spending now for some future payout is unthinkable. To Caterpillar's chairman and chief executive, Lee L. Morgan, however, it is common sense. "Our method might not work in Silicon Valley, but in our business the lead times are long," he explains. "It takes 10 years or more to develop and introduce a new product. To us, short-term planning means the next five years."

The same long-term approach has marked Caterpillar's attitude toward executive development. For example, where other companies are just now recognizing the fallacy of fast-track programs for newly minted MBAs, Caterpillar has always started its potential managers near the bottom, usually right on the production line. There are no overnight stars in the organization; indeed, ambitious climbers generally leave the company. Both Chairman Morgan, who holds an undergraduate degree in agriculture from the University of Illinois, and President Robert E. Gilmore, who never finished college, rose through the Caterpillar ranks via long, arduous apprenticeships—as did most other top executives and key managers.

The result has been a highly inbred and intensely loyal cadre of employees. "Most of our people develop a very sincere concern about the company. It evolves gradually, but [ultimately] the attitude comes that 'I want to be with Caterpillar for the rest of my life,'" Morgan maintains. Indeed, most high-level Caterpillar managers have been at the company for more than 25 years, and they have developed an ease in working together that is the envy of Caterpillar's competitors. "There is an informality to

Managers usually work their way up the ranks

decisions that is based on mutual trust between people," explains Lawrence Williams, a marketing manager. "We don't have the quagmire of rules that most big companies have."

Caterpillar does, of course, have guidelines. For instance, new product ideas must meet three tests before they are even considered for discussion. "Unless a product is highly capital-intensive, will benefit from high-level technology, and is marketable through our current distribution system, it won't fit our product-development strategy," explains Chapman, the top marketing man.

But the judgment as to whether a product meets those tests—and whether to proceed with its development—is made by consensus all the way up the line. A product-control department comprised of representatives from manufacturing, marketing, and engineering assesses potential competition and forecasts sales volume for five years. The final decision rests with a committee composed of Chairman Morgan, five executives from his office, and several key vice-presidents. "People begin bouncing ideas off one another, and after a series of meetings, the project finds its way into official status," Morgan says. "I am presumably the guy who makes the decision, but I'm heavily influenced by the consensus."

To arrive at that consensus, Morgan conducts informal discussions that explore all aspects of a project. "When our senior management meets, there are no minutes, and we never decide things by votes," the chairman explains. "Our whole management structure is as simple as we can make it. There is very little rigid structure."

An integral part of the informal communication process is the discussion of long-range plans—which is one reason Morgan has emphatically refused to set up corporate planning as a separate function. Caterpillar's main goal in its strategic plans is to foster product development in each of its businesses. "From our product plans, which are mapped out far in advance, flow facilities planning, financial plans, and human resources plans," Morgan explains.

Not surprisingly, the vast majority of research money is targeted directly toward product development, product improvement, and applied research. Caterpillar will undertake "pure" research only when it needs new materials or components that its suppliers cannot provide. For example, when the rubber industry failed to produce a tire that worked well for Caterpillar's big loaders, the company designed and manufactured a beadless tire that is now produced by Goodyear Tire & Rubber Co. for other customers under a licensing agreement.

With research geared almost exclusively to existing products, Caterpillar is rarely the first to come up with a new offering in its markets. But being on the leading edge has never been one of the company's goals. It has built its reputation by letting other companies go through the trial-and-error process of introducing new products. Caterpillar later jumps in with the most trouble-free product on the market.

Indeed, Caterpillar products do not usually even sport the lowest price tag. The company relies instead on its name for quality and reliable service to woo customers. "Market share for us is not an objective. Building sophisticated, durable, reliable products and providing good support is," maintains David S. Gould, vice-president of the fast-growing Engine Div.

The ability to provide such service comes from a massive distribution system that not only guarantees available parts for even brand-new products but also ensures replacement parts for any Caterpillar machine within 48 hours of a customer's order. The company has built in its own incentive for such service: If the parts are not delivered on its timetable, the customer gets them free.

Such stringent rules for parts availability serve a dual purpose. They have cemented Caterpillar's image among customers as a company that always responds to their needs. And they assure dealers that the company stands ready to provide backup support for its products from their inception, giving the dealers confidence to devote ample promotional dollars to new offerings. "We look at ourselves as a marketing arm trying to convince the customer that Caterpillar represents a continuing value for his investment," says G. L. Ward, manager of the huge Morton parts-distribution center.

Besides being an effective marketing tool, the parts operation is highly profitable in its own right. The Morton center, with its automated warehouse that carries a 60-day inventory of more than 200,000 parts, is the base of an elaborate computer network linking dealers and depots around the world. Sales of these parts provide earnings stability when demand for original equipment is

Considering and Choosing Strategies / 227

depressed. "They have such a huge base of machines in the field that parts are close to a razor-blade business," says Frank E. Manfredi, a construction equipment analyst at Dataquest Inc., a marketing research company in Cupertino, Calif. "Obviously, the vast volume helps them remain the low-cost producer."

Caterpillar's extensive distribution network is both its most formidable marketing tool and one of its greatest defenses against competition. Even though Komatsu's crawler tractors are perceived as well-made and carry a price tag 10% lower than comparable Caterpillar machines, for instance, many potential customers slip away because of the Japanese company's relatively small parts and service capability.

Conversely, Caterpillar's distribution ability has helped it make healthy inroads overseas. More than 57% of the company's sales are outside the U. S.; the European and African-Mideastern markets account for almost $1.3 billion

Caterpillar's backbone: A long dealer network

Caterpillar Tractor Co.'s mammoth dealer network is probably the biggest obstacle to competitors who try to breach Caterpillar's markets. The dealerships are all independently owned, but a competitor's chances of wooing any dealer into his own camp seem almost nonexistent. "Our average dealer can count on a steady income from service, maintenance, and used-machine business generated by at least several thousand machines operating in his territory, and competitors who don't have that base can't afford the investment it takes to provide first-class services," maintains E. C. Chapman, executive vice-president for marketing.

Indeed, the 93 domestic and 137 overseas dealerships have blossomed into rich and diversified companies in their own right. With the strong encouragement of Caterpillar, many have established related businesses, such as refurbishing tractor parts and rebuilding diesel engines, that add to both their service capability and their own bottom lines. Average sales of $100 million and a typical net worth approaching $4 million give the dealerships the financial muscle to expand selling and service capabilities at the same pace that Caterpillar expands its product line. During the past year, dealers spent more than $200 million to add new buildings and equipment.

"We approach our dealers as partners in the enterprise, not as agents or middlemen," says Caterpillar Chairman Lee L. Morgan. "We worry as much about their performance as they do themselves." The dealers themselves are effusive in their praise of relations with Caterpillar. "They have consistently supplied us with superior products and a high-quality program of parts and product information," says Frank O. Moyle, executive vice-president of Patten Industries Inc., a dealer in Chicago's Elmhurst suburb.

Strong customer relations. But the strength of the dealer system lies less in the relations with Caterpillar than in the dealers' relations with customers. "It is our people—not Caterpillar's—who have to understand the customer's business well enough to match his needs with the right equipment," Moyle says.

Patten comes close to being an archetypal Caterpillar dealer. Besides making routine sales calls to promote business, Patten has added branches in Rockford, Ill., and Hammond, Ind., since its founding in 1933. Today it has more than 400 employees, a production line to rebuild Caterpillar engines, and a shop that refurbishes track shoes and other tractor parts. Its customers can

Dealer Moyle: His Illinois operation, with 400 workers, rebuilds engines and tractor parts, in addition to selling.

buy rebuilt parts that last about 80% as long as new ones yet cost only half the price. Caterpillar loses some new-parts sales, but it encourages the practice because its equipment becomes more economical in the long run for the customer.

Caterpillar goes out of its way to make sure dealers' inventories are at the right level. There is a national computer network linking all dealers to the Morton (Ill.) distribution center, enabling them to order any part they need for delivery the next day. The company will buy back parts the dealers do not sell. And it tries to pace its introduction of new products according to dealers' capabilities. For example, because many dealers are still gearing up to handle the expansion of engine sales, Caterpillar will probably limit its new-product introductions over the next few years, although it has been developing a four-wheel-drive farm tractor.

The company also conducts dozens of training programs for dealers and product demonstrations for their customers. Last year it assembled a large group of dealers and company personnel in Europe to demonstrate the competitive advantages of Caterpillar's excavating equipment. And it invited 300 mining executives from eight countries to New Mexico for a demonstration of Caterpillar machines in mining operations.

The company even conducts a course in Peoria to encourage dealers' children to remain in the business. "We had a dealer's son who was studying for the ministry and had a secondary interest in music," Chapman recalls. "By the time we sent him home, he changed his career plan. He has become one of our most successful dealers."

apiece, and sales in Latin America and in the Asia-Pacific Basin area are each closing in on the $1 billion mark. Sales outside the U. S. last year surged 19.8%, compared with a gain of only 4.9% in the recession-torn domestic market. The company has just formed its first joint venture in Mexico, in cooperation with CYDSA Group of Monterrey, to produce earth-moving machines. For well over a decade it has participated in a highly profitable joint venture in Japan with Mitsubishi Heavy Industries Ltd., enabling it to garner close to 35% of a market that Komatsu understandably dominates. And recently it became the beneficiary of the first U. S. loan to be made to Moscow since the Soviet invasion of Afghanistan in 1979. First National Bank of Chicago is arranging a $25 million credit to the Russians to enable them to purchase either new Caterpillar tractors or parts.

Caterpillar continues to seek robust markets for its products at home as well. "There is still tremendous opportunity in our vehicular markets," Chairman Morgan insists. "We're not anywhere near the end of the product line that can be manufactured by us and sold and serviced through our dealers."

Most of the growth in future years will probably revolve around the company's engine division rather than around its heavy equipment. By 1980, after investing some $1.5 million to expand engine output, Caterpillar had built sales in nonconstruction markets such as standby electrical-generating and oil-field equipment to about $1.4 billion, and that volume has increased more than 20% since then. "We are counting very heavily on the engine business to keep us growing in the next 10 years as rapidly as we have in the past," says Morgan.

The increased volume has enabled Caterpillar to justify extensive modernization programs for its engine-manufacturing plants. A centerpiece of those programs was the 1978 addition to the 12-year-old Mapleton (Ill.) facility, which makes engine blocks and crankshafts. The addition brought one of the dirtiest jobs in the industry—melting iron, pouring it into molds, and cleaning off the cooled castings—into the electronic age. Factory robots are now venting molds and drying molded pieces, while workers in air-conditioned cabs operate manipulators that remove the castings.

The company is modernizing older plants as well. At the Decatur (Ill.) facility, a $357,000 computerized machining center just took the place of three antiquated machines. The new center can make some 80 different parts at a production rate of seven pieces per hour, triple the total output of the machines it replaced. Moreover, the new center requires only two operators instead of the five needed previously. "Our large volume allows us to use high-technology machining systems and automatic transfer lines to reduce unit costs and guarantee better quality," claims President Gilmore.

Friction on the assembly line

The automation program has done little to help the company with one of its major trouble spots, however: labor relations. The old-fashioned approach reflected in the emphasis on customers and dealers has brought with it a concomitant deemphasis on blue-collar workers. As a result, the fierce loyalty that Caterpillar has so consciously instilled in its white-collar staff does not extend to the assembly line. In 1979 the company and the UAW endured an unusually bitter strike that idled some 40,000 workers for more than 11 weeks at Peoria plants and more than 7 weeks at other U. S. sites. Although the company until recently managed to steer clear of huge layoffs, it began a cutback last summer that has resulted in 5,600 workers being laid off. "The relationship could be a lot better," says Robert L. Davidson, president of Peoria Local 974. And one plant manager admits that dealings with workers "have been going downhill for 30 years, and it's going to take at least 10 years to turn them around."

It is a problem that Caterpillar management does not take lightly. "There is friction," admits Morgan, "and to remain competitive, it must be addressed." Last year, Caterpillar started experimenting with quality circles, an approach that encourages assembly-line workers to form problem-solving groups to identify and analyze problems and recommend solutions. Dale W. Turnbull, head of the company's Towmotor Corp. forklift subsidiary, says the union has been "very much behind the concept."

Caterpillar is also using its employee newsletters and other internal communications vehicles to drive home to labor the point that foreign competition can affect their jobs. Turnbull notes that the publicity given to the troubles of Chrysler Corp., White Motor Corp., and others "have put a real concern and awareness to the average blue-collar worker of the vulnerability of American industry."

Caterpillar's trumpeting of the new foreign pressure is not just a ploy to spur its workers to greater productivity. Despite rivals' claims that the company is invincible, Caterpillar itself is deeply concerned about mounting competition.

A number of companies emerged from the 1970s with greater muscle for doing battle in the coming years. For example, Germany's IBH Holding Co., with the acquisition of two European companies last year plus the purchase of Terex Corp. from General Motors Corp., has established a broad machinery line and an extensive international dealer network that Chairman Horst Dieter Esch projects can bring IBH into a strong No. 2 spot behind Caterpillar (BW—Apr. 20). Tenneco Inc.'s JI Case Co. subsidiary greatly broadened its construction line in the past 12 years with the acquisitions of Drott Mfg., Davis Mfg. and 40% of Poclain, a large French excavator manufacturer. Case's construction equipment sales topped $1.5 billion last year, and it was second only to Caterpillar in the North American market. Deere & Co., with a strong base in the farm-implement business, already has more than a 25% share of the U. S. crawler market and is gearing up for aggressive expansion overseas. Its construction line inched over the $1 billion mark last year. And Germany's Daimler-Benz just acquired Euclid Inc., a manufacturer of off-highway hauling trucks, and has recently been rumored as a possible suitor for International Harvester's troubled construction-equipment unit.

More competition

Komatsu also is closing in. It has boosted its network to 60 dealers, compared with Caterpillar's 93. That move may soon pay off in the limited categories in which Komatsu competes—mostly crawler tractors and loaders, where it holds an estimated 5% to 8% U. S. share. What is more, at January's industry trade show, Komatsu signaled its plans to broaden its product offerings by exhibiting a huge off-highway hauler and a hydraulic shovel. "We believe we can increase our market share in the U. S. to about 20% within five years," says Takachika Anada, president of Komatsu's U.S. subsidiary.

So far, the mounting competition has done little to hurt Caterpillar in any of its markets. But the company's intense concern is a quintessential example of its long-view approach toward solving potential problems before they have a chance to cause major damage. It is that approach that causes competitors and analysts alike to see Caterpillar as invincible. "They have such an excellent organization I don't know how anyone can knock it," says Charles Weitz, president of IBH's Terex Unit. And Alexander Blanton, an analyst with Merrill Lynch, Pierce, Fenner & Smith Inc. who has watched the company closely for years, sums up: "If Caterpillar is vulnerable, I certainly don't see where the weakness is." ∎

Considering and Choosing Strategies / 229

WHY ESMARK SOLD A PROFITABLE SUBSIDIARY

University of Notre Dame basketball coach Richard "Digger" Phelps recently chided his friend, Esmark Inc. President Donald P. Kelly, about Esmark's plan to sell off its profitable Vickers Energy Corp., and Kelly responded with a characteristic one-liner. "We had a problem with a gas station in South Bend, so we decided to sell off the whole company," said Kelly. But while he was joking, the plan to auction off the capital-intensive energy subsidiary was nevertheless hatched suddenly earlier this year while Kelly was striving to relieve the strain that a long series of acquisitions had put on Esmark's balance sheet.

As Kelly recalls it, his first notion was to sell off another subsidiary—according to some sources, the $520 million International Playtex Inc. But when he noted the huge prices commanded on energy divestitures—such as Seagram Co.'s sale of its Texas Pacific Oil Co. to Sun Co. for $2.3 billion—he decided to put a for-sale sign on Vickers and its valuable TransOcean Oil Inc. subsidiary.

The decision was a quick way for Esmark to capitalize on frenzied interest in oil-producing properties and reserves. The sale would also generate badly needed cash to pay down its long-term debt, to cover some $250 million in write-offs on its fresh meat business, and to finance expansion of its consumer products and specialty chemicals businesses. Indeed, at $1.01 billion, the Vickers sale price is more than twice its book value of $500 million, and 50% more than Salomon Bros., Esmark's investment bankers, originally estimated.

Top performer. Still, the move is not without considerable risk. In selling off Vickers—which is made up of Vickers Petroleum Corp., a refining and marketing company, TransOcean Oil, an exploration and development company, and Doric Petroleum Inc., a gas processing company—Esmark is dropping its top-performing unit, which generated 42% of total operating earnings in 1979. Further, TransOcean holds 18.9 million bbl. of crude oil reserves, 237.9 billion cu. ft. of gas, and 2.3 million acres of undeveloped property, including 500,000 acres in the promising Rocky Mountain Overthrust Belt of Wyoming and Utah.

In defending the sale, Kelly explains: "We had to create additional funding. If we had held on to the energy business, we would have had to plow back such huge sums into exploration and development that it would have held down earnings growth anyway."

Esmark's decision to overhaul its operations began taking shape last December. Debt had reached 48% of total capitalization, and Kelly foresaw dangers to the company's credit rating and to planned acquisitions, particularly of Danskin Inc., with which discussions had already begun (they were successfully completed in April). At the same time, the company was searching for a way to drop its money-losing fresh meat business (BW—July 14).

On June 26, Kelly's plan was unveiled. Vickers would be auctioned off, the meat plants sold or shuttered, debt trimmed, and up to 50 of Esmark's common stock bought back. Kelly's long-term goal was a sounder base for continued acquisitions, one prime target being Louisville-based Reliance Universal Inc., a specialty chemicals maker.

Antitrust fears. Esmark initially aimed to sell Vickers in one chunk. But before the highly secretive Aug. 4–19 auction began in Dallas and Houston, it decided to break Vickers up into the three parts. The reason: Esmark feared that potential antitrust action aimed at breaking up overlapping operations might inhibit some companies from bidding for the Vickers operation as a whole.

In all, Esmark got 30 bids, with Mobil Corp. winning the biggest plum, TransOcean, for $740.1 million. Mobil's attraction to TransOcean was its huge onshore acreage, particularly in the Overthrust Belt where Mobil, among the oil majors, had been conspicuous by its absence. TransOcean thus fits into Mobil's shift back to onshore exploration and development in the U.S.

In a financing arrangement that could save Esmark up to $100 million in taxes, Mobil will make a tender offer for 12 million Esmark common shares, then exchange those shares with Esmark in a tax-free deal for TransOcean shares. Esmark will also receive a 10% royalty on oil and gas profits from unexplored TransOcean acreage—after Mobil accounts for its costs plus an undisclosed profit.

The other buyers. Of the remaining Vickers properties, Vickers Petroleum, which includes a refinery and 350 service stations, will be bought by Total Petroleum

The deal was a quick way to capitalize on the frenzy of interest in oil

(North America) Ltd. for $245 million in cash. And Doric Petroleum will be sold for $26.5 million in cash to Petro-Lewis Corp.

While the earnings potential of stripped-down Esmark remains to be seen, few shareholders are complaining. Since rumors of a restructuring began in the spring, Esmark's common stock has soared from the mid-$20 range to more than $57 recently. And Mobil's tender offer for Esmark shares is now pegged at $60 a share. If the tender offer is successful, Esmark common shares outstanding will shrink to just 10 million. As a result, figures Michael Steinberg, a partner in the New York investment firm of Sloate, Weisman, Murray & Co., the trimmed-down conglomerate "can earn $10 a share this year." Notes Kelly: "I didn't see anything that would have gotten the stock to $60 [without the Vickers sale]." ∎

KAISER STEEL:
The Strategic Question is Whether to Liquidate

A planned liquidation is difficult at any time. Managers' morale is low because of uncertainties over which operations will survive and which will be shut down. Labor unions worry about layoffs and dismissals. And management of existing operations becomes a major chore. For Kaiser Steel Corp., the problems are even more intense. When Chairman Edgar F. Kaiser Jr. suggested in his July 30 shareholders' report that he might liquidate the company because of continued losses in steel, not only did the announcement bring forth the usual problems, but because the liquidation itself is uncertain, there is even more confusion.

Says Frank M. Yans, a steel expert at Arthur D. Little Inc. (ADL), who is studying Kaiser's dual alternatives: "The simple fact is that you don't manage a company when you don't know whether it will survive. You have to make the fate of a company certain to attract people. You need a corporate commitment to a strategy."

The lack of that commitment has not been lost on its steelworkers. The possibility of liquidation is underscored by the fact that the company has already sold off some nonsteel assets—in ships and natural resources—in the past year. Moreover, Wall Street, expecting Kaiser to complete its sell-offs or seek a merger, has run the company's stock up as high as $50.75 per share from a 1979 low of about $18. So strongly do these actions point to some sort of end to Kaiser Steel that workers at Kaiser's fully integrated steel mill, the Fontana Works in California, are currently considering a wage cut of $1 per hour to encourage the company to stay in business.

Breathing room. Even if the workers agree to a $9 million to $10 million pay cut, there is no certainty that the company will remain in business. Edgar Kaiser, hardly optimistic, reported to stockholders: "It is impossible now to say with any certainty when or if there will be a turnaround." Kaiser's steel operation has experienced three successive years of losses: Last year it suffered an operating loss of $5 million on $738.6 million in sales, and in this year's first half an additional $4.6 million was lost.

What could give the company breathing room is the cash from the nonsteel operations it has sold. Hein Poulus, an assistant to Kaiser, suggests that the company's cash trove of $278 million has "bought time" to consider the options. And ADL's Yans says there may be an "intermediate position" between liquidation and business-as-usual for Kaiser to fall back on. There are expectations that ADL's analysis will be presented at the Sept. 5 directors' meeting, and while Yans will not telegraph his recommendations, the odds are that Kaiser will remain in business and continue to invest in the steel operations which do best, such as line pipe and steel plate.

Poor locations. One weight for remaining in business has been added to the scales: In mid-August the company won $97 million in contracts for steel pipe that will be used to transport natural gas from Canada to the U.S. Another boost could come from a host of energy projects now on the drawing boards of oil companies, including construction of huge synthetic fuels plants and stepped-up oil and gas drilling from the Rocky Mountains to the Pacific Coast. Kaiser is one of only two steelmakers west of the Mississippi, and it is the only integrated steel company on the West Coast.

Liquidation might thus be postponed or forgotten. In that event, Edgar Kaiser, the 38-year-old grandson of the company's founder, will have to find a viable means of competing in steel, which has dragged down profits. Last year the Oakland-based company earned $48.5 million on sales of $994.8 million, mainly because of an extraordinary gain of $112.3 million before taxes on the sale of its share in Hamersley Holdings Ltd., an Australian iron ore company. Similarly, in the first half of 1980, Kaiser netted $98.2 million on sales of $487.6 million, primarily from $117 million in extraordinary investment gains from Kaiser Resources Ltd. An extraordinary gain in the third quarter will come from the sale of four bulk cargo ships for $65 million, while steel operations continue their lag.

Kaiser's problems in steel are legion. It has long faced exceptionally high labor and raw materials costs and has had to cope with facilities that were poorly located. During World War II, Kaiser built its Fontana mill 45 mi. east of Los Angeles so that it would be out of range of Japanese fire. This meant that Kaiser would face higher costs than other steelmakers. The company's costs for iron ore and coal now run about $20 per ton, or $40 million per year, higher than if the minerals were purchased at a deep-water port.

Ironically, though Japanese guns never damaged Kaiser, its steel industry has. Imported steel, mostly from Japan, now has 46% of the market in the West.

Labor has caused Kaiser's other traditional cost squeeze. Since 1959, Kaiser has habitually started its negotiations with the United Steel Workers by accepting the terms agreed to by the Big Nine Eastern steelmakers. From that beginning, Kaiser locals have added additional benefits. During the last three years, Kaiser's labor costs have averaged 66¢ per hour more than the other companies, causing labor as a percent of production costs to reach 45%, compared with an industry average of 40%.

Edgar Kaiser has moved to correct a number of the company's disadvantages in the year that he has been chief executive. In labor negotiations in July, the company persuaded the union to accept lesser increases in fringe benefits than those won from other steelmakers. But these merely reduced Kaiser's labor disadvantage from 66¢ per hour higher than average to 58¢. In plant and equipment, Kaiser has pumped money into Fontana to build new basic oxygen furnaces and install efficient continuous casters. But it has failed to modernize fully its equipment for finishing steel. Not surprisingly, LTV Corp. and a Japanese steelmaker have investigated purchasing Kaiser's steel facilities during the last year but have decided against it. "LTV told me they found that the mill was worth less than zero," declares one industry source.

Demoralized management. Kaiser's board will have to decide whether Kaiser's new business prospects and the union's will-

Considering and Choosing Strategies / 231

ingness to accept substantial pay cuts could generate a turnaround. The evidence will have to be compelling, because Kaiser is now mainly a company of attractive liquid assets. In addition it has more than 1 billion tons of coal reserves in New Mexico and Utah that seem ripe for sale.

Even if Kaiser decides to keep its doors open, however, it will face more problems than just its steel operations. The company has been in a management "cutback position" since last September, says one company source. Some 1,000 jobs have been eliminated, mostly at the supervisory or management level. How the company will plan growth from this vitiated management position remains to be seen. In the meantime, political pressure is building. California Governor Jerry Brown has begun jawboning to prevent liquidation, which would eliminate 12,000 jobs. In any case, Kaiser must make its decision soon if it is to avoid further turmoil with managers, labor, and the government.

THE CHORES FACING POLAROID'S NEW CEO

For months little has gone right at Polaroid Corp., the company that invented instant photography. Earnings and employment have slumped while inventories and plant capacity have risen. So when Edwin H. Land, the company's 70-year-old founder, announced on Mar. 6 his intention to step aside as chief executive after 43 years, few tears of regret were shed. Instead, the news was greeted with sighs of relief from both Cambridge, Mass., where the company is based, and Wall Street. "His technical genius will be dearly missed," says one observer, "but this is the nicest thing that could have happened to Polaroid."

Although Land will remain chairman, many observers feel the top management change is likely to lead to a long-overdue revamping of the company's corporate strategy, including its marketing methods and its product mix. "I think you'll see a more pragmatic and efficient business approach," says Eugene G. Glazer, an analyst at Dean Witter Reynolds Inc. "Polaroid has been technology driven, but now there will be more emphasis on the controls side." Adds another analyst, "It won't get away from R&D entirely, but there'll be less focus on the R than on the D."

To be sure, Land cannot be blamed for all of the company's recent misfortunes. Insiders note that his successor, President William J. McCune Jr., a 41-year Polaroid veteran, has been de facto CEO for many months anyway. Yet Land's preoccupation with technological achievement over the years has left the company ill-equipped to deal with today's volatile business climate. "Polaroid has been run to further technology," asserts one analyst. "It has not been run as a profitable enterprise."

Nonconsumer markets. To achieve long-term growth, Polaroid will apparently need to shift steadily into both new consumer and nonconsumer markets. McCune, who will officially take the reins at the close of the annual stockholders' meeting on Apr. 22, is considered likely to accelerate inroads already made in new areas. As for new consumer products, analysts say opportunities in the post-Land era may include such areas as video players, long-life storage batteries, and electronic photography—one of the more promising nonsilver photo processes.

Although the consumer market for instant photography is maturing, there is considerable potential for instant photography and its technological byproducts in nonconsumer markets. Last year, Polaroid introduced several film products for use in medical imaging, and it established a 20-person medical marketing group. This month it began selling its sonar transducer—an automatic focusing device previously used only on its cameras—to nonphotographic users.

Hand in hand with a shift toward broadening its product mix, observers expect Polaroid to reexamine its marketing methods. Traditionally, Polaroid's efforts to sell its instant cameras and film have been aimed at the consumer. Now, Polaroid may have to follow the lead of Eastman Kodak Co., which controls nearly 40% of the instant photography market, and work more closely with retailers. "Land always felt his products could create their own market," says Glazer. "But nowadays you have to find out what the market wants first."

One Land invention consumers evidently do not want, for example, is Polavision, an instant movie system. Last year, Polaroid took a $68 million write-off on the product, and its earnings fell to $36 million from $118 million in 1978. At the same time sales slipped 1% to $1.36 billion.

Personnel slashed. Even so, the company's financial prospects are expected to improve somewhat this year because of a companywide retrenchment. Employment has been slashed about 12% from a year ago through layoffs and attrition. And just last month, Polaroid trimmed operations further by selling a partly built production facility in Andover, Mass., to Digital Equipment Corp.

Land's stepping down has renewed rumors that Polaroid may be a takeover target, but most analysts consider a merger unlikely. However, because McCune is 64, there is speculation that Polaroid will start looking for an outsider to groom for the top job. ∎

Considering and Choosing Strategies / 233

COULD BANKRUPTCY SAVE CHRYSLER?

When Lee A. Iacocca took over as president of Chrysler Corp. in November, 1978, the ensuing top-level management shuffle soon earned him the nickname of Lee Ayatollah. Now, one year and $800 million in losses later, Iacocca continues to live up to his moniker by virtually holding the U. S. government hostage. His ultimatum: Either give massive federal aid to keep Chrysler a full-line auto maker or face liquidation of the nation's 10th largest manufacturing company—one that employs 115,000 workers.

Chrysler executives claim to have ruled out all other options as unworkable. The company cannot pare back to a profitable core, as has American Motors Corp., they say, because Chrysler dealers need a complete line of cars to compete effectively with the wider choice of models offered by General Motors Corp. and Ford Motor Co. And Iacocca insists a reorganization under the new federal bankruptcy code would lead to total collapse, because car sales would screech to a halt as soon as the company filed for Chapter 11. "We've looked at all the alternatives," says one Chrysler vice-president, "and it's all or nothing."

But Congress, along with the company's own bankers, is increasingly skeptical that a simple infusion of cash will solve Chrysler's problems. As a result, each passing day increases the possibility that federal aid will not come in sufficient quantities or in time (the company is expected to run out of cash by mid-February) to keep the company afloat.

A white flag. As the prospect of Chrysler's bankruptcy becomes more real, there is now growing speculation about a reorganization strategy that would allow Chrysler to survive on its own and without federal aid. Many bankruptcy experts and auto industry observers insist that a bid to reorganize Chrysler would not inevitably lead the company into liquidation, as its executives claim. Says Professor Eugene E. Jennings, a management consultant at Michigan State University: "Chrysler needs a contingency plan that includes the intelligent use of bankruptcy."

Others believe Chrysler has to come up with a plan to undo the strategic mistakes of the past. While no conceivable restructuring is likely to preserve the auto maker's full-line status, these experts contend that a reorganization would give Iacocca a white flag under which he could hold off the company's creditors and halt interest payments while whittling the troubled No. 3 domestic car company down to a leaner and more viable core. Among various options, they suggest:

■ Building only what the car market is buying. This would mean discontinuing slow-selling full-sized and intermediate car lines and either shutting down big-car plants permanently or converting them so they can produce more popular models, such as Chrysler's front-wheel-drive Omni and Horizon subcompacts.

■ Selling off large chunks of the company. As a limited-line producer, Chrysler would have little need for its vast parts-making operations, which have been running in the red because of extensive underutilization. And, as a last resort, Chrysler might further support remaining auto operations by selling off all or some of its profitable units, including its tank business, Chrysler Financial Corp., its New Process Gear division, and its Huntsville (Ala.) electronics division.

■ Merging its nameplates. Chrysler could pull together its Chrysler-Plymouth and Dodge lines into a single line to simplify assembly, reduce costly inventory of duplicate parts, and streamline its selling operations.

■ Augmenting its lines with "niche" cars that would be unusual enough to warrant a high price, and high profit, even with such low sales volumes as 30,000 cars a year—a strategy that revived BMW, the German sports car manufacturer. Such a plan might allow Chrysler to trade on its strong suit. "People have great respect for Chrysler engineering, if it can find a way to capitalize on it," says one industry expert.

■ Affiliating with another auto maker. A cash-rich carmaker, such as Volkswagen of America Inc., might help it finance its programs while augmenting its lineup with foreign-designed cars.

Iacocca is so adamantly opposed to such restructuring schemes that company insiders predict that the Chrysler chairman would quit rather than manage the company through bankruptcy proceedings that, he is convinced, can only lead to liquidation anyway. Washington has been reluctant to challenge Iacocca's assessment. But Congress has stalled plans for federally guaranteed loans to Chrysler, and some observers say it now is trying to avoid blame for allowing Chrysler to fail by adding so many conditions to its aid package that it is becoming unworkable.

"They've been trying to sell us a pig in a poke," complains Senator Richard G. Lugar (R-Ind.), the prime architect of a three-year wage freeze built into the Senate version of the bailout bill. The bill would give Chrysler $1.3 billion in loan guarantees as part of a $4 billion assistance package. But it requires the United Auto Workers to accept a three-year wage freeze, saving $1.3 billion, and forces the company to raise the balance through asset sales and other nonguaranteed new financing.

Flagging support. The provisions could scuttle the rescue program altogether. The union, the company, and Treasury Secretary G. William Miller hotly oppose any freeze, and that alone could force Chrysler into bankruptcy. "If in the final bill, the UAW has to come up with $1 billion in concessions," admits a Chrysler official, "the ball game is over." Even Chrysler's banks began backpedaling from a show of support when flagging auto sales last fall worsened the Chrysler outlook.

So far Chrysler management refuses to swerve from the recovery plan it mapped out last September. That $13.6 billion program would revamp Chrysler's entire lineup of automobiles into three "platforms" of front-wheel-drive vehicles by 1985.

The 'orphan syndrome.' As the federal bailout package unravels, however, Chrysler may be forced to turn to the federal government for a different form of aid—protection from its creditors under the federal bankruptcy laws. But there is great dispute over what would happen in a Chapter 11. Says one knowledgeable source: "Its assembly plants could be converted, but it would be a monumentally expensive program. And who would want to buy the unused plants?"

But another argues that foreign auto makers, who have been thinking about U.S.-based plants, might be prospective buyers if the price were right.

Any strategy the company might devise to pull out of reorganization would first have to clear the hurdle of bankruptcy itself. Despite the revival of a $300-a-car rebate program, dealer inventories swelled to a 134-day backlog in November. "People even now are staying away from Chrysler because of the 'orphan syndrome,'" notes auto analyst David B. Healy of Drexel Burnham Lambert Inc. A formal declaration of bankruptcy would probably drive away all but die-hard Chrysler loyalists. At the same time, scores of Chrysler's 5,000 major suppliers would probably be dragged into bankruptcy themselves by a Chrysler collapse, because their trade debt would be tied up for years in reorganization.

All that does not have to happen, say some bankruptcy lawyers, who think Iacocca has been too hasty in discarding Chapter 11 as an option. Washington bankruptcy specialist Murray Drabkin argues that the company might be able to preserve an acceptable level of car sales during reorganization by launching a campaign aimed at convincing consumers that it is at last taking the drastic steps necessary to turn itself around. And with priority given to claims of suppliers and lenders who come to the aid of a company in reorganization, Chrysler might find it easier to raise capital after a Chapter 11 filing than before. "I just don't think liquidation is in the cards," says Drabkin, "if they give reorganization a good whack."

Reining in. Aside from public relations campaigns, observers suggest that Chrysler's best strategy in reorganization would be to close immediately all operations except those needed to turn out its Omni/Horizon models at Belvidere, Ill. While they suggest that the company try to hold on to its finance subsidiary and keep its profitable military and New Process Gear divisions going, observers think it should then begin a feverish selloff of its auto parts plants, which remain largely free of mortgage liens.

That would help the company marshal enough cash to pay for the rest of the costly retooling needed for its "K-body" car, a front-wheel-drive compact that will replace the Volaré and Aspen models. Due next fall, the K-body cars will compete directly with GM's hot-selling Chevrolet Citation. "If they could sell off their assets quickly and become a smaller company," concludes one large Chrysler lender, "it's conceivable they could pull something off."

Iacocca argues that such moves—plausible at first glance—will not give Chrysler the near-term help it needs to keep functioning, even in reorganization. The central problem is that Chrysler cannot gear up fast enough to produce the number of small cars needed to support its overhead, which—even if substantially reduced by the selloffs—would remain considerable.

The production of the Omni and Horizon cars illustrates the problem. Chrysler managed to bring those models to market earlier than otherwise possible by arranging to buy engine blocks from Volkswagen. But that deal limits the company to 300,000 engines per year. Chrysler's own four-cylinder engine plant will not come on line until next summer, and all of the 400,000 engines it will turn out are now earmarked for the K-body car.

Stymied strategies. Such limited small-car production, Chrysler says, could not cover its fixed costs, particularly because profit margins on these cars do not come close to equaling those on large cars. And even if more engines were available,

---

Investment figures of the week

The week saw the erratic pattern in interest rates continue—short-term rates higher, long rates mostly lower. But warnings of higher-than-expected inflation in 1980 have put new upward pressure on all rates.

Money market rates	Latest week	Previous week	Year ago
Federal funds	14.11%	13.78%	9.94%
New three-month Treasury bills	12.29%	11.67%	8.86%
Three-month commercial paper	12.90%	12.50%	10.25%
Stocks			
Average price/earnings ratio* (1,500 stocks)	8.64	8.40	8.76
Average dividend yield* (1,500 stocks)	5.14%	5.18%	4.97%
Dow Jones industrial average	833.70	824.91	814.97
Standard & Poor's 500 stock index	107.49	106.79	96.59
Value Line composite index	119.74	117.86	99.87
Lipper growth mutual fund index	117.02	115.67	93.81
Average daily NYSE volume (millions)	37.5	33.3	22.5
NYSE blocks (10,000 shares and over)	499	408	267
Bonds			
New Aaa utility bonds	10.85%	10.88%	9.20%
New Baa utility bonds	12.50%	12.75%	10.10%
New Aa industrial bonds	10.55%	10.50%	9.10%
U.S. government bonds (8½% issue of 1994-99)	10.25%	9.91%	8.79%
Bond Buyer municipal bond index (20 bonds)	7.17%	7.26%	6.29%

All figures are as of Tuesday, Dec. 11—except those marked*, which are from Friday, Dec. 7, and the Bond Buyer index from Thursday, Dec. 6, 1979.
Data: Salomon Bros., Standard & Poor's Compustat Services Inc., Lipper Analytical Services Inc.

it would take months for Chrysler to convert its other assembly plants to churn out more Omnis and Horizons. And the conversions would add hundreds of millions of dollars in costs that would squeeze small-car margins even tighter.

Chrysler also might find it all but impossible to get certain parts that it must obtain from outside suppliers, given the domino effect that a Chrysler bankruptcy might trigger. Even if most suppliers continued to ship on 30-day terms, the company says, failure to get a single critical component could paralyze assembly operations.

Any effort by Chrysler to hang on to its big-car models by merging its lines under a single name, while likely to save millions in long-term marketing and production costs, is dismissed by many observers as insufficient even to begin to salvage the company.

The biggest roadblock. Chrysler's chances of pursuing a far more lucrative course—linking up with a foreign auto maker—are viewed by most observers as remote. Any smart suitor, they suggest, would wait to pick up any Chrysler facilities it wants until the company sinks into liquidation. Quips one of Chrysler's lenders: "There may be a lot of people who don't want to visit the sickbed but who might like to attend the funeral."

The biggest roadblock to successful reorganization may well be Lee Iacocca himself. Despite his ascent to the presidency of Ford Motor—before being fired by Henry Ford II in 1978—Iacocca's reputation is based more on product development and marketing savvy than on management and financial skills.

While he will close the company's largest and oldest assembly plant at Hamtramck, Mich., on Jan. 4, he has not made the drastic reductions in excess parts and assembly capacity that many believe are now demanded by the sharply deteriorating situation. "It takes a different kind of mind-set at Chrysler," observes Robert J. Orsini, an automotive management consultant with A. T. Kearney Inc. "You need someone with a turnaround mentality."

"The problem is not that there aren't any alternatives," adds William J. McGrath Jr., a Kearney vice-president, "but rather the man at the helm. The trouble with super leaders is their super egos. Lee's in a race to show Henry [Ford] what he can do. And in the process, he's likely to become a General Custer." ■

QUESTIONS

An Oil Giant's Dilemma: Investing a Mountain of Cash before the Oil Runs Out:

1. What are some of the specific strategic choices facing SOHIO?

2. What are the most significant environmental threats and opportunities that will influence which strategies are chosen?

Deere: A Counter-Cyclical Expansion to Grab Market Share:

1. Describe Deere's strategy and explain how it capitalizes on the company's strengths.

2. Choosing a strategy requires the consideration and evaluation of numerous factors. Discuss these items in general terms, then specifically as they apply to the article.

LTV: On the Acquisition Trail Again, but Now in Aerospace and Energy:

1. Describe LTV's proposed future strategy and the goals it is designed to achieve.

2. Given the internal strengths and weaknesses of LTV and the existing environmental opportunities and threats, is the proposed strategy a viable one to pursue? Discuss.

Nabisco: Diversifying Again, but This Time Wholeheartedly:

1. What factors contributed to the failure of Nabisco's previous attempts at diversification?

2. Have any steps been taken to correct these past errors, and if so, are they sufficient to enable the new growth strategy to succeed?

Baker International: A Growth Wizard Divides to Conquer:

1. Discuss the impact that Chairman Clark has had on the strategy implemented by Baker International.

2. What type of growth strategy is proposed (external, horizontal, etc.) and how is it to be achieved?

Western International: A $1 Billion Expansion in the Face of Recession:

1. What is the attitude of Western International toward risk, and how has this had an impact on the strategy they chose to implement?

2. What are some of the major reasons Western International has decided to pursue a growth strategy despite the upcoming recession? Mention the environmental opportunities that exist and Western International's major internal strategic advantages.

Ramada Inns: Renovating Rooms and Pushing into Gambling:

1. What major obstacles must Ramada Inn overcome in order to establish itself in the hotel industry?

2. In light of these internal and external obstacles, can the proposed "gaming and refurbishing" strategy be effective?

Citibank: A Rising Giant in Computer Services:

1. What were the primary considerations in Citibank's selection of a diversification strategy?

2. Is this strategy consistent with the values of top management and Citibank's overall goals? Explain.

Caterpillar: Sticking to Basics to Stay Competitive:

1. Explain how Caterpillar's "single-minded focus" has facilitated emphasizing long-term instead of short-term objectives.

2. "Today management experts are recognizing that the 1970s techniques did little to bolster the U.S. economy or to keep foreign competitors from making devastating inroads in American markets." Explain this statement and relate it to the strategy adopted by Caterpillar.

Why Esmark Sold a Profitable Subsidiary:

1. How has the sale of its Vickers Energy Corp. subsidiary helped to position Esmark for the future?

2. What were the key factors that fostered Esmark's decision to divest itself of "its top performing unit"?

Kaiser Steel: The Strategic Question Is Whether to Liquidate:

1. What are the two major strategies that Kaiser Steel is considering? Discuss the advantages of pursuing each one.

2. Are the aforementioned the only viable grand strategies for Kaiser Steel to consider? Explain.

The Chores Facing Polaroid's New CEO:

1. Discuss some of the possible courses of action that Polaroid could pursue at the present time.

2. What type of grand strategy is called for? Explain.

Could Bankruptcy Save Chrysler?:

1. Given the present economic and competitive environments and Chrysler's financial position, a retrenchment strategy would be the best alternative to consider. Discuss. Prepare an argument either for or against this statement.

2. Discuss some of the major obstacles that will tend to hinder Chrysler's recovery, regardless of the strategy it chooses.

Seven.

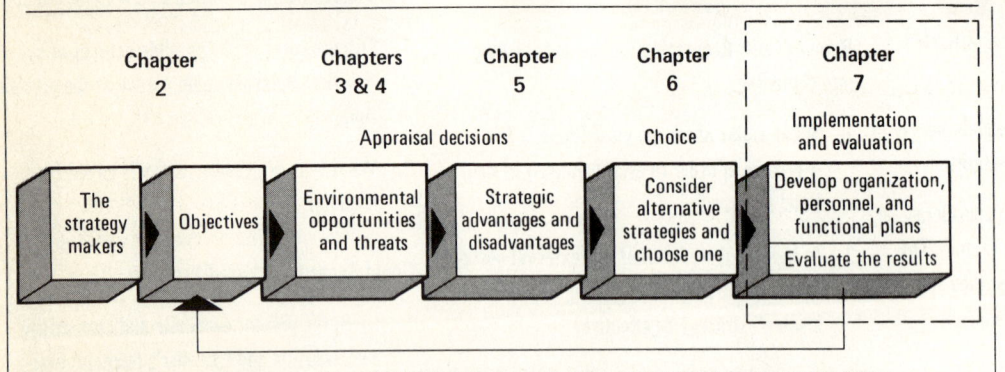

Exhibit 7-1: A MODEL OF THE BUSINESS POLICY AND STRATEGIC MANAGEMENT PROCESS.

Chapter 2	Chapters 3 & 4	Chapter 5	Chapter 6	Chapter 7
The strategy makers → Objectives	Appraisal decisions: Environmental opportunities and threats → Strategic advantages and disadvantages		Choice: Consider alternative strategies and choose one	Implementation and evaluation: Develop organization, personnel, and functional plans / Evaluate the results

In Chapter 6, the choice process was illustrated with examples of firms considering and/or choosing strategies. This chapter focuses on the final phase of the business policy and strategic management process—implementation of the choice and evaluation of the results. This is highlighted in Exhibit 7-1.

In the implementation phase, first the enterprise makes sure that it has developed an appropriate organization structure for the stage of development of the firm. For example, in earlier stages of development, firms tend to organize functionally. That is, vice presidents reporting to the president have responsibility for particular business functions and have titles such as vice president—marketing. If the firm's strategy leads it to grow in product/service scope and/or geographically, it tends to shift to a decentralized divisional organization. In this stage, the people reporting to the president lead product/service, geographic, or similar units. The functional units then report to these executives.

The second implementation step is to place in key positions executives with the background and motivation to make the new strategy successful. Then functional policy decisions must be made to bring the strategic choice to fruition.

Policies are decision guides to action that make the strategy work. They provide the means of carrying out strategic decisions. The critical part of policy formation is to factor the grand strategy into policies that are compatible and workable. It is not enough for managers to decide to change the strategy. They must decide how to get where they want to go, when they want to get there, and how efficiently they want to operate as they go. A manager does this by preparing policies to implement the grand strategy.

Policies must be developed for the key functional decisions in the following areas:

- Operations/production
- Finance/accounting
- Personnel
- Marketing and logistics
- Research and development

Thus, if the choice is to grow, policy decisions that are consistent with the growth strategy must be made. A sample list of policy questions in each of the functional areas follows:

1. Operations/Production

- Can we handle the added business with our present facilities and number of shifts?
- Must we add equipment, facilities, shifts? Where?
- Can we become more efficient by better scheduling?
- What is the firm's inventory safety level? How many suppliers does it need for major supplies?
- What level of productivity and costs should the firm seek to realize?
- How much emphasis should there be on quality control?
- How far ahead should we schedule production? Should we guarantee delivery?
- Are we going to be operations or production leaders with the latest equipment and methods?

2. Finance/Accounting

- Where will we get added funds to grow: internally or externally?
- If we get added funds externally, how do we get them? Where do we get them?
- What will the growth do to our cash flow?
- What accounting systems and policies do we use (for example, LIFO or FIFO)?
- What capital structure policy do we pursue: No debt or heavily leveraged structure? What policy do we pursue with regard to ownership?

Implementing and Evaluating the Strategic Decisions: The Policy Process

238 / Readings from *Business Week*

- How much cash and other assets do we keep on hand?

3. Personnel

- Will we have an adequate work force?
- How much hiring and retraining are necessary?
- What types of individuals do we need to recruit: College graduates? Minority groups? How do we recruit: advertise or personal contact?
- What will be the methods for selection: informal interview or very sophisticated testing?
- What will be the standards and methods for promotion: From within? By seniority?
- What payment, incentive plans, benefits, labor relations, policies, and so on will we have?
- Will we attain the satisfaction level desired on the attitude survey?

4. Marketing and Logistics

- Which specific products or services will be expanded? How? Will these be present or new products?
- Which channels will be used to market these products or services? Will we use exclusive dealerships or multiple channels?
- How will we promote these products or services? Is it our policy to use large amounts of TV advertising or no advertising? Heavy personal selling expenses or none? Price competition or nonprice competition?
- Do we have an adequate sales force?
- What distribution policies do we have? Guaranteed delivery with 3 days? Minimum shipments?

5. Research and Development

- What new projects are necessary to support our growth?
- Should we contract some of this out?
- How much should we spend on research and development (R & D)?

These are just examples of policy questions that must be answered before a grand strategy can be implemented successfully. Your ability to formulate and answer policy questions will be a good indicator of your ability to make the strategy work.

There is a time dimension in the policy formation process. Some policy decisions can be made and implemented immediately (for example, change from LIFO to FIFO, hiring unskilled workers). Others take long lead times to come to fruition (for example, research and development, building new plants). In effect, the enterprise creates a cascade of policies. The longer-range policies have a significant effect on medium- and short-range policy decisions, as seen in Exhibit 7-2.

After the strategy is implemented, the top managers must evaluate its effectiveness. Evaluation of strategy is that phase of the strategic planning process in which the top managers determine whether their strategic choice as implemented is meeting the objectives of the enterprise. The evaluation can be qualitative or quantitative. For example, some quantitative criteria are

Time	Policy Decisions
Greater than 3 years	Long-range policies, plans and programs
1 to 3 years	Medium-range policies, plans, and programs
Less than 1 year	Short-range policies, procedures, and programs

Exhibit 7-2: TIME DIMENSION OF POLICY DECISIONS.

- Net profit.
- Stock price.
- Dividend rates.
- Earnings per share.
- Return on capital.
- Return on equity.
- Market share.
- Growth in sales.
- Days lost per employee as a result of strikes.
- Production costs and efficiency.
- Distribution costs and efficiency.
- Employee turnover, absenteeism, and satisfaction indexes.

If the executives believe the strategy is working, they continue to implement it. If it is not, they shift to another strategy or adjust the current strategy to make it more effective.

This chapter contains *Business Week* examples of implementation and evaluation. The implementation articles include

- "Ashland Oil: Scrambling for Crude after a Premature Sell-Off"
- "Republic Air Takes On a New Merger Problem"
- "Volkswagen of America—Facing a Head-On Challenge from Detroit"
- "Anheuser's Plan to Flatten Miller's Lead"
- "Open for Business: IBM's Computer Store"
- "Hart Schaffner and Marx: Expanding Boldly from Class to Mass Markets"
- "AT & T's Fast Move on Baby Bell"
- "Washington Post: New Ventures Get Off to an Uncertain Start"
- "Beatrice Foods: Adding Tropicana for a Broader Nationwide Network"

The evaluation articles include

- "Why IBM Reversed Itself on Computer Pricing"
- "Quaker Oats Retreats to Its Food Lines"
- "American Can: Diversification Brings Sobering Second Thoughts"
- "McGraw-Edison: Paying the Price of the Studebaker Acquisition"
- "GE Moves to Correct Its Error in Chips"

The Policy Process / 239

ASHLAND OIL: Scrambling for Crude After a Premature Sell-off

The doubling of world oil prices last year has increased the profits of most U.S. oil companies to embarrassing levels. But the impact has not been even throughout the industry. Strategic plans of some companies have been proven sound, while others now seem lacking in foresight. At one end of the spectrum is the Canadian arm of Sun Co., Suncor Inc., which is finally reaping a bonanza on its Alberta oil sands after years of tribulation. But at Ashland Oil Inc., the higher value of crude brings into question the company's divestiture of its oil and gas properties.

Last March, Lear Petroleum Corp. paid Ashland Oil Inc. $17.8 million to obtain exploratory leases on 1.1 million acres in 19 states. Just two months later, Lear discovered natural gas south of Tyler, Tex., with its first exploratory well—a discovery large enough to guarantee a substantial drilling program. Says a happy David L. Paffett, Lear's vice-president for exploration: "The first well has paid for the entire bid, and that ain't just blowing smoke."

Lear's find was Ashland's loss. In fact, the modest price Ashland received is just one illustration of holes that are beginning to show in an oddly timed move by Ashland to sell off its oil and gas exploration and production business in the U.S., Canada, and the North Sea. Ashland's plan was to sell the properties, use the proceeds largely to enrich its shareholders and, finally, to reduce the company to a refiner and marketer that had some spare cash to make acquisitions outside of oil. Ashland began the divestiture program in mid-1978 and ended it just last November.

Beneficiaries. The company has indeed rewarded its stockholders. It received $1 billion for all of its oil and gas properties—including 81 million bbl. of proven oil reserves, 906.7 billion cu. ft. of gas, and 5.4 million acres of leases—and promptly launched a series of actions of the sort Wall Street adores. Ashland's dividends now are 65% higher than in June, 1978, while the per-share market value of its common stock has risen 110%, thanks largely to Ashland's repurchase of 15.6 million shares, more than one-third of those outstanding.

But Ashland, which only briefly considered a bid for NLT Corp. last year, has yet to make a major acquisition. And in 1979, when most oil companies saw their earnings leap because of the increased value of their crude oil, Ashland's earnings from operations rose a relatively modest 16% to $186 million on operating revenues of $6.7 billion. Most clearly, because Ashland failed to anticipate the likelihood that crude prices would rise, it badly underestimated the worth of its now-divested petroleum assets. Paffett, who was Ashland's vice-president of domestic exploration before moving to Lear, suggests that by waiting less than a year, Ashland could have received twice the price for its exploratory acreage. At Ashland, Vice-Chairman John R. Hall still defends the sale as a

Vice-Chairman Hall: The Energy Dept. should continue ensuring Ashland's allocation of oil from other companies.

"good decision," but he also concedes, "Sure, we might have gotten something more by selling today."

The rationale. Ashland's executives have little time to second-guess themselves. They are scrambling now to secure new sources of crude oil to keep the company's seven refineries running because, aside from selling properties that had produced 41,000 bbl. a day of oil, Ashland has suffered from the cutoff of crude deliveries from Iran. When Ashland Chairman Orin E. Atkins described his divestiture strategy to BUSINESS WEEK in August, 1978, he contended that the letting-go of captive reserves was safe on two grounds. "Right now," he declared, "you have a surplus of oil. We see that situation continuing for another two or three years." For the long term, Atkins said, if shortages occurred, Ashland could count on the Energy Dept. to order other oil companies to supply any amount of crude that Ashland was unable to secure in the marketplace.

Atkins was hardly in a position to know that 15 months later, a Presidential order would eliminate Ashland's 100,000 bbl. a day in oil shipments from Iran, and that shortages would occur much sooner, wiping out his first rationale. Atkins' second hope—that the government would fully ensure Ashland's oil supply—was, at the least, diminished in November. When Ashland asked the Energy Dept.'s Office of Hearings & Appeals to order replacement of the company's 100,000 bbl. a day from Iran, the agency ordered nine other oil companies to sell Ashland just 80,000 bbl., and only temporarily.

Not surprisingly, Ashland has quietly begun what appears to be a reversal of its crude-oil divestiture strategy. Without any of the fanfare that accompanied the sell-off, it has financed an exploratory venture by Patrick Petroleum Co. off the Texas coast, in which Ashland may spend up to $25 million in return for first call to buy any oil Patrick might find. Ashland also tentatively agreed in January with Basic Resources International of Luxembourg to search jointly for oil in Guatemala at a cost to Ashland of $10 million to $20 million this year.

Fluctuations. These new ventures, although modest, are cited by Ashland observers as proof that the sell-off was a poorly conceived plan for short-term gain. Former members of the company's exploration team, pared by resignations and early retirements, say the divestiture was the last step in a history of

240 / Readings from *Business Week*

erratic commitment to finding oil. Even before the oil property sales, charges former Senior Vice-President Burt E. Hamric, "our budget would fluctuate wildly from year to year, or within a year."

In a strangely self-deprecating manner, Ashland executives retort that their exploration arm had never been a key part of the company because it had never found much oil. The 41,000 bbl. a day from its oil-producing properties represents just 9% of Ashland's 475,000 bbl. a day of refining capacity at plants in Kentucky, Ohio, Minnesota, and New York. And because of its location, Ashland had been selling some of this oil rather than refining it. The divestiture, says Vice-Chairman Hall, simply meant that Ashland had finally decided it was "not big enough to play the elephant oil game." He portrays the new exploration effort as an attempt to secure oil only for Ashland's refineries rather than to build a crude surplus to sell.

Most oil analysts, pleased with the higher value of Ashland's shares, still defend the divestiture move. But the opinion is far from unanimous. Ashland's new hunt for oil, says one, means that the company "is saying that its complete withdrawal from the exploration business was at least premature and probably incorrect."

That sort of criticism pales next to the remarks of officials of other oil companies, who are livid about supplying Ashland's oil needs from their own sources.

Besides selling reserves, Ashland lost its crude supply from Iran

The companies forced to do so by the Energy Dept. responded with a suit that seeks to overturn the order and harshly attacks Ashland's planning. Gripes one oilman: "Ashland intentionally put itself in a position for its own profit, and when things didn't turn out the way it projected, it went to the government."

Having its way. Ashland's opponents, however, have been denied a temporary injunction to block the order. Ashland executives say they will petition the Office of Hearings & Appeals in February to win an extension of their guaranteed supply of 80,000 bbl. a day, which had been limited to 90 days. Outsiders say Ashland is likely to have its way. Federal policy has generally been drifting toward a government-controlled system of allocation of crude, regardless of its source (BW—Dec. 24, 1979). Beyond that, Ashland, despite its medium-size in oil company ranks, operates one of the most powerful lobbies in Washington.

Even so, Ashland's oil supply would appear tenuous. It is now running its refineries at 85% of capacity—not unusual given the industry's relatively tight crude supplies. But maintaining even that refining rate may be difficult over the long term because of the uncertainty of foreign supply. As a hedge, Ashland sold most of its oil properties under agreements that give the company the right to purchase crude produced from them. But some agreements will expire in two years, sending Ashland on a hunt for still more oil.

This makes it all the more important for Ashland to deploy its sale proceeds. "I suspect the future of this company," says one analyst, "will hinge on how successful its diversification is." ∎

REPUBLIC AIR TAKES ON A NEW MERGER PROBLEM

The problems of meshing equipment, seniority lists, and schedules make airline mergers particularly difficult to work out. But Republic Airlines Inc. wants to put together three lines at once. Formerly North Central Airlines Inc., Republic was formed when it merged with Southern Airways Inc. last July. Now, despite unexpected problems in meshing the two, Republic wants to acquire Hughes Airwest.

Airwest is 78% owned by Summa Corp., the corporate catchall for companies once controlled by Howard R. Hughes, the late eccentric billionaire, and 22% owned by the Hughes estate. It has been rumored to be for sale for several years, primarily because Summa management has its hands full developing its hotel, gambling casino, and real estate interests and cannot devote enough time and attention to the proper running of an airline. In fact, Airwest lost $21.6 million on revenues of $312 million last year—when it had a 61-day strike—and has been trying to retrench.

On a route map, Airwest looks like a perfect fit for Republic. Airwest provides blanket coverage from the Rocky Mountains west. With Republic's strong market dominance in the upper Midwest and Southeast, the merger would create a powerful nationwide airline with enormous growth potential. But that is one of the few attractive aspects about the proposed deal. Two airlines far stronger than Republic, Delta Air Lines Inc. and Allegheny Airlines Inc., now USAir Inc., looked at Airwest and walked away.

A problem with pilots. The Airwest deal would fit into the strategy of Republic's president, Bernard Sweet: tying together regional air networks with "bridge" routes that are designed to win more profitable long-haul traffic that otherwise goes to trunk lines. But, says E. Scott Thatcher, an airline analyst with the Minneapolis firm of Dain Bosworth Inc., "I wish Republic had waited longer on this one."

The problem is that Republic is still working out its earlier merger. The big difficulty, as it is in all airline mergers, is pilot seniority, which allows the oldest hands to fly the highest-paying flights. Fearful that former Southern pilots with high seniority will bump them off the best North Central flights or from proposed new, long-haul flights, former North Central pilots have resisted the combined company's efforts to find an amicable solution. The issue is now in arbitration, holding up Republic's post-merger scheduling plans.

Republic's losses. Even after a decision is reached, Republic faces contract negotiations with the merged pilot group that are likely to be long and costly. Union officers say the Air Line Pilots Assn. will seek to protect wages of pilots bumped to more junior flights. "Merging with Airwest would mean taking on a whole new set of labor problems before the others are resolved," one source argues.

In addition to its labor problems, Re-

How to digest Airwest? Difficulties with cash and turbulence with pilots

public was apparently caught by surprise at the condition of Southern's fleet. Virtually all of Southern's McDonnell Douglas DC-9s had unsuspected tail cracks, that have since been corrected, and the Republic management has decided to ground Southern's fleet of small, commuter-size Metroliner propjets.

Because of huge merger costs, Republic lost money in the fourth quarter of 1979 and is expected to show a loss again in the first quarter this year. Earnings for all of 1979 dropped 47% to only $13 million on revenues that increased 25% to $609 million. This was particularly distressing because the regional airline industry generally, of which Republic and Airwest are important parts, has been doing well lately. In addition, Republic is committed to spend $370 million in borrowed money tied to the now-lofty prime rate to acquire 32 new jets. Combining with Airwest is certain to add to its cash needs. ∎

VOLKSWAGEN OF AMERICA: FACING A HEAD-ON CHALLENGE FROM DETROIT

As most auto makers tell it, there are two indispensable ingredients for making money in the price-sensitive U.S. car business: volume and integration. By Detroit's gargantuan yardstick, economies of scale start at production of a million cars a year, or roughly 10% of the market. And unless an auto company can build about half of its own parts, conventional wisdom says it will never match General Motors, Ford, or even Chrysler on manufacturing costs—let alone the even lower-cost Japanese producers.

Given such strongly held beliefs, it is ironic that, except for GM and possibly American Motors Corp. (page 80), the only auto maker expected by analysts to turn a profit on U.S. car operations this year is tiny Volkswagen of America Inc. With its sole assembly plant in Westmoreland County, Pa., turning out only 225,000 vehicles a year, VWOA is building barely one-fifth of the industry's theoretical threshold volume. And while about a third of its parts are provided by its West German parent, auto giant Volkswagenwerk, VWOA must pay as much as a 30% premium for these components, because of exchange rates and transportation costs. "It isn't all roses," admits James W. McLernon, president of the wholly owned U.S. subsidiary. "But we still think building cars in the U.S. was the right idea."

Despite all of these handicaps, the new VWOA plant is a linchpin in the company's strategy for regaining the share of U.S. market it lost throughout much of the 1970s, as its aging Beetle was squeezed out by less expensive Japanese imports. As a result, VW's sales in the U.S. tumbled from a high of 590,000 units, or 5% of the American market, to a decade low of 202,000 units or 2% of the market in 1976.

By relying totally on imports from its German parent, VWOA was also losing money on every car sold in the U.S. because high production costs in Germany—combined with transportation costs and the erosion of the dollar against the mark—totally wiped out its margins. When the company decided in 1976 to spend $350 million to convert an unused Chrysler plant to produce VWs, becoming the first foreign-owned auto maker to build cars in the U.S., it did so primarily to reduce labor and other cost disadvantages.

So far, the strategy has worked extremely well. VWOA expects to be solidly in the black this year on sales of $3 billion. While it still imports 46% of its cars from Germany, its overall American sales, including Porsche and Audi models, are expected to rise to 375,000 cars and trucks this year, increasing its U.S. market share to 3.5%.

Another U.S. plant. Encouraged by that, the company has already decided to open its second U.S. plant in 1982. That will double the company's domestic production to around 450,000 units per year by 1985, when it expects to be importing another 150,000 models. Assuming both plants operate at capacity, the plan would still only return VWOA's market share in the U.S. to 5%, the level it achieved a decade ago. But this time, notes McLernon, "the way we're structured, a 5% share is enough for us to be profitable."

The low-volume domestic production is not only a vital part of VWOA's strategy in the U.S., it fits nicely with the German carmaker's strategy in the world car market. Clobbered by high production costs that were squeezing its models out of the low-price, small-car market, VW in the early 1970s undertook one of the most sweeping retoolings in the industry's history. Starting with its 1975 introduction of the Rabbit, the company has brought out a new line of precision-engineered, fuel-efficient small cars and priced them into the small-car elite. The company is gambling that it can make up in margins what it lacks in volume by attracting a coterie of affluent, well-educated customers willing to pay more for a quality car.

The average-priced Rabbit sells today for $5,700 but can easily top $7,000 with options, and its convertible version, introduced in the U.S. last fall, commands $9,000. That compares with less than $4,000 for a budget-equipped Toyota Tercel and $4,799 for a Chevrolet Citation. Despite such price tags, waiting lists for Rabbits in the U.S. now run as long as a year, while buyers are paying $1,000 over invoice to get the five-speed diesel model whose 42 mpg leads all cars sold in the U.S. in fuel economy.

The price contest. The question is whether VWOA can continue to succeed at such comparatively inflated sales prices. Company officials are hoping that as small cars grow to dominate the U.S. market, Detroit will be forced to make huge price increases on its subcompacts. And even if Japanese models remain cheap, VWOA is hoping that its technological innovations, such as the fuel-efficient turbo-charged engine due to be offered in the U.S. over the next two years, will enable it to maintain its higher prices.

Some observers, however, are skeptical that VWOA can keep enough of an edge to justify a stiff premium over the long haul. Chrysler's Omni and Horizon models already duplicate the Rabbit, and by the mid-1980s, all three of the big U.S. auto makers will be fielding products aimed squarely at VW's niche. "Volkswagen ultimately is going to have to take on GM in the equivalent car," says LeRoy H. Lindgren, vice-president of the Lexington (Mass.) management consulting firm of Rath & Strong Inc., "and if they don't go for a million cars a year [in the U.S.], they are going to have cost problems."

Cost cutting. Even with low volume, VWOA hopes to get economies of scale comparable to the Big Three by building a variety of similar vehicles off the basic Rabbit design. The Rabbit is the first in an emerging breed of multipurpose car designs that can be adapted to other configurations quickly and cheaply. At its Pennsylvania plant, the company last fall began building a minipickup truck whose front half is identical to the Rabbit car. Made on the same assembly line—every eighth unit a truck—the Alpha beat GM, Ford, and Chrysler to market with a U.S.-built minitruck by anywhere up to three years at a fraction of the billion-dollar costs of developing such a vehicle from the wheels up.

To get true production economies, however, McLernon agrees that VWOA must make a higher share of its own

---

The Big Three are all readying vehicles aimed at VW's market niche

---

components in the U.S. But for now, that effort is stymied by the U.S. fuel-economy law. If the company sources more than 75% of the U.S.-built Rabbit from domestic manufacturers, it could no longer be counted as an import. Since that would mean VWOA's other car imports would flunk the U.S. mileage requirements of 27.5 mpg by 1985, the company continues to import 40% of the Rabbit's components.

Complaints. Because of its cost constraints, VWOA appears to be making life miserable for those U.S. suppliers it does use. The vendors complain that it imposes slim margins and yet extraordinarily rigorous quality standards. Says one marketing manager with a major supplier: "Their attitude is: You *vill* perform, or else."

Such strains are but the first signs of the pressures to come. With all cars bound to get better fuel mileage, VWOA executives acknowledge that their efforts to hold on to a distinctive quality image will grow more difficult, yet more important. Concedes Noel Phillips, executive vice-president for sales and marketing: "If we don't, we've lost everything we stand for." ∎

ANHEUSER'S PLAN TO FLATTEN MILLER'S HEAD

Since 1970, Miller Brewing Co., a subsidiary of Philip Morris Inc., has blossomed from a seventh-place also-ran into a strong No. 2, employing massive advertising outlays and an innovative strategy of product and package segmentation to surge ahead. But now it is finding that its drive to the top is getting bumpier. Miller is being boxed in by an increasingly aggressive Anheuser-Busch Inc., which has undertaken sweeping marketing changes to protect its teetering crown. "In the last 20 years, a number of companies have taken tough runs at us, and none has succeeded," says Anheuser Chairman August A. Busch III. "If I were them [Miller], I would damn sure not be talking about becoming No. 1."

Busch's confidence is remarkable for someone who was caught flat-footed by Miller's huge success in identifying the low-calorie beer segment in 1974. The St. Louis-based brewer at first disregarded Miller's moves and then was crippled by a 95-day strike in 1976 that left its marketing network a shambles and its executives hamstrung by Miller's challenge.

Now, Anheuser has devised a strategy to regain the momentum. It has brought out several new products, repositioned others, and overhauled its marketing force. It is moving away from the popular-price beer segment into the faster growing and more profitable premium, super-premium, and import categories. The plan is to bracket and pinion each Miller entry in a particular category with two flanking Anheuser products.

For example, Busch Bavarian, long sold as a popular-price beer, has been reformulated and packaged to accompa-

The No. 1 brewer defends its crown with new beers and an $84 million ad budget

ny Budweiser, the country's largest selling premium beer. This supposedly will give a one-two punch to counter Miller's fast-gaining High Life, which sold 23.3 million bbl. last year to Budweiser's 30.6 million bbl. Likewise, in the low-calorie segment, Anheuser's Michelob Light and Natural Light together will try to daunt Miller's hugely successful Lite beer, which holds 60% of the market. Backing these and other products is a media spending budget that has grown 245% since the strike, to $84 million, estimates E. F. Hutton & Co. Miller's media budget is about $72 million.

The new moves are intended to shatter Miller's oft-stated goal of wresting the No. 1 spot from Anheuser. "We set a goal as a company to become No. 1," says Miller's president and chief operating officer, William K. Howell. "And we're determined somehow to become No. 1." But that "somehow" is getting more difficult.

August Busch, who seldom refers to Miller by name, preferring to call them "our friends in Milwaukee," or "the tobacco people," is backing up his merchandising strategies with increased capital spending. To blunt Miller's assault, Anheuser has spent more than $1 billion on new capacity in the past five years and will commit $2 billion more over the next five years to push capacity from 46 million bbl. to more than 65 million bbl. Meanwhile, Miller has earmarked $1.5 billion for plant expansion over the next five years to expand capacity 74% to 62 million bbl. Still, Emanuel Goldman, an analyst with Sanford C. Bernstein & Co., predicts that "Miller won't be able to close the gap. Since the strike, Anheuser has taken the right marketing steps."

These moves have slowed Miller's progress. Last year, Miller's 14.5% barrelage gain, to 35.8 million bbl., was down from the previous year's 29.1% growth rate and was 2 million bbl. short of its own target. Anheuser's beer sales grew 11.1% in 1979, to 46.2 million bbl., down from a 13.7% increase in 1978. Robert S. Weinberg, an industry consultant, figures that Anheuser, with a current 26.4% share of market, has recently made share gains against Miller in almost two-thirds of the 38 states reporting beer sales data.

Faster industry reaction. But no one is underestimating Miller, whose superior merchandising ability has rocketed its share of market from 4.2% over the past decade to 21%. Miller executives say that they are actively looking for new products. And they are wooing retailers and wholesalers across the country with an elaborate traveling show that highlights the company's achievements and future plans. Says Lauren S. Williams, Miller's executive vice-president: "We've always had an emphasis on merchandising. The others are trying now to catch up." But he concedes that "the industry is reacting to a lot of things we're doing in a quicker fashion. And that requires a lot of homework on our part."

The costly contest between the two giants has caused a massive shake-out in the industry, reducing the number of brewers from 92 in 1970 to 41. It is estimated that Anheuser and Miller will probably control 70% of the market by 1985, with Anheuser hoping to approach 40% by that date.

Still, industry observers believe the shake-out may have slowed, and that the other survivors will be largely strong, regional brewers such as Coors, Heileman, and Genesee. "The reaction of other brewers and ourselves has cut off the avenues of growth for Miller," claims Dennis P. Long, Anheuser's president and chief operating officer.

Part of that reaction is to take a leaf from Miller's playbook and to segment markets. Ironically, Miller, which first capitalized on segmentation, is now less specialized than Anheuser. Its most glaring weakness is in the super-premium category, where Anheuser successfully slowed Miller's Lowenbrau brand after charging that the beer was deceptively advertised and priced as an import when it was, in fact, domestically brewed. Despite a $15.6 million advertising outlay for Lowenbrau in 1979, the brand sold only about 1 million bbl.

By contrast, Anheuser spent $15.1 million on its super-premium Michelob and garnered sales of 8.3 million bbl. Gloats Busch: "They tried to enter the super-premium market, where we are dominant, using a vehicle that consumers felt deceived them."

The market where Anheuser is playing a furious game of catch-up is in low-calorie beers. The company entered the market belatedly in 1977 with Natural Light, a brand whose sales increased from only 1.5 million bbl. to 2.8 million bbl. in 1979. But together with Michelob Light, a super-premium brand introduced in 1978, Anheuser has managed to bracket Miller's Lite and snare 23% of the fast-growing market segment. Anheuser has had to repackage and reformulate its Natural Light, however, to improve its taste and customer recognition. To Anheuser's dismay, many drinkers, when ordering a beer, simply requested "Lite" and were served Miller's product. Now the company's ads stress that drinkers should request a "natural" instead of a "light" beer.

Mantle switches teams. Anheuser has also stung Miller by unleashing new commercials that feature five celebrated

The Policy Process / 245

athletes, including Mickey Mantle and Walt Frazier, who had previously touted Miller Lite, in humorous spots reminiscent of Miller's much acclaimed ad campaign. Miller's Williams bristles that the new ads are nothing more than a desperation move. "They wouldn't be changing their product and ads if they were doing well in the marketplace," he says.

To get off the defensive and on the offensive against Miller, Anheuser had to overhaul marketing systems that lacked coordination and cohesive brand management. A task force was created to go into areas needing immediate merchandising, sales, and distribution aid. A national accounts sales department was built to coordinate sales and distribution with large retail accounts, and a marketing services department was added to strengthen sales promotion and point-of-sale and incentive programs.

The cost in profits. Anheuser's desire to impede Miller has affected its profitability. Net profit margins have slipped from 4.1% to 3.8% over the past five years. And although annual sales have increased 60% to $3.3 billion, net earnings are up only 46%, to $124 million.

To improve the bottom line, the company is slowing down new products and seeking a boost in overseas beer sales, which account for only 1% of total volume. More important, Anheuser is diversifying into snack foods and soft drinks, where it can capitalize on its consumer franchise and distribution net-

Anheuser plays catch-up in light beers. A long lead in super-premiums

work. "The domestic beer business will one day become a cash cow," says Busch. "We've got to make sure we provide the avenues for the other businesses to use the cash." Within 10 years, he says, Anheuser's beer sales could be reduced from 92% of total sales to 70%.

The company's first major soft-drink foray, with Chelsea, failed to win favor and was abandoned last year. Anheuser has higher hopes for a new root beer beverage, called Root 66, that was introduced in test markets last fall.

Snack-food campaigns. The slow-growing $2 billion salted-snack market at which Anheuser is shooting also faces threats from entrenched national and regional rivals. With four of its test products—pretzels, cheese- and bacon-flavored corn curls, and tortilla chips—Anheuser is up against Frito-Lay Inc.'s formidable 7,200-person sales force. With its other product, honey-roasted peanuts, Anheuser will have to do battle with Standard Brands Inc.'s Planters peanuts, which commands 55% of the market. Undaunted, Anheuser plans to package the snack products in 2-oz. cans rather than the usual bags, and sell them at premium 50¢ and 75¢ prices.

Similarly, Anheuser's plan to take its beer business abroad faces mighty challenges, particularly from the deeply ingrained loyalties of foreign beer drinkers. Anheuser intends to avoid the mistake Jos. Schlitz Brewing Co. made more than a decade ago when it bought breweries abroad. The company will rely on foreign brewers to produce and distribute its beers—most likely the Budweiser and Michelob brands. To handle these products, Anheuser has been negotiating with BSN-Gervais Danone, a French company that has set up U.S. offices to sell its Kronenbourg brand, and Allied Breweries Ltd., Britain's second largest brewer.

But for now, Anheuser's principal attention is riveted on its nip-and-tuck leadership battle with Miller. Its success in that fight is likely to depend on how thoroughly Anheuser has shaken off the conservative marketing posture that defined the company for so long and left it vulnerable. ■

OPEN FOR BUSINESS: IBM'S Computer Store

In their battle to capture the small-business market, major computer and office-equipment vendors have been experimenting with a new merchandising channel: retail stores. Now the largest supplier of them all, International Business Machines Corp., has given the retail movement a big push. On Nov. 18 the computer giant opened its first office-products store in the U.S., a downtown Philadelphia facility of 4,400 sq. ft. "When IBM does something," notes Amy D. Wohl, president of Advanced Office Concepts Corp., "it sort of puts the papal seal on it."

Indeed, the small-business segment "is an emerging and important marketplace," observes J. Richard Young, president of IBM's Office Products Div. Although the company will continue to rely mainly on its large direct sales force, Young concedes that "we know there are opportunities that we may be missing by sticking to direct sales exclusively." By broadening its marketing avenues into retailing, IBM hopes to tap the more than 4 million small businesses in the U.S. with fewer than 200 employees and the 6 million offices run in the proprietor's home.

The cost of making direct sales calls on these prospects is prohibitive in relation to the cost of the products they buy. To reduce sales costs, IBM has been experimenting for some time with mass-merchandising techniques for its low-end products. In 1978 it opened a series of nationwide Business Computer Centers to pitch its small-business computer to a group of potential customers rather than selling to one at a time. It launched its retail program in April, 1979, when it opened stores in London and Buenos Aires, and it has since added seven outlets overseas.

Cautious start. The apparent success of these ventures is behind IBM's decision to begin expanding its retailing experiments to the U.S. market. A second store is scheduled to open in Baltimore on Dec. 2. Still, the company is proceeding with caution, saying it will wait and see how its current outlets fare before adding any more. That decision should come soon. "We should have some good intelligence by the end of the year," Young says. And if all goes according to plan, suggests Gideon I. Gartner, president of Gartner Group Inc., "there are going to be many more than two" IBM stores by the end of 1981.

Gartner and other analysts speculate that IBM may be making its retail thrust now to prepare a sales channel for its upcoming low-cost microcomputer. According to Gartner, the company will announce the development of such a computer within the next 18 months. George D. Elling, an analyst with Bear, Stearns & Co., adds that retail stores "will be the ideal way" to reach the small businesses and individual customers that would use the new computer.

IBM is not the first to move into computer retailing in the U.S. Xerox Corp. already has 10 office-products stores in the U.S. and elsewhere aimed directly at the small-business dollar (BW—Oct. 27), and it plans to add four more by yearend. The company says it expects to have 30 to 50 stores by the end of 1981 and "several hundred" by the mid-1980s. Similarly, Digital Equipment Corp. has 25 retail computer stores in the U.S., and Control Data Corp., which now has two retail outlets, plans 200 by the end of 1981. Even Tandy Corp., with its 100 Radio Shack Computer Centers, is broadening the appeal of its stores to small business. In addition to calculators and computers, it will sell office copiers early next year.

Learning. Despite all this activity, vendors are still feeling their way in mass-merchandising techniques—searching for the optimum store size, location, layout, and product mix. Digital Equipment, for example, closed two stores—one in lower Manhattan and another in Detroit—in October because they were not meeting sales goals.

Many industry experts predict that IBM, for all its savvy in selling big computers to big companies, may face rough sailing with its first U.S. outlets. While IBM's well-known brand name may lure browsers, industry watchers question whether it can attract enough paying customers for some of the higher-priced items to make the stores profitable. They point out that, while such lower-priced offerings as Selectric typewriters may sell briskly, more expensive products such as the $13,500 Displaywriter word processor and the $49,260 Series III, Model 40 copier may be harder to sell. "They undoubtedly will have a lot of problems," predicts Elling of Bear Stearns. He says: "IBM is going to get an unbelievable number of blind leads." ∎

HART SCHAFFNER & MARX: Expanding Boldly from Class to Mass Markets

Hart Schaffner & Marx, the venerable men's clothier, is discovering that a market niche, once filled, may offer little opportunity for growth even though it remains profitable. HSM makes and retails top-of-the-line men's suits, including Hickey-Freeman and Christian Dior brands, selling for as much as $500 each. By sticking mainly with these lines, HSM has held itself aloof from the competition raging among other tailoring companies for the popularly priced market.

But the limitations of this starchy strategy have grown increasingly clear: HSM's revenues in the last 10 years have grown at an average rate of just 6% per year, scarcely half the rate of comparable manufacturers. In 1979 sales increased only 4% to $630.8 million from a year earlier, and profits, although up 17% to $21 million, returned but a modest 7.8% on capital.

Now, however, Jerome S. Gore, president and chief executive, is rolling up his sleeves for a fight to expand from class to mass markets. In the past, HSM had dabbled lightly in making and selling inexpensive clothing—it went so far as to make some leisure suits from 1974 to 1976—but this year the company has changed from testing the water to launching a major effort.

It has already introduced a Playboy-brand line of men's suits that will retail for $115 to $155. And in August the company spent $12.5 million to acquire Country Miss Inc., a New York maker of medium-priced women's sportswear, suits, and dresses—HSM's first venture into women's wear manufacturing. Gore says that he will soon inaugurate a third tactic for growth: acquisition of chains of retail stores to add to HSM's stable of 275 existing stores, which sell both the company's products and those of other manufacturers.

A bigger base. Because demographics should work in the company's favor, Gore is buoyed by his chances of success. HSM's traditional customer base has come from men 35 to 55 years old, and the aging of the baby-boom generation ought to cause this demographic group to increase 28% in the next decade, compared with just 4% in the 1970s, he notes. Gore's objective is to use the company's strength with this growing segment to generate cash for the push into an even bigger market. Suits priced in the Playboy brand's range account for about one-third of all suits sold, much larger than the share for suits above $200. "The 1980s," Gore declares, "are the best opportunity we've seen in years."

The main barrier to Gore's plan is that so many others in his business have the same idea. Garment trade circles are buzzing about plans by Levi Strauss & Co. to introduce new lines of men's suits next spring that will retail for $115 to $145. Levi has occasionally offered expensive jackets and trousers under its David Hunter label, but sources say the new thrust will be more aggressive and sustained. Wool and wool-blended suits will be backed up by Levi's broad advertising, including television spots and in-store video cassettes to educate customers on how to assemble Levi suits from the combinations of "separates" it hopes to sell.

As if this weren't enough, Haggar Co., the nation's largest pants maker, has also made a new push into medium-priced separates that can be made into suits. "It's going to be rough," predicts Bruce Geller, executive vice-president for the Botany 500 unit of Rapid-American Corp. "There is no room in this market for all the companies that want to get in."

Leeway for borrowing. HSM executives say they are aware of this but are undaunted. Outside of marketing, the company will spend $55 million by 1982 on plant and equipment to buy its way into the popular market and expand retailing through internal development and acquisition, says Treasurer Mark J. Lies. This will almost double the spending of the prior three years. "We think this kind of financial commitment shows we're serious about growing," says Lies. It should also be relatively easy spending to arrange HSM's short- and long-term debt is just 19.7 of capital, allowing plenty of leeway for new borrowing.

The Chicago-based company was founded as a retail store in 1871 by brothers Harry and Max Hart. The business got along without much formal strategic planning until recently. Now it has a number of specific goals to implement the widening of its interests.

Some of its spending will be used in nearly doubling the capacity of its plant in Whiteville, N.C., which manufactures the Playboy suit line. Country Miss, whose brands include Handmacher women's suits, will also be nurtured. Gore hopes that women's wear will account for 10% of the company's manufacturing volume next year and 25% by 1982. Already, HSM sells women's clothing made by other companies in 64% of its stores.

The retailing expansion will be just as big a change. Right now, retailing accounts for 62% of the company's sales and about 45% of pretax earnings, and its importance could grow. In 1969, after HSM had gone on an acquisition spree, buying 40 men's stores in only four years, the Justice Dept. filed an antitrust action against the company, forcing a divestiture of some stores and prohibiting similar acquisitions. But that ban ended on June 30. On Sept. 25, Gore reacted by purchasing Bishop's, a men's store in Salem, Ore.

'Extra element.' Gore says he is now looking at an additional "three or four opportunities" to buy single stores or chains in the South, Southwest, or West Coast. Bishop's will be melded into the company's Klopfenstein's chain, based in Seattle. HSM operates 43 other chains, many of them well-positioned in their markets, including Wallachs on the East Coast; Baskin and Chas. A. Stevens in the Midwest, and Silverwoods and Hastings in California.

All of these plans have so far elicited approving—although less than rave—reviews from outsiders. The main plan, to trade down in men's fashion, "will give them an extra element of growth and help improve return on investment, so it's good," says Jeffrey B. Edelman, textile analyst with Dean Witter Reynolds Inc.

What may not be so good is the new competition: The company has no lock on good names in the middle market. HSM is hoping that the Playboy name, which it has licensed for suits, will be a major aid, selling at prices just below those of its Johnny Carson line, another proven brand. But Robert Siegel, president of Levi's Sportswear Div., counters: "We think the Levi name is pretty strong. We believe that we are going to become a leader in this business." ∎

The data processing business knew that it was going to have a towering new competitor in American Telephone & Telegraph Co. when the Federal Communications Commission this spring deregulated all of AT&T's business but basic telephone service. But most of the industry had expected that AT&T would not act until the FCC heard the industry's worried challenges to its decision. They got the surprise of their life, however, when AT&T announced on Aug. 20—just four months after the FCC decision—that it had commenced a massive reorganization aimed at splitting the $45 billion company in two.

The major part of AT&T will continue to offer basic telephone service under regulation, while a new subsidiary, already stuck with the nickname of Baby Bell, will compete with other companies in unregulated markets. Baby Bell will not only market existing products, such as telephones and switchboards, but, more important, it will move AT&T into a host of new data processing activities, such as data communications networks and computer terminals that the company has been prohibited from entering by a 1956 consent decree. "I'm surprised they did it now," says Daniel L. Tulis, an analyst with Shearson Loeb Rhoades Inc. "Over the years the telephone company typically has not made big moves until it had to."

Taking a chance. Making the timing of that AT&T move even more startling is the uncertainty on the Washington regulatory scene. The Justice Dept. and Congress, as well as the FCC, all have actions pending that are aimed at defining the future shape of the Bell System. By plunging ahead with its reorganization, AT&T is taking a chance that it will guess right on its new structure. "If they make the wrong move now, it could hurt them dearly later on," warns Harry Edelson, president of Edelson Technology Associates.

AT&T's uncharacteristic speed illustrates the company's determination to be more competitive. This aggressive new stance has been growing ever since Charles L. Brown was elected chairman nearly two years ago. "Once public policy trends became clear enough, we decided to act," Brown says, "and take hold of our future rather than just let it happen." By acting now, the telephone company will be in a better position to influence several government moves now under way that would affect its future structure, Washington observers predict.

That is precisely what is worrying some of Baby Bell's new competitors.

AT&T'S FAST MOVE ON BABY BELL

Datapoint Corp., a San Antonio producer of telecommunications and distributed processing equipment, for one, is calling for additional congressional hearings on deregulation legislation. "We have never in the history of this country deregulated a monopoly, and there are a lot of unknowns that need to be carefully scrutinized," says a Datapoint official.

The AT&T move has already won friends at the FCC. Charles D. Ferris, FCC chairman, commends Bell management for its fast action in taking the "first step toward reorganizing to become an effective but fair competitor in the new communications markets opening up in the 1980s." One FCC staffer takes the agency's warmer feelings one step further. "If in 18 months AT&T comes back to the FCC and says it can't comply with the March, 1982, deregulation deadline, the commission will be much more sympathetic because the company has already taken some action."

New legislation. AT&T's decision to go ahead with its reorganization could also help the company on Capitol Hill. "Tactically, they've positioned themselves very well," says one government offical. The latest version of the rewrite of the Communications Act of 1934, which is tougher than the FCC order in separating the regulated and nonregulated portions of AT&T's business, is dead at least for this year. Not only has the Senate leadership delayed its version of the bill, but the House decided to review its bill for the potential impact on the government's antitrust suit against the telephone company. When Congress reconvenes in January, AT&T can then lobby effectively for a law modeled after the reorganization that it has already initiated.

The Justice Dept.'s antitrust case against AT&T, which is scheduled to go to trial by the end of October, could be a different story. In fact, Winston E. Himsworth, an industry analyst at Salomon Bros. in New York, believes that AT&T's move "appears to be a step in the wrong direction as far as Justice is concerned." Even AT&T's Brown agrees that the company reorganization plan will have no influence on the case because "the Justice Dept. aims at nothing less than the complete disintegration of the Bell System." Yet at least one government official believes that AT&T's decision to consolidate its 33 pension programs into two nationwide plans "will integrate the company much more closely, and makes it tougher to divest parts of AT&T."

Stock purchase. As a first step to splitting the company in two, AT&T is consolidating much of its operations. It plans to purchase for about $1 billion in stock the shares that it does not already own in four of its operating companies and to set up a single international subsidiary. The regulated activities—primarily the local operating companies that provide the telephone lines to every phone and the Long Lines Dept. that runs the backbone network—will report to President

The Policy Process / 249

William M. Ellinghaus. Charged with setting up Baby Bell is Vice-Chairman James E. Olson. Brown emphasizes that the subsidiary's final form is still not firm, but he concedes that AT&T favors a single nationwide subsidiary that would be responsible for the marketing and service of all the terminal equipment as well as any moves into nonregulated markets. No date has been set yet for it to begin operations.

One thing is certain. When Baby Bell is born, it will be a giant. All 138 million telephones now leased to residential and business users, as well as all office switchboards and Teletype machines, will become assets of the new subsidiary. Together, this equipment represents total assets of $12 billion.

Brown estimates that the activities that will be transferred to the new subsidiary already account for some 15% of AT&T's annual revenues, or about $6.8 billion. And by 1985, when some of the new unregulated data communications services come on line, Baby Bell could easily reach $10 billion in annual revenues, predicts Martin W. Fletcher, an analyst with Dataquest Inc.

AT&T must also determine what to do with the two operating companies in which it holds a minority interest: Southern New England Telephone Co. and Cincinnati Bell Inc. It could mean the creation of two new independent phone companies. As Salomon's Himsworth puts it: "They either have to step up to 100% ownership or down to zero—and I think the latter is more likely."

AT&T is not being all that clear about what it will do with Western Electric Co., its manufacturing arm, and Bell Telephone Laboratories Inc., its research and development unit. For the time being both of them will report to Ellinghaus. But they could be split up as well between Baby Bell and the regulated operation. Brown, for example, says that it would be possible to divide Western Electric between the plants that turn out central-office switching equipment and other hardware for the regulated telephone network and those facilities that manufacture telephones, terminals, and other competitive products. But Philip S. Nyborg, general counsel of the Computer & Communications Industry Assn., says that AT&T's plan "should not be construed in any way to preempt the need for full divestiture of Western Electric and Bell Labs."

For AT&T, the reorganization may be the best possible plan at the best possible time. This may be "their last chance," says Howard Anderson, president of the Yankee Group. "If they don't do it now, they'll just be a utility," he adds. As far as Salomon's Himsworth is concerned, the plan has a good chance of succeeding. "It seems a practical balance of what they could get away with and what they'd like to do." ∎

WASHINGTON POST: New Ventures Get Off to an Uncertain Start

The conflict between quality and profits is often sharper in the publishing industry than in other fields. Traditionally, Washington Post Co., which publishes *The Washington Post* and *Newsweek,* has emphasized quality. Yet the company has not sacrificed profits. Both publications are solidly successful, contributing nearly 70% of the company's $80 million operating profit and some 80% of its sales of $593 million. In recent years its earnings growth has been superior in its industry. But the company has avoided new ventures. With the exception of a modest foray into two other small newspapers, Post Co. has relied on its flagship publications and its broadcasting operation for income.

In the last two years, however, the company has opted for expansion. One new magazine has been brought out and another is in the works. And the company has joined with 10 others to form a news data bank. But its new expansion efforts may be off to a rocky start.

Many media observers wonder whether Post Co. can bring its Midas touch to its newer publications. The *Trenton Times*, which Post Co. purchased in 1974, has been steadily losing circulation to its competitor, *The Trentonian*, owned by Ingersoll Publications. The first issue of *Inside Sports,* a monthly magazine aimed at the college-educated sports enthusiast, came out in April and has had difficulty making the 500,000 circulation guaranteed to advertisers. Another new magazine, *Focus,* that would cover a different subject in depth six times a year, also has problems. The company, fearing that the recession will continue, may just scrap the idea. The struggles that Post Co. is having with its newer publications may mean that, for the time being, the company will be hesitant to further expand those divisions.

Yet its only other possibility for growth is with its broadcasting division, which owns four TV stations. It has avoided cable TV systems. And while other media giants are branching out into nonjournalistic areas, such as timberlands and real estate, Post Co. has been more conservative, restricting itself to a small venture in TV programming and a 30% interest in a Virginia newsprint plant. Advertising remains the source of 75% of the company's revenues.

Whether Post Co.'s aggressiveness develops in the years ahead depends partly on who will be running its operations. During the next several months, Chairman and Chief Executive Officer Katharine Graham, 63, must find a president to replace Mark J. Meagher, who will leave at the end of the year. Graham has to find someone who can work both with her and independently of her—something her unpredictable management style has often precluded in the past. Indeed, industry scuttlebutt makes a telling point about Graham's demanding expectations: She is reportedly less than satisfied even with the successful *Post* and *Newsweek* operations.

Even so, the *Post* is weathering the recession well. Its daily advertising linage and circulation rose 5.3% and 0.5% respectively between March, 1979, and March, 1980. Although its competitor, Time Inc.'s *Washington Star,* showed slightly larger increases, the *Post's* share of ad lines in its market remains a dominant 73% and its share of total revenues an estimated 85%. The newspaper's 1979 revenues were $240.5 million out of newspaper division revenues of $272.7 million; net operating income for the division was $35.4 million.

Because the Washington metropolitan area is rapidly expanding and has a higher-than-ordinary demand for news, there is no doubt that the *Post* will continue to grow. About Sept. 29, the company's $65 million offset printing plant

Family control: Chairman and CEO Katharine Graham and her son, Donald, 35, publisher of *The Washington Post.*

in the Virginia suburbs will link up with a new high-technology editing system and a laser-driven platemaking device, increasing the newspaper's production capacity by about 30%. "We've felt ever since 1978 that our circulation was being constrained by our manufacturing capacity," says *Post* Publisher Donald E. Graham. The added production will permit the *Post* to increase its distribution in Maryland and Virginia, where the *Post* already has a higher circulation than any other daily newspaper.

But Graham and other *Post* executives have no intention of expanding indiscriminately. They view the *Post* as a local paper, and prefer to leave the national market to *The Wall Street Journal* and the new national edition of *The New York Times.* Says *Post* Executive Editor Benjamin C. Bradlee: "We are a metro paper, we're glad to be, and we're proud of it."

Magazines. Not only is the *Post* dealing with the recession handily but *Newsweek* also is withstanding the ravages of the economy. The weekly increased its circulation rate base in January by 50,000 to 2.95 million. That is still far behind *Time* magazine's circulation of 4.2 million, but *Newsweek* was almost entirely responsible for the 8% increase in the Post Co.'s magazine and book division revenues in the second quarter of 1980 over 1979.

That figure does not include the losses of *Inside Sports*, which totaled $3.7 million in the same period, thus raising the possibility that the new publication may cost the company more than the planned $8 million in 1980. Even aided by a $5 million advertising campaign, the magazine has not achieved its hoped-for 90/10 newsstand-to-subscription mix. Instead the ratio is closer to 70/30. That is a more costly combination, given the expense of mailing magazines.

The cost of soliciting subscriptions will come right off Post Co.'s bottom line this year because of a 1979 company accounting change that expenses, rather than amortizes, such costs. However, because the company's stock is largely controlled by the Graham family, management is less likely to be criticized when there is a drop in earnings. Although the Post Co.'s profits fell from $49.7 million in 1978 to $29.5 million in 1979, most of the drop came from the accounting change. But part came from the startup costs of *Inside Sports*.

Still, Graham says she would launch the magazine at the same time if she had to do it again. "When you develop a product, you ought to go ahead with it, not hold out for the economy," she says.
'Out of the nursery.' But the recession has made the company think twice about *Focus*, whose concept puzzles many in the magazine industry. Conventional wisdom suggests that a magazine's success comes from identifying and appealing to specialized audiences. But *Focus*, which intends to concentrate each issue on a different subject as diverse as space or movies, causes industry observers to question how it will build and hold an audience. In any case, no decision will be made on *Focus* until the economy improves and *Inside Sports* is more secure. "We are unlikely to bring out a new magazine until we get this baby out of the nursery," says Peter A. Derow, Newsweek Inc.'s president.

More significant than Post Co.'s new projects, however, are investments it has chosen not to make. In the early 1970s, Graham, fearful of its questionable future and high cost, decided not to follow other publishers into cable TV. Today she says, "I very much wish we'd gotten into cable . . . a few years ago."

Post Co. has even rejected growth opportunities in the business it knows. It pulled back from its intention of creating a small chain of newspapers after it bought the *Trenton Times* and in 1978 the *Everett Herald*, a fairly successful paper near Seattle. "We thought back in 1977, if we put together half a dozen small newspapers, they would have some impact [on profits]," says Meagher. "Then we backed off as prices exploded."

Post Co. did bid on several other newspapers up for sale, such as *The Wilmington* (Del.) *News-Journal*, which eventually was bought by Gannett Co. for $60 million. And it recently considered buying *The Denver Post*. While Graham and other Post Co. executives say that the company will continue to

Chairman Graham: 'You have to get your feet wet to know the problems'

look at available newspapers, they see little need to expand for the sake of expanding. In fact, the company in recent years has instead paid $86.2 million to buy back some 6 million shares, or 30% of its outstanding stock, on the theory that investing in itself produced a better return than would investing in another business.
'Time to move on.' Graham's immediate job is to replace Meagher, and she plans to look outside the company. Meagher, 48, says he never intended to stay longer than he has. "I was not asked to leave," he says. "It's time to move on to a new challenge." But some observers believe that Meagher may have been discouraged by Graham's tendency to run the show single-handedly, and by the fact that her son, Donald, 35, now *Post* publisher, will eventually take over.

This year, Graham was propelled into the presidency of the American Newspaper Publishers Assn. when her predecessor, Len H. Small, president of Small Newspapers Inc., was killed in an auto crash. That job often takes her away from her duties at the *Post*, and the remarkably lean corporate structure—there are seven executives above the operating divisions—leaves little depth to run things when she is elsewhere.

That structure also means that much of the new-product research is done at the divisional level. One of Post Co.'s only nonjournalistic ventures, TV program development, sprang from its broadcasting division, which runs four VHF stations. The Los Angeles office has 12 programs in production or development that could be sold to networks, cable, or for syndication, plus four programs already on the market.
The real test. But program development is a very small part of Post Co. The real test for the company in the next few years will be how it applies its newsgathering expertise to the information explosion. Post Co., along with 10 other newspapers, will participate in Compuserve, an information data base for libraries, homes, and corporations, but it has made no other commitments yet to what Graham wryly refers to as her fourth division.

In fact, Post Co. is already behind other such publishing giants as Knight-Ridder, Time, and New York Times in the new technology. Graham will have to overcome her traditional reluctance to experiment if she does not want to miss the boat again, as she did with cable. Indications are that she may be willing to move ahead. "From an offensive and a defensive point of view, no matter what you do [with the new technologies], you have to be aware of them and you have to try them out," she says. "You have to get your feet wet to know the problems as well as the opportunities." ■

BEATRICE FOODS:
Adding Tropicana for a Broader Nationwide Network

Beatrice Foods Co. has climbed to the pinnacle of the nation's processed foods industry by repeating one formula with uncanny consistency: It buys strong regional companies and then pushes their brand-name products into new markets.

The Chicago-based conglomerate is preparing to test that formula again, but on a much larger scale than in the past. This week, Beatrice signed a definitive agreement to buy Tropicana Products Inc., the leading marketer of fresh orange juice, for $490 million in cash and stock.

Until recently, Tropicana focused on the orange juice drinkers in the populous Northeast. But, enticed by established growth trends in other regions, the company has begun dipping into those markets—with a national campaign that no doubt will be speeded up with the aid of Beatrice's financial resources and national distribution network for dairy products.

Yet the Tropicana acquisition also represents a break with the traditional growth strategy at Beatrice. In the past, the $6.2 billion company has steered clear of commodity-type businesses, where prosperity can sometimes hinge on a single crop harvest. And despite its hundreds of acquisitions, it has rarely entered a business that competes directly with one of the nation's premier marketing companies. This, too, has changed because of Tropicana.

Challenge. The competition will come from Coca-Cola Co.'s Food Div., which owns Minute Maid, the top U. S. producer of orange juice that is made from frozen concentrate and then sold in bottles and cartons. Tropicana's "chilled juice," on the other hand, is squeezed from fresh oranges and then packaged. After testing in the Northeast since 1973, Minute Maid is now squaring off with Tropicana in a race to market chilled juice nationally. And the two companies are already competing nose to nose in such cities as Chicago and New York.

Today, the fast-growing chilled variety accounts for 31% of the $1.3 billion orange juice market, up from 20% a decade ago. Tropicana holds half of the chilled juice segment.

"But with Tropicana, Beatrice not only has to contend with the logistics of distributing the fresh product," notes one food company executive, "but it also now faces the brutal prospect of going head-on with Coca-Cola. That will be a challenge."

Though Beatrice leads the industry in sales and profits, it trails such companies as General Foods, Pillsbury, and General Mills in terms of marketing savvy. For the most part, Beatrice sells food and nonfood products that, by dint of either a quality image or an established position, have carved secure niches in national markets or dominate regional ones. Its Dannon yogurt, Louis Sherry ice cream, Peter Eckrich sausages, JBL stereo equipment, and Samsonite luggage are all examples.

Thus the Tropicana move seems to reflect a new emphasis at Beatrice on marketing and a willingness to take on the leading practitioners of that art. The change in the company's philosophy comes less than two years after Wallace N. Rasmussen became president and chief executive officer and seven months after a boardroom debate about the company's management and plans. That debate led to the resignation of William G. Mitchell, former chairman, who is now president of Chicago's Central Telephone & Utilities Corp.

Though neither Rasmussen nor other Beatrice executives would permit interviews, the new chairman, according to sources close to the company, is setting a course that calls for more rapid expansion than in the past. In private conversations, Rasmussen has reportedly said that he wants to lift the company's sales to near the $10 billion mark before he retires. Without some change in the corporate bylaws, Rasmussen, 64, must step down by June, 1979.

Acquisitions. During the past five years, Beatrice's sales have jumped 94%, to the $6.2 billion recorded in the last fiscal year, ended Feb. 28, 1978, while profits have climbed 96%, to $221 million. And in the past 14 months, Beatrice has engineered two acquisitions besides Tropicana: It bought Harman International Industries Inc., a $137 million manufacturer of hi-fi equipment, for $99 million, and it agreed to purchase Culligan International Co., a $93 million producer of water-softening equipment, for $54 million.

Beatrice is also on the move internally. For example, Dannon, the country's leading yogurt maker, will soon begin selling its products nationwide.

Its first acquisition that challenges a big rival. The market: $1.3 billion

For the upcoming growth drive, Rasmussen is committed to keeping the same management setup that has worked so effectively until now. That decision, however, is apparently what prompted Mitchell's departure.

Mitchell, the company's top acquisition scout and head of administration, argued that Beatrice needed a tighter rein on its 400 or so profit centers and more thorough reporting procedures before it embarked on a major new acquisition program. Rasmussen was opposed to these management and administrative changes. Mitchell then presented his proposal to the board—and lost.

Corporate setup. The company's management structure mirrors the classic model of the decentralized conglomerate. Accounting, legal, and administrative chores are handled at the Chicago corporate headquarters, while day-to-day operations and marketing are left to field managers.

But, unlike many conglomerates, Beatrice seems to have fine-tuned this setup to get the most from its 200-member corporate staff. "Beatrice takes all the front office problems back to Chicago, getting rid of a lot of overhead," says one investment banker. And analysts point to the efficiency of Beatrice's corporate management as one reason for its profitability. Last year the company's pretax profit margin of 7% was second only to that of General Mills Inc. among the nation's big food-processing companies.

But the marketing challenges posed by another round of expansion, not the management challenges, will be the acid test for Beatrice. For it would seem inevitable that, seeking growth, the company will enter more of the big urban markets it has often shunned in the past. In these markets the competition is stiffer, the operating costs are higher, and the advertising and promotion spending needed to win customer dollars is greater.

Tropicana is the first such big test; Beatrice has landed an attractive property that fits nicely with its current product offerings. Over the past five years, Tropicana's sales have climbed at an average yearly clip of 19%, to $244.5 million, while earnings rose 21%, to $22.4 million. Reflecting its strength, the company's earnings jumped 41% last year, despite a damaging frost that badly crimped supplies. "Tropicana is now growing twice as fast as Beatrice," notes Donald J. Lupa, a vice-president with Duff, Anderson & Clark, a Chicago securities firm. "And orange juice completes Beatrice's product line in the dairy case."

Marketing mix. After the Culligan and Harman deals, Rasmussen wanted to acquire a large food company to keep the mix of Beatrice's food to nonfood businesses at a 75%-25% ratio. Over the past few years, Beatrice executives had talked to Tropicana's 77-year-old chairman and founder, Anthony T. Rossi, about merging the companies.

Rossi was indifferent to these earlier Beatrice overtures. But after listening to dozens of other offers, Rossi agreed two months ago to merge with Beatrice, which had decided to pay 42% more than a recent bid by Kellogg Co.

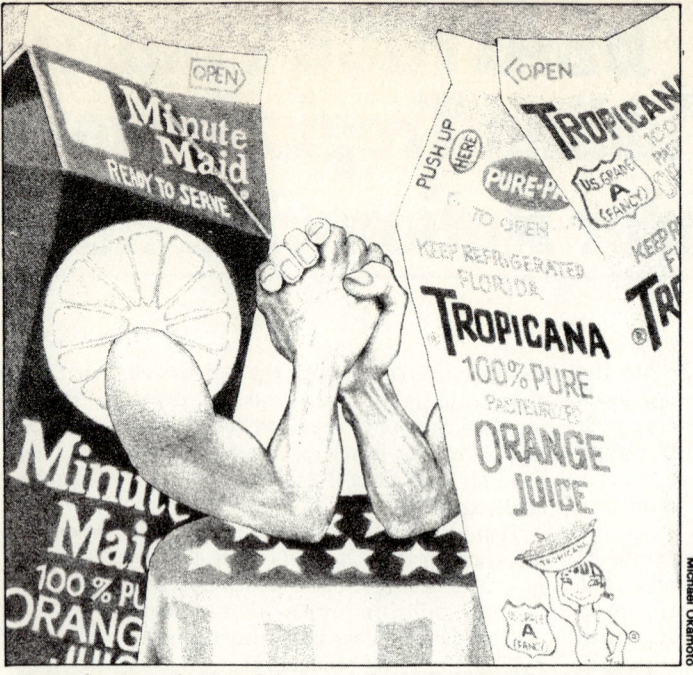

A coming test of strength between Coca-Cola and Beatrice Foods.

At the outset, the match-up between Tropicana and Minute Maid seems fairly even. Working to Minute Maid's advantage are the marketing knowhow that it can draw from Coca-Cola and its early jump in the national race. Minute Maid is now distributing its chilled juice in some big urban markets of the West and Southwest that Tropicana has as yet not touched.

"We are going to move into new areas as fast as our facilities and product can be made available," says Albert G. Munkelt, vice-president of marketing at Coca-Cola's frozen and chilled products unit in Houston.

Tropicana, on the other hand, holds a larger portion of overall chilled juice sales. It also sells fresh juice, rather than the reconstituted product Minute Maid offers. Considering the public affection for all things "natural," Tropicana will probably stress this difference between the two products in its ads, and that could help Tropicana.

A contender. Even without Beatrice, Tropicana has not shied from the competitive fray. "Tropicana has been an aggressive competitor in every market so far," Coca-Cola's Munkelt concedes. With Beatrice, its competitive clout will be greater. In fact, the company announced last month that the Federal Trade Commission is now reviewing any antitrust questions posed by the Beatrice-Tropicana marriage.

To attain truly national coverage, Minute Maid and Tropicana will eventually go into smaller towns as well as big urban centers. It is in these smaller markets that Beatrice can help Tropicana the most. Beatrice owns a bevy of regional dairies, which operate mostly in small towns. And some of its trucks have been carrying Tropicana juice for years. "Beatrice already understands the distribution of fresh products," notes one competitor. "I can't think of another food company that could better exploit Tropicana's potential."

How well Beatrice fares with Tropicana in the battle against Coca-Cola's Minute Maid remains to be seen. But whatever the outcome, the next year should tell much about Beatrice's abilities as a big-league national marketer—and whether Rasmussen's heady growth plans are workable prospects or just wishful thinking. ∎

COMMENTARY

By Robin Grossman

Why IBM reversed itself on computer pricing

When International Business Machines Corp. introduced its powerful 4300 series of mainframe computers a year ago, it knocked the computer industry on its ear. It set prices so low that it appeared that competitors would be hard-put to match the new price/performance standards. Indeed, at least one maker of plug-compatible computers—copycat machines that sell for less than IBM's but run on IBM software—was forced out of the market, and others were badly crippled. Long accustomed to operating under the protection of IBM's price umbrella, the industry, it seemed, was in for a new era of aggressive and perhaps profitless competition and, eventually, further consolidation.

So the industry was stunned again on Dec. 28 when IBM unfolded its umbrella again, raising prices by 5% to 7% on most of its data processing and word processing products. "IBM has taken a step backward on its march to offer price/performance improvements," observes L. Duane Kirkpatrick, head of the technology group at Dean Witter Reynolds Inc. in San Francisco. While the price boosts undoubtedly reflect increasing costs of doing business, as IBM claims, IBM-watchers say that the post-Christmas reversal is also a clear admission by the company that its original pricing for the 4300 series was too low—a mistake that IBM is now trying to rectify.

Profitability. Only the industry's customers are likely to lose by IBM's reversal. The Armonk giant has a lot to gain. No one expects the higher prices to reduce demand for the 4300 series, so profitability—badly needed to underwrite the company's ambitious manufacturing and leasing programs—will only be enhanced. "By the stroke of a pen, IBM has just increased revenue by $1 billion," figures S. S. "Tim" Tyler, a senior consultant at Input, a Palo Alto (Calif.) market research firm.

Pricing the new 4300 mainframes too low hurt earnings.

The episode, though, reflects a deep-seated business problem that, because of IBM's preeminence, must inevitably affect the future pace of product introductions. IBM has a huge customer base, and thus a huge potential for hurting itself each time it announces a new product. The giant walks a fine line between introducing attractively priced machines and milking its installed base.

After the medium-scale 4300 series was announced, for example, users of IBM's top-of-the-line 303X series of mainframes anticipated that the company's impending H series, to replace the 303X line, would echo the aggressive price/performance of the 4300. Expecting that the H series could appear as early as the end of 1979, they stopped buying the 303X machines, fearing that they would decline sharply in value.

As a result, just as IBM was trying to encourage customers to buy instead of lease to improve its cash flow, its 303X customers began to insist on leasing to protect themselves. This cost IBM doubly: Besides losing the purchase revenues, it had to finance a larger lease and rental base than it had planned for. While the company refuses to discuss the matter, "in retrospect, IBM wishes it had not priced so aggressively," says William R. Becklean, an analyst with Bache Halsey Stuart Shields Inc. in Boston. Becklean believes that the 4300 pricing boomerang was largely responsible for the 18% decline in IBM's third-quarter earnings last year. (Earnings for the year were off 3%.)

Those profit declines came at a bad time: when IBM needed money to expand production capacity for the 4300 series and to fund its lease base for the forthcoming H series. In October the company went outside for money for the first time, floating $1 billion in bonds. And in December it announced a $300 million loan from Saudi Arabia. The profit declines also worried IBM stockholders who have come to expect constant improvements in revenues and return on investment. "IBM needs growth to keep its stock at a premium multiple," says Kirkpatrick of Dean Witter.

Not as dramatic. Most industry observers expect to see IBM back on the growth track soon. "IBM has never had a profitability or cash flow problem before," notes H. Glen Haney, vice-president for worldwide marketing at Sperry Corp.'s Univac Div. "They'll work at this until they fix it." The year-end price increases may do the trick. They conspicuously excepted the purchase prices, though not the lease and rental rates, of the 303X series. And IBM customers, say the company's competitors, now will not expect the price/performance improvements of the H series to be as dramatic as those originally announced for the 4300 series. Thus they will step up their purchases of the 303X computers.

Meanwhile, by its price action, IBM has breathed new life into some troubled competitors. The chief beneficiaries are the plug-compatible manufacturers, but other full-line computer makers, such as Honeywell, Sperry, and Burroughs, may also be able to let out their pricing belts a notch. J. Roy Henry, executive vice-president for marketing at Burroughs Corp., is still analyzing the IBM move, but he says, "If it gives us room to raise our prices, we will do that." With the price umbrella up, observes Stephen T. McClellan, an analyst with Salomon Bros., "the industry can get under it comfortably and profitably again."

But IBM's competitors would do well not to make themselves too comfortable. By its aggressive pricing a year ago, the industry leader has shown that it intends to hold on to, if not raise, its massive share of the information processing market. Industry experts believe that if competition gets too tough in 1981 or 1982, particularly from the Japanese, IBM will not hesitate to slash its prices again.

QUAKER OATS RETREATS TO ITS FOOD LINES

The proliferation of private-label and generic grocery products and the constant flow of new food items and product-line extensions have brought the scramble for shelf space in supermarkets to a feverish pitch. One casualty has been Chicago's Quaker Oats Co., which has been preoccupied in recent years with a hectic drive to diversify. To perk up a lethargic earnings and growth record, Quaker tried to recast itself during the early 1970s from a mundane marketer of such staple foods as oatmeal and pancake mixes into a trendy marketer of toys and theme restaurants.

In the process, however, the company succeeded mainly in sapping its marketing prowess, management capabilities, and profits. A prolonged study that the company sponsored, completed last year, revealed serious deficiencies in Quaker's marketing operations. Sales calls took too long, fewer stores were serviced, and shelf space was not expanded. For example, Quaker's 100% Natural Cereal, a granola breakfast food that leads in its market segment, was found to have no more "facings" in the supermarkets than a competitor with half the market share. "If there's a battle for shelf space, we may just say we don't need Quaker," says an executive at a Midwestern supermarket chain, complaining that the company has reduced store margins on its products and, in effect, restricted promotional expenditures.

Chagrined by the losing battle for shelf space and by the unsuccessful results of its diversification efforts, Quaker is now striving to become what William D. Smithburg, its new president and chief operating officer, calls "a more aggressive marketing company." The sales force was expanded by 25% over the past year as a means of increasing supermarket exposure—the first such increase in 12 years. The advertising and promotional budget was expanded by 14%, and an energetic drive for new products has been launched.

Cutting back. The key to winning the fight for supermarket shelf space is introducing new grocery items. Immersed in its diversification programs, however, Quaker brought out only one major new product in the U.S. market during 1970-78—100% Natural Cereal. Now the company has retreated to its core businesses in food. It has dumped one of the two acquired toy companies and is trimming its restaurant and chemical operations, both of which expanded in scope but not in earnings. The focus now will be on developing innovative products in foods.

"You don't have the automatic growth built into the industry that you did in the 1960s," says Smithburg, 41, who became president in October when Kenneth Mason retired. "The premium on having something unique is much greater." As head of the U.S. Grocery Products Group for three years, Smithburg began reviving new-product development in that area and is now extending that approach to foreign grocery operations and to Quaker's surviving toy venture, Fisher-Price. (The other toy company, Louis Marx & Co., once an industry leader, turned sour under Quaker's ownership and was sold.)

"Part of our strategy is to take advantage of great old brand names and add on new products," says Robert D. Stuart Jr., Quaker's 63-year-old chairman and chief executive officer, who planned the company's uneven diversification.

So far, Quaker has scored heavily with two new products, both introduced during Smithburg's tenure as domestic grocery chief. In 1978, the Ken-L Ration pet food line brought out Tender Chunks. Positioned as the first dry, yet moist dog food, it quickly grabbed 8.5% of the $1 billion dry dog food market segment. Although the field now includes five competing products, Tender Chunks is outselling Moist & Chunky, introduced by Ralston Purina, the No. 1 dog food producer, by 2 to 1.

Quaker's other successful new product, Corn Bran cereal, capitalizes on the growing popularity of natural foods and is a departure from the usual wheat products on the market. Since its national introduction last year, the brand has grabbed a respectable 1.2% share of the $2 billion cold cereal market.

Now in test markets is Halfsies, which has half the sugar content of most presweetened cereals. Quaker's entry has raised hackles in the industry, which is defensive about growing consumer and government fears about excessive sugar use. "There's not a damned thing wrong with marketing presweetened cereals," bristles Arnold G. Langbo, president of Kellogg's U.S. Food Products Group. "The concept of playing upon the consumer's conception of presweetened as bad indicts all products on the market." Smithburg happily defends Halfsies. "The real fact of life is that the housewife is worried, and needs an alternative," he says.

Another food market that has aroused Quaker's interest is breakfast and snack food items for preparation in microwave ovens. Quaker believes that this market has a big potential, although household penetration of the ovens seems stuck at a 15% level, which is about half the number of users needed to stimulate major product activity.

Hard-pressed. Despite the stepup in new grocery products, Quaker's push lags behind Kellogg's, which introduced five new cereals last year. Still feeling the financial effects of a breakneck acquisition drive that plunged profits to a low of $31 million in 1975, Quaker simply lacks the resources to keep up with its main competitors. Last year profits were up to $99 million on sales of $2 billion, but the return on invested capital was 12.3%, a bit above the industry average but far behind Kellogg's 19.41%.

In playing the diversification game, CEO Stuart, a member of Quaker's founding family, aimed to reduce dependence on domestic staple grocery prod-

256 / Readings from *Business Week*

ucts from 69% of sales in 1969. The proportion has been brought down to 42% of total revenues through the acquisition of the Magic Pan crêpe restaurants, Celeste pizza, the toy business, and by the expansion of foreign grocery and chemical operations.

Most of these activities have been troubled by managerial and marketing problems. Profits have fallen for four consecutive years at the 93-unit Magic Pan chain. Celeste's share of the $620 million frozen pizza market has slipped from 9.7% to 8.9% over the past year and it is now repackaging the line. The chemical division, which makes grain-based furfurylalcohol (used as a binding agent by foundries) was knocked out of the market by cheaper oil-based agents after capacity was expanded in the U. S. and a new plant built in Belgium.

The situation has been more favorable in overseas groceries and at Fisher-Price. Foreign sales and earnings have grown 75% and 94% over the past five years. The company acquired a majority

Quaker is beefing up its promotional budget and adding new products

interest last year in Chiari & Forti, an Italian maker of edible oils and mixes, and is seeking expansion in pet foods in such high growth countries as West Germany and France.

New items. A dominant position in infant and preschool toys has increased Fisher-Price's sales tenfold to nearly $300 million since 1969. It returned 12% on sales last year vs. corporate's 9.2%. The division now wants to spread its franchise to older children by adding items such as audiovisual and electronic toys and expanding further into European markets. But moving into the older-age bracket it will face stiff competition from Mattel, Kenner Products, and Ideal Toy.

In Europe, Fisher-Price wants to alter its premium-priced image and is aiming for mass distribution of lower-priced toys. A new 75-person Quaker sales force has replaced local distributors, and a new plant will reduce imports from the U. S. and help ease pricing pressures.

Although stung by its earlier efforts, Quaker still appears enchanted by acquisitions and is searching for companies in the $30 million sales range. Negotiations are now under way to buy Brookstone Co., a small New Hampshire tool distributor. Quaker is also considering the purchase of home repair-center ventures. This time, however, the company is determined that diversification will be held to a scale that will not drain financial resources and managerial talent from the primary task of pushing out new grocery products and fighting for that valuable shelf space. ∎

AMERICAN CAN: Diversification Brings Sobering Second Thoughts

The indictments handed down on Feb. 28 against top officials of Sam Goody Inc. for allegedly dealing in counterfeit records and tapes have blown a gaping hole in the touted acquisition expertise of American Can Co. Successfully diversified into paper products, mail-order merchandise sales, and other fields, American Can in 1978 bought Goody, a record store chain, and placed it under the aegis of another subsidiary, Pickwick International Inc., a manufacturer and distributor of records. American Can had purchased Pickwick in 1977.

Both acquisitions—justified on financial grounds more than because of a business fit—came only after American supposedly made a sophisticated analysis. The company used insiders and outsiders to study the two businesses and says it hired detectives to make certain that the corruption that has often tainted the recording industry would never find its way to American Can's doorstep.

Instead, Goody; its president, George Levy; and vice-president, Sam Stolon, have been charged by a federal grand jury in Brooklyn, N. Y., with racketeering, interstate transportation of stolen property, and 12 counts of distribution of counterfeit recordings. The executives have pleaded innocent. But American, whose earnings of $127.3 million on sales of $4.5 billion last year make it second only to Continental Group Inc. in the container industry, has still been dragged into the web of recording piracy that industry associations estimate may cost legitimate companies $400 million to $1 billion this year alone.

Damaging publicity. And the indictments at Goody may be only a beginning. The Justice Dept. is also known to be delving into operations at Pickwick. At stake is a $500 million-a-year record empire embracing production, distribution, and marketing that American has built since 1977 through the two companies and other acquired record store chains, also operated under Pickwick. Arthur M. Stupay, a former corporate planner at American and now a container industry analyst at Prescott, Ball & Turben, a Cleveland brokerage house, says company officials have told him that only $1 million to $3 million worth of inventory is suspected of being counterfeit and therefore subject to confiscation. But publicity could be more damaging; counterfeits tend to be lower in quality, and customers may therefore shun American's 436 record stores. "I think American Can is in big trouble," says an executive of another container company.

At American Can headquarters in Greenwich, Conn., the indictments have had a sobering effect, especially on President William S. Woodside, the man picked to become chief executive this year when Chairman William F. May retires. Company officials reacted mainly with silence when the indictments occurred, but Woodside is now scrambling to explain.

On Mar. 6, he told BUSINESS WEEK that the counterfeit dealings apparently did occur, that American learned of them through an internal audit last November, and that the company promptly reported its findings to the FBI. The company made the same remarks in an internal memo dated Feb. 27—the day, ironically, that Stupay was in Greenwich to give American a Financial Analysts Federation award for openness in corporate reporting in 1979.

John H. Jacobs, executive assistant prosecutor of the organized crime strike force handling the investigation for the Justice Dept., confirms American did report its findings. But the company, although it was aware of the irregularities, still left Levy and Stolon in charge of Goody. Other executives, however, have quit or are being reshuffled. C. Charles Smith, who headed Pickwick, revealed plans to resign last September, shortly after American moved to place Pickwick under the supervision of Theodore J. Deikel, who heads another American subsidiary, Fingerhut, a mail-order house.

Shift. Woodside denies that Smith's resignation, effective Mar. 31, was forced or related to the scandal. But in another move higher in the company's executive echelons, American on Feb. 29 also relieved Lionel N. Sterling of his sector executive title, under which he supervised corporate finance plus all record industry operations. Sterling, 42 and now senior vice-president of finance, was regarded as the company's financial whiz kid, with a good shot at the presidency until the record scandal arose. As controller in 1977, Sterling engineered the purchase of Pickwick and boasted that it was a prime example of proper pre-acquisition financial screening and solid strategic planning. At the time, Sterling discounted Pickwick's modest $9.5 million profit on $265 million in sales because the company was in a growth industry, and he deprecated the notion that recordings were too far afield from the company's mainstay can business. He maintained that American's knowledge of consumer products, based on its existing diversification into Dixie cups and other paper products, was enough to enable it to manage a record and tape business.

The company says it stripped Sterling of his recording responsibilities only so he can attend better to unsettled financial markets. Woodside also defends American's pre-acquisition probe, but in doing so he indicts its subsequent management. "In a very detailed pre-purchasing investigation, we could find not a thing [about counterfeit sales]," Woodside declares. Instead, he adds in an oddly self-critical justification: "Actually, the dates on the indictments started about two weeks after we bought it [Goody] and ran on until November, 1978."

Such explanations do little to appease critics. A can company moving into records "didn't make rational sense" to begin with, snipes one competitor. "These indictments undermine investor confidence in American's ability to make sound judgments about acquisitions," adds Richard S. Palm, an analyst with Merrill Lynch Pierce, Fenner & Smith Inc.

Indeed, at Pickwick and its Sam Goody operations, even the alleged crime did not pay last year. Although the recording industry grew 12.1% annually from 1970 to 1978, sales flattened and profits were clobbered in 1979. Cost increases, stemming from surging vinyl prices, and a dearth of hit records combined last year with a newly discovered price elasticity to slash margins. "Records selling at more than $8 each began to turn people off," observes analyst Stupay. Pickwick, after garnering pretax earnings of about $30 million in 1978, finished 1979 with an operating loss of as much as $25 million on its $500 million in sales, Stupay says.

Few survivors. Pickwick's failures are sorely reminiscent of past errors in diversification at American. The company did well in 1957, when it moved into paper products with acquisitions of Dixie Cup Co. and Marathon Corp., whose brands include Northern, Aurora, Brawny, and Bolt paper towels, toilet tissue, and related products. But a decade after their purchase, American, observing that all its products involved printing of designs and labels, redefined itself as both a container company and the nation's largest printer. In the late 1960s,

258 / Readings from *Business Week*

it therefore bought its way into commercial printing with two acquisitions and into the manufacture of dress patterns. The company also moved into glass bottlemaking, although it had no background in glass. Of these ventures, only the dress patterns, including the Butterick, See & Sew, and Vogue brand names, remain; commercial printing and glass bottles quickly proved disappointing and were divested.

While American was diversifying, its stable of can manufacturing plants was aging. Since 1972, the company has had to sell or close an astonishing 105 factories that had produced $1.2 billion sales, and has taken write-downs totaling $300 million. These now have been replaced with a new system of 62 plants. Can and other packaging operations in 1979 contributed 53% of sales, and, despite all the attempts at diversification, 60% of $304.8 million in operating income.

Despite its modernization, American still has some problems in its can operation. For example, it is still behind the industry in the shift to aluminum and away from steel. Its proportion of steel can production is thought to be considerably above the industry average of 61%. Aluminum, increasingly popular for soft drinks and beer, saw its share rise 10.6%, while steel lost 6%, in 1979 alone.

Aluminum has been boosted by such events as the adoption in seven states of

Analyst Palm: American's ability to make sound acquisitions is now in doubt

mandatory deposit laws that favor aluminum cans for their recycling value.

Deposit laws, however, also threaten overall can production by promoting greater use of refillable bottles. In addition, canmakers have been hurt by a new trend toward self-manufacturing of cans by some large customers, while some basic aluminum producers, including Reynolds Metals Co., are vertically integrating their operations by beginning can fabrication, too. As a result, American's share of the U.S. food and beverage can market has dropped from 28% in 1971 to 18% last year.

Some winners. These events have made diversification of some sort wise for all canmakers. American's closest competitor, industry-leader Continental Group, has moved into insurance and natural gas production. And American has far from failed totally in its diversification attempts. Fingerhut, whose sales increased 14% to $250 million in 1979, also saw its operating income rise an estimated 10% to $26 million. Company officials expect mail order sales to continue to grow as shoppers recognize that the cost of gasoline must be added to their bills for retail goods from stores.

American is trying as well to introduce revolutionary new products. It has developed a pouch, made mainly of plastic, which it hopes will become price-competitive enough to replace cans for some foods on supermarket shelves. The company also is trying to back into the energy business by selling a patented process that would increase the yield of oil wells by flooding them with lignin, a byproduct of papermaking.

These operations, however, are overshadowed now by the furor over counterfeit recordings. Under Fingerhut's Deikel, regarded as a tough manager, American at least hopes to improve Pickwick's financial controls. As recently as last June, the company had been forecasting that Pickwick would be profitable in 1979. Woodside, meanwhile, admits that in the wake of the Goody indictments, certain diversification moves of his competitors are beginning to look good by comparison. "I would love to have an insurance company," he says wistfully, "that was as helpful to us as Continental's has been to it." ∎

McGRAW-EDISION: Paying the Price of the Studebaker Acquisition

When McGraw-Edison Co. moved boldly last summer to acquire Studebaker-Worthington Inc., it was clear that Edward J. Williams, McGraw's chairman, was preparing for nothing less than a change of corporate identity. Studebaker, with 1978 sales of $1.4 billion, was 22% larger than McGraw, and as a result the combined companies became more reliant on Studebaker's lines of industrial machinery and auto components than on McGraw's electrical equipment.

What was not so obvious then were the dangers of Williams' decision. Strongly influenced to make the acquisition by his newly hired president, O. E. "Odey" Powers, an erstwhile Studebaker executive, Williams changed not only his company's business mix but also a meticulously mapped strategy that had called for major investments in McGraw's existing household appliance business. To finance the $724 million purchase, Williams sold the appliances—pulling McGraw out of consumer products, which provided 28% of its 1978 sales of $1.2 billion—and scrapped a firm company bias against heavy debt first set by founder Max McGraw.

Soaring interest rates are now beginning to vindicate Max McGraw's attitude rather than Williams'. The company's total debt has leaped from $58 million, or 11% of capital in 1978, to $768 million, or 60% by the end of last year. Of that, $335 million is in short-term borrowings that must be rolled over this year at interest rates currently about five points higher than when the acquisition occurred, raising McGraw's estimated 1980 interest costs about 15% to $80 million. Beyond that, one of McGraw's biggest single product lines is now components for the ailing auto industry, including brakes and other parts made by Studebaker's largest division, Wagner Electric Corp., which had sales of $400 million last year.

Too soon to call. Outsiders are not ready to suggest that Williams erred in buying Studebaker—undoubtedly the most dramatic move ever at a company formed just 23 years ago in Elgin, Ill., by the merger of Max McGraw's McGraw Electric Co. and Thomas A. Edison Inc. They suggest it will take years of viewing how the new company works under different business cycles before conclusions can be made. "There is risk as far as getting through the current economic downturn, but I'm looking at what could be a veritable explosion of earnings in the next upturn," notes Horace P. Smith, an analyst with Kidder, Peabody & Co.

What is astounding to most observers, however, is the totality of Williams' strategic reversal. Just 20 months ago, Williams was plotting a renewed focus on the company's well-known but modestly profitable Speed Queen washers and dryers and Toastmaster kitchen appliances. It was more than mere talk. McGraw had quietly solicited a study of its appliance business by Booz, Allen & Hamilton Inc. and was preparing to make a $100 million capital infusion into appliances over a two-year period. McGraw executives had even talked with the makers of Frigidaire, Admiral, Norge, and Tappan appliance brands about selling out to McGraw. Says a former McGraw executive: "Ed comes into the office with different ideas on different days."

Indeed, it was less than a year after making his appliance plans that Williams decided to leave that business. In January, 1979, Williams hired Powers directly from Studebaker, and Powers, an aggressive operations man now viewed as a "trigger" behind decision-making at McGraw, almost immediately began pushing for the purchase of his former employer. Powers directly contacted Studebaker Chairman Derald H. Ruttenberg, at first about the acquisition of portions of the company and finally about complete merger.

At the same time, the McGraw two-some targeted their appliance business and several others, with sales totaling $400 million, for divestiture to help pay for the massive buyout. Speed Queen and Modern Maid appliance units were sold late last year to Raytheon Co. for $73 million. McGraw has now lined up buyers for its Toastmaster toasters and household fans, plus a restaurant-equipment business. Some Studebaker operations, including portable air compressors and machinery controls, also are being placed on the auction block.

Sensible sacrifice. With this help, Williams maintains he will be able to pare debt to 45% of capital by yearend, a big step toward his ultimate goal of 35%. Despite his earlier statements, Williams now contends the sacrifice of appliances for Studebaker makes sense. The product lines being sold, he notes, were "earning a return on investment of only 7%. Studebaker offered three times the business and a return of 13.6%."

McGraw, to be sure, might have had its problems turning appliances around. Williams now is having problems as well with Studebaker's businesses. Studebaker's profits exceeded McGraw's before the acquisition, but the combined companies in the fourth quarter of 1979 yielded profits of $19 million, up just 62% from the earnings a year earlier of McGraw alone.

And, because of the increasing slide of auto sales, McGraw is expected to show a decline in earnings in the first quarter of 1980. Sales should rise beyond $2.5 billion in 1980, but earnings will now depend largely on the depth of the auto downturn and on the fortunes of capital goods markets for McGraw's electrical products, ranging from transformers to fuses, and Studebaker's pumps, compressors, and turbines.

Troubles have arisen, too, in management transition. Powers' knowledge of Studebaker, plus that company's tradition of decentralized management, have reportedly helped, but employee morale has suffered from not knowing which operations McGraw would sell to help pay for the acquisition. Williams and Powers also have made dozens of new appointments to assert their management style. Studebaker's Ruttenberg has taken a director's seat, but has left management.

Marketing setback. The management shuffling, some observers say, has hurt Studebaker's marketing in some instances. "Since McGraw took over, we don't consider Worthington Pump [a Studebaker division] to be one of our prime competitors," says an executive at another pump company. He adds: "They've had so many personnel changes, it has weakened their organization, and their products have suffered."

McGraw officials suggest that these are simply temporary problems. And they note that by acquiring Studebaker, McGraw obtained participation in much more than just the auto industry. With Studebaker's pumps and compressors, McGraw now sells to the booming oil industry. Studebaker also owns Masoneilan International Inc., a $150 million-per-year supplier of valves and regulators to the petrochemical industry, and Onan Corp., a $250 million maker of small electric generators growing in popularity at hospitals and other institutions. Growth markets such as these, says analyst Cornell, could cause the company's earnings to double by 1983—provided an economic recovery begins next year. "McGraw has repositioned itself in better growth markets," says another Wall Street analyst. But he adds: "First, management will have to show it can hold the pieces together." ∎

GE MOVES TO CORRECT ITS ERROR IN CHIPS

Ever since General Electric Co. pulled out of the integrated circuit market a decade ago, it has become increasingly clear that it made a strategic mistake. This technology is mushrooming into one of the world's biggest industries, and it is penetrating virtually every GE product line.

Now GE is moving to rectify its error. On Sept. 4, it offered $237 million to buy Intersil Inc., a California semiconductor maker that is one of a dwindling number of such independent companies. In the past few months, GE has committed another $100 million for semiconductor facilities, including a new plant in North Carolina.

"With semiconductors so pervasive in everything electric and electronic, GE has a large internal demand and is back to needing an in-house supplier," says Wilfred J. Corrigan, former chairman of Fairchild Camera & Instrument Corp., which was acquired last year by Schlumberger Ltd. for partly the same reasons. A GE executive predicts that within five years, as semiconductors become more essential to his company's appliances and industrial equipment, "two-thirds of GE's sales will be impacted by the electronics content in our individual product lines."

Special designs. GE's appetite for in-house chip-making capability stems not only from its desire for a guaranteed supply but from its need for specialized, custom-designed devices that volume-oriented producers are less and less willing to make. GE finds Intersil so appealing, analysts say, because much of Intersil's chip technology is of the type GE needs to improve products from motors to light bulbs. Recently, for instance, Intersil started marketing a power transistor that can be used to make electric motors more energy-efficient.

Intersil also is said to be developing an integrated circuit that could be used to cut the electrical consumption of light bulbs, a product obviously desirable to bulb-king GE. Says Sal F. Accardo, an industry analyst at Shearson Loeb Rhoades Inc. in New York: "Intersil is strong in specialized circuits with high-technology engineering. GE has been desperate and frustrated for many years to get [this capability] in house." GE may eventually gobble up as much as 50% of Intersil's production, he adds.

Will size hurt? Ironically, the same overwhelming size that gives GE the muscle to make nine-figure investments in electronics could be a liability on the racetrack of Silicon Valley. Success in semiconductors comes from quick, intuitive decisions, industry insiders say, not from the management-by-committee found in large corporations.

But Orion L. Hoch, Intersil's president, says his company, which earned $10 million on sales of $140 million in the year ended last Sept. 30, has been promised substantial independence as a part of GE. "The objective is to grow Intersil into a major merchant market supplier. At the same time, we'll be able to serve GE," says Hoch. One boost GE can provide is to help Intersil meet capital needs for updating production equip-

More than $100 million is already committed to semiconductor facilities

ment. Intersil is now reinvesting an estimated 8.8% of semiconductor revenues into production equipment, compared with the industry leader average of 15%. "GE's resources and support are going to make Intersil become a big company faster," says Hoch.

One uncertainty is the possibility of counteroffers that could push the price above GE's $35-per-share bid. Gould Inc., which failed to buy two semiconductor concerns, is considered one likely suitor. Another is Northern Telecom Ltd., which owns 22% of Intersil. But a company official says: "We've said in the past we wouldn't buy more." ∎

QUESTIONS

Ashland Oil: Scrambling for Crude after a Premature Sell-Off:

1. What was Ashland's previous strategy, and what were the major policies used to implement this grand strategy?
2. What is Ashland's current strategy, and on what criteria did it base the strategic change?

Republic Air Takes On a New Merger Problem:

1. Evaluate Republic Air's strategy.
2. Propose a more viable strategy.

Volkswagen of America: Facing a Head-On Challenge from Detroit:

1. Answer the following questions as they apply to Volkswagen of America:
   a. What do they want to achieve? (Goals)
   b. How will they get where they want to go?
   c. When do they want to get there?
   d. How efficiently do they want to operate as they go?
2. Discuss some of the drawbacks VWOA faces as a result of being a division of a foreign corporation. How does this affect the successful implementation of their primary strategy?

Anheuser's Plan to Flatten Miller's Lead:

1. Describe Anheuser's strategy and the specific policies it has developed.
2. Which major functional area should be the focus of Anheuser's policy formation process? Explain.

Open for Business: IBM's Computer Store:

1. Has adequate attention been devoted to developing policies for each major functional area to ensure the successful implementation of IBM's new retailing endeavor? Discuss.
2. Discuss the advantages and disadvantages of IBM's conservative approach to strategy implementation.

Hart Schaffner and Marx: Expanding Boldly from Class to Mass Markets:

1. Discuss the policies HSM developed in each of the relevant functional areas.
2. What are some of the major reasons that HSM decided to implement their mass-market strategy?

AT&T's Fast Move on Baby Bell:

1. Describe the implementation process as it relates to AT&T's reorganization strategy.
2. What are the major corporate goals AT&T is trying to achieve through implementation of this strategy?

Washington Post: New Ventures Get Off to an Uncertain Start:

1. What impact does the conservatism of Washington Post Co.'s CEO and Chairman Graham have on the implementation of the firm's expansion strategy?
2. Discuss how Washington Post Co. plans to implement its strategy.

Beatrice Foods: Adding Tropicana for a Broader Nationwide Network:

1. Identify how the Tropicana acquisition deviated from traditional corporate strategy and its (the acquisition) implications for Beatrice as a whole.
2. Is the organization structure of Beatrice Foods appropriate, given the stage of development of the firm? Explain.

Why IBM reversed itself on computer pricing:

1. Did the strategy of reducing prices meet the desired objectives of IBM? Explain.
2. What changes were made in strategy as a result of the evaluation process?

Quaker Oats Retreats to Its Food Lines:

1. Explain how Quaker's diversification (growth) strategy was adjusted to make it more effective.
2. What were the primary factors contributing to the ineffectiveness of this previous strategy?

American Can: Diversification Brings Sobering Second Thoughts:

1. Discuss the topics of financial feasibility and internal consistency as they pertain to the American Can acquisition of Sam Goody Inc. and Pickwick International Inc.
2. Evaluate American Can's strategy of growth by diversification as a whole.

McGraw-Edison: Paying the Price of the Studebaker Acquisition:

1. What were the quantitative and qualitative criteria that McGraw-Edison used to evaluate the Studebaker acquisition?
2. Discuss both the positive and negative aspects of this acquisition.

GE Moves to Correct its Error in Chips:

1. How has GE's past strategy affected its present and future positions in the electronics industry?
2. Discuss the importance of the time dimension in the implementation of GE's acquisition strategy.

Eight.

This book has described a model of the business policy and strategic management process.

Exhibit 8-1 reminds you again that it consists of the interrelated decision processes of

- Appraisal
- Choice
- Implementation
- Evaluation

This book has examined what the process is, how the strategists influence the process, and who the strategists are. Then it described the subparts of the process.

The major method used to describe business policy was a series of *Business Week* articles which described how a number of companies coped with these crucial decisions.

There is a good deal of evidence that effective companies formalize their business policy and strategic management decisions.

It is hoped that this book provided insights to help you become a more effective executive.

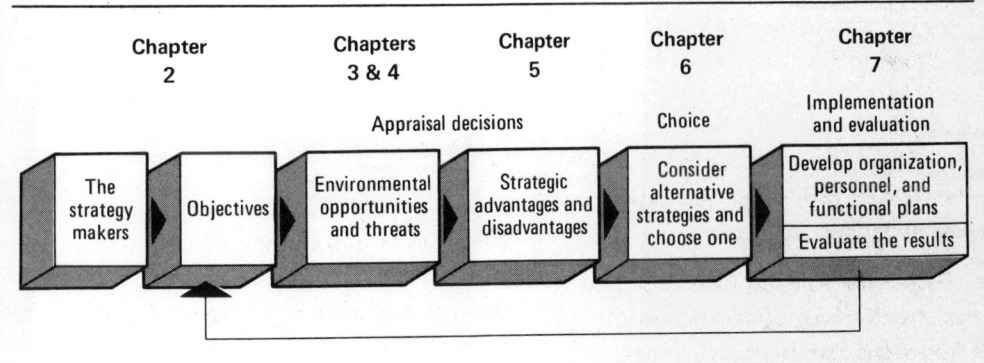

Chapter 2	Chapters 3 & 4	Chapter 5	Chapter 6	Chapter 7
	Appraisal decisions		Choice	Implementation and evaluation
The strategy makers	Objectives → Environmental opportunities and threats	Strategic advantages and disadvantages	Consider alternative strategies and choose one	Develop organization, personnel, and functional plans / Evaluate the results

Exhibit 8-1: A MODEL OF THE BUSINESS POLICY AND STRATEGIC MANAGEMENT PROCESS.

Summary and Conclusions

HD 70 .U5 R43